Major Problems
in American Women's History

MAJOR PROBLEMS IN AMERICAN HISTORY SERIES

GENERAL EDITOR

THOMAS G. PATERSON

Major Problems
in American Women's History

DOCUMENTS AND ESSAYS

EDITED BY
MARY BETH NORTON
CORNELL UNIVERSITY

D. C. HEATH AND COMPANY
Lexington, Massachusetts   Toronto

International Standard Book Number: 0-669-14490-8

Library of Congress Catalog Card Number: 88-80719

10   9   8   7   6   5   4

For Grael and Lia

Preface

The first books on women's history published in the United States appeared in the mid-nineteenth century, and yet as a subject of serious scholarly inquiry the field is barely two decades old. For generations the only authors who concerned themselves with women's past were women with no formal training in the discipline of history. Until the mid-1960s graduate education was open primarily to men, who tended to show little interest in studying the history of the other sex.

That pattern changed dramatically, as two interrelated developments had an enormous impact on the practice of history in this country: First, the modern feminist movement erupted in the general turmoil of that most turbulent decade, and women pressed for equality with men in all areas of life. Second, appreciable numbers of women began to enter the history profession, partly as a result of the new employment opportunities that had become available to them. The history that the first such women studied in graduate school was defined traditionally, focusing on politics, economics, and intellectual life. Yet historians' views of the past are always affected by their experiences in the present. The demonstrations, riots, and iconoclastic atmosphere of the 1960s helped to create a revolution in the history profession, bringing to the fore questions about ordinary people, their families, and their work lives, in what has come to be called the new social history.

The earliest works of social history, like those written on more traditional topics, concerned themselves almost exclusively with men. But by the mid-1970s an increasing number of books and articles examining women's experiences, most of them written by young female historians, began to appear in print. A new field was being born: courses on the subject proliferated in undergraduate and graduate curricula, journals were founded to publish articles on the new subject, and women's-studies programs were organized, most with a strong historical component. At long last, graduate and undergraduate women could study the history of their own sex in a formal educational setting, and men could learn the history of women just as women had long studied the history of men.

Today the field of American women's history is a lively one, full of fervent debates and hotly contested disputes. The essays and documents in this book, like those that appear in the other anthologies in the Heath Major Problems in American History Series, are intended to introduce the student to the most interesting and fundamental of those arguments. Currently, there is widespread agreement on basic interpretations of many important subjects in American women's history. Such topics include the history of women's education and the role of women in the nation's religious life. Accordingly, those issues are not central to this collection, although they are discussed in some of the selections. Rather, the focus of the book is on interpretive dialogues—subjects on which historians disagree. Sometimes the authors whose works are included here draw diametrically opposite conclusions from the same material; on other occasions they approach questions from diverse perspectives and thereby emphasize different aspects of women's experiences. In either case, these historians are engaging in perhaps their most important professional function: learning from and challenging each other's viewpoints so as to arrive at a better, more complete, and more accurate understanding of the past.

Each chapter in this book opens with a brief introduction to the topic at hand. There follows a selection of pertinent documents and either two or three essays examining the subject. The documents introduce key issues and reveal both the flavor of the times and the passionate spirit and conviction typically underlying the debate. The essays show how varying interpretations can be drawn from study of the same documents and phenomena. Headnotes, setting the readings in historical and interpretive perspective, introduce each chapter's documents and essays. The aim is to encourage readers to develop their own interpretations. For those who wish to explore topics in more depth, a list of books and articles for further reading appears at the end of each chapter.

For essential assistance in locating and copying documents and essays for this collection, I wish to thank Ruth M. Alexander and Peter Zinoman. For advice on the selection of materials, my thanks go to Joan Jacobs Brumberg, Nick Salvatore, Jane Caplan, and the reviewers of the draft outlines: Patricia Cline Cohen, Susan Estabrook Kennedy, Ann J. Lane, and Laurel Ulrich. Finally, I wish to acknowledge the assistance of Thomas Paterson of the University of Connecticut, general editor of the Major Problems in American History Series, of which this book is a part; and of Linda Halvorson, Sylvia Mallory, James Miller, Margaret Roll, and Bryan Woodhouse, all of the editorial department of D. C. Heath.

M.B.N.

Contents

CHAPTER 9
Victorian Sexuality
Page 225

CHAPTER 10
Suffrage and Social Reform
Page 255

CHAPTER 11
Work Culture in the Early Twentieth Century
Page 281

*Major Problems
in American Women's History*

What Is Women's History?

Historians of women, unlike scholars who work in more conventional fields, must confront a novel and challenging problem: defining what they are doing and why they are doing it. Every student of history automatically accepts the proposition that war, politics, diplomacy, and other aspects of life that have fallen primarily within the purview of men are important subjects for research. But women have, for the most part, been excluded from such spheres of action; and their own traditional activities have been devalued. Why, then, should we study women's history? What is its importance? To take some random examples, why should we want to know how many women worked for wages at a particular time in the past, what relationships women had with each other or with men, how they raised their children, why they married, or what they thought about their lives? And, most significant of all, what is the history of women, anyway, and how does it differ from or resemble the history of men or the history of families? These are the sorts of questions that women's historians have had to address in defining their field.

❖ E S S A Y S

The two essays reprinted here are attempts to answer such inquiries. In the first, Gerda Lerner of the University of Wisconsin, a pioneer in the field of American women's history, made one of the earliest systematic efforts to criticize traditional approaches to women's history and to sketch out possible alternative ways of thinking about the topic; her 1975 essay defines the conceptual framework within which women's studies had been developed, and goes on to present critical challenges to working within this framework. The second selection was written ten years later by Carol Ruth Berkin, a professor at Baruch College of the City University of New York. Berkin's essay provides a chronological exploration of the development of historical perspectives on women, and assesses the progress that had been made in the previous decade.

Placing Women in History

GERDA LERNER

In the brief span of five years in which American historians have begun to develop women's history as an independent field, they have sought to find a conceptual framework and a methodology appropriate to the task.

The first level at which historians, trained in traditional history, approach women's history is by writing the history of "women worthies" or "compensatory history." Who are the women missing from history? Who are the women of achievement and what did they achieve? The resulting history of "notable women" does not tell us much about those activities in which most women engaged, nor does it tell us about the significance of women's activities to society as a whole. The history of notable women is the history of exceptional, even deviant women, and does not describe the experience and history of the mass of women. This insight is a refinement of an awareness of class differences in history: Women of different classes have different historical experiences. To comprehend the full complexity of society at a given stage of its development, it is essential to take account of such differences.

Women also have a different experience with respect to consciousness, depending on whether their work, their expression, their activity is male-defined or woman-oriented. Women, like men, are indoctrinated in a male-defined value system and conduct their lives accordingly. Thus, colonial and early nineteenth-century female reformers directed their activities into channels which were merely an extension of their domestic concerns and traditional roles. They taught school, cared for the poor, the sick, the aged. As their consciousness developed, they turned their attention toward the needs of women. Becoming woman-oriented, they began to "uplift" prostitutes, organize women for abolition or temperance and sought to upgrade female education, but only in order to equip women better for their traditional roles. Only at a later stage, growing out of the recognition of the separate interests of women as a group, and of their subordinate place in society, did their consciousness become woman-defined. Feminist thought starts at this level and encompasses the active assertion of the rights and grievances of women. These various stages of female consciousness need to be considered in historical analysis.

The next level of conceptualizing women's history has been "contribution history": describing women's contribution to, their status in, and their oppression by male-defined society. Under this category we find a variety of questions being asked: What have women contributed to abolition, to reform, to the Progressive movement, to the labor movement, to the New

Gerda Lerner, "Placing Women in History: Definitions and Challenges," *Feminist Studies*, III, no. 1–2 (Fall 1975), 5–14. Reprinted by permission of Gerda Lerner.

Deal? The movement in question stands in the foreground of inquiry; women made a "contribution" to it; the contribution is judged first of all with respect to its effect on that movement and secondly by standards appropriate to men.

The ways in which women were aided and affected by the work of these "great women," the ways in which they themselves grew into feminist awareness, are ignored. Jane Addams' enormous contribution in creating a supporting female network and new structures for living are subordinated to her role as a Progressive, or to an interpretation which regards her as merely representative of a group of frustrated college-trained women with no place to go. In other words, a deviant from male-defined norms. Margaret Sanger is seen merely as the founder of the birth control movement, not as a woman raising a revolutionary challenge to the centuries-old practice by which the bodies and lives of women are dominated and ruled by man-made laws. In the labor movement, women are described as "also there" or as problems. Their essential role on behalf of themselves and of other women is seldom considered a central theme in writing their history. Women are the outgroup, Simone de Beauvoir's "other."

Another set of questions concern oppression and its opposite, the struggle for women's rights. Who oppressed women and how were they oppressed? How did they respond to such oppression?

Such questions have yielded detailed and very valuable accounts of economic or social oppression, and of the various organizational, political ways in which women as a group have fought such oppression. Judging from the results, it is clear that to ask the question—why and how were women victimized—has its usefulness. We learn what society or individuals or classes of people have done to women, and we learn how women themselves have reacted to conditions imposed upon them. While inferior status and oppressive restraints were no doubt aspects of women's historical experience, and should be so recorded, the limitation of this approach is that it makes it appear either that women were largely passive or that, at the most, they reacted to male pressures or to the restraints of patriarchal society. Such inquiry fails to elicit the positive and essential way in which women have functioned in history. Mary Beard was the first to point out that the ongoing and continuing contribution of women to the development of human culture cannot be found by treating them only as victims of oppression. I have in my own work learned that it is far more useful to deal with this question as one aspect of women's history, but never to regard it as the *central* aspect of women's history. Essentially, treating women as victims of oppression once again places them in a male-defined conceptual framework: oppressed, victimized by standards and values established by men. The true history of women is the history of their ongoing functioning in that male-defined world, *on their own terms.* The question of oppression does not elicit that story, and is therefore a tool of limited usefulness to the historian.

A major focus of women's history has been on women's-rights struggles, especially the winning of suffrage, on organizational and institutional history of the women's movements, and on its leaders. This, again, is an important aspect of women's history, but it cannot and should not be its central concern. . . .

"Contribution" history is an important stage in the creation of a true history of women. The monographic work which such inquiries produce is essential to the development of more complex and sophisticated questions, but it is well to keep the limitations of such inquiry in mind. When all is said and done, what we have mostly done in writing contribution history is to describe what men in the past told women to do and what men in the past thought women should be. This is just another way of saying that historians of women's history have so far used a traditional conceptual framework. Essentially, they have applied questions from traditional history to women, and tried to fit women's past into the empty spaces of historical scholarship. The limitation of such work is that it deals with women in male-defined society and tries to fit them into the categories and value systems which consider *man* the measure of significance. Perhaps it would be useful to refer to this level of work as "transitional women's history," seeing it as an inevitable step in the development of new criteria and concepts.

Another methodological question which arises frequently concerns the connection between women's history and other recently emerging fields. Why is women's history not simply an aspect of "good" social history? Are women not part of the anonymous in history? Are they not oppressed the same way as racial or class or ethnic groups have been oppressed? Are they not marginal and akin in most respects to minorities? The answers to these questions are not simple. It is obvious that there has already been rich cross-fertilization between the new social history and women's history, but it has not been nor should it be a case of subsuming women's history under the larger and already respectable field of social history.

Yes, women are part of the anonymous in history, but unlike them, they are also and always have been part of the ruling elite. They are oppressed, but not quite like either racial or ethnic groups, though some of them are. They are subordinate and exploited, but not quite like lower classes, though some of them are. We have not yet really solved the problems of definition, but it can be suggested that the key to understanding women's history is in accepting—painful though that may be—that it is the history of the *majority* of mankind. Women are essentially different from all the above categories, because they are the majority now and always have been at least half of mankind, and because their subjection to patriarchal institutions antedates all other oppression and has outlasted all economic and social changes in recorded history.

Social history methodology is very useful for women's history, but it must be placed within a different conceptual framework. For example, historians working in family history ask a great many questions pertaining to women, but family history is not in itself women's history. It is no longer sufficient to view women mainly as members of families. Family history has neglected by and large to deal with unmarried and widowed women. In its applications to specific monographic studies, such as the work of Philip Greven, family history has been used to describe the relationships of fathers and sons and the property arrangements between them. The relationships of fathers to daughters and mothers to their children have been ignored. The complex family-support patterns, for example, whereby the work and wages of daughters are used to sup port the education of brothers and to maintain aged parents, while that of sons is not so used, have been ignored.

Another way in which family history has been interpreted within the context of patriarchal assumptions is by using a vaguely defined "domestic power" of women, power within the family, as a measure of the societal status of women. In a methodologically highly sophisticated article, Daniel Scott Smith discovers in the nineteenth century the rise of something called "domestic feminism," expressed in a lowered birth rate from which he deduces an increasing control of women over their reproductive lives. One might, from similar figures, as easily deduce a desire on the part of men to curb their offspring due to the demands of a developing industrial system for a more highly educated labor force, hence for fewer children per family. Demographic data can indeed tell us something about female as well as male status in society, but only in the context of an economic and sociological analysis. Further, the status of women within the family is something quite different and distinct from their status in the society in general.

I learned in studying the history of black women and the black family that relatively high status for women within the family does not signify "matriarchy" or "power for women," since black women are not only members of families, but persons functioning in a larger society. The status of persons is determined not in one area of their functioning, such as within the family, but in several. The decisive historical fact about women is that the *areas* of their functioning, not only their status *within* those areas, have been determined by men. The effect on the consciousness of women has been pervasive. It is one of the decisive aspects of their history, and any analysis which does not take this complexity into consideration must be inadequate.

Then there is the impact of demographic techniques, the study of large aggregates of anonymous people by computer technology based on census data, public documents, property records. Demographic techniques have led to insights which are very useful for women's history. They have yielded revealing data on fertility fluctuations, on changes in illegitimacy patterns and sex ratios, and aggregate studies of life cycles. . . .

The compensatory questions raised by women's history specialists are proving interesting and valuable in a variety of fields. It is perfectly understandable that after centuries of neglect of the role of women in history, compensatory questions and those concerning woman's contribution will and must be asked. In the process of answering such questions it is important to keep in mind the inevitable limitation of the answers they yield. Not the least of these limitations is that this approach tends to separate the work and activities of women from those of men, even where they were essentially connected. As yet, synthesis is lacking. For example, the rich history of the abolition movement has been told as though women played a marginal, auxiliary, and at times mainly disruptive role in it. Yet female antislavery societies outnumbered male societies; women abolitionists largely financed the movement with their fundraising activities, did much of the work of propaganda-writing in and distribution of newspapers and magazines. The enormous political significance of women-organized petition campaigns remains unrecorded. Most importantly, no historical work has as yet taken the organizational work of female abolitionists seriously as an integral part of the antislavery movement.

Slowly, as the field has matured, historians of women's history have become dissatisfied with old questions and old methods, and have come up with new ways of approaching historical material. They have, for example, begun to ask about the actual *experience* of women in the past. This is obviously different from a description of the condition of women written from the perspective of male sources, and leads one to the use of women's letters, diaries, autobiographies, and oral history sources. This shift from male-oriented to female-oriented consciousness is most important and leads to challenging new interpretations.

Historians of women's history have studied female sexuality and its regulation from the female point of view, making imaginative use of such sources as medical textbooks, diaries, and case histories of hospital patients. Questions concerning women's experience have led to studies of birth control, as it affects women and as an issue expressing cultural and symbolic values; of the physical conditions to which women are prone, such as menarche and pregnancy and women's ailments; of customs, attitudes, and fashions affecting women's health and women's life experience. Historians are now exploring the impact of female bonding, of female friendship and homosexual relations, and the experience of women in groups, such as women in utopian communities, in women's clubs and settlement houses. There has been an interest in the possibility that women's century-long preoccupation with birth and with the care of the sick and dying have led to some specific female rituals.

Women's history has already presented a challenge to some basic assumptions historians make. While most historians are aware of the fact that their findings are not value-free and are trained to check their biases by a variety of methods, they are as yet quite unaware of their own sexist bias and, more importantly, of the sexist bias which pervades the value system, the culture, and the very language within which they work.

Women's history presents a challenge to the periodization of traditional history. The periods in which basic changes occur in society and which historians have commonly regarded as turning points for all historical development, are not necessarily the same for men as for women. This is not surprising when we consider that the traditional time frame in history has been derived from political history. Women have been the one group in history longest excluded from political power as they have, by and large, been excluded from military decision making. Thus the irrelevance of periodization based on military and political developments to their historical experience should have been predictable. . . .

What kind of periodization might be substituted for the periodization of traditional history, in order for it to be applicable to women? The answer depends largely on the conceptual framework in which the historian works. Many historians of women's history, in their search for a unifying framework, have tended to use the Marxist or neo-Marxist model supplied by Juliet Mitchell and recently elaborated by Sheila Rowbotham. The important fact, says Mitchell, which distinguished the past of women from that of men is precisely that until very recently sexuality and reproduction were inevitably linked for women, while they were not so linked for men. Similarly, child-bearing and child-rearing were inevitably linked for women and still are so linked. Women's freedom depends on breaking those links. Using Mitchell's categories we can and should ask of each historical period: What happened to the link between sexuality and reproduction? What happened to the link between child-bearing and child-rearing? Important changes in the status of women occur when it becomes possible through the availability of birth control information and technology to sever sexuality from inevitable motherhood. However, it may be the case that it is not the availability and distribution of birth control information and technology so much as the level of medical and health care which are the determinants of change. That is, when infant mortality decreases, so that raising every child to adulthood becomes the normal expectation of parents, family size declines.

The above case illustrates the difficulty that has vexed historians of women's history in trying to locate a periodization more appropriate to women. Working in different fields and specialities, many historians have observed that the transition from agricultural to industrializing society and then again the transition to fully developed industrial society entails important changes affecting women and the family. Changes in relations of production affect women's status as family members and as workers. Later, shifts in the mode of production affect the kinds of occupations women can enter and their status within them. Major shifts in health care and technological development, related to industrialization, also affect the lives of women. It is not too difficult to discern such patterns and to conclude that there must be a causal relationship between changes in the mode of production and the status of women. Here, the Marxist model seems to offer an immediately satisfying solution, especially if, following Mitchell, "sexuality" as a factor is added to such factors as class. But in the case of women, just as in the case of racial castes, ideology and prescription internalized by both women and men, seem to be as much a causative factor as are material changes in production relations. Does the entry of lower-class women into industrial production really bring them closer to "liberation"? In the absence of institutional changes such as the right to abortion and safe contraception, altered child-rearing arrangements, and varied options for sexual expression, changes in economic relations may become oppressive. Unless such changes are accompanied by changes in consciousness, which in turn result in institutional changes, they do not favorably affect the lives of women.

Is smaller family size the result of "domestic freedom" of choice exercised by women, the freedom of choice exercised by men, the ideologically buttressed coercion of institutions in the service of an economic class? Is it liberating for women, for men, or for corporations? This raises another difficult question: What about the relationship of upper-class to lower-class women? To what extent is the relative advance in the status of upper-class women predicated on the status loss of lower-class women? Examples of this are: the liberation of the middle-class American housewife in the mid-nineteenth century through the availability of cheap black or immigrant domestic workers; the liberation of the twentieth-century housewife from incessant drudgery in the home through agricultural stoop labor and the food-processing industry, both employing low paid female workers.

Is periodization then dependent as much on class as on gender? This question is just one of several which challenge the universalist assumptions of all previous historical categories. I cannot provide an answer, but I think the questions themselves point us in the right direction.

It appears to me that all conceptual models of history hitherto developed have only limited usefulness for women's history, since all are based on the assumptions of a patriarchal ordering of values. The structural-functionalist framework leaves out class and sex factors, the traditional Marxist framework leaves out sex and race factors as *essentials,* admitting them only as marginal factors. Mitchell's neo-Marxist model includes these, but slights ideas, values, and psychological factors. Still, her four-structures model and the refinements of it proposed by Bridenthal, are an excellent addition to the conceptual working tools of the historian of women's history. They should be tried out, discussed, refined. But they are not, in my opinion, the whole answer.

Kelly-Gadol offers the useful suggestion that attitudes toward sexuality should be studied in each historical period. She considers the constraints upon women's sexuality imposed by society a useful measure of women's true status. This approach would necessitate comparisons between pre-scribed behavior for women and men as well as indications of their actual sexual behavior at any given time. This challenging method can be used with great effectiveness for certain periods of history and especially for upper- and middle-class women. I doubt that it can be usefully employed as a general criterion, because of the difficulty of finding substantiating evidence, especially as it pertains to lower classes.

I raised the question of a conceptual framework for dealing with women's history in 1969, reasoning from the assumption that women were a subgroup in history. Neither caste, class, nor race quite fit the model for describing us. I have now come to the conclusion that the idea that women are some kind of a subgroup or particular is wrong. It will not do—there are just too many of us. No single framework, no single factor, four-factor or eight-factor explanation can serve to contain all that the history of women is. Picture, if you can, an attempt to organize the history of men by using four factors. It will not work; neither will it work for women.

Women are and always have been at least half of mankind and most of the time have been the majority of mankind. Their culturally determined and psychologically internalized marginality seems to be what makes their historical experience essentially different from that of men. But men have defined their experience as history and have left women out. At this time, as during earlier periods of feminist activity, women are urged to fit into the empty spaces, assuming their traditional marginal, "sub-group" status. But the truth is that history, as written and perceived up to now, is the history of a minority, who may well turn out to be the "subgroup." In order to write a new history worthy of the name, we will have to recognize that no single methodology and conceptual framework can fit the complexities of the historical experience of all women.

The first stage of "transitional history" may be to add some new categories to the general categories by which historians organize their material: sexuality, reproduction, the link between child-bearing and child-rearing; role indoctrination; sexual values and myths; female consciousness. Further, all of these need to be analysed, taking factors of race, class, ethnicity and, possibly, religion into consideration. What we have here is not a single framework for dealing with women in history, but new questions to all of universal history.

The next stage may be to explore the possibility that what we call women's history may actually be the study of a separate women's culture. Such a culture would include not only the separate occupations, status, experiences, and rituals of women but also their consciousness, which internalizes patriarchal assumptions. In some cases, it would include the tensions created in that culture between the prescribed patriarchal assumptions and women's efforts to attain autonomy and emancipation.

The questions asked about the past of women may demand interdisciplinary approaches. They also may demand broadly conceived group research projects that end up giving functional answers; answers that deal not with slices of a given time or society or period, but which instead deal with a functioning organism, a functioning whole, the society in which both men and women live.

A following stage may develop a synthesis: a history of the dialectic, the tensions between the two cultures, male and female. Such a synthesis could be based on close comparative study of given periods in which the historical experience of men is compared to that of women, their tensions and interactions being as much the subject of study as their differences. Only after a series of such detailed studies can we hope to find the parameters by which to define the new universal history. My guess is that no one conceptual framework will fit so complex a subject.

Methods are tools for analysis—some of us will stick with one tool, some of us will reach for different tools as we need them. For women, the problem really is that we must acquire not only the confidence needed for using tools, but for making new ones to fit our needs. We should do so relying on our learned skills and our rational scepticism of handed-down doctrine. The recognition that we had been denied our history came to many of us as a staggering flash of insight, which altered our consciousness irretrievably. We have come a long way since then. The next step is to face, once and for all and with all its complex consequences, that women are the majority of mankind and have been essential to the making of history. Thus, all history as we now know it, is merely prehistory. Only a new history firmly based on this recognition and equally concerned with men, women, the establishment and the passing away of patriarchy, can lay claim to being a truly universal history.

Clio in Search of Her Daughters/
Women in Search of Their Past

CAROL RUTH BERKIN

Clio, the Muse of History, is a woman with a gentle sense of humor. As I sat at my desk, surrounded by false starts and the crumpled papers that gave testimony to them, wondering how on earth to begin this talk, my four-year-old daughter, Hannah, interrupted me to share her delight in a magic trick. She shoved a newly arrived copy of her children's magazine under my nose, urging me to look at the magic face. There, on the page, was a visual trick familiar to all of us in this room: a drawing that, with the page right side up, was a male face; but, with the page inverted, became the face of a woman. Hannah's own face revealed the pleasure of finding the "hidden," of realizing there was always more than first meets the eye, and that it looked like her.

Those of us who do women's history share Hannah's delight. For my generation of American women scholars, the male face stared out at us throughout our graduate school years—and a solid, stern face it was. Few of us thought to turn the page upside down—although some peers with a Marxist perspective had been seen drawing irreverent mustaches on the frowning face. We women pursued our dissertation work on male political leaders, on male institutions, and male conflicts. Did we know something was missing? I cannot honestly say. As Gerda Lerner has put it: "The recognition that we had been denied our history came to many of us as a staggering flash of insight, which altered our consciousness irretrievably."

Perhaps a history of that staggering flash of insight is a good place for me to begin today. Women's historians are a product of the history we now write. As Kate Stimpson reminds us, we came to scholarship out of a gradual democratization of education; first, in the passing away of gender ideologies that would have debarred women from serious intellectual training because of weak or inferior brains and then from a subsequent elaboration of an ideology that acknowledged woman's intellectual capacities and urged her first to be taught and then to teach others in turn. It was a democratization by class as well, one which allowed students marginal to the middle class (like myself) into college and university settings. The desire of women to be, in Stimpson's words, "formal knowers," is revealed in one modern set of comparative statistics: in 1965, 10.5 percent of all doctorates went to women; in 1983, 33.6 percent were awarded to us.

If these familiar, broad transformations in our culture created a setting and an opportunity for women, the political events of the 1960s and 1970s created the framework and perspective for our discovery of woman's face and her presence in our collective past. We are daughters not only of Clio but of the women's movement, of feminism. Feminism, more than anything else, prepared us to see that woman's face and to recognize its importance when we found it. This is not to say that we are no more than crude propagandists, lurking in the halls of academe, making them one more outpost to be taken in the battle for liberation. Rather, the women's movement became the source of the questions that we as historians have sought to answer in our scholarship—a generative experience—and at the same time, our scholarship has served to clarify our political tasks, producing a rich unity of thought and action for many of us. . . .

The 1970s and 1980s, then, proved a fortuitous moment in time for Clio and her daughters to become acquainted. This collaboration between muse and scholars has been electrifying, disturbing, frustrating, and perplexing—not simply to others but to ourselves as well. Woman's curiosity has, after all, opened Pandora's box, but it has loosed as many demons upon us as upon our critics.

Again, a history is in order. In women's history, as in all the humanities, women have pursued several goals at once. We have hoped, through our scholarship, to "deconstruct error and banish falsehood"; to add knowledge about women for the enlightenment of our profession, ourselves, our students, and our children; and to build new theories, construct new paradigms of the past. Some of us have devoted our energies to one of these goals exclusively; others to one and then another of them as our work progressed or when it reached an impasse. There is a chronology, a rough one I admit, to our development of the corpus and its frameworks, and I will try to outline that for you today. But I urge you to remember that the deconstruction of error continues in one area while the construction of fact proceeds in another, and that the strategies for understanding and for pursuing women's history have often arisen in simultaneity and conflict, some to pass away but most to continue, whether favored by the majority or not, as others arise to be tested.

We began our search for Clio with that which outraged and saddened us most: the oppression and subordination of women throughout history. We sought the source of our wounds, and we took satisfaction in naming our oppressors. We found an ironic comfort in detailing the injustices done to our predecessors. In thinking about this phase, this cataloguing of injustices, it does not seem particularly surprising that this was our starting point. In black history or working class history, the point of beginning has also been the recognition and reiteration, as a litany, of sufferings.

Much of American women's history in these earlier years was focused on the nineteenth century and on the impact of industrialization on women. Believing that the problems faced by women today had their roots in the particular forms taken by patriarchy in the nineteenth century, we examined the legal status of white women, their place in the new industrial capitalism, and the ideologies of "true womanhood" and "guardians of the hearth" that seemed to elevate and at the same time isolate these white middle class women from the world taking shape around them. It was, of course, a class-based perspective: middle class women of the 1970s looking at the experiences of their counterparts a century before. Yet, this study of subordination spread quickly, and continues to spread to other time periods and other socio-economic groups and races. Backward and forward in time, up and down the social ladder, women are drawing a vivid picture of the restraints upon their sex's life.

Here, the subject, women's subordination, determined the method. In this history, women are generally acted upon rather than viewed as historical agents; their passivity is acute but it is, at least and at last, comprehensible. The exception that nevertheless proved the rule was found in a subgenre, the recovery of "lost women," or what various scholars have dubbed "contribution history." Contribution history gave to us a roll call of notable women, women who entered the mainstream of the historical flow as reformers, heroines in war or revolution, wielders of power or intellectual influence.

With these two related types of work, we managed to people what was then accepted as the historical landscape with women, and we forced into the historical record the subordination and oppression of women, offering analyses of that oppression's sources and suggesting the calibration of that oppression along class, racial, ethnic, and regional lines.

Yet, through this work we have constructed a duality—woman as victim and woman as achiever—giving voice no doubt to our own sense of women's limitations and potentialities in today's American society. The woman-as-victim was a collective, gender image; the woman as historical agent and achiever was a portrait of extraordinary women or extraordinary groups of women.

The tension of this duality was soon broken by a new conceptualization of women's historical experience. By placing women in a social universe composed of two separate gender worlds, a male and a female culture, we made it possible to see all women as actors and agents of historical change. And, because that change takes place in arenas removed, by force or choice, from dominant male institutions, with linguistic and ritual forms uniquely its own, women's historians have reinforced the social historian's proposal to redefine the very subject matter of history.

The recognition that history happens to non-elites as well as to elites, and the identification of a woman's culture that has internal dynamics and laws suitable for historical study, has generated new work and new techniques for historical excavation. The study of the female world requires attention to the everyday event, the acceptance that continuity, like change, is part of the historical fabric that women and men weave. New sources have been sought to reveal these everyday textures, and the tools of anthropology, linguistics, archeology, and psychoanalytic theory have been employed to reconstruct women's world.

Perhaps as importantly, this study has provided women scholars with a sense of connectedness between our own daily lives and the lives of our subjects that validates our own struggles and adds to our sense of self-worth as effectively as the earlier roll call of notable women had done. We have become secret sharers with generations before us of women as we explore the realm of reproduction, mothering, domestic chores, informal culture and speech, and the aesthetics of domestic crafts. This is not simply a romantic relationship, forged by unreflective sisterhood: this empathetic bond has allowed us to struggle to understand the differences between our subjects and ourselves without fear of alienation from them. It has helped us believe in, and respect, what Stimpson aptly calls our historical subject's "capacity for sincerity" in the telling and recording of her own life. This respect allows us to do battle against the historian's hubris, the Olympian posturing that turns our advantageous but fortuitous position *beyond* another's moment in time into a vantage point for passing judgment on choices made, actions taken or not taken during a human lifetime.

For others in our profession, we have provided a firm reminder that the collective memory of the past has, thus far, been a gender as well as a class-based memory and is, therefore, no more than a partial recollection. We have helped place what was once termed "the world" into its position of relativity and incompleteness and, thus, made it more accessible to analysis than ever before.

The insistence on separate male and female cultures places gender at the center of the historical process. A host of questions flow from this envisioning: do the two separate gender universes rotate at the same speed? Does time move at the same rate? Periodization—the base line of history—now seems in doubt. The categories used to demark change and continuity have been challenged by the need to graph shifts in reproductive patterns as carefully and clearly as alternations of Republican and Democratic regimes. The labels given to eras, that common coin of the chronological realm, seem inappropriate when applied to the female as well as the male collective experience of the period. Was the revolutionary era revolutionary? Does the Era of the Common Man characterize historical reality for *women* in antebellum America?

The separate male culture/female culture model has wreaked havoc with both the carefully constructed segments of our chronological line and with the rhythms and pace of movement along that line. In American history, the coming and going of wars beats one cadence for change in our society; but significant variations in reproductive patterns beat quite another. Reasonable, well-trained scholars can no longer agree on the most important events or ideas or decisions in a given historical moment; those "socially justified beliefs" described so effectively by Kenneth Bruffee as "knowledge" are challenged, and women's history produces that very "abnormal discourse" that Bruffee tells us prompts "a knowledge revolution, when consensus no longer exists with regard to rules, assumptions, goals, values, or mores."

Resistance to this abnormal discourse is strong and powerful. Women's history and the study of women in general have been attacked as subjective, propagandistic, and trivial. Male scholars, already burdened by demands to integrate the massive amounts of new data spewed up by the technological revolutions in research, and pressured by male colleagues to incorporate social history or to attend to class and race in their explanations of an era or an event, balk at adding yet another worrisome variable to those clamoring to enter the historical record. Enough! these scholars shout, and rely upon their own devaluation of women's traditional realm of home and private relationships and emotions in order to exclude the topic from their professional responsibilities. As "formal knowers," women have been judged as collectively second-rate, especially when they pursue women's subjects, and few have found it possible to secure institutional bases from which to share their knowledge. Their permanent presence in tenured positions among the knowledge communities would, of course, only strengthen their power to challenge "socially justified beliefs."

Despite its impact on Clio's disciples and the world they inhabit, academe, the women's culture/male culture paradigm has not ended the search by Clio and her daughters for one another. It has generated, instead, a host of controversies and challenges. First, a precise definition of women's culture has not been offered or agreed upon by those who employ it or attack it. Frequently, women's culture is confused with "women's sphere," a confusion that leads, I believe, to arguments among women scholars that are frustrating and perhaps fruitless. Women's sphere, I suggest, is the location, the environment—not simply physical, but legal and ideological—in which women's culture takes its shape. That sphere stands in a political relationship to the male sphere; that is, its creation and the maintenance of its boundaries involve questions of power and of governance. The parameters of women's sphere are drawn by a dominant male interest within the full society and its perimeters are policed by male institutions, laws, and manipulation and interpretation of the economic and ideological systems in which both men and women live.

What women make of their activities within that sphere, how they value those activities within their own gender community, and what space they find, or force, to create their own rituals and moral choices is one central concern of women's history. Indeed, the configuration of that space—psychic, physical, and moral—may well constitute women's culture at any given historical moment. But when women attempt to move the boundaries of their sphere, impose their understanding of their activities upon the world around them, reinterpret the importance of their moral vision in the hierarchy of existing social values, this aspect of women's history is the study of women's political engagement with the male society around them. So too is the attempt by women to abolish their sphere altogether by gaining the right to wield formal power, an independent access to economic and social resources, and personal autonomy.

This analysis insists that the relationship between women's sphere and women's culture is problematical, highly complex. Yet women historians have tended to stress either the antagonistic or congruent aspects of this relationship to the exclusion of others. Thus the polarized debate: does women's culture provide the strength by which women rebel against the limitations upon their autonomy, given form in women's sphere? Or does women's culture—women's separate and often secret psychic place—operate as an opiate of the gender, providing solace and satisfaction that deflect energies from the struggle for autonomy?

The historian's emotional commitment to and belief in the universality of women's culture, often appears to determine her judgment not only of its political role but also of the value of its study. Some historians insist that the *only* proper study of women is the language, the symbolism and rituals, and the intimate relationships among women that constitute women's culture. Others believe that the moments of concerted struggle against the confinement of women's sphere are the most compelling subjects for study. This is more than a conflict of strategies; it is an ideological battle. At stake here is the right to carry the banner of feminism into the fray.

Other historians, struggling to avoid this ideological battle, but unable to clarify its errors, have urged that women scholars take as their primary task the measurement of women's collective progress or regression vis-à-vis their male counterparts in American society. These historians focus upon the relationship between women's work roles within women's sphere and women's status in the larger society. Thus, the great "golden age" debate, which compares the status of women in agrarian, colonial America to their status in industrial America.

This effort to compare women's status within two socio-economic systems is an honest attempt to relate women to the dominant society around them while still maintaining the integrity of their gender identity. In the process of marching women in step with major transformations in the world around them, these historians hope to satisfy both the impulse to study women's experiences and to attend to the progress or setbacks of women's liberation from their subordinate sphere. One result has been rich, textured descriptions of many aspects of women's sphere, both in the nineteenth century and more recently in the colonial era.

Yet this compromise model proves ultimately unsuccessful. First, there is little apparent relationship between, as Elizabeth Fox-Genovese puts it, "the work women do and the regard in which they are held." Second, women historians now realize that few historical developments affect all women uniformly or simultaneously. Women's culture may or may not be affected by class and racial differences—that is, it may be universal—but women's sphere most surely is not. Finally, shifts like that from agrarian to industrial society do not lift women's sphere up whole, and move it forward or backward on some historical gameboard. Instead, in such transformations, the component parts of women's sphere seem to separate and regroup, to undergo alteration or maintain integrity, always at different rates, and in different patterns by race, class, and regional group. Industrial society, for example, decreased opportunities for women to serve as "surrogate patriarchs" within their families and communities; it reduced women's informal political influence by professionalizing and rationalizing political bureaucracies in which decisions were made; and it limited women's opportunity to participate in certain kinds of economic activities. Yet, the nineteenth-century white American woman found a new model of individualism to legitimate her demands for political and social equality, new techniques for production that diminished the significance of physiological differences between men and women in the workplace, scientific and medical advancements that favorably affected her health and offered control over reproduction, and educational opportunities unimaginable in the previous era.

Thus, even were we to agree upon what constitutes progress or improvement in women's status, it does not seem to proceed uniformly within women's sphere or among the women who inhabit that sphere. The most pressing historical problem is this: why the sphere itself continues. And, that question may lead us, helter skelter, back to the ideological debate over the relationship between women's culture and women's sphere.

Yet another group of historians have tried to finesse this ideological debate by working to *refine* the use of gender as a category of analysis. They do so by placing gender upon a grid with race and class as its intersecting lines. In reminding us that gender is not the only and always defining category *for women themselves,* these scholars break free of the women's culture/male culture dichotomy. They do not suggest the subordination of gender as a category—an ironic thought indeed. Rather they place women in a sexually integrated world by looking at two valid kinds of women's experiences: those they share with other women and those they share with men of their own immediate social group. Urging us to "pay close attention to the conditions under which women are likely to perceive of themselves as *primarily,* or even *significantly,* members of a gender which they share with other women," these scholars bring the debate back to historical process, where it surely belongs; they remind us that gender, like class, is a socially constructed category, with a historical evolution and elaboration that must be charted.

Appropriately, given women's history's early focus on nineteenth-century industrialization, historians of this school, like Elizabeth Fox-Genovese, put forward the theory that gender as a major category of self-identification and a base for group action is linked to the development of industrial capitalism. "It is very likely," Fox-Genovese argues, "that with the development of capitalism gender has assumed greater importance as a universal principle of social classification precisely because the formal importance of other forms of social classification have diminished." If she is correct, the banner of feminism belongs to neither camp in the debate over women's culture as source of strength for, or source of resistance to, feminism. Feminism is, instead, a response to a historical process that intensified gender identification and transformed the meaning and nature of women's culture itself.

This newest perspective on gender brings us back to Hannah's "magic face." For just as the woman's face and the man's occupy the same surface and indeed employ the same lines to shape their features, so women and men occupy the same historical space and create, or respond to the creation of, the same constellation of historical events and ideas. Differentiating their responses and roles as actors is one, indeed a major task of women's history, but exploring their linkages is another. In the end, these are the tasks for all historians who hope to engage Clio's support in finding the human past.

✣ *F U R T H E R   R E A D I N G*

Carol Ruth Berkin and Mary Beth Norton, eds., *Women of America: A History* (1979)

Berenice Carroll, ed., *Liberating Women's History* (1976)

Carl Degler, *At Odds: Women and the Family in America from the Revolution to the Present* (1980)

Ellen DuBois et al., *Feminist Scholarship* (1986)

Sharon Harley and Rosalyn Terborg-Penn, eds., *The Afro-American Woman* (1978)

Edward and Janet James, eds., *Notable American Women 1607–1950* (1971)

Joan Kelly, *Women, History, and Theory* (1984)

Gerda Lerner, *The Majority Finds its Past* (1979)

Alfredo Mirande and Evangelina Enriquez, *La Chicana* (1979)

Mary Ryan, *Womanhood in America*, 3d. ed. (1983)

Joan W. Scott, "Gender: A Useful Category of Analysis," *American Historical Review*, XCI (1986), 1053–75

Barbara Sicherman, ed., *Notable American Women: The Modern Period* (1980)

Carroll Smith-Rosenberg, "The New Woman and the New History," *Feminist Studies*, 3, no. 1/2 (Fall 1975), 185–98

Nancy Woloch, *Women and the American Experience* (1984)

The Status of White Women
in Seventeenth-Century America

The first residents of the first permanent English colony in mainland North America were males. Jamestown, Virginia, founded in 1607, had no white female residents for more than a decade, because Virginia was planned to be solely a trading and military outpost. Even so, the early settlers rapidly realized that the future of their colony lay in agriculture, specifically in the cultivation of tobacco, a crop native to the Americas. As the great tobacco boom began, the first English women finally arrived in Virginia (1619). But because of the traditional English sexual division of labor—which identified men as the most appropriate cultivators of crops—tobacco planters seeking indentured servants to work in their fields imported large numbers of male laborers but relatively few females. Accordingly, women long remained a minority of the population in Virginia, and also in Maryland, the second colony founded in the Chesapeake region (1634).

Farther north, in the Pilgrim and Puritan settlements in New England around Cape Cod and the great bay of Massachusetts, women came with their menfolk on the first ships in the 1620s. There the settlers intended from the beginning to establish farms and re-create, if possible, the social and economic structure they had left behind in England. The New Englanders were able to come close to accomplishing that goal because of their nearly balanced numbers of men and women, and because they quickly began subsistence farming rather than relying on the production and sale of a staple crop like tobacco.

The dramatic differences between the Chesapeake and New England colonies in the seventeenth century have attracted the attention of many historians. How, they have asked, did the migration from England affect the status of women? Were they better off in the Chesapeake, where they made up only a small proportion of the population, or in New England, where they were nearly half the settlers? And what was the impact of Puritan ideology and theology on women's lives? Were Puritan women more oppressed, or less so, than Anglicans, Catholics, or Quakers?

These important questions have proved difficult to answer because of a lack of readily accessible source material. Few of the Chesapeake settlers—men or women—could read and write, so most of the evidence for that region comes from public records. In New England, because Puritans believed that each person should be able to read the Bible, more people acquired literacy skills. Therefore, the residents of the northern colonies also produced sermons, letters, and diaries, most of them written by men. The nature of these sources has had a major impact on historians' discussions of the experiences of seventeenth-century white women.

❖ D O C U M E N T S

Anne Bradstreet (1612–1672) was the best-known woman writer in colonial America; the four poems that compose the first document, written after she moved to New England in 1630, express her views on women and writing, and on her family life. Bradstreet's ideas on women's intellectual activity stand in sharp contrast to those revealed in the second selection by John Winthrop, the governor of Massachusetts Bay; in his 1645 account, he comments on the insanity of the wife of another New England political leader. The third document, a selection from the famous sermon by Cotton Mather, *Ornaments for the Daughters of Zion* (1698), shows that Puritan men carefully defined female virtue; it included modesty, piety, and humility. In the fourth selection, written in 1666, George Alsop, a former indentured servant in Maryland, described the lives that men and women could expect to lead in that Chesapeake colony, and their prospects for advancement. For men, Alsop predicted success in farming or trade, for women success in finding a suitable husband. The remaining selections—all from the court records of Maryland—suggest the variety of circumstances women actually encountered there, and the treatment of women by the law. The fifth document is the prenuptial agreement arranged in 1654 by the widow Jane Moore and her fiancé Peter Godson. The sixth is the 1668 disposition of the estate of Richard Pinner, whose widow had remarried without a prenuptial settlement. The last selection is the official record of the 1661 bastardy trial of Elesabeth Lockett and Thomas Bright.

Four Poems by Anne Bradstreet, 1643–1669

The Prologue.

1.

To sing of Wars, of Captains, and of Kings,
Of Cities founded, Common-wealths begun,
For my mean pen are too superiour things:
Or how they all, or each their dates have run
Let Poets and Historians set these forth,
My obscure Lines shall not so dim their worth.

. . .

5.

I am obnoxious to each carping tongue
Who says my hand a needle better fits,
A Poets pen all scorn I should thus wrong,
For such despite they cast on Female wits:
If what I do prove well, it won't advance,
They'l say it's stoln, or else it was by chance.

6.

But sure the Antique Greeks were far more mild
Else of our Sexe, why feigned they those Nine
And poesy made, *Calliope's* own Child;
So 'mongst the rest they placed the Arts Divine,
But this weak knot, they will full soon untie,
The Greeks did nought, but play the fools & lye.

7.

Let Greeks be Greeks, and women what they are
Men have precedency and still excell,
It is but vain unjustly to wage warre;
Men can do best, and women know it well
Preheminence in all and each is yours;
Yet grant some small acknowledgement of ours.

An EPITAPH
On my dear and ever honoured Mother
Mrs. Dorothy Dudley,
who deceased **Decemb. 27. 1643.** *and of her age,* **61:**

Here lyes,
A Worthy Matron of unspotted life,
A loving Mother and obedient wife,
A friendly Neighbor, pitiful to poor,
Whom oft she fed, and clothed with her store;
To Servants wisely aweful, but yet kind,
And as they did, so they reward did find:
A true Instructer of her Family,
The which she ordered with dexterity.
The publick meetings ever did frequent,
And in her Closet constant hours she spent;
Religious in all her words and wayes,
Preparing still for death, till end of dayes:
Of all her Children, Children, liv'd to see,
Then dying, left a blessed memory.

To my Dear and loving Husband.

If ever two were one, then surely we.
If ever man were lov'd by wife, then thee;
If ever wife was happy in a man,
Compare with me ye women if you can.
I prize thy love more then whole Mines of gold,
Or all the riches that the East doth hold.
My love is such that Rivers cannot quench,
Nor ought but love from thee, give recompence.
Thy love is such I can no way repay,
The heavens reward thee manifold I pray.
Then while we live, in love lets so persever,
That when we live no more, we may live ever.

In memory of my dear grand-child
Anne Bradstreet.
Who deceased June 20. 1669. *being three years and*
seven Moneths old.

With troubled heart & trembling hand I write,
The Heavens have chang'd to sorrow my delight.
How oft with disappointment have I met,
When I on fading things my hopes have set?
Experience might 'fore this have made me wise,
To value things according to their price:
Was ever stable joy yet found below?
Or perfect bliss without mixture of woe.
I knew she was but as a withering flour,
That's here to day, perhaps gone in an hour;
Like as a bubble, or the brittle glass,
Or like a shadow turning as it was.
More fool then I to look on that was lent,
As if mine own, when thus impermanent.
Farewel dear child, thou ne're shall come to me,
But yet a while, and I shall go to thee;
Mean time my throbbing heart's chear'd up with this
Thou with thy Saviour art in endless bliss.

John Winthrop on Mistress Hopkins's Madness, 1645

Mr. Hopkins, the governor of Hartford upon Connecticut, came to Boston, and brought his wife with him, (a godly young woman, and of special parts,) who was fallen into a sad infirmity, the loss of her understanding and reason, which had been growing upon her divers years, by occasion of her giving herself wholly to reading and writing, and had written many books. Her husband, being very loving and tender of her, was loath to grieve her; but he saw his error, when it was too late. For if she had attended her household affairs, and such things as belong to women, and not gone out of her way and calling to meddle in such things as are proper for men, whose minds are stronger, etc., she had kept her wits, and might have improved them usefully and honorably in the place God had set her. He brought her to Boston, and left her with her brother, one Mr. Yale, a merchant, to try what means might be had here for her. But no help could be had.

Cotton Mather on the Virtuous Woman, 1698

The virtuous Woman counts the best Female favour to be deceitful, the best Female Beauty to be vain. By favour is meant, a comely Presence, an handsome carriage, a decent gesture, a ready wit agreeably expressing itself, with all other graceful motions, and what soever procures favour for a woman among her neighbors. The virtuous Woman is willing to have this favour so far as is consistent with virtue; she counts it a favour of God for

PAPER 1

one to be graced with it; But still she looks upon it as a deceitful thing. She is careful that she do not hereby deceive herself, or be contemptuous towards others. Careful she likewise is, lest hereby she deceive unwary men, into those Amours which bewitching looks and smiles so often betray the children of Men. . . .

By Beauty is meant, a good Proportion and Symmetry of the parts, and a skin well varnished, or that which Chrysostem calls, a good mixture of Blood and flegm spining through a good skin; with all the harmonious Air of the Countenance, which recommends itself, as a Beauty to the Eye of the Spectator. The virtuous woman is not unthankful for this Beauty, when the God of Nature has bestowed any of it on her; and yet she counts it no virtue for her to be very sensible of her being illustrated with such a Beauty. But still she looks upon it as a vain thing. She reckons it so vain, that she has no assurance for the continuance of it . . . for a thousand casualties may soon destroy that idol of the Amorites. And upon these thoughts, a virtuous woman takes heed of becoming so deceitful and vain, as many women are tempted by their Favour and Beauty to become. . . .

The Fear of God is that which the heart of a virtuous woman is under the power of. The Female sex is naturally the fearful sex; but the Fear of God is that which exceeds (and sometimes extinguishes) other fears in the virtuous woman. To state this matter aright, we are to know that the Fear of God is an Old Testament Expression, as the Love of God is a New Testament one. It may then be said of a virtuous woman, that she is a religious woman; that [she] has bound herself to that God, whom she had by the sin and the fall of her first mother [Eve] departed from; she has a love which does not cast out the fear that is no fault, but confirm and settle her in that Fear of God; that all kind of Piety and Charity is prevailing in her disposition; that sobriety and Righteousness and Godliness are visible in her whole Behaviour; and, that she does Justice, loves Mercy, and walks Humbly with her God.

George Alsop on the Lives of Servants in Maryland, 1666

They whose abilities cannot extend to purchase their own transportation over into Mary-Land, (and surely he that cannot command so small a sum for so great a matter, his life must needs be mighty low and dejected) I say they may for the debarment of a four years sordid liberty, go over into this Province and there live plentiously well. And what's a four years Servitude to advantage a man all the remainder of his dayes, making his predecessors happy in his sufficient abilities, which he attained to partly by the restrainment of so small a time?

Now those that commit themselves unto the care of the Merchant to carry them over, they need not trouble themselves with any inquisitive search touching their Voyage; for there is such an honest care and provision made for them all the time they remain aboard the Ship, and are sailing over, that they want for nothing that is necessary and convenient.

The Merchant commonly before they go aboard the Ship, or set themselves in any forwardness for their Voyage, has Conditions of Agreements drawn between him and those that by a voluntary consent become his Servants, to serve him, his Heirs or Assigns, according as they in their primitive acquaintance have made their bargain, some two, some three, some four years; and whatever the Master or Servant tyes himself up to here in England by Condition, the Laws of the Province will force a performance of when they come there: Yet here is this Priviledge in it when they arrive, If they dwell not with the Merchant they made their first agreement withall, they may choose whom they will serve their prefixed time with; and after their curiosity has pitcht on one whom they think fit for their turn, and that they may live well withall, the Merchant makes an Assignment of the Indenture over to him whom they of their free will have chosen to be their Master, in the same nature as we here in England (and no otherwise) turn over Covenant Servants or Apprentices from one Master to another. . . .

The Servants here in Mary-Land of all Colonies, distant or remote Plantations, have the least cause to complain, either for strictness of Servitude, want of Provisions, or need of Apparel: Five dayes and a half in the Summer weeks is the alotted time that they work in; and for two months, when the Sun predominates in the highest pitch of his heat, they claim an antient and customary Priviledge, to repose themselves three hours in the day within the house, and this is undeniably granted to them that work in the Fields.

In the Winter time, which lasteth three months (*viz.*) December, January, and February, they do little or no work or imployment, save cutting of wood to make good fires to sit by, unless their Ingenuity will prompt them to hunt the Deer, or Bear, or recreate themselves in Fowling, to slaughter the Swans, Geese, and Turkeys (which this Country affords in a most plentiful manner): For every Servant has a Gun, Powder and Shot allowed him, to sport him withall on all Holidayes and leasurable times, if he be capable of using it, or be willing to learn.

Now those Servants which come over into this Province, being Artificers, they never (during their Servitude) work in the Fields, or do any other imployment save that which their Handicraft and Mechanick endeavours are capable of putting them upon, and are esteem'd as well by their Masters, as those that imploy them, above measure. He that's a Tradesman here in Mary-Land (though a Servant), lives as well as most common Handicrafts do in London, though they may want something of that Liberty which Freemen have, to go and come at their pleasure; yet if it were rightly understood and considered, what most of the Liberties of the several poor Tradesmen are taken up about, and what a care and trouble attends that thing they call Liberty, which according to the common translation is but Idleness, and (if weighed in the Ballance of a just Reason) will be found to be much heavier and cloggy then the four years restrainment of a Mary-Land Servitude. He that lives in the nature of a Servant in this Province, must serve but four years by the Custom of the Country; and when the expiration of his time speaks him a Freeman, there's a Law in the Province, that enjoyns his Master whom he hath served to give him Fifty Acres of Land, Corn to serve him a whole year, three Sutes of Apparel, with things necessary to them, and

Tools to work withall; so that they are no sooner free, but they are ready to set up for themselves, and when once entred, they live passingly well.

The Women that go over into this Province as Servants, have the best luck here as in any place of the world besides; for they are no sooner on shoar, but they are courted into a Copulative Matrimony, which some of them (for aught I know) had they not come to such a Market with their Virginity, might have kept it by them untill it had been mouldy, unless they had let it out by a yearly rent to some of the Inhabitants of Lewknors-lane, or made a Deed of Gift of it to Mother Coney, having only a poor stipend out of it, untill the Gallows or Hospital called them away. Men have not altogether so good luck as Women in this kind, or natural preferment, without they be good Rhetoricians, and well vers'd in the Art of perswasion, then (probably) they may ryvet themselves in the time of their Servitude into the private and reserved favour of their Mistress, if Age speak their Master deficient.

In short, touching the Servants of this Province, they live well in the time of their Service, and by their restrainment in that time, they are made capable of living much better when they come to be free.

Prenuptial Agreement of Jane Moore and Peter Godson, 1654

Know all men by these presents that Whereas my Husband Richard Moore being Sick and weake upon his death bed did Call to his wife Jane Moore and desired her to bring him the will which he had formerly made and he perused it, and after that he Cancelled it and Caused it to be burnt and made his wife whole and Sole Executor to Sett and dispose of amongst her Children as She will, Richard Manship and Elizabeth Manship his wife being present at the Same time

Know all men by these presents that I Jane Moore the wife of Richard Moore deceased doe bind over the four hundred Acres of Land which we now live upon to be Equally Divided betwixt my three Sons, Viz. Richard Moore Roger Moore and Timothy Moore, and they to be of age when they are Come to Eighteen, and the Maids at fifteen, and fourteen head of female Cattell for Seven Children for their use with all the Increase, the Males being taken out of them and as they Come to age or Marry their Shares to be taken out proportionably, and if any of these Children Should dye the Cattell to goe amongst the rest, and for the Land She is to Enjoy it So Long as She the Said Jane doth Live, and then to Come to the Children

Teste Richard Recklesse   The marke of Jane O Moore
the marke of George W White

Know all men by these presents That Whereas I Peter Godson Chirurgeon intending to Intermarry with Jane Moore of Calvert County in the Province of Maryland widdow, have agreed and doe hereby Consent and agree (in Case the Said Marriage take Effect) not to lay any Clayme to or

Intermeddle with all or any part of the Estate late of Richard Moore deceased late husband of the Said Jane Moore mentioned in the within written Deed or Conveyance to be by the Said Jane disposed of to her Childrens use, but will Leave the Same to the Said Children accordingly   Wittness my hand this Sixt day of July 1654

Test Tho: Hatton   the Marke of Peter G Godson

Proceedings on the Estate of Richard Pinner, 1668

Whereas Ann Pinner alias Attkins the relict [widow] of Rich[d] Pinner late dec[d] had Administration Committed to her of the Goods & Chattles of the said Richard Pinner who dyed (as the Office was then inform'd) intestate since which there doth appear a will of the said Richard Pinners Wherefore upon information given the Court that Georg Attkins since marrying the said Relict and doth dayly imbezill & wast the Estate of the said Richard Pinners dec[d] whereby in time the said Pinners Orphants will be totally depriv'd of theire right thereto, It is Ordred that Administration be Committed to the said Ann Pinner alias Attkins wth the said will annexed upon the Estate of the said Richard Pinner deceased she being named Executrix in the said Will, and that her now husband George Attkins is not to have any Intrest in or to meddle with any part or parcell of the said Estate which shall be duely brought in and Administred upon by Vertue of the aforegoing Administration, neither is the said George Attkins to bee burdened withall or molested wth any of the debts that shall ensue thereon or which properly doth or which hereafter shall be accompted due from the Estate of the said Richard Pinner dec[d]

The Trial of Elesabeth Lockett and Thomas Bright, 1661

Robert Martine Junior sworne in the behalfe of Elesabeth Lockett
    Saith that he Cannot Remmember that thare wase any Munye broken betwext thomas Bright and the said Elesabeth to the best of his knowledg and farther saith not

Teste Me   Tobye wells Clk   the marke of Robert Я Martine

    The Examination of Fransis Nash sworne and examined in Court
    Saith that about the midell of summer thes deponant wase goinge with Robert martine and Thomas Bright towards goodman Martins house thes deponant heard the said Bright say th[t] theare wase a peace of Munye Broke betwext hime and Elesabeth lockett and further saith not

Jurat quorum Me   the mark of Fransis ИF Nash
    Will: Coursey

    Ann Doob Ann Hill & Catheren Gammer sworne in Court saith
    That Elesabeth Lockett begunn hur Laboure on teusday night and so Remained tell wensday night and about Cooke Crowing she wase Delivered

and all that ever she Confest wase that it wase thomas Brights Child and you[r] Deponants asked hur w[t] hur master Dide to hure in the husks in the tobaco house and she answered so well as she could that hur master Did butt tickell hur and we Cauld hur into the sheed wheare Mistres blunt and Ann Doob Examiened hure agayne and bade hure speak the Trewth and kathern Gammer heard us and all that Ever she Confest wase that she never knew any other mane in three quarters of a yeare and that she never knew hur Master but by his face and Hands and that the Child wase goote when hur Master wase att Severen wheare that night thomas Bright would not goe to beed butt lay upon the forme and when the sarvants wase aslepe he came to the beed to hur and that night the Child wase goote and when the Childs heed wase in the Birth M[rs] Blunt tooke the booke and swore hure & all that she said it wase thomas Brights Child and further saith not   signum

Ann ✝ Doobe
Catheren ᔔ Gammer
Ann 𝟴 Hill

Sarah Tourson sworne in Court
Saith That she cann Remmember nothing but that she still cried oute on thomas Bright and further saith not

the marke of Sarah SED Tourson

Elesabeth Lockett sworne in Court saith that Thomas Bright wase the father of hure Child and no other mane but himself and that theare wase a peace of Munny brooken betwext theme and that he promised hur Mariege before the Child wase gott and further saith not

the marke of Elesabeth 𝒲 Lockett

Whearas Elesabeth Lookett and thomas Bright hath binn plainly Convicted for basterdy the Court passinge Judgment that the said Elesabeth should have twenty lashes on hur backe well layd on she hath Craved the bennefett of the Act of Indemnity which the Court doth grant and doth order that Thomas Bright shall pay the Chargges that did Inshue by thayre unlawfull doinge and Cost of seut only the charge that Mrs. Conner hath benn at for keepinge of the child that the said Elesabeth shall pay or make sattisfaiction for

❖ *E S S A Y S*

In the first essay Lyle Koehler of the University of Cincinnati, relying heavily on writings by men like Mather and Winthrop, argues forcefully that Puritan ideology was especially oppressive to women, and that female New Englanders found themselves with a limited sphere of action in both theory and reality. The selection focuses on the influence of sex-role stereotyping on these patterns—an issue that is pertinent throughout these essays. Lois Green Carr, the historian of the St. Mary's City Commission in Maryland, and Lorena S. Walsh, a historical researcher at Colonial Williamsburg, Inc., see quite a different pattern in the early Chesapeake settlements, contending in the second essay that women gained power and stature in the society, primarily because they were so few in number. Finally, Mary Beth Norton's 1984 essay surveys the arguments on both sides and concludes that perhaps the issue was not as clear as it seemed and that the contrasts might have been overdrawn. In comparing the position of women in the New England and Chesapeake settlements, Norton shows that how one weighs the advantages for each group of women depends on the criteria by which their circumstances are evaluated.

The Oppression of Women in New England

LYLE KOEHLER

Like so many of their European contemporaries, New England's male Puritan leaders assumed that the obvious physical differences between the sexes had important social consequences. Throughout the seventeenth century these authorities argued and acted as if they believed anatomy alone determined destiny. In virtually all avenues of behavior Puritans affirmed the differences and deemphasized the similarities between the sexes—a practice which usually worked to the disadvantage of women. Because Puritan men had a high need to prove that they wielded some sort of power, in the face of the impotence inculcated in childhood and a theology of man's ultimate powerlessness before God, they tended to exaggerate prevailing notions of male superiority. While such men referred to themselves as the "Magnanimous, Masculine, and Heroicke sexe," every woman became a "poore fraile" creature—the "weaker sex." As Elnathan Chauncy scrawled in his commonplace book, "Y^e soule consists of two portions inferior and superior[;] the superior is masculine and aeternal. Y^e inferior foeminine and mortal." Custom meshed with psychological need for Puritans and non-Puritans alike—with sometimes bizarre results.

Beginning with conception and birth, profound developmental differences were assumed between male and female infants. Some physicians hypothesized that the male child was conceived earlier than the female because the male, as a higher, more sophisticated form of life, needed more time to develop in the womb. On the other hand, some religious leaders asserted that the male embryo, in recognition of its ultimate superiority, received his soul on the fortieth day, while the female embryo had to wait until the eightieth day before she acquired hers. When a woman had conceived twins of each sex, those twins supposedly occupied segregated uterine chambers to breathe into them the "laws of chastity." When the twins or a single child was ready to enter the outside world, the birth of a male was easier, according to the English obstetrical expert Thomas Raynalde. The reason for this was simple: babies were presumed to find their way into the outer world under their own power, and boys, being more vigorous than girls, got out faster. After delivery, the attending midwives cut a girl's navel string shorter than a boy's, "because they believe it makes . . . [females] modest, and their [genital] Parts narrower, which makes them more acceptable to their husbands."

Daughters were "less long'd for" than sons, perhaps in part because English obstetrical guides asserted that mothers who were carrying boys enjoyed fair complexions, red nipples, and white milk, while girls gave them "a pale, heavy, and swarth[y] countenance, a melancolique eye," black nipples, and watery bluish milk. At birth Puritan daughters, in particular, often received names which providentially reminded them of the limitations of their feminine destiny: Silence, Fear, Patience, Prudence, Mindwell, Comfort, Hopestill, and Be Fruitful. No Calvinist girl would ever bear an impressive name such as Freeborne, Fearnot, or Wrestling.

Puritan males, like so many of their English contemporaries, valued those characteristics in women which would insure submissiveness. The ideal woman blushed readily and chose "to be seen rather than Heard whenever she comes." She held her tongue until asked by her father or husband to speak; then only good, comforting words flowed from her mouth. "The greatest Nuisance in Nature," Joseph Beacon unequivocatingly wrote, "is an immodest impudent Woman." The ideal female displayed "an Eminence in Modesty, reserve, purity, temperance, humility, truth, meekness, patience, courtesie, affability, charity, goodness, mercy, [and] compassion," taking special care to avoid the "monstrous" decorative habit of painting the face with "varnish." Tender, consoling, and in need of careful direction, she was viewed as a defenseless creature, "that naked Sex that hath no arms but for imbraces."

In Puritan terms, women needed men, not only for physical protection and financial support but also to prevent themselves from going intellectually astray. Since the woman was presumed less able to ground her spiritual development in the cold logic of reason, Puritan divines told her to consult her father, her husband, or a minister whenever she wished to comprehend a theological issue. In fact, too much intellectual activity, on a theological or any other plane, might overtax her frail mind and thereby debilitate her equally weak body. In 1645 Emmanuel Downing claimed his wife, Lucy, made herself sick "by trying new Conclusions"; he suggested riding as a cure. In the same year Downing's brother-in-law, Massachusetts Governor John Winthrop, asserted that Ann Hopkins, the wife of the Connecticut governor, had lost her understanding and reason by giving herself solely to reading and writing. This statesman commented that if she "had attended her household affairs, and such things as belong to women, and had not gone out of her way and calling to meddle in such things as are proper for men, whose minds are stronger etc., she had kept her wits, and might have improved them usefully and honorably in the place God had set her."

Weak-minded women ostensibly had little talent for letters. Joseph Tompson included the poems of his sister Anna Hayden in a manuscript journal, since they had "love & . . . Christian spirit breathing in them," but at the same time he pointed out that her poems lacked literary merit. Some of Tompson's contemporaries were reluctant to extend Anne Bradstreet much recognition for her own obviously superior poetic efforts. Nathaniel Ward was quick to state that men—Du Bartas, Chaucer, and Homer—had laid the basis for the poetry of a thirty-eight-year-old "girl" whose achievement was notable, because women did not do "good" things; even though Ward recognized Bradstreet's talent, her finest efforts could only "half" revive him. "R. Q." wrote an introduction to the first volume of Bradstreet's poetry (1650) in which he rather snidely concluded that her verse seemed only superficially dangerous to male supremacy:

> Arme, arme, Soldado's arme, Horse, Horse, speed to your Horses,
> Gentle-women, make head, they vent their plots in verses;
> They write of Monarchies, a most seditious word,
> It signifies Oppression, Tyranny, and Sword:
> March amain to London, they'l rise, for there they flock,
> But stay a while, they seldome rise till ten a clock.

In the same year when Bradstreet's first edition appeared, Thomas Parker, the Newbury pastor, reacted to his own sister's writing with particular sharpness. "Your printing of a Book," he wrote, "beyond the custom of your sex, doth rankly smell."

The Puritan divines celebrated woman's divinely prescribed destiny to exist for and through man. William Secker emphatically explained God's design as follows: "She must be so much, and no less, and so much, and no more. Our Ribs were not ordained to be our Rulers: They are not made of the head to claim Superiority. . . . They desert the Author of nature that invert the order of nature. The Woman was made for the mans comfort, but the man was not made for the womans command. Those shoulders aspire too high, that content not themselves with a room below the head."

Many English and American Puritans believed the virtuous woman should walk in the shadow of her male masters from the cradle to the grave. A daughter owed almost complete allegiance to her father's wishes. He was to supervise whom she might choose as friends, direct her to the service of others, and remind her to keep constant watch over the state of her soul. He was expected to reprimand her for tending to become a "Busie-Body" or "Pragmatical." Whatever he commanded (with exception of something sinful), she was to obey. His pleasure was her goal, and "her heart would melt/ When she her Fathers looks not pleasant felt." The ideal daughter was like "a nun unprofest," a girl who never read lust-inducing plays and romances, who avoided the comb and the looking glass, and who relished serving her parents with a demeanor of "Virgin Modesty." When she reached a marriageable age, a daughter should "do nothing" without her father's approval; in marriage matters, she should be "very well contented . . . to submit to such condition[s]" as her parents "should see providence directing." In every familial relation the father, that "soul of the family," served as "governor of the governed." Apparently to emphasize the potency of such paternal overlordship, John Cotton in 1641 actually suggested hanging any maiden who allowed a lover to have sexual intercourse with her in her father's house.

In marriage the woman traded her father's surname for her husband's, in a symbolic transferral of the male right to "govern, direct, protect, and cherish" her. Her lack of an independent name accented the fact that she could not exist independent of men: as daughter she was to give "Reverence, subjection & Obedience" to her father, and as wife she was to give the same to her marital "master." Since he possessed more "quickness of witte . . . greater insight and forecast," that "Prince and chiefe Ruler" deserved her assistance, "reuerand awe," and silent submission—if not outright fear. Massachusetts Governor John Winthrop wrote, "a true wife accounts her subjection her honor and freedom, and would not think her condition safe and free, but in her subjection to her husband's authority, even if he were an unbeliever." A wife should so need to please her husband, Cotton Mather asserted, that she would utterly fear his frowns and be "loth in any way to grieve him, or cause an Head-ake in the Family by Ofending him." Her personal identity so completely depended upon him that for a "Woman to be Praised, is for her to be Married." She could shine only "with the Husbands Reyes," deserving no praise "except she frame, and compose herself, what may be, unto her husband, in conformity of manners."

Theologians directed the "true wife" to be constantly concerned for her husband's welfare, even at the expense of her own. In Cotton Mather's words:

> When she Reads, That Prince Edward in his Wars against the Turks, being stabbed with a poisoned Knife, his Princess did suck the Poison out of his Wounds, with her own Royal Mouth, she finds in her own Heart a principle disposing her to shew her own Husband as great a Love. When she Reads of a woman called Herpine, who having her Husband Apoplex'd in all his Limbs, bore him on her Back a thousand and three Hundred English Miles to a Bath, for his Recovery, she minds herself not altogether unwilling to have done the Like.

Mather urged the wife to address her husband by the appropriate title of "My Lord." If she felt any "passion" against her mate, she left it unexpressed; but when he was in a passion, she quickly strove to mollify it. The virtuous wife was to "carry her self so to her husband as not to disturb his love by her contention, nor to destroy his love by her alienation." She was to be at his beck and call, acting "as if there were but One Mind [His] in Two Bodies."

The utterly selfless Calvinist woman who aspired to carry her husband 1,300 miles to a bath was an economic asset; certainly she could be relied upon to maintain her husband's estate. Women who worked long and hard could advance their husbands financially, instead of being like despicable "Moths . . . spending when they should be sparing." Although wives received no direct remuneration for their services, Puritans expected them to assume the appearance of "labouring Bees" about the household hive, so that the home would exist as a functional economic unit, like a hive over-flowing with honey.

A wife's major purpose in life, besides working on religious salvation, was to minister to her husband's needs. Her personal identity and social rank were derived through him. She was his appendage, as Cotton Mather explained in a letter to his sister-in-law, Hannah Mather. To be the "best of women in the American World," he urged Mistress Mather, "Go on to love him [her husband], and serve him, and felicitate him, and become accessary to all the Good which *he* may do in the world."

The need to define all women as weak and dependent was so deeply embedded in the character of American Puritanism (and English conserva-tism in general) that even the anti-feminine prototypes could not exercise much self-direction, and what little they did exercise got them into trouble. A witch willfully signed, usually in blood, a covenant with Satan to acquire the power to kill by sorcery and to afflict individuals with awesome fits. Yet the being whence these powers supposedly derived was a male figure, who often appeared to the witch as a tall dark man and to whom, in return for such powers, she was to pledge her submission. Without Satan's presumed assistance there could be no fits, no mysterious deaths, and no witchly suspensions of the law of gravity. In addition, the status hierarchy of Satan's kingdom reflected the male-focused hierarchy of seventeenth-century soci-ety. Male witches, or wizards, were considered the closest confederates of the tall, dark man. They allegedly killed more people than the female witches could dream of, and presided over the large-scale gatherings of witches.

Quite in tune with the belief that women were dependent by nature was the Puritan contention that female activities ought to be largely limited to the home's safe environment, even though many non-Puritan women worked in various English agricultural pursuits. William Perkins wrote, "The woman is not to take libertie of wandring, and staying abroad from her owne house, without the man's knowledge and consent." Considering her an ineffective manager of "outward business and affairs," Puritan leaders urged the wife to busy herself with cooking, cleaning, spinning, child care, and other house-hold tasks. Indeed, worldly concerns constituted a potential threat to her health in a way that monotonous household activities did not. A woman achieved respect largely by the extent to which "She looks well to the Wayes of her Household." . . .

In the final analysis, the spokesmen for the several Biblical Common-wealths posited an ideology of female weakness, deference, patience, and nurturance. Sex roles were sharply separated, with the male viewed as the stronger, ruling sex, one more protective than nurturant. . . .

The skeptical scholar might argue that, in the "free aire" of the New World, deep-seated conventions faced severe tests and ultimate disruption, that women neither listened to what the authorities had to say nor drew the proper inferences from separation of the sexes. However, such a claim ignores the fact that an individual woman's identity is largely a product of her experiences in society. The person she becomes, and her response to events in her environment are highly conditioned by her cultural milieu. "Becoming a woman" was measured primarily by the degree to which females adopted or possessed the distinguishing characteristics that the Puritan community had defined as necessary for the status of womanhood.

Some sex-role changes occurred in New England between 1620 and 1700; however, such changes ought to be considered against Puritanism's potent, often immobilizing psychological impact on women. Puritan men, combatting a generalized sense of their own inadequacy, viewed disobedience on the part of a child, servant, or wife as a dire threat, a potentially mortal blow to the integrity and viability of the Biblical Commonwealth. As N. Ray Hiner has pointed out, "Puritans viewed enculturation, the process by which the central values of a culture are internalized by a child, as more critical than socialization, the process by which a child learns the ways of a society so that he can function within it." The repeated emphasis on guilt to compel both child and adult, male and female, to think, feel, and act in acceptable ways made female rejection of the ideal role very unlikely. Even if a woman thought for herself, she then had to confront the sheer force of her sex-role conditioning, community censure, the many legal checks on her behavior, and her lack of training for any occupation other than that of housewife and mother.

Puritan sex-role stereotyping had great impact. Young girls apparently felt that they should not actively pursue learning, for few girls attended the town schools in those regions where they were allowed to do so. At Northampton in 1674, for example, 30 or 40 boys but only 11 girls attended classes, while at Hatfield in 1700 only four girls—8.7 percent of the students—appeared on the schoolmaster's class list. Nor did most females obtain rudimentary educations through dame schools. The number of women who signed deeds with a mark, instead of a signature, suggests that female education in home or school was hardly adequate. William Kilpatrick has reported that 11 percent of the 179 men who made deeds in Suffolk County, Massachusetts, between 1653 and 1656 made marks, as did 11 percent of 199 men deeding property between 1686 and 1697. By contrast, 58 percent of 48 and 38 percent of 130 women in those time intervals signed deeds only with a mark. Kenneth Lockridge's examination of 75 women's wills (1650–70) in Massachusetts, Connecticut, New Hampshire, and Maine yields corroborative results. Fewer than one-third of the female but 60 percent of the male testators could sign their names.

Given their educational disadvantages, the prevailing censorship of the press, and the potency of their sex-role conditioning for non-intellectual activity, women chose not to seek fulfillment through writing. Only four women are among the authors of the 911 works published in seventeenth-century New England. Anne Bradstreet's *Several Poems Compiled with Great Variety of Wit and Learning* appeared in 1678. Four years later, Mary Rowlandson's account of her captivity among the Indians was published under the title *The Soveraignty & Goodness of God, Together With the Faithfulness of His Promises Displayed.* In 1694 M. Hooper's *Lamentations for Her Sons, Poisoned by Eating Mushrooms, August 1, 1693* was published. The fourth book, a *Valedictory and Monitory-Writing,* was a private journal kept by Sarah Goodhue of Ipswich, Massachusetts. It appeared in print only after her death (1682).

Women did not express themselves in print on any of the important issues of the day; nor did they keep private journals, like so many Puritan men, or attempt to write poems for their own private satisfaction. I have found only two women, Mistress Goodhue and Elizabeth White, who wrote accounts of their personal religious turmoil; in addition, only two of the fifty-seven seventeenth-century New Englanders listed in William Matthews's *American Diaries* were women. Of more than a hundred known poets, Anne Bradstreet and her sister Mercy Woodbridge are the only females. Women's lack of education indeed affected their desire to create and to wield influence through the pen.

The young woman looked to marriage for security and fulfillment, just as many ministers suggested she should. Maidens sometimes "toyed" with fortune-telling devices to find out "what trade their sweet harts should be of." They often rushed into marriage; statistics for Plymouth, Dedham, and Andover indicate that the typical bride was between 19 and 22.5 years old, five to eight years younger than her English counterpart. Men, on the other hand, wed at 25 to 27, like their English contemporaries. More than 99 percent of all women married at least once. Even the widow reportedly "has one Eye weeping for her Departed Husband, [while] she . . . has the other open to see, who comes next," since remarriage was often her only realistic alternative to poverty.

A mere handful of women possessed the will and means to become shopkeepers, doctors, schoolteachers, or innkeepers. Instead, most became housewives, for which they received great praise. Benjamin Tompson, for example, could think of no higher accolade for his deceased wife Mary than to accent her role in beautifying their house, and her charitable willingness to minister to the sick and the poor. Edward Taylor similarly boasted of his mate, "She was a neate good Huswife every inch."

Many wives deferred to their mates. Elizabeth, the wife of John Winthrop, Jr., described herself in a letter to her husband as "thy eaver loveing and kinde wife to comande in whatsoever thou plesest so long as the Lord shall be plesed to geve me life and strenge." Lucy Downing, a sister of the elder John Winthrop, ended her letters to her brother with a deferential "Your sister to commaund." Governor Winthrop's own wife, Margaret Tyndal, considered herself "faythfull and obedient" to him and felt she had "no thinge with in or with out" worthy of her husband. She depended completely upon his care for her own security; she valued herself only because he valued her. In one letter she told him, "I will be a seruant to wash the feete of my Lord, I will doe any seruice whearein I may please my good Husband." Tyndal blushed to hear herself commended by her mate and left all important decisions to him, even when she had definite preferences of her own.

Another Puritan wife, much later in the century, was equally obedient, although she did not consider her husband as Christ-like as Margaret Tyndal did. Boston printer Bartholomew Green's wife "was so exactly observant" to her husband's will "that he cou'd not be more ready to Command, then she was to obey." When some of Green's "Commands seem'd not to be as kind as she might have expected," she would obey them nevertheless, objecting only by asking him to extend humane "Compassion to a meek sufferer." Like Elizabeth Winthrop, Lucy Downing, and Margaret Tyndal, she put into practice the ideal of dutiful wifely compliance.

Female dependence was so much a part of Puritan life that women undergoing spiritual stress sometimes asked men to intercede with God on their behalf. In 1640 Mary Cole, plagued with a "corrupt hart, and strong inclinations to sinne, and weaknesse to resist temptation," asked John Winthrop to "plead hard with the lord for me." Similarly, Hannah Jones wrote in 1681 to Increase Mather: "Sometimes I feel myself so under the pres of unbeleav that it makes me cry, mournfully, More fath, more fath. O that the Lord would moue your hart & the harts of the rest of the desipills to intreat the Lord for me & many. more." Men in times of religious turmoil were much more inclined to work out their own reckoning with God; although they occasionally sought the comfort of other men, they did not ask those men to intercede with the Lord on their behalf.

A deferential attitude did not accord well with high self-esteem. Hannah Jones, for one, called herself "bold to present a few lynes" to the "worthy" Mather. She had to justify even writing her letter by explaining, "Now, S^r, tho I am a worm, not worthy to be regarded by God or by men, yet senc it is put into my heart to ventur to give you the trubell of these scrales [i.e., scrawls], exorsise pasience so far as to read them, & if you can desern anything of the spirit of God, I beleaue you will not reject it." Anne Bradstreet, in so many respects an unusual woman, also questioned her own "weak" abilities, when faced with the desire to imitate poetically the "sugared lines" of Guillaume Du Bartas. Bradstreet felt her pen was too "mean" to write of "superior things": songs "of wars, of captains, and of kings,/ Of cities founded, commonwealths begun,/ . . . / Or how they all, or each their dates have run." By her own admission too "simple" to write anything as well as Du Bartas, Anne Bradstreet told her readers that women could not compete poetically with men. Yet, at the same time, she urged men to extend to her and other poetesses a small measure of recognition:

> Let Greeks be Greeks, and women what they are
> Men have precedency and still excel,
> It is but vain unjustly to wage war;
> Men can do best, and women know it well.
> Preeminence in all and each is yours;
> Yet grant some small acknowledgement of ours.

Although she wrote ambitious poems about "masculine" subjects, Bradstreet was embarrassed to find the "ill-formed offspring of my feeble brain" published "by friends less wise than true." . . .

The fragmentary records of their lives suggest that many, if not most, Puritan women conformed to the ideological expectations of their culture and respected the institutional checks on female independence. Although we can draw no definitive conclusion about the extent to which the typical woman fulfilled the attributes of the ideal female role, we can reasonably speculate that Puritan women existed primarily through others, not as individuals who acted for themselves. As in more modern times, the woman spent a lifetime bestowing her energies, skills, talents, and services on her family or on society's needy. This is not to dismiss her impact on society, in the broadest sense; as homemaker, nurturer, and creator of the child's environment, the woman filled an important (but too often undervalued) function. However, that sole function was obscured, if not positively injured, by her need to maintain proper deference, dependency, and non-assertiveness. Puritan males, possessing the power needs of men of their religion and their century, would generally have it no other way. Puritan women, even more powerless than their male "overlords," may have acted in an ideal way; however, we cannot assume that they totally accepted the constraints on their behavior. The evidence is simply too sparse to allow such a claim. Still, enough material does exist to refute the widely reiterated contention that Puritanism served as a liberating experience for women; those women who struggled to express their freedom in seventeenth-century New England generally did so in spite of Puritanism, not because of it.

The Advantageous Position of White Women in Maryland

LOIS GREEN CARR AND LORENA S. WALSH

Four facts were basic to all human experience in seventeenth-century Maryland. First, for most of the period the great majority of inhabitants had been born in what we now call Britain. Population increase in Maryland did not result primarily from births in the colony before the late 1680s and did not produce a predominantly native population of adults before the first decade of the eighteenth century. Second, immigrant men could not expect to live beyond age forty-three, and 70 percent would die before age fifty. Women may have had even shorter lives. Third, perhaps 85 percent of the immigrants, and practically all the unmarried immigrant women, arrived as indentured servants and consequently married late. Family groups were never predominant in the immigration to Maryland and were a significant part for only a brief time at mid-century. Fourth, many more men than women immigrated during the whole period. These facts—immigrant predominance, early death, late marriage, and sexual imbalance—created circumstances of social and demographic disruption that deeply affected family and community life.

We need to assess the effects of this disruption on the experience of women in seventeenth-century Maryland. Were women degraded by the

Lois Green Carr and Lorena S. Walsh, "The Planter's Wife: The Experience of White Women in Seventeenth-Century Maryland," *William & Mary Quarterly*, 3rd ser. XXXIV (Oct. 1977), 542–71.

hazards of servitude in a society in which everyone had left community and kin behind and in which women were in short supply? Were traditional restraints on social conduct weakened? If so, were women more exploited or more independent and powerful than women who remained in England? Did any differences from English experience which we can observe in the experience of Maryland women survive the transformation from an immigrant to a predominantly native-born society with its own kinship networks and community traditions? The tentative argument put forward here is that the answer to all these questions is Yes. There were degrading aspects of servitude, although these probably did not characterize the lot of most women; there were fewer restraints on social conduct, especially in courtship, than in England; women were less protected but also more powerful than those who remained at home; and at least some of these changes survived the appearance in Maryland of New World creole communities. However, these issues are far from settled, and we shall offer some suggestions as to how they might be further pursued. . . .

Whatever their status, one fact about immigrant women is certain: many fewer came than men. Immigrant lists, headright lists, and itemizations of servants in inventories show severe imbalance. On a London immigrant list of 1634–1635 men outnumbered women six to one. From the 1650s at least until the 1680s most sources show a ratio of three to one. From then on, all sources show some, but not great, improvement. Among immigrants from Liverpool over the years 1697–1707 the ratio was just under two and one half to one.

Why did not more women come? Presumably, fewer wished to leave family and community to venture into a wilderness. But perhaps more important, women were not as desirable as men to merchants and planters who were making fortunes raising and marketing tobacco, a crop that requires large amounts of labor. The gradual improvement in the sex ratio among servants toward the end of the century may have been the result of a change in recruiting the needed labor. In the late 1660s the supply of young men willing to emigrate stopped increasing sufficiently to meet the labor demands of a growing Chesapeake population. Merchants who recruited servants for planters turned to other sources, and among these sources were women. They did not crowd the ships arriving in the Chesapeake, but their numbers did increase.

To ask the question another way, why did women come? Doubtless, most came to get a husband, an objective virtually certain of success in a land where women were so far outnumbered. The promotional literature, furthermore, painted bright pictures of the life that awaited men and women once out of their time; and various studies suggest that for a while, at least, the promoters were not being entirely fanciful. Until the 1660s, and to a less degree the 1680s, the expanding economy of Maryland and Virginia offered opportunities well beyond those available in England to men without capital and to the women who became their wives.

Nevertheless, the hazards were also great, and the greatest was untimely death. Newcomers promptly became ill, probably with malaria, and many died. What proportion survived is unclear; so far no one has devised a way of measuring it. Recurrent malaria made the woman who survived seasoning less able to withstand other diseases, especially dysentery and influenza. She was especially vulnerable when pregnant. Expectation of life for everyone was low in the Chesapeake, but especially so for women. A woman who had immigrated to Maryland took an extra risk, though perhaps a risk not greater than she might have suffered by moving from her village to London instead.

The majority of women who survived seasoning paid their transportation costs by working for a four- or five-year term of service. The kind of work depended on the status of the family they served. A female servant of a small planter—who through about the 1670s might have had a servant—probably worked at the hoe. Such a man could not afford to buy labor that would not help with the cash crop. In wealthy families women probably were household servants, although some are occasionally listed in inventories of well-to-do planters as living on the quarters—that is, on plantations other than the dwelling plantation. Such women saved men the jobs of preparing food and washing linen but doubtless also worked in the fields. In middling households experience must have varied. Where the number of people to feed and wash for was large, female servants would have had little time to tend the crops.

Tracts that promoted immigration to the Chesapeake region asserted that female servants did not labor in the fields, except "nasty" wenches not fit for other tasks. This implies that most immigrant women expected, or at least hoped, to avoid heavy field work, which English women—at least those above the cottager's status—did not do. What proportion of female servants in Maryland found themselves demeaned by this unaccustomed labor is impossible to say, but this must have been the fate of some. A study of the distribution of female servants among wealth groups in Maryland might shed some light on this question. Nevertheless, we still would not know whether those purchased by the poor or sent to work on a quarter were women whose previous experience suited them for field labor.

An additional risk for the woman who came as a servant was the possibility of bearing a bastard. At least 20 percent of the female servants who came to Charles County between 1658 and 1705 were presented to the county court for this cause. A servant woman could not marry unless someone was willing to pay her master for the term she had left to serve. If a man made her pregnant, she could not marry him unless he could buy her time. Once a woman became free, however, marriage was clearly the usual solution. Only a handful of free women were presented in Charles County for bastardy between 1658 and 1705. Since few free women remained either single or widowed for long, not many were subject to the risk. The hazard of bearing a bastard was a hazard of being a servant.

This high rate of illegitimate pregnancies among servants raises lurid questions. Did men import women for sexual exploitation? Does John Barth's Whore of Dorset have a basis outside his fertile imagination? In our opinion, the answers are clearly No. Servants were economic investments on the part of planters who needed labor. A female servant in a household where there were unmarried men must have both provided and faced temptation, for the pressures were great in a society in which men outnumbered women by three to one. Nevertheless, the servant woman was in the household to work—to help feed and clothe the family and make tobacco. She was not primarily a concubine.

This point could be established more firmly if we knew more about the fathers of the bastards. Often the culprits were fellow servants or men recently freed but too poor to purchase the woman's remaining time. Sometimes the master was clearly at fault. But often the father is not identified. Some masters surely did exploit their female servants sexually. Nevertheless, masters were infrequently accused of fathering their servants' bastards, and those found guilty were punished as severely as were other men. Community mores did not sanction their misconduct.

A female servant paid dearly for the fault of unmarried pregnancy. She was heavily fined, and if no one would pay her fine, she was whipped. Furthermore, she served an extra twelve to twenty-four months to repay her master for the "trouble of his house" and labor lost, and the fathers often did not share in this payment of damages. On top of all, she might lose the child after weaning unless by then she had become free, for the courts bound out bastard children at very early ages.

English life probably did not offer a comparable hazard to young unmarried female servants. No figures are available to show rates of illegitimacy among those who were subject to the risk, but the female servant was less restricted in England than in the Chesapeake. She did not owe anyone for passage across the Atlantic; hence it was easier for her to marry, supposing she happened to beome pregnant while in service. Perhaps, furthermore, her temptations were fewer. She was not 3,000 miles from home and friends, and she lived in a society in which there was no shortage of women. Bastards were born in England in the seventeenth century, but surely not to as many as one-fifth of the female servants.

Some women escaped all or part of their servitude because prospective husbands purchased the remainder of their time. At least one promotional pamphlet published in the 1660s described such purchases as likely, but how often they actually occurred is difficult to determine. Suggestive is a 20 percent difference between the sex ratios found in a Maryland headright sample, 1658–1681, and among servants listed in lower Western Shore inventories for 1658–1679. Some of the discrepancy must reflect the fact that male servants were younger than female servants and therefore served longer terms; hence they had a greater chance of appearing in an inventory. But part of the discrepancy doubtless follows from the purchase of women for wives. Before 1660, when sex ratios were even more unbalanced and the expanding economy enabled men to establish themselves more quickly, even more women may have married before their terms were finished.

Were women sold for wives against their wills? No record says so, but nothing restricted a man from selling his servant to whomever he wished. Perhaps some women were forced into such marriages or accepted them as the least evil. But the man who could afford to purchase a wife—especially a new arrival—was usually already an established landowner. Probably most servant women saw an opportunity in such a marriage. In addition, the shortage of labor gave women some bargaining power. Many masters must have been ready to refuse to sell a woman who was unwilling to marry a would-be purchaser.

If a woman's time was not purchased by a prospective husband, she was virtually certain to find a husband once she was free. Those famous spinsters, Margaret and Mary Brent, were probably almost unique in seventeenth-century Maryland. In the four counties of the lower Western Shore only two of the women who left a probate inventory before the eighteenth century are known to have died single. Comely or homely, strong or weak, any young woman was too valuable to be overlooked, and most could find a man with prospects.

The woman who immigrated to Maryland, survived seasoning and service, and gained her freedom became a planter's wife. She had considerable liberty in making her choice. There were men aplenty, and no fathers or brothers were hovering to monitor her behavior or disapprove her preference. This is the modern way of looking at her situation, of course. Perhaps she missed the protection of a father, a guardian, or kinfolk, and the participation in her decision of a community to which she felt ties. There is some evidence that the absence of kin and the pressures of the sex ratio created conditions of sexual freedom in courtship that were not customary in England. A register of marriages and births for seventeenth-century Somerset County shows that about one-third of the immigrant women whose marriages are recorded were pregnant at the time of the ceremony—nearly twice the rate in English parishes. There is no indication of community objection to this freedom so long as marriage took place. No presentments for bridal pregnancy were made in any of the Maryland courts.

The planter's wife was likely to be in her mid-twenties at marriage. . . . Because of the age at which an immigrant woman married, the number of children she would bear her husband was small. She had lost up to ten years of her childbearing life—the possibility of perhaps four or five children, given the usual rhythm of childbearing. At the same time, high mortality would reduce both the number of children she would bear over the rest of her life and the number who would live. One partner to a marriage was likely to die within seven years, and the chances were only one in three that a marriage would last ten years. In these circumstances, most women would not bear more than three or four children—not counting those stillborn—to any one husband, plus a posthumous child were she the survivor. The best estimates suggest that nearly a quarter, perhaps more, of the children born alive died during their first year and that 40 to 55 percent would not live to see age twenty. Consequently, one of her children would probably die in infancy, and another one or two would fail to reach adulthood. Wills left in St. Mary's County during the seventeenth century show the results. In 105 families over the years 1660 to 1680 only twelve parents left more than three children behind them, including those conceived but not yet born. The average number was 2.3, nearly always minors, some of whom might die before reaching adulthood.

For the immigrant woman, then, one of the major facts of life was that although she might bear a child about every two years, nearly half would not reach maturity. The social implications of this fact are far-reaching. Because she married late in her childbearing years and because so many of her children would die young, the number who would reach marriageable age might not replace, or might only barely replace, her and her husband or husbands as child-producing members of the society. Consequently, so long as immigrants were heavily predominant in the adult female population, Maryland could not grow much by natural increase. It remained a land of newcomers. . . .

However long they lived, immigrant women in Maryland tended to outlive their husbands—in Charles County, for example, by a ratio of two to one. This was possible, despite the fact that women were younger than men at death, because women were also younger than men at marriage. Some women were widowed with no living children, but most were left responsible for two or three. These were often tiny, and nearly always not yet sixteen.

This fact had drastic consequences, given the physical circumstances of life. People lived at a distance from one another, not even in villages, much less towns. The widow had left her kin 3,000 miles across an ocean, and her husband's family was also there. She would have to feed her children and make her own tobacco crop. Though neighbors might help, heavy labor would be required of her if she had no servants, until—what admittedly was usually not difficult—she acquired a new husband.

In this situation dying husbands were understandably anxious about the welfare of their families. Their wills reflected their feelings and tell something of how they regarded their wives. In St. Mary's and Charles counties during the seventeenth century, little more than one-quarter of the men left their widows with no more than the dower the law required—one-third of his land for her life, plus outright ownership of one-third of his personal property. If there were no children, a man almost always left his widow his whole estate. Otherwise there were a variety of arrangements.

During the 1660s, when testators begin to appear in quantity, nearly a fifth of the men who had children left all to their wives, trusting them to see that the children received fair portions. Thus in 1663 John Shircliffe willed his whole estate to his wife "towards the maintenance of herself and my children into whose tender care I do Commend them Desireing to see them brought up in the fear of God and the Catholick Religion and Chargeing them to be Dutiful and obedient to her." As the century progressed, husbands tended instead to give the wife all or a major part of the estate for her life, and to designate how it should be distributed after her death. Either way, the husband put great trust in his widow, considering that he knew she was bound to remarry. Only a handful of men left estates to their wives only for their term of widowhood or until the children came of age. When a man did not leave his wife a life estate, he often gave her land outright or more than her dower third of his movable property. Such bequests were at the expense of his children and showed his concern that his widow should have a maintenance which young children could not supply.

A husband usually made his wife his executor and thus responsible for paying his debts and preserving the estate. Only 11 percent deprived their wives of such powers. In many instances, however, men also appointed overseers to assist their wives and to see that their children were not abused or their property embezzled. Danger lay in the fact that a second husband acquired control of all his wife's property, including her life estate in the property of his predecessor. Over half of the husbands who died in the 1650s and 1660s appointed overseers to ensure that their wills were followed. Some trusted to the overseers' "Care and good Conscience for the good of my widow and fatherless children." Others more explicitly made overseers responsible for seeing that "my said child . . . and the other [expected child] (when pleases God to send it) may have their right Proportion of my Said Estate and that the said Children may be bred up Chiefly in the fear of God." A few men—but remarkably few—authorized overseers to remove children from households of stepfathers who abused them or wasted their property. On the whole, the absence of such provisions for the protection of the children points to the husband's overriding concern for the welfare of his widow and to his confidence in her management, regardless of the certainty of her remarriage. Evidently, in the politics of family life women enjoyed great respect. . . .

Remarriage was the usual and often the immediate solution for a woman who had lost her husband. The shortage of women made any woman eligible to marry again, and the difficulties of raising a family while running a plantation must have made remarriage necessary for widows who had no son old enough to make tobacco. One indication of the high incidence of remarriage is the fact that there were only sixty women, almost all of them widows, among the 1,735 people who left probate inventories in four southern Maryland counties over the second half of the century. Most other women must have died while married and therefore legally without property to put through probate.

One result of remarriage was the development of complex family structures. Men found themselves responsible for stepchildren as well as their own offspring, and children acquired half-sisters and half-brothers. Sometimes a woman married a second husband who himself had been previously married, and both brought children of former spouses to the new marriage. They then produced children of their own. The possibilities for conflict over the upbringing of children are evident, and crowded living conditions, found even in the households of the wealthy, must have added to family tensions. Luckily, the children of the family very often had the same mother. In Charles County, at least, widows took new husbands three times more often than widowers took new wives. The role of the mother in managing the relationships of half-brothers and half-sisters or stepfathers and stepchildren must have been critical to family harmony.

Early death in this immigrant population thus had broad effects on

Maryland society in the seventeenth century. It produced what we might call a pattern of serial polyandry, which enabled more men to marry and to father families than the sex ratios otherwise would have permitted. It produced thousands of orphaned children who had no kin to maintain them or preserve their property, and thus gave rise to an institution almost unknown in England, the orphans' court, which was charged with their protection. And early death, by creating families in which the mother was the unifying element, may have increased her authority within the household.

When the immigrant woman married her first husband, there was usually no property settlement involved, since she was unlikely to have any dowry. But her remarriage was another matter. At the very least, she owned or had a life interest in a third of her former husband's estate. She needed also to think of her children's interests. If she remarried, she would lose control of the property. Consequently, property settlements occasionally appear in the seventeenth-century court records between widows and their future husbands. Sometimes she and her intended signed an agreement whereby he relinquished his rights to the use of her children's portions. Sometimes he deeded to her property which she could dispose of at her pleasure. Whether any of these agreements or gifts would have survived a test in court is unknown. We have not yet found any challenged. Generally speaking, the formal marriage settlements of English law, which bypassed the legal difficulties of the married woman's inability to make a contract with her husband, were not adopted by immigrants, most of whom probably came from levels of English society that did not use these legal formalities.

The wife's dower rights in her husband's estate were a recognition of her role in contributing to his prosperity, whether by the property she had brought to the marriage or by the labor she performed in his household. A woman newly freed from servitude would not bring property, but the benefits of her labor would be great. A man not yet prosperous enough to own a servant might need his wife's help in the fields as well as in the house, especially if he were paying rent or still paying for land. Moreover, food preparation was so time-consuming that even if she worked only at household duties, she saved him time he needed for making tobacco and corn. The corn, for example, had to be pounded in the mortar or ground in a handmill before it could be used to make bread, for there were very few water mills in seventeenth-century Maryland. The wife probably raised vegetables in a kitchen garden; she also milked the cows and made butter and cheese, which might produce a salable surplus. She washed the clothes, and made them if she had the skill. When there were servants to do field work, the wife undoubtedly spent her time entirely in such household tasks. A contract of 1681 expressed such a division of labor. Nicholas Maniere agreed to live on a plantation with his wife and child and a servant. Nicholas and the servant were to work the land; his wife was to "Dresse the Victualls milk the Cowes wash for the servants and Doe allthings necessary for a woman to doe upon the s[ai]d plantation." . . .

If the demography of Maryland produced the effects here described, such effects should also be evident elsewhere in the Chesapeake. The four characteristics of the seventeenth-century Maryland population—immigrant predominance, early death, late marriage, and sexual imbalance—are to be found everywhere in the region, at least at first. The timing of the disappearance of these peculiarities may have varied from place to place, depending on date of settlement or rapidity of development, but the effect of their existence upon the experience of women should be clear. Should research in other areas of the Chesapeake fail to find women enjoying the status they achieved on the lower Western Shore of Maryland, then our arguments would have to be revised.

Work is also needed that will enable historians to compare conditions in Maryland with those in other colonies. Richard S. Dunn's study of the British West Indies also shows demographic disruption. When the status of wives is studied, it should prove similar to that of Maryland women. In contrast were demographic conditions in New England, where immigrants came in family groups, major immigration had ceased by the mid-seventeenth century, sex ratios balanced early, and mortality was low. Under these conditions, demographic disruption must have been both less severe and less prolonged. If New England women achieved status similar to that suggested for women in the Chesapeake, that fact will have to be explained. The dynamics might prove to have been different; or a dynamic we have not identified, common to both areas, might turn out to have been the primary engine of change. And, if women in England shared the status—which we doubt—conditions in the New World may have had secondary importance. The Maryland data establish persuasive grounds for a hypothesis, but the evidence is not all in.

New England and the Chesapeake Compared

MARY BETH NORTON

The England that the seventeenth-century migrants left behind was undergoing dramatic changes, many of which stemmed from a rapid rise in population that began early in the sixteenth century. As the population grew, the economy altered, social stratification increased, and customary modes of political behavior developed into new forms. England's ruling elites saw chaos everywhere, and they became obsessed with the problem of maintaining order in the evidently anarchic society around them. The large-scale migration of English people to America can itself be taken as an indication of the extent of these changes, for never before in the century-old history of European expansion had more than a small number of male adventurers chosen to emigrate to the New World. Within the overall context of change new forms of familial and religious organization were especially important for women. In late sixteenth- and early seventeenth-century England, Law-

Adapted from Mary Beth Norton, "The Evolution of White Women's Experience in Early America," *American Historical Review*, LXXXIX (June 1984), 595–601.

rence Stone has argued, patriarchal, nuclear family structures had recently become dominant, replacing an older, open-lineage system characterized by powerful lineal and collateral kin relationships. English families of the day increasingly turned inward on themselves, cutting the ties that had previously bound them to extended kin. In such nuclear households, power gravitated to the husband and father: he dominated his wife, children, and other dependents without fear of interference from kin or community. A wife was expected to defer to her husband, and he in turn expected to direct the lives of all his dependents—spouse, children, and servants alike. Reformation (and especially Puritan) theology, which was aggressively masculine in its orientation, reinforced this secular development. The rejection of Roman Catholicism included the abolition of the cult of the Virgin Mary and the removal of the convent option from women's lives. In addition, Puritanism stressed the religious role of the paterfamilias; he was responsible for the spiritual well-being of all members of his household, and they were consequently expected to defer to him in religious as well as secular matters.

The family pattern most familiar to the migrants, then, was nuclear, with authority ideally—if not always in reality—concentrated in the hands of the father. The conditions of migration further reinforced such tendencies by physically severing individuals and families from their wider English kin connections. In America, migrants were thrown on their own resources: the colonies lacked the web of traditional communal institutions that still governed many aspects of life in England, even though those institutions were beginning to lose much of their force. By migrating to America the colonists accelerated and intensified the effects on their own lives of the changes already evident in their homeland. Moreover, given their origins, they were especially concerned about the maintenance of social order. In the absence of other institutions, the family took on greater relative importance and had to bear heavier social responsibilities. Therefore, even more than in England, the family became the central focus of society.

The adult woman occupied a clearly defined place in the seventeenth-century family—so much so that she was seen more as part of that system and less as an autonomous person. Indeed, her authority derived from her role as mistress of the household. She directed the household's daily affairs (under her husband's supervision, of course), and in his absence she could act on his behalf. Thus, although his role and hers were defined in mutually exclusive terms, they involved some overlap of function. She was positioned below her husband in the hierarchy of sex, but above her children in the hierarchy of age, and considerably above her indentured servants, who lacked the essential attribute of freedom. The delineation of the female role was remarkably consistent throughout seventeenth-century Anglo-America. Robert V. Wells has perceptively suggested that such role stability may well have been a reaction to the uncertainties of life in the early colonies; when particular persons might not survive long enough to develop mutually understood relationships, clarity of role definition could help guide individual behavior.

Although gender-role expectations remained the same whatever the female migrants' American destination, the circumstances of their lives in the colonies varied considerably according to geography. Vastly different patterns of settlement developed in New England and the Chesapeake, defining the outer limits of demographic possibility. The early seventeenth-century colonies identified the range of variation along the spectrum; the experiences of later migrants to Britain's North American possessions fell somewhere between the two extremes. Thus, it is important to define those extremes with precision and to understand the way each affected the colonists' attempts to re-create English family forms in America.

In the Chesapeake—the first region to be colonized—environmental and economic factors conspired to prevent patriarchal family practices (as opposed to ideals) from taking root, at least during the first three-quarters of the century. Devastatingly high mortality rates and a heavily imbalanced sex ratio—the results, respectively, of a high-risk disease environment and the almost exclusive importation of young male laborers to cultivate tobacco—together produced a society with anomalous characteristics. High mortality rates for adults and children alike made specific families short-lived and ensured that membership in them changed repeatedly. Under such conditions, it was difficult for fathers to exercise much sustained control over their families. Members of the migrant generation—those who came from England primarily as isolated individuals—obviously governed their lives without paternal interference, and the members of the first American-born generations, often orphaned at an early age, may also have been largely free to determine their own futures. The relative lack of women meant that few men could marry at any one time but that widows remarried quickly, often to previously unmarried men, thus allowing more men to find spouses than would otherwise have been possible. In addition, native-born Chesapeake women were more likely to marry, and to do so at younger ages, than were English women. (Indeed, they married so young that a large age differential between themselves and their husbands was common.) More of them also experienced widowhood, and again at younger ages. Since such young widows accordingly were normally left with minor children to raise, their husbands bequeathed them greater proportions of their estates than was the case elsewhere in Anglo-America. These demographic circumstances led Maryland to grant widows more legal independence than any other colony yet investigated. And both Chesapeake colonies allowed widows to challenge their husbands' wills if the property they inherited was less than a stated minimum.

If the Chesapeake constitutes one demographic extreme, New England constitutes the other. There, the full impact of English patriarchal ideas and practices can be seen, for the early settlements in the Northeast, where the sex ratio was more nearly balanced, experienced low mortality and high nuptiality rates. Like their Chesapeake contemporaries, New England women were more likely to marry, and to marry at younger ages, than were English women of the day. But, since New England proved to be a healthy environment, marriages in the Northern colonies lasted longer and produced more children than those in the South. New England women were likely to be widowed only late in life and were unlikely to remarry frequently. In other words, they spent a longer part of their lives within a single patriarchal household than did their counterparts elsewhere in the English-speaking world. Indeed, the stability of their marital lives is remarkable, especially in contrast to their contemporaries in England—who married later—or the Chesapeake—who were widowed sooner. New England fathers arranged their daughters' marriages, and New England husbands expected to dominate their wives. Marylynn Salmon's investigation shows that civil law in the Northern colonies gave women less independence, in marriage and in widowhood, than did law in the Chesapeake colonies—or even in England. The civil code of the New England colonies embodied a concept of marital unity striking in its expression of the patriarchal ideal that women's private interests had to be subordinated to the greater familial whole.

Major variations in religion reinforced these demographic differences between the Chesapeake and New England. With the exception of a few Catholic migrants to early Maryland, all English settlers in America were Protestants. But the contrast between Southern and Northern religious practices was marked. Since transferring a vigorous Anglican parish structure to the seventeenth-century Chesapeake proved impossible, religion in Maryland and Virginia remained more a matter of personal piety than a constant institutional presence. In New England, however, Puritan church and state were closely entwined; each supported the other, and determining which was the superior authority (especially in the early years) was often difficult. Thus, New England women had to reckon with two strong institutions—the Puritan church and the stable patriarchal family—that Chesapeake women did not. The effects of these religious differences have not been explored as fully as those resulting from demography, but the case of Anne Hutchinson suggests that Puritanism in its formative stages offered women opportunities for religious leadership obviously denied Chesapeake residents with no comparable institutions. Although Puritan theology reinforced secular patriarchal tendencies, it also emphasized the spiritual equality of all souls before God and the ability of all believers (male or female) to interpret the scriptures. Hutchinson took advantage of the ambiguities in Puritan teachings and, for a time, established herself as one of the most powerful residents of Massachusetts Bay. Whether she saw herself as a spokeswoman for other females is unclear, but she certainly did not believe that her sex disqualified her from engaging in theological speculation or from influencing others in spiritual matters. The severity of both church and state reaction against her indicates the magnitude of the threat she posed to social order in the colony. Indeed, that threat was three-fold: political, for she threatened to divide Massachusetts Bay at a time when it was under attack by the Pequot; theological, for she challenged some of the basic tenets of Puritanism; and familial, for as a woman she violated patriarchal norms of behavior. Hutchinson was unique, yet early New England records yield many other lesser examples of female religious activism. And, as Laurel Ulrich has pointed out, when access to church membership is restricted and confers special status, considerable significance necessarily derives from women's ability to attain that status on an equal basis with men.

It is easier to describe the demographic and religious contrasts between New England and the Chesapeake than to assess their meaning for women. If the criteria [are the] ability to select marital partners and relative economic independence, then Chesapeake women were clearly better off. That is indeed the position taken by Lois Green Carr and Lorena S. Walsh, the two historians who have worked most directly on the topic. But if the criteria are instead the benefits of marital stability, better health, a smaller age differential between husband and wife, and possibilities for religious expression, New England women seem to have had the preferable lifestyle, at least in the first half-century of settlement. Some suggestive evidence from architectural remains and estate inventories appears to support the latter interpretation. If we assume that women were centrally concerned with the nature of their domestic environment and, therefore, that the shape and composition of that environment can reveal the extent of women's power in the family by measuring their impact on familial spending decisions, then seventeenth-century New England homes experienced considerably greater female influence than those in the Chesapeake. The houses themselves were better built and more spacious; the domestic work spaces were more efficiently organized; and families more quickly acquired a wider range of domestic amenities (like table linen). Since both methods of measuring seventeenth-century women's power—through men's wills and through material culture—are essentially inferential, the contradiction between the two cannot now be resolved.

The inquiry as to who was better off— New Englanders or Chesapeake residents—is misdirected, for it overlooks the underlying unities of women's lives in both regions. Tempting as it is to forget the similarities, which were many, and stress the differences, the important characteristic of colonial women's lives was alike, whatever the region: an adult woman's status was everywhere determined by her marital state. In the Chesapeake no less than in New England, a woman was seen chiefly as an adjunct of her husband. Her social standing depended on her husband's position in the colonial hierarchy; her primary role in family and community was as mistress of his household. Granted, the same was true of her English contemporaries. But two major differences separated the women of the Old World from those of the New. First, because of later marriage and longer widowhood, seventeenth-century English women most likely earned wages and lived independently of a paternal or marital household for a period of time at least as long as the terms of their marriages. In other words, they spent as much of their adult lives outside a marital household as inside one. Few American women had similar experiences: demographic constraints precluded long-term, independent lives in the colonies. Second, English women actively engaged in a market economy, exchanging goods and services with neighbors and working in shops alongside their husbands and fathers. The economic life of seventeenth-century English households, unlike that of colonial households, was highly interdependent.

Although some of the same patterns reappeared in America, they did so on a much more limited scale. The small colonial population was scattered over a wide geographic area, and so farmers and their wives had to strive for greater self-sufficiency than did the English. The American economy offered women few opportunities to work for wages, even had they had the time and inclination. Most of women's time was probably occupied with subsistence activities. The overall pattern is unmistakable: in the colonies, women's productive work took place primarily within the confines of their own households; in England, the reverse may well have been true. Economic conditions thus reinforced social trends that tended to make all American women more dependent on the family for the definition of their lives and roles than were their English counterparts. Consequently, the significance of the household roles of colonial women was increased. That was true in both New England and the Chesapeake, and the similarity may well have been far more important as a crucial determinant of the shape of their lives than varying demographic or religious experiences. It remains to be seen whether households in one of the two regions can be clearly identified as more dominated by patriarchal power than those in the other.

✤ FURTHER READING

Ben Barker-Benfield, "Anne Hutchinson and the Puritan Attitude toward Women," *Feminist Studies,* I (1972), 65–96

John P. Demos, *A Little Commonwealth: Family Life in Plymouth Colony* (1970)

Mary Maples Dunn, "Saints and Sisters: Congregational and Quaker Women in the Early Colonial Period," *American Quarterly,* XXX (1978), 582–601

David Galenson, *White Servitude in Colonial America* (1981)

Philip Greven, *The Protestant Temperament: Patterns of Religious Experience, Child-Rearing, and the Self in Early America* (1977)

N. E. H. Hull, *Female Felons: Women and Serious Crime in Colonial Massachusetts* (1987)

Lyle Koehler, "The Case of the American Jezebels: Anne Hutchinson and Female Agitation during the Years of Antinomian Turmoil, 1636–1640," *William and Mary Quarterly,* 3d ser., XXXI (1974), 55–78

Edmund S. Morgan, *The Puritan Family* (1966)

Mary Beth Norton, "Gender and Defamation in Seventeenth-Century Maryland," *William and Mary Quarterly,* 3d ser., XLIV (1987), 1–39

Kim Lacy Rogers, "Relicts of the New World: Conditions of Widowhood in Seventeenth-Century New England," in Mary Kelley, ed., *Woman's Being, Woman's Place* (1979)

Darrett and Anita Rutman, *A Place in Time: Middlesex County, Virginia, 1650–1750* (1984)

Marylynn Salmon, *Women and the Law of Property in Early America* (1986)

Linda Speth, "More than her 'Thirds': Wives and Widows in Colonial Virginia," *Women and History,* no. 4 (1982), 5–41

Julia Cherry Spruill, *Women's Life and Work in the Southern Colonies* (1938)

Thad W. Tate and David Ammerman, eds., *The Chesapeake in the Seventeenth Century* (1979)

Roger Thompson, *Women in Stuart England and America* (1974)

———, *Sex in Middlesex* (1986)

Laurel Thatcher Ulrich, *Good Wives: Image and Reality in the Lives of Women in Northern New England, 1650–1750* (1982)

CHAPTER
3

Witchcraft in

Seventeenth-Century America

The Salem witchcraft crisis of 1692–1693, in which a small number of adolescent girls and young women accused hundreds of older women (and a few men) of having bewitched them, has fascinated Americans ever since. It has provided material for innumerable books, plays, movies, and television productions. To twentieth-century Americans, the belief in witchcraft in the seventeenth-century colonies is difficult to explain or understand; perhaps that is why the Salem episode has attracted so much attention. For those interested in studying women's experiences, of course, witchcraft incidents are particularly intriguing. The vast majority of suspected witches were female, and so, too, were many of their accusers. Although colonial women rarely played a role on the public stage, in witchcraft cases they were the primary actors. What accounts for their prominence under these peculiar circumstances?

To answer that question, the Salem crisis must be placed into its proper historical and cultural context. People in the early modern world believed in witchcraft because it offered a rationale for events that otherwise seemed random and unfathomable. In the absence of modern scientific knowledge about such natural phenomena as storms and diseases, and clear explanations for accidents of various sorts, the evil actions of a witch could provide a ready answer to a person or community inquiring about the causes of a disaster.

Therefore, witchcraft accusations—and some large-scale ''witch hunts''—were not uncommon in Europe between the early fourteenth and late seventeenth centuries (1300 to 1700). In short, the immigrants to the colonies came from a culture in which belief in witchcraft was widespread and in which accusations could result in formal prosecutions and executions. Recent research has demonstrated that the Salem incident, though the largest and most important witch hunt in New England, was just one of a number of such episodes in the American colonies.

But why were witches women? Admittedly, historians have not yet answered that question entirely satisfactorily. Certain observations can be made: women gave birth to new life and seemed to have the potential to take life away. In Western culture, women were seen as less rational than men, more linked to the ''natural''

*world, in which magic held sway. Men, who dominated European society, defined
the characteristics of a "proper woman," who was submissive and accepted a subordinate position. The stereotypical witch, usually described as an aggressive and
threatening older woman, represented the antithesis of that image. These broad
categories need further refinement, and historians are currently looking closely at
the women who were accused of practicing witchcraft in order to identify the crucial
characteristics that set them apart from their contemporaries and made them a
target for accusations.*

❖ D O C U M E N T S

In 1654, in a little-known incident, an old woman was executed as a witch on a ship
en route to Maryland. She was killed because the sailors and some of the passengers believed that a storm that had afflicted them for weeks had been caused by a
malevolent power. The first two documents give three different accounts of that
incident: The first is Father Francis Fitzherbert's account of the voyage, which
mentions the incident but allows for the possibility that the old woman was not
guilty. In the second selection, the testimonies of two witnesses betray confusion
about how to take responsibility for the situation while on board the ship. At about
the same time, Mistress Elizabeth Godman, a contentious woman who lived in the
New Haven Colony, was likewise suspected of witchcraft. However, unlike the
woman executed at sea, the legal system afforded her some protection against her
accusers. The second group of documents are the records of a slander suit she filed
against a number of persons in 1653 and the proceedings at her 1655 trial for witchcraft. These accounts reveal the personal characteristics and behaviors common to
many of the women accused of practicing witchcraft in seventeenth-century New
England.

Execution of a Witch at Sea, 1654

Account of Father Francis Fitzherbert's Voyage to Maryland

Four ships sailed together from England, which a fearful storm overtook,
when carried beyond the Western Isles, and the ship in which the Father was
carried, the violent waves so shattered, that, springing a leak by the continued violence of the sea, it almost filled its hold. But in carrying away and
exhausting the water, the men, four at a time, not only of the ship's crew but
of the passengers, every one in his turn, sweated at the great pump in
ceaseless labor, day and night.

Wherefore, having changed their course, their intention was to make sail
towards the island, which the English call Barbados; but it could be accomplished by no art, by no labor; then the design was, having abandoned the
ship and its freight, to commit themselves to the long boat. But the sea,
swelling with adverse winds, and the huge mountainous waves, forbade.
Many a form of death presenting itself to the minds of all, the habit of terror,
now grown familiar, had almost excluded the fear of death. The tempest

lasted two months in all, whence the opinion arose, that it was not raised by the violence of the sea or atmosphere, but was occasioned by the malevolence of witches. Forthwith they seize a little old woman suspected of sorcery; and after examining her with the strictest scrutiny, guilty or not guilty, they slay her, suspected of this very heinous sin. The corpse, and whatever belonged to her, they cast into the sea. But the winds did not thus remit their violence, or the raging sea its threatenings. To the troubles of the storm, sickness was added, which having spread to almost every person, carried off not a few. Nevertheless, the Father remained untouched by all the contagion, and unharmed, except that in working and exercising at the pump too laboriously, he contracted a slight fever of a few days' continuance. Having passed through multiplied dangers, at length, by the favor of God, the ship, contrary to the expectation of all, reached the port of Maryland.

The Testimonies of Two Witnesses

The Deposition of mr Henry Corbyn of London Merchant aged about 25 years, Sworne and Examined in the Province of Maryland before the Governour & Councell there (whose Names are hereunto Subscribed) the 23ᵗʰ day of June Anno Domini 1654. Saith

That at Sea upon his this Deponents Voyage hither in the Ship called the Charity of London mʳ John Bosworth being Master and about a fortnight or three weeks before the Said Ships arrivall in this Province of Maryland, or before A Rumour amongst the Seamen was very frequent, that one Mary Lee then aboard the Said Ship was a witch, the Said Seamen Confidently affirming the Same upon her own deportment and discourse, and then more Earnestly then before Importuned the Said Master that a tryall might be had of her which he the Said Master, mʳ Bosworth refused, but resolved (as he Expressed to put her ashore upon the Barmudoes) but Cross winds prevented and the Ship grew daily more Leaky almost to desparation and the Chiefe Seamen often declared their Resolution of Leaving her if an opportunity offerred it Self which aforesaid Reasons put the Master upon a Consultation with mʳ Chipsham and this Deponent, and it was thought fitt, Considering our Said Condition to Satisfie the Seamen in a way of trying her according to the Usuall Custome in that kind whether She were a witch or Not and Endeavoured by way of delay to have the Commanders of other Ships aboard but Stormy weather prevented, In the Interime two of the Seamen apprehended her without order and Searched her and found Some Signall or Marke of a witch upon her, and then calling the Master mʳ Chipsham and this Deponent with others to See it afterwards made her fast to the Capstall betwixt decks, And in the Morning the Signall was Shrunk into her body for the Most part, And an Examination was thereupon importuned by the Seamen which this Deponent was desired to take whereupon She confessed as by her Confession appeareth, And upon that the Seamen Importuned the Said Master to put her to Death which as it Seemed he was unwilling to doe, and went into his Cabbinn, but being more Vehemently pressed to it, he tould them they might doe what they would and went into his Cabbinn, and Sometime before they were about that Action he desired this depon[t] to acquaint them that they Should doe no more then what they Should Justifie which they Said they would doe by laying all their hands in generall to the Execution of her, All which herein before Expressed or the Same in Effect this Depon[t] averreth upon his oath to be true, And further Sayth not

William Stone	Sworne before us the	Henry Corbyne
Tho: Hatton	day and year above written	
Job Chandler		

The Deposition of ffrancis Darby Gent Aged about 39 yeares Sworne and Examined in the Province of Maryland before the Governour and Councell there whose Names are hereunto Subscribed the 23 day of June Anno Domini 1654. Saith

That at Sea upon the Voyage hither about a fortnight or three weeks before the Arrivall of the Ship called the Charity of London in this Province of Maryland, whereof m[r] John Bosworth was then Master and upon the Same day that one Mary Lee was put to Death aboard the Said Ship as a witch he the Said m[r] Bosworth Seeing him this Deponent backward to Assist in the Examination of her asked this Depon[t] why? and tould him that he was perplext about the busieness Seeing he did not know how he might doe it by the Law of England afterwards this deponent being present in the Round house heard the Said m[r] Bosworth give Order that nothing Should be done concerning the Said Mary Lee without Speaking first with him, and after She was put to Death or Executed to the best of this Deponents remembrance he Said he knew nothing of it, And this Deponent Saith that the Said Bosworth was in the inner room of the Roundhouse, he this deponent being in the next room at the time they treated about the busieness And this Depon[t] could not perceive any thing either by word or Deed whereby he gave order for her Execution or putting to Death and after this he Commanded they Should doe Nothing without his Order and alsoe after the Execution, expressed he knew not of it for that this Deponent hearing these words (She is dead) ran out and asked who was dead, and it was replyed the witch then this Deponent Entred the next Room and Said they have hanged her and he the Said Bosworth thereupon as it were Speaking with trouble in a high Voyce replyed he knew not of it All which herein before Expressed or the Same in Effect this Deponent averreth upon his oath to be true, And further Sayth not.

Sworne before us the day and   Francis Darby
Yare abovewritten
    William Stone
    Tho: Hatton
    Job Chandler

The Trials of a Witch

Elizabeth Godman *v.* Goodwife Larremore *et al.*, 1653

The Examination of Elizabeth Godman, May 21ᵗʰ, 1653

Elizabeth Godman made complainte of Mʳ. Goodyeare, Mʳⁱˢ. Goodyeare, Mʳ. Hooke, Mʳⁱˢ. Hooke, Mʳⁱˢ. Bishop, Mʳⁱˢ. Atwater, Hanah & Elizabeth Lamberton, and Mary Miles, Mʳⁱˢ. Atwaters maide, that they have suspected her for a witch; she was now asked what she had against Mʳ. Hooke and Mʳⁱˢ. Hooke; she said she heard they had something against her aboute their soone. Mʳ. Hooke said hee was not wᵗhout feares, and hee had reasons for it; first he said it wrought suspition in his minde because shee was shut out at Mʳ. Atwaters upon suspition, and hee was troubled in his sleepe aboute witches when his boye, was sicke, wᶜh was in a vercy strang manner, and hee looked upon her as a mallitious one, and prepared to that mischeife, and she would be often speaking aboute witches and rather justifye them then condemne them; she said why doe they provoake them, why doe they not let them come into the church. Another time she was speaking of witches wᵗhout any occasion given her, and said if they accused her for a witch she would have them to the governor, she would trounce them. . . .

Mʳ. Hooke further said, that he hath heard that they that are adicted that way would hardly be kept away from yᵉ houses where they doe mischeife, and so it was wᵗh her when his boy was sicke, she would not be kept away from him, nor gott away when she was there, and one time Mʳⁱˢ. Hooke bid her goe away, and thrust her from yᵉ boye, but she turned againe and said she would looke on him. Mʳⁱˢ. Goodyeare said that one time she questioncd wᵗh Elizabeth Godman aboute yᵉ boycs sickness, and said what thinke you of him, is he not strangly handled, she replyed, what, doe you thinke hee is bewitched; Mʳⁱˢ. Goodyeare said nay I will keepe my thoughts to myselfe, but in time God will discover. . . .

Mʳ. Hooke further said, that when Mʳ. Bishop was married, Mʳⁱˢ. Godman came to his house much troubled, so as he thought it might be from some affection to him, and he asked her, she said yes; now it is suspitious that so soone as they were contracted Mʳⁱˢ Byshop fell into verey strang fitts wᶜh hath continewed at times ever since, and much suspition there is that she hath bine the cause of the loss of Mʳⁱˢ. Byshops children, for she could tell when Mʳⁱˢ. Bishop was to be brought to bedd, and hath given out that she kills her chilldren wᵗh longing, because she longs for every thing she sees, wᶜh Mʳⁱˢ. Bishop denies. . . .

The 24ᵗʰ of May, 1653

Mʳⁱˢ. Godman being examined, (Mʳ. Davenport being present,) she was asked why she said Mʳⁱˢ. Bishop longed allmost for every thing she see, and when she could not have it, that was the cause of her fainting fitts and yᵉ loss of her chilldren; she said she heard something of Mʳⁱˢ. Hooke to that purpose, that she longed for pease, but M^ris. Hooke being sent for denyed that ever she told her so, and Jane Hooke being present said M^ris. Godman told her that M^ris. Bishop was much given to longing and that was the reason she lost her chilldren, and Hanah Lamberton said M^ris. Godman told her so also, and M^ris. Bishop said another woman in ye towne told her that she had heard M^ris. Godman say as much, so that she could not denye it; she was told she hath much inquired after the time of M^ris. Bishops delivery of her chilldren, and would speake of it so as M^ris. Goodyeare and her daughters marveled how she could know, and Hanah Lamberton one time told her mother that M^ris. Godman kept her sisters count; she was asked the reason of this and of her saying M^ris. Bishop was so given to longing as it was a meanes to lose her chilldren when it was not so; she said she could give no reason, then she was told it was a high slander upon M^ris. Bishop, she said she can say nothing but must lye under it. . . .

June 16, 1653

Goodwife Thorp complained that M^ris. Godman came to her house and asked to buy some chickens, she said she had none to sell, M^ris. Godman said will you give them all, so she went away, and she thought then that if this woman was naught as folkes suspect, may be she will smite my chickens, and quickly after one chicken dyed, and she remembred she had heard if they were bewitched they would consume w^thin, and she opened it and it was consumed in ye gisard to water & wormes, and divers others of them droped, and now they are missing and it is likely dead, and she never saw either hen or chicken that was so consumed w^thin wth wormes. M^ris. Godman said goodwife Tichenor had a whole brood so, and M^ris. Hooke had some so, but for M^ris. Hookes it was contradicted presently. This goodwife Thorp thought good to declare that it may be considered wth other things.

Court of Magistrates, New Haven, August 4, 1653

M^ris. Elizabeth Godman accused goodwife Larremore that one time when she saw her come in at goodman Whitnels she said so soone as she saw her she thought of a witch. Goodwife Larremore said that one time she had spoken to that purpose at M^r. Hookes, and her ground was because M^r. Davenport aboute that time had occasion in his ministry to speake of witches, and showed that a froward discontented frame of spirit was a subject fitt for ye Devill to worke upon in that way, and she looked upon M^rs. Godman to be of such a frame of spirit, but for saying so at goodman Whitnels she denyes it. M^ris. Godman said, goodman Whitnels maid can testify it. The maid was sent, and when she came she said she heard M^ris. Godman and goodwife Larremore a talking, and she thinkes she heard goodwife Larremore say she thought of a witch in ye Bay when she see M^ris. Godman. Goodwife Larremore further said that M^ris. Godman had her before the governor for this, and the governor asked her if she thought M^rs. Godman was a witch, and she answered no.

M^{ris}. Godman was told she hath warned to the court divers psons, viz^d: M^r. Goodyeare, M^{ris}. Goodyeare, M^r. Hooke, M^{ris}. Hooke, M^{ris}. Atwater, Hanah & Elizabeth Lamberton, goodwife Larremore, goodwife Thorpe, &c., and was asked what she hath to charge them w^th, she said they had given out speeches that made folkes thinke she was a witch, and first she charged M^{ris}. Atwater to be ye cause of all, and to cleere things desired a wrighting might be read wch was taken in way of examination before ye magistrate, (and is hereafter entred,) wherein sundrie things concerning M^{ris}. Atwater is specifyed wch were now more fully spoken to, and she further said that M^{ris}. Atwater had said that she thought she was a witch and that Hobbamocke [the devil] was her husband, but could prove nothing, though she was told that she was beforehand warned to prepare her witnesses ready, wch she hath not done, if she have any. After sundrie of the passages in ye wrighting were read, she was asked if these things did not give just ground of suspition to all that heard them that she was a witch. She confessed they did, but said if she spake such things as is in M^r. Hookes relation she was not herselfe. She was told she need not say, if she spake them, for she did at the governo^rs before many witnesses confess them all as her words, though she made the same excuse that she was not in a right minde; but M^{ris}. Hooke now testifyed she was in a sober frame and spake in a diliberate way, as ordinarily she is at other times. Beside what is in the paper, M^{ris}. Godman was remembred of a passage spoken of at the governo^rs aboute M^r. Goodyeares falling into a swonding fitt after hee had spoken something one night in the exposition of a chapter, wch she (being present) liked not but said it was against her, and as soone as M^r. Goodyeare had done duties she flung out of the roome in a discontented way and cast a fierce looke upon M^r. Goodyeare as she went out, and imediately M^r. Goodyeare (though well before) fell into a swond, and beside her notorious lying in this buisnes, for being asked how she came to know this, she said she was present, yet M^r. Goodyeare, M^{ris}. Goodyeare, Hanah and Elizabeth Lamberton all affirme she was not in ye roome but gone up into the chamber.

After the agitation of these things the court declared to M^{ris}. Godman, as their judgment and sentence in this case, that she hath unjustly called heither the severall persons before named, being she can prove nothing against them, and that her cariage doth justly render her suspitious of witchcraft, wch she herselfe in so many words confesseth, therefore the court wisheth her to looke to her carriage hereafter, for if further proofe come, these passages will not be forgotten, and therefore gave her charge not to goe in an offensive way to folkes houses in a rayling manner as it seemes she hath done, but that she keepe her place and medle wth her owne buisnes.

New Haven *v.* Elizabeth Godman, *1655*

New Haven Town Court, August 7, 1655

Elizabeth Godman was called before the Court, and told that she lies under suspition for witchcraft, as she knowes, the grounds of which were examined in a former Court, and by herselfe confessed to be just grounds of suspition, wch passages were now read, and to these some more are since added, wch are now to be declared: . . .

Goodwife Thorpe informed the Court that concerning something aboute chickens she had formerly declared, wch was now read, after wch she one time had some speech wth M^{ris} Evance aboute this woman, and through the weakness of her faith she began to doubt that may be she would hurt her cowes, and that day one of her cowes fell sick in the herd, so as the keeper said he thought she would have dyed, but at night when she came into the yard was well and continewed so, but would never give milk nor bring calfe after that; therfore they bought another cow, that they might have some breed, but that cast calfe also; after that they gott another, and she continewed well aboute a fortnight, but then began to pine away and would give no milke and would sweat so as she would be all of a water wher-ever she lay, wthout or wthin; then she thought ther was some thing more then ordinary in it, and could not but thinke that she was bewitched. . . . Aboute a weeke after, she went by Mr Goodyeares, and there was Eliza: Godman pulling cherries in ye streete; she said, how doth Goody Thorpe? I am behoulden to Goody Thorpe above all the weomen in the Towne: she would have had me to the gallowes for a few chickens; and gnashed and grinned wth her teeth in a strang manner, wch she confesseth was true, but owned nothing aboute ye cowes. . . .

Allen Ball informed the Court that one time Eliza: Godman came to his house and asked his wife for some butter-milke; she refused, and bid her be gone, she cared not for her company: she replyed, what, you will save it for your piggs, but it will doe them no good; and after this his piggs all but one dyed, one after another, but the cause he knowes not. . . .

These things being declared, the Court told Elizabeth Godman that they have considered them wth her former miscariages, and see cause to Order that she be committed to prison, ther to abide the Courts pleasure, but because the matter is of weight, and the crime whereof she is suspected capitall, therefore she is to answer it at the Court of Magistrats in October next.

Court of Magistrates, New Haven, October 17, 1655

Elizabeth Godman was called before the court and told that upon grounds formerly declared, wch stand upon record, she by her owne confession remaines under suspition for witchcraft, and one more is now added, and that is, that one time this last summer, comeing to M^r. Hookes to beg some beare, was at first denyed, but after, she was offered some by his daughter which stood ready drawne, but she refused it and would have some newly drawne, wch she had, yet went away in a muttering discontented manner, and after this, that night, though the beare was good and fresh, yet the next morning was hott, soure and ill tasted, yea so hott as the barrell was warme w^thout side, and when they opened the bung it steemed forth; they brewed againe and it was so also, and so continewed foure or five times, one after another.

She brought divers persons to the court that they might say something to cleere her, and much time was spent in hearing them, but to litle purpose, the grounds of suspition remaining full as strong as before and she found full of lying, wherfore the court declared unto her that though the evidenc is not sufficient as yet to take away her life, yet the suspitions are cleere and many, wch she cannot by all the meanes she hath used, free herselfe from, therfore she must forbeare from goeing from house to house to give offenc, and cary it orderly in the family where she is, wch if she doe not, she will cause the court to comitt her to prison againe, & that she doe now presently upon her freedom give securitie for her good behaviour; and she did now before the court ingage fifty pound of her estate that is in M^r. Goodyeers hand, for her good behaviour, wch is further to be cleered next court, when M^r. Goodyeare is at home.

✤ *E S S A Y S*

Two recent books on witchcraft present sharply differing interpretations of the sorts of women most likely to be accused of that crime in seventeenth-century New England. The first essay is from the book by John Putnam Demos, a professor at Yale University, who is descended from the Putnam family of Salem, active accusers in the 1692–1693 crisis. Demos contends that witches were likely to be low-status widows with few or no children. The second selection, from the book by Carol Karlsen of the University of Michigan, agrees that witches were likely to be childless widows, but she puts a very different interpretation on their childlessness. Demos argues that a lack of children would make women relatively powerless and anomalous in a society in which five or six children were the norm. Karlsen, by contrast, focuses on the women's lack of sons, brothers, or other male relatives to inherit the family's lands. This, she argues, made such women potentially *powerful* and threatening in a society in which females were supposed to be subordinate to males and in which they did not usually own real estate. Thus these women were disproportionately represented among those accused of being witches.

The Poor and Powerless Witch

JOHN PUTNAM DEMOS

To investigate the witches as a biographical type is no easy task. With rare exceptions the record of their experience is scattered and fragmentary. Much of the surviving evidence derives from their various trial proceedings; in short, we can visualize them quite fully as *suspects,* but only here and there in other aspects of their lives. We lack, most especially, a chance to approach them directly, to hear their side of their own story. Most of what we do hear comes to us second- or third-hand, and from obviously hostile sources.

Abridged from *Entertaining Satan: Witchcraft and the Culture of Early New England,* 57–94, by John Putnam Demos. Copyright © 1982 by Oxford University Press, Inc. Reprinted by permission.

It is hard enough simply to count their number. Indeed, it is impossible to compile a complete roster of all those involved. We shall be dealing in what follows with 114 individual suspects. Of these people 81 were subject to some form of legal action for their supposed witchcraft, i.e., "examination" by magistrates and/or full-fledged prosecution. Another 15 were not, so far as we know, formally accused in court; however, their status as suspects is apparent from actions—for slander—which they themselves initiated. A final group of 18 (some not identified by name) are mentioned elsewhere in writings from the period.

Yet these figures certainly *under*-represent the total of witchcraft suspects in seventeenth-century New England. The court records are riddled with gaps and defects; it is possible, even probable, that important cases have been entirely lost from sight. . . .

But if our list of 114 is only the tip, its substantive and structural features still merit investigation. There is no reason to imagine any considerable difference between the known witches and their unknown counterparts. The former are presented here, as a group, in their leading biographical characteristics. Their (1) sex and (2) age have an obvious claim to attention. Thence the focus moves, successively, to their (3) background and early life, (4) marital and child-bearing status, (5) pattern of family relationships, (6) overall record of social and/or criminal "deviance," (7) occupational history, and (8) social and economic position. A final question concerns their (9) personal style and character, and their specific experiences as witches—that is, as objects of formal and informal sanction at the hands of their cultural peers.

Sex

There was no intrinsic reason why one sex should have been more heavily represented among New England witches than the other. The prevailing definitions of witchcraft—the performance of *maleficium* and "familiarity with the Devil"—made no apparent distinctions as to gender. Yet the predominance of women among those actually accused is a historical commonplace—and is confirmed by the present findings.

Females outnumbered males by a ratio of roughly 4:1. These proportions obtained, with some minor variations, across both time and space. Furthermore, they likely *under*state the association of women and witchcraft, as can be seen from a closer look at the males accused. Of the twenty-two men on the list, eleven were accused together with a woman. Nine of these were husbands of female witches, the other two were religious associates (*protégés* of the notorious Anne Hutchinson). There is good reason to think that in most, if not all, such cases the woman was the primary suspect, with the man becoming implicated through a literal process of guilt by association. Indeed this pattern conformed to a widely prevalent assumption that the transmission of witchcraft would follow the lines of family or close friendship. (There were at least two instances when a woman-witch joined in the charges against her own husband.) . . .

An easy hypothesis—perhaps too easy—would make of witchcraft a single plank in a platform of "sexist" oppression. Presumably, the threat of being charged as a witch might serve to constrain the behavior of women. Those who asserted themselves too openly or forcibly could expect a summons to court, and risked incurring the ultimate sanction of death itself. Hence the dominance of *men* would be underscored in both symbolic and practical terms. Male dominance was, of course, an assumed principle in traditional society—including the society of early New England. Men controlled political life; they alone could vote and hold public office. Men were also leaders in religion, as pastors and elders of local congregations. Men owned the bulk of personal property (though women had some rights and protections). Furthermore, the values of the culture affirmed the "headship" of men in marital and family relations and their greater "wisdom" in everyday affairs. Certainly, then, the uneven distribution of witchcraft accusations and their special bearing on the lives of women were consistent with sex-roles generally.

But was there *more* to this than simple consistency? Did the larger matrix of social relations enclose some dynamic principle that would energize actual "witch-hunting" so as to hold women down? On this the evidence—at least from early New England—seems doubtful. There is little sign of generalized (or "structural") conflict between the sexes. Male dominance of public affairs was scarcely an issue, and in private life there was considerable scope for female initiative. Considered overall, the relations of men and women were less constrained by differences of role and status than would be the case for most later generations of Americans. It is true that many of the suspects displayed qualities of assertiveness and aggressiveness beyond what the culture deemed proper. But these displays were not directed at men as such; often enough the targets were other women. Moreover, no single line in the extant materials raises the issue of sex-defined patterns of authority. Thus, if witches were at some level protesters against male oppression, they themselves seem to have been unconscious of the fact. As much could be said of the accusers, in their (putative) impulse to dominate.

Two possible exceptions should be noticed here. Anne Hutchinson was suspected of performing witchcraft, during and after her involvement with "antinomianism." And the ecclesiastical proceedings against her affirmed, among other things, the "natural" subordination of women to male authority. (Said Governor Winthrop at one point: "We do not mean to discourse with those of your sex.") Similarly, the convicted witch Anne Hibbens had been "cast out" of the Boston church for a variety of reasons, including this one: "she hath [violated] . . . the rule of the Apostle in usurping authority over him whom God hath made her head and husband." (According to John Cotton, the pastor, "some do think she doth but make a wisp of her husband.") Yet even in these cases there was no clear line of connection between the (alleged) witchcraft and the flouting of conventional sex-roles. With Mrs. Hutchinson heresy remained the central issue throughout. With

Mrs. Hibbens many years elapsed between her trial of excommunication (1640) and her conviction for witchcraft (1656). It is also well to remember numerous other New England women who would seem to qualify as sex-role "deviants." Their sins were many and various—assault on magistrates and constables, "wicked carriage and speeches" toward husbands, physical violence against husbands (and others), sexual harassment and abuse of men—yet most of them would never fall prey to charges of witchcraft.

And one final point in this connection: a large portion of witchcraft charges were brought against women *by* other women. Thus, if the fear of witchcraft expressed a deep strain of misogyny, it was something in which both sexes shared. It was also something in which other cultures have quite generally shared. . . .

Age

How old were the accused? At what age did their careers as suspected witches begin? These questions are difficult to answer with precision, in many individual cases; but it is possible to create an aggregate picture by analyzing a broad sample of age-estimates. . . .

The results converge on one time of life in particular: what we would call "midlife," or simply "middle age." The years of the forties and fifties account for the great mass of accused witches, whether considered at the time of prosecution (67 percent) or of earliest known suspicion (82 percent). It seems necessary to emphasize these figures in order to counteract the now familiar stereotype which makes witches out to be old. In fact, they were not old, either by their standards or by ours. (One victim, in her fits, was asked pointedly about the age of her spectral tormentors, and "she answered neither old nor young.") Contrary (once again) to currently prevalent understandings, the New Englanders construed the chronology of aging in terms not very different from our own. Their laws, their prescriptive writings, and their personal behavior expressed a common belief that old age begins at sixty. All but a handful of the witches were younger than this. Indeed, substantial majorities of both the groups considered above were age fifty or less (72 percent of the general sample, and 78 percent of the "major suspects"). . . .

One can scarcely avoid asking *why* this should have been so. What, for a start, was the meaning of midlife in that time and that cultural context? One point seems immediately apparent: midlife was *not* seen as one of several stages in a fully rounded "life-cycle." Early Americans spoke easily and frequently of "childhood," "youth," and "old age"—but not of "middle age." The term and (presumably) the concept, so familiar to us today, had little place in the lives of our forebears centuries ago. Instead of constituting a stage, midlife meant simply manhood (or womanhood) itself. Here was a *general* standard, against which childhood and youth, on the one side, and old age, on the other, were measured as deviations. Early life was preparatory; later life brought decline. The key element in midlife—as defined, for example, by the Puritan poet Anne Bradstreet—was the exercise of power, the use of fully developed capacity. The danger was *mis*use of power, the besetting sin an excess of "vaulting ambition." In fact, these conventions gave an accurate reflection of experience and behavior. In the average life the years from forty to sixty enclosed a high point of wealth, of prestige, of responsibility for self and others. This pattern can be demonstrated most clearly for *men* in midlife (from tax-lists, inventories, records of office-holding, and the like); but it must have obtained for women as well. A middle-aged woman was likely, for one thing, to have a full complement of children in her care and under her personal authority. The numbers involved could well reach eight or ten, and in some families there would be additional dependents—servants, apprentices, other children "bound out" in conditions of fosterage. With female dependents the authority of the "mistress" was particularly extensive; significantly, it appeared as an issue in at least one of the witchcraft cases. Listen to the words of Mercy Short, "in her fits" and addressing her spectral tormentors:

> What's that? Must the younger women, do ye say, hearken to the elder? They must be another sort of elder women than you then! They must not be elder witches, I am sure. Pray, do you for once hearken to me!

Beyond the cultural insistence that others "hearken" to her, a woman in midlife would enjoy considerable prestige in her village or neighborhood. She was likely by this time to be a church member—and, if her husband was well to do, to have a front-row seat in the meeting-house. Indeed, her status reflected her husband's quite generally, and his was probably higher than at any time previous. The point, in sum, is this. Midlife was associated, in theory and in fact, with power over others. Witchcraft was a special (albeit malign) instance of power over others. Ergo: most accused witches were themselves persons in midlife.

If this seems a bit too simple, there are indeed some additional—and complicating—factors. The accused were not, on the whole, well positioned socially. Their personal access to power and authority was, if anything, below the average for their age-group. They can therefore be viewed as representative of midlife status only in a very generalized sense. Perhaps it was the discrepancy between midlife norms and their own individual circumstances that made them seem plausible as suspects. Perhaps a middle-aged person who was poorly situated (relative to peers) could be presumed to want "power"—and, in some cases, to seek it by any means that came to hand.

To suggest this is to acknowledge elements of *dis*advantage—of deficit and loss—in generating suspicions of witchcraft. And one more such element must be mentioned, at least speculatively. Most of the accused were middle-aged women; as such they were subject to the menopausal "change of life." The old phrase sounds quaint and slightly off-key to modern ears, but in traditional society menopause brought more—at least more tangible—change than is the usual case nowadays. Its effects embraced biology, psychology, and social position, in roughly equal measure. This process will need further, and fuller, consideration in relation to the putative victims of witchcraft; for the moment we simply underscore its meaning as loss of function. The generative "power" of most women was by midlife visibly manifest in a houseful of children; yet that same power came suddenly to an end. There was a gap here between one mode of experience and another—past versus present—an additional kind of unsettling discrepancy. Was it, then, coincidental that witches appeared to direct their malice especially toward infants and very young children? . . .

Background

The most severe of all the deficiencies in the source materials relate to the early life of the witches. In what circumstances did they grow up? Was there something distinctive about their various families of origin? Were they orphaned, sent out into servitude, subject to illness, raised by disabled or insensitive parents, to any extent beyond the average for their cultural peers? Unfortunately, the material to answer such questions is not extant. . . .

Other elements of "background" deserve investigation. Were the witches anomalous in their ethnic and/or religious heritage? On this the evidence is clearer, and it supports a negative answer overall. An early suspect in the Hartford trials of 1662–63 was Dutch—Judith Varlet, daughter of a merchant and relative by marriage of Governor Peter Stuyvesant of New Netherland. (A leading victim in the case was given to "Dutch-toned discourse," when overtaken by fits.) The widow Glover, convicted and executed at Boston in 1688, was Irish and Catholic, and at her trial could speak only in Gaelic. Elizabeth Garlick of Easthampton apparently had one Huguenot parent. And Mary Parsons was the wife of a "papist" before her ill-starred second marriage and trial for witchcraft at Springfield. But otherwise the witches seem to have been of solidly English stock and mostly "Puritan" religion. . . .

Marriage and Child-Bearing

But what of the families in which witches lived as adults, the families they helped to create as spouses and parents? The results on this point seem generally unremarkable: there are no clear departures from the pattern of the culture at large. The portion of widows (10 percent) looks normal for the age-group most centrally involved, given the prevailing demographic regime. The never-marrieds (another 10 percent) include those few young men who virtually courted suspicion and also the several children of witches accused by "association." (John Godfrey was the only person past "youth" in this particular sub-group.) There was but one divorcée.

In sum, most witches were married persons (with spouses still living) when brought under suspicion. Most, indeed, had been married only once. Four were definitely, and two probably, in a second marriage; one had been married (also widowed) twice previously. Perhaps a few others belong in the previously married group, assuming some lost evidence; however, this would not alter the total picture. Again, the witches seem little different in their marital situation from their cultural peers.

As part of their marriages the accused would, of course, expect to bear and rear children. But in this their actual experience may have differed somewhat from the norm. The pertinent data (vital records, genealogies, and the like) are flawed at many points, and conclusions must be qualified accordingly. Still, with that understood, we may ponder the following. It appears that nearly one in six of the witches was childless—twice the rate that obtained in the population at large. Moreover, those who *did* bear children may have experienced lower-than-normal fecundity (and/or success in raising children to adulthood). In numerous cases (23 out of 62) the procedure of family reconstitution yields but one or two clearly identifiable offspring. Meanwhile, relatively few cases (7 of 62) can be associated with large complements of children, i.e. six or more per family. Fuller evidence would surely change these figures, reducing the former and raising the latter; but it would take a quite massive shift to bring the witches into line with the child-bearing and child-rearing norms of the time.

Connections between witchcraft and children emerge at many points in the extant record: children thought to have been made ill, or murdered, by witchcraft; mothers apparently bewitched while bearing or nursing children; witches alleged to suckle "imps" (in implicit parody of normal maternal function); witches observed to take a special (and suspicious) interest in other people's children; witches found to be predominantly of menopausal age and status; and so on. Thus the witches' own child-bearing (and child-rearing) is a matter of considerable interest. And if they were indeed relatively ill-favored and unsuccessful in this respect, their liability to witch-charges becomes, by so much, easier to understand.

Family Relationships

There is another, quite different way in which the witches may have been atypical. Briefly summarized, their domestic experience was often marred by trouble and conflict. Sometimes the witch and her (his) spouse squared off as antagonists. Jane Collins was brought to court not only for witchcraft but also for "railing" at her husband and calling him "gurley-gutted Devil." Bridget Oliver and her husband Thomas were tried, convicted, and punished for "fighting with each other," a decade before Bridget's first trial for witchcraft. (A neighbor deposed that she had "several times been called . . . to hear their complaints one of the other, and . . . further [that] she saw Goodwife Oliver's face at one time bloody and at other times black and blue, . . . and [Goodman] Oliver complained that his wife had given him several blows.") The witchcraft trials of Mary and Hugh Parsons called forth much testimony as to their marital difficulties. Mary was alleged to have spoken "very harsh things against him before his face . . . such things as are not ordinary for persons to speak one of another." Hugh, for his part, "never feared either to grieve or displease his wife any time"; once, by his own admission, he "took up a block [of wood] and made as if . . . [to] throw it at her head.'' A second Mary Parsons also quarreled frequently with her husband. The estrangement between Sarah Dibble and *her* husband was so bitter that he actively encouraged suspicions of her witchcraft; moreover, his general "carriage" toward her was "most inhumane, [e.g.] beating of her so that he caused the blood to settle in several places of her body." There was similar evidence about other suspects, including several of those tried at Salem.

In some cases the lines of conflict ran between parents and children. The Marblehead witch Jane James was chronically at odds with her son Erasmus; at least once the county court undertook an official arbitration of their differences. (On a separate occasion the same court examined and fined Erasmus "for giving his mother abusive language and carriage.") The witchcraft charges against William Graves seem to have developed out of a longstanding dispute with his daughter and son-in-law. Susannah Martin's household was disrupted by violent quarrels between her husband and son; the latter was brought to court and convicted of "high misdemeanors" in "abusing of his father, and throwing him down, and taking away his clothes."

This material cannot meaningfully be quantified; in too many cases the surviving evidence does not extend to any part of the suspect's domestic experience. But what does survive seems striking, if only by way of "impressionism." Harmony in human relations was a touchstone of value for early New Englanders, and nowhere more so than in families. A "peaceable" household was seen as the foundation of all social order. Hence domestic disharmony would invite unfavorable notice from neighbors and peers. A woman from Dorchester, Massachusetts, called to court in a lawsuit filed by her son, expressed the underlying issue with candor and clarity: "it is no small trouble of mind to me that there should be such recording up [of] family weaknesses, to the dishonor of God and grief of one another, and I had rather go many paces backward to cover shame than one inch forward to discover any." Yet the lives of witches—we are speculating—were often crossed with "family weaknesses." And perhaps these belonged to the matrix of factors in which particular suspicions originated.

Such weaknesses may have held other significance as well. The troubles in Rachel Clinton's family left her isolated and exposed to a variety of personal misadventures: her sheer vulnerability made a central theme in her story. Rachel was doubtless an extreme case, but not a wholly atypical one. Conflict with spouse, siblings, children had the effect of neutralizing one's natural allies and defenders, if not of turning them outright into adversaries. The *absence* of family was also a form of weakness. Widowhood may not by itself have invited suspicions of witchcraft; yet where suspicions formed on other grounds, it could become a serious disadvantage. Case materials from the trials of the widows Godman (New Haven), Holman (Cambridge), Hale (Boston), and Glover (Boston) implicitly underscore their vulnerable position.

The experience of Anne Hibbens (Boston) is particularly suggestive this way. Mrs. Hibbens had arrived in New England with her husband William in the early 1630s. Almost at once William established himself as an important and exemplary member of the community: a merchant, a magistrate, a member of the Court of Assistants. But Anne made a different impression. In 1640 she suffered admonition, then excommunication, from the Boston church; a still-extant transcript of the proceedings reveals most vividly her troubled relations with neighbors and peers. In 1656 she was tried in criminal court—and convicted—and executed—for witchcraft. The long interval between these two dates invites attention; and there is a third date to notice as well, 1654, when William Hibbens died. It seems likely, in short, that William's influence served for many years to shield her from the full force of her neighbors' animosity. But with his passing she was finally, and mortally, exposed.

Crime

Witchcraft was itself a crime, and witches were criminals of a special sort. Were they also criminals of other—more ordinary—sorts? Were they as a group disproportionately represented within the ranks of all defendants in court proceedings? Was there possibly some implicit affinity between witchcraft and other categories of crime?

Again, the extant records do not yield fully adequate information. Some 41 of the accused can be definitely associated with other (and prior) criminal proceedings; the remaining 73 *cannot* be so associated. The difficulty is that many in the latter group can scarcely be traced at all beyond their alleged involvement with witchcraft. Still, the total of 41 offenders is a considerable number, which serves to establish a minimum "crime rate"—of 36 percent—for the witches as a whole. Clearly, moreover, this is only a minimum. To concentrate on witches for whom there is some evidence of *ongoing* experience is to reduce the "at risk" population to no more than 65. (The latter, in short, form a sub-sample among the accused whose offences might plausibly have left some trace in the records; the rest are biographical phantoms in a more complete sense.) This adjustment yields an alternative rate (of offenders/witches) of some 63 percent.

The two figures, 36 and 63 percent, may be viewed as lower and upper bounds for the actual rate, and their midpoint as a "best guess" response to the central question. In short, approximately one half of the people accused of practicing witchcraft were also charged with the commission of other crimes. But was this a notably large fraction, in relation to the community at large? Unfortunately, there are no fully developed studies of criminal behavior in early America to provide firm standards of comparison, only scatter-shot impressions and partial analyses of two specific communities included in the current investigation. The latter may be summarized in a sentence. The overall "crime rate"—defined as a percentage of the total population charged with committing crimes at some point in a lifetime—was on the order of 10 to 20 percent.* Thus, even allowing for the possibility of substantial error, the link between witchcraft and other crime does look strong.

---

*The rate for *women only* was much lower, perhaps in the vicinity of 5 percent. And this may be a better "control group" for present purposes, since most witches were female. If so, the disparity between witch-behavior and prevailing norms appears even more pronounced.

There is more to ask about the other crime, particularly about its substantive range and distribution. Taken altogether, the witches accounted for fifty-two separate actions at court (apart from witchcraft itself). . . . Crimes of assaultive speech and theft are dramatically highlighted here. Together they account for 61 percent of all charges pressed against the witches, as opposed to 35 percent for the larger sample. Moreover, the fact that accused witches were predominantly female suggests a refinement in the sample population. If men are excluded—if, in short, the comparison involves witches versus *women* offenders generally—then the disparity becomes even larger, 61 percent and 27 percent.

Are there reasons why persons previously charged with theft and/or assaultive speech might be found, to a disproportionate extent, in the ranks of accused witches? Was there something which these two categories of offense shared (so to say) with witchcraft? Such questions point to the meaning of witchcraft in the minds of its supposed (or potential) victims. But consider what is common to crimes of theft and assaultive speech themselves. The element of loss, of undue and unfair taking away, seems patent in the former case, but it is—or was for early New Englanders—equally central to the latter one as well. Slander, for example, meant the loss of good name, of "face," of reputation, and thus was a matter of utmost importance. (The evidence against one alleged slanderer, who would later be charged as a witch, was summarized as follows: "She hath *taken away* their [i.e. the plaintiffs'] names and credits . . . which is *as precious as life itself."* [Emphasis added.]) "Filthy speeches" was a somewhat looser designation, but in most specific instances it described a similar threat. Even "lying"—a third category of crime, notably salient for witches—can be joined to this line of interpretation. A lie was, in a sense, a theft of truth, and seemed especially dangerous when directed toward other persons.

In sum, each of these crimes carried the inner meaning of theft. And so did witchcraft. Theft of property, theft of health (and sometimes of life), theft of competence, theft of will, theft of self: such was *maleficium,* the habitual activity of witches.

Occupations

. . . "Jane Hawkins, of Boston, midwife . . ." "Isabel Babson, of Gloucester, midwife . . ." "Wayborough Gatchell, of Marblehead, midwife . . ."; here was a special *woman's* occupation. That midwife and witch were sometimes (often?) the same person has long been supposed by historians; hence the evidence, for individual cases, deserves a most careful review. In fact, only two people in the entire suspect-group can be plausibly associated with the regular practice of midwifery. Otherwise the witches were not midwives, at least in a formal sense. It is clear, moreover, that scores of midwives carried out their duties, in many towns and through many years, without ever being touched by imputations of witchcraft.

However, this does not entirely dispose of the issue at hand. Witchcraft charges often did revolve in a special way around episodes of childbirth, and some of the accused were thought to have shown inordinate (and sinister) interest in the fate of the very young. Thus, for example, Eunice Cole of Hampton aroused suspicion by trying to intrude at the childbed (later death-bed) of her alleged victims. Others among the accused pressed medicines and advice on expectant or newly delivered mothers, or, alternatively, sought to take from the same quarter. Some may have displayed special skills in attending at childbirth, even without being recognized officially as midwives. (When Elizabeth Morse was tried for witchcraft, witnesses de-scribed her part in the delivery of a neighbor. First, she was deliberately kept away. Then, as "strong labor . . . continued . . . without any hopeful appearance," she was "desired to come"—but declined, evidently miffed at not being asked sooner. Eventually she relented, "and so at last . . . went, and quickly after her coming the woman was delivered.") Perhaps, at bot-tom, there was a link of antipathy: the midwife *versus* the witch, life-giving and life-taking, opposite faces of the same coin.

Recent scholarship of English witchcraft has spotlighted the activities of so-called "cunning folk." These were local practitioners of magic who spe-cialized in finding lost property, foretelling the future, and (most especially) treating illness. Usually they sided with moral order and justice; often enough their diagnoses served to "discover" witchcraft as the cause of particular sufferings. Yet their powers were mysterious and frightening: charms, incantations, herbal potions, a kind of second sight—all in exotic combination. Inevitably, it seemed, some of them would be tempted to apply such powers in the cause of evil. Thus they might move from the role of "discoverer" to that of suspect—in short, from witch-doctor to witch.

Were there also "cunning folk" among the transplanted Englishmen of North America? The extant evidence seems, at first sight, to yield a negative answer. There is little sign that individual persons achieved (or wanted) a public reputation of this sort, as was plainly the case in the mother country. The nomenclature itself rarely appears, and then only as a form of name-calling. ("What?" exclaimed one man of Goody Morse; "Is she a witch, or a cunning woman?") Almost certainly, the religious establishment of early New England set itself against such practice. Puritan leaders, on both sides of the Atlantic, associated it with the Devil—and, on this side, their views carried decisive influence.

And yet, while "cunning folk" did not present themselves as such, some of their ways (and character) may have survived in at least attenuated forms. For within the ranks of witches were several—perhaps many—women of singular aptitude for "healing." Not "physicians," not midwives, and not (publicly) identified by the pejorative term "cunning," they nonetheless proffered their services in the treatment of personal illness. For example: the widow Hale of Boston (twice a target of witchcraft proceedings) ran a kind of lodging-house where sick persons came for rest and "nursing." Anna Edmunds of Lynn (presented for witchcraft in 1673) was known locally as a "doctor woman"; references to her practice span at least two decades. (One prolonged court case showed her in implicit competition with a Boston physician. The physician had tried, and failed, to cure a young girl with a badly infected leg; and when the girl's parents turned next to Goody Ed-munds he vowed to "swallow a firebrand" if her treatment proved successful.) Elizabeth Garlick of Easthampton prescribed "dockweeds" and other herbal remedies for sick neighbors. Katherine Harrison played a similar part at Wethersfield; her therapies included "diet, drink, and plasters." A woman of Boston, not identified but suspected in the "affliction" of Margaret Rule "had frequently cured very painful hurts by muttering over them certain charms." . . .

What this and other evidence does make clear is a key association: between efforts of curing, on the one hand, and the "black arts" of witchcraft, on the other. Opposite though they seemed in formal terms, in practice they were (sometimes) tightly linked. "Power" in either direction could be suddenly reversed. We cannot discover how many New England women may have tried their hand at doctoring, but we know that some who did so brought down on themselves a terrible suspicion. Among the various occupations of premodern society this one was particularly full of hope—and of peril.

Social Position

There is a long-standing, and reasonably well attested, view of early America that makes the settlers solidly middle-class. To be sure, the notion of "class" is somewhat misleading when applied to the seventeenth century; "status" would be a better term in context. But "middle" does seem the right sort of qualifier. The movement of people from England to America included few from either the lowest or the highest ranks of traditional society—few, that is, from among the laboring poor (or the truly destitute) and fewer still from the nobility and upper gentry. Yet, with that understood, one cannot fail to notice how the middle range became itself divided and graded by lines of preference. The "planting" of New England yielded its own array of leaders and followers, of more and less fortunate citizens. Social distinction remained important, vitally so, to the orderly life of communities. . . .

The sorting attempted here posits three broad social groups—"high" (I), "middle" (II), and "low" (III)—of roughly equal size. Of course, all such categories are a matter of contrivance, conforming to no specific historical reality; but they do help to arrange the material for analysis.

Within our working roster of accused witches, some eighty-six can be classified according to this scheme. (For the other twenty-eight there is too little evidence to permit a judgement.) A substantial majority can be assigned directly to one or another of the basic rank-groups. Eighteen more occupy marginal positions (i.e., *between* groups), while seven seem distinctive in their mobility (up or down) and are on that account held for a separate category. . . . Witches were recruited, to a greatly disproportionate extent, among the most humble, least powerful of New England's citizens. As a matter of statistical probabilities, persons at the bottom of the sorting-scale were many times more likely to be accused and prosecuted than their counterparts at the top. Moreover, when the results of such accusation are figured in, the difference looks stronger still. Among all the suspects in categories, I, I/II, and II, only one was a *convicted* witch. (And of the remainder, few, if any, were seriously threatened by the actions taken against them.) The accused in categories II/III and III present quite another picture. Indeed they account for all convictions save the one above noted, and for the great bulk of completed trials.

Finally, the "mobile" group deserves special consideration. Five of them started life in a top-category position and ended near the bottom (e.g. Rachel Clinton). Two experienced equivalent change but in the opposite direction. None was convicted; all but one, however, were subject to full-scale prosecution. (Moreover, five were tried more than once.) In short; the mobile group, while not numerous, included people whose "witchcraft" was taken very seriously. To interpret this finding is difficult, without comparable information about the population at large. But there is the suggestion here of a significant relationship: between life-change and witchcraft, between mobility and lurking danger. Perhaps mobility seemed a threat to traditional values and order. And if so, it may well have been personally threatening to the individuals involved. As they rose or fell, moving en route past their more stable peers, they must at the least have seemed conspicuous. But perhaps they seemed *suspect* as well. To mark them as witches would, then, be a way of defending society itself.

Character

With the witches' sex, age, personal background, family life, propensity to crime, occupations, and social position all accounted for (as best we can manage), there yet remains one category which may be the most important of all. What were these people like—as people? What range of motive, of style, and of behavior would they typically exhibit? Can the scattered artifacts of their separate careers be made to yield a composite portrait, a model, so to speak, of witch-character? . . .

Witchcraft was *defined* in reference to conflict; and most charges of witchcraft grew out of specific episodes of conflict. Hence it should not be surprising that the suspects, as individuals, were notably active that way. . . .

What follows is a motley assemblage of taunts, threats, and curses attributed to one or another suspect:

> Mercy Disborough did say that it should be pressed, heaped, and running over to her.

> He [Hugh Parsons] said unto me, "Gammer, you need not have said anything. I spoke not to you, but I shall remember you when you little think on it.

> She [Goodwife Jane Walford] said I had better have done it; that my sorrow was great already, and it should be greater—for I was going a great journey, but should never come there.

> She [Elizabeth Godman] said, "How doth Goody Thorp? I am beholden to Goody Thorp above all the women in the town; she would have had me to the gallows for a few chickens."

Mercy Disborough told him that she would make him as bare as a bird's tail.

Then said he [Hugh Parsons], "If you will not abate it [i.e. a certain debt in corn] it shall be but as lent. It shall do you no good. It shall be but as wild fire in your house, and as a moth in your clothes." And these threatening speeches he uttered with much anger.

Goodwife Cole said that if this deponent's calves did eat any of her grass, she wished it might poison or choke them. . . .

Some suspects appeared to favor witchcraft and its alleged practitioners. Elizabeth Godman "would be often speaking about witches . . . without any occasion . . . and [would] rather justify them than condemn them"; indeed, "she said, 'why do they provoke them? why do they not let them come into the church?' " When her neighbor, Mrs. Goodyear, expressed confidence that God would ultimately "discover" and punish witches, "for I never knew a witch to die in their bed," Mrs. Godman disagreed. "You mistake," she said, "for a great many die and go to the grave in an orderly way." Hugh Parsons was suspected of holding similar views. According to his wife he could "not abide that anything should be spoken against witches." Indeed the two of them quarreled while discussing a witch trial in another community: Hugh was allegedly angered "because she wished the ruin of all witches." There were, in addition, postures of support for particular suspects (e.g. Alice Stratton for Margaret Jones, Elizabeth Seager for Goodwife Ayres, Mary Staples for Goodwife Knapp), which would also invite unfavorable notice.

Some of these statements and postures serve to raise a further question. Was the impulse to provoke others through leading references to witchcraft a manifestation of some larger characterological disturbance? Here, indeed, is the germ of an old supposition, that witches have usually been deranged persons, insane or at least deeply eccentric. For New England the situation was largely otherwise. . . .

Conclusion

From this long and somewhat tortuous exercise in prosopography a rough composite finally emerges. To recapitulate, the typical witch:

1. was female.
2. was of middle age (i.e. between forty and sixty years old).
3. was of English (and "Puritan") background.
4. was married, but was more likely (than the general population) to have few children—or none at all.
5. was frequently involved in trouble and conflict with other family members.
6. had been accused, on some previous occasion, of committing crimes— most especially theft, slander, or other forms of assaultive speech.
7. was more likely (than the general population) to have professed and practiced a medical vocation, i.e. "doctoring" on a local, quite informal basis.

8. was of relatively low social position.
9. was abrasive in style, contentious in character—and stubbornly resilient in the face of adversity.

The Potentially Powerful Witch

CAROL F. KARLSEN

Most observers now agree that witches in the villages and towns of late sixteenth- and early seventeenth-century England tended to be poor. They were not usually the poorest women in their communities, one historian has argued; they were the "moderately poor." Rarely were relief recipients suspect; rather it was those just above them on the economic ladder, "like the woman who felt she ought to get poor relief, but was denied it." This example brings to mind New England's Eunice Cole, who once berated Hampton selectmen for refusing her aid when, she insisted, a man no worse off than she was receiving it.

Eunice Cole's experience also suggests the difficulty in evaluating the class position of the accused. Commonly used class indicators such as the amount of property owned, yearly income, occupation, and political offices held are almost useless in analyzing the positions of women during the colonial period. While early New England women surely shared in the material benefits and social status of their fathers, husbands, and even sons, most were economically dependent on the male members of their families throughout their lives. Only a small proportion of these women owned property outright, and even though they participated actively in the productive work of their communities, their labor did not translate into financial independence or economic power. Any income generated by married women belonged by law to their husbands, and because occupations open to women were few and wages meager, women alone could only rarely support themselves. Their material condition, moreover, could easily change with an alteration in their marital status. William Cole, with an estate at his death of £41 after debts, might be counted among the "moderately poor," as might Eunice Cole when he was alive. But the refusal of the authorities to recognize the earlier transfer of this estate from husband to wife ensured, among other things, that as a widow Eunice Cole was among the poorest of New England's poor.

The distinction between the economic circumstances of wife and widow here may not seem particularly significant, but in other cases the problem is more complicated. How, for instance, do we classify the witch Ann Dolliver? The daughter of prominent Salem minister John Higginson, who was

Reprinted from "The Economic Basis of Witchcraft," Chapter 3 of *The Devil in the Shape of a Woman: Witchcraft in Colonial New England*, 77–83, 102–16, by Carol F. Karlsen, by permission of the author and W. W. Norton & Co., Inc. Copyright © 1987 by Carol F. Karlsen.

well above most of his neighbors in wealth and social status, she was also the deserted wife of William Dolliver, and lived out her life without the support of a husband, dependent first on her father and then on the town for her maintenance. Even if we were willing to assume that the accused shared the class position of their male relatives, the lack of information on so many of the families of witches makes it impossible to locate even the males on an economic scale.

Despite conceptual problems and sparse evidence, it is clear that poor women, both the destitute and those with access to some resources, were surely represented, and very probably overrepresented, among the New England accused. Perhaps 20 percent of accused women, including both Eunice Cole and Ann Dolliver, were either impoverished or living at a level of bare subsistence when they were accused. Some, like thirty-seven-year-old Abigail Somes, worked as servants a substantial portion of their adult lives. Some supported themselves and their families with various kinds of temporary labor such as nursing infants, caring for sick neighbors, taking in washing and sewing, or harvesting crops. A few, most notably Tituba, the first person accused during the Salem outbreak, were slaves. Others, like the once-prosperous Sarah Good of Wenham and Salem, and the never-very-well-off Ruth Wilford of Haverhill, found themselves reduced to abject poverty by the death of a parent or a change in their own marital status. Accused witches came before local magistrates requesting permission to sell family land in order to support themselves, to submit claims against their children or executors of their former husbands' estates for nonpayment of the widow's lawful share of the estate, or simply to ask for food and fuel from the town selectmen. Because they could not pay the costs of their trials or jail terms, several were forced to remain in prison after courts acquitted them. The familiar stereotype of the witch as an indigent woman who resorted to begging for her survival is hardly an inaccurate picture of some of New England's accused.

Still, the poor account for only a minority of the women accused. Even without precise economic indicators, it is clear that women from all levels of society were vulnerable to accusation. If witches in early modern England can accurately be described as "moderately poor," then New Englanders deviated sharply from their ancestors in their ideas about which women were witches. Wives, daughters, and widows of "middling" farmers, artisans, and mariners were regularly accused, and (although much less often) so too were women belonging to the gentry class. The accused were addressed as Goodwife (or Goody) and as the more honorific Mrs. or Mistress, as well as by their first names.

Prosecution was a different matter. Unless they were single or widowed, accused women from wealthy families—families with estates valued at more than £500—could be fairly confident that the accusations would be ignored by the authorities or deflected by their husbands through suits for slander against their accusers. Even during the Salem outbreak, when several women married to wealthy men were arrested, most managed to escape to the safety of other colonies through their husbands' influence. Married women from moderately well-off families—families with estates valued at between roughly £200 and £500—did not always escape prosecution so easily, but neither do they seem, as a group, to have been as vulnerable as their less prosperous counterparts. When only married women are considered, women in families with estates worth less than £200 seem significantly overrepresented among *convicted* witches—a pattern which suggests that economic position was a more important factor to judges and juries than to the community as a whole in its role as accuser.

Without a husband to act on behalf of the accused, wealth alone rarely provided women with protection against prosecution. Boston's Ann Hibbens, New Haven's Elizabeth Godman, and Wethersfield's Katherine Harrison, all women alone, were tried as witches despite sizeable estates. In contrast, the accusations against women like Hannah Griswold of Saybrook, Connecticut, Elizabeth Blackleach of Hartford, and Margaret Gifford of Salem, all wives of prosperous men when they were accused, were simply not taken seriously by the courts. The most notable exception to this pattern is the obliviousness of the Salem judges to repeated accusations against Margaret Thatcher, widow of one of the richest merchants in Boston and principal heir to her father's considerable fortune. Her unusual wealth and social status may have kept her out of jail in 1692, but more likely it was her position as mother-in-law to Jonathan Corwin, one of the Salem magistrates, that accounts for her particular immunity.

Economic considerations, then, do appear to have been at work in the New England witchcraft cases. But the issue was not simply the relative poverty—or wealth—of accused witches or their families. It was the special position of most accused witches vis-à-vis their society's rules for transferring wealth from one generation to another. To explain why their position was so unusual, we must turn first to New England's system of inheritance.

Inheritance is normally thought of as the transmission of property at death, but in New England, as in other agricultural societies, adult children received part of their father's accumulated estates prior to his death, usually at the time they married. Thus the inheritance system included both pre-mortem endowments and post-mortem distributions. While no laws compelled fathers to settle part of their estates on their children as marriage portions, it was customary to do so. Marriages were, among other things, economic arrangements, and young people could not benefit from these arrangements unless their fathers provided them with the means to set up households and earn their livelihoods. Sons' portions tended to be land, whereas daughters commonly received movable goods and/or money. The exact value of these endowments varied according to a father's wealth and inclination, but it appears that as a general rule the father of the young woman settled on the couple roughly half as much as the father of the young man.

Custom, not law, also guided the distribution of a man's property at his death, but with two important exceptions. First, a man's widow, if he left one, was legally entitled "by way of dower" to one-third part of his real property, "to have and injoy for term of her natural life." She was expected to support herself with the profits of this property, but since she held only a life interest in it, she had to see that she did not "strip or waste" it. None of the immovable estate could be sold, unless necessary for her or her children's maintenance, and then only with the permission of the court. A man might will his wife more than a third of his real property—but not less. Only if the woman came before the court to renounce her dower right publicly, and then only if the court approved, could this principle be waived. In the form of her "thirds," dower was meant to provide for a woman's support in widowhood. The inviolability of dower protected the widow from the claims of her children against the estate and protected the community from the potential burden of her care.

The second way in which law determined inheritance patterns had to do specifically with intestate cases. If a man died without leaving a will, several principles governed the division of his property. The widow's thirds, of course, were to be laid out first. Unless "just cause" could be shown for some other distribution, the other two-thirds were to be divided among the surviving children, both male and female. A double portion was to go to the eldest son, and single portions to his sisters and younger brothers. If there were no sons, the law stipulated that the estate was to be shared equally by the daughters. In cases where any or all of the children had not yet come of age, their portions were to be held by their mother or by a court-appointed guardian until they reached their majorities or married. What remained of the widow's thirds at her death was to be divided among the surviving children, in the same proportions as the other two-thirds.

Although bound to conform to laws concerning the widow's thirds, men who wrote wills were not legally required to follow the principles of inheritance laid out in intestate cases. Individual men had the right to decide for themselves who would ultimately inherit their property. As we shall see later, will-writers did sometimes deviate sharply from these guidelines, but the majority seem to have adhered closely (though not always precisely) to the custom of leaving a double portion to the eldest son. Beyond that, New England men seem generally to have agreed to a system of partible inheritance, with both sons and daughters inheriting.

When these rules were followed, property ownership and control generally devolved upon men. Neither the widow's dower nor, for the most part, the daughter's right to inherit signified more than *access to* property. For widows, the law was clear that dower allowed for "use" only. For inheriting daughters who were married, the separate but inheritance-related principle of coverture applied. Under English common law, "feme covert" stipulated that married women had no right to own property—indeed, upon marriage, "the very being or legal existence of the woman is suspended." Personal property which a married daughter inherited from her father, either as dowry or as a post-mortem bequest, immediately became the legal possession of her husband, who could exert full powers of ownership over it. A married daughter who inherited land from her father retained title to the land, which her husband could not sell without her consent. On her husband's death such land became the property of her children, but during his life her husband was entitled to the use and profits of it, and his wife could not devise it to her children by will. The property of an inheriting daughter who was single seems to have been held "for improvement" for her until she was married, when it became her dowry.

This is not to say that women did not benefit when they inherited property. A sizeable inheritance could provide a woman with a materially better life; if single or widowed, inheriting women enjoyed better chances for an economically advantageous marriage or remarriage. But inheritance did not normally bring women the independent economic power it brought men.

The rules of inheritance were not always followed, however. In some cases, individual men decided not to conform to customary practices; instead, they employed one of several legal devices to give much larger shares of their estates to their wives or daughters, many times for disposal at their own discretion. Occasionally, the magistrates themselves allowed the estate to be distributed in some other fashion. Or, most commonly, the absence of male heirs in families made conformity impossible. In all three exceptions to inheritance customs, but most particularly the last, the women who stood to benefit economically also assumed a position of unusual vulnerability. They, and in many instances their daughters, became prime targets for witchcraft accusations. . . .

A substantial majority of New England's accused females were women without brothers, women with daughters but no sons, or women in marriages with no children at all. Of the 267 accused females, enough is known about 158 to identify them as either having or not having brothers or sons to inherit: only sixty-two of the 158 (39 percent) did, whereas ninety-six (61 percent) did not. More striking, *once accused,* women without brothers or sons were even more likely than women with brothers or sons to be tried, convicted, and executed: women from families without male heirs made up 64 percent of the females prosecuted, 76 percent of those who were found guilty, and 89 percent of those who were executed.

These figures must be read with care, however, for two reasons. First, eighteen of the sixty-two accused females who *had* brothers or sons to inherit were themselves daughters and granddaughters of women who did not. If these eighteen females, most of whom were young women or girls, were accused because their neighbors believed that their mothers and grandmothers passed their witchcraft on to them, then they form a somewhat ambiguous group. Since they all had brothers to inherit, it would be inaccurate to exclude them from this category, yet including them understates the extent to which inheritance-related concerns were at issue in witchcraft accusations. At the same time, the large number of cases in which the fertility and mortality patterns of witches' families are unknown (109 of the 267 accused females in New England) makes it impossible to assess precisely the proportion of women among the accused who did not have brothers or sons. . . .

Numbers alone, however, do not tell the whole story. More remains to be said about what happened to these inheriting or potentially inheriting women, both before and after they were accused of witchcraft.

It was not unusual for women in families without male heirs to be accused of witchcraft shortly after the deaths of fathers, husbands, brothers, or sons. Katherine Harrison, Susanna Martin, Joan Penney, and Martha Carrier all exemplify this pattern. So too does elderly Ann Hibbens of Boston, whose execution in 1656 seems to have had a profound enough effect on some of her peers to influence the outcome of subsequent trials for years to come. Hibbens had three sons from her first marriage, all of whom lived in England; but she had no children by her husband William Hibbens, with whom she had come to Massachusetts in the 1630s. William died in 1654; Ann was brought to trial two years later. Although her husband's will has not survived, he apparently left a substantial portion (if not all) of his property directly to her: when she wrote her own will shortly before her execution, Ann Hibbens was in full possession of a £344 estate, most of which she bequeathed to her sons in England.

Similarly, less than two years elapsed between the death of Gloucester's William Vinson and the imprisonment of his widow Rachel in 1692. Two children, a son and a daughter, had been born to the marriage, but the son had died in 1675. Though William Vinson had had four sons (and three daughters) by a previous marriage, the sons were all dead by 1683. In his will, which he wrote in 1684, before he was certain that his last son had been lost at sea, William left his whole £180 estate to Rachel for her life, stipulating that she could sell part of the lands and cattle if she found herself in need of resources. After Rachel's death, "in Case" his son John "be Living and returne home agayne," William said, most of the estate was to be divided between John and their daughter Abigail. If John did not return, both shares were to be Abigail's.

Bridget Oliver (later Bridget Bishop) was brought into court on witchcraft charges less than a year after the death of her husband Thomas Oliver in 1679. He had died intestate, but since the estate was worth less than £40 after debts, and since Bridget had a child to raise, the court gave her all but £3 of it during her lifetime, stipulating that she could sell a ten-acre lot "towards paying the debts and her present supply." Twenty shillings went to each of her husband's two sons by his first wife, and twenty shillings to the Olivers' twelve-year-old daughter Christian, the only child of their marriage.

In other cases, many years passed between the death of the crucial male relative and the moment when a formal witchcraft complaint was filed. Twenty years had elapsed, for instance, between the death of Adam Hawkes of Lynn and the arrest of his widow and daughter. Adam had died in 1672, at the age of sixty-four, just three years after his marriage to the much-younger Sarah Hooper and less than a year after the birth of their daughter Sarah. He had died without leaving a will, but his two principal heirs—his widow and his son John from his first marriage—said they were aware of Adam's intentions concerning his £772 estate. The magistrates responsible for distributing

Adam's property took their word, allowing "certain articles of agreement" between the two to form the basis of the distribution. As a result, the elder Sarah came into full possession of 188 acres of land and one-third of Adam's movable property. Her daughter was awarded £90, "to be paid five pounds every two years until forty pounds is paid, and the fifty pounds at age or marriage."

It was just about the time young Sarah was due to receive her marriage portion that she and her mother, then Sarah Wardwell, were accused of witchcraft. Named with them as witches were the elder Sarah's second husband, carpenter Samuel Wardwell, their nineteen-year-old daughter Mercy, and the mother, two sisters, and brother of Francis Johnson, the younger Sarah's husband-to-be. It is not clear whether when Sarah Hawkes became Sarah Johnson she received the balance of her inheritance, but £36 of Sarah and Samuel Wardwell's property was seized by the authorities in 1692. Massachusetts passed a law at the height of the Salem outbreak providing attainder for "conjuration, witchcraft and dealing with evil and wicked spirits." Attainder meant the loss of civil, inheritance, and property rights for persons like Sarah Wardwell who had been sentenced to death. Not until 1711 was restitution made to Sarah Wardwell's children. . . .

Not all witches from families without male heirs were accused of conspiring with the Devil *after* they had come into their inheritances. On the contrary, some were accused prior to the death of the crucial male relative, many times before it was clear who would inherit. Eunice Cole was one of these women. Another was Martha Corey of Salem, who was accused of witchcraft in 1692 while her husband was still alive. Giles Corey had been married twice before and had several daughters by the time he married the widow Martha Rich, probably in the 1680s. With no sons to inherit, Giles's substantial land holdings would, his neighbors might have assumed, be passed on to his wife and daughters. Alice Parker, who may have been Giles's daughter from a former marriage, also came before the magistrates as a witch in 1692, as did Giles himself. Martha Corey and Alice Parker maintained their innocence and were hanged. Giles Corey, in an apparently futile attempt to preserve his whole estate for his heirs, refused to respond to the indictment. To force him to enter a plea, he was tortured: successively heavier weights were placed on his body until he was pressed to death.

What seems especially significant here is that most accused witches whose husbands were still alive were, like their counterparts who were widows and spinsters, over forty years of age—and therefore unlikely if not unable to produce male heirs. Indeed, the fact that witchcraft accusations were rarely taken seriously by the community until the accused stopped bearing children takes on a special meaning when it is juxtaposed with the anomalous position of inheriting women or potentially inheriting women in New England's social structure.

Witches in families without male heirs sometimes had been dispossessed of part or all of their inheritances before—sometimes long before—they were formally charged with witchcraft. Few of these women, however, accepted disinheritance with equanimity. Rather, like Susanna Martin, they

took their battles to court, casting themselves in the role of public challeng-
ers to the system of male inheritance. In most instances, the authorities
sided with their antagonists.

The experience of Rachel Clinton of Ipswich is instructive. As one of
five daughters in line to inherit the "above £500" estate of their father,
Richard Haffield, Rachel had been reduced to abject poverty at least eighteen years before she came before county magistrates in 1687 as a witch.
Richard Haffield had bequeathed £30 to each of his daughters just before his
death in 1639, but since Rachel was only ten at the time, and her sister Ruth
only seven, he stipulated that their shares were to be paid "as they shall com
to the age of sixteen yeares old." While he had not made other bequests, he
made his wife Martha executrix, and so the unencumbered portions of the
estate were legally at her disposal. In 1652, since Rachel and Ruth were still
unmarried (Rachel was twenty-three at the time), local magistrates ordered
Martha Haffield to pay one of her sons-in-law, Richard Coy, the £60 still due
Rachel and Ruth, to "improve their legacy."

When Martha Haffield wrote her own will in 1662, six years before her
death, she bequeathed the still-single Rachel the family farm, valued at £300,
with the proviso that she share the income it produced with her sisters, Ruth
(now Ruth White) and Martha Coy. The household goods were to be divided
among the three. Martha had effectively disinherited her two oldest children
(children of her husband's first marriage) with ten shillings apiece. This will,
though legal, would never be honored. In 1666, the county court put the
whole Haffield estate into the hands of Ruth's husband, Thomas White,
whom they named as Martha Haffield's guardian and whom they empowered to "receive and recover her estate." They declared Martha Haffield
"non compos mentis."

The issue that seems to have precipitated this court action was Rachel's
marriage to Lawrence Clinton several months before. Lawrence was an
indentured servant and fourteen years younger than his wife. Perhaps even
more offensive to community standards, Rachel had purchased Lawrence's
freedom for £21, with money she said her mother had given her. Once
Thomas White had control of the Haffield estate, he immediately sued Lawrence's former master, Robert Cross, for return of the £21.

Several issues were raised in the almost four years of litigation that
followed, but arguments focused on the legality of Rachel's access to and
use of the money. Never explicitly mentioned by White, but clearly more
important to him than the £21, was Rachel's sizeable inheritance. For
Rachel, the stakes were obvious: "my brother [in-law] White . . . is a
cheaten Rogue," she insisted, "and [he] goese about to undoe mee. He
keeps my portion from me, and strives to git all that I have." The case was
complicated by a number of factors, including Lawrence Clinton's desertion
of his wife. White did at last gain full control of the Haffield estate, however,
and retained it for the rest of his life.

Martha Haffield died in 1668. Shortly before, Rachel, then thirty-nine,
had been forced to petition the court for relief, "being destitute of money
and friends and skill in matters of Law." The house where she and her
mother had lived, she said, had been sold by White, and its contents seized.

Even her marriage portion, she averred, was still withheld from her "under pretence of emprovement." Giving up her attempt to claim her inheritance, she subsequently tried to make her estranged husband support her. Though the court made several halfhearted attempts to compel Lawrence to live with his wife, or at least to maintain her, by 1681 they had tired of the effort: "Rachel Clinton, desiring that her husband provide for her, was allowed 20 shillings," they declared, "she to demand no more of him." No doubt Rachel's adulterous involvement with other men influenced the court's decision, although Lawrence's sexual behavior had been even more flagrant. In 1677, Rachel had petitioned for, but had been denied, a divorce. When she appealed again in late 1681, it was granted her. From then on, she was a ward of the town. In 1687, and again in 1692, she was accused of malefic witchcraft. The second time she was tried and convicted. . . .

Aside from these many women who lived or had lived in families without male heirs, there were at least a dozen other witches who, despite the presence of brothers and sons, came into much larger shares of estates than their neighbors would have expected. In some cases, these women gained full control over the disposition of property. We know about these women because their fathers, husbands, or other relatives left wills, because the women themselves wrote wills, or because male relatives who felt cheated out of their customary shares fought in the courts for more favorable arrangements.

Grace Boulter of Hampton, one of several children of Richard Swain, is one of these women. Grace was accused of witchcraft in 1680, along with her thirty-two-year-old daughter, Mary Prescott. Twenty years earlier, in 1660, just prior to his removal to Nantucket, Grace's father had deeded a substantial portion of his Hampton property to her and her husband Nathaniel, some of which he gave directly to her.

Another witch in this group is Jane James of Marblehead, who left an estate at her death in 1669 which was valued at £85. While it is not clear how she came into possession of it, the property had not belonged to her husband Erasmus, who had died in 1660, though it did play a significant role in a controversy between her son and son-in-law over their rightful shares of both Erasmus's and Jane's estates. Between 1650 and her death in 1669, Jane was accused of witchcraft at least three times by her Marblehead neighbors.

A third woman, Margaret Scott of Rowley, had been left most of her husband Benjamin's small estate in 1671. The land and most of the cattle were hers only "dureing hir widowhood," but approximately one-third of the estate was "to be wholy hir owne." Margaret did not remarry. By the time she was executed as a witch in 1692, twenty-one years after her husband's death, she was seventy-five years old and little remained of the estate for the next generation to inherit.

In each of these last few cases, the women came into property through the decision of a father or husband. Only occasionally, however, do we find the courts putting property directly into the hands of women subsequently accused of witchcraft. Mary English's mother, Elinor Hollingworth, was one of these exceptions. In this situation, as in the others, the unusual decision of the magistrates can be attributed to the small size of the estate involved. These particular inheriting women were widows, usually with young children to support.

Looking back over the lives of these many women—most particularly those who did not have brothers or sons to inherit—we begin to understand the complexity of the economic dimension of New England witchcraft. Only rarely does the actual trial testimony indicate that economic power was even at issue. Nevertheless it is there, recurring with a telling persistence once we look beyond what was explicitly said about these women as witches. Inheritance disputes surface frequently enough in witchcraft cases, cropping up as part of the general context even when no direct link between the dispute and the charge is discernible, to suggest the fears that underlay most accusations. No matter how deeply entrenched the principle of male inheritance, no matter how carefully written the laws that protected it, it was impossible to insure that all families had male offspring. The women who stood to benefit from these demographic "accidents" account for most of New England's female witches.

The amount of property in question was not the crucial factor in the way these women were viewed or treated by their neighbors, however. Women of widely varying economic circumstances were vulnerable to accusation and even to conviction. Neither was there a direct line from accuser to material beneficiary of the accusation: others in the community did sometimes profit personally from the losses sustained by these women (Rachel Clinton's brother-in-law, Thomas White, comes to mind), but only rarely did the gain accrue to the accusers themselves. Indeed, occasionally there was no direct temporal connection: in some instances several decades passed between the creation of the key economic conditions and the charge of witchcraft; the charge in other cases even anticipated the development of those conditions.

Finally, inheriting or potentially inheriting women were vulnerable to witchcraft accusations not only during the Salem outbreak, but from the time of the first formal accusations in New England at least until the end of the century. Despite sketchy information on the lives of New England's early witches, it appears that Alice Young, Mary Johnson, Margaret Jones, Joan Carrington, and Mary Parsons, all of whom were executed in the late 1640s and early 1650s, were women without sons when the accusations were lodged. Elizabeth Godman, brought into court at least twice on witchcraft charges in the 1650s, had neither brothers nor sons. Decade by decade, the pattern continued. Only Antinomian and Quaker women, against whom accusations never generated much support, were, as a group, exempt from it.

The Salem outbreak created only a slight wrinkle in this established fabric of suspicion. If daughters, husbands, and sons of witches were more vulnerable to danger in 1692 than they had been previously, they were mostly the daughters, husbands, and sons of inheriting or potentially inheriting women. As the outbreak spread, it drew into its orbit increasing numbers of women, "unlikely" witches in that they were married to well-off and influential men, but familiar figures to some of their neighbors nonetheless.

What the impoverished Sarah Good had in common with Mary Phips, wife of Massachusetts's governor, was what Eunice Cole had in common with Katherine Harrison, and what Mehitabel Downing had in common with Ann Hibbens. However varied their backgrounds and economic positions, as women without brothers or women without sons, they stood in the way of the orderly transmission of property from one generation of males to another.

✢ FURTHER READING

Paul Boyer and Stephen Nissenbaum, *Salem Possessed* (1974)

Jon Butler, "Magic, Astrology, and the Early American Religious Heritage, 1600–1760," *American Historical Review*, LXXXIV (1979), 317–46

John P. Demos, "Underlying Themes in the Witchcraft of Seventeenth-Century New England," *American Historical Review*, LXXV (1970), 1311–26

Frederick C. Drake, "Witchcraft in the American Colonies," *American Quarterly*, XX (1968), 694–725

Barbara Ehrenreich and Dierdre English, *Witches, Midwives and Nurses* (1972)

Chadwick Hansen, *Witchcraft at Salem* (1969)

George Kittredge, *Witchcraft in Old and New England* (1929)

Christina Larner, *Enemies of God: The Witch-hunt in Scotland* (1981)

———, *Witchcraft and Religion* (1984)

Alan Macfarlane, *Witchcraft in Tudor and Stuart England* (1970)

Marion Starkey, *The Devil in Massachusetts* (1950)

Keith Thomas, *Religion and the Decline of Magic* (1971)

Richard Weisman, *Witchcraft, Magic, and Religion in 17th-Century Massachusetts* (1984)

The Impact of the
American Revolution

In many ways the American Revolution changed the course of history for the residents of what had been Britain's mainland North American colonies. In 1774 the Americans were colonials, subjects of a monarchy based thousands of miles away across the Atlantic Ocean and participants in a traditional political system. Less than a decade later they were successful revolutionaries, the founders of an independent republic—the first colonists in history to win their freedom and establish a nation of their own.

Such dramatic events, it could be argued, impinged primarily on men, not women. After all, men alone fought in the armies, voted in the new republic's elections, drafted state and national constitutions, and served in legislative bodies. Women traditionally did not take part in politics; their domain was the domestic sphere, whereas the public world was defined exclusively as men's arena. Did the Revolution, then, affect women? If so, what was its impact? Or can the Revolution be safely ignored by historians of women because it held so little meaning for their subjects?

❖ D O C U M E N T S

In March 1776, recognizing that the United States, which had already been at war with Great Britain for nearly a year, would soon declare independence, Abigail Adams wrote to her congressman husband John in Philadelphia, reminding him to "remember the ladies" in the nation's "new code of laws." She thus initiated the first-known exchange in American history on the subject of women's rights; the first document consists of the Adamses' comments to each other on the matter. Drawing on revolutionary ideas of women's equality with men, in 1779 Susanna Wright wrote a poem in praise of her friend, Elizabeth Norris, reprinted here as the second selection. The following year, after the Americans had suffered one of their worst defeats of the war when Charleston, South Carolina, fell to the British forces, a broadside entitled "The Sentiments of an American Woman" (the third document) proposed a nationwide Ladies Association to contribute to the welfare of the troops. Many years after the Revolution, Sarah Osborn, who had traveled with her husband and the American army, recalled her experiences, reprinted as the final selection, when she applied for a government pension in 1837.

Abigail and John Adams's "Remember the Ladies" Letters, 1776

Abigail Adams to John Adams:

Braintree March 31 1776

I long to hear that you have declared an independancy—and by the way in the new Code of Laws which I suppose it will be necessary for you to make I desire you would Remember the Ladies, and be more generous and favourable to them than your ancestors. Do not put such unlimited power into the hands of the Husbands. Remember all Men would be tyrants if they could. If perticuliar care and attention is not paid to the Laidies we are determined to foment a Rebelion, and will not hold ourselves bound by any Laws in which we have no voice, or Representation.

That your Sex are Naturally Tyrannical is a Truth so thoroughly established as to admit of no dispute, but such of you as wish to be happy willingly give up the harsh title of Master for the more tender and endearing one of Friend. Why then, not put it out of the power of the vicious and the Lawless to use us with cruelty and indignity with impunity. Men of Sense in all Ages abhor those customs which treat us only as the vassals of your Sex. Regard us then as Beings placed by providence under your protection and in immitation of the Supreem Being make use of that power only for our happiness.

John to Abigail:

Ap. 14. 1776

As to Declarations of Independency, be patient. Read our Privateering Laws, and our Commercial Laws. What signifies a Word.

As to your extraordinary Code of Laws, I cannot but laugh. We have been told that our Struggle has loosened the bands of Government every where. That Children and Apprentices were disobedient—that schools and Colledges were grown turbulent—that Indians slighted their Guardians and Negroes grew insolent to their Masters. But your Letter was the first Intimation that another Tribe more numerous and powerfull than all the rest were grown discontented.—This is rather too coarse a Compliment but you are so saucy, I wont blot it out.

Depend upon it, We know better than to repeal our Masculine systems. Altho they are in full Force, you know they are little more than Theory. We dare not exert our Power in its full Latitude. We are obliged to go fair, and softly, and in Practice you know We are the subjects. We have only the Name of Masters, and rather than give up this, which would compleatly subject Us to the Despotism of the Peticoat, I hope General Washington, and all our brave Heroes would fight. I am sure every good Politician would plot, as long as he would against Despotism, Empire, Monarchy, Aristocracy, Oligarchy, or Ochlocracy,—A fine Story indeed. I begin to think the Ministry as deep as they are wicked. After stirring up Tories, Landjobbers, Trimmers, Bigots, Canadians, Indians, Negroes, Hanoverians, Hessians, Russians, Irish Roman Catholicks, Scotch Renegadoes, at last they have stimulated the   to demand new Priviledges and threaten to rebell.

Abigail to John:

B[raintre]e May 7 1776

I can not say that I think you very generous to the Ladies, for whilst you are proclaiming peace and good will to Men, Emancipating all Nations, you insist upon retaining an absolute power over Wives. But you must remember that Arbitrary power is like most other things which are very hard, very liable to be broken—and notwithstanding all your wise Laws and Maxims we have it in our power not only to free our selves but to subdue our Masters, and without violence throw both your natural and legal authority at our feet—

> "Charm by accepting, by submitting sway
> Yet have our Humour most when we obey."

Susanna Wright's "To Eliza Norris—at Fairhill," c. 1779

> Since Adam, by our first fair Mother won
> To share her fate, to taste, & be undone,
> And that great law, whence no appeal must lie,
> Pronounc'd a doom, that he should rule & die,
> The partial race, rejoicing to fulfill
> This pleasing dictate of almighty will
> (With no superior virtue in their mind),
> Assert their right to govern womankind.
> But womankind call reason to their aid,
> And question when or where that law was made,
> That law divine (a plausible pretence)
> Oft urg'd with none, & oft with little sense,
> From wisdom's source no origin could draw,
> That form'd the man to keep the sex in awe;

Extract from poem by Susanna Wright, "To Eliza Norris—at Fairhill," in Pattie Cowell, ed., *Signs,* VI (1980–81), 799–800. Reprinted by permission of The University of Chicago Press.

Say Reason governs all the mighty frame,
And Reason rules in every one the same,
No right has man his equal to control,
Since, all agree, there is no sex in soul;
Weak woman, thus in agreement grown strong,
Shakes off the yoke her parents wore too long;
But he, who arguments in vain had tried,
Hopes still for conquest from the yielding side,
Soft soothing flattery & persuasion tries,
And by a feign'd submission seeks to rise,
Steals, unperceiv'd, to the unguarded heart,
    And there reigns tyrant.

. . .

Indulge man in his darling vice of sway,
He only rules those who of choice obey;
When strip'd of power, & plac'd in equal light,
Angels shall judge who had the better right,
All you can do is but to let him see
That woman still shall sure his equal be,
By your example shake his ancient law,
And shine yourself, the finish'd piece you draw.

The Sentiments of an American Woman, 1780

On the commencement of actual war, the Women of America manifested a firm resolution to contribute as much as could depend on them, to the deliverance of their country. Animated by the purest patriotism, they are sensible of sorrow at this day, in not offering more than barren wishes for the success of so glorious a Revolution. They aspire to render themselves more really useful ; and this sentiment is universal from the north to the south of the Thirteen United States. Our ambition is kindled by the fame of those heroines of antiquity, who have rendered their sex illustrious, and have proved to the universe, that, if the weakness of our Constitution, if opinion and manners did not forbid us to march to glory by the same paths as the Men, we should at least equal, and sometimes surpass them in our love for the public good. I glory in all that which my sex has done great and commendable. I call to mind with enthusiasm and with admiration, all those acts of courage, of constancy and patriotism, which history has transmitted to us : The people favoured by Heaven, preserved from destruction by the virtues, the zeal and the revolution of Deborah, of Judith, of Esther ! The fortitude of the mother of the Macchabees, in giving up her sons to die before her eyes : Rome saved from the fury of a victorious enemy by the efforts of Volumnia, and other Roman Ladies : So many famous sieges where the Women have been seen forgeting the weakness of their sex, building new walls, digging trenches with their feeble hands, furnishing arms to their defenders, they themselves darting the missile weapons on the enemy, resigning the ornaments of their apparel, and their fortune, to fill the public treasury, and to hasten the deliverance of their country ; burying themselves under its ruins ; throwing themselves into the flames rather than submit to the disgrace of humiliation before a proud enemy.

Born for liberty, disdaining to bear the irons of a tyrannic Government, we associate ourselves to the grandeur of those Sovereigns, cherished and revered, who have held with so much splendour the scepter of the greatest States, The Batildas, the Elizabeths, the Maries, the Catharines, who have extended the empire of liberty, and contented to reign by sweetness and justice, have broken the chains of slavery, forged by tyrants in the times of ignorance and barbarity. The Spanish Women, do they not make, at this moment, the most patriotic sacrifices, to encrease the means of victory in the hands of their Sovereign. He is a friend to the French Nation.   They are our allies.   We call to mind, doubly interested, that it was a French Maid who kindled up amongst her fellow-citizens, the flame of patriotism buried under long misfortunes :   It was the Maid of Orleans who drove from the kingdom of France the ancestors of those same British, whose odious yoke we have just shaken off ; and whom it is necessary that we drive from this Continent.

But I must limit myself to the recollection of this small number of atchievements.   Who knows if persons disposed to censure, and sometimes too severely with regard to us, may not disapprove our appearing acquainted even with the actions of which our sex boasts ?   We are at least certain, that he cannot be a good citizen who will not applaud our efforts for the relief of the armies which defend our lives, our possessions, our liberty ?   The situation of our soldiery has been represented to me; the evils inseparable from war, and the firm and generous spirit which has enabled them to support these.   But it has been said, that they may apprehend, that, in the course of a long war, the view of their distresses may be lost, and their services be forgotten.   Forgotten ! never ; I can answer in the name of all my sex. Brave Americans, your disinterestedness, your courage, and your constancy will always be dear to America, as long as she shall preserve her virtue.

We know that at a distance from the theatre of war, if we enjoy any tranquility, it is the fruit of your watchings, your labours, your dangers. If I live happy in the midst of my family ;   if my husband cultivates his field, and reaps his harvest in peace ;   if, surrounded with my children, I myself nourish the youngest, and press it to my bosom, without being affraid of seeing myself separated from it, by a ferocious enemy ;   if the house in which we dwell ;   if our barns, our orchards are safe at the present time from the hands of those incendiaries, it is to you that we owe it. And shall we hesitate to evidence to you our gratitude   ? Shall we hesitate to wear a cloathing more simple   ; hair dressed less elegant, while at the price of this small privation, we shall deserve your benedictions. Who, amongst us, will not renounce with the highest pleasure, those vain ornaments, when she shall consider that the valiant defenders of America will be able to draw some advantage from the money which she may have laid out in these   ; that they will be better defended from the rigours of the seasons, that after their painful toils, they will receive some extraordinary and unexpected relief ; that these presents will perhaps be valued by them at a greater price, when they will have it in their power to say : *This is the offering of the Ladies.* The time is arrived to display the same sentiments which animated us at the beginning of the Revolution, when we renounced the use of teas, however agreeable to our taste, rather than receive them from our persecutors ; when we made it appear to them that we placed former necessaries in the rank of superfluities, when our liberty was interested ; when our republican and laborious hands spun the flax, prepared the linen intended for the use of our soldiers ; when exiles and fugitives we supported with courage all the evils which are the concomitants of war. Let us not lose a moment ; let us be engaged to offer the homage of our gratitude at the altar of military valour, and you, our brave deliverers, while mercenary slaves combat to cause you to share with them, the irons with which they are loaded, receive with a free hand our offering, the purest which can be presented to your virtue,

By an AMERICAN WOMAN
[Esther DeBerdt Reed]

Sarah Osborn's Narrative, 1837

That she was married to Aaron Osborn, who was a soldier during the Revolutionary War. That her first aquaintance with said Osborn commenced in Albany, in the state of New York, during the hard winter of 1780. That deponent then resided at the house of one John Willis, a blacksmith in said city. That said Osborn came down there from Fort Stanwix and went to work at the business of blacksmithing for said Willis and continued working at intervals for a period of perhaps two months. Said Osborn then informed deponent that he had first enlisted at Goshen in Orange County, New York. That he had been in the service for three years, deponent thinks, about one year of that time at Fort Stanwix, and that his time was out. And, under an assurance that he would go to Goshen with her, she married him at the house of said Willis during the time he was there as above mentioned, to wit, in January 1780. . . .

That after deponent had married said Osborn, he informed her that he was returned during the war, and that he desired deponent to go with him. Deponent declined until she was informed by Captain Gregg that her husband should be put on the commissary guard, and that she should have the means of conveyance either in a wagon or on horseback. That deponent then in the same winter season in sleighs accompanied her husband and the forces under command of Captain Gregg on the east side of the Hudson river to Fishkill, then crossed the river and went down to West Point. . . .

Deponent further says that she and her husband remained at West Point till the departure of the army for the South, a term of perhaps one year and a

Sarah Osborn, Narrative, 1837, in John Dann, ed., *The Revolution Remembered*, 1980, 241–246, The University of Chicago Press.

half, but she cannot be positive as to the length of time. While at West Point, deponent lived at Lieutenant Foot's, who kept a boardinghouse. Deponent was employed in washing and sewing for the soldiers. Her said husband was employed about the camp. . . .

When the army were about to leave West Point and go south, they crossed over the river to Robinson's Farms and remained there for a length of time to induce the belief, as deponent understood, that they were going to take up quarters there, whereas they recrossed the river in the nighttime into the Jerseys and traveled all night in a direct course for Philadelphia. Deponent was part of the time on horseback and part of the time in a wagon. Deponent's said husband was still serving as one of the commissary's guard. . . .

They continued their march to Philadelphia, deponent on horseback through the streets, and arrived at a place towards the Schuylkill where the British had burnt some houses, where they encamped for the afternoon and night. Being out of bread, deponent was employed in baking the afternoon and evening. Deponent recollects no females but Sergeant Lamberson's and Lieutenant Forman's wives and a colored woman by the name of Letta. The Quaker ladies who came round urged deponent to stay, but her said husband said, "No, he could not leave her behind." Accordingly, next day they continued their march from day to day till they arrived at Baltimore, where deponent and her said husband and the forces under command of General Clinton, Captain Gregg, and several other officers, all of whom she does not recollect, embarked on board a vessel and sailed down the Chesapeake. There were several vessels along, and deponent was in the foremost. . . . They continued sail until they had got up the St. James River as far as the tide would carry them, about twelve miles from the mouth, and then landed, and the tide being spent, they had a fine time catching sea lobsters, which they ate.

They, however, marched immediately for a place called Williamsburg, as she thinks, deponent alternately on horseback and on foot. There arrived, they remained two days till the army all came in by land and then marched for Yorktown, or Little York as it was then called. The York troops were posted at the right, the Connecticut troops next, and the French to the left. In about one day or less than a day, they reached the place of encampment about one mile from Yorktown. Deponent was on foot and the other females above named and her said husband still on the commissary's guard. Deponent's attention was arrested by the appearance of a large plain between them and Yorktown and an entrenchment thrown up. She also saw a number of dead Negroes lying round their encampment, whom she understood the British had driven out of the town and left to starve, or were first starved and then thrown out. Deponent took her stand just back of the American tents, say about a mile from the town, and busied herself washing, mending, and cooking for the soldiers, in which she was assisted by the other females; some men washed their own clothing. She heard the roar of the artillery for a number of days, and the last night the Americans threw up entrenchments, it was a misty, foggy night, rather wet but not rainy. Every soldier threw up for himself, as she understood, and she afterwards saw and went into the entrenchments. Deponent's said husband was there throwing up entrenchments, and deponent cooked and carried in beef, and bread, and coffee (in a gallon pot) to the soldiers in the entrenchment.

On one occasion when deponent was thus employed carrying in provisions, she met General Washington, who asked her if she "was not afraid of the cannonballs?"

She replied, "No, the bullets would not cheat the gallows," that "It would not do for the men to fight and starve too."

They dug entrenchments nearer and nearer to Yorktown every night or two till the last. While digging that, the enemy fired very heavy till about nine o'clock next morning, then stopped, and the drums from the enemy beat excessively. . . .

All at once the officers hurrahed and swung their hats, and deponent asked them, "What is the matter now?"

One of them replied, "Are not you soldier enough to know what it means?"

Deponent replied, "No."

They then replied, "The British have surrendered."

Deponent, having provisions ready, carried the same down to the entrenchments that morning, and four of the soldiers whom she was in the habit of cooking for ate their breakfasts.

Deponent stood on one side of the road and the American officers upon the other side when the British officers came out of the town and rode up to the American officers and delivered up [their swords, which the deponent] thinks were returned again, and the British officers rode right on before the army, who marched out beating and playing a melancholy tune, their drums covered with black handkerchiefs and their fifes with black ribbands tied around them, into an old field and there grounded their arms and then returned into town again to await their destiny. . . .

On going into town, she noticed two dead Negroes lying by the market house. She had the curiosity to go into a large building that stood nearby, and there she noticed the cupboards smashed to pieces and china dishes and other ware strewed around upon the floor, and among the rest a pewter cover to a hot basin that had a handle on it. She picked it up, supposing it to belong to the British, but the governor came in and claimed it as his, but said he would have the name of giving it away as it was the last one out of twelve that he could see, and accordingly presented it to deponent, and she afterwards brought it home with her to Orange County and sold it for old pewter, which she has a hundred times regretted.

❖ *E S S A Y S*

In the first essay, written in 1976, Joan Hoff-Wilson of Indiana University contends that the effect of the Revolution on women, if there could be said to have been one, was chiefly negative: the war, she argued, brought few or no benefits to women, whose prewar situation was so circumscribed that they could not take advantage of the opportunities that the war presented to their male contemporaries. After reading hundreds of women's and men's letters and diaries from that period, Mary Beth Norton reached the opposite conclusion. The second selection consists of excerpts from Norton's 1980 book *Liberty's Daughters,* in which she contends that the Revolution was, at least to a limited extent, "liberating" for women.

The Negative Impact of the American Revolution

JOAN HOFF-WILSON

I will argue that certain types of female functions, leading either to the well-known exploitation of working women or to the ornamental middle-class housewife of the nineteenth century, were abetted by the American Revolution, although not caused by it.

This occurred because the functional opportunities open to women between 1700 and 1800 were too limited to allow them to make the transition in attitudes necessary to insure high status performance in the newly emerging nation. In other words, before 1776 women did not participate enough in conflicts over land, religion, taxes, local politics, or commercial transactions. They simply had not come into contact with enough worldly diversity to be prepared for a changing, pluralistic, modern society. Women of the postrevolutionary generation had little choice but to fill those low status functions prescribed by the small minority of American males who *were* prepared for modernization by enough diverse activities and experiences.

As a result, the American Revolution produced no significant benefits for American women. This same generalization can be made for other powerless groups in the colonies—native Americans, blacks, probably most propertyless white males, and indentured servants. Although these people together with women made up the vast majority of colonial population, they could not take advantage of the overthrow of British rule to better their own positions, as did the white, propertied males who controlled economics, politics, and culture. By no means did all members of these subordinate groups support the patriot cause, and those who did, even among whites, were not automatically accorded personal liberation when national liberation was won. This is a common phenomenon of revolution within subcultures which, because of sex, race, or other forms of discrimination or deprivation of the members, are not far enough along in the process toward modernization to express their dissatisfaction or frustration through effectively organized action.

Given the political and socioeconomic limitations of the American Revolution, this lack of positive societal change in the lives of women and other

Excerpts from Joan Hoff-Wilson, "The Illusion of Change: Women and the American Revolution," in Alfred Young, ed., *The American Revolution: Explorations in the History of American Radicalism,* 386–401, 419–431. Copyright 1976 by Northern Illinois University Press. Reprinted with permission of the publisher.

deprived colonials is to be expected. It is also not surprising that until recently most historians of the period have been content to concentrate their research efforts on the increased benefits of Lockean liberalism that accrued to a relatively small percent of all Americans and to ignore the increased sexism and racism exhibited by this privileged group both during and after the Revolution. They have also tended to ignore the various ways in which the experience of the Revolution either hastened or retarded certain long-term eighteenth-century trends already affecting women.

What has been called in England and Europe "the transformation of the female in bourgeois culture" also took place in America between 1700 and 1800. This process would have occurred with or without a declaration of independence from England. It produced a class of American bourgeoises who clearly resembled the group of middle-class women evident in England a century earlier. However, the changing societal conditions leading up to this transformation in American women were much more complex than they had been for seventeenth-century British women because of the unique roles, that is, functions, that colonial women had originally played in the settlement and development of the New World. The American Revolution was simply one event among many in this century-long process of change. It was a process that ultimately produced two distinct classes of women in the United States—those who worked to varying degrees exclusively in their homes and those who worked both inside and outside of their homes. . . .

It is true, however, for most of the period up to 1750 that conditions *out of necessity* increased the functional independence and importance of all women. By this I mean that much of the alleged freedom from sexism of colonial women was due to their initial numerical scarcity and the critical labor shortage in the New World throughout the seventeenth and eighteenth centuries. Such increased reproductive roles (economic as well as biological) reflected the logic of necessity and *not any fundamental change* in the sexist, patriarchal attitudes that had been transplanted from Europe. Based on two types of scarcity (sex and labor), which were not to last, these enhanced functions of colonial women diminished as the commercial and agricultural economy became more specialized and the population grew.

A gradual "embourgeoisement" of colonial culture accompanied this preindustrial trend toward modern capitalism. It limited the number of high status roles for eighteenth-century American women just as it had for seventeenth-century English and European women. Alice Clark, Margaret George, Natalie Zemon Davis, and Jane Abray have all argued convincingly that as socioeconomic capitalist organization takes place, it closes many opportunities normally open to women both inside and outside of the family unit in precapitalist times. The decline in the status of women that accompanied the appearance of bourgeois modernity in England, according to Margaret George, "was not merely a relative decline. Precapitalist woman was not simply relatively eclipsed by the great leap foward of the male achiever; she suffered rather, an absolute setback."

In the New World this process took longer but was no less debilitating. Before 1800 it was both complicated and hindered by the existence of a severe labor shortage and religious as well as secular exhortations against the sins of idleness and vanity. Thus, colonial conditions demanded that all able-bodied men, women, and children work, and so the ornamental, middle-class woman existed more in theory than in practice.

The labor shortage that plagued colonial America placed a premium on women's work inside and outside the home, particularly during the war-related periods of economic dislocation between 1750 and 1815. And there is no doubt that home industry was basic to American development both before and after 1776. It is also true that there was no sharp delineation between the economic needs of the community and the work carried on within the preindustrial family until after the middle of the eighteenth century. Woman's role as a household manager was a basic and integral part of the early political economy of the colonies. Hence she occupied a position of unprecedented importance and equality within the socioeconomic unit of the family.

As important as this function of women in the home was, from earliest colonial times, it nonetheless represented a division of labor based on sex-role stereotyping carried over from England. Men normally engaged in agricultural production; women engaged in domestic gardening and home manufacturing—only slave women worked in the fields. Even in those areas of Massachusetts and Pennsylvania that originally granted females allotments of land, the vestiges of this practice soon disappeared, and subsequent public divisions "simply denied the independent economic existence of women." While equality never extended outside the home in the colonial era, there was little likelihood that women felt useless or alienated because of the importance and demanding nature of their domestic responsibilities.

In the seventeenth and eighteenth centuries spinning and weaving were the primary types of home production for women and children (of both sexes). This economic function was considered so important that legal and moral sanctions were developed to insure it. For example, labor laws were passed, compulsory spinning schools were established "for the education of children of the poor," and women were told that their virtue could be measured in yards of yarn. So from the beginning there was a sex, and to a lesser degree a class and educational, bias built into colonial production of cloth, since no formal apprenticeship was required for learning the trade of spinning and weaving.

It has also been recognized that prerevolutionary boycotts of English goods after 1763 and later during the war increased the importance of female production of textiles both in the home and in the early piecework factory system. By mid-1776 in Philadelphia, for example, 4,000 women and children reportedly were spinning under the "putting out system" for local textile plants. . . .

American living standards fluctuated with the unequal prosperity that was especially related to wars. Those engaging in craft production and commerce were particularly hard hit after 1750, first by the deflation and depression following the French and Indian War (1754–1763), and then by the War for Independence. In fact, not only were the decades immediately preceding and following the American Revolution ones of economic dislocation, but the entire period between 1775 and 1815 has been characterized as one of "arrested social and economic development." These trends, combined with increased specialization, particularly with the appearance of a nascent factory system, "initiated a decline in the economic and social position of many sections of the artisan class." Thus with the exception of the innkeeping and tavern business, all of the other primary economic occupations of city women were negatively affected by the periodic fluctuations in the commercial economy between 1763 and 1812.

Women artisans and shopkeepers probably suffered most during times of economic crisis because of their greater difficulty in obtaining credit from merchants. Although research into their plight has been neglected, the documents are there—in the records of merchant houses showing women entrepreneurs paying their debts for goods and craft materials by transferring their own records of indebtedness, and in court records showing an increased number of single women, especially widows sued for their debts, or in public records of the increased number of bankrupt women who ended up on poor relief lists or in debtors' prisons or who were forced to become indentured servants or earn an independent living during hard times.

It was also a difficult time for household spinners and weavers, about whom a few more facts are known. First, this all-important economic function increasingly reflected class distinctions. In 1763 one British governor estimated that only the poor wore homespun clothes, while more affluent Americans bought English imports. Second, it was primarily poor women of the northern and middle colonies who engaged in spinning and weaving for pay (often in the form of credit rather than cash), while black slave women and white female indentured servants performed the same function in the South. Naturally women in all frontier areas had no recourse but to make their own clothing. Beginning with the first boycotts of British goods in the 1760s, women of all classes were urged to make and wear homespun. Several additional "manufactory houses" were established as early as 1764 in major cities specifically for the employment of poor women. Direct appeals to patriotism and virtue were used very successfully to get wealthier women to engage in arduous home-spinning drives, but probably only for short periods of time.

Thus all classes of women were actively recruited into domestic textile production by male patriots with such pleas as, "In this time of public distress you have each of you an opportunity not only to help to sustain your families, but likewise to call your mite into the treasury of the public good." They were further urged to "cease trifling their time away [and] prudently employ it in learning the use of the spinning wheel." Beyond any doubt the most well-known appeal was the widely reprinted 9 November 1767 statement of advice to the "Daughters of Liberty" which first appeared in the *Massachusetts Gazette*. It read in part:

> First then throw aside your high top knots of pride
> Wear none but your own country linen.
> Of economy boast. Let your pride be the most
> To show cloaths of your make and spinning.

Peak periods in prerevolutionary spinning and weaving were reached during every major boycott from 1765 to 1777. But the war and inflation proved disruptive. For example, we know that the United Company of Philadelphia for Promoting American Manufactures, which employed 500 of the City's 4,000 women and children spinning at home, expired between 1777 and 1787, when it was revived. The record of similar organizations elsewhere was equally erratic.

It is common for developing countries with a labor shortage to utilize technological means to meet production demands. After the war, the new republic proved no exception, as the inefficiency and insufficiency of household spinners became apparent. Ultimately the "putting out" system was replaced entirely by the factory that employed the same women and children who had formerly been household spinners. It took the entire first half of the nineteenth century before this process was completed, and when it was, it turned out to be at the expense of the social and economic status of female workers. . . .

Why didn't the experiences of the Revolution result in changing the political consciousness of women? Part of the answer lies in the socialized attitudes among female members of the revolutionary generation that set them apart from their male contemporaries. Their attitudes had been molded by the modernization trends encountered by most women in the course of the eighteenth century. Out of the necessity wrought by the struggle with England, women performed certain tasks that appeared revolutionary in nature, just as they had performed nonfamilial tasks out of necessity throughout the colonial period. But this seemingly revolutionary behavior is not necessarily proof of the acceptance of abstract revolutionary principles.

Despite their participation in greater economic specialization, despite their experiences with a slightly smaller conjugal household where power relations were changing, despite a limited expansion of the legal rights and somewhat improved educational opportunities for free, white women, the revolutionary generation of females were less prepared than most men for the modern implications of independence. Their distinctly different experiential level, combined with the intellectually and psychologically limiting impact of the Great Awakening and the Enlightenment on women, literally made it impossible for even the best educated females to understand the political intent or principles behind the inflated rhetoric of the revolutionary era. Words like virtue, veracity, morality, tyranny, and corruption were ultimately given public political meanings by male revolutionary leaders that were incomprehensible or, more likely, misunderstood by most women.

As the rhetoric of the revolution began to assume dynamic, emotional proportions, its obsession with "virtue" versus "corruption" struck a particularly responsive chord among literate women, as evidenced for example, in their patriotic statements as individuals and in groups when supporting the boycott of English goods between 1765 and 1774. While these statements are impressive both in number and intensity of feeling, it can be questioned whether the idea of taking "their country back on the path of virtue" and away from "the oppression of corrupt outside forces" was understood in the same way by female and male patriots, when even men of varying Whig persuasions could not agree on them. Virtue and morality for the vast majority of Americans, but particularly women, do not appear to have had the modernizing implications of pluralistic individualism, that is, of the "acceptance of diversity, the commitment to individual action in pursuit of individual goals, the conception of politics as an arena where these goals contest and the awareness of a national government which is at once the course of political power and the framework for an orderly clash of interest." These are characteristics of "modern man."

How does one prove such a generalization about attitudes behind the behavior of women during the Revolution? Few poor white or black women left records revealing how they felt about the war. Such women, whether Loyalists or patriots, conveyed their sentiments silently with their physical labor. Among the more articulate and educated women there is written testimony to at least an initial sense of pride and importance involved in their participation in the war effort. Thus a young Connecticut woman named Abigail Foote wrote in her diary in 1775 that carding two pounds of whole wool had made her feel "Nationly," while others recorded their contributions in similarly patriotic terms.

But the question remains: did their supportive actions prepare them to accept a vision of society anywhere near the version ultimately conveyed by James Madison's Federalist Number Ten in the fight over the Constitution of 1787? To date there is little evidence that this type of sophisticated political thought was present, either in the writings of women about the Revolution and its results or in the appeals made to them during or immediately following the war. From the popular 1767 statement of advice to the Daughters of Liberty to the 1787 one urging women to use "their influence over their husbands, brothers and sons to draw them from those dreams of liberty under a simple democratic form of government, which are so unfriendly to . . . order and decency," it is difficult to conclude that women were being prepared to understand the political ramifications of the Revolution.

The same lack of political astuteness appears to underlie even the least traditional and most overtly political activities of women, such as the fifty-one who signed the anti-tea declaration in Edenton, North Carolina, on 25 October 1774 (later immortalized in a London cartoon). The same could be said of the more than 500 Boston women who agreed on 31 January 1770 to support the radical male boycott of tea; of the Daughters of Liberty in general; and of the 1,600 Philadelphia women who raised 7,500 dollars in gold for the Continental Army. Even Mercy Otis Warren never perceived the modern political system that evolved from the Revolution. Instead she viewed the war and its aftermath as the "instrument of Providence that sparked a world movement, changing thought and habit of men to complete the divine plan for human happiness" largely through the practice of virtue.

Perhaps the most important aspect of the supportive activities among women for the patriot cause was the increase in class and social distinctions they symbolized. For example, it appears unlikely that poor white or black women joined Daughters of Liberty groups, actively boycotted English goods, or participated in any significant numbers in those associations of "Ladies of the highest rank and influence," who raised money and supplies for the Continental Army. On the contrary, it may well have been primarily "young female spinsters" from prominent families and well-to-do widows and wives who could afford the time or the luxury of such highly publicized activities. The vast majority, however, of middle-class female patriots (and, for that matter, Loyalists), whether single or married, performed such necessary volunteer roles as seamstresses, nurses, hostesses, and sometime spies, whenever the fighting shifted to their locales, without any undue fanfare or praise.

The same is true of poorer women, with one important difference: they had no choice. They had all they could do to survive, and although this did lead a few of them to become military heroines, they could not afford the luxury of either "disinterested patriotism" or the detached self-interest and indulgences that some of the richer women exhibited. The very poorest, particularly those in urban areas, had no resources to fall back on when confronted with the personal or economic traumas caused by the War for Independence. As noted above, this was especially evident in the case of women wage earners who, regardless of race or class, had apparently always received lower pay than free men or hired-out male slaves, and who had suffered severely from runaway inflation during the war. Women's services were more likely to be paid for in Continental currency than with specie. Fees for male "doctors," for example, according to one Maryland family account book, were made in specie payment after the middle of 1780, while midwives had to accept the depreciated Continental currency for a longer period of time. Thus, the American Revolution hastened the appearance of greater class-based activities among "daughters of the new republic," with poor women undertaking the least desirable tasks and suffering most from the inflationary spiral that plagued the whole country. It is easy to imagine the impact that inflation had on the rural and urban poor, but it even affected those middle- and upper middle-class women who were left at home to manage businesses, estates, plantations, or farms. Their activities often meant the difference between bankruptcy and solvency for male revolutionary leaders.

Probably the classic example of housewifely efficiency and economic shrewdness is found in Abigail's management of the Adams's family and farm during John's long absences. But in this respect Abigail Adams stands in direct contrast to the women in the lives of other leading revolutionaries like Jefferson, Madison, and Monroe—all of whom were bankrupt by public service in part because their wives were not as capable at land management as she was. This even proved true of the most outspoken of all revolutionary wives, Mercy Otis Warren. Numerous lesser well-known women, however, proved equal to the increased domestic responsibilities placed upon them. Only the utterly impoverished could not resort to the traditional colonial task of household manager.

As the months of fighting lengthened into years, more and more poverty-stricken women left home to join their husbands, lovers, fathers, or other male relatives in the army encampments. Once there, distinctions between traditional male and female roles broke down. While a certain number of free white and black slave women were needed to mend, wash, and cook for officers and care for the sick and wounded, most enlisted men and their women took care of themselves and fought beside each other on many occasions. Moreover, unlike the English, German, and French commanders, American military leaders were often morally offended or embarassed by the presence of these unfortunate and destitute women, "their hair flying, their brows beady with the heat, their belongings slung over one sholder [sic], chattering and yelling in sluttish shrills as they went and spitting in the gutters."

This puritanical, hostile attitude on the part of patriot army officers toward such a common military phenomenon insured that camp followers of the American forces were less systematically provided for than those of foreign troops. Aside from its class overtones (after all Martha Washington, Catherine Greene, and Lucy Knox were accepted as respectable camp followers), it is difficult to explain this American attitude, except that in the prevailing righteous rhetoric of the Revolution and of later historians these women were misrepresented as little better than prostitutes. In reality they were the inarticulate, invisible poor whose story remains to be told from existing pension records based on oral testimony. At any rate there is pathos and irony in the well-preserved image of Martha Washington, who visited her husand at Valley Forge during the disastrous winter of 1777–1778, copying routine military communiques and presiding over a sewing circle of other officers' wives, while the scores of combat-hardened women, who died along with their enlisted men, have been conveniently forgotten.

These camp followers, as well as the women who stayed at home, complained about their plight privately and publicly, and on occasion they rioted and looted for foodstuffs. Women rioting for bread or other staples never became a significant or even a particularly common revolutionary act in the New World as it did in Europe, largely because of the absence of any long-term, abject poverty on the part of even the poorest colonials. The most likely exception to this generalization came during the extreme inflation that accompanied the war. Then there is indeed some evidence of what can be called popular price control activity by groups of women who had a definite sense of what were fair or legitimate marketing practices. At the moment we have concrete evidence of only a half-dozen seemingly spontaneous instances of "a corps of female infantry" attacking merchants. Other examples will probably be discovered as more serious research into the "moral economy of the crowd" is undertaken by American historians.

What is interesting about the few known cases is that the women involved in some of them did not simply appear to be destitute camp followers passing through towns stripping the dead and looting at random for food. A few at least were women "with Silk gownes on," who were offering to buy sugar, salt, flour, or coffee for a reasonable price with Continental currency. When a certain merchant insisted on payment with specie or with an unreasonable amount of paper money, the women then, and only then, insisted on "taking" his goods at their price. These appear, therefore, to be isolated examples of collective behavior by women where there was, at the least, a very strongly held cultural notion of a moral economy.

Nevertheless, there is still no clear indication of an appreciable change in the political consciousness of such women. Perhaps it was because even the poorest who took part in popular price control actions primarily did so, like the Citoyennes Républicaines Révolutionnaires during the French Revolution, out of an immediate concern for feeding themselves and their children and not for feminist reasons growing out of their age-old economic plight as women in a patriarchal society. In addition, except for camp followers and female vagabonds, the principal concern of most members of this generation of primarily rural women remained the home and their functions there. During the home-spinning drives and during the war when their men were away, their domestic and agricultural duties became all the more demanding, but not consciousness-raising. . . .

Lastly, in explaining the failure of the equalitarian ideals of the Revolution to bear even limited fruit for women, one must analyze the narrow ideological parameters of even those few who advocated women's rights, persons such as Abigail Adams, Judith Sargent Murray, Elizabeth Southgate Bowne, Elizabeth Drinker, and Mercy Otis Warren.

These women . . . were not feminists. Like most of the better organized, but no less unsuccessful Républicaines of France, they seldom, if ever, aspired to complete equality with men except in terms of education. Moreover, none challenged the institution of marriage or defined themselves "as other than mothers and potential mothers." They simply could not conceive of a society whose standards were not set by male, patriarchal institutions, nor should they be expected to have done so. Instead of demanding equal rights, the most articulate and politically conscious American women of this generation asked at most for privileges and at least for favors—not for an absolute expansion of their legal or political functions, which they considered beyond their proper womanly sphere. Man was indeed the measure of equality to these women, and given their societal conditioning, such status was beyond their conception of themselves as individuals.

Ironically it is this same sense of their "proper sphere" that explains why the most educated female patriots did not feel obliged to organize to demand more from the Founding Fathers. It is usually overlooked that in the famous letter of 31 March 1776 where Abigail asks John Adams to "Remember the Ladies," she justified this mild request for "more generous and favourable" treatment on the grounds that married women were then subjected to the "unlimited power" of their husbands. She was not asking him for the right to vote, only for some legal protection of wives from abuses under common law practices. "Regard us then," she pleaded with her husband, "as Beings placed by providence under your protection and in imitation of the Supreme Being make use of that power only for our happiness." Despite an earlier statement in this letter about the "Ladies" being "determined to foment a Rebellion" and refusing to be "bound by any Laws in which we have no voice, or Representation," Abigail Adams was not in any sense demanding legal, let alone political or individual, equality with men at the beginning of the American Revolution. If anything, her concept of the separateness of the two different spheres in which men and women operated was accentuated by the war and the subsequent trials of the new republic between 1776 and 1800.

This idea that men and women existed in two separate spheres or orbits was commonly accepted in the last half of the eighteenth century as one of the natural laws of the universe. While European Enlightenment theories adhered strictly to the inferiority of the natural sphere that women occupied, in colonial America they were tacitly challenged and modified by experience—as were so many other aspects of natural law doctrines. On the other hand, the degree to which educated, upper-class women in particular thought that their sphere of activity was in fact equal, and the degree to which it actually was accorded such status by the male-dominated culture, is all important. Historians have tended to place greater emphasis on the former rather than the latter, with misleading results about the importance of the roles played by both colonial and revolutionary women.

It is true that Abigail Adams was an extremely independent-minded person who firmly criticized books by foreign authors who subordinated the female sphere to that of the male. Writing to her sister Elizabeth Shaw Peabody in 1799, she said that "I will never consent to have our sex considered in an inferior point of light. Let each planet shine in their own orbit, God and nature designed it so—if man is Lord, woman is *Lordess*—that is what I contend for." Thus, when her husband was away she deemed it was within her proper sphere to act as head of the household on all matters, including the decision to have her children inoculated against smallpox without his permission. At the same time, however, she always deferred to his ambitions and his inherent superiority, because the equality of their two separate orbits did not make them equal as individuals. In general Abigail Adams and other women of her class accepted the notion that while they were mentally equal to men their sphere of activity was entirely private in nature, except on those occasions when they substituted for their absent husbands. "Government of States and Kingdoms, tho' God knows badly enough managed," she asserted in 1796, "I am willing should be solely administered by the lords of creation. I should contend for Domestic Government, and think that best administered by the female." Such a strong belief in equal, but separate, spheres is indeed admirable for the times, but it should not be confused with feminism. . . .

Only unusual male feminists like Thomas Paine asked that women be accorded "the sweets of public esteem" and "an equal right to praise." It was Paine—not the female patriots—who also took advantage of American revolutionary conditions to attack the institution of marriage. Later, in the 1790s, only a few isolated women in the United States supported Mary Wollstonecraft's demand for the right to public as well as private fulfillment on the grounds that "private duties are never properly fulfilled unless the understanding enlarges the heart and that public virtue is only an aggregate of private. . . ." Her criticisms of marital bondage were never seriously considered by American women in this postrevolutionary decade.

The reasons for this unresponsiveness to the feminism of both Paine and

Wollstonecraft are complex, for it was not only opposed by the sexist Founding Fathers, but by most women. Again we must ask—why?

The physical and mental hardships that most women had endured during the war continued to varying degrees in the economic dislocation that followed in its wake. Sheer personal survival, not rising social or material expectations, dominated the thinking and activities of lower and even some middle- and upper-class women. Probably more important, the few well-educated American women, fortunate to have the leisure to reflect, clearly realized the discrepancy that had occurred between the theory and practice of virtue in the course of the war and its aftermath. While it was discouraging for them to view the corruption of morals of the society at large and particularly among men in public life, they could take some satisfaction in the greater consistency between the theory and practice of virtue in their own private lives. Such postrevolutionary women found their familial duties and homosocial relationships untainted by the corruption of public life. They considered themselves most fortunate and they *were,* compared to their nineteenth-century descendants, who had to pay a much higher price for similar virtuous consistency and spiritual purity.

It was natural, therefore, for the educated among this generation to express disillusionment with politics, as they saw republican principles corrupted or distorted, and then to enter a stage of relative quiescence that marked the beginning of the transitional period between their war-related activities and a later generation of female reformers who emerged in the 1830s. They cannot be held responsible for not realizing the full extent of the potentially debilitating features of their withdrawal to the safety of modern domesticity—where virtue becomes its own punishment instead of reward.

A final factor that helps to explain the absence of feminism in the behavior of women during the Revolution and in their attitudes afterward is related to the demographic changes that were taking place within the family unit between 1760 and 1800. Middle- and upper-class women were increasingly subjected to foreign and domestic literature stressing standards of femininity that had not inhibited the conduct of their colonial ancestors. While the rhetoric of this new literature was that of the Enlightenment, its message was that of romantic love, glamorized dependence, idealized motherhood, and sentimentalized children within the ever-narrowing realm of family life. At poorer levels of society a new family pattern was emerging as parental control broke down, and ultimately these two trends would merge, leaving all women in lower status domestic roles than they had once occupied.

In general it appears that the American Revolution retarded those societal conditions that had given colonial women their unique function and status in society, while it promoted those that were leading toward the gradual "embourgeoisement" of late eighteenth-century women. By 1800 their economic and legal privileges were curtailed; their recent revolutionary activity minimized or simply ignored; their future interest in politics discouraged; and their domestic roles extolled, but increasingly limited.

Moreover, at the highest *and* lowest levels of society this revolutionary generation of women was left with misleading assumptions: certain educated women believing strongly in the hope that immediate improvement for themselves and their children would come with educational reform, and some lower-class women believing that improvement would come through work in the "manufactories." Both admitted, according to Mercy Otis Warren, that their "appointed subordination" to men was natural, if for no other reason than "for the sake of Order in Families." Neither could be expected to anticipate that this notion would limit their participation in, and understanding of, an emerging modern nation because the actual (as opposed to idealized) value accorded their postrevolutionary activities was not yet apparent.

A few, like Priscilla Mason, the valedictorian of the 1793 graduating class of the Young Ladies' Academy of Philadelphia, might demand an equal education with men and exhort women to break out of their traditional sphere, but most ended up agreeing with Eliza Southgate Bowne when she concluded her defense of education for women by saying: "I believe I must give up all pretension to *profundity,* for I am much more at home in my female character." And the dominate male leadership of the 1790s could not have agreed more.

For women, the American Revolution was over before it ever began. Their "disinterested" patriotism (or disloyalty, as the case may be) was accorded identical treatment by male revolutionaries following the war: conscious neglect of female rights combined with subtle educational and economic exploitation. The end result was increased loss of function and authentic status for all women whether they were on or under the proverbial pedestal.

The Positive Impact of the American Revolution

MARY BETH NORTON

Women could hardly have remained aloof from the events of the 1760s and early 1770s even had they so desired, for, like male Americans, they witnessed the escalating violence of the prerevolutionary decade. Into their letters and diary entries—which had previously been devoted exclusively to private affairs—crept descriptions of Stamp Act riots and "Rejoicings" at the law's repeal, accounts of solemn fast-day observances, and reports of crowd actions aimed at silencing dissidents. The young Boston shopkeeper Betsy Cuming, for instance, was visiting a sick friend one day in 1769 when she heard "a voilint Skreeming Kill him Kill him" and looked out the window to see John Mein, a printer whose publications had enraged the radicals, being chased by a large crowd armed with sticks and guns. Later that evening Betsy watched "ful a thousand Man & boys" dragging around the city "a Kart [on which] a Man was Exibited as . . . in a Gore of Blod." At

Excerpted from Chapters 6 and 7 of *Liberty's Daughters: The Revolutionary Experience of American Women, 1750–1800,* 156–69, 212–27, by Mary Beth Norton. Copyright © 1980 by Mary Beth Norton. By permission of Little, Brown and Company.

first Betsy believed Mein had been caught, but she then learned that the victim was an unfortunate customs informer who had fallen into the crowd's hands after Mein made a successful escape.

Betsy herself confronted an angry group of Bostonians only a few weeks later. She and her sister Anne had just unpacked a new shipment of English goods when "the Comitey wated" on them, accusing them of violating the nonimportation agreement. "I told them we have never antred into eney agreement not to import for it was verry trifling owr Business," Betsy explained to her friend and financial backer Elizabeth Murray Smith. She charged the committeemen with trying "to inger two industrious Girls who ware Striving in an honest way to Git there Bread," resolutely ignoring their threat to publish her name in the newspaper as an enemy to America. In the end, Betsy and Anne discovered, the publicity "Spirits up our Friends to Purchess from us," and they informed Mrs. Smith that they ended the year with "mor custom then before."

Despite their bravado the Cuming sisters had learned an important political lesson: persons with their conservative beliefs were no longer welcome in Massachusetts. As a result, they emigrated to Nova Scotia when the British army evacuated Boston in 1776. Patriot women, too, learned lessons of partisanship. Instead of being the targets of crowds, they actively participated in them. They marched in ritual processions, harassed female loyalists, and, during the war, seized essential supplies from merchants whom they believed to be monopolistic hoarders. In addition, they prepared food for militia musters and, in the early days of September 1774—when the New England militia gathered in Cambridge in response to a false rumor that British troops were mounting an attack on the populace—they were reported by one observer to have "surpassed the Men for Eagerness & Spirit in the Defense of Liberty by Arms." As he rode along the road to Boston, he recounted later, he saw "at every house Women & Children making Cartridges, running Bullets, making Wallets, baking Biscuit, crying & bemoaning & at the same time animating their Husbands & Sons to fight for their Liberties, tho' not knowing whether they should ever see them again."

The activism of female patriots found particular expression in their support of the colonial boycott of tea and other items taxed by the Townshend Act of 1767. Male leaders recognized that they needed women's cooperation to ensure that Americans would comply with the request to forgo the use of tea and luxury goods until the act was repealed. Accordingly, newspaper essays urged women to participate in the boycott, and American editors frequently praised those females who refused to drink foreign Bohea tea, substituting instead coffee or local herbal teas. . . .

In a marked departure from the tradition of feminine noninvolvement in public affairs, women occasionally formalized their agreements not to purchase or consume imported tea. Most notably, the *Boston Evening Post* reported in February 1770 that more than three hundred "Mistresses of Families" had promised to "totally abstain" from the use of tea, "Sickness excepted." Their statement showed that they understood the meaning of their acts: the women spoke of their desire to "save this abused Country from Ruin and Slavery" at a time when their "invaluable Rights and Privileges are attacked in an unconstitutional and most alarming Manner." In the South, groups of women went even further by associating themselves generally with nonimportation policies, not confining their attention to the tea issue alone. The meeting satirized in the famous British cartoon of the so-called Edenton Ladies' Tea Party fell into this category. The agreement signed in October 1774 by fifty-one female North Carolinians—among them two sisters and a cousin of Hannah Johnston Iredell—did not mention tea. Instead, the women declared their "sincere adherence" to the resolves of the provincial congress and proclaimed it their "duty" to do "every thing as far as lies in our power" to support the "publick good."

This apparently simple statement had unprecedented implications. The Edenton women were not only asserting their right to acquiesce in political measures, but they were also taking upon themselves a "duty" to work for the common good. Never before had female Americans formally shouldered the responsibility of a public role, never before had they claimed a voice—even a compliant one—in public policy. Accordingly, the Edenton statement marked an important turning point in American women's political perceptions, signaling the start of a process through which they would eventually come to regard themselves as participants in the polity rather than as females with purely private concerns.

Yet the North Carolina meeting and the change it embodied aroused amusement among men. The same tongue-in-cheek attitude evident in the satirical drawing of the grotesque "Ladies" was voiced by the Englishman Arthur Iredell in a letter to his emigrant brother James. He had read about the Edenton agreement in the newspapers, Arthur wrote, inquiring whether his sister-in-law Hannah's relatives were involved in the protest. "Is there a Female Congress at Edenton too?" he continued. "I hope not," for "Ladies ... have ever, since the Amazonian Era, been esteemed the most formidable Enemies." If they choose to attack men, "each wound They give is Mortal. . . . The more we strive to conquer them, the more are Conquerd!"

Iredell thus transformed a serious political gesture that must have been full of meaning for the participants into an occasion for a traditional reference to women's covert power over men. Like many of his male contemporaries, he dismissed the first stirrings of political awareness among American women as a joke, refusing to recognize the ways in which their concept of their role was changing. In an Englishman, such blindness was understandable, but the similar failure of perception among American men must be attributed to a resolute insistence that females remain in their proper place. The male leaders of the boycott movement needed feminine cooperation, but they wanted to set the limits of women's activism. They did not expect, or approve, signs of feminine autonomy.

Nowhere was this made clearer than in a well-known exchange between Abigail and John Adams. . . . Abigail asked her husband in March 1776* to ensure that the new nation's legal code included protection for wives against the "Naturally Tyrannical" tendencies of their spouses. In reply John declared, "I cannot but laugh" at "your extraordinary Code of Laws." Falling back upon the same cliché employed by Arthur Iredell, he commented, "[O]ur Masculine systems . . . are little more than Theory. . . . In Practice you know We are the subjects. We have only the Name of Masters." Adams, like Iredell, failed to come to terms with the implications of the issues raised by the growing interest in politics among colonial women. He could deal with his wife's display of independent thought only by refusing to take it seriously.

American men's inability to perceive the alterations that were occurring in their womenfolk's self-conceptions was undoubtedly heightened by the superficially conventional character of feminine contributions to the protest movement. Women participating in the boycott simply made different decisions about what items to purchase and consume; they did not move beyond the boundaries of the feminine sphere. Likewise, when colonial leaders began to emphasize the importance of producing homespun as a substitute for English cloth, they did not ask women to take on an "unfeminine" task: quite the contrary, for spinning was the very role symbolic of femininity itself. But once the context had changed, so too did women's understanding of the meaning of their traditional tasks. . . .

The first months of 1769 brought an explosion in the newspaper coverage of women's activities, especially in New England. Stories about spinning bees, which had been both rare and relegated to back pages, suddenly became numerous and prominently featured. The *Boston Evening Post,* which carried only one previous account of female domestic industry, printed twenty-eight articles on the subject between May and December 1769, and devoted most of its front page on May 29 to an enumeration of these examples of female patriotism. The editor prefaced his extensive treatment of women's endeavors with an enthusiastic assessment of their significance: "[T]he industry and frugality of American ladies must exalt their character in the Eyes of the World and serve to show how greatly they are contributing to bring about the political salvation of a whole Continent."

It is impossible to know whether the increased coverage of spinning bees in 1769 indicated that women's activities expanded at precisely that time, or whether the more lengthy, detailed, and numerous stories merely represented the printers' new interest in such efforts. But one fact is unquestionable: the ritualized gatherings attended by women often termed Daughters of Liberty carried vital symbolic meaning both to the participants and to the editors who reported their accomplishments.

The meetings, or at least the descriptions of them, fell into a uniform pattern. Early in the morning, a group of eminently respectable young ladies (sometimes as many as one hundred, but normally twenty to forty), all of them dressed in homespun, would meet at the home of the local minister. There they would spend the day at their wheels, all the while engaging in enlightening conversation. When they stopped to eat, they had "American produce prepared which was more agreeable to them than any foreign Dainties and Delicacies," and, of course, they drank local herbal tea. At nightfall, they would present their output to the clergyman, who might then deliver a sermon on an appropriate theme. For example, the Reverend Jedidiah

Jewell, of Rowley, Massachusetts, preached from Romans 12:2, "Not sloth-ful in business, fervent in spirit, serving the Lord," and the Reverend John Cleaveland of Ipswich told the seventy-seven spinners gathered at his house, "[T]he women might recover to this country the full and free enjoyment of all our rights, properties and privileges (which is more than the men have been able to do)" by consuming only American produce and manufacturing their own clothes.

The entire community became involved in the women's activities. Large numbers of spectators—Ezra Stiles estimated that six hundred persons watched the bee held at his house in 1769—encouraged the spinners in their work, supplied them with appropriate American foodstuffs, and sometimes provided entertainment. The occasional adoption of a match format, in which the women competed against each other in quality and quantity, must have further spurred their industry. And they must have gloried in being the center of attention, if only for the day. In reporting a Long Island spinning bee, the *Boston Evening Post* captured the spirit of the occasion with an expression of hope that "the ladies, while they vie with each other in skill and industry in their profitable employment, may vie with the men in con-tributing to the preservation and prosperity of their country and equally share in the honor of it."

"Equally share in the honor of it": the idea must have been exceedingly attractive to any eighteenth-century American woman raised in an environ-ment that had previously devalued both her and her domestic sphere. Those involved in the home manufacture movement therefore took great pride in their newfound status, demonstrating that fact unequivocably when satirical essayists cast aspersions on their character.

Late in 1767, "Mr. Squibo" of Boston joked that the spinners were so patriotic they consumed only "New-England Rum . . . the principal and almost only manufacture of this country." Shortly thereafter, "A Young American" hinted that women discussed only "such triffling subjects as Dress, Scandal and Detraction" during their spinning bees. Three female Bostonians responded angrily to both letters, which they declared had "scandalously insulted" American women. Denying that gossip engrossed their thoughts or that rum filled their glasses, they pronounced themselves so committed to the patriot cause that they would even endure the unmerited ridicule of "the little wits and foplings of the present day" in order to continue their efforts. "Inferior in abusive sarcasm, in personal invective, in low wit, we glory to be," they concluded; "but inferior in veracity, honesty, sincerity, love of virtue, of liberty and of our country, we would not willingly be to any." Significantly, the Bostonians made a special point of noting that women had been "addressed as persons of consequence, in the present oeconomical regulations." They thereby revealed the novelty and impor-tance of that designation in their own minds. Having become established as "persons of consequence" in American society, women would not relin-quish that position without a fight.

The formal spinning groups had a value more symbolic than real. They do not seem to have met regularly, and in most cases their output appears to have been donated to the clergyman for his personal use. The women might not even have consistently called themselves Daughters of Liberty, for many newspaper accounts did not employ that phrase at all. But if the actual production of homespun did not motivate the meetings, they were nonetheless purposeful. The public attention focused on organized spinning bees helped to dramatize the pleas for industry and frugality in colonial households, making a political statement comparable to men's ostentatious wearing of homespun on public occasions during the same years. The spinning bees were ideological showcases: they were intended to convince American women that they could render essential contributions to the struggle against Britain, and to encourage them to engage in increased cloth production in the privacy of their own homes. Sometimes the newspaper accounts made this instructional function quite explicit. The fact that many of the participants came from "as *good families* as any in town," one editor remarked, showed that "it was no longer a disgrace for one of our fair sex to be catched at a spinning wheel." . . .

Wives of ardent patriots and loyalists alike were left alone for varying lengths of time while their spouses served in the army or, in the case of loyalists, took refuge behind the British lines. Although women could stay with their soldier husbands and earn their own keep by serving as army cooks, nurses, or laundresses, most did not find this an attractive alternative. Life in the military camps was hard, and army commanders, while recognizing that female laborers did essential work, tended to regard them as a hindrance rather than an asset. Only in rare cases—such as the time when the laundresses attached to General Anthony Wayne's regiment staged a strike in order to ensure that they would be adequately paid—were camp followers able to ameliorate their living and working conditions. Consequently, most women who joined the army probably did so from necessity, lacking any other means of support during their husbands' absence.

At least, though, patriot women had a choice. For the most part, loyalists were not so fortunate. From the day they and their spouses revealed their loyalty to the Crown, their fate was sealed. Like other eighteenth-century women, their lives had focused on their homes, but because of their political beliefs they lost not only those homes but also most of their possessions, and they had to flee to alien lands as well. Understandably, they often had difficulty coping with their problems. Only those women who had had some experience beyond the household prior to the war were able to manage their affairs in exile in England, Canada, or the West Indies with more than a modicum of success.

Female loyalists' claims petitions are particularly notable because the women frequently commented on their lack of a network of friends and relatives. The laments convey a sense of an entire familiar world that had been irretrievably lost. Many women submitted claims after the deadline, each giving a similar reason in her request for special consideration: there had been "no person to advise her how to proceed," she "was destitute of advice and Assistance," or "she had nobody to advise with & that she did not know how to do it." Even when some of a woman loyalist's friends were

also exiles her situation was little better; as one southerner poin[...]
claims commission, "[T]hose Friends and Acquaintances to w[...]
other circumstances she could look up to for comfort and Assistan[...]
equally involved in the Calamities which overwhelm" her. . . .

The importance of friendship networks and a familiar environment for
women left alone is further confirmed when the focus shifts from widowed
loyalists to the patriots who called themselves temporary widows—those
women whose husbands had joined the American army. In contrast to the
distressed, disconsolate refugee loyalists, who often complained of their
inability to deal effectively with their difficulties, patriot women who
managed the family property in the absence of their menfolk tended to find
the experience a positive one. Although they had to shoulder a myriad of
new responsibilities, they did so within a well-known and fully understood
context: that of their own households. Accordingly, aided by friends and
relatives, they gained a new sense of confidence in themselves and their
abilities as they learned to handle aspects of the family affairs that had
previously fallen solely within their husbands' purview. And the men, in
turn, developed a new appreciation of their wives' contributions to the family's welfare. . . .

Patriot men found it difficult to avoid service in the militia or the Continental Army. They accordingly had to leave their wives behind to take
charge of their affairs for months or years at a time. Most sets of wartime
correspondence that survive today come from the families of officers or
congressmen—in other words, from those patriots of some wealth or prominence who also tended to experience the longest separations—but the scattered evidence available for couples of lesser standing suggests that the same
process was at work in poor, middling, and well-to-do households alike. As
the months and years passed, women became more expert in their handling
of business matters and their husbands simultaneously more accustomed to
relying on their judgment.

A standard pattern emerges from the sequences of letters, some of
which will shortly be examined in greater detail. Initially, the absent husband instructed his wife to depend upon male friends and relatives for advice
and assistance. In 1776, for example, Edward Hand, a Pennsylvania officer,
told his wife, Kitty, to have one neighbor invest money for her and to ask
another to estimate the value of two horses he had sent home for sale.
Women, for their part, hesitated to venture into new areas. "In some partic-
ulars I have been really puzzled how to act," a South Carolinian informed
her spouse, a private soldier; and in 1777 Esther Reed, asking Joseph
whether she should plant some flax, explained, "[A]s I am not famous for
making good Bargains in things out of my Sphere I shall put it off as long as
possible, in hopes you may be at home before it is too late."

But as time went on, women learned more about the family's finances
while at the same time their husbands' knowledge became increasingly outdated and remote. Accordingly, whereas men's letters early in the war were
filled with specific orders, later correspondence typically contained statements like these: "I Can't give any Other Directions About Home more than

what I have Done but must Leave all to your good Management'' (1779); ''Apply [the money] to such as you think proper'' (1780); draw on a neighbor for ''any Sums you may choose, for providing things necessary & comfortable for yourself & the little Folks & Family for the approaching Season, in doing which I am sure you will use the greatest discretion'' (1779). By the same token, women's letters showed their increasing familiarity with business and their willingness to act independently of their husbands' directions. . . .

The diary of the Philadelphian Sally Logan Fisher provides an especially illuminating example of this process. Thomas Fisher was among the Quakers arrested and sent into exile in Virginia by the patriots just prior to the British conquest of Philadelphia in September 1777. Then nearly eight months pregnant with her daughter Hannah, Sally at first found ''this fiery triall'' almost more than she could bear. Nine days after the men had been forcibly carried off, she commented, ''I feel forlorn & desolate, & the World appears like a dreary Desart, almost without any visible protecting Hand to gaurd us from the ravenous Wolves & Lions that prowl about for prey.'' Sally became so depressed that she failed to write in her diary for several weeks, and when she resumed her daily entries in mid-October she observed, ''[N]o future Days however calm & tranquil they may prove, can ever make me forget my misery at this time.''

Soon thereafter, though, Mrs. Fisher became too busy to be able to allow herself the luxury of debilitating depression. A long entry on November 1 reflected her changed role in its detailed attention to household financial affairs and at the same time signaled the end of her period of incapacitating despair. ''I have to think & provide every thing for my Family, at a time when it is so difficult to provide anything, at almost any price, & cares of many kinds to engage my attention,'' she wrote revealingly. After Hannah's birth six days later Sally remarked, ''[I have] been enabled to bear up thro' every triall & difficulty far beyond what I could have expected.'' Although in succeeding months she continued to lament Tommy's absence, her later reflections differed significantly from her first reaction to her situation. Instead of dwelling upon her despondency, Sally wrote of ''the fond, the delightfull Hope'' that her husband would return to love her as before. ''Oh my beloved, how Ardently, how tenderly how Affectionately, I feel myself thine,'' she effused in February 1778, describing ''the anxiety I feel for thee, the longing desire to be with thee, & the impatience I feel to tell thee I am all thy own''—but not indicating any sense of an inability to cope with problems in his absence. When Tommy returned in late April 1778, she welcomed him gladly, but she did not revert completely to her former role of ignorance about monetary matters. Her diary subsequently noted several consultations with him about household finances, a subject they had not discussed before his exile.

Although Mary Bartlett, the wife of a New Hampshire congressman, left no similar record of her feelings about her husband's extended stays in Philadelphia during the war, she nevertheless subtly disclosed the fact that her role had undergone a comparable change. When Josiah Bartlett first went to Congress in the fall of 1775, he told Mary he hoped she would have "no Great trouble about my out Door affairs," and he continued to write to her about "my farming Business." In 1776 she accepted his terminology, reporting on "Your farming business," but during Josiah's second stint in Congress in 1778 that phrase became "our farming business" in her letters. No longer was the farm simply "his": she had now invested too much effort in it for that. The distinction between male and female spheres she had once accepted without question had been blurred by her own experience.

Although Josiah Bartlett's persistent use of "my farm" implies that he did not recognize the way in which his wife's role had altered, other patriot men separated from their spouses for long periods revealed changing attitudes toward their womenfolk in their correspondence. The differences are especially apparent in the case of a New Englander, Timothy Pickering, because he began with a severely limited conception of his wife's capability. . . .

Pickering adopted a patronizing tone in his early letters to his wife, Rebecca White. In November 1775, before their marriage, he told her he wanted to "instruct" her and went on to quote the same poem other Americans cited in discussions of children's education: " 'Tis a 'Delightful task to rear the tender thought, / To teach the fair idea how to shoot.' " Like a father teaching a daughter, he encouraged her to write to him, saying, "[F]requent writing will improve your hand." Unremarkably, Pickering's condescension continued during the early years of their marriage, after he had joined the Continental Army's quartermaster corps. When he sent home a lame horse in June 1777, he told her to consult male friends "for advice and direction" in caring for it, then apologized for asking her to undertake a task that was "entirely out of [her] sphere." Even his praise contained an evident patronizing note. "Your conduct in domestic affairs gives me the highest satisfaction," he told her in July 1778, spoiling it by adding, "even if you had done wrong I could not find fault; because I know in every action you aim at the best good of our little family: and knowing this: it would be cruel and unreasonable to blame you." In other words, he was telling her she would be judged on the basis of her intentions, not her actual performance, because he feared she could not meet the higher standard.

For the Pickerings matters changed in October 1780 after Rebecca acted as Timothy's agent in a complex arrangement for the repayment of a debt. "I am very glad you made me fully acquainted with it," she told him. "It is a satisfaction to me to pa[r]take of any thing that gives you Concern. I know my Dear you would make me happy in telling me any thing that had a tendency to make you so." After the successful resolution of the debt problem and her verbalization of her desire to assist him with their financial affairs, Timothy began to rely more heavily upon her. When the family rented a farm in 1782, she ably shouldered the responsibility for managing it despite her fears of "not being acquainted with farming business." Five years later, after they had moved to the frontier community of Wilkes-Barre, Pennsylvania, and Timothy's post required him to be in Philadelphia, she not only supervised the building of their new house but also oversaw the harvest, all the while nursing their newest baby. Timothy continued to apologize for the burdens he was placing on her (as well he should have), but he no longer mentioned her "sphere." Rebecca Pickering, like Mary Bartlett before her, began to speak in her letters of "our business" and "our crops." Timothy had already revealed his new attitude as early as August 1783: "This war which has so often & long separated us, has taught me how to value you," he told her then. . . .

The war dissolved some of the distinctions between masculine and feminine traits. Women who would previously have risked criticism if they abandoned their "natural" feminine timidity now found themselves praised for doing just that. The line between male and female behavior, once apparently so impenetrable, became less well defined. It by no means disappeared, but requisite adjustments to wartime conditions brought a new recognition of the fact that traditional sex roles did not provide adequate guidelines for conduct under all circumstances. When Betsy Ambler Brent looked back on her youth from the perspective of 1810, she observed, "[N]ecessity taught us to use exertions which our girls of the present day know nothing of. We Were forced to industry to appear genteely, to study Manners to supply the place of Education, and to endeavor by amiable and agreeable conduct to make amends for the loss of fortune."

The realization that they had been equally affected by the war led some women to expect equal treatment thereafter and, on occasion, to apply to their own circumstances the general principles promulgated by the revolutionaries. "I have Don as much to Carrey on the warr as meney that Sett Now at ye healm of government & No Notice taken of me," complained the New Jersey widow Rachel Wells as she protested to the Continental Congress in 1786 about a technicality that deprived her of interest payments on the money she had invested in state bonds during the war. "If she did not fight She throw in all her mite which bought ye Sogers food & Clothing & Let them have Blankets," she explained, asking only for the "justice" due her. "Others gits their Intrust & why then a poor old widow be put of[f]?" Mrs. Wells asked. "Now gentelmen is this Liberty?"

Mary Willing Byrd's social standing was much higher than that of Rachel Wells, but she advanced a similar argument when she contended in 1781 that Virginia had treated her unfairly. She claimed the right to redress of grievances "as a female, as the parent of eight children, as a virtuous citizen, as a friend to my Country, and as a person, who never violated the laws of her Country." Byrd's recital of her qualifications was peculiarly feminine in its attention to her sex and her role as a parent (no man would have included such items on a list describing himself), but it was also sexless in its references to her patriotism and her character as a "virtuous citizen." In developing the implications of the latter term, Byrd arrived at her most important point. "I have paid my taxes and have not been Personally, or Virtually represented," she observed. "My property is taken from me and I have no redress."

The echoes of revolutionary ideology were deliberate. Mary Byrd wanted the men she addressed to think about the issue of her status as a woman, and she adopted the revolutionaries' own language in order to make her point. The same tactic was employed by Abigail Adams in her most famous exchange with her husband.

In March 1776, after admonishing John to "Remember the Ladies" and to offer them legal protection from "the unlimited power" of their husbands, Abigail issued a warning in terms that John must have found exceedingly familiar. "If perticular care and attention is not paid to the Laidies," Abigail declared, "we are determined to foment a Rebelion, and will not hold ourselves bound by any Laws in which we have no voice, or Representation." On one level, she was speaking tongue-in-cheek; she did not mean her husband to take the threat seriously. Yet she chose to make a significant observation about women's inferior legal status by putting a standard argument to new use and by applying to the position of women striking phraseology previously employed only in the male world of politics. Like Mary Willing Byrd, Abigail Adams thus demonstrated an unusual sensitivity to the possible egalitarian resonances of revolutionary ideology and showed an awareness of implications that seem to have escaped the notice of American men.

✤ FURTHER READING

Ruth H. Bloch, "American Feminine Ideals in Transition: The Rise of the Moral Mother, 1785–1815," *Feminist Studies,* IV, no. 2 (June 1978), 100–26

——, "The Gendered Meanings of Virtue in Revolutionary America," *Signs,* XIII (1987), 37–58

Richard and Joy Buel, *The Way of Duty: A Woman and Her Family in Revolutionary America* (1984)

Nancy Cott, "Divorce and the Changing Status of Women in Massachusetts," *William and Mary Quarterly,* 3d ser., XXXIII (1976), 586–614

Linda Grant DePauw and Conover Hunt, *"Remember the Ladies": Women in America 1750–1815* (1976)

Joan R. Gunderson, "Independence, Citizenship, and the American Revolution," *Signs,* XIII (1987), 59–77

Ronald Hoffman and Peter Albert, eds., *Women in the Age of the American Revolution* (1988)

Linda K. Kerber, *Women of the Republic* (1980)

Barbara Lacey, "Women in the Era of the American Revolution: The Case of Norwich, Connecticut," *New England Quarterly,* LIII (1980), 527–43

Jan Lewis, "The Republican Wife: Virtue and Seduction in the Early Republic," *William and Mary Quarterly,* 3d ser., XLIV (1987), 689–721

Mary Beth Norton, "Eighteenth-Century American Women in Peace and War: The Case of the Loyalists," *William and Mary Quarterly,* 3d ser., XXXIII (1976), 386–409

The Cult of Domesticity

If one concept seems essential to understanding the circumstances of middle-class white women in nineteenth-century America, that concept is the "cult of domesticity"—the phrase historians have coined to describe the ideology of women's place that was advanced in thousands of publications appearing over many decades. All commentators agreed that woman's proper sphere was the home; females were uniquely suited to raise children, care for the needs of their menfolk, and devote their lives to the creation of a nurturing home environment. They argued that women were inherently more pious, gentle, instinctive, and submissive than men; therefore, they had no place in the public world outside the home. They should concentrate their energies on their households and not seek to enter the world of men by agitating for the vote or for other modes of participating in public life.

Yet this doctrine, seemingly confining, subverted its own intent. If women were so uniquely suited to caring for young children, Catharine Beecher contended, then they should do so as teachers in schools as well as in their own homes. If women were naturally religious, they should join foreign missions and work in domestic charitable organizations. If their lives and roles were so different from those of men, they could logically form close, long-lasting relationships with other women—relationships that our era might perhaps deem "lesbian."

Ever since the dimensions of the "cult of domesticity" and its inherent ambiguities were first explored by historians, they have been arguing over where to place the emphasis: on the limitations of domestic ideology, or on the opportunities it presented to creative and innovative women who understood how to turn its tenets to their own advantage? The matter is by no means resolved. What are the advantages and disadvantages of each approach?

✤ DOCUMENTS

In 1850, Lydia H. Sigourney, one of the most popular female authors of the nineteenth century, published a book entitled *Whisper to a Bride,* which included the first document reprinted here, a sentimental discourse called "Home." In 1845 *Godey's Lady's Book,* the most widely read women's magazine of the time, printed both the second selection, a poem by its editor, Sarah Josepha Hale, and the third document, a statement entitled "Maternal Instruction," also probably by Hale. In 1863 Catharine Beecher, author of several household advice books, published

"Words of Comfort for a Discouraged Housekeeper," the fourth selection. Over a period of several decades, Sarah Alden Ripley, one of the middle-class women who made up the audience for Hale's magazine and the books by Sigourney and Beecher, wrote a series of letters to her female relatives and friends; the final document consists of excerpts from some of these letters.

Lydia H. Sigourney's "Home," 1850

Home!—sweet word and musical!—keytone of the heart, at whose melody, as by the harp of Orpheus, all the trees in its garden are moved, holy word! refuge from sadness, and despair, best type of that eternal rest, for which we look, when the journey of life is ended!

Home,—blessed spot!—for which the sick yearn, and the stranger sigheth, among people of a strange speech, where none taketh him by the hand, who seeth casements glimmer through the evening storm, and firesides sparkle,—but not for him! . . .

Blessed Bride,—thou art about to enter this sanctuary, and to become a priestess at its altar. When thy foot first presseth its threshold, ask in thy secret soul, wisdom from above, to make the place of thy rest, fair and holy.

Bring with thee the perennial flowers of a pure affection; and however humble may be thine abode, beautify it by neatness, and order, and the ministries of love. Desire that it shall be thine own, and choose not to dwell under the roof of another, that thou mayest avoid care.

In the thronged hotel, a married man hath not his true pre-eminence. At the table of another, he misseth the honor that belongeth unto the head of a household. He is subordinate, and may not show that hospitality which God commendeth.

For his sake, therefore, acquaint thyself with the knowledge that appertaineth unto a wife and a housekeeper. If thou art deficient in this knowledge, rest not, till thou hast acquired it. It cometh readily to an attentive mind, and groweth with experience.

He, who chose thee, above all others, to bear his name, and to share his fortunes, hath a right to expect of thee such knowledge. Defraud him not, by continuing in ignorance, nor make thy beloved a stranger to the comforts of home, that thou mayst fold thy hands in indolence.

For the Apostle hath said, that "no man liveth unto himself." More especially should a woman, when she hath promised to be no longer her own, renounce self, as the aim of her existence. . . .

Consider the sphere in which thou art placed, as the one in which God willeth thee to be; and show kindness, and do good to all, according to thine ability.

Count thy husband's relatives as thy own; and if he hath parents show them the respect and tenderness of a true daughter. Be grateful to them for the culture of his virtue, whose fruits thou art gathering, and under the shadow of whose branches thou dost repose in peace.

Should his, or thine own parents, reside under the same roof with thee, give thanks for the privilege. For so thou mayest have opportunity to repay some portion of the affection of their cradle-watchings, and tender care, and patience of hope.

Whatever service their feeble years may require, render willingly, and with a cheerful countenance. Covet their prayers more than gold; and by filial piety, win their blessing. . . .

Forgive me, Oh Bride, if in the time of thy joy, I have spoken too gravely unto thee of life's cares. Yet in these very cares lies the secret of woman's happiness, more than in the haunts of pleasure, or the giddiness of mirth.

And in thy faithful efforts to make home beautiful and holy, the wings of guardian spirits shall enfold thy bosom, and give thee strength from above.

Sarah Josepha Hale's "Empire of Woman," 1845

1.

Woman's Empire defined.

The outward World, for rugged Toil design'd,
    Where Evil from true Good the crown hath riven,
    Has been to Man's dominion ever given;
But Woman's empire, holier, more refin'd,
Moulds, moves and sways the fall'n but God-breath'd mind,
    Gifting the earth-crushed heart to hope and heaven:
As plants put forth to Summer's gentle wind,
    And 'neath the sweet, soft light of starry even,
Those treasures which the tyrant Winter's sway
    Could never wrest from Nature,—so the soul
Will Woman's sweet and gentle power obey—
    Thus doth her summer smile its strength control;
Her love sow flowers along life's thorny way;
    Her star-bright faith lead up toward heaven's goal.

2.

The Daughter.

The iron cares that load and press men down
    A father can, like school-boy tasks, lay by,
    When gazing in his Daughter's loving eye,
Her soft arm like a spell around him thrown:
The passions that, like Upas' leaves, have grown
    Most deadly in dark places, which defy
Earth, heaven and human will, even these were shown
    All powerless to resist the pleading cry
Which pierced a savage but a father's ear,
    And shook a soul where pity's pulse seemed dead:
When Pocahontas, heeding not the fear
    That daunted boldest warriors, laid her head
Beside the doomed! Now with our country's fame,
Sweet forest Daughter, we have blent thy name.

3.

The Sister.

Wild as a colt, o'er prairies bounding free,
  The wakened spirit of the Boy doth spring,
  Spurning the rein authority would fling,
And striving with his peers for mastery;
But in the household gathering let him see
  His Sister's winning smile, and it will bring
A change o'er all his nature; patiently,
  As caged bird, that never used its wing,
He turns him to the tasks that she doth share—
  His better feelings kindle by her side—
Visions of angel beauty fill the air,—
  And she may summon such to be his guide:
—Our Saviour listened to a Sister's prayer,
  When, "Lazarus, from the tomb come forth!" he cried.

4.

The Wife.

The Daughter from her father's bosom goes—
  The Sister drops her brother's clasping hand—
  For God himself ordained a holier band
Than kindred blood on human minds bestows;
That stronger, deeper, dearer tie she knows,
  The heart-wed Wife; as heaven by rainbow spann'd,
Thus bright with hope life's path before her glows—
  Proves it like mirage on the desert's sand?
Still in her soul the light divine remains—
  And if her husband's strength be overborne
By sorrow, sickness, or the felon's chains,—
  Such as by England's noblest son were worn,—
  Unheeding how her own poor heart is torn,
She, angel-like, his sinking soul sustains.

5.

The Mother.

Earth held no symbol, had no living sign
  To image forth the Mother's deathless love;
  And so the tender care the righteous prove
Beneath the ever-watching eye divine,
Was given a type to show how pure that shrine,
  The Mother's heart, was hallowed from above;
And how her mortal hopes must intertwine
  With hopes immortal,—and she may not move
From this high station which her Saviour sealed,
When in maternal arms he lay revealed.

> Oh! wondrous power, how little understood,
> Entrusted to the Mother's mind alone,
>   To fashion genius, form the soul for good,
> Inspire a West, or train a Washington!

"Maternal Instruction," 1845

It takes a long time for the world to grow wise. Men have been busying themselves these six thousand years nearly to improve society. They have framed systems of philosophy and government, and conferred on their own sex all the advantages which power, wealth and knowledge could bestow. They have founded colleges and institutions of learning without number, and provided themselves teachers of every art and science; and, after all, the mass of mankind are very ignorant and very wicked. Wherefore is this? Because the *mother,* whom God constituted the first teacher of every human being, has been degraded by men from her high office; or, what is the same thing, been denied those privileges of education which only can enable her to discharge her duty to her children with discretion and effect. God created the woman as a *help-meet* for man in every situation; and while he, in his pride, rejects her assistance in his intellectual and moral career, he never will succeed to improve his nature and reach that perfection in knowledge, virtue and happiness, which his faculties are constituted to attain.

If half the effort and expense had been directed to enlighten and improve the minds of females which have been lavished on the other sex, we should now have a very different state of society. Wherever a woman is found excelling in judgment and knowledge, either by natural genius or from better opportunities, do we not see her children also excel? Search the records of history, and see if it can be found that a great and wise man ever descended from a weak and foolish mother. So sure and apparent is this maternal influence, that it has passed into an axiom of philosophy, it is acknowledged by the greatest and wisest of men; and yet, strange to say, the inference which ought to follow, namely, that in attempting to improve society, the first, most careful and continued efforts should be to raise the standard of female education, and qualify woman to become the educator of her children, has never yet been acted upon by any legislators, or acknowledged and tested by any philanthropists.

What is true of the maternal influence respecting sons is, perhaps, more important in the training of daughters. The fashionable schools are a poor substitute for such example and instruction as a thoroughly educated and right principled mother would bestow on her daughters. The best schools in the world will not, in and of themselves, make fine women. The tone of *family education* and of society needs to be raised. This can never be done till greater value is set on the cultivated female intellect. Young ladies must be inspired with high moral principles, noble aims, and a spirit of self-improvement to become what they ought to be. Maternal instruction is the purest and safest means of opening the fountain of knowledge to the young mind.

Catharine Beecher's "Words of Comfort for a Discouraged Housekeeper," 1863

For those who wish they *could* become systematic, neat, and thorough housekeepers, and would like to follow out successfully the suggestions found in this work, and for those who have tried, or will try, and find themselves baffled and discouraged, these words of comfort are offered.

Perhaps you find yourself encompassed by such sort of trials as these. Your house is inconvenient, or destitute of those facilities for doing work well which you need, and you cannot command the means to supply these deficiencies. Your domestics are so imperfectly qualified that they never can do anything *just right,* unless you stand by and attend to everything yourself, and you cannot be present in parlor, nursery, and kitchen all at once. Perhaps you are frequently left without any cook, or without a chambermaid, and sometimes without any hands but your own to do the work, and there is constant jostling and change from this cause. And perhaps you cannot get supplies, either from garden or market, such as you need, and all your calculations fail in that direction.

And perhaps your children are sickly, and rob you of rest by night, or your health is so poor that you feel no energy, or spirits to make exertions. And perhaps you never have had any training in domestic affairs, and cannot understand how to work yourself, nor how to direct others. And when you go for aid to experienced housekeepers, or cookery books, you are met by such sort of directions as these: "Take a *pinch* of this, and a *little* of that, and *considerable* of the other, and cook them till they are done *about right.*" And when you cannot succeed in following such indefinite instructions, you find your neighbors and husband wondering how it is, that when you have one, two, or three domestics, there should be so much difficulty about housekeeping, and such constant trouble, and miscalculation, and mistake. And then, perhaps, you lose your patience and your temper, and blame others, and others blame you, and so everything seems to be in a snarl.

Now the first thing to be said for your comfort is, that you *really have* great trials to meet; trials that entitle you to pity and sympathy, while it is the fault of others more than your own, that you are in this very painful and difficult situation. You have been as cruelly treated as the Israelites were by Pharaoh, when he demanded bricks without furnishing the means to make them.

You are like a young, inexperienced lad, who is required to superintend all the complicated machinery of a manufactory, which he never was trained to understand, and on penalty of losing reputation, health, and all he values most.

Neither your parents, teachers, or husband have *trained* you for the place you fill, nor furnished you with the knowledge or assistance needed to enable you to meet all the complicated and untried duties of your lot. A young woman who has never had the care of a child, never done housework, never learned the numberless processes that are indispensable to keep domestic affairs in regular order, never done anything but attend to books, drawing, and music, at school, and visiting and company after she left school, such an one is as unprepared to take charge of a nursery, kitchen, and family establishment, as she is to take charge of a *man-of-war*. And the chief blame rests with those who placed her *so unprepared* in such trying circumstances. Therefore, you have a right to feel that a large part of these evils are more your misfortune than your fault, and that they entitle you to sympathy rather than blame.

The next word of comfort is, the assurance that you *can* do *every one* of your duties, and do them well, and the following is the method by which you can do it. In the first place, make up your mind that it never is your *duty* to do anything more than you *can,* or in any better manner than *the best you can.* And whenever you have done the best you can, you have done *well,* and it is all that man *should* require, and certainly all that your Heavenly Father *does* require.

The next thing is, for you to make out an inventory of all the things that *need* to be done, in your whole establishment. Then calculate what things you find you *cannot* do, and strike them off the list, as what are not among your *duties*. Of those that remain, select a certain number that you think you can do *exactly as they need to be done,* and among these be sure that you put the making of *good bread*. This every housekeeper *can* do, if she will only determine to do it.

Make a selection of certain things that you will *persevere* in having done *as well as they can be done,* and let these be only so many as you feel sure you can succeed in attempting. Then make up your mind that all the rest must go along as they do, until you get more time, strength, and experience, to increase the list of things that you determine shall always be well done.

By this course, you will have the comfort of feeling that in *some* respects you are as good a housekeeper as you can be, while there will be a cheering progress in gaining on all that portion of your affairs, that are left at loose ends. You will be able to measure a gradual advance, and be encouraged by success. Many housekeepers fail entirely, by expecting to do *everything well at first,* when neither their knowledge or strength is adequate, and so they fail everywhere, and finally give up in despair.

Sarah Alden Ripley's Letters, 1809–1810 and 1859

To Mary Emerson, c. 1809:

Dear, Dear Mary,—

I am afraid you will hear no more about satiety and disgust of life. With every rising dawn your idea is associated. The day no longer presents in prospect an unvaried tasteless round of domestic duties. Bright gleams of hope illumine the dull perspective. The mellow rays of the declining sun sweep the chords of love. Oh that they ceased to vibrate with the gentle touch! Your idea intrudes too often on the hallowed hours. But it will not be always thus. The affection whose object is so pure, so heavenly, cannot, will not, forever militate with devotion. Once convinced the chains are riveted, suspicion, dread to have disgusted or offended, will give place to calm reposing satisfaction. How delightful the thought that our religion sanctions friendship! How docs worldliness dry up every spring of pure affection, chill every generous, glowing emotion! I was bantered a little at tea about violent romantic attachments. I was bold in the defense of disinterested friendship. My mother considers it a delusion, innocent as to its object, rather dangerous as to its effects, making me unsteady, as she terms it. But you told me once you hated sentimental epistles. May everything that can make life's journey pleasant be yours in perfection!

To Miss Allyn, 1810:

Miss Emerson has left Boston for an uncertain time. You know how I dislike writing; yet I have already written to her. It was the condition on which I am to expect her letters; and if they are of as much benefit to me as I hope her society has been, I shall be abundantly compensated. Do not be jealous of her, my best friend. My affection for you and her are very different: there is too much of reverential respect mingled with the former to admit of that unreserved confidence which is so strong a bond of union between *us*. Can an acquaintance of a few months, where there is disparity of years and difference in pursuits, be weighed in the balance with a friendship of years, cemented by union in studies as well as sentiment?

To Mary Emerson, 1810:

Dear Mary,—

I have begun Stewart. (Oh, how you have multiplied my sources of enjoyment!) By bringing into view the various systems of philosophers concerning the origin of our knowledge, he enlarges the mind, and extends the range of our ideas, while he traces to their source those torrents of error, skcpticism, and infidelity that have for ages inundated this fair field of science; clearly distinguishing between proper objects of inquiry and those that must forever remain inexplicable to man in the present state of his faculties. Reasonings from induction are delightful. I have read but few works on these subjects. Oh, how I envy the scholar, the philosopher, whose business, whose profession, is science! Continually making new discoveries in this boundless region, where every object bears the impress of Divinity, Linnæus could trace with equal wonder and delight the strokes of a divine, unrivaled pencil, as Newton the omnipotent arm that first gave motion to the planetary system. Even the humble dandelion exhibits an order and regularity of parts admirable as the harmony of spheres. Yet, as much as I am pleased with your philosophical speculations, I should not be willing to renounce for them entirely the poets of Greece and Rome. Opening Virgil the other night after I was in bed, his fine description of Æneas's descent into the lower regions held imagination entranced for hours. . . . In pathos of sentiment he is unrivaled: he is acquainted with every avenue to the heart. His epic abounds with the most affecting pictures of filial love and heroic friendship. I have almost a mind to blot this long eulogium. I am continually introducing you to one or another of my old friends, that you do not care a fig for, who meet with so much more agreeable society of your own age. I am afraid you will never be rid of their intrusions till you absolutely command them to stay at home. Do call me a good girl for writing again so soon. Good-by.

Yours with affection, SARAH.

To Mary Emerson, 1810:

Dear Mary,—

I have just received your valuable letter, and would answer it while warm with gratitude for the affectionate interest it expresses in my welfare. Your caution against an undue devotion to literary pursuits is, I fear, too necessary. Perhaps not more time is allotted to them than conscience would permit for innocent amusements. But their dominion over the affections is the danger. I fear, if called to relinquish them entirely or desert some positive duty, the sacrifice would be made with reluctance. Yet, when I experience how much more easy is the transition to serious meditation from an evening spent in study than one spent in society, where vanity may have been excited or pride flattered, I am inclined to consider them, if not directly tending to produce, at least not unfavorable to, piety. How ready we are to excuse a favorite passion! It is my constant prayer that my affections may be purified, and with advantages for improvement my sphere of usefulness may also be enlarged. My friend, I should not write thus to any one but yourself. I am almost ashamed when I see that I have as yet been the only subject. Do tell me if you think me vain or presuming.

. . . You are the only person who ever thought me of any consequence, and I am pretty well convinced other folks are more than half right. I want you to love me, but you must do as you please about it.

To Sophia Bradford, Her Sister-in-Law, Undated

Dear Sophia,—

Phœbe reports you not well. Do take care of yourself and expel the cough. Hearing that you are not well reminds me what it would be to lose your loving society. We have kept step together through a long piece of road in the weary journey of life: we have loved the same beings and wept together over their graves. I have not your faith to console me, as they drop one after another from my side; yet my will, I trust, is in harmony with the divine order, and resigned where light is wanting. The sun looks brighter and my home more tranquil as the evening of life draws near. Would to heaven that the lives of the dear ones that remain could be insured to me till its end! Then I could fold my hands in perfect peace, ready, if such is the law of finite existence, to breathe the last breath of consciousness into the infinite source of light and love whence it came.

You cannot think how much I expect to enjoy a visit from you, now that I am a spare hand and so have plenty of leisure to walk and talk and sympathize with those with whom I have gone hand in hand through so many years of joy and sorrow.

To Sophia Bradford, 1859:

Dear Sophia,—

Can there be a possible chance that I may never look upon your dear face again! Am I to stand on the declivity of life, while one after another drops from my side of those who have been so long parts of myself? You are the vision of my nights; you appear to me for the first time in the little parlor of the house in South Street, a graceful and bright being of sixteen or seventeen, with a becoming straw hat and a most agreeable smile. I still see the corner of the room where you sat, though I see nothing else connected with the visit. Then the scene changes to your uncle Blake's, where I found you one morning practicing on the guitar before the family had arisen from their beds. After your closer connection with us as a family, our interviews so crowd together in the background of the past that I am kept awake as if solving a mathematical problem to arrange them in their proper time and place as they press in confusion upon the scene. How much we enjoyed those evening rides to Cambridge, to the house you had planned and built, where we forgot, for an hour or two, the school bondage of home! How much you did to soften the pillow of decline and death for the father I loved and respected so much! How can I recall or arrange the happy meetings we have had together as a family in Waltham or Lowell! How much you were to dear Margaret! How much Martha has always enjoyed, and still enjoys, your society! Do you wonder that I should desire to see you now? Still, I should not be willing to see you at the risk of exciting and doing you harm. So I will try to content myself with thinking of you with hope when I can. But sorrow, not hope, is the color of old age.

Your Sister.

✤ *E S S A Y S*

In 1966 Barbara Welter of Hunter College examined scores of books and magazines aimed at a middle-class female audience and for the first time outlined in detail the dimensions of what she called the "cult of true womanhood," now more frequently termed the "cult of domesticity." In the first essay, Welter decries the effects of this limited definition of women's sphere. Nine years later Carroll Smith-Rosenberg of the University of Pennsylvania celebrated its positive aspects—those that brought women together in a specifically female world—in the second selection. Still more recently, as the third essay reveals, Richard A. Meckel, who teaches at Brown University, pointed out the ways in which women could use certain tenets of the "cult of domesticity"—in this case an emphasis on their maternal function—to seek to change their own lives and those of other women.

The Cult of True Womanhood, 1820–1860

BARBARA WELTER

The nineteenth-century American man was a busy builder of bridges and railroads, at work long hours in a materialistic society. The religious values of his forebears were neglected in practice if not in intent, and he occasionally felt some guilt that he had turned this new land, this temple of the chosen people, into one vast countinghouse. But he could salve his conscience by reflecting that he had left behind a hostage, not only to fortune, but to all the values which he held so dear and treated so lightly. Woman, in the cult of True Womanhood presented by the women's magazines, gift annuals and religious literature of the nineteenth century, was the hostage in the home. In a society where values changed frequently, where fortunes rose and fell with frightening rapidity, where social and economic mobility provided instability as well as hope, one thing at least remained the same—a true woman was a true woman, wherever she was found. If anyone, male or female, dared to tamper with the complex of virtues which made up True Womanhood, he was damned immediately as an enemy of God, of civilization and of the Republic. It was a fearful obligation, a solemn responsibility, which the nineteenth-century American woman had—to uphold the pillars of the temple with her frail white hand.

The attributes of True Womanhood, by which a woman judged herself and was judged by her husband, her neighbors and society could be divided into four cardinal virtues—piety, purity, submissiveness and domesticity. Put them all together and they spelled mother, daughter, sister, wife—woman. Without them, no matter whether there was fame, achievement or wealth, all was ashes. With them she was promised happiness and power.

Religion or piety was the core of woman's virtue, the source of her strength. Young men looking for a mate were cautioned to search first for piety, for if that were there, all else would follow. Religion belonged to woman by divine right, a gift of God and nature. This "peculiar susceptibility" to religion was given her for a reason: " the vestal flame of piety, lighted up by Heaven in the breast of woman" would throw its beams into the naughty world of men. So far would its candle power reach that the "Universe might be Enlightened, Improved, and Harmonized by WOMAN!!" She would be another, better Eve, working in cooperation with the Redeemer, bringing the world back "from its revolt and sin." The world would be reclaimed for God through her suffering, for "God increased the cares and sorrows of woman, that she might be sooner constrained to accept the terms of salvation." A popular poem by Mrs. Frances Osgood, "The Triumph of the Spiritual Over the Sensual" expressed just this sentiment, woman's purifying passionless love bringing an erring man back to Christ.

Dr. Charles Meigs, explaining to a graduating class of medical students

Barbara Welter, "The Cult of True Womanhood: 1820–1860," *American Quarterly*, XVIII (1966), 151–74, copyright 1966, American Studies Association.

why women were naturally religious, said that "hers is a pious mind. Her confiding nature leads her more readily than men to accept the proffered grace of the Gospel." Caleb Atwater, Esq., writing in *The Ladies' Repository*, saw the hand of the Lord in female piety: "Religion is exactly what a woman needs, for it gives her that dignity that best suits her dependence." And Mrs. John Sandford, who had no very high opinion of her sex, agreed thoroughly: "Religion is just what woman needs. Without it she is ever restless or unhappy. . . ." Mrs. Sandford and the others did not speak only of that restlessness of the human heart, which St. Augustine notes, that can only find its peace in God. They spoke rather of religion as a kind of tranquilizer for the many undefined longings which swept even the most pious young girl, and about which it was better to pray than to think.

One reason religion was valued was that it did not take a woman away from her "proper sphere," her home. Unlike participation in other societies or movements, church work would not make her less domestic or submissive, less a True Woman. In religious vineyards, said the *Young Ladies' Literary and Missionary Report,* "you may labor without the apprehension of detracting from the charms of feminine delicacy." Mrs. S. L. Dagg, writing from her chapter of the Society in Tuscaloosa, Alabama, was equally reassuring: "As no sensible woman will suffer her intellectual pursuits to clash with her domestic duties" she should concentrate on religious work "which promotes these very duties."

The women's seminaries aimed at aiding women to be religious, as well as accomplished. Mt. Holyoke's catalogue promised to make female education "a handmaid to the Gospel and an efficient auxiliary in the great task of renovating the world." The Young Ladies' Seminary at Bordentown, New Jersey, declared its most important function to be "the forming of a sound and virtuous character." In Keene, New Hampshire, the Seminary tried to instill a "consistent and useful character" in its students, to enable them in this life to be "a good friend, wife and mother" but more important, to qualify them for "the enjoyment of Celestial Happiness in the life to come." And Joseph M' D. Mathews, Principal of Oakland Female Seminary in Hillsborough, Ohio, believed that "female education should be preeminently religious."

If religion was so vital to a woman, irreligion was almost too awful to contemplate. Women were warned not to let their literary or intellectual pursuits take them away from God. Sarah Josepha Hale spoke darkly of those who, like Margaret Fuller, threw away the "One True Book" for others, open to error. Mrs. Hale used the unfortunate Miss Fuller as fateful proof that "the greater the intellectual force, the greater and more fatal the errors into which women fall who wander from the Rock of Salvation, Christ the Saviour. . . ."

One gentleman, writing on "Female Irreligion" reminded his readers that "Man may make himself a brute, and does so very often, but can woman brutify herself to his level—the lowest level of human nature—without exerting special wonder?" Fanny Wright, because she was godless, "was no woman, mother though she be." A few years ago, he recalls, such women would have been whipped. In any case, "woman never looks

lovelier than in her reverence for religion'' and, conversely, ''female irreligion is the most revolting feature in human character.''

Purity was as essential as piety to a young woman, its absence as unnatural and unfeminine. Without it she was, in fact, no woman at all, but a
member of some lower order. A ''fallen woman'' was a ''fallen angel,''
unworthy of the celestial company of her sex. To contemplate the loss of
purity brought tears; to be guilty of such a crime, in the women's magazines
at least, brought madness or death. Even the language of the flowers had
bitter words for it: a dried white rose symbolized ''Death Preferable to Loss
of Innocence.'' The marriage night was the single great event of a woman's
life, when she bestowed her greatest treasure upon her husband, and from
that time on was completely dependent upon him, an empty vessel, without
legal or emotional existence of her own.

Therefore all True Women were urged, in the strongest possible terms,
to maintain their virtue, although men, being by nature more sensual than
they, would try to assault it. Thomas Branagan admitted in *The Excellency
of the Female Character Vindicated* that his sex would sin and sin again,
they could not help it, but woman, stronger and purer, must not give in and
let man ''take liberties incompatible with her delicacy.'' ''If you do,'' Branagan addressed his gentle reader, ''You will be left in silent sadness to bewail
your credulity, imbecility, duplicity, and premature prostitution.''

Mrs. Eliza Farrar, in *The Young Lady's Friend*, gave practical logistics
to avoid trouble: ''Sit not with another in a place that is too narrow; read not
out of the same book; let not your eagerness to see anything induce you to
place your head close to another person's.''

If such good advice was ignored the consequences were terrible and
inexorable. In *Girlhood and Womanhood: Or Sketches of My Schoolmates,*
by Mrs. A. J. Graves (a kind of mid-nineteenth-century *The Group*), the bad
ends of a boarding school class of girls are scrupulously recorded. The worst
end of all is reserved for ''Amelia Dorrington: The Lost One.'' Amelia died
in the almshouse ''the wretched victim of depravity and intemperance'' and
all because her mother had let her be ''high-spirited not prudent.'' These
girlish high spirits had been misinterpreted by a young man, with disastrous
results. Amelia's ''thoughtless levity'' was ''followed by a total loss of virtuous principle'' and Mrs. Graves editorializes that ''the coldest reserve is
more admirable in a woman a man wishes to make his wife, than the least
approach to undue familiarity.''

A popular and often-reprinted story by Fanny Forester told the sad tale
of ''Lucy Dutton.'' Lucy ''with the seal of innocence upon her heart, and a
rose-leaf on her cheek'' came out of her vine-covered cottage and ran into a
city slicker. ''And Lucy was beautiful and trusting, and thoughtless: and he
was gay, selfish and profligate. Needs the story to be told? . . . Nay, censor,
Lucy was a child—consider how young, how very untaught—oh! her innocence was no match for the sophistry of a gay, city youth! Spring came and
shame was stamped upon the cottage at the foot of the hill.'' The baby died;
Lucy went mad at the funeral and finally died herself. ''Poor, poor Lucy
Dutton! The grave is a blessed couch and pillow to the wretched. Rest thee

there, poor Lucy!'' The frequency with which derangement follows loss of virtue suggests the exquisite sensibility of woman, and the possibility that, in the women's magazines at least, her intellect was geared to her hymen, not her brain. . . .

Purity, considered as a moral imperative, set up a dilemma which was hard to resolve. Woman must preserve her virtue until marriage and marriage was necessary for her happiness. Yet marriage was, literally, an end to innocence. She was told not to question this dilemma, but simply to accept it.

Submission was perhaps the most feminine virtue expected of women. Men were supposed to be religious, although they rarely had time for it, and supposed to be pure, although it came awfully hard to them, but men were the movers, the doers, the actors. Women were the passive, submissive responders. The order of dialogue was, of course, fixed in Heaven. Man was "woman's superior by God's appointment, if not in intellectual dowry, at least by official decree." Therefore, as Charles Elliott argued in *The Ladies' Repository,* she should submit to him "for the sake of good order at least." In *The Ladies Companion* a young wife was quoted approvingly as saying that she did not think woman should "feel and act for herself" because "When, next to God, her husband is not the tribunal to which her heart and intellect appeals—the golden bowl of affection is broken." Women were warned that if they tampered with this quality they tampered with the order of the Universe.

The Young Lady's Book summarized the necessity of the passive virtues in its readers' lives: "It is, however, certain, that in whatever situation of life a woman is placed from her cradle to her grave, a spirit of obedience and submission, pliability of temper, and humility of mind, are required from her."

Woman understood her position if she was the right kind of woman, a true woman. "She feels herself weak and timid. She needs a protector," declared George Burnap, in his lectures on *The Sphere and Duties of Woman.* "She is in a measure dependent. She asks for wisdom, constancy, firmness, perseverance, and she is willing to repay it all by the surrender of the full treasure of her affections. Woman despises in man every thing like herself except a tender heart. It is enough that she is effeminate and weak; she does not want another like herself." Or put even more strongly by Mrs. Sandford: "A really sensible woman feels her dependence. She does what she can, but she is conscious of inferiority, and therefore grateful for support." . . .

The true woman's place was unquestionably by her own fireside—as daughter, sister, but most of all as wife and mother. Therefore domesticity was among the virtues most prized by the women's magazines. "As society is constituted," wrote Mrs. S. E. Farley, on the "Domestic and Social Claims on Woman," "the true dignity and beauty of the female character seem to consist in a right understanding and faithful and cheerful performance of social and family duties." Sacred Scripture re-enforced social pressure: "St. Paul knew what was best for women when he advised them to be domestic," said Mrs. Sandford. "There is composure at home; there is something sedative in the duties which home involves. It affords security not only from the world, but from delusions and errors of every kind."

From her home woman performed her great task of bringing men back to God. *The Young Ladies' Class Book* was sure that "the domestic fireside is the great guardian of society against the excesses of human passions." *The Lady at Home* expressed its convictions in its very title and concluded that "even if we cannot reform the world in a moment, we can begin the work by reforming ourselves and our households—It is woman's mission. Let her not look away from her own little family circle for the means of producing moral and social reforms, but begin at home."

Home was supposed to be a cheerful place, so that brothers, husbands and sons would not go elsewhere in search of a good time. Woman was expected to dispense comfort and cheer. In writing the biography of Margaret Mercer (every inch a true woman) her biographer (male) notes: "She never forgot that it is the peculiar province of woman to minister to the comfort, and promote the happiness, first, of those most nearly allied to her, and then of those, who by the Providence of God are placed in a state of dependence upon her." Many other essays in the women's journals showed woman as comforter: "Woman, Man's Best Friend," "Woman, the Greatest Social Benefit," "Woman, A Being to Come Home To," "The Wife: Source of Comfort and the Spring of Joy." . . .

In the home women were not only the highest adornment of civilization, but they were supposed to keep busy at morally uplifting tasks. Fortunately most of housework, if looked at in true womanly fashion, could be regarded as uplifting. Mrs. Sigourney extolled its virtues: "The science of housekeeping affords exercise for the judgment and energy, ready recollection, and patient self-possession, that are the characteristics of a superior mind." According to Mrs. Farrar, making beds was good exercise, the repetitiveness of routine tasks inculcated patience and perseverance, and proper management of the home was a surprisingly complex art: "There is more to be learned about pouring out tea and coffee, than most young ladies are willing to believe." Godey's went so far as to suggest coyly, in "Learning vs. Housewifery" that the two were complementary, not opposed: chemistry could be utilized in cooking, geometry in dividing cloth, and phrenology in discovering talent in children. . . .

The debate over women's education posed the question of whether a "finished" education detracted from the practice of housewifely arts. Again it proved to be a case of semantics, for a true woman's education was never "finished" until she was instructed in the gentle science of homemaking. Helen Irving, writing on "Literary Women," made it very clear that if women invoked the muse, it was as a genie of the household lamp. "If the necessities of her position require these duties at her hands, she will perform them nonetheless cheerfully, that she knows herself capable of higher things." The literary woman must conform to the same standards as any other woman: "That her home shall be made a loving place of rest and joy and comfort for those who are dear to her, will be the first wish of every true woman's heart." Mrs. Ann Stephens told women who wrote to make sure they did not sacrifice one domestic duty. "As for genius, make it a domestic plant. Let its roots strike deep in your house. . . ."

The fear of "blue stockings" (the eighteenth-century male's term of derision for educated or literary women) need not persist for nineteenth-century American men. The magazines presented spurious dialogues in which bachelors were convinced of their fallacy in fearing educated wives. One such dialogue took place between a young man and his female cousin. Ernest deprecates learned ladies ("A *Woman* is far more lovable than a *philosopher*") but Alice refutes him with the beautiful example of their Aunt Barbara who "although she *has* perpetrated the heinous crime of writing some half dozen folios" is still a model of "the spirit of feminine gentleness." His memory prodded, Ernest concedes that, by George, there was a woman: "When I last had a cold she not only made me a bottle of cough syrup, but when I complained of nothing new to read, set to work and wrote some twenty stanzas on consumption."

The magazines were filled with domestic tragedies in which spoiled young girls learned that when there was a hungry man to feed French and china painting were not helpful. According to these stories many a marriage is jeopardized because the wife has not learned to keep house. Harriet Beecher Stowe wrote a sprightly piece of personal experience for *Godey's,* ridiculing her own bad housekeeping as a bride. She used the same theme in a story "The Only Daughter," in which the pampered beauty learns the facts of domestic life from a rather difficult source, her mother-in-law. Mrs. Hamilton tells Caroline in the sweetest way possible to shape up in the kitchen, reserving her rebuke for her son: "You are her husband—her guide—her protector—now see what you can do," she admonishes him. "Give her credit for every effort: treat her faults with tenderness; encourage and praise whenever you can, and depend upon it, you will see another woman in her." He is properly masterful, she properly domestic and in a few months Caroline is making lumpless gravy and keeping up with the darning. Domestic tranquillity has been restored and the young wife moralizes: "Bring up a girl to feel that she has a responsible part to bear in promoting the happiness of the family, and you make a reflecting being of her at once, and remove that lightness and frivolity of character which makes her shrink from graver studies." These stories end with the heroine drying her hands on her apron and vowing that *her* daughter will be properly educated. . . .

Marriage was seen not only in terms of service but as an increase in authority for woman. Burnap concluded that marriage improves the female character "not only because it puts her under the best possible tuition, that of the affections, and affords scope to her active energies, but because it gives her higher aims, and a more dignified position." *The Lady's Amaranth* saw it as a balance of power: "The man bears rule over his wife's person and conduct. She bears rule over his inclinations: he governs by law; she by persuasion. . . . The empire of the woman is an empire of softness . . . her commands are caresses, her menaces are tears."

Woman should marry, but not for money. She should choose only the high road of true love and not truckle to the values of a materialistic society. A story "Marrying for Money" (subtlety was not the strong point of the ladies' magazines) depicts Gertrude, the heroine, rueing the day she made her crass choice: "It is a terrible thing to live without love. . . . A woman who dares marry for aught but the purest affection, calls down the just judgments of heaven upon her head."

The corollary to marriage, with or without true love, was motherhood, which added another dimension to her usefulness and her prestige. It also anchored her even more firmly to the home. "My Friend," wrote Mrs. Sigourney, "If in becoming a mother, you have reached the climax of your happiness, you have also taken a higher place in the scale of being . . . you have gained an increase of power." The Rev. J. N. Danforth pleaded in *The Ladies' Casket*, "Oh, mother, acquit thyself well in thy humble sphere, for thou mayest affect the world." A true woman naturally loved her children; to suggest otherwise was monstrous.

America depended upon her mothers to raise up a whole generation of Christian statesmen who could say "all that I am I owe to my angel mother." The mothers must do the inculcating of virtue since the fathers, alas, were too busy chasing the dollar. Or as *The Ladies' Companion* put it more effusively, the father "weary with the heat and burden of life's summer day, or trampling with unwilling foot the decaying leaves of life's autumn, has forgotten the sympathies of life's joyous springtime. . . . The acquisition of wealth, the advancement of his children in worldly honor—these are his self-imposed tasks." It was his wife who formed "the infant mind as yet untainted by contact with evil . . . like wax beneath the plastic hand of the mother." . . .

The American woman had her choice—she could define her rights in the way of the women's magazines and insure them by the practice of the requisite virtues, or she could go outside the home, seeking other rewards than love. It was a decision on which, she was told, everything in her world depended. "Yours it is to determine," the Rev. Mr. Stearns solemnly warned from the pulpit, "whether the beautiful order of society . . . shall continue as it has been" or whether "society shall break up and become a chaos of disjointed and unsightly elements." If she chose to listen to other voices than those of her proper mentors, sought other rooms than those of her home, she lost both her happiness and her power—"that almost magic power, which, in her proper sphere, she now wields over the destinies of the world."

But even while the women's magazines and related literature encouraged this ideal of the perfect woman, forces were at work in the nineteenth century which impelled woman herself to change, to play a more creative role in society. The movements for social reform, westward migration, missionary activity, utopian communities, industrialism, the Civil War—all called forth responses from woman which differed from those she was trained to believe were hers by nature and divine decree. The very perfection of True Womanhood, moreover, carried within itself the seeds of its own destruction. For if woman was so very little less than the angels, she should surely take a more active part in running the world, especially since men were making such a hash of things. . . .

The Female World of Love and Ritual

CARROLL SMITH-ROSENBERG

The female friendship of the nineteenth century, the long-lived, intimate, loving friendship between two women, is an excellent example of the type of historical phenomenon that most historians know something about, few have thought much about, and virtually no one has written about. It is one aspect of the female experience which, consciously or unconsciously, we have chosen to ignore. Yet an abundance of manuscript evidence suggests that eighteenth- and nineteenth-century women routinely formed emotional ties with other women. Such deeply felt same-sex friendships were casually accepted in American society. Indeed, from at least the late eighteenth through the mid-nineteenth century, a female world of varied and yet highly structured relationships appears to have been an essential aspect of American society. These relationships ranged from the supportive love of sisters, through the enthusiasms of adolescent girls, to sensual avowals of love by mature women. It was a world in which men made but a shadowy appearance.

Defining and analyzing same-sex relationships involves the historian in deeply problematical questions of method and interpretation. This is especially true since historians, influenced by Freud's libidinal theory, have discussed these relationships almost exclusively within the context of individual psychosexual development or, to be more explicit, psychopathology. Seeing same-sex relationships in terms of a dichotomy between normal and abnormal, they have sought the origins of such apparent deviance in childhood or adolescent trauma and detected the symptoms of "latent" homosexuality in the lives of both those who later became "overtly" homosexual and those who did not. Yet theories concerning the nature and origins of same-sex relationships are frequently contradictory or based on questionable or arbitrary data. In recent years such hypotheses have been subjected to criticism, both from within and without the psychological professions. Historians who seek to work within a psychological framework, therefore, are faced with two hard questions: Do sound psychodynamic theories concerning the nature and origins of same-sex relationships exist? If so, does the historical datum exist which would permit the use of such dynamic models?

I would like to suggest an alternative approach to female friendships—one that would view them within a cultural and social setting rather than from an exclusively individual psychosexual perspective. Only by thus altering our approach will we be in the position to evaluate the appropriateness of particular dynamic interpretations. Intimate friendships between men and men and women and women existed in a larger world of social relations and

Extracts from Carroll Smith-Rosenberg, "The Female World of Love and Ritual: Relations between Women in Nineteenth-Century America," *Signs*, I (1975), 1–29. Reprinted by permission of The University of Chicago Press.

social values. To interpret such friendships more fully, one must relate them to the structure of the American family and to the nature of sex-role divisions and of male-female relations, both within the family and in society generally. The female friendship must not be seen in isolation; it must be analyzed as one aspect of women's overall relations with one another. The ties between mothers and daughters, sisters, female cousins, and friends, at all stages of the female life cycle, constitute the most suggestive framework the historian can use to begin an analysis of intimacy and affection between women. Such an analysis would not only emphasize general cultural patterns rather than the internal dynamics of a particular family or childhood; it would shift the focus of the study from a concern with deviance to that of defining configurations of legitimate behavioral norms and options. . . .

Several factors in American society between the mid-eighteenth and the mid-nineteenth centuries may well have permitted women to form a variety of close emotional relationships with other women. American society was characterized in large part by rigid gender-role differentiation within the family and within society as a whole, leading to the emotional segregation of women and men. The roles of daughter and mother shaded imperceptibly and ineluctably into each other, while the biological realities of frequent pregnancies, childbirth, nursing, and menopause bound women together in physical and emotional intimacy. It was within just such a social framework, I would argue, that a specifically female world did indeed develop, a world built around a generic and unself-conscious pattern of single-sex or homosocial networks. These supportive networks were institutionalized in social conventions or rituals that accompanied virtually every important event in a woman's life, from birth to death. Such female relationships were frequently supported and paralleled by severe social restrictions on intimacy between young men and women. Within such a world of emotional richness and complexity, devotion to and love of other women became a plausible and socially accepted form of human interaction.

An abundance of printed and manuscript sources exists to support such a hypothesis. Etiquette books, advice books on child-rearing, religious sermons, guides to young men and young women, medical texts, and school curricula all suggest that late-eighteenth- and most nineteenth-century Americans assumed the existence of a world composed of distinctly male and female spheres, spheres determined by the immutable laws of God and nature. The unpublished letters and diaries of Americans during this same period concur, detailing the existence of sexually segregated worlds inhabited by human beings with different values, expectations, and personalities. Contacts between men and women frequently partook of a formality and stiffness quite alien to twentieth-century America, and which today we tend to define as "Victorian." Women, however, did not form an isolated and oppressed subcategory in male society. Their letters and diaries indicate that women's sphere had an essential integrity and dignity that grew out of women's shared experiences and mutual affection and that, despite the profound changes that affected American social structure and institutions between the 1760s and the 1870s, retained a constancy and predictability. The ways in which women thought of and interacted with one another remained unchanged. Continuity, not discontinuity, characterized this female world. . . .

Friends did not form isolated dyads but were normally part of highly integrated networks. Knowing one another, perhaps related to one another, they played a central role in holding communities and kin systems together. Especially when families became geographically mobile, women's long visits to one another and their frequent letters filled with discussions of marriages and births, illnesses and deaths, descriptions of growing children, and reminiscences of times and people past provided an important sense of continuity in a rapidly changing society. Central to this female world was an inner core of kin. The ties between sisters, first cousins, aunts, and nieces provided the underlying structure upon which groups of friends and their network of female relatives clustered. Although most of the women within this sample would appear to be living within isolated nuclear families, the emotional ties between nonresidential kin were deep and binding and provided one of the fundamental existential realities of women's lives. Twenty years after Parke Lewis Butler moved with her husband to Louisiana, she sent her two daughters back to Virginia to attend school, live with their grandmother and aunt, and be integrated back into Virginia society. The constant letters between Maria Inskeep and Fanny Hampton, sisters separated in their early twenties when Maria moved with her husband from New Jersey to Louisiana, held their families together, making it possible for their daughters to feel a part of their cousins' network of friends and interests. The Ripley daughters, growing up in western Massachusetts in the early 1800s, spent months each year with their mother's sister and her family in distant Boston; these female cousins and their network of friends exchanged gossip-filled letters and gradually formed deeply loving and dependent ties.

Women frequently spent their days within the social confines of such extended families. Sisters-in-law visited one another and, in some families, seemed to spend more time with one another than with their husbands. First cousins cared for one another's babies—for weeks or even months in times of sickness or childbirth. Sisters helped one another with housework, shopped and sewed for one another. Geographic separation was borne with difficulty. A sister's absence for even a week or two could cause loneliness and depression and would be bridged by frequent letters. Sibling rivalry was hardly unknown, but with separation or illness the theme of deep affection and dependency re-emerged.

Sisterly bonds continued across a lifetime. In her old age, a rural Quaker matron, Martha Jefferis, wrote to her daughter Anne concerning her own half-sister, Phoebe: "In sister Phoebe I have a real friend—she studies my comfort and waits on me like a child. . . . She is exceedingly kind and this to all other homes (set aside yours) I would prefer—it is next to being with a daughter." Phoebe's own letters confirmed Martha's evaluation of her feelings. "Thou knowest my dear sister," Phoebe wrote, "there is no one . . . that exactly feels [for] thee as I do, for I think without boasting I can truly say that my desire is for thee."

Such women, whether friends or relatives, assumed an emotional centrality in one another's lives. In their diaries and letters they wrote of the joy and contentment they felt in one another's company, their sense of isolation and despair when apart. The regularity of their correspondence underlines the sincerity of such words. Women named their daughters after one another and sought to integrate dear friends into their lives after marriage. As one young bride wrote to an old friend shortly after her marriage, "I want to see you and talk with you and feel that we are united by the same bonds of sympathy and congeniality as ever." After years of friendship, one aging woman wrote of another, "Time cannot destroy the fascination of her manner . . . her voice is music to the ear. . . ." Women made elaborate presents for one another, ranging from the Quakers' frugal pies and breads to painted velvet bags and phantom bouquets. When a friend died, their grief was deeply felt: Martha Jefferis was unable to write to her daughter for three weeks because of the sorrow she felt at the death of a dear friend, and such distress was not unusual. A generation earlier, a young Massachusetts farm woman filled pages of her diary with her grief at the death of her "dearest friend" and transcribed the letters of condolence other women sent her. She marked the anniversary of Rachel's death each year in her diary, contrasting her faithfulness with that of Rachel's husband, who had soon remarried.

These female friendships served a number of emotional functions. Within this secure and empathetic world women could share sorrows, anxieties, and joys, confident that other women had experienced similar emotions. One mid-nineteenth-century rural matron, in a letter to her daughter, discussed this particular aspect of women's friendships: "To have such a friend as thyself to look to and sympathize with her—and enter into all her little needs and in whose bosom she could with freedom pour forth her joys and sorrows—such a friend would very much relieve the tedium of many a wearisome hour. . . ." A generation later Molly more informally underscored the importance of this same function in a letter to Helena: "Suppose I come down . . . [and] spend Sunday with you quietly," she wrote Helena, ". . . that means talking all the time until you are relieved of all your latest troubles, and I of mine. . . ." These were frequently troubles that apparently no man could understand. When Anne Jefferis Sheppard was first married, she and her older sister Edith (who then lived with Anne) wrote in detail to their mother of the severe depression and anxiety they experienced. Moses Sheppard, Anne's husband, added cheerful postscripts to the sisters' letters—which he had clearly not read—remarking on Anne's and Edith's contentment. Theirs was an emotional world to which he had little access.

This was, as well, a female world in which hostility and criticism of other women were discouraged, and thus a milieu in which women could develop a sense of inner security and self-esteem. As one young woman wrote to her mother's long-time friend: " I cannot sufficiently thank you for the kind unvaried affection & indulgence you have ever shown and expressed both by words and actions for me. . . . Happy would it be did all the world view me as you do, through the medium of kindness and forbearance." They valued one another. Women, who had little status or power in the larger world of male concerns, possessed status and power in the lives and worlds of other women.

An intimate mother-daughter relationship lay at the heart of this female world. The diaries and letters of both mothers and daughters attest to their closeness and mutual emotional dependency. Daughters routinely discussed their mothers' health and activities with their own friends, expressed anxiety when their mothers were ill and concern for their cares. Expressions of hostility which we would today consider routine on the part of both mothers and daughters seem to have been uncommon indeed. On the contrary, this sample of families indicates that the normal relationship between mother and daughter was one of sympathy and understanding. Only sickness or great geographic distance was allowed to cause extended separation. When marriage did result in such separation, both viewed the distance between them with distress. Something of this sympathy and love between mothers and daughters is evident in a letter Sarah Alden Ripley, at age sixty-nine, wrote her youngest and recently married daughter: "You do not know how much I miss you, not only when I struggle in and out of my mortal envelop and pump my nightly potation and no longer pour into your sympathizing ear my senile gossip, but all the day I muse away, since the sound of your voice no longer rouses me to sympathy with your joys or sorrows. . . . You cannot know how much I miss your affectionate demonstrations." A dozen aging mothers in this sample of over thirty families echoed her sentiments.

Central to these mother-daughter relations is what might be described as an apprenticeship system. In those families where the daughter followed the mother into a life of traditional domesticity, mothers and other older women had carefully trained daughters in the arts of housewifery and motherhood. Such training undoubtedly occurred throughout a girl's childhood but became more systematized, almost ritualistic, in the years following the end of her formal education and before her marriage. At this time a girl either returned home from boarding school or no longer divided her time between home and school. Rather, she devoted her energies to two tasks: mastering new domestic skills and participating in the visiting and social activities necessary to finding a husband. Under the careful supervision of their mothers and of older female relatives, such late-adolescent girls temporarily took over the household management from their mothers, tended their young nieces and nephews, and helped in childbirth, nursing, and weaning. Such experiences tied the generations together in shared skills and emotional interaction. . . .

At some point in adolescence, the young girl began to move outside the matrix of her mother's support group to develop a network of her own. Among the middle class, at least, this transition toward what was at the same time both a limited autonomy and a repetition of her mother's life seemed to have most frequently coincided with a girl's going to school. Indeed, education appears to have played a crucial role in the lives of most of the families in this study. Attending school for a few months, for a year, or longer was common even among daughters of relatively poor families, while middle-class girls routinely spent at least a year in boarding school. These school years ordinarily marked a girl's first separation from home. They served to wean the daughter from her home, to train her in the essential social graces, and, ultimately, to help introduce her into the marriage market. It was not infrequently a trying emotional experience for both mother and daughter.

In this process of leaving one home and adjusting to another, the mother's friends and relatives played a key transitional role. Such older women routinely accepted the role of foster mother; they supervised the young girl's deportment, monitored her health, and introduced her to their own network of female friends and kin. Not infrequently, women who had been friends from their own school years arranged to send their daughters to the same school, so that the girls might form bonds paralleling those their mothers had made. For years Molly and Helena wrote of their daughters' meeting and worried over each other's children. When Molly finally brought her daughter east to school, their first act on reaching New York was to meet Helena and her daughters. Elizabeth Bordley Gibson virtually adopted the daughters of her school chum, Eleanor Custis Lewis. The Lewis daughters soon began to write Elizabeth Gibson letters with the salutation "Dearest Mama." Eleuthera DuPont, attending boarding school in Philadelphia at roughly the same time as the Lewis girls, developed a parallel relationship with her mother's friend, Elizabeth McKie Smith. Eleuthera went to the same school as and became a close friend of the Smith girls, and eventually married their first cousin. During this period she routinely called Mrs. Smith "Mother." Indeed, Eleuthera so internalized the sense of having two mothers that she casually wrote her sisters of her "Mamma's" visits at her "mother's" house—that is, at Mrs. Smith's.

Even more important to this process of maturation than their mother's friends were the female friends young women made at school. Young girls helped one another overcome homesickness and endure the crises of adolescence. They gossiped about beaux, incorporated one another into their own kinship systems, and attended and gave teas and balls together. Older girls in boarding school "adopted" younger ones, who called them "Mother." Dear friends might indeed continue this pattern of adoption and mothering throughout their lives; one woman might routinely assume the nurturing role of pseudo-mother, the other the dependency role of daughter. The pseudo-mother performed for the other woman all the services we normally associate with mothers; she went to absurd lengths to purchase items her "daughter" could have obtained from other sources, gave advice, and functioned as an idealized figure in her "daughter's" imagination. Helena played such a role for Molly, as did Sarah for Jeannie. Elizabeth Bordley Gibson bought almost all Eleanor Parke Custis Lewis's necessities—from shoes and corset covers to bedding and harp strings—and sent them from Philadelphia to Virginia, a procedure that sometimes took months. Eleanor frequently asked Elizabeth to take back her purchases, have them redone, and argue with shopkeepers about prices. These were favors automatically asked and complied with. Anne Jefferis Sheppard made the analogy very explicitly in a letter to her own mother written shortly after Anne's marriage, when she was feeling depressed about their separation: "Mary Paulen is truly kind, almost acts the part of a mother and trys to aid and *comfort me,* and also to *lighten my new cares.*"

A comparison of the references to men and women in women's letters is striking. Boys were obviously indispensable to rate courtship ritual girls engaged in. In these teen-age letters and however, boys appear distant and warded off—an effect produced by the girl's sense of bonding and by a highly developed and deprecatory whimsy. Girls joked among themselves about the conceit, poor looks, or affectations of suitors. Rarely, especially in the eighteenth and early nineteenth centuries, were favorable remarks exchanged. Indeed, although hostility and criticism of other women were so rare as to seem almost tabooed, young women permitted themselves to express a great deal of hostility toward peer-group men. If unacceptable suitors appeared, girls might even band together to harass them. When one such unfortunate came to court Sophie DuPont, she hid in her room, first sending her sister Eleuthera to entertain him and then dispatching a number of urgent notes to her neighboring sister-in-law, cousins, and a visiting friend, who all came to Sophie's support. A wild female romp ensued, ending only when Sophie banged into a door, lacerated her nose, and retired, with her female cohorts, to bed. Her brother and the presumably disconcerted suitor were left alone. These were not the antics of teen-agers but of women in their early and mid-twenties.

Even if young men were acceptable suitors, girls referred to them formally and obliquely: "The last week I received the unexpected intelligence of the arrival of a friend in Boston," Sarah Ripley wrote in her diary of the young man to whom she had been engaged for years and whom she would shortly marry. Harriet Manigault assiduously kept a lively and gossipy diary during the three years preceding her marriage, yet did not once comment upon her own engagement or, indeed, make any personal references to her fiancé—who was never identified as such but always referred to as Mr. Wilcox. The point is not that these young women were hostile to young men. Far from it: they sought marriage and domesticity. Yet in these letters and diaries men appear as an other or out group, segregated into different schools, supported by their own male network of friends and kin, socialized to different behavior, and coached to a proper formality in courtship behavior. As a consequence, relations between young women and men frequently lacked the spontaneity and emotional intimacy that characterized the young girls' ties to one another. . . .

Marriage followed adolescence. With increasing frequency in the nineteenth century, marriage involved a girl's traumatic removal from her mother and her mother's network. It involved, as well, adjustment to a husband, who, because he was male, came to marriage with both a different world view and vastly different experiences. Not surprisingly, marriage was an event surrounded by supportive, almost ritualistic, practices. (Weddings are one of the last female rituals remaining in twentieth-century America.) Young women routinely spent the months preceding their marriage almost exclusively with other women—at neighborhood sewing bees and quilting parties or in a round of visits to geographically distant friends and relatives. Ostensibly they went to receive assistance in the practical preparations for their new homes—sewing and quilting trousseaux and linen—but, of equal importance, they appear to have gained emotional support and reassurance. Sarah Ripley spent over a month with friends and relatives in Boston and Hingham before her wedding; Parke Custis Lewis exchanged visits with her aunts and first cousins throughout Virginia. Anne Jefferis, who married with some hesitation, spent virtually half a year in endless visiting with cousins, aunts, and friends. Despite their reassurance and support, however, she would not marry Moses Sheppard until her sister Edith and her cousin Rebecca moved into the groom's home, met his friends, and explored his personality. The wedding did not take place until Edith wrote to Anne, "I can say in truth I am entirely willing thou shouldst follow him even away in the Jersey sands believing if thou are not happy in thy future home it will not be any fault on his part. . . ."

Sisters, cousins, and friends frequently accompanied newlyweds on their wedding night and wedding trip, which often involved additional family visiting. Such extensive visits presumably served to wean the daughter from her family of origin. As such they often contained a note of ambivalence. Nelly Custis, for example, reported homesickness and loneliness on her wedding trip. "I left my Beloved and revered Grandmamma with sincere regret," she wrote Elizabeth Bordley. "It was some time before I could feel reconciled to traveling without her." Perhaps they also functioned to reassure the young woman herself, and her friends and kin, that though marriage might alter it would not destroy old bonds of intimacy and familiarity.

Married life too was structured about a host of female rituals. Childbirth, especially the birth of the first child, became virtually a *rite de passage,* with a lengthy seclusion of the woman before and after delivery, severe restrictions on her activities, and finally a dramatic re-emergence. This seclusion was supervised by mothers, sisters, and loving friends. Nursing and weaning involved the advice and assistance of female friends and relatives. So did miscarriage. Death, like birth, was structured around elaborate, unisexed rituals. When Nelly Parke Custis Lewis rushed to nurse her daughter who was critically ill while away at school, Nelly received support, not from her husband, who remained on their plantation, but from her old school friend Elizabeth Bordley. Elizabeth aided Nelly in caring for her dying daughter, cared for Nelly's other children, played a major role in making arrangements for the elaborate funeral (which the father did not attend), and frequently visited the girl's grave at the mother's request. For years Elizabeth continued to be the confidante of Nelly's anguished recollections of her lost daughter. These memories, Nelly's letters make clear, were for Elizabeth alone. "Mr. L. knows nothing of this" was a frequent comment. Virtually every collection of letters and diaries in my sample contained evidence of women turning to one another for comfort when facing the frequent and unavoidable deaths of the eighteenth and nineteenth centuries. While mourning for her father's death, Sophie DuPont received eloquent letters and visits of condolence—all from women. No man wrote or visited Sophie to offer sympathy at her father's death. Among rural Pennsylvania Quakers, death and mourning rituals assumed an even more extreme same-sex form, with men or women largely barred from the deathbeds of the other sex.

Women relatives and friends slept with the dying woman, nursed her, and prepared her body for burial.

Eighteenth- and nineteenth-century women thus lived in emotional proximity to one another. Friendships and intimacies followed the biological ebb and flow of women's lives. Marriage and pregnancy, childbirth and weaning, sickness and death, involved physical and psychic trauma which comfort and sympathy made easier to bear. Intense bonds of love and intimacy bound together those women who, offering one another aid and sympathy, shared such stressful moments.

These bonds were often physical as well as emotional. An undeniably romantic and even sensual note frequently marked female relationships. This theme, significant throughout the stages of a woman's life, surfaced first during adolescence. As one teen-ager from a struggling pioneer family in the Ohio Valley wrote in her diary in 1808, "I laid with my dear R[ebecca] and a glorious good talk we had until about 4[A.M.]—O how hard I do *love* her. . . ." Only a few years later, Bostonian Eunice Callender carved her initials and Sarah Ripley's into a favorite tree, along with a pledge of eternal love, and then waited breathlessly for Sarah to discover and respond to her declaration of affection. The response appears to have been affirmative. A half-century later, urbane and sophisticated Katherine Wharton commented upon meeting an old school chum: "She was a great pet of mine at school & I thought as I watched her light figure how often I had held her in my arms—how dear she had once been to me." Katie maintained a long, intimate friendship with another girl. When a young man began to court this friend seriously, Katie commented in her diary that she had never realized "how deeply I loved Eng and how fully." She wrote over and over again in that entry, "Indeed I love her!," and only with great reluctance left the city that summer, since it meant also leaving Eng with Eng's new suitor.

Peggy Emlen, a Quaker adolescent in Philadelphia in the 1760s, expressed similar feelings about her first cousin, Sally Logan. The girls sent love poems to each other (not unlike the ones Elizabeth Bordley wrote to Nelly Custis a generation later), took long, solitary walks together, and even haunted the empty house of the other when one was out of town. Indeed, Sally's absences from Philadelphia caused Peggy acute unhappiness. So strong were Peggy's feelings that her brothers began to tease her about her affection for Sally and threatened to steal Sally's letters, much to both girls' alarm. In one letter that Peggy wrote the absent Sally, she elaborately described the depth and nature of her feelings:

> I have not words to express my impatience to see My Dear Cousin, what would I not give just now for an hours sweet conversation with her, it seems as if I had a thousand things to say to thee, yet when I see thee, everything will be forgot thro' joy. . . . I have a very great friendship for several Girls yet it dont give me so much uneasiness at being absent from them as from thee. . . . [Let us] go and spend a day down at our place together and there unmolested enjoy each others company.

Sarah Alden Ripley, a young, highly educated woman, formed a similar intense relationship, in this instance with a woman somewhat older than herself. The immediate bond of friendship rested on their atypically intense scholarly interests, but it soon involved strong emotions, at least on Sarah's part. "Friendship," she wrote Mary Emerson, "is fast twining about her willing captive the silken hands of dependence, a dependence so sweet who would renounce it for the apathy of self-sufficiency?" Subsequent letters became far more emotional, almost conspiratorial. Mary visited Sarah secretly in her room, or the two women crept away from family and friends to meet in a nearby wood. Sarah became jealous of Mary's other young woman friends. Mary's trips away from Boston also thrust Sarah into periods of anguished depression. Interestingly, the letters detailing their love were not destroyed but were preserved and even reprinted in a eulogistic biography of Sarah Alden Ripley. . . .

How, then, can we ultimately interpret these long-lived intimate female relationships and integrate them into our understanding of Victorian sexuality? Their ambivalent and romantic rhetoric presents us with an ultimate puzzle: the relationship along the spectrum of human emotions between love, sensuality, and sexuality.

One is tempted, as I have remarked, to compare Molly, Peggy, or Sophie's relationship with the friendships adolescent girls in the twentieth century routinely form—close friendships of great emotional intensity. Helena Deutsch and Clara Thompson have both described these friendships as emotionally necessary to a girl's psychosexual development. But, they warn, such friendships might shade into adolescent and postadolescent homosexuality.

It is possible to speculate that in the twentieth century a number of cultural taboos evolved to cut short the homosocial ties of girlhood and to impel the emerging women of thirteen or fourteen toward heterosexual relationships. In contrast, nineteenth-century American society did not taboo close female relationships but, rather, recognized them as a socially viable form of human contact—and, as such, acceptable throughout a woman's life. Indeed, it was not these homosocial ties that were inhibited but, rather, heterosexual leanings. While closeness, freedom of emotional expression, and uninhibited physical contact characterized women's relationships with one another, the opposite was frequently true of male-female relationships. One could thus argue that within such a world of female support, intimacy, and ritual it was only to be expected that adult women would turn trustingly and lovingly to one another. It was a behavior they had observed and learned since childhood. A different type of emotional landscape existed in the nineteenth century, one in which Molly and Helena's love became a natural development.

Of perhaps equal significance are the implications we can garner from this framework for the understanding of heterosexual marriages in the nineteenth century. If men and women grew up, as they did, in relatively homogeneous and segregated sexual groups, then marriage represented a major problem in adjustment. From this perspective we could interpret much of the emotional stiffness and distance that we associate with Victorian marriage as a structural consequence of contemporary sex-role differentiation and gender-role socialization. With marriage both women and men had to adjust to life with a person who was, in essence, a member of an alien group.

I have thus far substituted a cultural or psychosocial for a psychosexual interpretation of women's emotional bonding. But there are psychosexual implications in this model which I think it only fair to make more explicit. Despite Sigmund Freud's insistence on the bisexuality of us all, or the recent American Psychiatric Association decision on homosexuality, many psychiatrists today tend explicitly or implicitly to view homosexuality as a totally alien or pathological behavior—as totally unlike heterosexuality. I suspect that in essence they may have adopted an explanatory model similar to the one used in discussing schizophrenia. As a psychiatrist can speak of schizophrenia and of a borderline schizophrenic personality as both ultimately and fundamentally different from a normal or a neurotic personality, so they also think of both homosexuality and latent homosexuality as states totally different from heterosexuality. With this rapidly dichotomous model of assumption, "latent homosexuality" becomes the indication of a disease in progress—seeds of a pathology which belie the reality of an individual's heterosexuality.

Yet, at the same time, we are well aware that cultural values can affect choices in the gender of a person's sexual partner. We, for instance, do not necessarily consider homosexual-object choice among men in prison, on shipboard, or in boarding schools a necessary indication of pathology. I would urge that we expand this relativistic model and hypothesize that a number of cultures might well tolerate or even encourage diversity in sexual and nonsexual relations. Based on my research into this nineteenth-century world of female intimacy, I would further suggest that, rather than seeing a gulf between the normal and the abnormal, we view sexual and emotional impulses as part of a continuum or spectrum of affect gradations strongly affected by cultural norms and arrangements, a continuum influenced in part by observed and thus learned behavior. At one end of the continuum lies committed heterosexuality, at the other uncompromising homosexuality; between, a wide latitude of emotions and sexual feelings. Certain cultures and environments permit individuals a great deal of freedom in moving across this spectrum. I would like to suggest that the nineteenth century was such a cultural environment. That is, the supposedly repressive and destructive Victorian sexual ethos may have been more flexible and responsive to the needs of particular individuals than those of the mid-twentieth century.

A Ministry of Mothers

RICHARD A. MECKEL

To the social and moral reformers and ideologues who made antebellum America a hothouse of schemes to perfect and regulate the young republic's citizenry, few targets for reform seemed more promising than America's

---

Richard Meckel, "Educating a Ministry of Mothers: Evangelical Maternal Associations, 1815–1860," article originally published in *Journal of the Early Republic*, Vol. 2, No. 4 (Winter 1982), 403–423.

mothers. An ideology and a rhetoric had developed since the revolution defining the civic responsibility of women and recognizing their changing parental roles. Antebellum reformers, aware that mothers were becoming virtually the sole arbiters of family and child life and increasingly convinced of the formative importance of early childhood, credited the nation's mothers with a formidable ability to shape the future character of the American populace. "Mothers," declared John S. C. Abbott in 1833, "have as powerful an influence over the welfare of future generations, as all other earthly causes combined."

In granting such power to maternal influence, reformers necessarily made the education of mothers a critical tool of reform. If mothers could be enlightened about their responsibilities and instructed in proper child management, then the influence they possessed could be channeled toward social and moral good. As Samuel Jennings explained early in the century: "If every woman were properly qualified and would faithfully perform her duty in bringing up children; their virtuous affection might be so confirmed, their disposition to vice so effectively subdued, that the greatest revolution in the morals and health of the world would be a consequence." To encourage such a revolution, most maternal reformers turned to what had long been in America a primary vehicle for popular education—didactic literature. The result aided in no small way by a printing revolution was an unprecedented deluge of domestic and child rearing advice literature. . . .

While several networks and channels operated in early nineteenth century America to provide women with access to published advice on child rearing and domesticity, perhaps none enjoyed either the success or the reach of those created by the nationwide formation of maternal associations and the subsequent publication of maternal association journals. Like the occupational and vocational associations which proliferated in antebellum America, those composed of actual or prospective mothers were organized on the principle that information and communication were essential for self-improvement and competency in the performance of one's duties. Consequently, maternal associations provided their members with access to information and ideas pertaining to motherhood and thus served as surprisingly effective channels for the dissemination of maternal reform literature. By institutionalizing the circulation of published advice on child rearing, motherhood, and domesticity, these voluntary associations were one of the preeminent forces in the diffusion of the rhetoric of maternal and domestic reform beyond the parlors of a literate northeastern elite.

Certainly such diffusion seems to have been the aim of the most pervasive of these maternal organizations, the ones associated with evangelical Presbyterian, Congregational, and Baptist churches. First appearing in the second decade of the century, these evangelical maternal associations spread throughout the nation before fading from the American scene in the years immediately following the Civil War. As one of the more prominent forms of association for married women in antebellum America, these organizations have not been overlooked by historians. Yet because they were organized at the local level and often left no lasting records, their influence as the basis of a significant social and cultural movement may be still somewhat underestimated. The evidence suggests that the numbers were immense, although it is impossible to determine exactly how many maternal associations were formed or how many women were involved in them. In 1836, for instance, two rural New Hampshire counties alone contained 38 maternal associations with a combined membership of over one thousand women. Especially among the Congregationalists and Presbyterians, it seems that wherever an evangelical church existed there was a maternal association connected with it. . . .

The ground in which maternal associations were planted and flourished was well cultivated by the complementary growth and proliferation after 1800 of voluntary associations and female religious activism. The appearance and spread of maternal associations must be viewed within the larger context of voluntary activity among women during and following the Second Great Awakening. Yet maternal associations were not mere replications of the benevolent and missionary societies which prepared the way for them. Although borrowing from those societies the principle of voluntary organization, a commitment to female activism, and a spirit of benevolence born of millennial optimism, they charted for themselves a course of action which was unprecedented. The women who formed maternal associations did not join together to bring relief to the poor or the word of God to the heathen. Though supportive of these activities, the focus of their concern was directed inward rather than outward as they turned their attention to promoting piety in their children and to fostering Christian motherhood.

In directing their evangelical energies toward themselves and their children, the women who formed maternal associations did not, however, abandon the millennial hope that the world could be transformed. Rather, they proposed that the theater of action most important to that transformation and to the advance of Christian civilization was not necessarily the foreign or domestic mission but was closer at hand—in the nursery of every home. It was, they believed, as mothers and instructors of the young that Christian women could do most to revolutionize humanity and usher in the glorious era when all could know the Lord. In a promotional circular sent out in 1832, the New York Maternal Association noted that mothers had played central roles in the Book of Genesis and in the birth of Christianity, and proclaimed that once again they were positioned to affect profoundly the course of history:

> A third moral revolution remains, in which mothers will have a conspicuous part to perform, viz: the introduction of the *Millen[n]ium.* When every nursery shall become a little sanctuary, and not before, will the earth be filled with the knowledge and glory of the Lord. Through the instrumentality of mothers, "out of the mouths of babes, and sucklings," God ordains strength; and were Christian mothers faithful, we believe that even in infancy, they would be the spiritual, as well as the natural parents of their children.

To accomplish such a revolution, however, demanded both an awareness of the responsibilities inherent in Christian motherhood and a familiarity with the best means by which those responsibilities might be met. Such, at least, was the reasoning of maternal association members who banded together, as the preamble of the Portland association's constitution proclaimed, "for the purpose of devising and adopting such measures as may seem best calculated to assist us in the right performance of [our] duty."

The major reformative thrust of maternal associations thus was aimed at the members themselves, and constituted an effort to produce a class of Christian mothers qualified to fulfill their roles as molders of the young and architects of the future of Christianity. As envisioned by maternal associations, each member was expected to seek guidance through prayer so that she might have the strength and inspiration to carry out the duties entrusted to her. She was also expected to go beyond prayer, to seek advice and "to suggest to her sister members such hints as her own experience may furnish, or circumstances seem to render necessary." The typical maternal association meeting, therefore, included a significant portion of time devoted to the free discussion of topics pertaining to motherhood and the rearing of children. "In this way," explained the secretary of a Massachusetts association in 1841, "we gain from the fruits of each other's experience much practical knowledge." Such mutual counsel was from the beginning a central function of maternal associations and, serving as it did either to formalize existing networks of advice among women or to provide them where they were absent, probably explains much of the attraction of these organizations. In discussing the growth of the New Ipswich Maternal Association, its founder recalled that she and many other early members, burdened and isolated by the cares of running large households, found that meeting together once a month allowed them to share those cares and benefit from the experiences of others in similar circumstances. . . .

To encourage the growth of this ministry of mothers, *The Mother's Magazine* [founded in 1833] successfully supported and promoted the spread of maternal associations. As the magazine's circulation quickly grew, reaching ten thousand by 1837, so too did the number of maternal associations throughout the country. In 1836, for instance, the New York City Maternal Association (an umbrella organization for various metropolitan associations) reported that there was a maternal association in every Presbyterian church in the city. Similarly, at a general meeting in Keene, New Hampshire, the next year it was ascertained that in the 22 towns of the county there were 17 maternal associations encompassing 437 mothers and 1,427 children. Moreover, by 1840 *The Mother's Magazine* was regularly publishing reports and correspondence from maternal associations located in every state and territory in America, as well as in several foreign countries.

Such was the popularity of *The Mother's Magazine* and the movement it promoted that soon two other maternal association periodicals began publication. In 1836 the maternal associations connected with the Baptist churches in and around Utica started *The Mother's Journal* under the editorship of Eliza C. Allen. Five years later, the Boston maternal associations began publishing *The Mother's Assistant and Young Lady's Friend*. Both these periodicals quickly rivaled *The Mother's Magazine* in circulation and devoted themselves with equal vigor to the promotion of maternal associations and the education of Christian mothers. In 1841 *The Mother's Journal* listed 138 agents in 135 towns and cities and noted that several hundred other women served as unofficial agents. If one assumes that each of the listed agents and most of those not named represented separate and distinct maternal associations, one begins to understand the immense scope of maternal association activity in the 1830s and 1840s.

One also begins to appreciate how dynamic and far-reaching the information network was which maternal associations could join by subscribing to these magazines. At a cost of only one dollar a year, *The Mother's Magazine, The Mother's Journal,* and *The Mother's Assistant* were available to even the smallest and most remote maternal associations, thereby providing members of these associations with "readers' digests" of domestic, maternal, and child rearing reform literature. Moreover, despite the evangelical orientation of these magazines, they contained surprisingly eclectic and inclusive material. One finds essays by Locke and Rousseau on infant and child education, by William Dewees and Andrew Combe on child health, and by Hannah Moore and Daniel Webster on the importance of maternal education interspersed with the main fare—pieces on early religious training and moral reform. Occasionally the magazines were well ahead of their time. As early as 1836, *The Mother's Magazine* published a special piece on Pestalozzian educational theory, significantly before the educational reformer or his theories had become familiar among even America's educated elites. Thus, while principally committed to the spread of Christian piety, the magazines also served to expose maternal association members to a body of literature and ideas which many historians have assumed circulated, if at all, among only the upper reaches of antebellum American society.

In bringing such literature to their members, maternal associations and the periodicals they inspired recognized that changing parental roles had significantly added to the child rearing responsibilities attached to motherhood. Although American women had always shouldered a greater share of daily child care than had men, early nineteenth century changes in the organization of work tended to increase that share even more. For the evangelical women who constituted the membership of maternal associations, this greater responsibility carried with it an extra concern. Evangelical revision of Calvinist doctrines, particularly those pertaining to predestination and innate depravity, placed a heavy burden on mothers by emphasizing the efficacy of free will and the importance of early religious and moral training in attaining piety and salvation. Locating themselves somewhere between the philosophies of Jonathan Edwards and Horace Bushnell, most early nineteenth century evangelists supported the necessity of conversion but contended that the young child could be early disposed toward it if molded correctly from infancy. Consequently, if a child were ultimately damned, it was not solely because God willed it so; it was also because the mother failed in her duty to lead it in the right direction. As the secretary of the Utica Baptist Maternal Association reminded readers of *The Mother's Magazine:*

> *You are the stewards of the Lord.* To you he has committed treasures which outweigh the *world!* To your charge he has given the tender buds of endless being; yours it is to expose them to the Sun of righteousness that they may so bloom on earth as to bear fruit in heaven. God will hold you in a measure responsible, should they be blighted in your hands. How fearful is your trust!

As educators and molders of the young, evangelical mothers thus bore on their shoulders almost sole responsibility for the salvation of their children. And it was to assist them in carrying that burden that maternal associations directed most of their educational efforts.

Maternal reformers also were quick to remind their readers and listeners that the fearful responsibility of motherhood carried with it a great deal of power and potential for substantial reward. If mothers were faithful in carrying out their duties, they would "reap the approving smile of the Heavenly Father" and shape the course of Christianity, because in molding the rising generation they could shape the future of the world. "If any one thing is more essential than everything else for the redemption of the world," argued Josiah Holbrook in 1838, "it is early religious education. If any one class of the human family can alone accomplish that work, that class is mothers." . . .

It was, then, as vehicles for relieving that isolation and for providing mothers with necessary information and instruction that members viewed maternal associations. They were not alone, of course, in their conviction that motherhood demanded special preparation. American female education reformers from Emma Willard through Catharine Beecher were advancing the same argument. Maternal associations were unique, nevertheless, in the extent to which they institutionalized maternal education and in the degree to which they maintained channels of communication below the upper reaches of American society for the dissemination of child rearing information. Unlike most antebellum maternal reform movements, maternal associationism appeared to receive much of its support from the lower middle class. The membership of the Utica Maternal Association, for instance, was dominated by the wives of artisans and mechanics. As a promotional circular sent out by a Boston association made clear, maternal associations seemed to attract those women "whose occupations are so constant and pressing" that their educational "opportunities for mental cultivation are extremely limited." Burdened by the myriad responsibilities of overseeing households which often included several children and frequently a boarder or two, these women had precious little time or money to devote to leisure reading and were not the audience which historians generally assume were reached by expert advice on child rearing. But reached they were. Motivated by piety, a concern for the salvation of their children, and the desire to share their burdens with others in similar situations, they joined maternal associations by the thousands and there found "the best works on education collected and explained."

✧ *FURTHER READING*

Norma Basch, *In the Eyes of the Law: Women, Marriage, and Property in Nineteenth-Century New York* (1982)
Lee Virginia Chambers-Schiller, *Liberty, A Better Husband: Single Women in America, The Generations of 1780–1840* (1984)

Nancy Cott, *The Bonds of Womanhood* (1977)

Ann Douglas, *The Feminization of American Culture* (1977)

John Mack Faragher, *Women and Men on the Overland Trail* (1979)

Harvey Green, *The Light of the Home: An Intimate View of the Lives of Women in Victorian America* (1983)

Karen Halttunen, *Confidence Men and Painted Women: A Study of Middle-Class Culture in America, 1830–1870* (1982)

Julie Jeffrey, *Frontier Women: The Trans-Mississippi West, 1840–1880* (1979)

Mary Kelley, *Private Woman, Public Stage: Literary Domesticity in Nineteenth-Century America* (1984)

Suzanne Lebsock, *The Free Women of Petersburg* (1984)

Mary P. Ryan, *Cradle of the Middle Class: The Family in Oneida County, New York, 1790–1865* (1981)

Kathryn Kish Sklar, *Catharine Beecher* (1973)

Carroll Smith-Rosenberg, "The Hysterical Woman: Sex Roles and Role Conflict in Nineteenth-Century America," *Social Research*, XXXIX (1972), 652–78

Christine Stansell, *City of Women: Work, Sex, and Class in New York 1789–1860* (1987)

The Family Lives
of Enslaved Women

❖

Studying the family lives of enslaved African-Americans is difficult, and for many years scholars rarely attempted to investigate the topic. Very few slaves were literate, and only a small number of those produced accounts of their experiences. Accordingly, many of the major pieces of surviving evidence are the letters, diaries, and plantation records of white slaveowners dating from the pre–Civil War years, which must be used with extreme caution because of their inherent bias. Historians can also rely on slave narratives collected in the 1930s by researchers from the Federal Writers' Project, who traveled through the South talking with aged former slaves about their lives before emancipation. But because even the youngest interviewees were in their late seventies when they were asked to tell their stories, users of the narratives must always be aware that the memories of very old people can be faulty.

 condensending!

Further, because slaves could not legally marry under the laws of the southern states, historians have to define ''marriage'' before slave families can be studied. What constituted a slave marriage? How can a modern researcher tell whether an enslaved couple regarded themselves as married or not, or whether the community regarded their children as legitimate? And does the very act of asking such a question impose twentieth-century white values on nineteenth-century black people?

Yet however slave families are defined, it is obvious that the kin connections of enslaved African-Americans played crucial roles in their lives. In circumstances in which marriages and parent-child relationships could be broken not only by death but also by sale or by enforced mobility, extended family ties among slaves grew particularly strong. If parents could no longer care for children, then aunts and uncles could; if a marriage was broken by sale, the remaining partner could be assisted by other kin.

Recently historians have begun to try to assess the position of women within this web of kin relationships. What were the relationships between women and their husbands or children? How did the actions of slaveowners affect the family lives of slave women? Were enslaved women able to control any aspects of their family lives?

✣ *D O C U M E N T S*

The first three documents are all narratives of former slaves. The first, the recollections of Cornelia, a Tennessean, was collected by a researcher from Fisk University. The other two come from work done by the Federal Writers' Project: the
second selection is an interview with Rose Williams, of Texas; and the third is an
interview with Fannie Moore, who grew up in South Carolina. These accounts provide glimpses of the strength of slave women during times of extreme adversity.
The last document consists of two letters from literate slave wives to their husbands; they are rare, direct, contemporary testimonies of the anguish of women
forcibly separated from their spouses by being sold.

Cornelia's Life on a Tennessee Farm

I began to exist in the year 1844, in a small town in Tennessee. Eden,
Tennessee, was between Nashville and Memphis. . . .

   I was the personal property of Mr. Jennings, who was a well-polished
southern man. He was portly in build, lively in step, and dignified in manner.
Mr. Jennings was a good man. There was no disputing that. . . .

   Master Jennings had a small farm. We did not cultivate any cotton; we
raised corn, oats, hay and fruits. Most of Master Jennings' slaves were hired
out. He had four families of slaves, that is, Aunt Caroline's family, Uncle
Tom's family, Uncle Dave's family, and the family of which I was a member. None of these others were related by blood to us. My father had several
brothers who lived on other places.

   Aunt Caroline, a big mulatto woman, was very quiet and good-natured. I
don't remember ever hearing her fuss. Each family had a cabin, and there
were but four cabins on the place. Aunt Mary, my mother's aunt, stayed
with us in our cabin. She had never married or had any children.

   My mother was the smartest black woman in Eden. She was as quick as
a flash of lightning, and whatever she did could not be done better. She could
do anything. She cooked, washed, ironed, spun, nursed and labored in the
field. She made as good a field hand as she did a cook. I have heard Master
Jennings say to his wife, "Fannie has her faults, but she can outwork any
nigger in the country. I'd bet my life on that."

   My mother certainly had her faults as a slave. She was very different in
nature from Aunt Caroline. Ma fussed, fought, and kicked all the time. I tell
you, she was a demon. She said that she wouldn't be whipped, and when she
fussed, all Eden must have known it. She was loud and boisterous, and it
seemed to me that you could hear her a mile away. Father was often the prey
of her high temper. With all her ability for work, she did not make a good
slave. She was too high-spirited and independent. I tell you, she was a
captain.

"Cornelia," in Bert S. Loewenberg and Ruth Bogin, eds. *Black Women in Nineteenth-Century
American Life,* 48–53, 1976. Reprinted by permission of Fisk University Library and The
Pennsylvania State University Press.

The one doctrine of my mother's teaching which was branded upon my senses was that I should never let anyone abuse me. "I'll kill you, gal, if you don't stand up for yourself," she would say. "Fight, and if you can't fight, kick; if you can't kick, then bite." Ma was generally willing to work, but if she didn't feel like doing something, none could make her do it. At least, the Jennings couldn't make, or didn't make her. . . .

I was the oldest child. My mother had three other children by the time I was about six years old. It was at this age that I remember the almost daily talks of my mother on the cruelty of slavery. I would say nothing to her, but I was thinking all the time that slavery did not seem so cruel. Master and Mistress Jennings were not mean to my mother. It was she who was mean to them. . . .

One day my mother's temper ran wild. For some reason Mistress Jennings struck her with a stick. Ma struck back and a fight followed. Mr. Jennings was not at home and the children became frightened and ran upstairs. For half hour they wrestled in the kitchen. Mistress, seeing that she could not get the better of ma, ran out in the road, with ma right on her heels. In the road, my mother flew into her again. The thought seemed to race across my mother's mind to tear mistress' clothing off her body. She suddenly began to tear Mistress Jennings' clothes off. She caught hold, pulled, ripped and tore. Poor mistress was nearly naked when the storekeeper got to them and pulled ma off.

"Why, Fannie, what do you mean by that?" he asked.

"Why, I'll kill her, I'll kill her dead if she ever strikes me again."

I have never been able to find out the why of the whole thing. My mother was in a rage for two days, and when pa asked her about it and told her that she shouldn't have done it, it was all that Aunt Caroline could do to keep her from giving him the same dose of medicine.

"No explaining necessary. You are chicken-livered, and you couldn't understand." This was all ma would say about it.

Pa heard Mr. Jennings say that Fannie would have to be whipped by law. He told ma. Two mornings afterwards, two men came in at the big gate, one with a long lash in his hand. I was in the yard and I hoped they couldn't find ma. To my surprise, I saw her running around the house, straight in the direction of the men. She must have seen them coming. I should have known that she wouldn't hide. She knew what they were coming for, and she intended to meet them halfway. She swooped upon them like a hawk on chickens. I believe they were afraid of her or thought she was crazy. One man had a long beard which she grabbed with one hand, and the lash with the other. Her body was made strong with madness. She was a good match for them. Mr. Jennings came and pulled her away. I don't know what would have happened if he hadn't come at that moment, for one man had already pulled his gun out. Ma did not see the gun until Mr. Jennings came up. On catching sight of it, she said, "Use your gun, use it and blow my brains out if you will."

Master sent her to the cabin and he talked with the man for a long time. I had watched the whole scene with hands calmly clasped in front of me. I felt no urge to do anything but look on.

That evening Mistress Jennings came down to the cabin. She stopped at the door and called my mother. Ma came out.

"Well, Fannie," she said, "I'll have to send you away. You won't be whipped, and I'm afraid you'll get killed. They have to knock you down like a beef."

"I'll go to hell or anywhere else, but I won't be whipped," ma answered. . . .

About a week later, she called me and told me that she and pa were going to leave me the next day, that they were going to Memphis. She didn't know for how long.

"But don't be abused, Puss." She always called me Puss. My right name was Cornelia. I cannot tell in words the feelings I had at that time. My sorrow knew no bound. My very soul seemed to cry out, "Gone, gone, gone forever." I cried until my eyes looked like balls of fire. I felt for the first time in my life that I had been abused. How cruel it was to take my mother and father from me, I thought. My mother had been right. Slavery was cruel, so very cruel.

Thus my mother and father were hired to Tennessee. The next morning they were to leave. I saw ma working around with the baby under her arms as if it had been a bundle of some kind. Pa came up to the cabin with an old mare for ma to ride, and an old mule for himself. Mr. Jennings was with him.

"Fannie, leave the baby with Aunt Mary," said Mr. Jennings very quietly.

At this, ma took the baby by its feet, a foot in each hand, and with the baby's head swinging downward, she vowed to smash its brains out before she'd leave it. Tears were streaming down her face. It was seldom that ma cried, and everyone knew that she meant every word. Ma took her baby with her.

With ma gone, there was no excitement around the place. Aunt Mary was old and very steady in her ways; Aunt Caroline was naturally quiet, and so were all the rest. I didn't have much to do around the place, and I thought about ma more than anyone around there knew. Yes, ma had been right. Slavery was chuck full of cruelty and abuse. During this time I decided to follow my mother's example. I intended to fight, and if I couldn't fight I'd kick; and if I couldn't kick, I'd bite. The children from the big house played with my brothers, but I got out of the bunch. I stopped playing with them. I didn't care about them, so why play with them. At different times I got into scraps with them. Everyone began to say, "Cornelia is the spit of her mother. She is going to be just like Fannie." And I delighted in hearing this. I wanted to be like ma now.

An uneventful year passed. I was destined to be happily surprised by the return of my mother and father. They came one day, and found me sitting by the roadside in a sort of trance. I had not seen them approaching; neither was I aware of their presence until ma spoke. Truly, I had been thinking of ma and pa at the time. I had dreams of seeing them again, but I thought that I would have to go to them. I could hardly believe that ma and pa were standing before my very eyes. I asked myself if I was still dreaming. No, I was not dreaming. They were standing over me. Ma was speaking to me.

"Puss, we've come back, me and pa, and we've come to stay."

"Oh, Ma," I exclaimed, "I was a praying to see you."

She and pa embraced and caressed me for a long time. . . .

Ma had on new clothes, and a pair of beautiful earrings. She told Aunt Mary that she stayed in Memphis one year without a whipping or a cross word.

Rose Williams's Forced Marriage in Texas

What I say am the facts. If I's one day old, I's way over ninety, and I's born in Bell County, right here in Texas, and am owned by Massa William Black. He owns Mammy and Pappy, too. Massa Black has a big plantation, but he has more niggers than he need for work on that place, 'cause he am a nigger trader. He trade and buy and sell all the time.

Massa Black am awful cruel, and he whip the colored folks and works 'em hard and feed 'em poorly. We-uns have for rations the corn meal and milk and 'lasses and some beans and peas and meat once a week. We-uns have to work in the field every day from daylight 'til dark, and on Sunday we-uns do us washing. Church? Shucks, we-uns don't know what that mean.

I has the correct memorandum of when the war start. Massa Black sold we-uns right then. Mammy and Pappy powerful glad to git sold, and they and I is put on the block with 'bout ten other niggers. When we-uns gits to the trading block, there lots of white folks there what come to look us over. One man shows the interest in Pappy. Him named Hawkins. He talk to Pappy, and Pappy talk to him and say, "Them my woman and childs. Please buy all of us and have mercy on we-uns." Massa Hawkins say, "That gal am a likely-looking nigger; she am portly and strong. But three am more than I wants, I guesses."

The sale start, and 'fore long Pappy am put on the block. Massa Hawkins wins the bid for Pappy, and when Mammy am put on the block, he wins the bid for her. Then there am three or four other niggers sold before my time comes. Then Massa Black calls me to the block, and the auction man say, "What am I offer for this portly, strong young wench. She's never been 'bused and will make the good breeder."

I wants to hear Massa Hawkins bid, but him say nothing. Two other men am bidding 'gainst each other, and I sure has the worriment. There am tears coming down my cheeks 'cause I's being sold to some man that would make separation from my mammy. One man bids $500, and the auction man ask, "Do I hear more? She am gwine at $500." Then someone say, "$525," and the auction man say, "She am sold for $525 to Massa Hawkins." Am I glad and 'cited! Why, I's quivering all over.

Massa Hawkins takes we-uns to his place, and it am a nice plantation. Lots better than Massa Black's. There is 'bout fifty niggers what is growed and lots of children. The first thing Massa do when we-uns gits home am give we-uns rations and a cabin. You must believe this nigger when I says them rations a feast for us. There plenty meat and tea and coffee and white flour. I's never tasted white flour and coffee, and Mammy fix some biscuits and coffee. Well, the biscuits was yum, yum, yum to me, but the coffee I doesn't like.

The quarters am pretty good. There am twelve cabins all made from logs and a table and some benches and bunks for sleeping and a fireplace for cooking and the heat. There am no floor, just the ground.

Massa Hawkins am good to he niggers and not force 'em work too hard. There am as much difference 'tween him and Old Massa Black in the way of treatment as 'twixt the Lord and the devil. Massa Hawkins 'lows he niggers have reasonable parties and go fishing, but we-uns am never tooken to church and has no books for larning. There am no education for the niggers.

There am one thing Massa Hawkins does to me what I can't shunt from my mind. I knows he don't do it for meanness, but I always holds it 'gainst him. What he done am force me to live with that nigger, Rufus, 'gainst my wants.

After I been at he place 'bout a year, the massa come to me and say, "You gwine live with Rufus in that cabin over yonder. Go fix it for living." I's 'bout sixteen year old and has no larning, and I's just ignomus child. I's thought that him mean for me to tend the cabin for Rufus and some other niggers. Well, that am start the pestigation for me.

I's took charge of the cabin after work am done and fixes supper. Now, I don't like that Rufus, 'cause he a bully. He am big and 'cause he so, he think everybody do what him say. We-uns has supper, then I goes here and there talking, till I's ready for sleep, and then I gits in the bunk. After I's in, that nigger come and crawl in the bunk with me 'fore I knows it. I says, "What you means, you fool nigger?" He say for me to hush the mouth. "This am my bunk, too," he say.

"You's teched in the head. Git out, I's told him, and I puts the feet 'gainst him and give him a shove, and out he go on the floor 'fore he know what I's doing. That nigger jump up and he mad. He look like the wild bear. He starts for the bunk, and I jumps quick for the poker. It am 'bout three feet long, and when he comes at me I lets him have it over the head. Did that nigger stop in he tracks? I's say he did. He looks at me steady for a minute, and you could tell he thinking hard. Then he go and set on the bench and say, "Just wait. You thinks it am smart, but you am foolish in the head. They's gwine larn you something."

"Hush your big mouth and stay 'way from this nigger, that all I wants," I say, and just sets and hold that poker in the hand. He just sets, looking like the bull. There we-uns sets and sets for 'bout an hour, and then he go out, and I bars the door.

The next day I goes to the missy and tells her what Rufus wants, and Missy say that am the massa's wishes. She say, "You am the portly gal, and Rufus am the portly man. The massa wants you-uns for to bring forth portly children."

I's thinking 'bout what the missy say, but say to myself, "I's not gwine live with that Rufus." That night when him come in the cabin, I grabs the poker and sits on the bench and says, "Git 'way from me, nigger, 'fore I bust your brains out and stomp on them." He say nothing and git out.

The next day the massa call me and tell me, "Woman, I's pay big money for you, and I's done that for the cause I wants you to raise me childrens. I's put you to live with Rufus for that purpose. Now, if you doesn't want whipping at the stake, you do what I wants."

I thinks 'bout Massa buying me offen the block and saving me from being separated from my folks and 'bout being whipped at the stake. There it am. What am I's to do? So I 'cides to do as the massa wish, and so I yields. . . .

I never marries, 'cause one 'sperience am 'nough for this nigger. After what I does for the massa, I's never wants no truck with any man. The Lord forgive this colored woman, but he have to 'scuse me and look for some others for to 'plenish the earth.

Fannie Moore's Memories of a South Carolina Childhood

Nowadays when I heah folks a'growlin an' a'grumblin bout not habbin this an' that I jes think what would they done effen they be brought up on de Moore plantation. De Moore plantation b'long to Marse Jim Moore, in Moore, South Carolina. De Moores had own de same plantation and de same niggers and dey children for yeahs back. . . .

Marse Jim own de bigges' plantation in de whole country. Jes thousands acres ob lan'. An de ole Tiger Ribber a runnin' right through de middle ob de plantation. On one side ob de ribber stood de big house, whar de white folks lib and on the other side stood de quarters. De big house was a purty thing all painted white, a standin' in a patch o' oak trees. . . .

De quarters jes long row o' cabins daubed wif dirt. Ever one in de family lib in one big room. In one end was a big fireplace. Dis had to heat de cabin and do de cookin too. We cooked in a big pot hung on a rod over de fire and bake de co'n pone in de ashes or else put it in de skillet and cover de lid wif coals. We allus hab plenty wood to keep us warm. Dat is ef we hab time to get it outen de woods.

My granny she cook for us chillens while our mammy away in de fiel. Dey wasn't much cookin to do. Jes make co'n pone and bring in de milk. She hab big wooden bowl wif enough wooden spoons to go 'roun'. She put de milk in de bowl and break it up. Den she put de bowl in de middle of de flo' an' all de chillun grab a spoon.

My mammy she work in de fiel' all day and piece and quilt all night. Den she hab to spin enough thread to make four cuts for de white fo'ks ebber night. Why sometime I nebber go to bed. Hab to hold de light for her to see by. She hab to piece quilts for de white folks too. Why dey is a scar on my arm yet where my brother let de pine drip on me. Rich pine war all de light we ebber hab. My brother was a holdin' de pine so's I can help mammy tack de quilt and he go to sleep and let it drop.

I never see how my mammy stan' sech ha'd work. She stan' up fo' her chillun tho'. De ol' overseeah he hate my mammy, case she fight him for beatin' her chillun. Why she git more whuppins for dat den anythin' else. She hab twelve chillun. . . .

My mammy grieve lots over brothah George, who die wif de fever. Granny she doctah him as bes' she could, evah time she git way from de white folks kitchen. My mammy nevah git chance to see him, 'cept when she git home in de evenin'. George he jes lie. One day I look at him an' he had sech a peaceful look on his face, I think he sleep and jes let him lone. Long in de evenin I think I try to wake him. I touch him on de face, but he was dead. Mammy nebber know til she come at night. Pore mammy she kneel by de bed an' cry her heart out'. Ol' uncle Allen, he make pine box for him an' carry him to de graveyard over on de hill. My mammy jes plow and cry as she watch 'em put George in de groun'.

Two Letters from Enslaved Wives, 1840 and 1852

Richmond Va. october 27 1840

Dear Husband—
this is the third letter that I have written to you, and have not received any from you; and dont no the reason that I have not received any from you. I think very hard of it. the trader has been here three times to Look at me. I wish that you would try to see if you can get any one to buy me up there. if you dont come down here this Sunday, perhaps you wont see me any more. give my love to them all, and tell them all that perhaps I shan't see you any more. give my love to your mother in particular, and to mamy wines, and to aunt betsy, and all the children; tell Jane and Mother they must come down a fortnight before christmas. I wish to see you all, but I expect I never shall see you all—never no more.

I remain your Dear and affectionate Wife,
Sargry Brown.

Charlottesville Oct. 8, 1852
Dear Husband   I write you a letter to let you know of my distress   my master has sold Albert to a trader on Monday court day and myself and other child is for sale also and I want you to let [me] hear from you very soon   before next cort if you can   I don't know when   I don't want you to wait till Chrismas   I want you to tell Dr. Hamilton your master if either will buy me they can attend to it know and then I can go afterwards

I don't want a trader to get me   they asked me if I had got any person to buy me and I told them no   they told me to the court house too   they never put me up   A man buy the name of brady bought albert and is gone   I don't know whare   they say he lives in scottsville   my things is in several places   some is in stanton and if I would be sold I don't know what will become of them   I don't expect to meet with the luck to get that way till I am quite heart sick   nothing more   I am and ever will be your kind wife

Marie Perkins

❖ *E S S A Y S*

In the early 1970s, scholars began to try to describe the functioning of the slave family from the standpoint of the slaves themselves. But most such studies, among them one by John W. Blassingame (which is not included here), focused on male slaves.* Although they mentioned women briefly, these authors saw the slave family solely from the viewpoint of the husband and father. In the first selection, entitled "Wives and Mothers," taken from his book *Roll, Jordan, Roll* (1974), Eugene Genovese, of the University of Rochester, tried to remedy these deficiencies. But Christie Farnham, a young scholar at Indiana University, was dissatisfied with Genovese's efforts, for reasons that she makes abundantly clear in the second essay.

Wives and Mothers   *Leftist*

EUGENE GENOVESE

The women field hands generally had a longer day than their men. Even the critical Fanny Kemble thought that the middle-aged men did not appear overworked but that the women did. She particularly drew attention to the effects of hard field work in combination with childbearing. Ex-slaves said much more. In addition to the usual work load, the women had to cook for their families, put the children to bed, and often spin, weave, and sew well into the night. On many plantations masters and overseers released them from field work early to attend to their household chores, but on many others they did not, except perhaps on Saturday to get the week's washing done. Many of the women rose early to feed their men, although most masters sensibly preferred to arrange for communal preparation of the morning's meal. Harrison Beckett of Texas grimly recalled his mother's coming in exhausted from the fields and having to cook for her husband and children: "Lots of times she's so tired she go to bed without eatin' nothin' herself."

Usually men, not women, plowed on the large plantations, but when the minority of plantation women who did plow are added to those on smaller units who had to work alongside their men or even alone, it would appear that the rigors of plowing engaged the efforts of a substantial minority of southern slave women. On many plantations the women proved superior to the men in picking cotton; in general, men and women did about equally well. Not unusually a woman would rate as the most valuable field hand on the place or as the single most physically powerful individual. Some excelled in such exacting roles as logrollers and even lumberjacks. And if the men often helped their wives to keep up with their tasks, the roles could be reversed. "My daddy was a field hand," recalled Pierce Harper, who had

---

*John W. Blassingame, *The Slave Community*, 2d ed. (New York: Oxford University Press, 1979), especially pp. 172–81.

Excerpt from Eugene D. Genovese, "Wives and Mothers," in *Roll, Jordan, Roll: The World the Slaves Made*, 495–501. Reprinted by permission of Pantheon Books, a Division of Random House, Inc.

been a slave in North Carolina, "and my mother worked in the field, too, right 'longside my daddy, so she could keep him lined up." Her mother had a reputation as the best field hand on the place and her father as the worst. "My mother," she explained, "used to say he was chilesome."

White southerners, who usually knew better, sometimes pretended that black mothers cared little about children. The whites might have been referring to that stoicism toward the death of an infant which appears in all societies with high infant mortality, especially among the poor; yet even upper-class southern whites suffered too often from the death of their own infants not to understand the necessity for a certain amount of fatalism and self-control. They did not confuse their own self-discipline with lack of grief. The white women and even the men frequently commented on the grief felt by particular slave parents when they lost a child. The sadistic mistress who whipped a slave girl to death fully appreciated the maternal affection of her slaves: she sent for the girl's mother to watch her die.

The calmness of many slave mothers and fathers in the face of the death of their infants and young children recalls that of many other peoples who simply had to live with the probability of losing some of their children. Keith Thomas writes: "In Tudor and Stuart England men were fully accustomed to disease and a low expectation of life. Parents were slower to recognize the individuality of their children, for they well knew that they might lose them in their infancy." Philippe Ariès adds that such conditions existed in France well into the nineteenth century: "Nobody thought, as we ordinarily think today, that every child already contained a man's personality. Too many of them died."

Mrs. Kemble, commenting on the apparent indifference of parents to the death of a boy, recounted a telling incident: "The mother merely repeated over and over again, 'I've lost a many; they all goes so'; and the father, without a word or comment, went out to his enforced labor." This self-protective hardening of parents' attitudes toward their children, reinforced under slavery by fear of sale, did not appear in the quarters any more noticeably than elsewhere under conditions of high infant mortality; it may even have appeared less often. Most black women welcomed their babies as a joy, loved them, and braced themselves for inevitable losses and heartaches.

Some slave women took little interest in their children either because they succumbed to the terrific pressures of overwork, insufficient time for child care, and general demoralization or because they did not want to raise them as slaves. But much of what has been called indifference was no more than the effects of exhaustion on women who loved the children they could not always find patience for. Women who had been forced into cohabitation might especially have resented the children of these unions; yet there is no evidence that even they usually did so.

Women who did not want children knew how to abort or to arrange to have a child die soon after birth. With childbirth deaths so common from natural causes, the deed could not easily be detected. But birth and reproduction rates remained high. Slave abortions, much less infanticide, did not become a major problem for the slave holders or an ordinary form of "resistance" for the slaves. Infanticide occurred, but so far as the detected cases reveal anything, only in some special circumstance. The white citizens of Virginia petitioned in 1822 to spare a slave condemned to death for killing her infant. The child's father was a respectable, married white man, and the woman insisted she would not have killed a child of her own color. Lou Smith, an ex-slave from South Carolina, recalled a woman who had had one child after another sold away from her. Finally, she poisoned her next child and swore to have no more. The other slaves knew what she had done but protected her. For the most part, however, the slaves recognized infanticide as murder. They loved their children too much to do away with them; courageously, they resolved to raise them as best they could, and entrusted their fate to God. Nothing like the widespread infanticide of, say, nineteenth-century Japan, with its economic rationale, ever swept the quarters.

Particularly humane or closely calculating masters released their slave women from field work for a full month before and after childbirth, but many fell short of this model. Normally, the women would have their tasks lightened or cut in half during the last month of pregnancy and then would not be expected back at work until a month after delivery.

Plantation midwives usually attended the deliveries, although mistresses sometimes helped. Slaveholders turned to physicians rarely, but the substantial fees recorded in physicians' account books suggest that they regularly attended the difficult cases. The women often complained bitterly that they needed more time before and after delivery, but they may have been more concerned about the care of their infants than about their own health. The slaveholders thought a month's rest after delivery ample and pointed out, accurately, that the peasant and working-class women of Europe had no such good fortune.

Black women supposedly needed less consideration than the weaker white women anyway, but the statistics on death in childbed as well as on disease and deformity following childbirth provide no support for this rationalization. Nor did lectures on the superiority of their treatment relative to that of, say, English peasant and working-class women who had to endure the physical and psychological hardships attendant upon pregnancy, delivery, and nursing. Kenneth Stampp, admittedly working from shaky data, plausibly estimates many more spontaneous abortions and stillbirths in black women than in white. Whatever the precise differential, the slave women's particular vulnerability to this group of maladies largely resulted from overwork, inadequate prenatal care, and enforced performance of tasks beyond their strength.

The women complained especially about the inadequate conditions for nursing. Landon Carter permitted his slaves to leave the fields three times a day to attend to their babies; the women thought five times would be proper and caused themselves no little trouble by lying or trying to maneuver the overseer into giving them more time. During the nineteenth century three or four times became standard. On M. W. Philips's plantation in Hinds County, Mississippi, the women went into the cookhouse to nurse at breakfast, at

9:30 A.M., at noon, and once during the afternoon. On some plantations mothers could remain with their infants for two hours at midday. Often, the nurses brought the children to their mothers in the field. Overseers and nurses had instructions to keep mothers from nursing their children for fifteen minutes or so after they had stopped working in hot weather or had walked the long distance from the fields. Such instructions could not readily be enforced; too often, hot and tired mothers picked their children up eagerly and nursed them under conditions that might easily have done psychological and physical damage.

If slave mothers viewed their infants with indifference as many slaveholders claimed, they had some strange ways of showing it. Notwithstanding the objective difficulties in nursing, they showed, by more recent standards, a marked unwillingness to wean them early. "We sucked till we was a fair size," said Mary Reynolds of Louisiana in expressing a common view. The Gullah slaves, like the West Africans to whom they remained culturally closer than did other slaves, nursed their children two or three years and even longer. The slaves' practice did not vary greatly from southern practice in general, especially that of the lower classes. Mrs. Kemble, Olmsted, and others were taken aback at the prolonged nursing among the whites. The little evidence we have indicates that the blacks followed the same course and nursed their babies as long as they reasonably could.

Many women saw their children only for a few minutes at night and then on weekends. That some became indifferent ought to cause no surprise; and yet, clearly, most did not.

> My mammy [recalled Fannie Moore of South Carolina] she work in de field all day and piece and quilt all night. . . . I never see how my mammy stand such hard work. She stand up for her chillen though. De old overseer he hate my mammy, 'cause she fought him for beatin' her chillen. Why she get more whippin' for dat dan anythin' else.

Fannie Moore's mother had plenty of company in slave mothers who forcibly defended their children against white abuse.

Although often accused of indifference to their children, slave mothers could hardly have made a deeper impression on the children themselves. The lifelong love of the children, male and female, for their mothers shines through the narratives, as it does through the earlier writings of successful runaways and the occasional observations of whites. Martha Schofield recorded in her diary the dying words of her male cook: "Lord forgive them. I am coming mother, I am coming. Oh! This is pleasant, my mother's grave." William Wells Brown reflected on his mother's having been sold south and on the probability of her early death: "As I thought of my mother, I could not but feel that I had lost, 'The glory of my life / My blessing and my pride! / I half forgot the name of slave / When she was by my side.' " Josiah Henson wrote of the mother from whom he was separated by sale only to be reunited by repurchase after he had fallen ill:

> We had been in the main very happy. She was a good mother to us, a woman of deep piety, anxious above all things to touch our hearts with a sense of religion. . . . Now, I was once more with my best friend on earth, and under her care. . . .

George Teamoh of Virginia recalled his mother in a letter to Carter G. Woodson that might have spoken for numerous others:

> My mother—whom I well remember—bore the common name "Winnie." She died when I was quite small. My father, who was not her husband by the usages of custom died some time after. She was the mother of three or four children, whether all by the same man I am not prepared to say, but what I do know is, she was a kind and affectionate mother and true to her offspring. She was raised with my old mistress, to whom we both belonged.

These were not occasional pronouncements. When added to the powerful image of the mother that comes through the spirituals, as well as to the overwhelming evidence of maternal devotion in the plantation records and the slave narratives, they compel the conclusion that the children felt loved and experienced their mothers' tenderness and warmth. In view of how much conspired to thwart the maternal instincts of these black women, their achievement reached heroic proportions.

The story of the slave women as wives requires indirect examination. To deduce from it an assumption that the man was a guest in the house will not do. A review of the actual position of the men as husbands and fathers suggests that the position of the women was much more complex than usually credited. The women's attitude toward house work, especially cooking, and toward their own femininity by itself belies the conventional wisdom according to which the women unwittingly helped ruin their men by asserting themselves in the home, protecting their children, and assuming other normally masculine responsibilities.

A remarkable number of women did everything possible to strengthen their men's self-esteem and to defer to their leadership. What has usually been viewed as a debilitating female supremacy was in fact a closer approximation to a healthy sexual equality than was possible for whites and perhaps even for many postbellum blacks. The men did not play the provider for their families in a full and direct sense, but they did everything they could to approximate it. They could have scored few successes without the sympathetic cooperation of their women, many—by no means all—of whom yielded their own prerogatives. This female deference represented an effort by the women to support their men—an effort that could only have flowed from a judgment on what men ought to be and an awareness of the terrible ravages being wrought by slavery. On whatever level of consciousness, many women—perhaps a substantial majority—understood that the degradation of their men represented their own degradation as black women and that of their children. They wanted their boys to grow up to be men and knew perfectly well that, to do so, they needed the example of a strong black man in front of them.

The struggle of the women to define a feminine role for themselves and to strengthen their men's sense of their own masculinity came to fruition after the war when the women so readily deferred to their men without surrendering their own opinions and activities, which were often militant. Black people found themselves in a brutal battle for genuine freedom in a postwar world in which certain norms reigned. They knew that in order to win, they would have to accommodate to those norms—specifically, the norms according to which men, not women, controlled the political process and supported the family. The ease with which black men and women made that transition, when not prevented by forces beyond their control, demonstrates how well prepared they already were.

The slave family had, however, rested on a much greater equality between men and women than had the white family. It had bred strong women. The strength of the women did not necessarily undermine the men; often, it supported them. It took enormous strength for a woman to keep her man from avenging an insult or a beating she had suffered and to convince him that the test of his masculinity was self-restraint, not some action that would deprive her of a husband and her children of a father. He needed that assurance to survive, and only she could give it to him. But with freedom the women had to strengthen their men in ways that separated themselves from some of the major sources of their own strength, especially their place in the economy. Their withdrawal from field work undoubtedly would have gone much further if new systems of exploitation had not forced many of them to help their tenant-farmer and sharecropper husbands. The subsequent history of the black family is another matter. New conditions of oppression made it difficult for black men and women to build on their past and create the new and more sexually equitable family inherent in it.

The postbellum record should not be projected backward. A substantial number of black women came out of slavery just as strong as some historians insist. But, in a sense, they had always been even stronger: strong enough to know that their own dignity required having strong men who could meet their responsibilities; strong enough to support their men in those very aspirations.

The Position of Women in the Slave Family

CHRISTIE FARNHAM

The question of dominance in the black family became a national issue in 1965 with the publication of *The Negro Family in America: The Case for National Action,* by Daniel Patrick Moynihan, who attributed the problems of the black urban poor to a "tangle of pathology" resulting from the "disorganization" of the black family. The term "disorganization," by which Moynihan meant the presence of female-headed households whose origins he claimed to find in slavery, is significant. It is a value-laden term that has become part of the jargon of social science; it implies that female-headed households are inherently disorderly because there is no male to impose his

authority over the woman and her children. Female-headed households constituted for Moynihan *ipso facto* evidence of the existence of matriarchy
and were by definition contrary to nature, since "the very essence of the
male animal, from the bantam rooster to the four-star general, is to strut."
This report is but the most prominent example of what has been termed the
pathological school of black family studies, which accepts the white, middle-
class nuclear family as the norm and assumes that all groups should assimilate its values. From this perspective the black family is seen as deviant,
being characterized by high rates of illegitimacy, the absence of fathers, and
welfare dependency—all of which are thought to undermine female–male
relationships and produce adverse effects on the personality development of
the children. These views have come under increasing attack from scholars
with a commitment to a pluralistic society, such as R. H. Hill and Andrew
Billingsley, who emphasize the strengths of the black family, especially its
coping strategies in a racist society. However, the growth of female-headed
families from 17.6 percent in 1950 to 40.2 percent in 1980 (compared with 8.5
and 14.6 percent for whites)—in conjunction with statistics showing that "a
Black child is twice as likely as a white child to live with neither parent,
three times as likely as a white child to be born to a teenage mother, seven
times as likely to have parents who separate, and three times as likely to see
his or her father die"—has kept the question of dominance in the black
family alive more than twenty years after Moynihan first focused national
attention on this issue.

However, the question of power relationships in the slave family cannot
be understood apart from the African context, particularly as it affected
women's work roles. Although earlier scholars rejected Melville Herskovits'
emphasis on African cultural transfers, there is now a general consensus
that, whereas links to African culture are not nearly so strong among Afro-
Americans as among their counterparts in Latin America, such retentions
are nevertheless not only numerous but fundamental to the formation of
Afro-American culture. Contemporary scholars have delineated an important substratum of African retentions in such areas as music, dance, religion,
folklore, and family life.

African societies were many and varied; therefore, generalizations must
be made with caution. Nevertheless, there appears to have been a basic
similarity in family structures. Whether they were organized as matri-
lineages or patrilineages, Niara Sudarkasa makes the case for a fundamental
distinction between African forms consisting of extended families—built
around consanguineal cores of same-sex adult siblings with their spouses
and children, living together in compounds—and Euro-American patterns of
isolated households based on the husband-wife-children bond. She terms
this distinction the difference between consanguinity and conjugality. Although the nuclear family may not have been so typical as it was once
thought to be, these two models are useful for highlighting cultural differences that influenced the development of the black family under slavery.

One of the most important differences to flow from these two models lies
in the work roles of women. Most African societies were polygynous. A

bride moved into the compound of her husband's kin or her husband moved into hers. In either case the lineage or kin group was of paramount importance. It was lineage elders, not husbands, who parceled out farmland to women for their individual use. Although in some parts of West Africa both men and women engaged in agriculture, elsewhere in the region, as well as in most areas to the south, farming was considered women's work. In short, there is no reason to suspect that in precolonial times women did not perform most of the agricultural labor.

Women's role in cultivation derived from a sexual division of labor that assigned women the responsibility for feeding their husbands and children. Since the land was given to women for their own use, the surplus they produced often belonged to them. For example, a French missionary to the eighteenth-century Bakongo living north of the Zaire River described how "each woman has her own hut, fields, gardens, and slaves over which the husband has no rights after she takes care of his needs." Such customs continued into the nineteenth century. A German, describing the Bakongo living on the Loango coast, observed that "when they have satisfied the needs of their husband, the produce that remains from the fields and from animal husbandry is their own." During that same period it is reported that the Bakalai women of Gabon "are expected to feed their husbands . . . but to what is left or not needed of the fruits thus raised the men have no right. The women sell and keep for themselves the articles received." Where women controlled the agricultural surplus, internal trade markets came to form a central part of their world. Maintaining property and profits separate from those of their husbands facilitated a tradition of female entrepreneurship in which a few women even achieved wealth and status.

The fact that the women of the compound were numerous and bound together by intimate ties facilitated organization in support of common interests. Women of the villages and towns, all wives of a local lineage, usually formed associations. The Igbo women of eighteenth-century Onitsha, for example, organized for the purpose of regulating trade, arranging the cooking for village meetings, and the like. Strength in numbers also provided them with some leverage in female-male relationships, enabling them to insist upon the proper treatment of wives.

Polygyny, women's organizations, and the support extended by one's blood kin tended to dilute the emotional importance of marriage, which was essentially an economic transaction between two families rather than a love match that established an all-encompassing relationship, as in the conjugal model. Although some societies, like the Hausa of present-day Nigeria, required virginity in brides, most accepted premarital sex. The overarching concern of the lineage for perpetuation and the strength that numbers bring gave procreation a central focus in African life. Sterility was a calamity. The primacy of lineage and the organization of family life into collectivities of blood relatives and their spouses also meant that childbearing lacked the exclusivity attached to the conjugal model. Although biological parents had the primary responsibility for their children, there were no rigid boundaries; the parenting role was exercised by all adults, and children were taught to identify themselves as daughters and sons of the lineage rather than as cousins.

The work roles of women and the sexual division of labor are in marked contrast to those of the conjugal model, whose characteristics were sharpened during the Victorian period under consideration and idealized in what Barbara Welter has termed the "cult of true womanhood," which emphasized piety, purity, submissiveness, and domesticity. The nuclear family epitomized the notion of exclusivity. Spouses were emotionally dependent on each other; resources were pooled and decisions made jointly or by the husband for the entire unit. Wives were isolated in the home, often separated from close kin and bearing sole responsibility for child care; husbands were providers and protectors, mediating between the home and the outside world. In striking contrast to the African view of sex as normal and healthy was the Victorian ambivalence, tinged with guilt and burdened with a Western cultural heritage that tended to dichotomize women into two types: the good, who were pure and passionless like the Virgin Mary; and the bad, who were sinful and seductive like Eve.

Separate decision-making, property, and incomes, combined with the power that resided in women's organizations and the allies available in natal villages, provided the traditional African woman with the space to be self-reliant. Self-reliance should never be confused with equality between the sexes, however. Although many traditional societies operated with dual sex systems in which each sex managed its own affairs and maintained its own hierarchies of power and position, such systems were meant to be complementary, not parallel—which says nothing about the relative balance of power and prestige between women and men. Separate is not equal. In general, the world that women inhabited offered labor-intensive work that largely involved taking care of the physical needs of men and children. That this work was organized and regulated by the women themselves does not erase the subordinate character of the enterprise.

What happened when the consanguineal and conjugal models collided on American plantations? Reaction to the Moynihan report had the positive effect of spurring research into the slave family. Although conscious attempts were made to avoid the previous error of viewing the black family through the prism of white middle-class norms, the thrust of the research has been an effort to refute Moynihan's position by documenting the presence of males in the household. The major factor underlying this approach seems to have been a desire to substantiate the importance of the family in Afro-American culture and to attack the negative stereotype of blacks as promiscuous. Laudable as these goals are, they have had the unfortunate effect of trivializing the importance of the female-headed household.

The most important study to respond to Moynihan's allegations is Herbert Gutman's book *The Black Family in Slavery and Freedom, 1750–1925*. Documenting premarital sexual norms and naming patterns, Gutman demonstrates that Afro-American culture was not a mimetic version of white forms. He also presents evidence of a shockingly high rate of forced separations. However, he does not use this high rate to support Moynihan's contention that the separation of spouses by planters resulted in a legacy of family disorganization. On the contrary, he counters this finding with evidence demonstrating that most slaves lived in double-headed families, thereby emphasizing how slaves clung to this form of family organization despite the exigencies of the slave system.

The term "double-headed," however, calls forth an image similar to that of the two-parent nuclear family and obscures the fact that many men were not the biological fathers of all the children present in the family. Such usage avoids the issue of serial monogamy, yet serial monogamy can produce at least temporary and often permanent female-headed households. Gutman seems to share Moynihan's view that female-headed families are aberrant. When he finds, for example, that "nearly one in five children born in families that started before 1855 grew up in households headed by women who had all their children by unnamed fathers" on the Stirling plantation in Louisiana, he considers the situation "important" but "far from common." Since some of these women had large families and were never sold, these facts suggest to him that "far from revealing the legitimacy of the single-parent household, such behavior may have represented deviation from the community's norm." Nevertheless, he also finds evidence of female-headed households elsewhere—for example, eight of them on the Bennehan-Cameron plantation were established before 1830. And 9 percent of those who fled to Camp Becker during the Civil War listed themselves as single parents—and some of them were in their thirties, not teenage mothers living with their families of origin. Gutman's study attempts to demonstrate the continuance of double-headed families into the twentieth century, but although he insists that the "typical black household . . . had in it two parents," he again documents numerous exceptions.

Recent research demonstrates the ubiquitousness of female-headed families in northern urban areas in the late nineteenth century, and a newly discovered 1878 survey of a portion of Dinwiddie County, Virginia, provides evidence that serial monogamy and the presence of children from pre- and extramarital unions were characteristic of the post-Emancipation family. Figures from this survey show that of those who had been married during slavery, 29.8 percent had been married more than once and 7 percent more than twice. These statistics are virtually identical to those indicating that by 1878 31.1 percent married more than once and 7.7 percent more than twice, thus demonstrating that serial marriage was common in slave times and remained substantially unchanged after emancipation. A study of ex-slave narratives finds that 18 percent remembered having lived in single-parent households. This finding is corroborated by Paul D. Escott's work, which shows that one-fifth of the ex-slaves interviewed reported having experienced at least partial breakup of their families. Orville Vernon Burton finds in his study of slavery in Edgefield, South Carolina, that "there was an accepted pattern of divorce among the slaves: long periods of relations between two slaves were replaced by alliances with others." He estimates the frequency of such divorce at 25 percent. Although Burton places little importance on African retentions as an explanation for slave society's acceptance of "divorce," the fact that it was practiced within a dominant culture to which divorce was anathema, whereas traditional African societies accepted the practice, argues for African continuities. Furthermore, since it is unlikely that both spouses would find new mates simultaneously, the potential for the formation of significant numbers of female-headed households is obvious. Thus the existence of such households is sufficiently extensive to warrant their inclusion among Afro-American cultural institutions.

There are two difficulties in dealing with female-headed households: the definition of the term and the significance of the form. Are only those households to be included in which the woman never married? But since slave marriages had no legal standing, what constitutes a marriage? Despite more than fifteen years of feminist scholarship, the female-headed family has yet to be viewed as a significant institution under slavery. Contemporary scholars of all persuasions have regarded the female-headed family as transitory: a young woman will soon "settle" into marriage, giving her children a father; teenage mothers remain with their families of origin until marriage, so there is a father figure present to provide a role model; if a woman is widowed or separated from her spouse, her previous marriage constitutes evidence that she does not reject the institution. Those instances of women who never married—such as the mother of William Wells Brown, who had seven children by seven men, both black and white—are dismissed as aberrant cases that existed for the benefit of the master.

Susanne Lebsock has taken a different view of female-headed families among free blacks in antebellum Petersburg, Virginia, half of whose households were headed by women. She sees this phenomenon as a rational response to the fact that single women retained ownership of their property, whereas married women's property reverted to their husbands: "The possibility remains that some free black women valued their relative equality and did their best to maintain it." The large numbers of female-headed families under slavery indicate that for some women the maintenance of a single-parent family was an inventive approach to conditions common to the slave system and represented an expansion of women's choices. Obviously, slavery was a brutal and coercive system, and the concept of choice does not apply to those spouses torn asunder by death or forced separation, nor does it imply that the available choices included an ideal one. Nevertheless, in a system where basic needs were provided by the master, the option of heading a family offered a small measure of autonomy that some women may have found preferable to other possible arrangements. To see this choice as aberrant is to interpret female-headed families within an androcentric framework and to ignore the attempts of some women to enlarge the confines of the cage of slavery.

If female heads of households have been cast as matriarchs, the wives in double-headed families have not altogether escaped a similar charge of being "Sapphires." Named after the wife of the Kingfish on the popular *Amos 'n'*

Andy radio show of the 1930s, Sapphires wore the pants in the family and treated men with contempt. Stanley M. Elkins, for example, analyzed the slave family as one in which the " 'real' father was virtually without authority over his child, since discipline, parental responsibility, and control of rewards and punishments all rested in other hands." Thus the role of the slave mother was more important than that of the father. Since the father could not protect his family from the lash, Elkins saw the cardinal components of the conjugal family's conception of manhood—provision and protection—as being undermined. But Africans did not view manhood in those terms. The lineage was the basic means of protection, and women themselves had a large role in providing for the family through their obligation to raise food. Yet if one conceptualizes the black family in terms of the nuclear middle-class white family, the slave mother is seen to slip into the power vacuum created by the emasculating effects of the slave system on the father, in consequence of which her power is unnaturally enhanced.

This view of the emasculated male which was popularized by Moynihan resulted in a particularly angry reaction, coming as it did in the midst of the Black Power movement, a movement which emphasized self-defense and pride in manhood. To counteract this interpretation, scholars sensitive to black nationalism have searched for evidence of male supremacy in both precolonial African and antebellum American societies. John Blassingame characterizes African societies as patriarchal; but, accepting the view of manhood which requires men to provide for and protect their families, he emphasizes the efforts fathers made to furnish their cabins and supplement the family diet through barter and hunting. Nevertheless, their status within the family, which Blassingame sees as resting on the authority of the husband over his wife and children, was reduced by slavery: "They could no longer exercise the same power over their families as they did in Africa." The bedrock of such a conception of manhood is the determination to stand and fight, which leads Blassingame to describe the plantation as "a battlefield where slaves fought masters for physical and psychological survival. Although unlettered, unarmed, and outnumbered, slaves fought in various ways to preserve their *manhood*" (emphasis mine). Thus, for Blassingame, Sapphire is banished, and the slave experience becomes synonymous with the male experience.

The feminist movement began to impinge upon this conceptualization of the problem of dominance in the 1970s, with curious results. Eugene Genovese, for example, describes cornshucking parties in *Roll, Jordan, Roll: The World the Slaves Made*. Slaves gathered from neighboring plantations for an evening of feasting, singing, and storytelling designed to make the mountain of corn disappear faster. The men did the shucking and were served by the women. Since Genovese can find no evidence that the women complained about being excluded from the party, he concludes that "they seem to have grasped the opportunity to underscore a division of labor and authority in the family and support the pretensions of their men." He believes that "on whatever level of consciousness"—his explanation for the lack of explicit documentation—women attempted "to strengthen their men's self-esteem and to defer to their leadership." He concludes that "what has usually been viewed as a debilitating female supremacy was in fact a closer approxima-tion to a healthy sexual equality than was possible for whites." Unlike Blassingame, who agrees with Elkins that husbands had lost some of their power under slavery and consequently struggled to rise to a position of parity with their wives, Genovese sees the wives as being conscious, at some level, of their unseemly superiority and therefore as attempting to reduce themselves to the level of their husbands by becoming deferential and increasing the division of labor in slave society.

By 1979, Blassingame had joined Genovese in viewing the slave family as essentially egalitarian in structure. He extolled "the transportation of African familial roles [which] led to the creation of America's first demo-cratic family in the quarters, where men and women shared authority and responsibility." Thus, in the short space of about a decade, the picture of the slave family changed from one in which the wife exceeded her husband in power and authority to a situation characterized by egalitarian relationships. This new-found democratic family was based largely on evidence drawn from the labor force participation of black women: from the beginning of slavery most female slaves had been agricultural laborers, doing even such heavy work as plowing, cutting wood, and building fences, roads, and ca-nals. This interpretation of the family may have been influenced by the movement of American women into the work force in ever larger numbers in the 1970s and by the emphasis of the women's movement on the right of women to enter previously male-dominated professions. Many analyses in anthropology and other disciplines delineated the split between the public and private spheres of life, demonstrating how power and prestige inhered in the public sphere, from which women were traditionally excluded.

However, the field was not a forum for slave power, either female or male. Furthermore, the fact that women worked in both the public and private spheres—that is, the field and the house—whereas men were active primarily in only one, the field, did not represent equality. Scholars have recently attempted to rectify this analysis by constructing the notion of the egalitarian slave family on a two-way movement in the division of labor. Angela Davis insists that not only did women labor in the fields but "men executed important domestic duties"; thus "the salient theme emerging from domestic life in the slave quarters is one of sexual equality." She points to the fact that "men would sometimes work in the cabin and women might tend the garden and perhaps even join the hunt." The argument that women gardened and hunted is but another instance of women participating in what white society considered to be men's work. The reverse situation—men working in the home—is but a "sometimes" activity. Thomas Webber makes the most ambitious attempt to document the presence of males in the domestic sphere. He concludes that "while it is true that in most slave households women did the cooking, washing, sewing, and cleaning and men did the gardening, constructing, and hunting roles were reversed often enough to suggest this was more a convenient division of labor than an expression of a societal norm that favored one sex over the other." He fails to explain, however, on what grounds he considers the assignment of household tasks to women to be "more convenient."

The ex-slave narratives make abundantly clear that women had responsibility for what has traditionally been seen as women's work. There is no evidence, for example, that men engaged in spinning, a job that occupied much of the women's time in the evenings. More typical of the life of the ordinary slave woman is the description by the former slave Henry Baker: ". . . de wimmin plowed jes lack de men. On Wednesday night dey had tuh wash en aftuh dey washed dey had tuh cook suppah. De nex' mornin' dey would get up wid de men en dey had tuh cook breakfus 'fore dey went tuh de fiel' en had tuh cook dinner [the noon meal] at dc same time en take hit wid 'em." Even husbands in cross-owner marriages, who saw their wives only on weekends, did not do their own laundry. A white man living in Georgia described how, on "Saturday night, the roads were . . . filled with men on their way to the 'wife house,' each pedestrian or horseman bearing his bag of soiled clothes." The movement of women into agricultural labor did not engender egalitarian relationships, since the public sphere (if such it can be termed) was a source of neither wealth nor power. Although women took pride in their strength and competence, their labor in the public sphere meant double duty, not power parity.

Sarah Fitzpatrick, a slave born in Alabama in 1838, observed: "Love is a won'erful thing. A mother al'ays loves her chillun. Don't care whut dey do. Dey may do 'rong but it's stil' her chile. Den dere is de love uv'va 'oman fer her man, but it ain't nut'in lack a mother's love fer her chillun. I loves a man when he treats me right but I ain't never had no graveyard love fer no man." Inasmuch as protection and provision were not as salient to the concept of manhood in the consanguineal model as they were in the conjugal model, it is unlikely that slaves brought from Africa insisted upon these qualities in a relationship. The slave experience itself inhibited the development of this conception, since shelter and basic provisions were provided by the masters, who also controlled to a large extent the use of physical force on the plantation. Thus there is little in the historical record to indicate that slave women considered their husbands to be unmanly. With no property to transmit or lineages to maintain, it is reasonable to suppose that companionship became a major attribute in the choice of a spouse. This may have been less true of men, however, since both consanguineal and conjugal models require women to take care of their husbands' physical needs. Robert Smalls, a former slave, explained to a congressional committee that in slavery "the colored men in taking wives always do so in reference to the service the women will render."

Della Promise, a resident of rural Macon County, Alabama, explained in the early 1900s that "everybody don't git married, and if I can't git the one I want I don't want to git married. I never seen but one boy I thought I could marry, and me and him had ways too much alike, and I knowed we couldn't git along, so I just has my chillun and raises 'em myself." Della Promise was exercising an option that some white professional women have only recently begun to choose. Although not universally applauded, the decision of single white professional women to raise families alone is sometimes seen as a positive approach to the problem of the paucity of men in their age and status categories, whereas the same choice by some black women—under slavery and later—has been castigated. Certainly, to be the female head of a family was not the ideal of slave society any more than it is the ideal of today's white professional women. But slaves, perhaps more than others, recognized that life is not always ideal. Of course, for many women—such as those separated from spouses by force or death—circumstances, not choice, brought them to the heads of their families. Nevertheless, a significant if small number of women appear to have chosen not to marry at all.

Black women were able to develop the alternative of female-headed families when it seemed in their interest to do so, given the constraints of slavery, because neither the slave community nor the planter class raised sanctions against it. The female-headed family, while different from the matricentric cell of the polygynous African family, was sufficiently similar in physical structure—a woman and her children living together in a separate residence—that this phenomenon would not have appeared altogether alien to slave society.

Despite occasional instances of polygamy, this form of marriage did not take root in America; nevertheless, the consanguineal model formed a general perspective toward marriage and family which could become the basis of patterns of behavior developed to meet the exigencies of slavery. Of these, the prime example is the fictive kin networks, which provided slaves—many of them torn from their blood relatives—with feelings of belonging and the protection previously provided by the lineage.

The development of a unique Afro-American culture grew out of attempts to retain what was feasible from African values and institutions. In the process, new forms were created. Female-headed families were viable under slavery because the planter provided the cabin, clothing, and food rations. Slave women understood that this arrangement was not a gift; they knew that their labor paid for their upkeep and that their children increased the value of their masters' estates. Since African women fed their families and Afro-American women continued to be agricultural laborers, the fact that slave women were ultimately responsible for feeding their children would not have seemed inappropriate.

Female-headed families were also viable in terms of child care, since the fictive kinship system, designed in part to replace the lineages of West African society, continued the practice of the socialization of children by the group rather than by parents alone. All adults felt some responsibility for the children on the plantation, and this arrangement had the added benefit of providing male role models in abundance. Furthermore, child-care arrangements were imposed upon all mothers, not just single heads of families, so that women would be free to labor in the fields. The designation of elderly women and older children to provide child care while the mothers worked removed a major obstacle that contemporary working mothers face. In fact, it was this very communal nature of the socialization of children—especially the assistance of grandmothers in caring for children resulting from the custom of prebridal pregnancy, and the assistance of older women while younger ones worked in the field—that made it possible to split off sexual relations from reproduction, much as access to the pill has separated sex from pregnancy in contemporary American society, thereby facilitating a change in sexual mores.

Blassingame points out that premarital sex was accepted among many African peoples as a normal part of courtship. Although the religious significance of sex was lost in the move to the American slave system, and Christianization developed ambivalent attitudes toward sex outside of marriage for many, the belief remained that sex is a natural act largely unconnected with sin. Such a view of sexuality permitted the slave community to be more accepting of female-headed families than was possible in white society. Although null evidence is seldom reported, the fact that slave communities did not shun such women or their children supports this interpretation of slave society. In fact, their full inclusion in the community argues strongly for the acceptance of this family form.

If female-headed families did not seem totally alien or threatening to Afro-American slave society, neither did they disturb the rationale for slavery developed by the master class. Reproduction, however achieved, added to a planter's wealth. Furthermore, the female-headed family did not adversely affect the labor supply, since female heads of families were forced to work in the fields or big house in the same manner as wives. Finally, slave indifference to the white middle-class standards of female purity idealized by Victorian America appeared to corroborate negative stereotypes of black women as promiscuous, thereby making it easier for white women as well as white men to blame the exploitation of black women on the victims.

It is useful to compare the development of the female-headed family under slavery with the development of a similarly small population of single white women in America during the nineteenth century. Because the norms of white middle-class society insisted on celibacy outside of marriage, these women were never in a position to become heads of families—a tragic deprivation for some of them. The prevalent animosity toward self-reliant women required them to accept Victorian notions of purity and self-sacrifice. It was only by extending these ideals to society generally, in what has been termed social housekeeping, that they were able to maintain a precarious existence. Slave women, on the other hand, through the redefinition of certain West African cultural forms that also meshed with the interests of the planter class, were able to raise a family alone. Unmarried white women, despite the image of single blessedness, were trivialized by a society that mocked them as man-hating old maids whom no man found attractive, but there is nothing in the historical record to indicate that the slave community treated female heads of families as pariahs or stigmatized their children as the illegitimate fruit of illicit unions.

"Sapphire" and "matriarch" are derogatory labels that have in common the image of women "lording it" over men. Yet black women in both double-headed and female-headed families were slaves to a double work load—both field and domestic labor. Perhaps what is so threatening, especially to a society based on conjugality, is not their power and privilege (for they had little) but their self-reliance, for self-reliance implies not so much ruling over men as the ability to manage without them.

❖ FURTHER READING

Dorothy Burnham, "The Life of the Afro-American Women in Slavery," *International Journal of Women's Studies,* I (1978), 366–77

Catherine Clinton, *The Plantation Mistress* (1982)

Angela Y. Davis, *Women, Race, and Class* (1981)

Richard S. Dunn, "A Tale of Two Plantations: Slave Life at Mesopotamia in Jamaica and Mount Airy in Virginia, 1799 to 1828," *William and Mary Quarterly,* 3d ser., XXXIV (1977), 34–65

Herbert S. Gutman, *The Black Family in Slavery and Freedom, 1750–1925* (1976)

Jacqueline Jones, *Labor of Love, Labor of Sorrow: Black Women, Work and the Family from Slavery to the Present* (1985)

Gerda Lerner, ed., *Black Women in White America* (1972)

Robert Starobin, "Privileged Bondsmen and the Process of Accommodation: The Role of Houseservants and Drivers as Seen in Their Own Letters," *Journal of Social History,* V (1971–72), 46–70

Filomina Chioma Steady, ed., *The Black Woman Cross-Culturally* (1981)

Richard Steckel, "Slave Marriage and the Family," *Journal of Family History,* V (1980), 406–21

James Trussell and Richard Steckel, "The Age of Slaves at Menarche and Their First Birth," *Journal of Interdisciplinary History,* VIII (1977–78), 477–505

Deborah Gray White, *Arn't I a Woman? Female Slaves in the Plantation South* (1985)

CHAPTER
7

Work and Protest
in Antebellum New England

The great paradox of the early nineteenth century is that the same period that witnessed the development of the cult of domesticity also saw the first movement by American white women into industrial employment—seemingly the very antithesis of domesticity. The first factories in the United States were the cotton textile mills of New England, and their labor force was largely female. As the production of cloth increasingly became mechanized, the farmers' daughters who had worked in their own homes producing clothing for their families moved into factories to take on the same tasks on a much larger scale. Rather than spinning wheels and hand looms, they now worked with spinning jennies and weaving equipment run by water power.

Yet in this early phase of industrialization, not all work for wages took place in large factories in mill towns. Some New England industries greatly expanded production not by building such manufacturing centers but rather by incorporating traditional work performed in the household, like shoemaking or straw-hat weaving, into a more efficient system through the use of what was called "putting out." In such a system of production, a boss sent materials to individual contractors, who then made items in their homes, returning the finished product to the supplier. Although in preindustrial America the work of artisans had been largely the province of men, the new system, especially in shoemaking, led to the increasing involvement of women in the manufacturing process.

These developments did not take place without protest and resistance from the workers involved. Historians have long been intrigued by the beginnings of industrial capitalism in the United States and by the nearly simultaneous origins of protest against the new system. Although it was once thought that women took little part in these processes, it is now apparent that their participation was central to both industrialization and resistance. What were some of the advantages of industrialization that propelled women into the work force? What conditions led them to protest? How did the values and circumstances of female factory workers versus those of home workers influence the protest movement?

❖ D O C U M E N T S

The Lowell Offering, a magazine produced by the women who worked in the textile mills, often carried essays written by young women about their experiences. The first document consists of two such essays from the issue of December 1840. Mary Paul, an operative at Lowell in the 1840s, wrote letters home describing her life in the mills; excerpts from them constitute the second selection. In the third document, a description of the work of female shoebinders precedes extracts from the laconic diary of one of the shoebinders, Sarah Trask, of Lynn, Massachusetts. These documents illustrate the wide range of women's responses to the economic changes influencing their lives.

Two Essays from *The Lowell Offering,* 1840

Defence of Factory Girls

"She has worked in a factory, is sufficient to damn to infamy the most worthy and virtuous girl."

So says Mr. Orestes A. Brownson; and either this horrible assertion is true, or Mr. Brownson is a slanderer. I assert that it is *not* true, and Mr. B. may consider himself called up to prove his words, if he can. . . .

And whom has Mr. Brownson slandered? A class of girls who in this city alone are numbered by thousands, and who collect in many of our smaller towns by hundreds; girls who generally come from quiet country homes, where their minds and manners have been formed under the eyes of the worthy sons of the Pilgrims, and their virtuous partners, and who return again to become the wives of the free intelligent yeomanry of New England, and the mothers of quite a proportion of our future republicans. Think, for a moment, how many of the next generation are to spring from mothers doomed to infamy! "Ah," it may be replied, "Mr. Brownson acknowledges that you may still be worthy and virtuous." Then we must be a set of worthy and virtuous idiots, for no virtuous girl of common sense would choose for an occupation one that would consign her to infamy. . . .

Whence has arisen the degree of prejudice which has existed against factory girls, I cannot tell; but we often hear the condition of the factory population of England, and the station which the operatives hold in society there, referred to as descriptive of *our* condition. As well might it be said, as say the *nobility* of England, that *labor itself* is disgraceful, and that all who work should be consigned to contempt, if not to infamy. And again: it has been asserted that to put ourselves under the influence and restraints of corporate bodies, is contrary to the spirit of our institutions, and to that love of independence which we ought to cherish. There is a spirit of independence which is averse to social life itself; and I would advise all who wish to cherish it, to go far beyond the Rocky Mountains, and hold communion with none but the untamed Indian, and the wild beast of the forest. We are under restraints, but they are voluntarily assumed; and we are at liberty to withdraw from them, whenever they become galling or irksome.

Neither have I ever discovered that any restraints were imposed upon us, but those which were necessary for the peace and comfort of the whole, and for the promotion of the design for which we are collected, namely, to get money, as much of it and as fast as we can; and it is because our toil is so unremitting, that the wages of factory girls are higher than those of females engaged in most other occupations. It is these wages which, in spite of toil, restraint, discomfort, and prejudice, have drawn so many worthy, virtuous, intelligent, and well-educated girls to Lowell, and other factories; and it is the wages which are in a great degree to decide the characters of the factory girls as a class. . . . The avails of factory labor are now greater than those of many domestics, seamstresses, and school-teachers; and strange would it be, if in money-loving New England, one of the most lucrative female employments should be rejected because it is toilsome, or because some people are prejudiced against it. Yankee girls have too much *independence* for *that*.

But it may be remarked, "You certainly cannot mean to intimate, that all factory girls are virtuous, intelligent," &c. No, I do not; and Lowell would be a stranger place than it has ever been represented, if among eight thousand girls there were none of the ignorant and depraved. Calumniators have asserted, that *all* were vile, because they knew *some* to be so; and the sins of *a few* have been visited upon *the many*. While the mass of the worthy and virtuous have been unnoticed, in the even tenor of their way, the evil deeds of a few individuals have been trumpeted abroad, and they have been regarded as specimens of factory girls. It has been said, that factory girls are not thought as much of any where else as they are in Lowell. If this be true, I am very glad of it, it is quite to our credit to be most respected where we are best known. Still, I presume, there are girls here who are a disgrace to the city, to their sex, and to humanity. But *they* do not fix the tone of public sentiment, and their morals are not the standard. . . . Our well filled churches and lecture halls, and the high character of our clergymen and lecturers, will testify that the state of morals and intelligence is not low.

Mr. Brownson, I suppose, would not judge of our moral characters by our church-going tendencies; but as many do, a word on this subject may not be amiss. That there are many in Lowell who do not regularly attend any meeting; is as true as the correspondent of the Boston Times once represented it; but for this there are various reasons. There are many who come here for but a short time, and who are willing for a while to forego every usual privilege, that they may carry back to their homes the greatest possible sum they can save. There are widows earning money for the maintenance and education of their children; there are daughters providing for their aged and destitute parents; and there are widows, single women, and girls, endeavoring to obtain the wherewithal to furnish some other home than a factory boarding-house. Pew rent, and the dress which custom has wrongly rendered essential, are expenses which they cannot afford, and they spend their Sabbaths in rest, reading, and meditation. There may also be many other motives to prevent a regular attendance at church, besides a disinclination to gratify and cultivate the moral sentiments.

There have also been nice calculations made, as to the small proportion which the amount of money deposited in the Savings Bank bears to that earned in the city; but this is not all that is saved. Some is deposited in Banks at other places, and some is put into the hands of personal friends. Still, much that is earned is immediately, though not foolishly, spent. Much that none but the parties concerned will ever know of, goes to procure comforts and necessaries for some lowly home, and a great deal is spent for public benevolent purposes. The fifteen hundred dollars which were collected in one day for Missionary purposes by a single denomination in our city, though it may speak of what Mrs. Gilman calls the "too great tendency to overflow in female benevolence," certainly does not tell of hearts sullied by vice, or souls steeped in infamy. And it is pleasing to view the interest which so many of the factory girls take in the social and religious institutions of this place, who do not call Lowell aught but a temporary home. Many of them stay here longer than they otherwise would, because these institutions have become so dear to them, and the letters which they send here after they do leave, show that the interest was too strong to be easily eradicated. I have known those who left homes of comfort and competence, that they might here enjoy religious privileges which country towns would not afford them. And the Lowell Offering may prove to all who will read it, that there are girls here whose education and intellect place them above the necessity of pursuing an avocation which will inevitably connect them with the ignorant and vicious. . . .

Pleasures of Factory Life

Pleasures there are, even in factory life; and we have many, known only to those of like employment. To be sure it is not so convenient to converse in the mills with those unaccustomed to them; yet we suffer no inconvenience among ourselves. But, aside from the talking, where can you find a more pleasant place for contemplation? There all the powers of the mind are made active by our animating exercise; and having but one kind of labor to perform, we need not give all our thoughts to that, but leave them measurably free for reflection on other matters.

The subjects for pleasurable contemplation, while attending to our work, are numerous and various. Many of them are immediately around us. For example: In the mill we see displays of the wonderful power of the mind. Who can closely examine all the movements of the complicated, curious machinery, and not be led to the reflection, that the mind is boundless, and is destined to rise higher and still higher; and that it can accomplish almost any thing on which it fixes its attention!

In the mills, we are not so far from God and nature, as many persons might suppose. We cultivate, and enjoy much pleasure in cultivating flowers and plants. A large and beautiful variety of plants is placed around the walls of the rooms, giving them more the appearance of a flower garden than a workshop. It is there we inhale the sweet perfume of the rose, the lily, and geranium; and, with them, send the sweet incense of sincere gratitude to the bountiful Giver of these rich blessings. And who can live with such a rich and pleasant source of instruction opened to him, and not be wiser and better, and consequently more happy.

Another great source of pleasure is, that by becoming operatives, we are often enabled to assist aged parents who have become too infirm to provide for themselves; or perhaps to educate some orphan brother or sister, and fit them for future usefulness. And is there no pleasure in all this? No pleasure in relieving the distressed and removing their heavy burdens? And is there no pleasure in rendering ourselves by such acts worthy of the confidence and respect of those with whom we are associated?

Another source is found in the fact of our being acquainted with some person or persons that reside in almost every part of the country. And through these we become familiar with some incidents that interest and amuse us wherever we journey; and cause us to feel a greater interest in the scenery, inasmuch as there are gathered pleasant associations about every town, and almost every house and tree that may meet our view.

Let no one suppose that the 'factory girls' are without guardian. We are placed in the care of overseers who feel under moral obligations to look after our interests; and, if we are sick, to acquaint themselves with our situation and wants; and, if need be, to remove us to the Hospital, where we are sure to have the best attendance, provided by the benevolence of our Agents and Superintendents.

In Lowell, we enjoy abundant means of information, especially in the way of public lectures. The time of lecturing is appointed to suit the convenience of the operatives; and sad indeed would be the picture of our Lyceums, Institutes, and scientific Lecture rooms, if all the operatives should absent themselves.

And last, though not least, is the pleasure of being associated with the institutions of religion, and thereby availing ourselves of the Library, Bible Class, Sabbath School, and all other means of religious instruction. Most of us, when at home, live in the country, and therefore cannot enjoy these privileges to the same extent; and many of us not at all. And surely we ought to regard these as sources of pleasure.

Mary Paul's Letters, 1845–1848

[Woodstock, Vt.] Saturday Sept. 13th 1845

Dear Father . . .

I want you to consent to let me go to Lowell if you can. I think it would be much better for me than to stay about here. I could earn more to begin with than I can any where about here. I am in need of clothes which I cannot get if I stay about here and for that reason I want to go to Lowell or some other place. We all think if I could go with some steady girl that I might do well. I want you to think of it and make up your mind. Mercy Jane Griffith is going to start in four or five weeks. Aunt Miller and Aunt Sarah think it would be a good chance for me to go if you would consent—which I want you to do if possible. I want to see you and talk with you about it. . . .

Mary

Lowell Nov 20th 1845

Dear Father

An opportunity now presents itself which I improve in writing to you. I started for this place at the time I talked of which was Thursday. . . . On Saturday after I got here Luthera Griffith went round with me to find a place but we were unsuccessful. On Monday we started again and were more successful. We found a place in a spinning room and the next morning I went to work. I like very well have 50 cts first payment increasing every payment as I get along in work have a first rate overseer and a very good boarding place. I work on the Lawrence Corporation. Mill is No 2 spinning room. . . . It cost me $3.25 to come. Stage fare was $3.00 and lodging at Windsor, 25 cts. Had to pay only 25 cts for board for 9 days after I got here before I went into the mill. Had 2.50 left with which I got a bonnet and some other small articles. . . .

excuse bad writing and mistakes
This from your own daughter
Mary

Lowell Dec 21st 1845

Dear Father

I received your letter on Thursday the 14th with much pleasure. I am well which is one comfort. My life and health are spared while others are cut off. Last Thursday one girl fell down and broke her neck which caused instant death. She was going in or coming out of the mill and slipped down it being very icy. The same day a man was killed by the [railroad] cars. Another had nearly all of his ribs broken. Another was nearly killed by falling down and having a bale of cotton fall on him. Last Tuesday we were paid. In all I had six dollars and sixty cents paid $4.68 for board. With the rest I got me a pair of rubbers and a pair of 50.cts shoes. Next payment I am to have a dollar a week beside my board. We have not had much snow the deepest being not more than 4 inches. It has been very warm for winter.

Perhaps you would like something about our regulations about going in and coming out of the mill. At 5 o'clock in the morning the bell rings for the folks to get up and get breakfast. At half past six it rings for the girls to get up and at seven they are called into the mill. At half past 12 we have dinner are called back again at one and stay till half past seven. I get along very well with my work. I can doff as fast as any girl in our room. I think I shall have frames before long. The usual time allowed for learning is six months but I think I shall have frames before I have been in three as I get along so fast. I think that the factory is the best place for me and if any girl wants employment I advise them to come to Lowell. . . .

This from
Mary S Paul

Lowell April 12th 1846

Dear Father

You wanted to know what I am doing. I am at work in a spinning room and tending four sides of warp which is one girls work. The overseer tells me that he never had a girl get along better than I do and that he will do the best he can by me. I stand it well, though they tell me that I am growing very poor. I was paid nine shillings a week last payment and am to have more this one. . . .

I have a very good boarding place have enough to eat and that which is good enough. The girls are all kind and obliging. The girls that I room with are all from Vermont and good girls too. Now I will tell you about our rules at the boarding house. We have none in particular except that we have to go to bed about 10. o'clock. At half past 4 in the morning the bell rings for us to get up and at five for us to go into the mill. At seven we are called out to breakfast are allowed half an hour between bells and the same at noon till the first of May when we have three quarters [of an hour] till the first of September. We have dinner at half past 12 and supper at seven. . . .

Yours affectionately
Mary S Paul

Lowell Nov 5th 1848

Dear Father

Doubtless you have been looking for a letter from me all the week past. I would have written but wished to find whether I should be able to stand it—to do the work that I am now doing. I was unable to get my old place in the cloth room on the Suffolk or on any other corporation. I next tried the dressrooms on the Lawrence Cor[poration], but did not succe[e]d in getting a place. I almost concluded to give up and go back to Claremont, but thought I would try once more. So I went to my old overseer on the Tremont Cor. I had no idea that he would want one, but he *did,* and I went to work last Tuesday—warping—the same work I used to do.

It is *very* hard indeed and sometimes I think I shall not be able to endure it. I never worked so hard in my life but perhaps I shall get used to it. I shall try hard to do so for there is no other work that I can do unless I spin and that I shall not undertake on any account. I presume you have heard before this that the wages are to be reduced on the 20th of this month. It is *true* and there seems to be a good deal of excitement on the subject but I can not tell what will be the consequence. The companies pretend they are losing immense sums every *day* and therefore they are obliged to lessen the wages, but this seems perfectly absurd to me for they are constantly making *repairs* and it seems to me that this would not be if there were really any danger of their being obliged to *stop* the mills.

It is very difficult for any one to get into the mill on any corporation. All seem to be very full of help. I expect to be paid about two dollars a week but it will be dearly earned. I cannot tell how it is but never since I have worked in the mill have I been so very tired as I have for the last week but it may be owing to the long rest I have had for the last six months. . . .

(Monday Eve) I have been to work today and think I shall manage to get along with the work. I am not so tired as I was last week. I have not yet found out what wages I shall get but presume they will be about $2.00 per week exclusive of board. . . .

Write soon. Yours affectionately
Mary S Paul

David Johnson's Description of Shoebinding, 1880

The shoe-binder of Lynn performed a very important part in the domestic economy of the household thirty, or more, years ago. The shoemaker's wife and daughters—if he had any—were often his best bowers, enabling him to weather many a financial tempest—on a small scale—and were often the chief reliance when the head of the family, through sickness, or other causes, could no longer work to support the family. As the wife and daughters "bound" the shoes made by the workmen of the family, the "uppers," all ready to "bind," with the needful silk, cotton and thread, and sometimes beeswax, made part of the load carried home in the "little cart," or in some other way, from the boss' shop. Then there would be a little delay, perhaps, until a shoe was bound, with which to start off the new lot.

But, generally, before the "jour" got his "stock" seasoned, one or two "uppers" were ready, and enough were usually bound ahead to keep all hands at work. And so, now and then, the order would be heard—"Come, John, go and see if your mother has got a shoe bound; I 'm all ready to last it." It may be well to notice here that the "jours" often called the "uppers" *shoes,* and the soles *"stuffs."* Accordingly, one would hear the remark— "The 'boss' did n't give me 'stuffs' enough"—meaning soles—or, "Come, William, go over to Isaiah's and get me a lot of shoes and 'stuffs.' " The dictionaries do not recognize this use of the word "stuffs," but the shoemakers did.

The style of "uppers" in vogue some forty years ago, and later, was a "foxed" boot. This foxing was of kid, with lasting top, and the boot laced in front. A few years later the "gaiter boot" came into fashion, which usually had a lower foxing, and the "lace" on the side. These were usually made "right" and "left." The binding of these boots, when it was done well, was quite a nice job. The price of binding ranged from seventeen to twenty-five cents a pair, and a smart woman could bind four pairs a day, and sometimes even more.

It will be seen that such help was no small item in maintaining the family. Many a little home was earned by "all hands," father and mother, boys and girls, who worked for years, cheered by the hope of paying off the mortgage, so that they could have a "house of their own."

Sarah Trask's Diary, 1849

Jan 25   Stay down to C. [Sarah's friend Catherine], all night for her to show me about my shoes, but did not do much, but I will try and see what I can do, for I cannot afford to make a coat for, 33, Cts. for, L. O. Hale, if I can get anny thing else to do.

Mary H. Blewett, "I Am Doom to Disapointment: The Diaries of a Beverly, Massachusetts, Shoebinder, Sarah E. Trask, 1849–51" *Essex Institute Historical Collections,* CXVII (1981), 200–204. Reprinted by permission of the Essex Institute, Salem, Massachusetts.

Jan 26   Stitched on three pairs of shoes, have I not done bravely, hope I shall do more than that, tomorrow, or I shall have to go to California, to seek my fortune, oh California for that all I hear, most every one is going there and I fear many will go that will never come back to their friends again. I am glad that I have not anny friends gone there.

Jan 31   . . . winter seem so dull. At home all day and in the evening. Oh my shoes they do go of so slow only four pairs and a half today, I wish they were all done, but what is the use of that it will not get them done anny sooner; so I must not despair. . . .

Feb 20   . . . Just for fun I counted the stiches in a shoe, the size was fives, 719 in the whole, 250 on the top, 173 in the filling, 120, on the side seams or 65 in one side, 69 in the closeing or 23 on a seam, 58 in the lineing, or 29, on a side, 99 on the surgeing. . . .

March 7   At home all day, in the evening went down to Hannah, and Mary Ellen, for it seem as though I must see her before I went to [prayer meeting], she was binding shoes four Cts. a pair and thread found, that is very good I think for thoes kind.

March 14   Another wedding last night one of our shop girls, all getting married. Mr. Shale will not have anny to work for him, if they go [off] so fast as they have done, this two or three years. It is three years last Novemeber [*sic*] since I went [to work binding shoes], there as been 20 Married. . . .

April 10   My shoes are not done yet, I begin to think that I am Lazy, and yet I try to do all I can, Mother tells that I run about [too] much, to do anny work, I can't think so, but I suppose I shall have to. . . .

April 17   today I have had another lot of shoes come, although I have not got my others done, but I hope I shall soon. . . .

April 21   This day I have been trying to finish my shoes, and have got them done and I am so glad. . . .

April 23   This day I have begun my gaiter boots, I have not finish anny tonight but hope I shall tomorrow. L.A.B. came in with her work a little while, and we saw a large bark come down the Southern way and go into Salem, we like so well to look at it, that we did not so much work as we ought to. . . .

April 26   This day [I] have finished four pairs of boots, just fifty cents this week, I hope I shall do four pair more before Saterday.

April 28   At home today, finishing my week work eight pairs of boots one dollar; how smart, beside my housework, and last tuesday I work for Lizzy, so there the duty of the week. I almost think I shall make my fortune soon. . . .

May 10   At home all day, housework and shoes have been my work to-day. . . .

✧ E S S A Y S

Thomas Dublin, who teaches at the State University of New York at Binghamton, argues in the first essay that the traditional values of antebellum New England helped to contribute to the protest movements among female operatives in the Lowell mills. But in the second essay Mary Blewett, of the University of Lowell, looks at female shoebinders in the same era and finds that for them the opposite was true: the traditional family loyalties of women who worked in the context of their own homes hindered the development of gender-based protest. Why did these two authors arrive at opposite conclusions? Can the impetus to generate, or not generate, protest movements be attributed to differences in background between these two groups or to differences in working conditions, or to some other cause?

The Solidarity of Women in the Lowell Mills

THOMAS DUBLIN

In the years before 1850 the textile mills of Lowell, Massachusetts were a celebrated economic and cultural attraction. Foreign visitors invariably included them on their American tours. Interest was prompted by the massive scale of these mills, the astonishing productivity of the power-driven machinery, and the fact that women comprised most of the workforce. Visitors were struck by the newness of both mills and city as well as by the culture of the female operatives. The scene stood in sharp contrast to the gloomy mill towns of the English industrial revolution.

Lowell, was, in fact, an impressive accomplishment. In 1820, there had been no city at all—only a dozen family farms along the Merrimack River in East Chelmsford. In 1821, however, a group of Boston capitalists purchased land and water rights along the river and a nearby canal, and began to build a major textile manufacturing center. Opening two years later, the first factory employed Yankee women recruited from the nearby countryside. Additional mills were constructed until, by 1840, ten textile corporations with thirty-two mills valued at more than ten million dollars lined the banks of the river and nearby canals. Adjacent to the mills were rows of company boarding houses and tenements which accommodated most of the eight thousand factory operatives.

As Lowell expanded, and became the nation's largest textile manufacturing center, the experiences of women operatives changed as well. The increasing number of firms in Lowell and in the other mill towns brought the pressure of competition. Overproduction became a problem and the prices of finished cloth decreased. The high profits of the early years declined and so, too, did conditions for the mill operatives. Wages were reduced and the pace of work within the mills was stepped up. Women operatives did not accept these changes without protest. In 1834 and 1836 they went on strike

---

Thomas Dublin, "Women, Work, and Protest in the Early Lowell Mills: The Oppressing Hand of Avarice Would Enslave Us," *Labor History,* XVI (1975), 99–116.

to protest wage cuts, and between 1843 and 1848 they mounted petition campaigns aimed at reducing the hours of labor in the mills.

These labor protests in early Lowell contribute to our understanding of the response of workers to the growth of industrial capitalism in the first half of the nineteenth century. They indicate the importance of values and attitudes dating back to an earlier period and also the transformation of these values in a new setting.

The major factor in the rise of a new consciousness among operatives in Lowell was the development of a close-knit community among women working in the mills. The structure of work and the nature of housing contributed to the growth of this community. The existence of community among women, in turn, was an important element in the repeated labor protests of the period. . . .

The textile corporations made provisions to ease the adjustment of new operatives. Newcomers were not immediately expected to fit into the mill's regular work routine. They were at first assigned work as sparehands and were paid a daily wage independent of the quantity of work they turned out. As a sparehand, the newcomer worked with an experienced hand who instructed her in the intricacies of the job. The sparehand spelled her partner for short stretches of time, and occasionally took the place of an absentee. One woman described the learning process in a letter reprinted in the *Offering*:

> Well, I went into the mill, and was put to learn with a very patient girl. . . . You cannot think how odd everything seems. . . . They set me to threading shuttles, and tying weaver's knots, and such things, and now I have improved so that I can take care of one loom. I could take care of two if only I had eyes in the back part of my head. . . .

After the passage of some weeks or months, when she could handle the normal complement of machinery—two looms for weavers during the 1830s —and when a regular operative departed, leaving an opening, the sparehand moved into a regular job. . . .

Living conditions also contributed to the development of community among female operatives. Most women working in the Lowell mills of these years were housed in company boarding houses. In July 1836, for example, more than 73 percent of females employed by the Hamilton Company resided in company housing adjacent to the mills. Almost three-fourths of them, therefore, lived and worked with each other. Furthermore, the work schedule was such that women had little opportunity to interact with those not living in company dwellings. They worked, in these years, an average of 73 hours a week. Their work day ended at 7:00 or 7:30 P.M., and in the hours between supper and the 10:00 curfew imposed by management on residents of company boarding houses there was little time to spend with friends living "off the corporation."

Women in the boarding houses lived in close quarters, a factor that also played a role in the growth of community. A typical boarding house accommodated twenty-five young women, generally crowded four to eight in a bedroom. There was little possibility of privacy within the dwelling, and pressure to conform to group standards was very strong (as will be discussed below). The community of operatives which developed in the mills it follows, carried over into life at home as well.

The boarding house became a central institution in the lives of Lowell's female operatives in these years, but it was particularly important in the initial integration of newcomers into urban industrial life. Upon first leaving her rural home for work in Lowell, a woman entered a setting very different from anything she had previously known. One operative, writing in the *Offering,* described the feelings of a fictional character: ". . . the first entrance into a factory boarding house seemed something dreadful. The room looked strange and comfortless, and the women cold and heartless; and when she sat down to the supper table, where among more than twenty girls, all but one were strangers, she could not eat a mouthful."

In the boarding house, the newcomer took the first steps in the process which transformed her from an "outsider" into an accepted member of the community of women operatives.

Recruitment of newcomers into the mills and their initial hiring was mediated through the boarding house system. Women generally did not travel to Lowell for the first time entirely on their own. They usually came because they knew someone—an older sister, cousin, or friend—who had already worked in Lowell. The scene described above was a lonely one— but the newcomer did know at least one boarder among the twenty seated around the supper table. The Hamilton Company Register Books indicate that numerous pairs of operatives, having the same surname and coming from the same town in northern New England, lived in the same boarding houses. If the newcomer was not accompanied by a friend or relative, she was usually directed to "Number 20, Hamilton Company," or to a similar address of one of the other corporations where her acquaintance lived. Her first contact with fellow operatives generally came in the boarding houses and not in the mills. Given the personal nature of recruitment in this period, therefore, newcomers usually had the company and support of a friend or relative in their first adjustment to Lowell.

Like recruitment, the initial hiring was a personal process. Once settled in the boarding house a newcomer had to find a job. She would generally go to the mills with her friend or with the boarding house keeper who would introduce her to an overseer in one of the rooms. If he had an opening, she might start work immediately. More likely, the overseer would know of an opening elsewhere in the mill, or would suggest that something would probably develop within a few days. In one story in the *Offering,* a newcomer worked on some quilts for her house keeper, thereby earning her board while she waited for a job opening.

Upon entering the boarding house, the newcomer came under pressure to conform with the standards of the community of operatives. Stories in the *Offering* indicate that newcomers at first stood out from the group in terms of their speech and dress. Over time, they dropped the peculiar "twang" in their speech which so amused experienced hands. Similarly, they purchased clothing more in keeping with urban than rural styles. It was an unusual and

strongwilled individual who could work and live among her fellow operatives and not conform, at least outwardly, to the customs and values of this
larger community.

The boarding houses were the centers of social life for women operatives after their long days in the mills. There they ate their meals, rested,
talked, sewed, wrote letters, read books and magazines. From among fellow
workers and boarders they found friends who accompanied them to shops,
to Lyceum lectures, to church and church-sponsored events. On Sundays or
holidays, they often took walks along the canals or out into the nearby
countryside. The community of women operatives, in sum, developed in a
setting where women worked and lived together, twenty-four hours a day.

Given the all-pervasiveness of this community, one would expect it to
exert strong pressures on those who did not conform to group standards.
Such appears to have been the case. . . .

To the extent that women could not have completely private lives in the
boarding houses, they probably had to conform to group norms, whether
these involved speech, clothing, relations with men, or attitudes toward the
ten-hour day. Group pressure to conform, so important to the community of
women in early Lowell, played a significant role in the collective response of
women to changing conditions in the mills.

In addition to the structure of work and housing in Lowell, a third factor,
the homogeneity of the mill workforce, contributed to the development of
community among female operatives. In this period the mill workforce was
homogeneous in terms of sex, nativity, and age. Payroll and other records of
the Hamilton Company reveal that more than 85 per cent of those employed
in July, 1836, were women and that over 96 per cent were native-born.
Furthermore, over 80 per cent of the female workforce was between the ages
of 15 and 30 years old; and only ten per cent was under 15 or over 40.

Workforce homogeneity takes on particular significance in the context
of work structure and the nature of worker housing. These three factors
combined meant that women operatives had little interaction with men during their daily lives. Men and women did not perform the same work in the
mills, and generally did not even labor in the same rooms. Men worked in
the picking and initial carding processes, in the repair shop and on the
watchforce, and filled all supervisory positions in the mills. Women held all
sparehand and regular operative jobs in drawing, speeding, spinning, weaving and dressing. A typical room in the mill employed eighty women tending
machinery, with two men overseeing the work and two boys assisting them.
Women had little contact with men other than their supervisors in the course
of the working day. After work, women returned to their boarding houses,
where once again there were few men. Women, then, worked and lived in a
predominantly female setting.

Ethnically the workforce was also homogeneous. Immigrants formed
only 3.4 per cent of those employed at Hamilton in July, 1836. In addition,
they comprised only 3 per cent of residents in Hamilton company housing.
The community of women operatives was composed of women of New
England stock drawn from the hill-country farms surrounding Lowell. Consequently, when experienced hands made fun of the speech and dress of

newcomers, it was understood that they, too, had been "rusty" or "rustic" upon first coming to Lowell. This common background was another element shared by women workers in early Lowell.

The work structure, the workers' housing, and workforce homogeneity were the major elements which contributed to the growth of community among Lowell's women operatives. To best understand the larger implications of community it is necessary to examine the labor protests of this period. For in these struggles, the new values and attitudes which developed in the community of women operatives are most visible.

In February, 1834, 800 of Lowell's women operatives "turned-out"—went on strike—to protest a proposed reduction in their wages. They marched to numerous mills in an effort to induce others to join them; and, at an outdoor rally, they petitioned others to "discontinue their labors until terms of reconciliation are made. Their petition concluded:

> Resolved, That we will not go back into the mills to work unless our wages are continued . . . as they have been.
> Resolved, That none of us will go back, unless they receive us all as one.
> Resolved, That if any have not money enough to carry them home, they shall be supplied.

The strike proved to be brief and failed to reverse the proposed wage reductions. Turning-out on a Friday, the striking women were paid their back wages on Saturday, and by the middle of the next week had returned to work or left town. Within a week of the turn-out, the mills were running near capacity.

This first strike in Lowell is important not because it failed or succeeded, but simply because it took place. In an era in which women had to overcome opposition simply to work in the mills, it is remarkable that they would further overstep the accepted middle-class bounds of female propriety by participating in a public protest. The agents of the textile mills certainly considered the turn-out unfeminine. . . .

Certainly a prime motive for the strike was outrage at the social implications of the wage cuts. In a statement of principles accompanying the petition which was circulated among operatives, women expressed well the sense of themselves which prompted their protest of these wage cuts:

UNION IS POWER

> Our present object is to have union and exertion, and we remain in possession of our unquestionable rights. We circulate this paper wishing to obtain the names of all who imbibe the spirit of our Patriotic Ancestors, who preferred privation to bondage, and parted with all that renders life desirable—and even life itself—to procure independence for their children. The oppressing hand of avarice would enslave us, and to gain their object, they gravely tell us of the pressure of the time, this we are already sensible of, and deplore it. If any are in want of assistance, the Ladies will be compassionate and assist them; but we prefer to have the disposing of our charities in our own hands; and as we are free, we would remain in possession of what kind Providence has bestowed upon us; and remain daughters of freemen still.

At several points in the proclamation the women drew on their Yankee heritage. Connecting their turn-out with the efforts of their "Patriotic Ancestors" to secure independence from England, they interpreted the wage cuts as an effort to "enslave" them—to deprive them of their independent status as "daughters of freemen."

Though very general and rhetorical, the statement of these women does suggest their sense of self, of their own worth and dignity. Elsewhere, they expressed the conviction that they were the social equals of the overseers, indeed of the millowners themselves. The wage cuts, however, struck at this assertion of social equality. These reductions made it clear that the operatives were subordinate to their employers, rather than equal partners in a contract binding on both parties. By turning-out the women emphatically denied that they were subordinates; but by returning to work the next week, they demonstrated that in economic terms they were no match for their corporate superiors.

In point of fact, these Yankee operatives were subordinate in early Lowell's social and economic order, but they never consciously accepted this status. Their refusal to do so became evident whenever the mill owners attempted to exercise the power they possessed. This fundamental contradiction between the objective status of operatives and their consciousness of it was at the root of the 1834 turn-out and of subsequent labor protests in Lowell before 1850. The corporations could build mills, create thousands of jobs, and recruit women to fill them. Nevertheless, they bought only the workers' labor power, and then only for as long as these workers chose to stay. Women could always return to their rural homes, and they had a sense of their own worth and dignity, factors limiting the actions of management.

Women operatives viewed the wage cuts as a threat to their economic independence. This independence had two related dimensions. First, the women were self-supporting while they worked in the mills and, consequently, were independent of their families back home. Second, they were able to save out of their monthly earnings and could then leave the mills for the old homestead whenever they so desired. In effect, they were not totally dependent upon mill work. Their independence was based largely on the high level of wages in the mills. They could support themselves and still save enough to return home periodically. The wage cuts threatened to deny them this outlet, substituting instead the prospect of total dependence on mill work. Small wonder, then, there was alarm that "the oppressing hand of avarice would enslave us." To be forced, out of economic necessity, to lifelong labor in the mills would have indeed seemed like slavery. The Yankee operatives spoke directly to the fear of a dependency based on impoverishment when offering to assist any women workers who "have not money enough to carry them home." Wage reductions, however, offered only the *prospect* of a future dependence on mill employment. By striking, the women asserted their actual economic independence of the mills and their determination to remain "daughters of freemen still."

While the women's traditional conception of themselves as independent daughters of freemen played a major role in the turn-out, this factor acting alone would not necessarily have triggered the 1834 strike. It would have led women as individuals to quit work and return to their rural homes. But the turn-out was a collective protest. When it was announced that wage reductions were being considered, women began to hold meetings in the mills during meal breaks in order to assess tactical possibilities. Their turn-out began at one mill when the agent discharged a woman who had presided at such a meeting. Their procession through the streets passed by other mills, expressing a conscious effort to enlist as much support as possible for their cause. At a mass meeting, the women drew up a resolution which insisted that none be discharged for their participation in the turn-out. This strike, then, was a collective response to the proposed wage cuts—made possible because women had come to form a "community" of operatives in the mill, rather than simply a group of individual workers. The existence of such a tight-knit community turned individual opposition to the wage cuts into a collective protest.

In October, 1836, women again went on strike. This second turn-out was similar to the first in several respects. Its immediate cause was also a wage reduction; marches and a large outdoor rally were organized; again, like the earlier protest, the basic goal was not achieved; the corporations refused to restore wages; and operatives either left Lowell or returned to work at the new rates.

Despite these surface similarities between the turn-outs, there were some real differences. One involved scale: over 1500 operatives turned out in 1836, compared to only 800 earlier. Moreover, the second strike lasted much longer than the first. In 1834 operatives stayed out for only a few days; in 1836, the mills ran far below capacity for several months. Two weeks after the second turn-out began, a mill agent reported that only a fifth of the strikers had returned to work: "The rest manifest *good 'spunk'* as they call it." Several days later he described the impact of the continuing strike on operations in his mills: "we must be feeble for months to come as probably not less than 250 of our former scanty supply of help have left town." These lines read in sharp contrast to the optimistic reports of agents following the turn-out in February, 1834.

Differences between the two turn-outs were not limited to the increased scale and duration of the later one. Women displayed a much higher degree of organization in 1836 than earlier. To co-ordinate strike activities, they formed a Factory Girls' Association. According to one historian, membership in the short-lived association reached 2500 at its height. The larger organization among women was reflected in the tactics employed. Strikers, according to one mill agent, were able to halt production to a greater extent than numbers alone could explain; and, he complained, although some operatives were willing to work, "it has been impossible to give employment to many who remained." He attributed this difficulty to the strikers' tactics: "This was in many instances no doubt the result of calculation and contrivance. After the original turn-out they, [the operatives] would assail a particular room—as for instance, all the warpers, or all the warp spinners, or all the speeder and stretcher girls, and this would close the mill as effectually as if all the girls in the mill had left."

Now giving more thought than they had in 1834 to the specific tactics of the turn-out, the women made a deliberate effort to shut down the mills in order to win their demands. They attempted to persuade less committed operatives, concentrating on those in crucial departments within the mill. Such tactics anticipated those of skilled mulespinners and loomfixers who went out on strike in the 1880s and 1890s.

In their organization of a Factory Girl's Association and in their efforts to shut down the mills, the female operatives revealed that they had been changed by their industrial experience. Increasingly, they acted not simply as "daughters of freemen" offended by the impositions of the textile corporations, but also as industrial workers intent on improving their position within the mills.

There was a decline in protest among women in the Lowell mills following these early strike defeats. During the 1837–1843 depression, textile corporations twice reduced wages without evoking a collective response from operatives. Because of the frequency of production cutbacks and lay-offs in these years, workers probably accepted the mill agents' contention that they had to reduce wages or close entirely. But with the return of prosperity and the expansion of production in the mid-1840s, there were renewed labor protests among women. Their actions paralleled those of working men and reflected fluctuations in the business cycle. Prosperity itself did not prompt turn-outs, but it evidently facilitated collective actions by women operatives.

In contrast to the protests of the previous decade, the struggles now were primarily political. Women did not turn-out in the 1840s; rather, they mounted annual petition campaigns calling on the State legislature to limit the hours of labor within the mills. These campaigns reached their height in 1845 and 1846, when 2,000 and 5,000 operatives respectively signed petitions. Unable to curb the wage cuts, or the speed-up and stretch-out imposed by mill owners, operatives sought to mitigate the consequences of these changes by reducing the length of the working day. Having been defeated earlier in economic struggles, they now sought to achieve their new goal through political action. The Ten Hour Movement, seen in these terms, was a logical outgrowth of the unsuccessful turn-outs of the previous decade. Like the earlier struggles, the Ten Hour Movement was an assertion of the dignity of operatives and an attempt to maintain that dignity under the changing conditions of industrial capitalism. . . .

The women's Ten Hour Movement, like the earlier turn-outs, was based in part on the participants' sense of their own worth and dignity as daughters of freemen. At the same time, however, [it] also indicated the growth of a new consciousness. It reflected a mounting feeling of community among women operatives and a realization that their interests and those of their employers were not identical, that they had to rely on themselves and not on corporate benevolence to achieve a reduction in the hours of labor. One woman, in an open letter to a State legislator, expressed this rejection of middle-class paternalism: "Bad as is the condition of so many women, it would be much worse if they had nothing but your boasted protection to rely upon; but they have at last learnt the lesson which a bitter experience teaches, that not to those who style themselves their 'natural protectors' are they to look for the needful help, but to the strong and resolute of their own sex.'' Such an attitude, underlying the self-organizing of women in the ten-hour petition campaigns, was clearly the product of the industrial experience in Lowell.

Both the early turn-outs and the Ten Hour Movement were, as noted above, in large measure dependent upon the existence of a close-knit community of women operatives. Such a community was based on the work structure, the nature of worker housing, and workforce homogeneity. Women were drawn together by the initial job training of newcomers; by the informal work sharing among experienced hands, by living in company boarding houses, by sharing religious, educational, and social activities in their leisure hours. Working and living in a new and alien setting, they came to rely upon one another for friendship and support. Understandably, a community feeling developed among them.

This evolving community as well as the common cultural traditions which Yankee women carried into Lowell were major elements that governed their response to changing mill conditions. The pre-industrial tradition of independence and self-respect made them particularly sensitive to management labor policies. The sense of community enabled them to transform their individual opposition to wage cuts and to the increasing pace of work into public protest. In these labor struggles women operatives expressed a new consciousness of their rights both as workers and as women. Such a consciousness, like the community of women itself, was one product of Lowell's industrial revolution.

The experiences of Lowell women before 1850 present a fascinating picture of the contradictory impact of industrial capitalism. Repeated labor protests reveal that female operatives felt the demands of mill employment to be oppressive. At the same time, however, the mills provided women with work outside of the home and family, thereby offering them an unprecedented opportunity. That they came to challenge employer paternalism was a direct consequence of the increasing opportunities offered them in these years. The Lowell mills both exploited and liberated women in ways unknown to the pre-industrial political economy.

The Divisions Among Female Shoebinders

MARY BLEWETT

This essay examines the relationship between gender and work in the shoe industry in Essex County, Massachusetts before the Civil War. Large numbers of men and women were employed in the putting-out system of domestic production as the boot and shoe industry of New England expanded prior

Mary Blewett, "Work, Gender, and the Artisan Tradition in New England Shoemaking, 1780–1860," *Journal of Social History*, XVII (1983–84), 221–248. Reprinted by permission of the author.

to 1860. Pre-industrial methods of shoemaking involved an initially close relationship between work and family, production and the home, in which the interrelationships of gender and work can be observed. Men and women shared the work and traditions of artisan life in the family, but each gender experienced work, culture and consciousness in different ways. What were the attitudes of male artisans toward women who worked in shoe production and how did these attitudes shape artisan ideology? Did the cultural traditions and ideology of artisan life reflect or serve the interests of pre-industrial women workers who were drawn into production in the early nineteenth century? How did the differences in gender and work affect the ability of artisans to protest the rise of industrialization? . . .

The motive for the recruitment of women in shoemaking families to new work appears to have been made in the context of a shift in the control of profits as production expanded between 1780 and 1810. Production was expanded by merchant capitalists who bought leather and provided it to shoemakers. The merchant capitalist owned the shoes and marketed them. This control over raw materials meant control of profits as all cordwainers knew, and master shoemakers borrowed capital if they could to purchase leather. Those shoemakers who owned no leather and who accepted work from capitalists had only their labor from which to profit. They divided up the work among the men in their shops and augmented their wage income from labor by recruiting additional family members for work: their women. The male head of the shoemaking family disciplined and controlled women's work in the home. The merchant capitalist, who had no control over the assignment of work in the artisan shop or family, welcomed the new potential for production. As entrepreneurs, they paid no wages directly to women workers and did not need to supervise their work. By adapting to the new work, women added their traditional household labor to their family's income in ways which continued to permit them to combine family and work roles.

Why didn't the apprentices do the sewing of uppers to meet the needs of expanded production? They had learned the skill as part of their apprenticeship, and some did sew uppers whenever bottlenecks in production occurred. Specialization in sewing uppers, however, would have disrupted the apprenticeship system as an orientation to the male world of the artisan and to its work, rituals and hierarchy of subordination and dominance, as well as limiting the various services apprentices provided for the master and journeymen. To use apprentices would not have solved the labor shortage in an expanding market, for in a few years apprentices would become journeymen, no longer available to sew seams. Some more dependable source of new labor was needed, one which the capitalist would accept in the interests of expanded production, yet would not have to pay wages or supervise. The utilization of women in shoemaking families was a solution that would avoid changes in the apprentice system, meet the needs of both capitalist and artisan and threaten no alteration in the traditional patterns of gender formation. The origins of the sexual division of labor in the shoemaking craft was a conscious decision made by artisans and accepted by merchant capitalists to expand production.

Historians of the New England shoe industry have regarded the recruitment of female labor in the late eighteenth century as the natural evolution
or inevitable outgrowth of women's involvement in household work or as
the fitting of an excess female population in Essex County into a work
process which drew on their abilities as needleworkers. The recruitment of
women in shoemaking families was instead a carefully controlled assignment
of work designed to fit the role of women and to maintain gender relationships in the family, while preserving the artisan training system in its social
as well as its craft aspect. Women were recruited to only a small part of the
work, the sewing of the upper part of the shoe, and not to the craft itself.
They were barred from apprenticeships and group work and isolated from
the center of artisan life: the shoe shop. The artisan shop has come to be
seen by historians as the center of pre-industrial political and cultural life for
New England shoemakers and the source of the ideology and consciousness
which many regard as representing the origins of the American working
class. It was a world of men and boys.

The introduction of the sexual division of labor into an artisan craft
represented a major change in the mode of production. Work was redefined
and relocated, new words were coined and new procedures devised for
supervision. The work assigned to women took on social meanings appropriate to their gender. Female family members adapted their traditional needle
skills to hand sew the leather uppers of shoes in their kitchens without
disrupting their domestic duties or their child care tasks. Needle work on
leather uppers, a relatively clean part of the job, was accompanied by a new
tool designed exclusively for women's work: the shoe clamp. The woman
shoeworker would not have to straddle a shoemaker's bench, but would use
a long, flexible wooden clamp which rested on the floor and which she held
between her knees, holding the pieces of shoe upper together and freeing her
hands to ply her needle. Her work was given a new name: shoebinding,
which became a major category of women's work in the early nineteenth
century.

Binders in shoemaking families earned no wages between the 1780s and
the 1810s, but they did contribute their labor to family production and to the
wage it commanded. The emergence of shoebinding testified to the adaptabil-
ity and persistence of women's labor in household production. At this time,
women in Essex County had few alternatives to hard, seasonal agricultural
work or barter to add income to their families. The introduction of the sexual
division of labor into an artisan craft was carefully controlled, guaranteeing
the subordinate role of women by separating the work of shoebinding from
any knowledge of the other various skills of the craft and by maintaining
separate work places for men and women. These patterns survived the
transformation of the industry into the factory system and, therefore, constituted a fundamental social dimension of work.

Although shoebinders worked in their kitchens where domestic tasks
and child care continued, the artisan shop and its demands for work in-
truded. No work in the shop could proceed without a few pairs of sewn
uppers. The binder's work in her kitchen was essential to the timing and

pace of production in the shop, and she had to keep ahead of the requirements of the shop workers with a ready supply of sewn uppers. Her kitchen
was transformed into a workplace where external demands from the ten
footer shaped her time and tasks. The collective nature of men's work in the
shoe shop, the locus of artisan culture, supported a militant tradition of
resistance to the reorganization of production. This tradition did not mirror
the experience of women workers who had no craft status and did not share
in the political and religious discussions in the shop. The relationship of
binders to this tradition was limited by their isolation from group production
and mediated through their role in the family. . . .

By the 1830s shoe manufacturers had assumed much of the responsibility for hiring binders for wages and replaced husbands and fathers as employers. Even if her husband made shoes, a binder might work on uppers for
ladies' boots while her spouse made coarse work shoes for Southern slaves.
This disassociation of women's work from the family labor system affected
the ability of the shoemaker to coordinate the work process. The shoe boss
assumed responsibility not only for hiring female workers, often from non-
shoemaking families, but also directed and coordinated the work process
from his central shop. The shoemaker had to wait, sometimes for hours, for
the shoe boss to provide him with bound uppers. The shift in the coordination of the work of binding and making to the central shop represented a
decline in the power of artisans to exert control over the work process. . . .

By 1833 there were about 1,500 women in Lynn who earned wages as
shoebinders. A wage cut prompted over half of them to organize the "Female Society of Lynn and vicinity for the protection and promotion of Female Industry." In their public statements, the shoebinders voiced the
mechanics' ideology, blending it with expressions of their grievances as
wage earners and using it as a defense of the worth of their labor as female
members of artisan families. Most important, however, was their claim to
new rights: the right to public action as women and the right to support
themselves respectably and independently on their wages, independently in
the sense of making a significant contribution to the family wage economy.

The Lynn binders who organized the Female Society met at the Friends'
Meetinghouse on December 30, 1833 where, as the *Lynn Record* noted,
women as well as men could speak freely in public. They were joined a few
days later by 125 binders who met at the Methodist church in neighboring
Saugus and adopted the same objectives, ideology and constitution. In the
preamble to the society's constitution, the Lynn binders pointed to ". . . a
manifest error, a want of justice, and reasonable compensation to the females; which calls imperiously for redress. While the prices of their labour
have been reduced, the business of their *employers* has appeared to be
improving, and prosperous, enabling them to increase their wealth. *These
things ought not so to be!*" Their demand for higher wages was based on the
labor theory of value. As workers, they believed they were not earning a just
compensation; their independence and respectability was threatened. Furthermore, this economic injustice enriched the shoe boss. This was a violation of the dignity of their labor and a "moral outrage."

To redress their grievances, the shoebinders of Lynn demanded an extension of the equal rights doctrine of the artisan tradition to women. "Equal rights should be extended to all—to the weaker sex as well as the stronger." Many of the women who attended the society's first meeting on December 30, 1833, the preamble claimed, either supported themselves or their families on their earnings as binders and had become dependent on their wage labor. The disadvantages that women experienced "by nature and custom" should not be aggravated by "unnecessary and unjust" treatment as workers. The preamble expressed the belief that ". . . women as well as men, have certain inalienable rights, among which is the right at all times of 'peaceably assembling to consult upon the common good.' " In this, the Lynn binders were responding to criticism that they were forming a combination against the manufacturers which endangered the town's prosperity. They replied that the shoe bosses combined together themselves to hold down wages and to pay the binders in store orders for goods. The women in the Lynn society equated their interests as workers with the interests of the community, regarding the welfare of the town as consisting, ". . . not in the aggrandizement of a few individuals, but in the general prosperity and welfare of the industrious and laboring classes."

The preamble went on to criticize the recent reduction in wages for shoebinding which prevented them from obtaining "a comfortable support." This concept represented the shoebinders' claim to a just wage, a feminine version of the "competency" sought by artisans, an income sufficient to support their families and permit a little savings for old age. However, in computing the wage which would earn them their comfortable support, the shoebinders used as a measure—not their work in production—but their duties and responsibilities as female members of artisan families. The shoebinders used their gender roles as the wives, daughters and widows of New England mechanics to insist upon a wage level that would confer dignity and independence on them. They calculated the price of the household services that a wife performed as a seamstress, washwoman, nurse and maid and demanded a wage high enough to cover these expenses. By extending the analogy of wage work into their domestic sphere, the wives of mechanics who bound shoes were bridging over the gap between work and domesticity. For a daughter, wages should be high enough to cover room, board and personal upkeep so as not to constitute a drain upon her father's income nor induce her to leave home for factory work. As for a mechanic's widow with dependents, her wage level should ensure a livelihood without the necessity of applying to the town for poor relief.

To be effective the Lynn shoebinders' society had to organize all working women in the local industry, whatever their attachment to the mechanic's family or dependence on their earnings. However, the ideology which the society's members borrowed from the artisan tradition and which they reshaped to their experiences of gender hierarchy within the family betrayed a contradiction between their demands for equal rights for men and women workers and the calculations of a just wage for women. Equal rights for women as workers suggested the primacy of work; wages computed on the expenses of household services indicated that, in family terms, domestic duties were primary for women. For the Lynn shoebinders, their gender role in the family and in artisan ideology transformed the labor theory of value into a measure of their domestic work. . . .

Shoebinders did not face a shift of production out of the home, but an assignment of new work for women in the home and its intensification in the outwork system. The sexual division of labor in shoe production reinforced the idea of a separate sphere for women and provided a class basis for the cult of domesticity among working women. By the 1830s, however, the family labor system had given way to the employment of women directly by the shoe boss in the outwork system. Sharing the bonds of womanhood both in work and in their domestic sphere, shoebinders in 1834 tried to organize themselves in terms of a female community of workers committed to self improvement and the improvement of society. Mary Russell actively sought to extend the idea of sisterhood as an organizing principle, but the shoebinders of Lynn could only respond hesitantly. The conditions under which many shoebinders labored—isolated from each other, employed by the shoe boss outside a group labor system and combining wage work with domestic responsibilities—discouraged collective activity. The tensions between their relationship to the artisan system and its equal rights ideology and their subordinate role as females in the family were exposed by their arguments for a just wage for women. Neither the social relations of the artisan family nor the realities of working as a woman for a shoe boss encouraged the shoebinder of Lynn to identify with her working sister in the Lowell mills or conceive of herself as a worker capable of supporting herself who could unite with her peers to protest mistreatment.

The efforts of the Lynn Female Society had limited success in 1834. Payments in store orders were temporarily suspended, but wages for binding shoes never even approached the wages offered to women workers in textile factories. Instead of raising wages to local shoebinders, shoe bosses in Eastern Massachusetts built networks of rural outworkers throughout the region extending into New Hampshire and Maine. By 1837, more women (15,366) were involved in shoe production in Massachusetts than female workers (14,759) in cotton textile factories. The decline in the importance of the shoemaking family as a work unit left wives increasingly dependent on their shoemaker husbands for economic support. As the shoe bosses became more important to the coordination of production and the recruitment of binders, the relationship between the shoemaker and his employer changed. The shoemaker was regarded less and less as a middle-man in the recruitment of outwork for the boss, who now ran the central shop and directed the work of both binder and maker. This change in the relationship between shoeworker and shoe boss plus the pressure on the family wage economy may be underlying reasons for the outbursts of collective activity among Essex County shoemakers in the 1840s.

The decade of the 1840s represented a high point of activism among shoemakers in Eastern Massachusetts, who organized on a regional basis and held conventions with other working men and women. The Cordwainers' Mutual Benefit Society of Lynn began to publish a labor paper, The *Awl*, in 1844 and tried to summon support for the society among women including shoebinders. In the first issue of the *Awl* on July 17, 1844, the editors developed a constituency and a set of objectives which limited and subordinated women's relationship to their organization. Oblivious to the implications for women of the disassociation of shoebinding from the family labor system and into a vulnerable isolation from group work and artisan ideology, the shoemakers' society in the 1840s perceived women as persons whose lives were defined primarily by family and morality. . . .

In the December 21 issue of the *Awl,* the editors published under the title, "Woman," a special appeal for female support which illustrated how they viewed the nature of women and the limits this view placed on women's involvement in the activities of the society. Women were perceived as moral beings and were called upon to "hallow and enoble" the objectives of the society. The appeal to them was based on their capacity for self-sacrifice. The editors sought to enlist their energies to serve the interests of others; "the poor and down-trodden" and "her lovely sisters toiling . . . to gain a scanty subsistence." Earlier, the *Awl* had reassured women that it was as moral for them to meet with the cordwainers every Saturday night as to attend church on Sunday. Indeed, their presence at these meetings would guarantee their propriety. The *Awl* regarded women's power as moral, unselfish and spiritual, not as material, self-interested or political. These attitudes seemed to blind the cordwainers' society to the vulnerability and isolation of shoebinders.

The appeal of the *Awl* for female participation was deeply ambivalent. If women were seen as essentially moral and spiritual, characteristics that suggested gentility and the pious, private virtues that historians have identified as the cult of true womanhood, the ideology of the cordwainers' society pointedly rejected the values of the genteel, non-working classes who by their unearned wealth and leisured lives threatened the basic values of artisan culture. This side of their attitudes toward women revealed a fear of genteel or middle-class social behavior in females within their own families which would unfit them for the useful life of a mechanic's wife. . . .

The depression years of the late 1850s created a crisis in the rapidly changing New England shoe industry. The crisis involved a collapse in the pre-industrial wage patterns of the family economy as shoe manufacturing moved toward mechanization, centralization and the factory system. In the early 1850s an expanding market for boots and shoes in the developing West had drawn additional male workers into the process of bottoming: the attachment by hand of machine or hand-sewn uppers to soles. Heeling and finishing operations were reorganized and performed separately along with cutting operations in the central shops. Groups of workmen in the surrounding towns of Essex County served by a network of teamsters bottomed shoes for Lynn and Haverhill shoe bosses, but an even more extensive rural outwork system, reaching into Central New Hampshire and Southern Maine and served by railroad, supplied additional male workers for bottoming.

Machine productivity by female factory operatives increased the demand for bottomers, and Irish and German immigrants as well as migrants from New England came to the shoe towns of Massachusetts, crowding the local labor market. While the numbers of men who worked as bottomers increased, stimulated by machine productivity, the sex ratio of male to female shoeworker sharply reversed. The numbers of women employed in Massachusetts shoe production dropped off steadily in the 1850s. In Lynn the number of females employed on shoes shrank sharply by 41% between 1850 and 1860. The mechanization of women's work intensified the hard conditions of labor for both men and women involved in outwork in Essex County. The productivity of the new machine stitchers had stimulated the demand for bottomers, while cutting the demand for shoebinders. By contemporary estimates, one factory girl at her stitching machine could supply enough work for twenty bottomers, while replacing eleven binders. The woman who operated a sewing machine at home still faced the custom of "furnishing," that is, providing thread, needles and lining materials. A considerable gap developed after 1855 between the wages of factory operatives and the wages of women working at home whether by hand or by machine.

Downward pressure on wages during the hard times after 1857 cut sharply into the shoemaker's family wage and helped precipitate the largest American demonstration of labor protest prior to the Civil War. A regional strike, beginning in February 1860 and spearheaded by activities in Natick and Lynn, disrupted production. The values and patterns of the pre-industrial family economy confronted the emerging factory system. This confrontation divided not only the workers and their employers, but also divided the strikers into groups promoting the family wage economy through the artisan tradition and groups of female factory operatives whose place in centralized production and whose status as temporary residents of the shoe city created a different set of interests in the 1860 strike.

The strikers in Lynn, led by the bottomers, hoped to organize the country shoemakers to refuse outwork, while they simultaneously halted production in the Lynn shops. Important to this strategy was the interruption of teamster activities which carried sewn uppers and cut soles to country workshops. Significantly, the first serious conflict in Lynn involved express teams which carried shoe uppers machine-sewn by female factory workers to Marblehead bottomers for the John Wooldredge Company. Wooldredge had pioneered both the adoption of the Singer sewing machine in 1852 and the introduction of steam power in 1858 for heeling and stitching operations. His firm symbolized the emerging factory system.

The strike leadership in Lynn had been considering the organization of the 3,000 shoebinders and stitchers as an auxiliary force to encourage community support and boycott uncooperative shoe bosses. Their decision to organize women workers was made after a violent incident on February 23 between strikers and expressmen which provoked widespread regional criticism in the press, precipitated the arrival of outside police forces and threatened to undermine the crucial support of shoemakers in the neighboring towns of Essex County for the strike. In 1860 the Lynn strike committee attempted to utilize the moral stature of women for the same family and community purposes as had the Lynn cordwainers' society in the 1840s. Women's participation would restore morality to the strike, help generate community support in Lynn and throughout Essex County and mitigate criticism. The involvement of local women would erase the images of violence and disorder and emphasize the nature of the strike as a defense of the New England family.

The strike committee in Lynn was not, however, prepared to acknowledge or represent the interests of the female factory operatives whose leaders quickly seized control of the women's meetings. The interests of these women workers, who were nearly 40% of the female work force in Lynn by 1860, conflicted with artisan conception of the family wage economy. The factory operatives disagreed with the advancement of the wages of male shoeworkers as the only objective in the strike and convinced the women workers of Lynn to strike for higher wages as binders and stitchers. They also began to organize women workers in the neighboring towns of Danvers, Newburyport and Marblehead. Realizing the importance of their strategic position to stop work in centralized production, the factory girls in Lynn proposed a coalition with female homeworkers to raise wages in both categories of work: homework for wives and mothers and factory work for single girls. This alliance of gender represented a bridge between the pre-industrial patterns of women's work and the developing factory system. Unity as a gender would protect the wages of the married and the unmarried, the homeworkers and the shop girls, by linking the cause of working women to the new sources of wages and power in factory work. Mechanization and centralization of women's work had meant higher wages for factory workers, but reduced the numbers of women employed, relegated wives and mothers to homework and depressed the wages of outworkers. For homeworkers, an alliance with the young factory girls represented a real chance in 1860 for women working at home to make a valuable connection with the new industrial workers. In return, factory girls could anticipate marriage and a chance to work at home for decent wages. The family wage economy would be protected by a coalition of women workers acting together on behalf of their own interests.

The factory girls, led by twenty-one-year-old Clara Brown, a native of Massachusetts, who boarded in Lynn with a shoemaker's family, won several crucial votes on raising women's wages in the strike meetings held by Lynn women. They challenged the male strike committee for leadership of the women workers and to articulation of their interests. The factory girls identified with other women in the industry as workers and as a gender, not unlike the brothers of the craft. The ideology of artisan life did not figure in their vision of an alliance of women workers at home and in the shops, nor did they identify with the bottomers on familial or on ideological grounds. Conscious of the power of factory stitchers in this alliance whose productivity could shut down production in the industry and halt outwork, Clara Brown declared: "Girls of Lynn, . . . strike at once . . . Don't work your machines; let them lie still until we get all we ask." At a later meeting she challenged: ". . . we've got the bosses where we can do as we please with 'em. If we don't take the work, what can the bosses do?"

The male strike committee quickly moved to oppose this unwelcome development. The committee members failed, however, to persuade the women at a meeting on February 28 to reconsider the list of wage demands which had been adopted the night before, a wage list which in the eyes of the striking shoemakers overvalued factory stitching and jeopardized homework. They feared that if the women's wages were raised, all stitching of uppers would be centralized in factories and homework eliminated. For the bottomers, the best protection for the family wage lay in obtaining higher wages for men's work and maintaining homework for women. In a bold move, the strike committee and its supporters among the women homeworkers ignored the high wage list adopted by votes taken at several of the women's meetings and substituted a lower list of wages which they circulated as the official wage list for the women workers of Lynn to sign. On March 2 the supporters of the men's strike committee and the factory girls confronted each other at a tumultuous meeting. James Dillon, representing the bottomers, pleaded for the support of the women as wives and mothers of shoemakers and appealed to them not to alienate the bosses of the stitching shops by demanding an "unfair" increase in wages. Other speakers dismissed the shop girls as interested only in money and in "the right to switch a long-tailed skirt [extravagant dress]." Wage decisions, it was argued at the March 2 meeting, should be made by "sober, and discreet women" and not by "laughing" and "thoughtless girls." Clara Brown countered by insisting that the machine girls of Lynn had the power to protect homeworkers, but that the factory girls would only strike for "something worth having." She pointed out that the low wage list prepared by the homeworkers actually cut wages on factory work. Despite her warnings, representatives of the bottomers' committee persuaded the majority of the women at the meeting to reject the high wage list and the factory girls, accept their recommendations on behalf of the family and community in Lynn and join the striking men in great show of community support for the strike.

The legendary parade of striking women on a snowy March day through the streets of Lynn represented a great victory for the defenders of decentralized production and for the artisan tradition in Lynn. The images of the women's procession printed in the pages of *Frank Leslie's Illustrated Newspaper* have come to epitomize the involvement of women in the 1860 strike, but these sketches obscured the battle which took place over the relationship of women workers to the strike. The political stance of the majority of the women workers who rejected the strategy of the factory girls and supported the bottomers was reflected in the familial values on one of their banners:

> Weak in physical strength but strong in moral courage, we dare to battle for the right, shoulder to shoulder with our fathers, husbands and brothers.

The decision of the homeworkers to support the men's strike committee was taken at the risk of ignoring the implications of mechanization, the factory system and the potential of the shop girls who, as workers in centralized production, represented the reorganization of industrial life in Lynn. Many

Lynn women continued to support the bottomers until the strike slowly fell apart in late March, while the factory girls who boarded in Lynn returned to work or to their homes.

The bottomers of Lynn had fought in 1860 to maintain the traditions and ideology of decentralized production, including women's work in the home. The artisan ideology had operated successfully to unite the heterogeneous work force of male workers—rural migrants, Irish, Germans and shoemakers in country shops and shoe towns—in the 1850s, but cut off the new female factory workers from contributing to labor protest. The leaders of the Lynn strike failed to perceive or respond to the strategic potential of female machine operators in centralized production and had ignored and opposed their articulated interests. The perceptions which shoemaking artisans had developed of work and gender made it difficult for them to regard women as fellow-workers outside of family relationships, to include them in the ideology and politics built on artisan life or see in the experience of working women what awaited all workers as capitalism in the New England shoe industry moved toward the factory system.

Historiography in the 1970s on women's work was dominated by a lively debate on the impact of economic change on women and their relationship to the family. Two major interpretations emerged. Joan Scott, Louise Tilly, Jane Humphries and Leslie Tentler emphasized the limitations of changes in women's lives as a result of industrialization, and they regarded the family as primary in defining the work and social roles of women employed at home or in the factory. Edward Shorter, Patricia Branca, Thomas Dublin and Heidi Hartmann have argued for a variety of levels of change in women's lives as a result of new work. All acknowledge the sexual division of labor as a fundamental condition of women's work in the nineteenth century.

This overview of changes in women's work in New England shoe production and the relationship of women shoeworkers to the artisan tradition suggests that tension between women workers and the family values of artisan culture remained constant and unresolved as work reorganized during the shift toward industrialization from 1780 to 1860. Contradictions between perceptions of the proper gender role for women in the family and their consciousness as workers in production prolonged these tensions for women workers into the early factory system and the 1860 strike. This struggle, most visible during moments of labor protest, had been initiated by the recruitment of women into production in the artisan system and maintained by the differences in the location of work and the exposure of the individual worker to the increasing control of the work process by the employer. For the most part, women shoeworkers negotiated those tensions between family and work within the value system of artisan ideology, but in doing so they built limits into their consciousness as workers and into their ability to act together as women to defend their interests or claim new rights. The gender perceptions of artisan ideology as articulated by male shoeworkers in ante bellum New England defined the role of women primarily as family members and as moral agents in society. Gender-based ideology and work experience cut women off from the most vital tradition of collective resistance in the early nineteenth century.

❖ FURTHER READING

Sandra Addickes, "Mind among the Spindles: An Examination of Some of the Journals, Newspapers, and Memoirs of the Lowell Female Operatives," *Women's Studies,* I (1973), 279–87

Mary H. Blewett, *Men, Women, and Work: A Study of Class, Gender, and Protest in the Nineteenth-Century New England Shoe Industry* (1988)

Milton Cantor and Bruce Laurie, eds., *Class, Sex, and the Woman Worker* (1977)

Thomas Dublin, *Women at Work: The Transformation of Work and Community in Lowell, Massachusetts, 1820–1860* (1979)

Carol Groneman and Mary Beth Norton, eds., *"To Toil the Livelong Day": America's Women at Work, 1790–1980* (1987)

Susan Estabrook Kennedy, *If All We Did Was to Weep at Home: A History of White Working-Class Women in America* (1979)

Alice Kessler-Harris, *Out to Work: A History of Wage-Earning Women in the United States* (1982)

Gerda Lerner, "The Lady and the Mill Girl," *American Studies,* X, no. 1 (spring 1969), 5–15

Christine Stansell, *City of Women: Work, Sex and Class in New York City, 1789–1860* (1986)

Carole Turbin, "And We Are Nothing but Women: Irish Working Women in Troy," in Carol Berkin and Mary Beth Norton, eds., *Women of America: A History* (1979), 202–22

Barbara Miller Wertheimer, *We Were There: The Story of Working Women in America* (1977)

CHAPTER
8

Varieties of Nineteenth-Century Feminism

The roots of today's feminist movement lie in the 1840s and 1850s, for it was then that white American women, building on the traditions of the female charitable and reform associations of the earlier years of the century, first organized themselves to advance their own position within American society. The crucial date is July 1848, when a group of male and female activists, many of them Quakers and veterans of other reform movements, met at Seneca Falls, in upstate New York, to adopt a "Declaration of Sentiments" calling for women's equality. A number of similar conventions followed, but not until the late 1860s did the supporters of women's rights create formal organizations to promote their cause. Throughout the century, such groups remained quite small, failing to appeal to a significant number of American women.

The mid-1870s, by contrast, saw the founding of what was to become by far the largest women's organization of the day. The Women's Christian Temperance Union (WCTU) appealed to women of different classes and races as it embarked on an ambitious program of reform that rested firmly on unrelenting opposition to the consumption of alcohol. The WCTU's initially limited goals expanded to encompass a wide range of reform activity, eventually including demands for women's suffrage under the rubric of "Home Protection." (The WCTU argued that women needed the vote to protect their homes and families from the many problems caused by drunken men.) Thus what began as a conservative movement later took on radical characteristics. But does that mean that the WCTU too should be called a "feminist" organization, despite having held beliefs that today would not be defined as such? Historians disagree sharply in their response to that question. What are some of the similarities and differences between the WCTU and other groups of the same time period who defended women's rights? Why was it easier for the WCTU to rally support for its cause?

❖ D O C U M E N T S

In 1838, Sarah Grimké, a South Carolina Quaker, became one of the first Americans to publish essays in support of women's rights. Her observations entitled "Legal Disabilities of Women," the twelfth of her *Letters on the Equality of the Sexes,* is the first document. The most famous and important nineteenth-century statement on women's rights was the "Declaration of Sentiments" (the second selection) adopted by the Seneca Falls convention in July 1848. Nearly three years later, the eloquent black abolitionist Sojourner Truth spoke at another women's rights convention; the only account of her speech, that written by Frances Gage, is the third document. Yet not all female activists supported suffrage demands. Notable among the nay-sayers were Catharine Beecher and her novelist sister Harriet Beecher Stowe, who in 1869 included an antisuffrage statement in their best-selling book, *The American Woman's Home*; this statement is reprinted here as the fourth selection. More female reformers put their energies into the temperance movement than worked for women's rights. The fifth document is an 1855 poem calling on the "Sisters of Temperance" to support prohibition laws like the one passed in Maine. That women responded to such appeals is demonstrated by the last two documents. The sixth selection is a speech Mary C. Vaughan delivered at the 1852 meeting of the New York Daughters of Temperance. The seventh is an account of a Syracuse woman's attack on a tavern that served liquor to her drunken husband.

Sarah Grimké on the Legal Disabilities of Women, 1838

There are few things which present greater obstacles to the improvement and elevation of woman to her appropriate sphere of usefulness and duty, than the laws which have been enacted to destroy her independence, and crush her individuality; laws which, although they are framed for her government, she has had no voice in establishing, and which rob her of some of her *essential rights*. Woman has no political existence. With the single exception of presenting a petition to the legislative body, she is a cipher in the nation; or, if not actually so in representative governments, she is only counted, like the slaves of the South, to swell the number of law-makers who form decrees for her government, with little reference to her benefit, except so far as her good may promote their own. . . .

Blackstone, in the chapter entitled 'Of husband and wife,' says:—

> By marriage, the husband and wife are one person in law; that is, *the very being, or legal existence of the woman* is suspended during the marriage, or at least is incorporated and consolidated into that of the husband under whose wing, protection and cover she performs everything. . . .

Here now, the very being of a woman, like that of a slave, is absorbed in her master. All contracts made with her, like those made with slaves by their owners, are a mere nullity. Our kind defenders have legislated away almost all our legal rights, and in the true spirit of such injustice and oppression, have kept us in ignorance of those very laws by which we are governed. They have persuaded us, that we have no right to investigate the laws, and that, if we did, we could not comprehend them; they alone are capable of understanding the mysteries of Blackstone, &c. But they are not backward to make us feel the practical operation of their power over our actions.

> The husband is bound to provide his wife with necessaries by law, as much as himself; and if she contracts debts for them, he is obliged to pay for them; but for anything besides necessaries, he is not chargeable.

Yet a man may spend the property he has acquired by marriage at the ale-house, the gambling table, or in any other way that he pleases. Many instances of this kind have come to my knowledge; and women, who have brought their husbands handsome fortunes, have been left, in consequence of the wasteful and dissolute habits of their husbands, in straitened circumstances, and compelled to toil for the support of their families. . . .

> The husband, by the old law, might give his wife moderate correction, as he is to answer for her misbehavior. The law thought it reasonable to entrust him with this power of restraining her by domestic chastisement. The courts of law will still permit a husband to restrain a wife of her liberty, in case of any gross misbehavior.

What a mortifying proof this law affords, of the estimation in which woman is held! She is placed completely in the hands of a being subject like herself to the outbursts of passion, and therefore unworthy to be trusted with power. Perhaps I may be told respecting this law, that it is a dead letter, as I am sometimes told about the slave laws; but this is not true in either case. The slaveholder does kill his slave by moderate correction, as the law allows; and many a husband, among the poor, exercises the right given him by the law, of degrading women by personal chastisement. And among the higher ranks, if actual imprisonment is not resorted to, women are not unfrequently restrained of the liberty of going to places of worship by irreligious husbands, and of doing many other things about which, as moral and responsible beings, *they* should be the *sole* judges. . . .

And farther, all the avails of her labor are absolutely in the power of her husband. All that she acquires by her industry is his; so that she cannot, with her own honest earnings, become the legal purchaser of any property. If she expends her money for articles of furniture, to contribute to the comfort of her family, they are liable to be siezed for her husband's debts: and I know an instance of a woman, who by labor and economy had scraped together a little maintenance for herself and a do-little husband, who was left, at his death, by virtue of his last will and testament, to be supported by charity. I knew another woman, who by great industry had acquired a little money which she deposited in a bank for safe keeping. She had saved this pittance whilst able to work, in hopes that when age or sickness disqualified her for exertion, she might have something to render life comfortable, without being a burden to her friends. Her husband, a worthless, idle man, discovered this hid treasure, drew her little stock from the bank, and expended it all in extravagance and vicious indulgence. . . .

As these abuses do exist, and women suffer intensely from them, our brethren are called upon in this enlightened age, by every sentiment of honor, religion and justice, to repeal these unjust and unequal laws, and restore to woman those rights which they have wrested from her. Such laws approximate too nearly to the laws enacted by slaveholders for the government of their slaves, and must tend to debase and depress the mind of that being, whom God created as a help meet for man, or 'helper like unto himself,' and designed to be his equal and his companion. Until such laws are annulled, woman never can occupy that exalted station for which she was intended by her Maker.

The "Declaration of Sentiments" of the Seneca Falls Convention, 1848

When, in the course of human events, it becomes necessary for one portion of the family of man to assume among the people of the earth a position different from that which they have hitherto occupied, but one to which the laws of nature and of nature's God entitle them, a decent respect to the opinions of mankind requires that they should declare the causes that impel them to such a course.

We hold these truths to be self-evident: that all men and women are created equal; that they are endowed by their Creator with certain inalienable rights; that among these are life, liberty, and the pursuit of happiness; that to secure these rights governments are instituted, deriving their just powers from the consent of the governed. Whenever any form of government becomes destructive of these ends, it is the right of those who suffer from it to refuse allegiance to it, and to insist upon the institution of a new government, laying its foundation on such principles, and organizing its powers in such form, as to them shall seem most likely to effect their safety and happiness. Prudence, indeed, will dictate that governments long established should not be changed for light and transient causes; and accordingly all experience hath shown that mankind are more disposed to suffer, while evils are sufferable, than to right themselves by abolishing the forms to which they were accustomed. But when a long train of abuses and usurpations, pursuing invariably the same object evinces a design to reduce them under absolute despotism, it is their duty to throw off such government, and to provide new guards for their future security. Such has been the patient sufferance of the women under this government, and such is now the necessity which constrains them to demand the equal situation to which they are entitled.

The history of mankind is a history of repeated injuries and usurpations on the part of man toward woman, having in direct object the establishment of an absolute tyranny over her. To prove this, let facts be submitted to a candid world.

He has never permitted her to exercise her inalienable right to the elective franchise.

He has compelled her to submit to laws, in the formation of which she had no voice.

He has withheld from her rights which are given to the most ignorant and degraded men—both natives and foreigners.

Having deprived her of this first right of a citizen, the elective franchise, thereby leaving her without representation in the halls of legislation, he has oppressed her on all sides.

He has made her, if married, in the eye of the law, civilly dead.

He has taken from her all right in property, even to the wages she earns.

He has made her, morally, an irresponsible being, as she can commit many crimes with impunity, provided they be done in the presence of her husband. In the covenant of marriage, she is compelled to promise obedience to her husband, he becoming, to all intents and purposes, her master— the law giving him power to deprive her of her liberty, and to administer chastisement.

He has so framed the laws of divorce, as to what shall be the proper causes, and in case of separation, to whom the guardianship of the children shall be given, as to be wholly regardless of the happiness of women—the law, in all cases, going upon a false supposition of the supremacy of man, and giving all power into his hands.

After depriving her of all rights as a married woman, if single, and the owner of property, he has taxed her to support a government which recognizes her only when her property can be made profitable to it.

He has monopolized nearly all the profitable employments, and from those she is permitted to follow, she receives but a scanty remuneration. He closes against her all the avenues to wealth and distinction which he considers most honorable to himself. As a teacher of theology, medicine, or law, she is not known.

He has denied her the facilities for obtaining a thorough education, all colleges being closed against her.

He allows her in Church, as well as State, but a subordinate position, claiming Apostolic authority for her exclusion from the ministry, and, with some exceptions, from any public participation in the affairs of the Church.

He has created a false public sentiment by giving to the world a different code of morals for men and women, by which moral delinquencies which exclude women from society, are not only tolerated, but deemed of little account in man.

He has usurped the prerogative of Jehovah himself, claiming it as his right to assign for her a sphere of action, when that belongs to her conscience and to her God.

He has endeavored, in every way that he could, to destroy her confidence in her own powers, to lessen her self-respect, and to make her willing to lead a dependent and abject life.

Now, in view of this entire disfranchisement of one-half the people of this country, their social and religious degradation—in view of the unjust laws above mentioned, and because women do feel themselves aggrieved, oppressed, and fradulently deprived of their most sacred rights, we insist that they have immediate admission to all the rights and privileges which belong to them as citizens of the United States.

In entering upon the great work before us, we anticipate no small amount of misconception, misrepresentation, and ridicule; but we shall use every instrumentality within our power to effect our object. We shall employ agents, circulate tracts, petition the State and National legislatures, and endeavor to enlist the pulpit and the press in our behalf. We hope this Convention will be followed by a series of Conventions embracing every part of the country.

Frances Gage's Account of Sojourner Truth's Address to the Akron Women's Rights Convention, 1851

There were very few women in those days who dared to "speak in meeting"; and the august teachers of the people were seemingly getting the better of us, while the boys in the galleries, and the sneerers among the pews, were hugely enjoying the discomfiture, as they supposed, of the "strong-minded." Some of the tender-skinned friends were on the point of losing dignity, and the atmosphere betokened a storm. When, slowly from her seat in the corner rose Sojourner Truth, who, till now, had scarcely lifted her head. "Don't let her speak!" gasped half a dozen in my ear. She moved slowly and solemnly to the front, laid her old bonnet at her feet, and turned her great speaking eyes to me. There was a hissing sound of disapprobation above and below. I rose and announced "Sojourner Truth," and begged the audience to keep silence for a few moments.

The tumult subsided at once, and every eye was fixed on this almost Amazon form, which stood nearly six feet high, head erect, and eyes piercing the upper air like one in a dream. At her first word there was a profound hush. She spoke in deep tones, which, though not loud, reached every ear in the house, and away through the throng at the doors and windows.

"Wall, chilern, whar dar is so much racket dar must be somethin' out o' kilter. I tink dat 'twixt de niggers of de Souf and de womin at de Norf, all talkin' 'bout rights, de white men will be in a fix pretty soon. But what's all dis here talkin' 'bout?

"Dat man ober dar say dat womin needs to be helped into carriages, and lifted ober ditches, and to hab de best place everywhar. Nobody eber helps me into carriages, or ober mud-puddles, or gibs me any best place!" And raising herself to her full height, and her voice to a pitch like rolling thunder, she asked. "And a'n't I a woman? Look at me! Look at my arm! (and she bared her right arm to the shoulder, showing her tremendous muscular power). I have ploughed, and planted, and gathered into barns, and no man could head me! And a'n't I a woman? I could work as much and eat as much as a man—when I could get it—and bear de lash as well! And a'n't I a woman? I have borne thirteen chilern, and seen 'em mos' all sold off to slavery, and when I cried out with my mother's grief, none but Jesus heard me! And a'n't I a woman?

"Den dey talks 'bout dis ting in de head; what dis dey call it?" ("Intellect," whispered some one near). "Dat's it, honey. What's dat got to do wid womin's rights or nigger's rights? If my cup won't hold but a pint, and yourn holds a quart, wouldn't ye be mean not to let me have my little half-measure full?" And she pointed her significant finger, and sent a keen glance at the minister who had made the argument. The cheering was long and loud.

"Den dat little man in black dar, he say women can't have as much rights as men, 'cause Christ wan't a woman! Whar did your Christ come from?'' Rolling thunder couldn't have stilled that crowd, as did those deep, wonderful tones, as she stood there with outstretched arms and eyes of fire. Raising her voice still louder, she repeated, "Whar did your Christ come from? From God and a woman! Man had nothin' to do wid Him." Oh, what a rebuke that was to that little man.

Turning again to another objector, she took up the defense of Mother Eve. I can not follow her through it all. It was pointed, and witty, and solemn; eliciting at almost every sentence deafening applause; and she ended by asserting: "If de fust woman God ever made was strong enough to turn de world upside down all alone, dese women togedder (and she glanced her eye over the platform) ought to be able to turn it back, and get it right side up again! And now dey is asking to do it, de men better let 'em." Long-continued cheering greeted this. " 'Bleeged to ye for hearin' on me, and now ole Sojourner han't got nothin' more to say."

Amid roars of applause, she returned to her corner, leaving more than one of us with streaming eyes, and hearts beating with gratitude. She had taken us up in her strong arms and carried us safely over the slough of difficulty turning the whole tide in our favor. I have never in my life seen anything like the magical influence that subdued the mobbish spirit of the day, and turned the sneers and jeers of an excited crowd into notes of respect and admiration. Hundreds rushed up to shake hands with her, and congratulate the glorious old mother, and bid her God-speed on her mission of "testifyin' agin concerning the wickedness of this 'ere people."

Catharine Beecher and Harriet Beecher Stowe on Why Women Should Not Seek the Vote, 1869

Many intelligent and benevolent persons imagine that the grand remedy for the heavy evils that oppress our sex is to introduce woman to political power and office, to make her a party in primary political meetings, in political caucuses, and in the scramble and fight for political offices; thus bringing into this dangerous *melée* the distinctive tempting power of her sex. Who can look at this new danger without dismay? . . .

Let us suppose that our friends have gained the ballot and the powers of office: are there any real beneficent measures for our sex, which they would enforce by law and penalties, that fathers, brothers, and husbands would not grant to a united petition of our sex, or even to a majority of the wise and good? Would these not confer what the wives, mothers, and sisters deemed best for themselves and the children they are to train, very much sooner than they would give power and office to our sex to enforce these advantages by law? Would it not be a wiser thing to *ask* for what we need, before trying so circuitous and dangerous a method? God has given to man the physical power, so that all that woman may gain, either by petitions or by ballot, will be the gift of love or of duty; and the ballot never will be accorded till benevolent and conscientious men are the majority—a millennial point far beyond our present ken.

"Rise, Sisters of Temperance," 1855

Rise, sisters of temperance!—we must not delay—
Our mission is holy, and we must away;
We'll gird on our armor tho' frail it may be,
And trust that the "Maine Law" will soon set us free.

Rise, daughters of temperance! your force we will meet,
And though we can't vote, we'll make drunkards retreat,
Though hard is the struggle, and long it may be,
We trust that the "Maine Law" will soon set us free.

Rise, mothers of temperance, to you it is given,
To point out to youth, the bright pathway to heaven,
Though aged or feeble or weary you be,
Faint not—for the "Maine Law" will soon set us free.

We'll go to the senate where noble have gone,
And temperance laurels are yet to be won;
We'll ask not for laurels, we'll ask not for fee—
But plead that the "Maine law" may soon set us free.

ANONYMIA.

Mary C. Vaughan's Address to the New York Daughters of Temperance, 1852

We have met to consider what we, as women, can do and may do, to forward the temperance reform. We have met, because, as members of the human family, we share in all the sufferings which error and crime bring upon the race, and because we are learning that our part in the drama of life is something beside inactive suffering and passive endurance. We would act as well as endure; and we meet here to-day because many of us have been trying to act, and we would combine our individual experiences, and together devise plans for the future, out of which shall arise well-based hopes of good results to humanity. We are aware that this proceeding of ours, this calling together of a body of women to deliberate publicly upon plans to carry out a specified reform, will rub rather harshly upon the mould of prejudice, which has gathered thick upon the common mind.

. . . There are plenty of women, as well as men, who can labor for reforms without neglecting business or duty. It is an error that clings most tenaciously to the public mind, that because a part of the sex are wives and mothers and have absorbing duties, that all the sex should be denied any other sphere of effort. To deprive every unmarried woman, spinster, or widow, or every childless wife, of the power of exercising her warm sympathies for the good of others, is to deprive her of the greatest happiness of which she is capable; to rob her highest faculties of their legitimate operation and reward; to belittle and narrow her mind; to dwarf her affections; to turn the harmonies of her nature to discord; and, as the human mind must be active, to compel her to employ hers with low and grovelling thoughts, which lead to contemptible actions.

There is no reform in which woman can act better or more appropriately than temperance. I know not how she can resist or turn aside from the duty of acting in this; its effects fall so crushingly upon her and those whose interests are identical with her own; she has so often seen its slow, insidious, but not the less surely fatal advances, gaining upon its victim; she has seen the intellect which was her dearest pride, debased; the affections which were her life-giving springs of action, estranged; the children once loved, abused, disgraced and impoverished; the home once an earthly paradise, rendered a fit abode for lost spirits; has felt in her own person all the misery, degradation, and woe of the drunkard's wife; has shrunk from revilings and cowered beneath blows; has labored and toiled to have her poor earnings transferred to the rum-seller's ill-gotten hoard; while her children, ragged, fireless, poor, starving, gathered shivering about her, and with hollow eyes, from which all smiles had fled, begged vainly for the bread she had not to bestow. Oh! the misery, the utter, hopeless misery of the drunkard's wife!

. . . We account it no reason why we should desist, when conscience, an awakened sense of duty, and aroused heart-sympathies, would lead us to show ourselves something different than an impersonation of the vague ideal which has been named, Woman, and with which woman has long striven to identify herself. A creature all softness and sensibility, who must necessarily enjoy and suffer in the extreme, while sharing with man the pleasures and the ills of life; bearing happiness meekly, and sorrow with fortitude; gentle, mild, submissive, forbearing under all circumstances; a softened reflex of the opinions and ideas of the masculines who, by relationship, hold mastery over her; without individualism, a mere adjunct of man, the chief object of whose creation was to adorn and beautify his existence, or to minister to some form of his selfishness. This is nearly the masculine idea of womanhood, and poor womanhood strives to personify it. But not all women. This is an age of iconoclasms; and daring hands are raised to sweep from its pedestal, and dash to fragments, this false image of woman. We care not how soon, if the true woman but take its place. This is also, and most emphatically, an age of progress. One old idea, one mouldering form of prejudice after another, is rapidly swept away. Thought, written and spoken, acts upon the mass of mind in this day of railroads and telegraphs, with a thousandfold more celerity than in the days of pillions and slow coaches. Scarce have the lips that uttered great thoughts ceased to move, or the pen which wrote them dropped from the weary hand, ere they vibrate through the inmost recesses of a thousand hearts, and awaken deep and true responses in a thousand living, truthful souls. Thence they grow, expand, fructify, and the result is Progress.

A Temperance Activist, 1853

A HEROIC WOMAN.—Mrs. Margaret Freeland, of Syracuse, was recently arrested upon a warrant issued on complaint of Emanuel Rosendale, a rum-seller, charging her with forcing an entrance to his house, and with stones and clubs smashing his doors and windows, breaking his tumblers and bottles, and turning over his whisky barrels and spilling their contents. Great excitement was produced by this novel case. It seems that the husband of Mrs. Freeland was a drunkard—that he was in the habit of abusing his wife, turning her out of doors, etc., and this was carried so far that the police frequently found it necessary to interfere to put a stop to his ill-treatment of his family. Rosendale, the complainant, furnished Freeland with the liquor which turned him into a demon. Mrs. Freeland had frequently told him of her sufferings and besought him to refrain from giving her husband the poison. But alas! she appealed to a heart of stone. He disregarded her entreaties and spurned her from his door. Driven to desperation she armed herself, broke into the house, drove out the base-hearted landlord and pro ceeded upon the work of destruction.

She was brought before the court and demanded a trial. The citizens employed Charles B. Sedgwick, Esq., as her counsel, and prepared to justify her assault upon legal grounds. Rosendale, being at once arrested on complaint of Thomas L. Carson for selling liquor unlawfully, and feeling the force of the storm that was gathering over his head, appeared before the Justice, withdrew his complaint against Mrs. Freeland, paid the costs, and gave bail on the complaint of Mr. Carson, to appear at the General Sessions, and answer to an indictment should there be one found.

Mrs. Freeland is said to be "the pious mother of a fine family of children, and a highly respectable member of the Episcopal Church."

✣ *E S S A Y S*

Ellen DuBois, a professor at the University of California at Los Angeles, argues forcefully in the first essay that the only true feminists of the nineteenth century were those women who agreed with Elizabeth Cady Stanton and Susan B. Anthony in rejecting the claim of the family on women's lives and insisting that women should be seen as individual citizens equal to men in all respects. By contrast, Ruth Bordin, a scholar affiliated with the Bentley Library in Michigan, contends in the second essay that the WCTU should also been seen as a "feminist" organization in spite of its goal of family protection and its rejection of many of Stanton and Anthony's ideas. How should "feminism" be defined? What activities and attitudes does that term properly encompass?

The Radicalism of the Woman Suffrage Movement: Notes Toward the Reconstruction of Nineteenth-Century Feminism

ELLEN DUBOIS

I would like to suggest an interpretation of nineteenth-century suffragism that reconciles the perceived radicalism of the woman suffrage movement with the historical centrality of the family to women's condition. My hy-

Reprinted from Ellen DuBois, "The Radicalism of the Woman Suffrage Movement," *Feminist Studies*, III, no. 1/2 (Fall 1975), 63–71. Used by permission of Ellen DuBois, Professor of History at UCLA.

pothesis is that the significance of the woman suffrage movement rested precisely on the fact that it bypassed women's oppression within the family, or private sphere, and demanded instead her admission to citizenship, and through it admission to the public arena. By focusing on the public sphere, and particularly on citizenship, suffragists demanded for women a kind of power and a connection with the social order not based on the institution of the family and their subordination within it.

Recent scholarship has suggested that the sharp distinction between public and private activities is a relatively modern historical phenomenon. . . . In seventeenth-century New England, all community functions—production, socialization, civil government, religious life—presumed the family as the basic unit of social organization. The whole range of social roles drew on familial roles. The adult male's position as producer, as citizen, as member of the church, all flowed from his position as head of the family. Similarly, women's exclusion from church and civil government and their secondary but necessary role in production coincided with their subordinate position within the family. A few women enjoyed unusual economic or social privileges by virtue of their family connections, but as Gerda Lerner has pointed out, this further demonstrated women's dependence on their domestic positions for the definition of their roles in community life.

By the nineteenth century, this relationship between family and society had undergone considerable change. Although the family continued to perform many important social functions, it was no longer the sole unit around which the community was organized. The concept of the "individual" had emerged to rival it. In the nineteenth century, we can distinguish two forms of social organization—one based on this new creature, the individual, the other based on the family. These overlapping but distinct structures became identified respectively as the public sphere and the private sphere. The emergence of a form of social organization not based on the family meant the emergence of social roles not defined by familial roles. This was equally true for women and men. But because women and men had different positions *within* the family, the existence of nonfamilial roles had different implications for the sexes. For women, the emergence of a public sphere held out the revolutionary possibility of a new way to relate to society not defined by their subordinate position within the family. . . .

The contradiction between the alternative to familial roles that activity in the public sphere offered and the exclusion of women from such activity was particularly sharp with respect to civil government. In seventeenth-century New England, citizenship was justified on the basis of familial position; the freeholder was at once the head of the household and a citizen. By contrast, nineteenth-century citizenship was posed as a direct relationship between the individual and his government. In other words, patriarchy was no longer the *official* basis of civil government in modern industrial democracy. However, in reality only men were permitted to become citizens. The exclusion of women from participation in political life in the early nineteenth century was so absolute and unchallenged that it did not require explicit proscription. It was simply assumed that political "persons" were male. The

U.S. Constitution did not specify the sex of citizens until the Fourteenth Amendment was ratified in 1869, after women had begun actively to demand the vote. Prior to that, the equation between "male" and "person," the term used in the Constitution, was implicit. The same by the way was true of the founding charter of the American Anti-Slavery Society. Written in 1833, it defined the society's membership as "persons," but for six years admitted only men into that category. . . .

Although suffragists accepted the peculiarly feminine character of the private sphere, their demand for the vote challenged the male monopoly on the public arena. This is what gave suffragism much of its feminist meaning. Suffragists accepted women's "special responsibility" for domestic activity, but refused to concede that it prohibited them from participation in the public sphere. Moreover, unlike the demand that women be admitted to trades, professions, and education, the demand for citizenship applied to all women and it applied to them all of the time—to the housewife as much as to the single, self-supporting woman. By demanding a permanent, public role for all women, suffragists began to demolish the absolute, sexually defined barrier marking the public world of men off from the private world of women. Even though they did not develop a critical analysis of domestic life, the dialectical relationship between public and private spheres transformed their demand for admission to the public sphere into a basic challenge to the entire sexual structure. Thus, although she never criticized women's role in the family, Stanton was still able to write: "One may as well talk of separate spheres for the two ends of the magnet as for man and woman; they may have separate duties in the same sphere, but their true place is together everywhere."

Suffragists' demand for a permanent, public role for all women allowed them to project a vision of female experience and action that went beyond the family and the subordination of women which the family upheld. Citizenship represented a relationship to the larger society that was entirely and explicitly outside the boundaries of women's familial relations. As citizens and voters, women would participate directly in society as individuals, not indirectly through their subordinate positions as wives and mothers. Mary Putnam Jacobi identified this as the revolutionary core of suffragism. The American state, she explained, is based on "individual cells," not households. She went on: "Confessedly, in embracing in this conception as women, we do introduce a change which, though in itself purely ideal, underlies all the practical issues now in dispute. In this essentially modern conception, women also are brought into direct relations with the state, independent of their 'mate' or 'brood'." Without directly attacking women's position within the private sphere, suffragists touched the nerve of women's subordinate status by contending that women might be something other than wives and mothers. "Womanhood is the great fact in her life," Stanton was fond of saying; "wifehood and motherhood are but incidental relations."

On one level, the logic behind the demand for women suffrage in a country professing republican principles is obvious, and suffragists made liberal use of the tradition and rhetoric of the Revolution. Yet this is not sufficient to explain why suffrage became the core of a *feminist* program, why enfranchisement was perceived as the key to female liberation. I hypothesize that because enfranchisement involved a way for women to relate to society independent of their familial relations, it was the key demand of nineteenth-century feminists. It was the cornerstone of a social movement that did not simply catalogue and protest women's wrongs in the existing sexual order, but revealed the possibility of an alternate sexual order. Unlike the tradition of female protest, from the moral reformers of the 1830s to the temperance women of the 1880s, which was based in the private sphere and sought to reinterpret women's place within it, suffragism focused squarely on the public sphere.

In part, the feminist, liberating promise of enfranchisement rested on the concrete power that suffragists expected to obtain with the vote. Suffragists expected women to use the ballot to protect themselves and to impose their viewpoint on political issues. They anticipated that by strategic use of their political power women would break open new occupations, raise the level of their wage scales to that of men, win strikes, and force reforms in marriage and family law in order to protect themselves from sexual abuse, the loss of their children, and the unchecked tyranny of their husbands. The demand for suffrage drew together protest against all these abuses in a single demand for the right to shape the social order by way of the public sphere. No longer content either with maternal influence over the future voter's character or an endless series of petitions from women to law makers, suffragists proposed that women participate directly in the political decisions that affected their lives. "Like all disfranchised classes, they began by asking to have certain wrongs redressed," Stanton wrote. But suffragism went beyond what she called "special grievances" to give women's protest "a larger scope.". . .

Even granted the greater power of the individual voter over political decisions that would affect her or his life, suffragists did not understand the ballot as merely a weapon with which to protect their interests in the political process. They also expected enfranchisement to transform woman's consciousness, to reanchor her self-image, not in the subordination of her familial role, but in the individuality and self-determination that they saw in citizenship. This was a particularly important aspect of the political thought of Elizabeth Cady Stanton, the chief ideologue of nineteenth-century suffragism. It is developed most fully in "Solitude of Self," the speech she thought her best. She wrote there: "Nothing strengthens the judgment and quickens the conscience like individual responsibility. Nothing adds such dignity to character as the recognition of one's self-sovereignty." Elsewhere, she wrote that, from the "higher stand-point" of enfranchisement, woman would become sensitive to the daily indignities which, without due appreciation for her own individuality, she ignored and accepted. She developed the theme of the impact of enfranchisement on women's self-concept most fully in a speech simply titled, "Self-Government the Best Means of Self-Development."

Given the impact on consciousness that suffragists expected from the vote, they generally refused to redirect their efforts toward such partial enfranchisements as municipal or school suffrage. Although these limited suffrages would give women certain political powers, they were suffrages designed especially for women and justified on the basis of women's maternal responsibilities. Their achievement would not necessarily prove women's right to full and equal participation in the public sphere. Suffragists did not simply want political power; they wanted to be citizens, to stand in the same relation to civil government as men did. As a result, it was primarily clubwomen who worked for school and municipal suffrage, while those who identified themselves as suffragists continued to concentrate on the admission of women to full citizenship.

An important index to the nature and degree of suffragism's challenge to the nineteenth-century sexual order was the kind and amount of opposition that it inspired. Antisuffragists focused on the family, its position *vis-à-vis* the state, and the revolutionary impact of female citizenship on that relation. In response to suffragists' demand that modern democracy include women, antisuffragists tried to reinstate a patriarchal theory of society and the state. The family, they contended, was the virtual, if not the official unit of civil government, and men represented and protected the women of their families in political affairs. Antisuffragists regularly charged that the enfranchisement of women would revolutionize the relations of the sexes and, in turn, the character and structure of the home and women's role within it. The 1867 New York Constitutional Convention expressed this fear for the future of the family when it rejected suffrage because it was an innovation "so revolutionary and sweeping, so openly at war with a distribution of duties and functions between the sexes as venerable and pervading as government itself, and involving transformations so radical in social and domestic life."

Most suffragists were much more modest about the implications of enfranchisement for women's position within the family. They expected reform of family law, particularly of the marriage contract, and the abolition of such inequities as the husband's legal right to his wife's sexual services. They also anticipated that the transformation in woman's consciousness which enfranchisement would bring would improve the quality of family relations, particularly between wife and husband. Stanton argued that once women were enfranchised they would demand that democracy be the law of the family, as well as of the state. Her comment suggests that, by introducing women into a form of social organization not based on patriarchal structures, she expected enfranchisement to permit women a much more critical perspective on the family itself. However, suffragists regularly denied the antisuffragists' charge that woman suffrage meant a revolution in the family.

Suffragists worked hard to attract large numbers of women to the demand for the vote. They went beyond the methods of agitational propaganda which they had learned as abolitionists, and beyond the skills of lobbying which they had developed during Radical Reconstruction, to become organizers. As suffragists' efforts at outreach intensified, the family-bound realities of most women's lives forced more and more domestic imagery into their rhetoric and their arguments. Yet suffrage remained a distinctly minority movement in the nineteenth century. The very thing that made suffragism the most radical aspect of nineteenth-century feminism—its focus on the public sphere and on a nonfamilial role for women—was the cause of its failure to establish a mass base. It was not that nineteenth-century women were content, or had no grievances, but that they understood their grievances in the context of the private sphere. The lives of most nineteenth-century women were overwhelmingly limited to the private realities of wifehood and motherhood, and they experienced their discontent in the context of those relations. The enormous success of the Women's Christian Temperance Union, particularly as contrasted with the nineteenth-century suffrage movement, indicates the capacity for protest and activism among nineteenth-century women, and the fact that this mass feminism was based in the private sphere. The WCTU commanded an army in the nineteenth century, while woman suffrage remained a guerrilla force.

Unlike the woman suffrage movement, the WCTU took as its starting point woman's position within the home; it catalogued the abuses she suffered there and it proposed reforms necessary to ameliorate her domestic situation. As the WCTU developed, its concerns went beyond the family to include the quality of community life, but its standard for nonfamilial relations remained the family and the moral values women had developed within it. The WCTU spoke to women in the language of their domestic realities, and they joined in the 1870s and 1880s in enormous numbers. Anchored in the private realm, the WCTU became the mass movement that nineteenth-century suffragism could not.

The WCTU's program reflected the same social reality that lay beyond suffragism—that the family was losing its central place in social organization to nondomestic institutions, from the saloon to the school to the legislature, and that woman's social power was accordingly weakened. Yet the WCTU, Luddite-like, defended the family and women's traditional but fast-fading authority within it. Its mottos reflected this defensive goal: "For God and Home and Native Land"; "Home Protection." In 1883, the WCTU formally endorsed the demand for female enfranchisement, but justified its action as necessary to protect the home and women within it, thus retaining its family-based analysis and its defensive character. The first resolutions introduced by Frances Willard in support of suffrage asked for the vote for women in their roles as wives and mothers, to enable them to protect their homes from the influence of the saloon. This was the woman suffrage movement's approach to female oppression and the problem of spheres stood on its head—women entering the public arena to protect the primacy of the private sphere, and women's position within it. Yet, the very fact that the WCTU had to come to terms with suffrage and eventually supported it indicates that the woman suffrage movement had succeeded in becoming the defining focus of nineteenth-century feminism, with respect to which all organized female protest had to orient itself. Even though the WCTU organized and commanded the forces, the woman suffrage movement had defined the territory.

Suffrage became a mass movement in the twentieth century under quite different conditions, when women's position *vis-à-vis* the public and private spheres had shifted considerably. Despite, or perhaps because of, the home-based ideology with which they operated, the WCTU, women's clubs, and other branches of nineteenth-century feminism had introduced significant numbers of women to extradomestic concerns. Charlotte Perkins Gilman noted the change among women in 1903: "The socialising of this hitherto subsocial, wholly domestic class, is a marked and marvellous event, now taking place with astonishing rapidity." Similarly, Susan B. Anthony commented at the 1888 International Council of Women: "Forty years ago women had no place anywhere except in their homes, no pecuniary independence, no purpose in life save that which came through marriage. . . . [I]n later years the way has been opened to every avenue of industry—to every profession. . . . What is true in the world of work is true in education, is true everywhere." At the point that it could attract a mass base, suffragism no longer opened up such revolutionary vistas for women; they were already operating in the public world of work and politics. The scope and meaning of twentieth-century suffragism requires its own analysis, but the achievement of nineteenth-century suffragists was that they identified, however haltingly, a fundamental transformation of the family and the new possibilities for women's emancipation that this revealed.

The Temperance Crusade as a Feminist Movement

RUTH BORDIN

Although temperance was not a new cause for women in the last quarter of the nineteenth century, the character of women's participation changed drastically in the 1870s, as did their relationship to the temperance movement as a whole. Temperance became a cause that large numbers of women actively embraced, and women in turn became the most important force in the temperance movement. Also, by the 1880s temperance had become the issue that drew tens of thousands of women to rally behind general women's and reformist causes and demand a more equal share in the political process. Through temperance, which women saw as protection of the home, women from many social and economic strata were caught up in feminist goals. Women joined the Woman's Christian Temperance Union, the major temperance organization for women, in numbers that far surpassed their participation in any other women's organization in the nineteenth century and that made the WCTU the first women's mass movement.

Ruth Bordin, *Woman and Temperance,* 3–14, 156–62. Copyright © 1981 by Temple University. Reprinted by permission of Temple University Press.

By 1892 the WCTU had nearly 150,000 dues-paying members. Including auxiliaries, such as the Young Woman's Christian Temperance Union (known as the Y's), its membership was well over 200,000. In 1892 only 20,000 women were affiliated with the General Federation of Women's Clubs, and in 1893 there were roughly 13,000 dues-paying members of the National American Woman Suffrage Association. Temperance was clearly the cause women found most attractive in the late nineteenth century. The WCTU was the largest organization of women that had existed until that time, and the size and influence of other women's groups were not comparable. . . .

Why did women flock in such impressive numbers to the temperance cause in the mid-1870s? Why this sudden acceleration in commitment? The answer requires first of all some explanation of the general attractiveness of temperance as a women's issue in the nineteenth century.

There seems little doubt that the temperance movement developed in response to a social evil that was both real and widespread. Nineteenth-century Americans were heavy users of strong drink, and alcohol was believed to be necessary as food, as a beverage, and as a generally available medicinal drug and anesthetic. Water in urban areas was frequently scarce or unsafe, and milk was dangerous, carrying tuberculosis, undulant fever, and other diseases even when it was fresh. Milk was also expensive. Distilled spirits were cheap. Alcohol was also thought to be necessary for supplying the energy for hard physical labor and providing the internal warmth that made outdoor work bearable in cold northern winters. Spirits were the most commonly available anesthetic and analgesic, and alcohol's place in the pharmacopeoia was generally accepted by the medical profession. In other words, strong drink was an accepted part of nineteenth-century life. . . .

Alcohol abuse was a real and pressing personal and social problem. It was also perceived as a problem from which women suffered disproportionately although they were not the offenders. In the late nineteenth century serious drinking was considered a male prerogative, and the American saloon, except for hangers-on like prostitutes, was almost exclusively a male institution. At the same time, women saw the saloon as a pervasive and pernicious influence on their lives. This perception was based on reality. The nineteenth-century drunkard's reputation as a wife beater, child abuser, and sodden, irresponsible nonprovider was not undeserved. Susan B. Anthony, addressing the National American Woman Suffrage Association at its meeting in Chicago in 1875, emphasized that women were the greatest sufferers from drunkenness, and graphically pictured the virtuous woman in legal subjection to a drunken husband. Anthony was repeating a widely held belief, echoing what was considered a truism at the time. Any reading of letters, diaries, newspaper articles, and books written by women in the 1870s shows that it was as victims of alcohol abuse that women were attracted to the temperance movement even before they had their own temperance organizations.

A woman also suffered severe legal disadvantages in the 1870s that left her especially vulnerable to the abuses of an alcoholic husband. Women did not usually control their own wages and had no claim on their husbands' earnings. A husband could not only drink up his pay, but anything a wife might earn as well. Although between 1839 and 1850 most states had passed some kind of legislation that recognized the right of married women to own property, this legislation did not remove all legal restrictions, and previous gains were sometimes lost in the courts. An 1879 Ohio decision stated outright that a husband had a property interest in his wife. She was not entitled to her own wages and must rely solely on her husband's pledge and promise to support her. As late as 1900, in thirty-seven states, a woman possessed no rights to her children, and all her possessions were her husband's property. Nowhere in the 1870s did women possess full suffrage, although some women could vote in school elections in Kentucky and Kansas. Given a woman's limited legal rights, the drunkard as head of the household was seen as a true oppressor of his wife and family. The drunken husband epitomized the evils of a society in which women were second-class citizens, in ways that no sober (however tyrannical) husband and father could.

Although women were attracted to the temperance cause from its beginnings because they were frequent victims of alcohol abuse, other factors contributed to the enthusiasm with which they flocked to its banners. Not unimportant was the congeniality of temperance as a cause with the nineteenth century's dominant sexual ideology, the doctrine of spheres. Men functioned in the world of politics and commerce; women presided over the spiritual and physical maintenance of home and family. Woman, as the protector of the home and the nurturer of children, had a compelling duty to save these sacred trusts from external threat. In the early temperance movement she was expected to exercise this duty through practicing moral suasion and setting a good example. The emphasis of the early temperance movement was on individual redemption and personal abstinence, and women were expected to use their influence at home to convert their husbands, sons, and brothers from drinking. However, in a sense the drink issue was itself to prove subversive to the maintenance of a strict division between the sexual spheres. As soon as the temperance movement began to look to coercive legal solutions such as local option or prohibition, moral suasion was admitted to be an ineffective weapon, and it became apparent that if women were to continue their commitment to temperance, their role must inevitably move into the public realm. At the same time the old concept provided the rationale for this leap into the outer world. If the saloon was a threat to home and hearth, was it not a woman's duty to invade the public sphere to defend what was universally acceded to be her special area of responsibility? To many temperance women, therefore, participation in the post–Civil War movement took place on a basis that did not fundamentally alter the ideology that held women responsible for the welfare of the home.

Jill Conway has pointed out that while women activists were achieving a real change in female behavior after the Civil War, this new activism did not for most of them result in a similarly new view of the female temperament or women's sphere. They still accepted women's role as one of nurturant domesticity. They wielded power, but their conceptions of what women could do did not immediately change to fit this new-found power. In the temperance movement women could view themselves as protecting the home. In this sense it was a maternal struggle. If they committed public acts, took public stands, it was only in their role as nurturant mothers who must insure a good environment for those dependent on them. The WCTU was a "safe" women's movement. But its members nonetheless were never completely sure about the nature of their public role. They frequently avowed their complete disinterest in activism for anything but altruistic purposes, and at the same time they pointed with pride to the widening spheres of women. These women were much like the settlement-house women who followed them, moralists and idealists who believed literally in their responsibility to help their fellow human beings—in this case by removing them from contact with the evils of drink.

June Sochen has labeled women who joined organizations like the WCTU "pragmatic feminists," in contrast to the ideologists. They identified specific grievances from which women suffered and tried to do something about them. They did not want to change traditional sex roles. They did not argue, at least at first, for women's rights as such. They were firm believers in "true womanhood," but they did push for widening spheres. They marked out an area that they felt concerned them deeply, the evils of drink, and directly attempted to do something about it. Frances Willard could describe the WCTU as an organization whose "broad sympathies . . . ministered to all good and true women who are willing to clasp hands in one common effort to protect their homes and loved ones from the ravages of drink . . . without a peer among the sisterhoods that have grouped themselves around the cross of Christ."

Another factor that no doubt contributed to the ease with which women flocked to temperance in the 1870s was the presence of an already existing network through which women could function in the temperance cause. The missionary societies of the several Protestant denominations, as well as the churches themselves, provided already functioning female networks that could be converted into WCTU chapters. The temperance movement, the WCTU in particular, was ecumenical from the beginning, and in this it differed from church groups such as missionary societies; but the WCTU was certainly church-oriented, and almost all of its members were church-going Protestants. . . .

By the last decades of the century a clear line had been drawn between the proper sphere of economic activities for poor women and their middle and upper-class sisters. As industrialization removed the urban worker from the home-related store or workshop, the working-class woman remained part of the work force, but the owner-entrepreneur-manager, even the clerk, left the women of his family at home solely occupied with domestic duties. The middle-class woman was no longer expected to make a direct contribution to family income. She was to be supported by her male relatives. Being able to support women in relative leisure and not to depend on their wages became a significant criterion of a man's movement into the middle class. The immigrant who had prospered to the point where his wife and daughters no longer went out to work for wages had moved up the social ladder. For the first time, rearing children and managing the household became a full-time job for large numbers of women. Housekeeping and parenting have considerable economic value, as anyone who has purchased these services outside the family well knows; still, by the last quarter of the nineteenth century, middle and upper-class urban women had lost their role as direct financial contributors to family income.

It is easy to exaggerate the degree of leisure that resulted. However, this relinquishing of economic responsibility was accompanied by ready availability of servants who provided relief from much of the sheer drudgery of household tasks. Aileen Kraditor believes the feminist movement was at least in part a result of the mass Irish migration that began in the mid-nineteenth century, providing American middle-class women with a large measure of domestic service for the first time and giving them the leisure to participate in reform activities. This service was performed for urban middle-class Southern women by freed blacks who had left the plantations after the Civil War. The availability of servants also left the young mother less closely confined by the care of small children. Women had some hours in the afternoon when they were free of immediate household responsibility.

Moreover, the birth rate was falling. The average number of children born to a white woman fell from 7.04 in 1800 to 4.24 in 1880 to 3.56 in 1900. Since women were having fewer children, less time was absorbed by pregnancy and the care of infants and young children, which increased their leisure and left them with more energy for outside concerns.

The number of women enjoying this leisure had to be large enough to support a mass movement. Thousands of presidents, secretaries, and superintendents were necessary to staff the WCTU's many chapters at the local level. Anyone who has participated in an activist, reformist, volunteer club knows how much time leadership, even on the local level, can require. By the 1870s enough women had the necessary leisure.

Also, they were gathered in urban areas where they could associate easily. Over six million people lived in urban places by 1860, nearly ten million by 1870, over fourteen million by 1880, and thirty million by 1900. Most of these towns and cities could easily be canvassed on foot. This made possible easy interaction and collaboration by women with a common cause. While many of the women now congregated in urban areas worked for a living, some of their middle-class sisters were probably in need of meaningful occupation. Women whose services were less visibly essential to the family's economic well-being would have a void to fill. They would search for and be easily enlisted in activities that were complementary and appropriate to the sphere in which they were expected to function, the home. And the problems the WCTU attacked were closely related especially at first to the domestic sphere, although this base rapidly broadened. The Industrial Revolution had created a class of women with leisure who were likely to be receptive to new ideas and activities. Simultaneously it created a society with glaring social evils to which women responded by urging reform— women who had time to see, investigate, and respond to these problems.

Another factor that promoted the mass growth of the WCTU was the marked increase in the number of women exposed to at least a common school education. There was by the 1870s an educated clientele for a mass movement. As early as 1850 more than 50 percent of school-age white females were attending school. What probably is equally important, most United States elementary schools were coeducational. As the number of children exposed to a common school education came to represent a major segment of the United States population, more and more women reached adulthood having already shared a common experience with men outside the home. Although both sexes received the same schooling, as adults women were not accepted on equal terms as potential leaders in organizations where they shared membership privileges with men. The WCTU offered them opportunities for creative service and self-fulfillment that they were unlikely to find elsewhere. The National American Woman Suffrage Association had male officers as well as male members. Men clearly played a major part in managing its affairs. The right of women to take leadership roles in Protestant churches was severely limited. But not in the WCTU. Here the women themselves were exclusively in charge. . . .

The Woman's Christian Temperance Union was unquestionably the first mass movement of American women. It had no competitors in size of membership or breadth and depth of local organization. It cut across sectional, racial, and ethnic boundaries, sheltering under its broad umbrella women from nearly every sector of American life. The Union penetrated into small towns and large cities. Among its members were seamstresses and the wives of artisans and clerks; women physicians, lawyers, clerics, and educators joined its ranks; the wives of business and professional men flocked to its banners. The Union also pioneered in being the first sizable organization controlled exclusively by women. Although women were major participants in church and charitable activities by the 1870s, that participation, except perhaps on the local level, was expected to stop short of leadership or control: women supplied the membership and men exercised the authority. From its beginning the Union excluded males from voting membership. As a result men never competed for leadership roles, and women ran the entire organization, including its affiliated business enterprises. Because the WCTU was entirely a women's institution, unlike the National American Woman Suffrage Association and the foreign missionary society movement, it became the major vehicle for active leadership by women on the local, state, and national levels. Frances Willard became a national heroine. The activities of the WCTU received national press coverage, and thousands of women in local Unions found their cause and their own contributions commented on from the hometown pulpit and reported in the local press. Through the WCTU, women became visible as leaders in communities and cities from coast to coast. . . .

Starting with the Crusade itself, the Union became one of the most powerful instruments of women's consciousness-raising of all time. Through the Union women learned of their legal and social disabilities, gained confidence in their strengths and talents, and became certain of their political power as a group and as individuals. The Union elevated the personal and civil consciences of large numbers of women and provided the underpinning for the surge of interest in woman's suffrage after 1900 that made the Nineteenth Amendment possible. Before 1873 most Union women had worked only in their churches. By 1900 they had a full generation's experience behind them in political action, legislation, lobbying, and running private charitable institutions.

In 1870 the suffrage movement was more advanced in its demands than many women were prepared to venture. The movement asked for equal rights and the vote, a clear call for a place in public life. Most suffragists, especially the radical wing led by Elizabeth Cady Stanton and Susan B. Anthony, rebelled against the ideology of separate spheres of life for the sexes, and asked women to support changes in role and self-image that were radically different from existing norms. The immediate result for the suffrage movement was that it could not and did not succeed in attracting mass support for its goals until another kind of woman's movement had bridged the gap between the way most women perceived themselves and the equal rights stance of the militant suffragists. In discussing this aspect of the WCTU's role, Janet Zollinger Giele called the temperance woman a consolidator and the suffragist a pioneer. This assessment is partly true. Temperance women were slower than suffragists to ask for the vote, but nineteenth-century Union activism in crucial ways made success possible for suffrage in the twentieth century. Most of all, the WCTU pioneered in local organization. As WCTU members, women learned how to organize, and eventually they put this knowledge to work in the campaign for the vote. And the Union was not always a follower. The suffrage movement advocated the woman's ballot earlier, but the Union was quicker to ally itself with organized labor, endorse the kindergarten, and advocate safer working conditions for women.

Ellen DuBois has argued that the WCTU's coming to terms with woman suffrage in the early 1880s demonstrates that the suffrage movement succeeded in making the woman's ballot the focus of nineteenth-century feminism. Because suffragists explicitly demanded that women be admitted to the political sphere in the 1870s, they challenged the nineteenth-century concept that the public sphere was an exclusively male domain. DuBois among others has pointed out that the WCTU was able to join the suffragists in their goals while avoiding the issue of spheres through its emphasis on the home-protection ballot. It is true that WCTU women, as had Catharine Beecher's teachers before them, entered the public sphere in the 1870s (and some as late as the 1880s) only as guardians of the home. However, the union did not stay at this transitional phase for long. By the 1890s natural rights replaced home protection in the WCTU's arguments for the ballot. The Union's support of a dozen political and social causes put it clearly in the public sphere, and in fact it was a pioneer in its support of broad social reform movements that the suffrage movement for tactical reasons would not touch. Perhaps instead of being criticized for its oblique approach to the suffrage question, the Union should be credited with putting the focus of feminism on reform, on social feminism rather than the ballot, on emphasizing suffrage as only the means to a broader end. Indeed, to the extent that these broad aims were lost sight of in the first decades of the twentieth century, the ballot proved a sterile victory. The larger social and economic disabilities of women remained untouched, and the battle had to be fought all over again two generations later. But in the nineteenth century the WCTU did succeed in fastening its definition of social feminism on the woman's movement, and with its tens of thousands of members it did provide the mass base from which the twentieth-century suffrage movement could take off. Without the Union's legacy of activism and political experience, the suffrage cause could never have expanded as rapidly in its final two decades. . . .

The WCTU was not only a mass movement that made substantial contributions to both the goals and the accomplishments of the nineteenth-century woman's movement; it also widely embraced diverse ethnic, sectional, and racial groups. Although thin in numbers, the mere presence of blacks, native Americans, and immigrants, and southerners too (who were numerically more important), contributed to the Union's claim to represent American womanhood. And like the conservative southerners, representatives from these minority groups attended conventions and were introduced from platforms, listened to in debate, and appointed to office. The evidence also confirms that while the Union was essentially middle and upper-class in its national leadership, lower-class women were able to find a meaningful niche in the Union. A black washerwoman occupied the position of Superintendent of Colored Work in Indiana in 1884. Skilled tradesmen's wives joined the Ohio Crusaders in 1873. A grocery clerk's wife shared responsibility with the wives of San Diego's leading businessmen in managing a facility for indigent women and children in the 1880s. The *Union Signal*'s pages contain communications from many ordinary housewives in modest circumstances with no particular talents, as well as reports on the activities of their more gifted sisters. The more deeply one looks at the membership of the WCTU the more one perceives its diversity. Temperance touched a chord that united women of many backgrounds.

The demographic characteristics of the leadership of the WCTU have been examined several times. While membership in the WCTU covers a broad spectrum, all studies agree that the women who led the WCTU in the nineteenth century were primarily white, well-educated, economically prosperous native-born Protestants of Anglo-Saxon ancestry. With the possible exception of religious affiliation (the WCTU had a larger proportion of women who participated in enthusiastic religious sects, such as Methodism) Union leaders differ little from what we know of the leaders of other women's reform groups of the time. . . .

That temperance was chosen as the focal point of the only major woman's movement that grew spectacularly in the nineteenth century and attracted a substantial measure of mass support, is only partially explained by the social respectability of the temperance cause and its widespread acceptance among the Protestant churches. Temperance is primarily a problem of control. The inebriate has lost control, and it is difficult for either the alcoholic or those around him to reestablish that control. Women suffered from this lack of control in more than one way. A drunken relative might put their lives in disarray, but they also had no legal and political control over their own destinies. Ohio women who took to the streets in the Crusade of 1873–74 could not vote on the constitutional provisions that would regulate the liquor trade, and they were restive under that disability.

Perhaps the WCTU's success represented a symbolic crusade. Joseph Gusfield coined that phrase to describe the century-long temperance campaign that resulted in passage of the Eighteenth Amendment. He argues that temperance advocates used the temperance movement to legislate personal behavior for groups that were threatening the status and power of the dominant majority. He speculates about the loss of political control experienced by a native-born rural Protestant population that was being rapidly outnumbered by a massive wave of immigration from central and eastern Europe at the same time that its economic and social clout was threatened by the new industrial urban society.

However, the words "symbolic crusade" can be used in another way. Women's attraction to temperance in the last quarter of the nineteenth century can be explained in terms of symbolism. Nothing was as destructive to a powerless woman's existence as a drunken husband. He could destroy both her and her family. Most of the fiction in the *Union Signal* repeats the same story over and over again: A woman and her children are abused and destroyed by a husband and father addicted to drink. The wife and mother has no legal remedies. She has no political remedies. She is forced to suffer from this lack of control. In the Crusade first, and later in the WCTU, women *were* taking control. The women who marched in Ohio shut down saloons. Mary Hunt and her cohorts successfully compelled legislatures to enact laws that required temperance education in the schools. Local option to close saloons became an alternative in hundreds of communities because of laws the Union shepherded through state legislatures. The WCTU was the major vehicle for the women's movement in the last quarter of the nineteenth century not only because of its impressively large membership, but also because it got things done. Women were taking real control over a part of their lives and the society to which they belonged. In this sense a symbolic crusade was under way. Temperance became the medium through which nineteenth-century women expressed their deeper, sometimes unconscious, feminist concerns.

FURTHER READING

Barbara Berg, *The Remembered Gate: Origins of American Feminism* (1978)

Ruth Bordin, *Frances Willard* (1987)

Ellen DuBois, *Feminism and Suffrage: The Emergence of an Independent Women's Movement in America, 1848–1869* (1978)

Barbara Epstein, *The Politics of Domesticity: Women, Evangelism, and Temperance in Nineteenth-Century America* (1980)

Eleanor Flexner, *Century of Struggle* (1959)

Elisabeth Griffith, *In Her Own Right: The Life of Elizabeth Cady Stanton* (1984)

Blanche Hersh, *The Slavery of Sex: Feminist-Abolitionists in Nineteenth-Century America* (1978)

William Leach, *True Love and Perfect Union: The Feminist Reform of Sex and Society* (1980)

Keith Melder, *Beginnings of Sisterhood: The American Women's Rights Movement, 1800–1850* (1977)

William O'Neill, *Everyone Was Brave: The Rise and Fall of Feminism in America* (1968)

Peggy Rabkin, *Fathers to Daughters: The Legal Foundations of Female Emancipation* (1980)

Kathryn Kish Sklar, *Catharine Beecher* (1973)

CHAPTER
9

Victorian Sexuality

Nineteenth-Century Americans—especially physicians—produced innumerable volumes of advice on sexual behavior addressed to men and women. Many authors contended that women felt little or no sexual passion; such a belief accorded well with the tenets of the ''cult of domesticity'' on the subject of women's natural purity. By contrast, the experts acknowledged men's sexual desires but nonetheless promoted the view that the excessive loss of sperm through masturbation or sexual intercourse would deprive men of strength needed for other, more important endeavours, including preserving their own health or advancing their careers. The primary message of the sexual advice literature was, then, that both men and women should engage in sexual activity only in moderation, even in marriage.

These themes pervade the published materials. But are such widely studied tracts representative of Victorian thinking about sexuality? Some have argued not, asserting that other lesser-known but equally popular works presented their readers with more realistic views. In any event, the historian's main problem is to determine what relationship the ideology bore to reality, since even in diaries nineteenth-century Americans revealed little about their sexual behavior, that most private aspect of their lives. Did white middle-class Americans actually follow the advice in such tracts? Can we know anything about the sexual lives of working-class people? And finally, what of same-sex relationships, particularly among women, which the authors of the advice literature never mentioned at all until the very end of the century?

❖ DOCUMENTS

In the first document, written in 1839, the American Female Moral Reform Society warned mothers about the dangers that masturbation posed for their children. That same decade (1833), Dr. Sylvester Graham lectured young men on the importance of sexual self-control, even within marriage; his advice appears as the second selection. In the 1890s Clelia Duel Mosher, a doctor, began asking some of her female patients about their sexual practices. Although she never formally analyzed her findings, historians have come to rely heavily on her survey of forty-five women; four extracts from longer questionnaires are included here as the third document.

M. Carey Thomas, later president of Bryn Mawr College, recorded in her journal in the 1870s comments on her love for other young women she met while attending school and later Cornell University; the fourth selection consists of excerpts from her journal. These documents suggest some discrepancies between the attitudes toward sex in prescriptive literature and actual attitudes and behaviors among nineteenth-century women.

A Warning to Mothers from the
Female Moral Reform Society, 1839

Beloved Sisters,

Will you permit an associated band, most of whom share responsibilities similar to your own, and know with yourselves the deep yearnings of maternal love, to call your attention, for a few moments, to a forbidding, but most important subject. Be assured that nothing but the fixed conviction that it is a subject affecting the temporal and eternal well-being of the young immortals committed to your care, would induce us to commend it to your consideration through the Press. We refer to a species of licentiousness from which neither age nor sex is exempt; a vice that has done its work of ruin, physical, mental, and moral, when no eye but that of Omniscience could behold it, a vice that has been practised in ten thousand instances, without a correct knowledge of its consequences, or its guilt, until it has paved the way for the most revolting excesses in crime. . . .

Recently it has pleased, our Heavenly Father to bring before our minds a flood of light, by which we have been solemnly convinced, that in nine cases out of ten, "solitary vice" [masturbation] is the first cause of social licentiousness, and the foundation and hidden source of the present corrupt state of society. . . .

The dangers to which all classes of the rising generation are exposed, are great beyond expression, they are dangers, too, that may stain the soul with guilt, and yet elude the vigilance of the most watchful parent, unless obviated *from the cradle,* by proper training and correct instruction. . . .

"A pupil in a select school, a child but ten years of age, confessed to her teacher, that she had been guilty of the sin alluded to for years, although she had never been taught it, and knew not that any one living practised it but herself. Her mind was fast sinking, she was wholly unable to reckon even small sums. This child had been religiously educated, but she was reared where the table was made a snare. Rich and high seasoned food, and abundance of dainties were given her, bathing was neglected, and a precocious development of the passions, and their consequent indulgence, was, in this case, the result."

"A child, under 12 years of age, whose morals in every respect had been carefully guarded, and who had never, except in one instance, been exposed, to the influence of an evil associate; on being questioned by her mother, confessed with tears that the sin had been taught her by the suspected individual."

"A son of a highly respectable physician, under three years of age, with no teacher but depraved instinct, had become so addicted to this pernicious habit, that the mother was obliged to provide a close night dress, and watch his waking hours with unceasing care." . . .

"A theological student, of superior mind and high attainments, deservedly beloved by numerous friends, and eminently fitted to be the centre of attraction in the highest circles of refinement, became a subject of this debasing vice. Presently his health failed, and abused reason deserted his throne. He was carried from the seminary to his friends, a maniac, and after lingering a few days, was ushered into the presence of his Judge."

A physician, who has long had an extensive practice in this city, confidently affirms that most of the young men in feeble health, who go south, to escape or recover from consumption, are the victims of this body and soul-destroying sin. . . .

Sylvester Graham's Advice to Young Men on Chastity, 1833

All kinds of stimulating and heating substances; high-seasoned food; rich dishes; the free use of flesh; and even the excess of aliment; all, more or less,—and some to a very great degree—increase the concupiscent excitability and sensibility of the genital organs, and augment their influence on the functions of organic life, and on the intellectual and moral faculties. . . .

The convulsive paroxysms attending venereal indulgence, are connected with the most intense excitement, and cause the most powerful agitation to the whole system, that it is ever subject to. The brain, stomach, heart, lungs, liver, skin—and the other organs—feel it sweeping over them, with the tremendous violence of a tornado. The powerfully excited and convulsed heart drives the blood, in fearful congestion, to the principal viscera,—producing oppression, irritation, debility, rupture, inflammation, and sometimes disorganization;—and this violent paroxysm is generally succeeded by great exhaustion, relaxation, lassitude, and even prostration.

These excesses, too frequently repeated, cannot fail to produce the most terrible effects. The nervous system, even to its most minute filamentary extremities, is tortured into a shocking state of debility, and excessive irritability, and uncontrolable mobility, and aching sensibility: and the vital contractility of the muscular tissues throughout the whole system, becomes exceedingly impaired, and the muscles generally, become relaxed and flaccid; and consequently, all the organs and vessels of the body, even to the smallest capillaries, become extremely debilitated; and their functional power, exceedingly feeble. . . .

Though every young man, of any correct moral discipline, must consider a promiscuous and unrestrained commerce between the sexes, as equally destructive to sound morality, and social peace, and civil welfare; yet most young men are apt to think, that if it were not for the moral, and social, and civil disadvantages, such a state of lawless intercourse were exceedingly desirable. But they who entertain this sentiment, are not aware, that moral and civil laws, so far as they are right and proper, are only the verbal forms of laws which are constitutionally established in our nature. They do not consider, that, however destitute society might be, of all moral and civil restraints, in regard to sexual commerce; yet, there are fixed and permanent laws, established in their very constitutions, which they cannot violate, without inevitably incurring penalty;—and that, in the present depraved state of man's instinctive propensities, such a lawless commerce, would, with the certainty of necessity, lead to the most calamitous and loathsome diseases and sufferings, that human nature is capable of enduring! Many of the most terrible plagues which have swept over the earth, and threatened to depopulate it, have been connected with such excesses! . . .

Marriage—or a permanent and exclusive connexion of one man with one woman—is an institution founded in the constitutional nature of things, and inseparably connected with the highest welfare of man, as an individual and as a race! And so intimately associated are the animal and moral sensibilities and enjoyments of man, that, besides the physical and social evils which result from illicit commerce between the sexes, the chaste and delicate susceptibilities of the moral affections are exceedingly depraved, and the transgressor renders himself incapable of those pure and exalted enjoyments which are found in connubial life, where perfect chastity has been preserved. . . .

The mere fact that a man is married to one woman, and is perfectly continent to her, will by no means prevent the evils which flow from sexual excess, if his commerce with her exceeds the bounds of that connubial chastity which is founded on the real wants of the system. Beyond all question, an immeasurable amount of evil results to the human family, from sexual excess within the precincts of wedlock. Languor, lassitude, muscular relaxation, general debility and heaviness, depression of spirits, loss of appetite, indigestion, faintness and sinking at the pit of the stomach, increased susceptibilities of the skin and lungs to all the atmospheric changes, feebleness of circulation, chilliness, head-ache, melancholy, hypochondria, hysterics, feebleness of all the senses, impaired vision, loss of sight, weakness of the lungs, nervous cough, pulmonary consumption, disorders of the liver and kidneys, urinary difficulties, disorders of the genital organs, weakness of the brain, loss of memory, epilepsy, insanity, apoplexy,—and extreme feebleness and early death of offspring,—are among the too common evils which are caused by sexual excesses between husband and wife. . . .

It is, therefore, impossible to lay down a precise rule, which will be equally adapted to all men, in regard to the frequency of their connubial commerce. But as a general rule, it may be said, to the healthy and robust; it were better for you, not to exceed in the frequency of your indulgencies, the number of months in the year; and you cannot exceed the number of weeks in the year, without impairing your constitutional powers, shortening your lives, and increasing your liability to disease and suffering; if indeed, you do not thereby actually induce disease of the worst and most painful kind; and at the same time transmit to your offspring an impaired constitution, with strong and unhappy predispositions. . . .

Extracts from the Mosher Survey, 1892–1913

Number 1

(Respondent Number 1 was twenty-five when interviewed in 1892. A former music teacher, she had been married for two and one-half years and had one child, age six months.)

What knowledge of Sexual Physiology had you before marriage?
Knew process of ovulation & menstruation in fairly well-defined way. [Hence] knew when conception was likely to take place & why. Very little about male sexual physiology. Knew, in regard to intercourse, condition of man at time [hence] necessity also need of self-control; danger of its occurring too often; time when woman was supposed to desire intercourse, if ever; best time for conception, as regards health of mother & child; several means of preventing conception. Realized little how important it is to a man and how much self-control it may entail. Did not suppose it was often desired by women. Considered that it sh'd be regulated largely by the woman.

Did conception occur by choice or by accident?
Accident.

Habit of intercourse? Average number of times per month?
Two or three times. Before conception, once or at most twice per month.

Was intercourse held during pregnancy?
No.
  Did you desire it at this period?
  Occasionally during first months. Not at all, during last half—or more.

At other times have you any desire for intercourse?
Yes.
  How often?
  Once or twice a month.
  At what time in relation to your menses?
  Immediately after. Occasionally just before—and rarely at some other time. Except in 1st case, it is scarcely ever except when there is some outside exciting cause.

Is intercourse agreeable to you or not?
Usually.

Do you always have a venereal orgasm?
No.

What do you believe to be the purpose of intercourse?
  Necessity to the man?
  Yes.
  To the woman?
  No.
  Reproduction?
  Yes. Primarily.

Have you ever used any means to prevent conception? If so, what? What was the effect on your health?
Thin rubber covering for man. Depended on so-called "safety week" at first.
I have not perceived any effect on my health.

Number 10

(Respondent Number 10 was twenty-six, married for two and one-half years, when interviewed in 1894. She had two children.)

What knowledge of sexual physiology had you before marriage?
Very slight.
   How did you obtain it?
   Mostly from *Tokology* [a popular sexual guide].

Did conception occur by choice or accident?
First conception by choice. Second by accident.

Habit of intercourse, average number of times?
1st time 5 months after marriage. Then not until 7 mos. after our first child was born. After that twice a week usually.

Was intercourse held during pregnancy? If so, how often?
Not during first pregnancy. Yes during second pregnancy. Once or twice a week until 6th or 7th month. Not after that.
   Had you any desire for it during this period?
   Yes, at times.

At other times have you any desire for intercourse?
Yes.
   At what time in relation to your menses?
   Immediately after menstruation.

Is intercourse agreeable to you or not?
Yes.

Do you always have a venereal orgasm?
No, but usually.
   When you do,
   Effect immediately afterwards?
   I think there is more exhaustion.

What do you believe to be the true purpose of intercourse?
   Necessity to man? to woman?
   No. [The woman's single negative response applied to both sexes.]
   Pleasure?
   Not solely.
   Reproduction?
   What other reasons beside reproduction are sufficient to warrant intercourse?

I think to the man and woman married from love, it may be used *temperately*, as one of the highest manifestations of love, granted us by our Creator.

Have you ever used any means to prevent conception?
Yes.
  If so, what?
  Sulphate of zinc. It is not infallible.
  Effect on your health?
  None.

What, to you, would be an ideal habit?
Occasional intercourse, with control over conception (?), everything to be absolutely mutual.

Number 35

(Respondent Number 35 was interviewed in 1897, when she was fifty-three. She had had six children and six miscarriages—twelve pregnancies in all— during more than twenty-eight years of marriage.)

What knowledge of sexual physiology had you before marriage?
Slight from girls. Mother taught her that such things were not only not talked about but also not thought of. School child at 14 told [her] what intercourse was. [She] was shocked and didn't believe it.

Habit of intercourse, average number of times per week?
[Average once a week,] sometimes oftener, sometimes less often.

Was intercourse held during pregnancy? If so, how often?
About average. Not so often during last 2 mo.
  Had you any desire for it during this period?
  [Often] more desire than at other times, and she needed it. "Nothing would ease my nervous condition but that."

At other times have you any desire for intercourse?
Yes. Very soon after period, [it is] more agreeable. Sometimes just before [period]. Much of time could have blotted [it] out and never missed it. Then another time wanted it. [She prefers intercourse] when not too tired, just before and just after [menses].

Is intercourse agreeable to you or not?
Yes, when not too tired & conditions are right.

Do you always have a venereal orgasm?
Always when she desires. Many times not.
  When you do,
  Effect immediately afterwards?
  Sleepy, relaxed, less nervous, good.
  Effect next day?
  Feels well.

When you do not,
Effect immediately afterwards?
Nervous strung up not sleepy.
Effect next day?
No effect.

What do you believe to be the true purpose of intercourse?
   Necessity to man? to woman?
   [Yes] Because many [who are] unmarried are too nervous & do not recognize what the cause is.
   Pleasure?
   [Yes] for purpose of bringing about [reproduction].
   Reproduction?
   [Yes] highest purpose.
   What other reasons beside reproduction are sufficient to warrant intercourse?
   Individual health: a normal desire and a rational use of it tends to keep people healthier.

Have you ever used any means to prevent conception? If so, what?
Withdrawal sometimes.
   Effect on your health?
   None in either [husband or wife?]

What, to you, would be an ideal habit?
Once a week or [once every] ten days. When both want it.

Number 44

(Respondent No. 44 was forty-two when interviewed in 1913. She had had two children and two miscarriages. The length of time she had been married was not recorded.)

What knowledge of sexual physiology had you before marriage? (b) How did you obtain it?
No knowledge. Did not know what marriage meant.

1st intercourse how long after marriage?
2 or 3 days after marriage.

Did conception occur by choice or accident?
1st by choice. All others accidental.

Habit of intercourse, average number of times per week?
Formerly 2 [times] weekly. Now once in 2–3 wks. Depends on whether they have leisure.

Was intercourse held during pregnancy? If so, how often?
Rarely with 1st [child] during [entire pregnancy]. Not with 2nd [child].
   Had you any desire for it during this period?
   With 2nd one yes, not with 1st.

At other times have you any desire for intercourse?
Yes.
  At what time in relation to your menses?
  Following or preceding menstruation.

Is intercourse agreeable to you or not?
Yes.

Do you always have a venereal orgasm?
No. Conscious of suppression on part of woman. Time reaction slower.
  When you do,
  Effect immediately afterwards?
  Rests better when she has orgasm. Temperamental uplift.
  When you do not,
  Effect immediately afterwards?
  Very little difference.

What do you believe to be the true purpose of intercourse?
  Necessity to man?
  Yes.
  To woman?
  Yes.
  Pleasure?
  Very strong. Psychological 2nd.
  Reproduction?
  Yes 1st.
  What other reasons beside reproduction are sufficient to warrant inter-
  course?
  If women enjoyed intercourse, the demands on them would be much less.
  Males [have] less desire when [they are] more perfectly satisfied. Intellec-
  tual work on part of husband—less leisure. [Intercourse produces]
  oneness [and is] uplifting like music. [There is] very little that is animal
  about it. The comradeship of it. [Remainder of response is unintelligible.]

Have you ever used any means to prevent conception? a) if so, what?
After known miscarriage because husband did not wish her to conceive
again until she was strong. Douches of bichloride.
  Effect on your health?
  No effect.

What, to you, would be an ideal habit?
When desired by both.

M. Carey Thomas on Loving Other Women, 1872–1877

March 14 [1872]
  The first of this month I got my allowance[:]$5.00 a month for ribbons,
cuffs, collars, etc. Rex has one too. Oh Bessie and I have changed our

The Papers of M. Carey Thomas (microfilm reels #1 & #2), Bryn Mawr College Archives.

names. I call her Rex and she calls me Rush and I suppose we'll call each
other by them all our lives.

Yesterday was the Sewing Meeting, the last one I guess, and we had a
real nice time, none of those horrid boys nor Lea [?] were there, and so after
the supper we went up in the Meeting house by ourselves.

It was so still . . . We walked up and down the aisle, we talked of what
we wanted to be and do and formed plans how after we had come home from
Vassar having taken bright honors we would do everything, we would devote ourselves to study and live together, have a library with all the splendid
books, with a bright wood fire always burning, dark crimson curtains and
furniture, great big easy chairs where we could sit lost in books for days
together, a great large table covered with papers for we would be authors.
Adjoining this should be a laboratory where far into the night we would pour
over Crucibles, mixing our mystic engredients and perhaps making discoveries which should effect the whole world and there we would live loving
each other so and urge each other on to every high and noble deed or action
and all who passed should say "Their example arouses me, their books
enoble me, their deeds inspire me and behold they are women!" Of course,
these were only the wildest fancies, but oh if only some of them might come
true. Why can't two girls love each other and live together and help each
other in life's struggle just as well as a man and a woman! But I suppose one
of us'll have to go and fall in love or something or other horrid. The more I
see of lovers the more thoroughly I despise the whole lot so I don't think it
will be me at any rate.

April 27
. . . Now I must give my thoughts on things in general. 1st Anna—I like her
ever so much. She is just too nice for any thing. She is real smart and
interested in every thing. Next to Rex she is the jolliest girl I know. . . . I
think I must feel towards Anna for instance like a boy would for I admire her
so not any particular thing but just an undefined sense of admiration and then
I like to touch her and the other morning I woke up and she was asleep and I
admired her hair so much that I kissed it. I never felt it so much with any
body else.

[Spring 1873]
I took up my journal today though with the intention of writing about a
friendship of last term in case it should never be renewed that at least I may
have *some* remembrance. It was with Libbie Conkey—we got acquainted
how I hardly know. The girls said we "smashed" on each other or "made
love," I don't know. I only know it was elegant—she called me "her boy,"
her "liebe knabe" and she was my "Elsie." . . .

June 12, 1877
. . . Well I began to see more and more of Miss H. She got in the habit of
coming and reading me her mother's letters and of bidding me good night.
We used to go and study some time in Caskadilla woods and when it would
get dark we would sit under her blue shawl and talk. Then we came across
Swinburne's "Atlanta in Calydon" and Miss Hicks would come in in her

wrapper after I was in bed and we would read it out loud and we learned several of the choruses. One night we had stopped reading later than usual and obeying a sudden impulse I turned to her and asked "do you love me?" She threw her arms around me and whispered "I love you passionately." She did not go home that night and we talked and talked. She told me she had been praying that I might care for her. That was the beginning and from that time, it was the Fall of '75 till June '77, we have been inseparable. I put this all down because I cannot understand it. I am sure it is not best for people to care about each other so much. . . .

In fact I just fell in love with her and I did it gradually too (not that adoring worship I had for Libbie, nor the equal fun and earnest loving devoted friendship Carrie and I have) but that Atlanta night I knew I did not care as much as she did and so it went on, I getting fonder and fonder of her until it was as I say—all the time against my better judgment and yet I cannot tell why it was, she is lovely, in many, many ways much better than I am.

❖ E S S A Y S

In the first essay, Carl N. Degler, a professor at Stanford University, analyzes the unique Mosher Survey, the only known systematic investigation of the sexual practices of middle-class Americans in the nineteenth century. Nancy Sahli, an archivist and historical researcher, in the second selection examines the phenomenon of "smashes" among young college women, and the redefinition of such relationships in the writings of sexologists at the end of the century. Carol Z. Stearns and Peter N. Stearns, of the Western Psychiatric Institute and Carnegie-Mellon University, respectively, call in the third essay for a reconsideration of Degler's work and a return to a more traditional view of Victorian sexuality.

Women's Sexuality as Revealed by the Mosher Survey

CARL N. DEGLER

Any systematic knowledge of the sexual habits of women is a relatively recent historical acquisition, confined to the surveys of women made in the 1920s and 1930s and culminating in the well-known Kinsey report. Until recently no even slightly comparable body of evidence for nineteenth-century women was known to exist. In the Stanford University Archives, however, are questionnaires completed by a group of women testifying to their sexual habits. The questionnaires are part of the papers of Dr. Clelia Duel Mosher (1863–1940), a physician at Stanford University and a pioneer in the study of women's sexuality. Mosher began her work on the sexual habits of married women when she was a student at the University of Wisconsin prior to 1892. That year she transferred for her senior year to Stanford, where she received an A.B. degree in 1893 and an M.A. in 1894. In

Carl N. Degler, "What Ought to Be and What Was: Women's Sexuality in the Nineteenth Century," *American Historical Review*, LXXIX (1974), 1479–90. Reprinted by permission of Carl N. Degler, Stanford University.

1900 she earned an M.D. degree from Johns Hopkins University. After a decade of private practice she joined the Stanford faculty as a member of the department of hygiene and medical adviser to women students. Her published work dealt with the physical capabilities of women; she was a well-known advocate of physical exercise for women. Mosher's questionnaires are carefully arranged and bound in volume 10 of her unpublished work, "Hygiene and Physiology of Women." Mosher, however, apparently never drew more than a few impressionistic conclusions from the highly revealing questionnaires. She did not even publish the fact of their existence, and so far as can be ascertained no use has heretofore been made of this manuscript source. Yet the amount and kind of information on sexual habits and attitudes of married women in the late nineteenth century contained in these questionnaires are unique.

The project, which spanned some twenty years, was begun at the University of Wisconsin when Mosher was a student of biology in the early 1890s. She designed the questionnaire when asked to address the Mother's Club at the university on the subject of marriage. In later years she added to her cases and used the information when giving advice to women about sexual and hygienic matters. This initiative, as well as the kind of questions she asked, reveals that Mosher was far ahead of her time. She amassed information on women's sexuality that none of the many nineteenth-century writers on the subject studied in any systematic way at all. . . .

Since the evidence in this questionnaire, which I call the Mosher Survey, has never been used before, it is first worthwhile to examine the social background of the women who answered the questionnaires. All told there are forty-six useable questionnaires, but since two of the questionnaires seem to have been filled out by the same woman at an interval of twenty-three years, the number of women actually surveyed is forty-five. In the aggregates that follow I have counted only forty-five questionnaires. The questionnaires, it ought to be said, were not administered at the same time, but at three different periods at least; moreover the date of administration of nine questionnaires cannot be ascertained. Of those that do provide that information, seventeen were completed before 1900, fourteen were filled out between 1913 and 1917, and five were answered in 1920.

More important than the date of administration of the questionnaires are the birth dates of the respondents. All but one of the forty-four women who provided their dates of birth were born before 1890. In fact thirty-three, or seventy per cent of the whole group, were born before 1870. And of these, seventeen, or slightly over half, were born before the Civil War. For comparative purposes it might be noted that in Alfred Kinsey's survey of women's sexuality the earliest cohort of respondents was only born in the 1890s. In short, the attitudes and practices to which the great majority of the women in the Mosher Survey testify were those of women who grew up and married within the nineteenth century, regardless of when they may have completed the questionnaires.

An important consideration in evaluating the responses, of course, is the social origins of the women. From what class did they come, and from what sections of the country? The questionnaire, fortunately, provides some information here, but not with as much precision as one might like. Since the great majority of the respondents attended college or a normal school (thirty-four out of forty-five, with the education of three unknown), it is evident that the group is not representative of the population of the United States as a whole. The remainder of the group attended secondary school, either public or private, a pattern that is again not representative of a general population in which only a tiny minority of young people attended secondary school. But for purposes of evaluating the impact of the prescriptive or marital-advice literature upon American women this group is quite appropriate. For inasmuch as their educational background identifies them as middle- or upper-class women, it can be said that they were precisely those persons to whom that advisory literature was directed and upon whom its effects ought to be most evident.

In geographical origin the respondents to the Mosher Survey seem to be somewhat more representative, if the location of parents, birthplaces, and colleges attended can be taken as a measure, albeit impressionistic, of geographical distribution. Unfortunately there is no other systematic or more reliable information on this subject. The colleges attended, for example, are located in the Northeast (Cornell [6], Smith, Wellesley, and Vassar [2]), in the Middle West (Ripon, Iowa State University, and Indiana), and in the Far West (Stanford [9], the University of California, and the University of the Pacific). The South is not represented at all among the colleges attended.

Although the emphasis upon prestigious colleges might make one think that these were women of the upper or even leisure class, rather than simply middle class, a further piece of information suggests that in fact they were not. One of the questions asked concerned working experience prior to marriage. Although seven of the respondents provided no data at all on this point, and eight reported that they had married immediately after completing their education, thirty of the women reported that they had worked prior to marriage. As a side light on the opportunities available to highly educated women in the late nineteenth century, it is worth adding that twenty-seven of the thirty worked as teachers. On the basis of their working experience it seems reasonable to conclude that the respondents were principally middle- or upper-middle-class women rather than members of a leisure class.

Despite the high level of education of these women, they confessed to having a pretty poor knowledge, by modern standards, of sexual physiology before marriage. Only eleven said that they had much knowledge on that subject, obtained from female relatives, books, or courses in college, while another thirteen said that they had some knowledge. The remainder—slightly over half—reported that they had very little or no knowledge. No guidelines were given in the questionnaire for estimating the amount of knowledge. The looseness of the definition is shown by the fact that three of the respondents who said that they had no knowledge at all named books on women's physiology that they had read. From other titles mentioned in passing it is clear that a number of these women had direct acquaintance with the prescriptive and advisory literature of the time. How did it affect their behavior? Did they repress their sexual impulses or deny them, as some of the prescriptive literature advised? Were they in fact without sexual desire? Or were they motivated toward personal sexual satisfaction as the medical literature quoted in this article advised?

The Mosher Survey provides a considerable amount of evidence to answer these and other questions. To begin with, thirty-five of the forty-five women testified that they felt desire for sexual intercourse independent of their husband's interest, while nine said they never or rarely felt any such desire. What is more striking, however, is the number who testified to orgasmic experience. According to the standard view of women's sexuality in the nineteenth century, women were not expected to feel desire and certainly not to experience an orgasm. Yet it is striking that in constructing the questionnaire Dr. Mosher asked not only whether the respondents experienced an orgasm during intercourse but whether "you *always* have a venereal orgasm?" (my italics). Although that form of the question makes quite clear Mosher's own assumption that female orgasms were to be expected, it unfortunately confuses the meaning of the responses. (Incidentally, only two of the forty-five respondents failed to answer this question.) Five of the women, for instance, responded "no" without further comment. Given the wording of the question, however, that negative could have meant "not always, but almost always" as well as "never" or any response in between these extremes. The ambiguity is further heightened when it is recognized that in answer to another question, three of the five negatives said that they had felt sexual desire, while a fourth said "sometimes but not often," and the fifth said sex was "usually a nuisance." Luckily, however, most of the women who responded to the question concerning orgasm made more precise answers. The great majority of them said that they had exierenced orgasms. . . .

In sum, thirty-four of the women experienced orgasm, with the possibility that the figure might be as high as thirty-seven if those who reported "no" but said they had felt sexual desire are categorized as "sometimes." (Interestingly enough, of nine women out of the forty-five who said they had never felt any sexual desire, seven said that they had experienced orgasms.) Moreover, sixteen or almost half of those who experienced orgasms did so either "always" or "usually." As we have seen, in the whole group of forty-five, all but two responded to the question asking if an orgasm was always experienced. Of those forty-three, thirty-four were born before 1875. Five answered "no" to that question without any further comment. One other woman responded "never," and two others said "once or twice." If the "noes" and the "never" are taken together, the proportion of women born before 1875 who experienced at least one orgasm is eighty-two per cent. If the "noes" are taken to mean "sometimes" or "once or twice," as they might well be, given the wording of the question, then the proportion rises to ninety-five per cent. . . .

Much more interesting and valuable than the bare statistics are the comments or rationales furnished by the women, which provide an insight into the sexual attitudes of middle-class women. As one might expect in a population by its own admission poorly informed on sexual physiology, the sexual adjustment of some of these women left something to be desired. Mosher, for example, in one of her few efforts at drawing conclusions from the Survey, pointed out that sexual maladjustment within marriage sometimes began with the first intercourse. "The woman comes to this new experience of life often with no knowledge. The woman while she may give mental consent often shrinks physically." From her studies Mosher had also come to recognize that women's "slower time reaction" in reaching full sexual excitement was a source of maladjustment between husband and wife that could kill off or reduce sexual feelings in some women. Women, she recognized, because of their slower timing were left without "the normal physical response. This leaves organs of women over congested." At least one of her respondents reported that for years intercourse was distasteful to her because of her "slow reaction," but "orgasm [occurs] if time is taken." On the other hand, the respondent continued, "when no orgasm, [she] took days to recover." Another woman spoke of the absence of an orgasm during intercourse as "bad, even disastrous, nerve-wracking—unbalancing, if such conditions continue for any length of time." Still a third woman, presumably referring to the differences in the sexual rhythms of men and women, said, "Men have not been properly trained." One of the women in the Mosher Survey testified in another way to her recognition of the differences in the sexuality of men and women. "Every wife submits when perhaps she is not in the mood," she wrote, "but I can see no bad effect. It is as if it had not been. But my husband was absolutely considerate. I do not think I could endure a man who forced it." And her response to a question about the effects of an orgasm upon her corroborate her remark: "a general sense of well being, contentment and regard for husband. This is true Doctor," she earnestly wrote.

Mosher's probing of the attitudes of women toward their sexuality went beyond asking about orgasms. Several of her questions sought to elicit the reactions of women to sexual intercourse. What is the purpose of sex, she asked? Is it a necessity for a man or for a woman? Is it for pleasure, or is it for reproduction? Only two of the women failed to respond in some fashion to these questions. Nine thought sex was a necessity for men, while thirteen thought it was a necessity for both men and women. Fifteen of the respondents thought it was not a necessity for either sex. Twenty-four of the forty-five thought that it was a pleasure for both sexes, while only one thought it was exclusively a pleasure for men. Given the view generally held about sexual attitudes in the nineteenth century, it comes as something of a surprise to find that only thirty marked "reproduction" as the primary purpose of sex. In fact, as we shall see in a moment, some of the women thought reproduction was not as important a justification for intercourse as love.

As one might expect, this particular series of questions was usually answered with a good deal of explanation. One woman who emphasized reproduction as the principal justification took the opportunity to condemn those couples she apparently had heard of who did not want children. "I cannot recognize as true marriage that relation unaccompanied by a strong desire for children." She thought it was close to "legalized prostitution." She admitted that because of her love for her husband she "cultivated the passion to effect the 'compromise' in this direction that must come in every other [area] when people marry.'' She went on to say that she did not experience orgasm until the fifth or sixth year of her marriage and that even at the time of her response to the questionnaire—the early 1890s—she still did not reach a sexual climax half of the time. A second woman was also apparently out of phase with her husband's sexual interests, for she thought a woman's needs for sex occurred ''half as often as a man's.'' It is revealing of her own feelings that though she said ''half as often,'' the figures she used to illustrate her point—twice a week for a man and twice a month for a woman—are actually in the ratio of one to four rather than of one to two as she said. Her true attitude was also summed up in the remark that since she was always in good health and intercourse ''did not hurt me, . . . I always meant to be obliging.''

But, as the earlier statistical breakdown makes evident, the women who only tolerated intercourse were in a decided minority. A frank and some-times enthusiastic acceptance of sexual relations was the response from most of the women. Sexual intercourse ''makes more normal people,'' said a woman born in 1857. She was not even sure that children were necessary to justify sexual relations within marriage. ''Even if there are no children, men love their wives more if they continue this relation, and the highest devotion is based upon it, a very beautiful thing, and I am glad nature gave it to us.'' Since marriage should bring two people close together, said one woman born in 1855, sexual intercourse is the means that achieves that end. ''Living relations have a right to exist between married people and these cannot exist in perfection without sexual intercourse to a moderate degree. This is the result of my experience,'' she added. A woman born in 1864 described sexual relations as ''the gratification of a normal healthy appetite.'' The only respondent who was divorced and remarried testified in 1913 that at age fifty-three ''my passionate feeling was declined somewhat and the orgasm does not always occur,'' but intercourse, she went on, was still ''agreeable'' to her.

Several of the women even went so far as to reject reproduction as sufficient justification for sex. Said one woman, ''I consider this appetite as ranking with other natural appetites and like them to be indulged legitimately and temperately; I consider it illegitimate to risk bringing children into the world under any but most favorable circumstances.'' This woman was born before the Compromise of 1850 and made her comment after she had been married ten years. Another woman, also born a decade before the Civil War, denied that reproduction ''alone warrants it at all; I think it is only warranted as an expression of true and passionate love. This is the prime condition for a happy conception, I fancy.'' To her, too, the pleasure derived from sexual intercourse was ''not sensual pleasure, but the pleasure of love.''

A third woman born before 1861 doubted that sex was a necessity in the same sense as food or drink, but she had no doubt that ''the desire of both husband and wife for this expression of their union seems to me the first and highest reason for intercourse. The desire for offspring is a secondary, inci-dental, although entirely worthy motive but could never to me make inter-course right unless the mutual desire were also present.'' She saw a clear conflict between the pleasure of intercourse and reproduction. "My husband and I," she said in 1893,

> believe in intercourse for its own sake—we wish it for ourselves and spiritually miss it, rather than physically, when it does not occur, because it is the highest, most sacred expression of our oneness. On the other hand, even a slight risk of pregnancy, and then we deny ourselves the intercourse, feeling all the time that we are losing that which keeps us closest to each other.

Another woman, in describing the ideal of sexual relations, said that she did not want intercourse to occur at any time when conception was likely, for conception should not occur by accident. Instead it ought to be the result of

> deliberate design on both sides in time and circumstances most favorable physically and spiritually for the accomplishment of an immensely important act. It amounts to separating times and objects of intercourse into (a) that of expression of love between man and woman (that act is frequently simply the extreme caress of love's passion, which it would be a pity to limit . . . to once in two or three years) and (b) that of carrying on a share in the perpetuation of the race, which should be done carefully and prayerfully.

It seems evident that among these women sexual relations were neither rejected nor engaged in with distaste or reluctance. In fact for them sexual expression was a part of healthy living and frequently a joy. Certainly the prescriptive literature that denigrated sexual feelings or expression among women cannot be read as descriptive of the behavior or attitude of these women. Nevertheless this is not quite the same as saying that the marriage handbooks had no effect at all. To be sure, there is no evidence that the great majority of women in the Mosher Survey felt guilty about indulging in sex because of what they were told in the prescriptive literature. But in two cases that literature seems to have left feelings of guilt. One woman said that sexual relations were "apparently a necessity for the *average* person" and that it was "only [the] superior individuals" who could be "independent of sex relations with no evident ill-results." To her, as to St. Paul and some of the marriage-advice books, it was better to indulge than to burn, but it was evidently even better to be free from burning from the beginning. A more blatant sign of guilt over sex came from the testimony of a woman who quite frankly thought the pleasure of sex was a justification for intercourse, but, she added "not necessarily a legitimate one."

Dr. Mosher herself obliquely testified to the effects of the prescriptive literature. She attributed the difficulties some women experienced in reaching orgasm to the fact that "training has instilled the idea that any physical response is coarse, common and immodest which inhibits [women's] proper part in this relation." That was the same point that some of the medical writers in the nineteenth century had made in explaining the coldness of some women toward their husbands.

The advice literature, for men as well as for women, generally warned against excessive sexual activity. The emphasis upon limits is reflected in the remarks of some of the women in the Mosher Survey. One woman said, for example, that "the pleasure is sufficient warrant" for sexual relations, but only if "people are extremely moderate and do not allow it to injure their health or degrade their best feelings toward each other." Another woman had concluded that "to the man and woman married from love," sexual intercourse "may be used temperately as one of the highest manifestations of love granted us by our Creator." A third woman who had no doubt that sexual relations were "necessary to marital happiness," nonetheless said she believed "in temperance in it." But temperance, another one of the women in the Mosher Survey reminds us, should not be confused with repugnance or distaste. Although this respondent did not think the ideal sexual relation should occur more often than once a month, she did think it ought to take place "during the menstrual period . . . and in the daylight." The fact is that this woman, in answer to other questions, indicated that she experienced sexual desire about once a week, but with greatest intensity "before and during menses." She was, in short, restricting her own ideal to what she considered an acceptable frequency of indulgence. Her description of her feelings after orgasm suggests where she learned that limits on frequency might be desirable or expected: "Very sleepy and comfortable. No disgust, as I have heard it described."

This examination of the literature, the popular advice books, and particularly the Mosher Survey makes clear that historians are ill-advised to rely upon the marital-advice books as descriptions either of the sexual behavior of women or of general attitudes toward women's sexuality. It is true that a literature as admittedly popular as much of the prescriptive or normative literature was could be expected to have some effect upon behavior as well as attitudes. But those effects were severely limited. Most people apparently did not follow the prescriptions laid down by the marriage and advice manuals. Indeed some undoubtedly found that advice wrong or misleading when measured against experience. Through some error or accident the same woman was apparently interviewed twice in the Mosher Survey, twenty-three years apart. As a result we can compare her attitudes at the beginning of her marriage in 1896 and her attitude in 1920. After one year of marriage she thought that sexual relations ought to be confined to reproduction only, but when asked the same question in 1920, she said that intercourse ought not to be confined to reproduction, though she thought it should be indulged in only when not pressed with work and when there was time for pleasure. Another woman in the Mosher Survey changed her mind about sexual relations even earlier in her sexual life. She said,

> My ideas as to the reason for [intercourse] have changed materially from what they were before marriage. I then thought reproduction was the only object and that once brought about, intercourse should cease. But in my experience the habitual bodily expression of love has a deep psychological effect in making possible complete mental sympathy, and perfecting the spiritual union that must be the lasting "marriage" after the passion of love has passed away with years.

These remarks were made in 1897 by a woman of thirty after one year of marriage.

Her comments make clear once again that historians need to recognize that the attitudes of ordinary people are quite capable of resisting efforts to reshape or alter them. That there was an effort to deny women's sexual feelings and to deny them legitimate expression cannot be doubted in the light of the books written then and later about the Victorian conception of sexuality. But the many writings by medical men who spoke in a contrary vein and the Mosher Survey should make us doubt that the ideology was actually put into practice by most men or women of the nineteenth century, even among the middle class, though it was to this class in particular that the admonitions and ideology were directed. The women who responded to Dr. Mosher's questions were certainly middle- and upper-middle-class women, but they were, as a group, neither sexless nor hostile to sexual feelings. The great majority of them, after all, experienced orgasm as well as sexual desire. Their behavior in the face of the antisexual ideology pressed upon them at the time offers testimony to the truth of Alex Comfort's comment that "the astounding resilience of human commonsense against the anxiety makers is one of the really cheering aspects of history."

Loving Relationships Among Women

NANCY SAHLI

Carroll Smith-Rosenberg has shown that a network of intimate, supportive relationships existed among American women during much of the eighteenth and nineteenth centuries. This network was subjected to increasing stress after about 1875. Prescriptions for female behavior changed; indeed, a new definition of what constituted "normal" female relationships developed in both America and Europe. Middle-class women, specifically feminists and college-educated women, would logically be among the first either to be affected by or to initiate new types of relationships. Luckily, this class also provides readily accessible primary source material. However, the behavior and attitudes described in this article were not atypical and should not be regarded as such by historians trying to understand late nineteenth-century American women.

One of the problems encountered in writing about women's relationships is that of terminology. Words such as "lesbian" and "homosexual" did not come into use until the last decade of the nineteenth century, and even then there was much confusion about whether they referred to emotional or sexual behavior or both. This article uses the word "lesbian" in the same sense as it was used by Blanche Cook in her recent article on female support networks in the early twentieth century:

> Women who love women, who choose women to nurture and support and to create a living environment in which to work creatively and independently, are lesbians.

Nancy Sahli, "Smashing: Women's Relationships before the Fall," *Chrysalis,* no. 8 (Summer 1979), 17–27. Reprinted by permission of the author.

Until about 1875, intimate, supportive relationships with a high degree of emotional, sensual, and even sexual content existed freely among both single and married women in America. . . .

New types of organizations, such as alumnae groups and sororities, resulted from the entrance of women into higher education. In 1881 the Association of Collegiate Alumnae—known today as the American Association of University Women—was formed, largely because of the alienation from the mainstream of social life which many women college graduates felt. The association's first research committee, that on physical education, was organized after a paper on that topic was read at the first regular meeting, early in 1882, by Dr. Adaline S. Whitney. The best-known result of this committee's activity was its 1885 report on *Health Statistics of Women College Graduates,* which disproved the contemporary theory that the rigors of academic life resulted in poor health among women students. . . .

A primary focus of the preliminary committee meetings was the emotional rather than the physical condition of women undergraduates, specifically something called "smashing." One description of this practice can be found in an 1873 letter to the *Yale Courant:*

> There is a term in general use at Vassar, truly calculated to awaken within the ima penetralia of our souls all that love for the noble and the aesthetic of which our natures are capable. The term in question is "smashing." When a Vassar girl takes a shine to another, she straightway enters upon a regular course of bouquet sendings, interspersed with tinted notes, mysterious packages of "Ridley's Mixed Candies," locks of hair perhaps, and many other tender tokens, until at last the object of her attentions is captured, the two become inseparable, and the aggressor is considered by her circle of acquaintances as—smashed. . . .

M. Carey Thomas, president of Bryn Mawr College for nearly thirty years, mutually smashed with another student during her boarding-school days at the Howland Institute in the early 1870's, thereby causing extreme annoyance and jealousy on the part of Bessie King, one of her Baltimore friends who was also attending the school. Mary Whitall Thomas, while cautioning her daughter to tone down the intensity of her emotions, nevertheless acknowledged their validity: "I guess thy feeling is quite natural. I used to have the same romantic love for my friends. It is a real pleasure." She took a much dimmer view, however, of her daughter's playing male roles, dressed in men's clothes, at school functions: "It is repugnant to my taste. I do suppose it is great fun but I think it is not nice. It would be simply disgusting if any men were present and I don't like it anyhow."

One of the members of the Association of Collegiate Alumnae committee was Alice Stone Blackwell, daughter of pioneer women's rights leader Lucy Stone and in her own right a prominent leader in the women's movement. A graduate of Boston University in 1881, Blackwell commented on the committee discussions in an early 1882 letter: The committee

> gave it as their strong opinion that one thing which damaged the health of the girls seriously was "smashes"—an extraordinary habit which they have of falling violently in love with each other and suffering all the pangs of unrequited

attachment, desperate jealousy &c &c, with as much energy as if one of them were a man. I could hardly have believed that the things they told were not exaggerations, if Maria Mitchell hadn't told me, when I was visiting at Vassar, what a pest the "smashing" was to the teachers there—how it kept the girls from studying, & sometimes made a girl drop behind her class year after year. Miss Brown, of our committee, told us her own experience, evidently not without some embarrassment, but for the general good; how she, at Smith, though not at all given to that sort of thing, had been a victim. "A veteran smasher" attacked her & captured her, & soon deserted her for someone else; & she used to cry herself to sleep night after night, & wake up with a headache in the morning. And they write each other the wildest love letters, & send presents, confectionery, all sorts of things, like a real courting of the Shaksperian style. If the "smash" is mutual, they monopolize each other & "spoon" continually, & sleep together & lie awake all night talking instead of going to sleep; & if it isn't mutual the unrequited one cries herself sick & endures pangs unspeakable. I listed with undisguised curiosity & amazement, for we had very little of that sort of thing at B.U. My theory is that it comes of massing hundreds of nervous young girls together, & shutting them up from the outside world. They are just at the romantic age, they see only each other, & so their sentimentality has no other outlet. The coeducational colleges don't suffer much from "smashes." . . . There are plenty of cases of "particular friends," but few or none of "smashes."

Significantly, the committee's final report, published in 1885, contained no mention of smashing, although there were general references to such conditions as "weakness of the nervous system," "emotional strain," and "worriment . . . either over studies or personal affairs." The report also noted that "only a few of the students were so situated as to be able to enter into society other than the companionship of their fellow-students." . . .

One of the most interesting aspects of the history of sexuality is the development of psychiatric and other prescriptive literature on homosexuality and lesbianism, beginning in 1869 with the publication of Westphal's clinical description of two cases, one male and one female, in the *Archiv für Psychologie,* a German professional journal. The published *Index-Catalogue of the Library of the Surgeon-General's Office, United States Army,* gives an idea of the extent to which this question was being discussed by both European and American writers.

The first sixteen-volume series of the *Index-Catalogue* appeared between 1880 and 1895. The index category most closely related to the topic under discussion in this article was "sexual instinct." Under this general heading, 17 books and nine articles were listed. Its only subheading, "sexual instinct (perversion and disorders of)," included 30 books and 106 articles, the earliest of which was published in 1740. Generally, the term "inversion" was used to describe homosexuality and lesbianism, while "perversion" included these topics as well as such exotic variations as fetishism and necrophilia.

The second series of the catalog appeared between 1896 and 1916 and included entries primarily for materials published subsequent to the first series. The change between these two series, particularly as it related to women's sexual behavior, is startling. The category "women," for instance, which in the first series was simply that, was now broken down into a remarkably detailed set of subheadings and cross-references, including "masturbation in the female," "nymphomania," "sapphism," "sexual instinct (inversion of)," and "sexual instinct (perversion of)." A volume-by-volume, term-by-term comparison of both series' entries pertaining to women's health reveals no difference in the methods of indexing. Obviously, then, the late-nineteenth-century medical world was focusing more and more attention on sexuality. Now, in addition to the general category "sexual instinct," with 28 books and 38 articles, there were no fewer than 17 subheadings. The subheading "sexual instinct (inversion of)" listed 36 books and 228 articles. The other relevant category, "sexual instinct (perversion of)," contained 26 books and 300 articles.

Despite all this interest, few cases of female homosexuality ever came to the attention of researchers. For example, in their 1883 review article in *The Journal of Nervous and Mental Disease,* New York psychiatrists J. C. Shaw and G. N. Ferris observed that out of a total of 19 homosexual case histories described in both European and American literature since 1869, only two were female. Those women who did come to the attention of professionals were likely to be labeled sexual perverts or inverts, not because they engaged in any variant sexual activities, but simply because they felt emotionally attracted to women or engaged in such suspicious practices as dressing in men's clothing. For example, a translation of Krafft-Ebing's 1884 article, "Perversion of the Sexual Instinct—Report of Cases," appeared in the *Alienist and Neurologist,* one of the United States' most influential psychiatric journals, in 1888. The one female case cited reported that she enjoyed dressing in men's clothing because it was "more convenient." Krafft-Ebing presented no evidence that she engaged in any sort of sexual activity with women, simply stating that "her friendship and self-sacrifices towards those she loved were boundless." The subject also disliked the idea of establishing relationships with men and "was carrying on a purely Platonic love affair with a young woman and wrote her tender love-letters." Is this really homosexual behavior?

Or is it a pejorative labeling directed more at evidence of a woman's autonomy than at her sexual activity?

Perhaps the culmination of this tendency to define women's love relationships as perversions, regardless of the sexual activity involved, was in Havelock Ellis's 1897 book *Sexual Inversion.* Ellis's definition and descriptions are worth more than passing notice, particularly when they are placed in the context of both nineteenth-century feminism and the specific examples of behavior in this article. Ellis used the words "homosexuality" and "lesbianism" interchangeably to describe women's love relationships that did not necessarily include either physical involvement or actual genital contact. According to Ellis, women who loved women were abnormal, and they should more appropriately feel the pangs of guilt than the joy of innocence in contemplating their condition. Writing about his Case 29, for example, Ellis first let her talk about her own feelings:

> "Love is with me a religion. The very nature of my affection for my friends precludes the possibility of any element entering into it which is not absolutely pure and sacred."

Ellis then commented:

> Miss M. can see nothing wrong in her feelings; and, until a year ago, [when] she came across the translation of Krafft-Ebing's book, she had no idea "that feelings like mine" were "under the ban of society" as he puts it, or were considered unnatural and depraved. She is reticent regarding the details of her relationships, but it is evident that specific physical gratification plays no part in them.

Intense friendships among schoolgirls, or between them and their teachers, were particularly suspect: "conventional propriety recognizes a considerable degree of physical intimacy between girls, thus at once encouraging and cloaking the manifestations of homosexuality." . . .

In the late nineteenth century a very definite change was occurring in definitions of normal patterns of women's relationships. There was a great deal of pressure against the intense, emotional, sensual, even sexual commitment between women that had existed without censure during the earlier part of the century, and we can reasonably expect that many women adjusted their behavior to conform to the new standards. Those who refused to conform, for whatever reason, were risking the disapproval, condemnation, and persecution of both society and their own potentially divided selves.

The question now is why. Why, during the first two-thirds of the nineteenth century, were relationships between women allowed to exist with the intensity that we have seen? Why was this a viable option? Why did this begin to change in the late nineteenth century, at a time when there was an active feminist movement, development of higher education for women, and a scientific-medical interest in the question of homoemotional and homosexual behavior?

One characteristic of the first generation of feminists, such as Susan B. Anthony and Anna E. Dickinson, was their intense religiosity—their internalization of Christian principles through either childhood training or later evangelical conversion. Whether one chooses to call it inner light, Garrisonian radical Christianity, or romantic evangelicalism, its essential features were the same. . . . By defining their love for other women as a spiritual force, women were, in many cases, able to sublimate any sexual feelings they may have had and make the intensity of their relationships acceptable to society.

In a sense, the feminist movement itself subverted the heightened emotional commitment which had typified women's relationships during most of the nineteenth century. As women began to be perceived by themselves and others as being capable of rational, intellectual thought, it seems evident that they would want to use this ability, rather than their emotions, to make decisions advancing their position *vis à vis* the male world, and, in their search for equality with men, that they would perceive this capacity as being on a higher status scale than that of the emotions. For example, in 1888, at an Association of Collegiate Alumnae meeting in Boston, Sarah L. Miner argued that among the qualities a woman gained by college training were

> the ability to be controlled by correct judgment and sense of right instead of by impulse, the ability to plan for herself, a knowledge of relative values, a knowl-

edge of the difference between means and ends, thoroughness, system, concentration, and power of reflection.

Another alumna commented that the college woman "learns to subordinate personal prejudice to impartial logic."

This downplaying of emotion by the first generation of college women was observed by Jane Addams, herself a member of this group, who noted that they had

> departed too suddenly from the active, emotional life led by their grandmothers and great-grandmothers. . . . somewhere in the process of "being educated" they had lost that simple and almost automatic response to the human appeal, that old healthful reaction resulting in activity from the mere presence of suffering or of helplessness.

Likewise, Gail Parker says that Carrie Chapman Catt, one of the second generation of suffrage leaders, "never really believed in the inner light or the potential sublimity of women's souls."

At the same time, members of the growing professional scientific, medical, psychiatric, and social scientific communities assumed the roles of definers and arbiters of acceptable and desirable—i.e., normal—behavior. Female friendships now began to be seen not only as purely spiritual unions but as sexual ones as well, even if only on an unconscious level. . . .

As long as women loved each other as they did for much of the nineteenth century, without threatening the system itself, their relationships either were simply ignored by men or were regarded as an acceptable part of the female sphere. Feminists, college graduates, and other independent women, however, were a real threat to the established order, and one way to control these sexless termites, hermaphroditic spinsters, or whatever one might call them, was to condemn their love relationships—the one aspect of their behavior which, regardless of their other social, political, or economic activities, posed a basic threat to a system where the fundamental expression of power was that of one sex over another.

A Traditional View of Victorian Sexuality

CAROL Z. STEARNS AND PETER N. STEARNS

Starting with Carl Degler's path-breaking article in the *American Historical Review* in 1974, and following with the publication of the now widely cited Mosher report, in 1980, we have been told that Victorian women, far from being revolted or frightened by sex, took it as a normal and pleasurable part of married life and were often orgasmic. Most recently the sexual revisionists have been joined by Peter Gay, who in his *The Bourgeois Experience,*

Carol Z. Stearns and Peter N. Stearns, "Victorian Sexuality: Can Historians Do it Better?" *Journal of Social History,* XVIII (1984–85), 626–33. Reprinted by permission of the *Journal of Social History,* copyright Peter N. Stearns.

Victoria to Freud, Education of the Senses, uses the material from the Mosher report and adds compelling corroboration from the diary of Mabel Loomis Todd. This lady, who recorded her sexual encounters with a short-hand that includes notation for orgasms, enjoyed a heady and successful relationship for many years with her husband, and then went on to employ the same sexual athleticism in a long-lasting affair with Austin Dickinson, Emily's brother.

The Mosher report, unpublished in Mosher's own time, was the result of a survey by a female physician on the sexuality of her comperes. Based on questionnaires answered by 45 women, 70% born before 1870, the forms were completed between 1892–1920. Most of those who answered were upper middle class college graduates, and as such not necessarily typical of Victorian females. The fact that they replied to the survey at all also suggests that they may not have been typical. Still, neither Degler nor Gay is naive, and they are far from making the claim that all Victorian women had a great time in bed. Nonetheless, they are both asking us, on the basis of just the type of evidence we have cited, to revise our views of Victorian female sexuality. Thus, Degler:

> A frank and sometimes enthusiastic acceptance of sexual relations was the response from most of the women . . . [intercourse was seen as part] of healthy living and frequently a joy . . . the great majority of them . . . experienced orgasm as well as sexual desire.

And thus again, Gay:

> the answers Dr. Mosher elicited carry conviction and have a meaning beyond the group of forty-five . . . they have the authenticity of awkwardness. Their artless and earnest candor is a clue to desires and fulfillments of which they were only partially aware . . . it is congruent with other, more informal testimony . . . Mabel Todd, in short, spoke for a substantial population of married middle-class women.

Degler read Mosher to say that 35% of the respondents usually or always had orgasms in intercourse, and another 40% sometimes did. Gay reads this to mean that a third almost always did and another 40% were only marginally less satisfied.

Neither Gay nor Degler dismisses all traces of a distinctive Victorianism. Degler notes, from Mosher, the women who had to abstain from sex during periods when conception could not be risked. Gay rather approvingly discusses the hypocrisy of Victorian culture, which said one thing about sex while doing another. But both interpretations present actual sexual behavior and values in a strikingly modern guise. It would be easy, reading them, to assume that Victorianism barely existed, describing 19th-century sexuality no more than, say, papal pronouncements describe the birth control attitudes and practices of contemporary American Catholics.

For the most part, the response of the historical community to this revisionist view has been favorable. To be sure, the new interpretation is still ignored by those who enjoy using Victorianism as a foil for a critique of modern males and modern medicine. But few critics have actually attacked the central findings about middle-class sexual behavior. There are several reasons for this. Historians learned some time ago that Victorianism was not as pervasive as once believed. It never described mainstream working-class sexuality during most of the 19th century, and indeed was partly directed at some fairly accurate perceptions of working-class indulgence in premarital sex and rising rates (to 1870) of illegitimacy. It does not come as a total surprise, then, to find the Victorian code even less descriptive than this first modification allowed.

And historians do like revisions. We may have grown bored with the stereotype of uptight Victorians and open to a newer and hence more interesting stereotype. Some implicit dismay about contemporary sexuality, which derives part of its justification from ringing attacks on Victorian prudery (see Gay Talese for a recent example), may also fuel the revision. A statement that Victorians were, in the main, sexually healthy might restrain contemporary penchants for sexual experimentation. Certainly it is a useful corrective for some exaggerations to know that Victorianism was partly invented in order to make 20th-century sexual achievements look good. Scholars like Carl Degler, sympathetic to feminism, may have been uncomfortable with the notion that female sexuality could have been so totally annihilated by a repressive culture as historians like Cominos had claimed. Or a Freudian true believer like Gay can enjoy the idea that biology or anatomy, even female biology/anatomy, must override culture; certainly a large portion of Gay's particular interpretation rests on assumptions of psychological constants such that history, rather than seriously testing a particular theory, must simply confirm it.

But, however attractive, revisionism often goes too far. In this case, we believe that significant interpretive problems remain which have not yet been addressed with any seriousness. It is amusing to reverse images, and we would certainly agree that some modification of the older conventions is now essential. But several problems remain, before we abandon Victorianism as an ill-tempered artifact.

Three avenues of inquiry tend to shed some doubt on the idea of the sexy middle-class Victorian. One, most obvious, is the evidence that Gay has chosen to ignore, and Degler to minimize, about Victorian preachments. Two, which follows in part, is what we know or suspect about the way children's sexuality is socially influenced. Three is the accumulated wisdom we have about rates of sexual dissatisfaction among contemporary women, which raises vital questions about the relationship between 19th-century sexuality and more recent trends. Let us examine each of these areas.

First we have the problem of the massive literature the Victorians published on the lack of female sexuality. These views were not buried in academic treatises or even medical journals; they entered into popular manuals, magazines and fiction. Female sexuality was seen by many Victorian physicians, clergymen and novelists as abnormal. To be sure, Acton himself, the most noted proponent of the asexual view of women, has been overquoted. Degler and Gay discuss authors such as Dr. George H. Napheys and Dr. Elizabeth Blackwell who believed quite differently, arguing that female sexuality was normal and expected. A large middle ground embraced authorities who admitted the possibility of female sexual pleasure but found the female sex drive, nevertheless, much less vigorous than the male, and usefully so in keeping sexuality within proper bounds. In sum, the Actonites themselves were hardly silent, and their views were echoed in part by a still larger group. Without pretending to know exactly which school of thought was most popular, it is fair to note that the few who really undertook a more radical view of female sexuality knew full well that they were bucking the mainstream. So if we are going to revise our views of Victorian female sexuality, we need to explain how it was that a substantial literature existed which denied that the sexuality existed, supplemented by other works which were only slightly less extreme in judging women's sexual needs. What was the function of this literature in its culture? . . .

Victorian views on sexuality—if not always rigorously Actonite—certainly went beyond intellectual discourse alone. They affected, indeed largely determined, longstanding legislation on censorship and the publicity of birth control, both of which could influence actual sexual behavior. And a similar Victorianism pervaded middle-class childrearing, such that well into the twentieth century school authorities, listing problems with female charges, attended to sexual issues above all. During the Victorian period itself, we still have every reason to believe that girls were taught about the horrors of masturbation, frightened about bodily functions such as menstruation, and denied frank discussions about female anatomy and the prerequisites of sexual satisfaction. And we have every reason to believe that this childrearing style is a good way to inhibit the enjoyment of adult sexuality. Degler and Gay give us no indication that they challenge the historical wisdom in this area, which is that Victorian girls would have been forcibly corrected if caught fondling themselves; that they would not have been encouraged to examine their own bodies or to discuss the sexual functions of their own bodies; that nobody would have taught them about the pleasures or necessity of foreplay. In helping women who are sexually dysfunctional today, Masters and Johnson and others have stressed the importance of undoing just these Victorian deficiencies. Self-examination of the female organs, then masturbation and learning to reach orgasm are now seen as important waystations toward orgasmic satisfaction with a partner. How did Victorian women manage to function so well when they were forbidden from childhood to do exactly what we think women need to do in order to function well today? If Degler and Gay know, they certainly do not explain.

Finally, there is the issue of the ongoing problem of female sexuality even in our own more open society—an issue easy enough to understand if we assume a genuine Victorian legacy in childrearing, but far harder if we are to believe in widespread female satisfaction a century ago. Shere Hite gained national attention in 1976 by claiming that more than two thirds of married women never achieve orgasm with sexual intercourse alone, and by recounting the great difficulty with which many others managed to achieve that potential for pleasure. Hite was widely criticized for taking a sample of women who had a complaint to typify all women, and in fact her problem was not unlike that of Dr. Mosher years earlier: how do we know if the women who answer a survey are typical of women in general? But in the contemporary case, more scientifically organized inquiries into the question of female orgasmic dysfunction have produced startling results not dissimilar to those of Hite. Three University of Pittsburgh researchers inquired about sexual function from 100 predominantly white, well-educated couples defining themselves as happily married. The questions relating to sexual adjustment were a small part of a large questionnaire covering many aspects of marriage. The project was specifically designed so as to avoid selecting for those who had a particular sexual axe to grind, as Hite's respondents may have had. This study, published in the *New England Journal of Medicine* in 1978, revealed that 46% of the women had difficulty, and an additional 15% reported a complete inability to have an orgasm—in total 63% reporting some difficulty with orgasm. Since these researchers did not discuss the method used to reach orgasm, it is possible that those who easily attained orgasm with intercourse alone may have been even fewer than the remaining 37%. In short, although disagreeing on the importance of sexual difficulties in marriage, this scientific study was in substantial accord with Hite's findings on the specific subject of the statistics of orgasmic achievement.

Obviously, this accord, juxtaposed with the new reading of the Victorian experience, raises fascinating interpretive problems. For women, at least, the twentieth century becomes not even a tentative step forward, but a massive regression in terms of sexual pleasure and orgasmic ability. Here is a reversal, not only of standard teachings about Victorianism, but of successive twentieth-century proclamations of sexual revolutions or at least increasing sexual freedom, stretching from the Bloomer girls of the late nineteenth century to the flappers to the premarital adepts among middle-class girls of the 1960s. Could it really be true that for all our hype about the sexual revolution, and the undeniable improvements in middle-class birth control knowledge and technology, the female majority, at least, is less orgasmic than their Victorian great-grandmothers? The prospect is worth considering, if only because of excessive brainwashing about our sexual prowess today. It can feed some recent feminist complaints that the current sexual revolution is actually male-dominated, for all the public concern about greater equality of pleasure. And the possibility of a sexual reversal, as against our ingrained expectations of progress in this area at least, is genuine; it cannot be dismissed out of hand. But possibility does not make certainty; the problem must be discussed, particularly in light of the undeniably different sexual culture and probably somewhat different socialization of the Victorian period. It is odd and unsatisfactory that the historians who have rediscovered Victorian sexuality not only have not offered a plausible interpretation of the Victorian-contemporary relationship, but do not seem to have noticed what a strange problem they have created for our understanding of ourselves. . . .

Without pretending to have all the answers to the new questions raised about Victorian sexuality, we do confess some hesitation in totally reversing the commonplace assumptions about the contemporary relationship to past sexuality. And there are two other, possibly related ways to deal with the Victorian evidence.

One approach to the newly discussed sources, particularly the Mosher report, is to question that these women meant the same thing we do when they talked about orgasm. In our reading of Mosher, of those who say they "always" had an orgasm, we find more than half (10/18) difficult to take at face value. We doubt that these women mean the same thing modern women mean by orgasm when we find that they consistently wish for a lower frequency of sex, are skeptical that pleasure is an important part of the sexual relationship, and are either silent or strikingly unenthusiastic in describing how orgasm makes them feel. We know that many of Hite's women report being uncertain as to what an orgasm is and are often confused as to whether they have had one or not. Seymour Fisher also attested to the great variety of experience which is actually encompassed when women use the word orgasm. It is clear that Mosher's respondents were trained to think of sex as part of a total marital experience, and that it was very important to them to view that marital experience as satisfactory. We wonder, then, if they did not overestimate rather than underestimate in their claims to orgasm. Their precision may also have been hampered by embarrassment at dealing with sexuality at all openly, even though their survey participation was voluntary.

What we can surmise about Victorian sexual practices is certainly in accord with our doubts. Marriage manuals and childhood training would certainly have prepared neither husband nor wife to think in terms of lengthy foreplay and clitoral stimulation, especially during the act of coitus. (Interestingly, even doctors daringly interested in female orgasm seemed confused about the functioning of the clitoris.) How can it be that Hite's subjects so often have needed clitoral stimulation during coitus, while Mosher's, reporting no concommitant clitoral stimulation, had less difficulty? Interestingly enough, those few of Mosher's subjects who do discuss the need for foreplay or difficulties of timing, also seem more frank in answering that they don't "always" but do "sometimes" reach orgasm. They also seem to have more to say about what an orgasm does for them than those who claim "perfect" satisfaction.

It is unpleasant to assume the role of sexual interrogator to the Mosher women, but one cannot help wondering if there was not a self-deluding quality in some of their responses. There is always reason for skepticism about what people say about themselves on surveys, and Degler and Gay have been surprisingly naive in their reading of this one, admittedly fascinating, Victorian approximation of survey data. . . .

A note of caution must assuredly be introduced into the "new" interpretation of Victorian sexuality, and more complicated questions explored than have been undertaken to date. Victorian culture cannot be dismissed too lightly. It had purpose, not only as a lament against modernity (which it was for some advocates), but also an encouragement to birth control and a protest against lower-class behavior patterns. The impact of prescriptive literature—repressive in the Victorian period, permissive and sometimes even erotic during the past three decades—poses a difficult interpretive problem, but one that must be faced. If it is true that early histories of Victorianism simplified the prescriptive literature and took it too much at face value, scholars like Gay and Degler have gone too far in the other direction. In fact, we know that prescriptions had real impact on some individuals, like the Frenchwoman described by Theodore Zeldin who tried to divorce her husband for seemingly modest sexual advances, or the many parents who punished masturbation. The Mosher report certainly suggests that the number of middle-class women who took Victorianism literally may have been limited. But we argue that it also suggests that, compared to contemporary expectations of orgasm, the attitudes of most such women also incorporated a large slice of modified Victorianism, which made them look at their sexual experience in distinctive ways. To be sure, another minority undoubtedly defied Victorianism altogether, and wrote diaries to prove it. But the most interesting group, the complex majority, must be sought with subtlety, through evidence that includes prescriptive advice and socialization, evaluative language as well as apparently measurable experience.

❖ *FURTHER READING*

Ben Barker-Benfield, *The Horrors of the Half-Known Life: Male Attitudes Toward Women and Sexuality in Nineteenth-Century America* (1976)

Blanche Wiesen Cook, "Female Support Networks and Political Activism: Lillian Wald, Crystal Eastman, Emma Goldman," *Chrysalis,* no. 3 (1977), 43–61

Nancy Cott, "Passionlessness: An Interpretation of Victorian Sexual Ideology, 1790–1850," *Signs,* IV (1978–79), 219–36

Lawrence Foster, *Religion and Sexuality: Three American Communal Experiments of the Nineteenth Century* (1981)

John Haller, "From Maidenhood to Menopause: Sex Education for Women in Victorian America," *Journal of Popular Culture,* VI (summer 1972), 46–69

John and Robin Haller, *The Physician and Sexuality in Victorian America* (1974)

David Pivar, *Purity Crusade: Sexual Morality and Social Control, 1868–1900* (1973)

Charles Rosenberg, "Sexuality, Class, and Role in Nineteenth-Century America," *American Quarterly,* XXV (1973), 131–54

William Shade, " 'A Mental Passion': Female Sexuality in Victorian America," *International Journal of Women's Studies,* I (1978), 13–29

Daniel Scott Smith, "Family Limitation, Sexual Control, and Domestic Feminism in Victorian America," *Feminist Studies,* I (1973), 40–57

Carroll Smith-Rosenberg and Charles Rosenberg, "The Female Animal: Medical and Biological Views of Woman and Her Role in Nineteenth-Century America," *Journal of American History,* LX (1973), 332–56

Ann Snitow et al., eds., *Powers of Desire: The Politics of Sexuality* (1983)

CHAPTER
10

Suffrage and Social Reform

In the decades around the turn of the century, a large number of women's organizations actively pursued a variety of ends—suffrage, prohibition, child-labor legislation, pure food and drug acts, city beautification, labor organizing, consumer protection, and many other similar goals. The feminist movement, as embodied in the National American Woman Suffrage Association (NAWSA), the umbrella organization created in 1890, has subsequently been criticized for focusing its aims too narrowly on obtaining the vote itself and for overemphasizing the ballot's importance. Yet American women in general more actively and successfully sought social reforms in this era than perhaps in any other, before or since. And regardless of the area at which one looks, one is struck by the uniformity of approach adopted by the female reformers. Unlike their antebellum predecessors, some of whom stressed the ways in which women resembled men and others the ways in which women and men differed, the women of the Progressive Era accepted the latter tenet. Admitting that women and men had diverse roles in life, they contended that women's special qualities and skills were needed in the public as well as in the private realm. How did this way of viewing women facilitate the change from "justice" to "expediency" in seeking the right to vote? What were the benefits and limits to this view of women regarding their efforts in social reform? How did it help women to consolidate forces? And to what extent did it prove necessary for them to work with men?

❖ DOCUMENTS

At a women's suffrage convention in 1890, Charlotte Perkins Stetson (later Gilman) explained how obtaining the vote would improve women's capabilities as mothers; the first selection is from her talk. Eight years later in the same forum, the Reverend Anna Garlin Spencer described (in the second document) how the government would benefit from women's voting. Mary Church Terrell, the president of the National Federation of Colored Women's Clubs, in 1901 praised the reform efforts of organizations composed entirely of black women in an essay excerpted in the third selection. In the fourth document, dating from 1906, Jane Addams told a suffrage convention why urban women in particular needed the vote. And in 1890 Ellen H.

Richards, a promoter of education in home economics for college women, demonstrated in her description of the New England Kitchen (the fifth selection) how women's traditional skills could be applied to societal problems. These documents suggest that despite the widely held view that women were different from men, there was a great diversity of approaches to women's rights and other social issues around the turn of the century.

Charlotte Perkins Stetson on the Effects of the Ballot on Mothers, 1890

What is the suffrage going to do for motherhood? Women enter upon this greatest function of life without any preparation, and their mothers permit them to do it because they do not recognize motherhood as a business. We do not let a man practice as a doctor or a druggist, or do anything else which involves issues of life and death, without training and certificates; but the life and death of the whole human race are placed in the hands of utterly untrained young girls. The suffrage draws the woman out of her purely personal relations and puts her in relations with her kind, and it broadens her intelligence. I am not disparaging the noble devotion of our present mothers—I know how they struggle and toil—but when that tremendous force of mother love is made intelligent, fifty per cent. of our children will not die before they are five years old, and those that grow up will be better men and women. A woman will no longer be attached solely to one little group, but will be also a member of the community. She will not neglect her own on that account, but will be better to them and of more worth as a mother.

Anna Garlin Spencer on the Effects of Women on Government, 1898

The Rev. Anna Garlin Spencer (R. I.) considered the Fitness of Women to Become Citizens from the Standpoint of Moral Development.

Government is not now merely the coarse and clumsy instrument by which military and police forces are directed; it is the flexible, changing and delicately adjusted instrument of many and varied educative, charitable and supervisory functions, and the tendency to increase the functions of government is a growing one. . . . The truth of this is shown in the modern public school system; in the humane and educative care of dependent, defective and wayward children; in the increasingly discriminating and wise treatment of the insane, the pauper, the tramp and the poverty-bound; in the provisions for public parks, baths and amusement places; in the bureaus of investigation and control and the appointment of officers of inspection to secure better sanitary and moral conditions; in the board of arbitration for the settlement of political and labor difficulties; and in the almost innumerable committees and bills, national, State and local, to secure higher social welfare for all classes, especially for the weaker and more ignorant. Government can never again shrink and harden into a mere mechanism of military and penal control.

It is, moreover, increasingly apparent that for these wider and more delicate functions a higher order of electorate, ethically as well as intellectually advanced, is necessary. Democracy can succeed only by securing for its public service, through the rule of the majority, the best leadership and administration the State affords. Only a wise electorate will know how to select such leadership, and only a highly moral one will authoritatively choose such. . . .

Wherever the State touches the personal life of the infant, the child, the youth, or the aged, helpless, defective in mind, body or moral nature, there the State enters "woman's peculiar sphere," her sphere of motherly succor and training, her sphere of sympathetic and self-sacrificing ministration to individual lives. If the service of women is not won to such governmental action (not only through "influence or the shaping of public opinion," but through definite and authoritative exercise), the mother-office of the State, now so widely adopted, will be too often planned and administered as though it were an external, mechanical and abstract function, instead of the personal, organic and practical service which all right helping of individuals must be.

In so far as motherhood has given to women a distinctive ethical development, it is that of sympathetic personal insight respecting the needs of the weak and helpless, and of quick-witted, flexible adjustment of means to ends in the physical, mental and moral training of the undeveloped. And thus far has motherhood fitted women to give a service to the modern State which men can not altogether duplicate. . . .

The earth is ready, the time is ripe, for the authoritative expression of the feminine as well as the masculine interpretation of that common social consciousness which is slowly writing justice in the State and fraternity in the social order.

Mary Church Terrell, "Club Work of Colored Women," 1901

Should anyone ask me what special phase of the Negro's development makes me most hopeful of his ultimate triumph over present obstacles, I should answer unhesitatingly, it is the magnificent work the women are doing to regenerate and uplift the race. Though there are many things in the Negro's present condition to discourage him, he has some blessings for which to be thankful: not the least of these is the progress of our women in everything which makes for the culture of the individual and the elevation of the race.

For years, either banding themselves into small companies or struggling alone, colored women have worked with might and main to improve the condition of their people. The necessity of systematizing their efforts and working on a larger scale became apparent not many years ago, and they decided to unite their forces. Thus it happened that in the summer of 1896 the National Association of Colored Women was formed by the union of two large organizations, from which the advantage of concerted action had been learned. From its birth till the present time its growth has been steady. Interest in the purposes and plans of the National Association has spread so rapidly that it has already been represented in twenty-six states. Handicapped though its members have been, because they lacked both money and experience, their efforts have for the most part been crowned with success.

Kindergartens have been established by some of its organizations, from which encouraging reports have come. A sanitarium with a training school for nurses has been set on such a firm foundation by the Phyllis Wheatley Club of New Orleans, Louisiana, and has proved itself to be such a blessing to the entire community, that the municipal government of that Southern city has voted it an annual appropriation of several hundred dollars. By the members of the Tuskegee branch of the association the work of bringing the light of knowledge and the gospel of cleanliness to their poor benighted sisters on the plantations in Alabama has been conducted with signal success. Their efforts have thus far been confined to four estates, comprising thousands of acres of land, on which live hundreds of colored people yet in the darkness of ignorance and in the grip of sin, and living miles away from churches and schools.

Plans for aiding the indigent orphaned and aged have been projected, and in some instances have been carried into successful execution. One club in Memphis, Tenn., has purchased a large tract of land on which it intends to erect an Old Folks' Home, part of the money for which has already been raised. Splendid service has been rendered by the Illinois Federation of Colored Women's Clubs, through whose instrumentality schools have been visited, truant children looked after, parents and teachers urged to co-operate with each other, rescue and reform work engaged in, so as to reclaim unfortunate women and tempted girls, public institutions investigated, and garments cut, made and distributed to the needy poor.

Questions affecting our legal status as a race are sometimes agitated by our women. In Tennessee and Louisiana colored women have several times petitioned the legislature of their respective states to repeal the obnoxious Jim Crow car laws. . . .

Homes, more homes, better homes, purer homes, is the text upon which our sermons have been and will be preached. There has been a determined effort to have heart-to-heart talks with our women, that we may strike at the root of evils, many of which lie at the fireside. If the women of the dominant race, with all the centuries of education, culture and refinement back of them, with all the wealth of opportunity ever present with them, feel the need of a Mothers' Congress, that they may be enlightened upon the best methods of rearing their children and conducting their homes, how much more do our women, from whom shackles were stricken but yesterday, need information on the same vital subjects! And so the Association is working vigorously to establish mothers' congresses on a small scale, wherever our women can be reached.

From this brief and meagre account of the work which has been and is still being accomplished by colored women through the medium of clubs, it is easy to observe how earnest and effective have been our efforts to elevate the race. No people need ever despair whose women are fully aroused to the duties which rest upon them, and are willing to shoulder responsibilities which they alone can successfully assume. The scope of our endeavors is constantly widening. Into the various channels of generosity and benefi- cence the National Association is entering more and more every day.

Some of our women are urging their clubs to establish day nurseries, a charity of which there is an imperative need. The infants of wage-earning mothers are frequently locked alone in a room from the time the mother leaves in the morning until she returns at night. Not long ago I read in a Southern newspaper that an infant thus locked alone in the room all day had cried itself to death. When one reflects on the slaughter of the innocents which is occurring with pitiless persistency every day, and thinks of the multitudes who are maimed for life or are rendered imbecile, because of the treatment received during their helpless infancy, it is evident that by estab- lishing day nurseries colored women will render one of the greatest services possible to humanity and to the race. . . .

Nothing lies nearer the heart of colored women than the cause of the children. We feel keenly the need of kindergartens, and are putting forth earnest efforts to honeycomb this country with them from one extreme to the other. The more unfavorable the environments of children the more necessary is it that steps be taken to counteract baleful influences upon innocent victims. How imperative is it then, that, as colored women, we inculcate correct principles and set good examples for our own youth, whose little feet will have so many thorny paths of prejudice, temptation and injus- tice to tread. . . .

And so, lifting as we climb, onward and upward we go, struggling, striving and hoping that the buds and blossoms of our desires will burst into glorious fruition ere long. With courage born of success achieved in the past, we look forward to a future large with promise and hope. Seeking no favors because of our color, nor patronage because of our needs, we knock at the bar of Justice and ask for an equal chance.

Jane Addams on the Political Role of Urban Women, 1906

It has been well said that the modern city is a stronghold of industrialism quite as the feudal city was a stronghold of militarism, but the modern cities fear no enemies and rivals from without and their problems of government are solely internal. Affairs for the most part are going badly in these great new centres, in which the quickly-congregated population has not yet learned to arrange its affairs satisfactorily. Unsanitary housing, poisonous sewage, contaminated water, infant mortality, the spread of contagion, adulterated food, impure milk, smoke-laden air, ill-ventilated factories, dangerous occupations, juvenile crime, unwholesome crowding, prostitution and drunkenness are the enemies which the modern cities must face and overcome, would they survive. Logically their electorate should be made up of those who can bear a valiant part in this arduous contest, those who in the past have at least attempted to care for children, to clean houses, to prepare foods, to isolate the family from moral dangers; those who have traditionally taken care of that side of life which inevitably becomes the subject of municipal consideration and control as soon as the population is congested. To test the elector's fitness to deal with this situation by his ability to bear arms is absurd. These problems must be solved, if they are solved at all, not from the military point of view, not even from the industrial point of view, but from a third, which is rapidly developing in all the great cities of the world—the human-welfare point of view. . . .

City housekeeping has failed partly because women, the traditional housekeepers, have not been consulted as to its multiform activities. The men have been carelessly indifferent to much of this civic housekeeping, as they have always been indifferent to the details of the household. . . . The very multifariousness and complexity of a city government demand the help of minds accustomed to detail and variety of work, to a sense of obligation for the health and welfare of young children and to a responsibility for the cleanliness and comfort of other people. Because all these things have traditionally been in the hands of women, if they take no part in them now they are not only missing the education which the natural participation in civic life would bring to them but they are losing what they have always had.

Ellen H. Richards on the New England Model Kitchen, 1890

Let each young college graduate begin her house-keeping in a simple way, feeling keenly that all her future happiness and the welfare of her family depend on the thoroughness with which she masters at the very beginning the essentials of a home.

But not only in her own home is there a call for this knowledge of the fundamental principles of healthful living and domestic economy. In all work for the amelioration of the condition of mankind, philanthropic and practical, there must be a basis of knowledge of the laws and forces which science has discovered and harnessed for our use.

An example of this kind of work undertaken by college women may now be found in Boston. It is a little shop called the New England Kitchen,—a college settlement of a somewhat novel sort,—a place for the cooking and sale of certain typical foods. The cooking is done on scientific principles, and in sight of the customers as an object lesson in methods and cleanliness. It is also a kind of household experiment station, where new apparatus may be tested and frank opinions expressed; a place to which many perplexed house-keepers bring their problems, to find comfort in their despair, if not relief in their troubles. The Kitchen was started primarily in order to learn how the people really live, how they cook, what they buy ready cooked, and what peculiar tastes and prejudices they have. As a means of doing this, it was determined to study the methods of cooking two things,—the cheaper cuts of beef and the cereals,—and to offer for sale the results of the experiments, the proof of this pudding being the selling.

There have been many attempts on the part of sanitary cranks to induce people to eat what was good for them; there have been many attempts on the part of business men to utilize some hygienic theory for a profitable manufacture; but here was an attempt to educate the people to like what was good and nutritious by serving it day by day. The successful issue did not come at once. Each dish was perfected only by the co-operation of the whole neighborhood, after repeated tasting and commenting, so that finally what might be called a cosmopolitan flavor was obtained; and for eight months at noon each day there has been a procession of pitchers, pails, and cans brought by men, women, and children of many nationalities, for pea soup or beef stew, as a witness to the fact that a really good food is appreciated and will be purchased. Here at last is a possible rival to the saloon. When food can be as easily obtained as drink, many a man will take the food in preference.

In this experiment, the training of the college woman showed. No mere enthusiasm would have patiently waited, understanding that success is reached only through failure and after a most careful study of every detail, and is maintained only by constant vigilance. I believe that there is opened up a whole new field of work for college women in this idea. The ease with which they can disseminate practical knowledge over the business counter, the readiness of the people to learn, when once they are convinced that business and not charity rules the establishment, prove that this is one way at least to reach the masses. The greatest lesson learned has been that the people of our cities best worth helping are the most self-respecting and least willing to receive anything in the way of charity.

The scientific work done at the Kitchen has helped greatly in this respect. A special preparation of beef broth for invalids, and a kind of evaporated milk, practically sterilized, and yet obtainable at a price within reach of all, have been approved by many physicians, and have furnished texts for many a lesson in the food of babies and invalids. The fact that every child put on a diet of this milk during the summer has been saved, would alone justify the existence of the Kitchen. . . .

❖ *E S S A Y S*

In the opening piece, Aileen Kraditor of Boston University examines the arguments made by supporters of woman suffrage at the turn of the century, pointing out that they stressed the ways in which women and men differed. Kraditor implies that this "argument from expediency" was a regrettable development, as suffragists abandoned their commitment to principles of "justice." In the second essay, Estelle Freedman, a professor at Stanford University, looks at a wide range of women's organizations in the same period and finds the same phenomenon but views it in a more positive light; it was, she argues, the source of women's success. Finally, in the third selection, a detailed study of Hull House, Kathryn Kish Sklar, who teaches at the State University of New York at Binghamton, cautions that female reformers could not have succeeded in achieving their goals if they had not worked with men inside a male-dominated system. All of these essays deal with the ramifications of the strategy of stressing the differences between women and men.

The Two Major Types of Suffragist Argument

AILEEN KRADITOR

From the early days of the woman's rights movement to 1920 when the Nineteenth Amendment was ratified, American society underwent drastic changes that were reflected in the thinking of the movement. In the middle of the nineteenth century the United States, with the exception of the slave South, was a nation of relative class fluidity, a nation in which men believed themselves equal, if not in fortune, certainly in natural right. The task of the pioneers of women's rights was to prove that this equality applied to women too. A half century later the nation was attempting to understand the implications of the growth of trusts, the influx of immigrants from unfamiliar cultures, the acquisition of colonies populated by "inferior" races, the class strife of the 1890s, and the sharpening demarcation between city and country. The equality of all men was no longer taken for granted, and those to whom it remained a fundamental principle began to see it not as a statement of present fact but as an ideal to be realized in the future. The meaning of the claim that all women were created equal to men altered accordingly.

In the earlier period suffragists had based their demand for political equality with men on the same ground as that on which their men had based their demand for political equality with their English rulers two generations before. If all men were created equal and had the inalienable right to consent to the laws by which they were governed, women were created equal to men and had the same inalienable right to political liberty. In asserting that natural right applied also to women, the suffragists stressed the ways in which men and women were identical. Their common humanity was the core of the suffragist argument. By the end of the century, however, many men of the older American stock were questioning the validity of the principle of "the consent of the governed" as it applied to the new immigrants, the populations of the islands acquired by the United States in 1898, and the workers in the cities. The suffragists, belonging to the same native-born, white, Anglo-Saxon, Protestant, middle class as the men who were rethinking the meaning of natural right, also began to put less emphasis on the

Aileen Kraditor, "The Two Major Types of Suffragist Argument," excerpted from *The Ideas of the Women Suffrage Movement,* 43–46, 52–56, 66–71. Copyright 1965 Columbia University Press, Copyright 1978 Aileen S. Kraditor. Reprinted by permission of author.

common humanity of men and women. At the time when the men of their group were taking new cognizance of the ways in which men differed from each other, new arguments for suffrage evolved, emphasizing the ways in which women differed from men. If the justice of the claim to political equality could no longer suffice, then the women's task was to show that expediency required it. The claim of women to the vote as a natural right never disappeared from the suffragist rationale, but the meaning of natural right changed in response to the new realities, and new arguments enumerating the reforms that women voters could effect took their places alongside the natural right principle that had been the staple plea of the suffragists in the early days of the movement. In 1894 Mrs. Stanton wrote a pamphlet entitled *Suffrage a Natural Right*; in 1918 Mrs. Catt said that she did not know what it was, a right, a duty, or a privilege, but that "whatever it is, the women want it." Mrs. Catt's remark illustrates in two ways the change from justice to expediency. First, she was recognizing the validity of claims to the vote other than natural right and justice. Second, the fact that she could ask for the vote on whatever grounds might bring the most favorable response was itself an indication of the triumph of expediency. This double meaning of the expediency argument appeared time and again. Some suffragists used the expediency argument because social reform was their principal goal and suffrage the means. Other suffragists used the same expediency argument because the link of woman suffrage to reform seemed to be the best way to secure support for their principal goal: the vote. To these women the expediency argument was itself an expedient. The difference between Mrs. Stanton's and Mrs. Catt's standpoints was the difference between not only two generations of suffragist spokesmen but also two periods of American history. . . .

The start of the twentieth century may be taken as the turning point in the change from justice to expediency as the chief argument of the suffragists, but the transition came about gradually, forms of the expediency doctrine having appeared even before Mrs. Stanton wrote "The Solitude of Self." In a period in which, as Merriam has observed, political liberty was becoming linked with political capacity, women could prove their capacity either as members of the "superior race" or as women. In that context they found that the "best" argument of native-born, white, middle-class women was one which would prove their own capacity but not that of men or women of other sections of the population. The decline of arguments on the basis of principles that must logically be universal in application was accompanied by the ever more frequent claim by many suffragists, including Mrs. Stanton herself, that their own enfranchisement could counteract the votes of the undesirable part of the electorate. When even Mrs. Stanton acknowledged the right of legislatures to define the electorate by barring illiterates from the polls, the natural right argument for woman suffrage lost much of its cogency.

The antis did not fail to note the contradiction between the suffragists' claim to the vote as a natural right and their frequent appeals to legislatures, in the late 1890s, to limit the franchise to the desirable elements in the population. Suffragists occasionally in this period complained of the declining faith in democracy, which was becoming an obstacle to women's enfranchisement. If appeals to the principles of democracy fell on deaf ears, then women seeking the vote would have to use other arguments. Hence, declining faith in democracy may have been a cause of the relative decline in importance of suffragist arguments based on the principles of democracy, in two ways: the women shared their men's skepticism as to the capacity of workers and nonwhites for self-government; and whether they shared that skepticism or not, they were forced to use arguments which could find a favorable hearing from the men from whom they sought their political liberty. . . .

To show that the ballot would help create that concrete equality that was woman's natural right, the later suffragists had to discuss specifically what the vote would do for woman and what woman would do with the vote. In this manner, the logic of the natural right claim itself and the transference of equality from the present to the future compelled them to discuss the utility of the ballot. The vote, contended the suffragists, would enlarge woman's interests and intellect by placing upon her part of the responsibility of running the government; it would make her a better mother by enabling her to teach her children from firsthand experience the meaning of citizenship; it would make her a better wife by permitting her to become her husband's equal, thus destroying the warped relationship that bred servility in one spouse and tyranny in the other. In these and other ways political equality would be good for woman, but woman would also be good for government; the development of this proposition dominated their propaganda from about the turn of the century until victory crowned their efforts twenty years later. . . .

The suffrage rationale no longer emphasized what benefits women could derive from the vote, or what the government could do for them. A new argument appeared, stressing what enfranchised women could do for the government and their communities. When the state ceased being regarded as a mere restrainer of men's interference with one another's rights and became a social welfare agency, woman suffrage ceased to be advocated primarily *as* a reform and became in addition a *means to* reform. To the WCTU, it had, of course, been a means to individual reformation. To the last generation of suffragists it became in addition a means to the reform of society. Hence, the new era saw a change from the emphasis by suffragists on the ways in which women were the same as men and therefore had the *right* to vote, to a stress on the ways in which they differed from men, and therefore had the *duty* to contribute their special skills and experience to government.

That this was more than simply a rationalization is proved by the new activities in which the federal and state governments engaged around the turn of the century. Whereas in the middle of the nineteenth century women spun, wove, and sewed the clothing for their families, churned their own butter, baked their own bread, and generally grew their own food, a generation later all these functions had become social activities and by the dawn of the Progressive era had become the subjects of legislation. Many men were performing traditional feminine tasks, as chefs, laundry operators, bakers, garment workers, and food processors. Thousands of women in fact followed these activities out of their homes and into the factories and mills. More and more Americans were living in cities and buying their food and clothing without knowledge of the sanitary conditions under which they had been produced. Their children were attending public schools administered by men who were not responsible to the mothers of their charges.

At a time when large numbers of women were entering professions, working in factories and offices, and earning college degrees, suffragists acknowledged gladly that the home was indeed woman's sphere, but they insisted that the spheres of men and women were not as separate as they had hitherto been. The historic sphere of woman was more and more influenced by political life, as governments passed laws concerning food, water, the production of clothing, and education. Thus the statement that the home was woman's sphere was now an argument not against woman suffrage but in favor of it, for government was now "enlarged housekeeping," and needed the experience of the nation's housekeepers. As the functions which they had previously performed as isolated individuals at home became social functions, women's claim to political equality changed from a demand for the right to protect themselves as individuals to an assertion of their duty to serve society as women. They assumed that their training as cooks, seamstresses, house cleaners, and mothers qualified them to help in legislation concerned with food inspection, sweatshop sanitation, street-cleaning, and public schools.

Just as Mrs. Stanton's "The Solitude of Self" embodied the philosophy of suffragism at the start of our thirty-year period, Jane Addams's "Why Women Should Vote," first published in 1909 in the *Ladies' Home Journal*, may be considered the ideal expression of the new philosophy. Miss Addams began by stating that many women were failing to discharge their duties to their own households simply because they did not perceive that as society grew more complicated it was necessary that women should extend their sense of responsibility to many things outside their own homes if they wanted to continue to preserve their homes. A woman's simplest duty, said Miss Addams, was to keep her house clean and wholesome and feed her children properly. Yet if she lived in an apartment house her efforts to fulfill these duties depended entirely upon the city administration. . . . Miss Addams went on to explain that the ready-made clothing that city women bought was frequently manufactured in germ-ridden sweatshops, and that the purchasers could control the conditions under which it was made only by participating in the lawmaking process. She illustrated her thesis by the example of a woman living in a comfortable house in a neighborhood that was becoming a slum. The woman kept aloof from the immigrants who were her new neighbors, believing that the problems of sanitation rapidly growing critical were no concern of hers. Her daughters came home from college at a time when typhoid was sweeping the area owing to the bad plumbing; one of them died and the other was sick for two years. The tragedy struck this family not because the mother was not devoted to her children but because the individual devotion of one woman to her isolated family was no longer enough to protect them.

In a book written in the same period, Miss Addams gave her thesis an historical background by arguing that cities had originally been formed for common defense against aggression, and their problems of government had then been those of relations with potential external enemies. In that era, she wrote, it was fair that the fighters should decide policies; but modern cities no longer fight, and the ancient test of an elector is no longer valid. The modern city is a stronghold of industrialism, involved in problems like child labor, unsanitary housing, infant mortality, adulterated food, and so on, problems that women from experience are prepared to deal with. "May we not say," she asked, "that city housekeeping has failed partly because women, the traditional housekeepers, have not been consulted as to its multiform activities?"

Miss Addams's argument may be contrasted with one used by Alice Stone Blackwell in the *Woman's Journal,* July 25, 1891. Miss Blackwell had written that women as well as men had the right to vote in municipal government because they breathed the same polluted air, drank the same contaminated water, and suffered the same long-range effects of saloons permitted by city law and therefore should have the same degree of political influence. Miss Addams, on the other hand, instead of arguing that women should have an equal influence because they suffered equally, declared that women ought to have the vote because they were specially fitted for modern municipal business, inasmuch as that business was large-scale housekeeping. Here is an excellent example of the change from justice to expediency as an argument for suffrage with the identical facts used for support in both cases. The suffragists who argued as Miss Addams did emphasized the need for municipal suffrage, although they also favored full suffrage. The functions of government in which they desired women's participation were taken over first in municipalities, and it is not merely coincidental that the Progressive movement realized its objectives most fully in the reform administrations in cities. . . .

The Benefits of Separate Female Organizations

ESTELLE FREEDMAN

In nineteenth-century America, commercial and industrial growth intensified the sexual division of labor, encouraging the separation of men's and women's spheres. While white males entered the public world of wage labor, business, the professions and politics, most white middle-class women re-

Reprinted from Estelle Freedman, "Separatism as Strategy: Female Institution Building and American Feminism, 1870–1930," *Feminist Studies,* V (1979), 512–29, by permission of the publisher, *Feminist Studies,* Inc., c/o Women's Studies Program, University of Maryland, College Park, MD 20742.

mained at home where they provided the domestic, maternal, and spiritual care for their families and the nation. These women underwent intensive socialization into their roles as "true women." Combined with the restrictions on women which denied them access to the public sphere, this training gave American women an identity quite separate from men's. Women shared unique life experiences as daughters, wives, childbearers, childrearers, and moral guardians. They passed on their values and traditions to their female kin. They created what Smith-Rosenberg has called "The Female World of Love and Ritual," a world of homosocial networks that helped these women transcend the alienation of domestic life.

The ideology of "true womanhood" was so deeply ingrained and so useful for preserving social stability in a time of flux that those few women who explicitly rejected its inequalities could find little support for their views. The feminists of the early women's rights movement were certainly justified in their grievances and demands for equal opportunity with men. The Seneca Falls Declaration of Sentiments of 1848, which called for access to education, property ownership, and political rights, has inspired many feminists since then, while the ridicule and denial of these demands have inspired our rage. But the equal rights arguments of the 1850s were apparently too radical for their own times. Men would not accept women's entry into the public sphere, but more importantly, most women were not interested in rejecting their deeply rooted female identities. Both men and women feared the demise of the female sphere and the valuable functions it performed. The feminists, however, still hoped to reduce the limitations on women within their own sphere, as well as to gain the right of choice—of autonomy—for those women who opted for public rather than private roles.

Radical feminists such as Elizabeth Cady Stanton and Susan B. Anthony recognized the importance of maintaining the virtues of the female world while eliminating discrimination against women in public. As their political analysis developed at mid-century, they drew upon the concepts of female moral superiority and sisterhood, and they affirmed the separate nature of woman. At the same time, their disillusionment with even the more enlightened men of the times reinforced the belief that women had to create their own movement to achieve independence. The bitterness that resulted when most male abolitionists refused to support women's rights in the 1860s, and when they failed to include Woman Suffrage in the Fifteenth Amendment (as well as the inclusion of the term "male citizen" in the Fourteenth Amendment) alienated many women reformers. When Frederick Douglass proclaimed in defense that "This is the Negro's Hour," the more radical women's rights advocates followed Stanton and Anthony in withdrawing from the reform coalition and creating a separatist organization. Their National Woman Suffrage Association had women members and officers; supported a broad range of reforms, including changes in marriage and divorce laws; and published the short-lived journal, *The Revolution*. The radical path proved difficult, however, and the National Woman Suffrage Association merged in 1890 with the more moderate American Woman Suffrage Association. Looking back on their disappointment after the Civil War, Stanton and Anthony wrote prophetically in 1881:

> Our liberal men counselled us to silence during the war, and we were silent on our own wrongs; they counselled us to silence in Kansas and New York (in the suffrage referenda), lest we should defeat "Negro Suffrage," and threatened if we were not, we might fight the battle alone. We chose the latter, and were defeated. But standing alone we learned our power: we repudiated man's counsels forevermore; and solemnly vowed that there should never be another season of silence until woman had the same rights everywhere on this green earth, as man. . . .
>
> We would warn the young women of the coming generation against man's advice as to their best interests. . . . Woman must lead the way to her own enfranchisement. . . . She must not put her trust in man in this transition period, since while regarded as his subject, his inferior, his slave, their interests must be antagonistic.

The "transition period" that Stanton and Anthony invoked lasted from the 1870s to the 1920s. It was an era of separate female organization and institution building, the result on the one hand, of the negative push of discrimination in the public, male sphere, and on the other hand, of the positive attraction of the female world of close, personal relationships and domestic institutional structures. These dual origins characterized, for instance, one of the largest manifestations of "social feminism" in the late nineteenth century—the women's club movement.

The club movement illustrated the politicization of women's institutions as well as the limitations of their politics. The exclusion of women reporters from the New York Press Club in 1868 inspired the founding of the first women's club, Sorosis. The movement then blossomed in dozens and later hundreds of localities, until a General Federation of Women's Clubs formed in 1890. By 1910, it claimed over one million members. Although club social and literary activities at first appealed to traditional women who simply wanted to gather with friends and neighbors, by the turn of the century women's clubs had launched civic reform programs. Their activities served to politicize traditional women by forcing them to define themselves as citizens, not simply as wives and mothers. The clubs reflected the societal racism of the time, however, and the black women who founded the National Association of Colored Women in 1896 turned their attention to the social and legal problems that confronted both black women and men.

The Women's Christian Temperance Union had roots in the social feminist tradition of separate institution building. As Ellen DuBois has argued, the WCTU appealed to late nineteenth-century women because it was grounded in the private sphere—the home—and attempted to correct the private abuses against women, namely, intemperance and the sexual double standard. Significantly, though, the WCTU, under Frances Willard's leadership, became a strong prosuffrage organization, committed to righting all wrongs against women, through any means, including the vote.

The women's colleges that opened in these same decades further attest to the importance of separate female institutions during this "transition period." Originally conceived as training grounds of piety, purity, and domesticity, the antebellum women's seminaries, such as Mary Lyon's Mt. Holyoke and Emma Willard's Troy Female Academy, laid the groundwork for the new collegiate institutions of the postwar era. When elite male institutions refused to educate women, the sister colleges of the East, like their counterparts elsewhere, took on the task themselves. In the process they encouraged intimate friendships and professional networks among educated women. At the same time, liberal arts and science training provided tools for women's further development, and by their examples, female teachers inspired students to use their skills creatively. As Barbara Welter noted when she first described the "Cult of True Womanhood," submissiveness was always its weakest link. Like other women's institutions, the colleges could help subvert that element of the Cult by encouraging independence in their students.

The most famous example of the impact of women's colleges may be Jane Addams's description of her experience at Rockford Seminary where she and other students were imbued with the mission of bringing their female values to bear on the entire society. While Addams later questioned the usefulness of her intellectual training in meeting the challenges of the real world, other women did build upon academic foundations when increasingly, as reformers, teachers, doctors, social workers, and in other capacities they left the home to enter public or quasi-public work. Between 1890 and 1920, the number of professional degrees granted to women increased 226 percent, at three times the rate of increase for men. Some of these professionals had attended separate female institutions such as the women's medical colleges in Philadelphia, New York, and Boston. The new female professionals often served women and children clients, in part because of the discrimination against their encroachment on men's domains, but also because they sincerely wanted to work with the traditional objects of their concern. As their skills and roles expanded, these women would demand the right to choose for themselves where and with whom they could work. This first generation of educated professional women became supporters of the suffrage movement in the early twentieth century, calling for full citizenship for women.

The process of redefining womanhood by the extension, rather than by the rejection, of the female sphere may be best illustrated by the settlement house movement. Although both men and women resided in and supported these quasi-public institutions, the high proportion of female participants and leaders (approximately three-fifths of the total), as well as the domestic structure and emphasis on service to women and children, qualify the settlements as female institutions. Mary P. Ryan has captured the link which these ventures provided between "true womanhood" and "new womanhood" in a particularly fitting metaphor: "Within the settlement houses, maternal sentiments were further sifted and leavened until they became an entirely new variety of social reform." Thus did Jane Addams learn the techniques of the political world through her efforts to keep the neighborhood clean. So too did Florence Kelley of Hull House welcome appointment as chief factory inspector of Illinois, to protect women and children workers;

and Julia Lathrop, another Hull House resident, entered the public sphere as director of the United States Children's Bureau; while one-time settlement resident Katherine Bement Davis moved from the superintendency of the Bedford Hills reformatory for women to become in 1914 the first female commissioner of corrections in New York City. Each of these women, and other settlement workers who moved on to professional and public office, eventually joined and often led branches of the National American Woman Suffrage Association. They drew upon the networks of personal friends and professional allies that grew within separate female institutions when they waged their campaigns for social reform and for suffrage.

Separate female organizations were not limited to middle-class women. Recent histories have shown that groups hoping to bridge class lines between women existed within working-class or radical movements. In both the Women's Trade Union League and the National Consumers League, middle-class reformers strived for cooperation, rather than condescension, in their relationships with working women. Although in neither organization were they entirely successful, the Women's Trade Union League did provide valuable services in organizing women workers, many of whom were significant in its leadership. The efforts of the Consumers League, led by Florence Kelley, to improve working conditions through the use of middle-class women's buying power was probably less effective, but efforts to enact protective legislation for women workers did succeed. Members of both organizations turned to suffrage as one solution to the problems workers faced. Meanwhile, both in leftist organizations and in unions, women formed separate female organizations. Feminists within the Socialist Party met in women's groups in the early twentieth century, while within the clothing trades, women workers formed separate local unions which survived until the mid-1920s.

As a final example of female institution building, I want to compare two actual buildings—the Woman's Pavillion at the 1876 Centennial Exposition in Philadelphia, analyzed recently by Judith Paine, and the Woman's Building at the 1893 World Columbian Exposition in Chicago. I think that the origins and functions of each illustrate some of the changes that occurred in the women's movement in the time interval between those two celebrations.

Originally, the managers of the 1876 Centennial had promised "a sphere for woman's action and space for her work" within the main display areas. In return women raised over $100,000 for the fair, at which point the management informed the Women's Centennial Executive Committee that there would not be any space for them in the main building. The women's response surprised the men: they raised money for a separate building, and although they hoped to find a woman architect to design it, there was no such professional at the time. From May through October, 1876, the Woman's Pavillion displayed achievements in journalism, medicine, science, art, literature, invention, teaching, business, and social work. It included a library of books by women; an office that published a newspaper for women; and an innovative kindergarten annex, the first such day school in the country. Some radical feminists, however, boycotted the building. Elizabeth

Cady Stanton claimed that the pavillion "was no true exhibit of woman's art" because it did not represent the product of industrial labor or protest the inequalities of "political slavery."

By 1893, there was less hesitation about the need for a woman's building and somewhat less conflict about its functions. Congress authorized the creation of a Board of Lady Managers for the Columbian Commission, and the women quickly decided on a separate Woman's Building, to be designed by a woman architect chosen by nationwide competition. Contests were also held to locate the best women sculptors, painters, and other artists to complete the designs of the building. The Lady Managers also planned and provided a Children's Building that offered nursery care for over ten thousand young visitors to the fair. At this exposition, not only were women's artistic and professional achievements heralded, but industrial organizations were "especially invited to make themselves known," and women's industrial work, as well as the conditions and wages for which they worked, were displayed. Feminists found this exhibit more agreeable; Antoinette Brown Blackwell, Julia Ward Howe, and Susan B. Anthony all attended, and Anthony read a paper written by Elizabeth Cady Stanton at one of the women's symposia. The Board of Lady Managers fought long and hard to combine their separate enterprise with participation in the rest of the fair. They demanded equal representation of women judges for the exhibitions and equal consideration of women's enterprises in all contests. While they had to compromise on some goals, their efforts are noteworthy as an indication of a dual commitment to separate female institutions, but only if they had equal status within the society at large.

The separate institution building of the late nineteenth century rested on a belief in women's unique identity which had roots in the private female sphere of the early nineteenth century. Increasingly, however, as its participants entered a public female world, they adopted the more radical stance of feminists such as Stanton and Anthony who had long called for an end to political discrimination against women.

The generation that achieved suffrage, then, stood on the border of two worlds, each of which contributed to its ideology and politics. Suffragists argued that women needed the vote to perform their traditional tasks—to protect themselves as mothers and to exert their moral force on society. Yet they also argued for full citizenship and waged a successful, female-controlled political campaign to achieve it.

The suffrage movement succeeded by appealing to a broad constituency—mothers, workers, professionals, reformers—with the vision of the common concerns of womanhood. The movement failed, however, by not extending fully the political strengths of woman bonding. For one thing, the leadership allowed some members to exploit popular racist and nativist sentiments in their prosuffrage arguments, thus excluding most black and immigrant women from a potential feminist coalition. They also failed to recognize that the bonds that held the constituency together were not "natural," but social and political. The belief that women would automatically use the vote to the advantage of their sex overlooked both the class and racial lines that separated women. It underestimated the need for continued political organization so that their interests might be united and realized. . . .

Women Reformers and Hull House

KATHRYN KISH SKLAR

What were the sources of women's political power in the United States in the decades before they could vote? How did women use the political power they were able to muster? This essay attempts to answer these questions by examining one of the most politically effective groups of women reformers in U.S. history—those who assembled in Chicago in the early 1890s at Hull House, one of the nation's first social settlements, founded in 1889 by Jane Addams and Ellen Gates Starr. Within that group, this study focuses on the reformer Florence Kelley (1859–1932). Kelley joined Hull House in 1891 and remained until 1899, when she moved to Lillian Wald's Henry Street Settlement on the Lower East Side of New York, where she lived for the next twenty-seven years. According to Felix Frankfurter, Kelley "had probably the largest single share in shaping the social history of the United States during the first thirty years of this century," for she played "a powerful if not decisive role in securing legislation for the removal of the most glaring abuses of our hectic industrialization following the Civil War." It was in the 1890s that Kelley and her colleagues at Hull House developed the patterns of living and thinking that guided them throughout their lives of reform, leaving an indelible imprint on U.S. politics. This essay attempts to determine the extent to which their political power and activities flowed from their collective life as coresidents and friends and the degree to which this power was attributable to their close affiliation with male reformers and male institutions.

The effects of both factors can be seen in one of the first political campaigns conducted by Hull House residents—the 1893 passage and the subsequent enforcement of pathbreaking antisweatshop legislation mandating an eight-hour day for women and children employed in Illinois manufacturing. This important episode reveals a great deal about the sources of this group's political power, including their own collective initiative, the support of other women's groups, and the support of men and men's groups. Finally, it shows how women reformers and the gender-specific issues they championed helped advance class-specific issues during a time of fundamental social, economic, and political transition.

One of the most important questions asked by historians of American women today is, To what degree has women's social power been based on separate female institutions, culture, and consciousness, and to what degree has it grown out of their access to male spheres of influence, such as higher education, labor organization, and politics? This essay advances the com-

Kathryn Kish Sklar, "Hull House in the 1890s: A Community of Women Reformers," *Signs*, X (1985), 657–77. Reprinted by permission of The University of Chicago Press.

monsense notion that women's social power in the late nineteenth century depended on both sources of support. Women's institutions allowed them to enter realms of reality dominated by men, where, for better or for worse, they competed with men for control over the distribution of social resources. Thus although their own communities were essential to their social strength, women were able to realize the full potential of their collective power only by reaching outside those boundaries.

The community of women at Hull House made it possible for Florence Kelley to step from the apprenticeship to the journeyman stage in her reform career. A study of the 1893 antisweatshop campaign shows that the community provided four fundamental sources of support for her growth as a reformer. First, it supplied an emotional and economic substitute for traditional family life, linking her with other talented women of her own class and educational and political background and thereby greatly increasing her political and social power. Second, the community at Hull House provided Kelley with effective ties to other women's organizations. Third, it enabled cooperation with men reformers and their organizations, allowing her to draw on their support without submitting to their control. Finally, it provided a creative setting for her to pursue and develop a reform strategy she had already initiated in New York—the advancement of the rights and interests of working people in general by strengthening the rights and interests of working women and children.

As a community of women, Hull House provided its members with a lifelong substitute for family life. In that sense it resembled a religious order, supplying women with a radical degree of independence from the claims of family life and inviting them to commit their energies elsewhere. When she first crossed the snowy threshold of Hull House "sometime between Christmas and New Year's," 1891, Florence Kelley Wischnewetzky was fleeing from her husband and seeking refuge for herself and her three children, ages six, five, and four. "We were welcomed as though we had been invited," she wrote thirty-five years later in her memoirs. . . .

One source of the basic trust established among the three major reformers at Hull House in the 1890s—Jane Addams, Julia Lathrop, and Florence Kelley—was similarity of family background. Not only were they all of the upper middle class, but their fathers were politically active men who helped Abraham Lincoln found and develop the Republican Party in the 1860s. John Addams served eight terms as a state senator in Illinois, William Lathrop served in Congress as well as in the Illinois legislature, and William Kelley served fifteen consecutive terms in Congress. All were vigorous abolitionists, and all encouraged their daughters' interests in public affairs. As Judge Alexander Bruce remarked at the joint memorial services held for Julia Lathrop and Florence Kelley after their deaths in 1932, "Both of them had the inspiration of great and cultured mothers and both had great souled fathers who, to use the beautiful language of Jane Addams in speaking of her own lineage, 'Wrapped their little daughters in the large men's doubtlets, careless did they fit or no.' "

These three remarkable women were participating in a political tradition that their fathers had helped create. While they were growing up in the 1860s and 1870s, they gained awareness through their fathers' experience of the mainstream of American political processes, thereby learning a great deal about its currents—particularly that its power could be harnessed to fulfill the purposes of well-organized interest groups.

Although Hull House residents have generally been interpreted as reformers with a religious motivation, it now seems clear that they were instead motivated by political goals. In that regard they resembled a large proportion of other women social settlement leaders, including those associated with Hull House after 1900, such as Grace and Edith Abbot, whose father was Nebraska's first lieutenant governor, or Sophonisba Breckinridge, daughter of a Kentucky congressman. Women leaders in the social settlement movement seem to have differed in this respect from their male counterparts, who were seeking alternatives to more orthodox religious, rather than political, careers. In, but not of, the Social Gospel movement, the women at Hull House were a political boat on a religious stream, advancing political solutions to social problems that were fundamentally ethical or moral, such as the right of workers to a fair return for their labor or the right of children to schooling.

Another source of the immediate solidarity among Addams, Lathrop, and Kelley was their shared experience of higher education. Among the first generation of American college women, they graduated from Rockford College, Vassar College, and Cornell University, respectively, in the early 1880s and then spent the rest of the decade searching for work and for a social identity commensurate with their talents. Addams tried medical school; Lathrop worked in her father's law office; Kelley, after being denied admission to graduate study at the University of Pennsylvania, studied law and government at the University of Zurich, where she received a much more radical education than she would have had she remained in Philadelphia. In the late 1880s and early 1890s, the social settlement movement was the right movement at the right time for this first generation of college-educated women, who were able to gain only limited entry to the male-dominated professions of law, politics, or academics. . . .

About thirty women's organizations combined forces and entered into local politics in 1888 through the Illinois Women's Alliance, organized that year by Elizabeth Morgan and other members of the Ladies Federal Union no. 2073 in response to a crusading woman journalist's stories in the *Chicago Times* about "City Slave Girls" in the garment industry. The alliance's political goals were clearly stated in their constitution: "The objects of the Alliance are to agitate for the enforcement of all existing laws and ordinances that have been enacted for the protection of women and children—as the factory ordinances and the compulsory education law. To secure the enactment of such laws as shall be found necessary. To investigate all business establishments and factories where women and children are employed and public institutions where women and children are maintained. To procure the appointment of women, as inspectors and as members of boards of education, and to serve on boards of management of public institutions." Adopting the motto "Justice to Children, Loyalty to Women," the alliance acted as a vanguard for the entrance of women's interests into municipal and state politics, focusing chiefly on the passage and enforcement of compulsory education laws. One of its main accomplishments was the agreement of the city council in 1889 "to appoint five lady inspectors" to enforce city health codes.

The diversity of politically active women's associations in Chicago in the late 1880s was reflected in a list of organizations associated with the alliance. Eight bore names indicating a religious or ethical affiliation, such as the Woodlawn branch of the Women's Christian Temperance Union and the Ladies Union of the Ethical Society. Five were affiliated with working women or were trade unions, such as the Working Women's Protective Association, the Ladies Federal Union no. 2703, and (the only predominantly male organization on the list) the Chicago Trades and Labor Assembly. Another five had an intellectual or cultural focus, such as the Hopkins Metaphysical Association or the Vincent Chatauqua Association. Three were women's professional groups, including the Women's Press Association and the Women's Homeopathic Medical Society. Another three were female auxiliaries of male social organizations, such as the Lady Washington Masonic Chapter and the Ladies of the Grand Army of the Republic. Two were suffrage associations, including the Cook County Suffrage Association; another two were clubs interested in general economic reform, the Single Tax Club and the Land Labor Club no. 1; and one was educational, the Drexel Kindergarten Association. . . .

The close relationship between Hull House and other groups of women in Chicago was exemplified in Kelley's interaction with the Chicago Women's Club. The minutes of the club's first meeting after Kelley's arrival in Chicago show that on January 25, 1892, she spoke under the sponsorship of Jane Addams on the sweating system and urged that a committee be created on the problem. Although a Reform Department was not created until 1894, minutes of March 23, 1892, show that the club's Home Department "decided upon cooperating with Mrs. Kelly [*sic*] of Hull House in establishing a Bureau of Women's Labor." Thus the club took over part of the funding and the responsibility for the counseling service Kelley had been providing at Hull House since February. (Initially Kelley's salary for this service was funded by the settlement, possibly with emergency monies given by Mary Rozet Smith.) In this way middle- and upper-middle-class clubwomen were drawn into the settlement's activities. In 1893 Jane Addams successfully solicited the support of wealthy clubwomen to lobby for the antisweatshop legislation: "We insisted that well-known Chicago women should accompany this first little group of Settlement folk who with trade-unionists moved upon the state capitol in behalf of factory legislation." Addams also described the lobbying Hull House residents conducted with other voluntary associations: "Before the passage of the law could be secured, it was necessary to appeal to all elements of the community, and a little group of us addressed the open meetings of trades-unions and of benefit societies, church organizations, and social clubs literally every evening for three months.'' Thus Hull House was part of a larger social universe of voluntary organizations, and one important feature of its political effectiveness was its ability to gain the support of middle-class and working-class women.

In 1893 the cross-class coalition of the Illinois Women's Alliance began to dissolve under the pressure of the economic depression of that year, and in 1894 its leaders disbanded the group. Hull House reformers inherited the fruits of the alliance's five years of agitation, and they continued its example of combining working-class and middle-class forces. In 1891 Mary Kenney, a self-supporting typesetter who later became the first woman organizer to be employed by the American Federation of Labor, established the Jane Club adjacent to the settlement, a cooperative boardinghouse for young working women. In the early 1890s Kenney was a key figure in the settlement's efforts to promote union organizing among working women, especially bookbinders. Thus the combination of middle-class and working-class women at Hull House in 1892–93 was an elite version of the type of cross-class association represented by the Illinois Women's Alliance of the late 1880s—elite because it was smaller and because its middle-class members had greater social resources, familiarity with American political processes, and exposure to higher than average levels of education, while its working-class members (Mary Kenney and Alzina Stevens) were members of occupational and organizational elites.

By collectivizing talents and energies, this community made possible the exercise of greater and more effective political power by its members. A comparison of Florence Kelley's antisweatshop legislation, submitted to the Illinois investigative committee in February 1893, with that presented by Elizabeth Morgan dramatically illustrates this political advantage. The obvious differences in approach indicate that the chief energy for campaigning on behalf of working women and children had passed from working-class to middle-class social reformers. Both legislative drafts prohibited work in tenement dwellings, Morgan's prohibiting all manufacturing, Kelley's all garment making. Both prohibited the labor of children under fourteen and regulated the labor of children aged fourteen to sixteen. Kelley's went beyond Morgan's in two essential respects, however. Hers mandated an eight-hour day for women in manufacturing, and it provided for enforcement by calling for a state factory inspector with a staff of twelve, five whom were to be women. The reasons for Kelley's greater success as an innovator are far from clear, but one important advantage in addition to her greater education and familiarity with the American political system was the larger community on which she could rely for the law's passage and enforcement.

Although Elizabeth Morgan could draw on her experience as her husband's assistant in his work as an attorney and on the support of women unionists, both resources were problematic. Thomas Morgan was erratic and self-centered, and Elizabeth Morgan's relationship with organized women workers was marred by sectarian disputes originating within the male power structure of the Chicago Trades and Labor Assembly. For example, in January 1892, when she accused members of the Shirtwaist Union of being controlled by her husband's opposition within the assembly, ''a half dozen women surrounded [her] seat in the meeting and demanded an explanation. She refused to give any and notice was served that charges would be preferred against her at the next meeting of the Ladies' Federation of Labor." Perhaps Morgan's inability to count on a supportive community explains her failure to provide for adequate enforcement and to include measures for workers over the age of sixteen in her legislative draft. Compared to Kelley's, Morgan's bill was politically impotent. It could not enforce what it endorsed, and it did not affect adults.

Kelley's draft was passed by the Illinois legislature in June 1893, providing for a new office of enforcement and for an eight-hour day for women workers of all ages. After Henry Demarest Lloyd declined an invitation to serve as the state's first factory inspector, reform governor John Peter Altgeld followed Lloyd's recommendations and appointed Kelley. Thus eighteen months after her arrival in Chicago, she found herself in charge of a dedicated and well-paid staff of twelve mandated to see that prohibitions against tenement workshops and child labor were observed and to enforce a pathbreaking article restricting the working hours of women and children.

Hull House provided Kelley and other women reformers with a social vehicle for independent political action and a means of bypassing the control of male associations and institutions, such as labor unions and political parties; at the same time they had a strong institutional framework in which they could meet with other reformers, both men and women. The drafting of the antisweatshop legislation revealed how this process worked. In his autobiography, Abraham Bisno, pioneer organizer in the garment industry in Chicago and New York, described how he became a regular participant in public discussions of contemporary social issues at Hull House. He joined "a group . . . composed of Henry D. Lloyd, a prominent physician named Bayard Holmes, Florence Kelley, and Ellen G. [Starr] to engage in a campaign for legislation to abolish sweatshops, and to have a law passed prohibiting the employment of women more than eight hours a day." Answering a question about the author of the bill he endorsed at the 1893 hearings, Bisno said, "Mrs. Florence Kelly [*sic*] wrote that up with the advice of myself, Henry Lloyd, and a number of prominent attorneys in Chicago." Thus as the chief author of the legislation, Florence Kelley drew on the expertise of Bisno, one of the most dedicated and talented union organizers; of Lloyd, one of the most able elite reformers in the United States; and, surely among the "prominent attorneys," of Clarence Darrow, one of the country's most able reform lawyers. It is difficult to imagine this cooperative effort between Bisno, Kelley, and Lloyd without the existence of the larger Hull House group of which they were a part. Their effective collaboration exemplified the process by which members of this remarkable community of women reformers moved into the vanguard of contemporary reform activity, for they did so in alliance with other groups and individuals. . . .

Historians of women have tended to assume that protective labor legislation was imposed on women workers by hostile forces beyond their control—especially by men seeking to eliminate job competition. To some degree this was true of the 1893 legislation since, by closing tenement dwellings to garment manufacture and by depriving sweatshop contractors of the labor of children under fourteen, the law reduced the number of sweatshops, where women and children predominated, and increased the number of garment workers in factories, where men prevailed. Abraham Bisno was well aware of the widespread opposition to the law and took time to talk with offenders, "to educate the parents who sent their children to work, and the employers of these children, the women who were employed longer than eight hours a day, and their employers." Jane Addams also tried to help those who were deprived of work by the new law: "The sense that the passage of the child labor law would in many cases work hardship, was never absent from my mind during the earliest years of its operation. I addressed as many mothers' meetings and clubs among working women as I could, in order to make clear the objective of the law and the ultimate benefit to themselves as well as to their children."

Did the children benefit? While further research is needed on this question, recent scholarship pointing to the importance of working-class support for the schooling of working-class children has revised earlier estimates that children and their families did not benefit. At best the law was a halfway measure that encouraged but could not force parents to place their children in school. Nevertheless, Florence Kelley was pleased with the compliance of parents and school officials. As she wrote Henry Demarest Lloyd, "Out of sixty-five names of children sent to the Board of Education in our first month of notifying it when we turned children under 14 yrs. of age out of factories, twenty-one were immediately returned to school and several others are known to be employed as nursegirls and cashgirls i.e. in non-prohibited occupations. This is good co-operation." While schools were inadequate and their teachers frequently prejudiced against immigrants, education was also an important route out of the grinding poverty that characterized immigrant neighborhoods. Thus it is not surprising that a large minority of parents complied with the law by enrolling their children in school.

The chief beneficiaries of the law, apart from those children who gained from schooling, were garment workers employed in factories. Most of these were men, but about one in four were women. The 1893 law was designed to prevent the erosion of this factory labor force and its replacement by sweatshop labor. Bisno described that erosion in his testimony before the state investigating committee early in 1893, stating, "Joseph Beifeld & Company have had three hundred and fifty employees some eleven or twelve years ago inside, and they have only eighty now to my knowledge, and they have increased their business about six times as much as it was eleven years ago." This decline of the factory population inevitably caused a decline of union membership since it was much more difficult to organize sweatshop workers. Thus as a union official Bisno was defending his own interests, but these were not inimical to all women workers.

Demonstrating the support of women unionists for the law's enforcement, members of the Women's Shoemakers Union chastized the Chicago Trades and Labor Assembly in February 1894 for their lukewarm support of the by-then-beleaguered eight-hour restriction. They "introduced resolutions, strongly condemning the manufacturers of this City for combining to nullify the state laws. . . . The resolutions further set forth that the members of the Women's Shoemakers Union effected as they were by the operation of the Eight hour Law unanimously approved the Law and for the benefit of themselves, for their sister wage workers and the little children, they pleaded for its maintenance and Enforcement.'' Although some women workers—particularly those who headed households with small children—must have opposed the law's enforcement, others, especially single women and mothers able to arrange child care, stood to gain from the benefits of factory employment. In a study completed for the Illinois Bureau of Labor Statistics in 1892, Florence Kelley found that 48 percent of Chicago working women lacked the "natural protectors" of fathers or husbands. Viewing them as a permanent feature of the paid labor force, she pointed to the importance of their wages to their families, thereby refuting the notion that all working women were supported by male wage earners. Although the historical evidence does not reveal how many, some young women who had formerly worked in sweatshops and whose families relied heavily on their wages doubtlessly benefited from the legislation by moving into larger factories with better working conditions.

The 1893 statute made it possible for women as well as men to move from exploitative, low-paying sweatshops into larger shops and factories with power machinery, unions, and higher wages. While the law's prohibition of tenement manufacturing obviously enabled such mobility, its eight-hour clause was no less instrumental since it attacked the basic principles of the sweating system—long hours and low wages. The average working day in the garment industry was about ten hours, but in some sweatshops it could be as long as twelve, thirteen, or fourteen hours. Reducing the working day from ten to eight hours did not significantly decrease production in factories with electric or steam-powered machinery since productivity could be raised by increasing a machine's speed or a worker's skill level. However, the eight-hour law drove many subcontractors or "sweaters" out of business since it eliminated the margin of profit created by workers' long hours at foot-powered sewing machines. From the sweatshop workers' perspective, it reduced wages even further since they were paid by the piece and could finish a much smaller amount of goods in eight hours. The wages of factory workers, by contrast, were likely to remain the same since negotiations between employers and employees customarily included a consideration of what it cost to sustain life, a factor absent from the sweaters' calculations. . . .

What conclusions can be drawn about the Hull House community from this review of their activities on behalf of antisweatshop legislation? First, and foremost, it attests to the capacity of women to sustain their own institutions. Second, it shows that this community's internal dynamics promoted a creative mixture of mutual support and individual expression. Third, these talented women reformers used their institution as a means of allying with male reformers and entering the mainstream of the American political process. In the tradition of earlier women's associations in the United States, they focused on the concerns of women and children, but these concerns were never divorced from those of men and of the society as a whole. Under the leadership of Florence Kelley, they pursued gender-specific reforms that served class-specific goals.

In these respects the Hull House community serves as a paradigm for women's participation in Progressive reform. Strengthened by the support of women's separate institutions, women reformers were able to develop their capacity for political leadership free from many if not all of the constraints that otherwise might have been imposed on their power by the male-dominated parties or groups with which they cooperated. Building on one of the strengths of the nineteenth-century notion of "women's sphere"—its social activism on behalf of the rights and interests of women and children—they represented those rights and interests innovatively and effectively. Ultimately, however, their power encountered limits imposed by the male-dominated political system, limits created more in response to their class-specific than to their gender-specific reform efforts.

✣ *FURTHER READING*

Joyce Antler, "After College, What? New Graduates and the Family Claim," *American Quarterly*, XXXII (1980), 409–34

G. J. Barker-Benfield, "Mother Emancipator: The Meaning of Jane Addams' Sickness and Cure," *Journal of Family History*, IV (1979), 395–420

Karen Blair, *The Clubwoman as Feminist* (1980)

Jill K. Conway, "Women Reformers and American Culture, 1870–1930," *Journal of Social History*, V (1971–72), 164–77

Allen Davis, *American Heroine: The Life and Legend of Jane Addams* (1973)

——, *Spearheads for Reform: The Social Settlements and the Progressive Movement, 1890–1914* (1967)

Roberta Frankfort, *Collegiate Women: Domesticity and Career in Turn-of-the-Century America* (1977)

Paula Giddings, *When and Where I Enter: The Impact of Black Women on Race and Sex in America* (1984)

Dolores Hayden, *The Grand Domestic Revolution: A History of Feminist Design for American Homes, Neighborhoods, and Cities* (1981)

Ellen Lageman, *A Generation of Women: Education in the Lives of Progressive Reformers* (1979)

Gerda Lerner, "Early Community Work of Black Club Women," *Journal of Negro History*, LIX (1974), 158–67

David Morgan, *Suffragists and Democrats* (1972)

Sheila Rothman, *Woman's Proper Place* (1978)

John Rousmaniere, "Cultural Hybrid in the Slums: The College Woman and the Settlement House, 1889–1914," *American Quarterly*, XXII (1970), 45–66

Margaret Gibbons Wilson, *The American Woman in Transition: The Urban Influence, 1870–1920* (1979)

Allis R. Wolfe, "Women, Consumerism, and the National Consumers' League in the Progressive Era, 1900–1923," *Labor History*, XVI (1975), 378–92

Marlene Stein Wortman, "Domesticating the Nineteenth-Century American City," *Prospects*, III (1977), 531–72

CHAPTER

11

Work Culture in the

Early Twentieth Century

In the early years of the twentieth century, the patterns of women's employment in
this country changed dramatically. During the nineteenth century, the majority of
wage-earning women in the United States worked as domestic servants. But the
expansion of the service and bureaucratic sectors of the American economy in the
last two decades of the nineteenth century opened up many new job opportunities
for females. The new department stores that served growing numbers of affluent
middle- and upper-class women needed sales clerks. Even more important, the
expanding offices of America's industries required secretaries trained to operate
that novel machine, the typewriter. At the same time, many more young women
were attending high school and afterward seeking white-collar employment before
marriage.

Because these young women did not want to work in factories or domestic
service—even though sometimes their wages in such positions would have been
higher—they flocked to the new jobs, creating sex- and age-segregated workplace
environments that, some historians have argued, had a profound impact on their
consciousness. Factory jobs, like those in the Lowell mills a century earlier, also followed the same pattern of age and sex segregation. The trend toward increasing
employment for women, even in such limited circumstances, aroused considerable
comment among contemporaries. What opportunities, or lack thereof, both inside
and outside the workplace, served to reinforce traditional gender-related behaviors
in working women? How did group loyalty help or hinder working women regarding both defending their rights and personal ambition?

❧ DOCUMENTS

As early as 1891, the number of young women working in clerical positions in major
cities had risen so dramatically that *Cosmopolitan* magazine noted the trend in the
lengthy article reprinted here as the first document. Although most people did not
object to the employment of single women, many commentators disapproved of
wage-earning by married women; a representative example of such reasoning is the

1906 statement by Samuel Gompers, leader of the American Federation of Labor, that appears here as the second selection. Some authors, like Harriet Brunkhurst, writing in the *Ladies Home Journal* in 1910, sympathized with the difficulties that working daughters encountered at home, as the third document shows. Yet, as Fannie Barrier Williams pointed out in the fourth selection, written in 1903, the new opportunities were open only to white women; black women still could rarely find jobs in fields other than domestic service. Although increasing numbers of young women sought employment, they encountered many obstacles on the road to a successful work career, particularly if they planned to work after marrying.

Clara Lanza, "Women Clerks in New York," 1891

The close of the nineteenth century brings us face to face with many noteworthy progressive movements that point triumphantly to the promotion of free thought; but perhaps none is more vital and significant than the progress that is based upon a high standard of womanly independence and is the direct outcome of a purely feminine inspiration. With the increase of educational advantages has come a corresponding evolution in habits and manners. Old-time prejudices lie buried. Work has become fashionable. By work, I do not mean dilettante dalliance with the implements of labor, but actual exercise of brain and muscle as a means of livelihood. Feminine dignity is nowadays in nowise imperilled by legitimate employment used as a means of existence. It is an accepted fact, and one that is wholly in accordance with a proper American spirit of democracy, that girls should be educated with a view to earning their own living. . . .

Among the woman workers in New York there are none who afford a more interesting study than the vast army of clerks; the work of a clerk being admirably adapted to the sex. You may count almost on the fingers of one hand the number of years that have elapsed since the women clerks appeared. Yet so prevalent have they become in all our large cities, that one might say they have entirely superseded the men in this particular department. Nine employers out of ten prefer women as clerks. If this statement appears to be a sweeping one, it can be verified by the fact that the demand for women as clerical workers is steadily on the increase, while men stand a comparatively poor chance of securing positions. The circumstance is amply justified by many reasons, not the least of these being the superior quality of the work performed by women.

Speaking, not long ago, to the head of a large publishing house where women were employed as cashiers and book-keepers, I ventured to ask whether the women compared favorably with men in the fulfilment of their respective duties.

"Women," was the answer, "are much to be preferred for a number of reasons. They are capable and industrious, and, so far as my personal experience goes, absolutely reliable. Besides, a woman is more conscientious about her work. . . .

Men are troublesome. They complain about trifles that a woman wouldn't notice. The office boys don't suit, or the temperature of the building is too hot or too cold, or the light is not properly adjusted. Then, if they have a slight headache, they stay at home. Most of them are married, and their wives fall ill, or their mother-in-law comes on a visit, and all these things are made an excuse for absence. The women come whether they have headaches or not. They never want a day off to attend a baseball match. They undertake the work with a full understanding of what is required of them, and they are steadfast in the performance of their duties. We treat them well and never refuse to grant them any trifling favor. There is only one thing we exact over and above their business qualifications. We do not employ a woman unless she lives at home with her family.

"This has the appearance of injustice, but if you reflect a moment you will recollect that the temptations to which a woman living by herself is exposed in a great city are manifold and dangerous, and for our own sake we find it necessary that our clerks, like Caesar's wife, should be above suspicion as to character and antecedents. We must know all about them and their families." . . .

The above proved conclusively that capability and a readiness to work did not in every instance insure a desirable occupation to the woman who sought it. A girl who had no "family," and who was obliged to depend upon her individual exertions for the food she ate and the clothes she wore, could not hope to get any position of trust. A woman who handles large sums of money that do not belong to her must be surrounded on all sides by a definite respectability; and while it sounds a bit quixotic to insist that she must have family connections over and above all her other virtues, it is perfectly just in the abstract. Unfortunately, respectable relations cannot be manufactured to order; therefore she who has them not would better become a typewriter, a stenographer, or a telegraph operator.

The large schools of stenography and typewriting turn out annually hundreds of women who rank easily with the most accomplished men clerks. Typewriting, being in great demand, is perhaps the most lucrative of the minor employments open to women. It is claimed that the market is decidedly overstocked with typewriters, and that there are not half enough positions for the largely increasing number of candidates. But this is a mistake. The market may be overcrowded with women who claim to be typewriters and stenographers, but in reality there is not a sufficient number of well-trained and capable clerks to supply the demand.

"By far the greatest difficulty I have to contend with," says Miss Seymour, who presides over the Union School of stenography and typewriting, "is to keep my best operators with me. Although I pay them liberal salaries and do everything I can to secure their services permanently, they are in constant receipt of offers that men would be glad to receive. Many pupils of the school receive offers of positions at salaries varying from eight to twelve dollars a week before they have finished the six months' course of instruction. I mention this for the purpose of showing how popular the employment of women clerks has become, that is, if they are properly trained for the work. It is positive that an intelligent woman is especially fitted for clerical work. If she does not succeed her failure is due to faulty training. Business men tell me they prefer women as shorthand amanuenses for one particular reason. It is because, contrary to accepted tradition, women are less likely than men to disclose the business secrets of their employers. Then, too, they are more faithful and more apt to remain for a long period in the service of one employer.

"Of course, a number of employers engage women under the prevailing impression that they will work for lower wages; but while this is true in the majority of cases, it is equally true that efficient women can command as high salaries as men, particularly if they refuse to work for less, which is usually the case."

Typewriting and stenography are not of themselves very difficult of comprehension or execution, and it does not take long in order to familiarize one's self with either; but a clerk who wishes to succeed must know many more things. She must possess a ready knowledge of English composition and orthography. She must be able to punctuate properly, and above all, be quick to grasp an idea. Large numbers of girls spend their last penny in an attempt to fit themselves for clerical work, only to discover that, owing to their rudimentary education and total inaptitude, it is impossible for them to fill any responsible position. A few study and persevere, contenting themselves with a meagre salary, five or six dollars a week perhaps, and thus gradually work themselves up to a higher rung of the ladder. But there are scores of discouraged plodders who have not the spirit of hopeful aspiration to guide them, and these fall by the wayside and sink into obscurity, while their braver sisters pass on to victory. . . .

Most clerks have comfortable homes with their parents, and numbers of them enjoy not only the ordinary necessaries of life, but a considerable portion of its luxuries. As a rule, the clerk's entire salary is at her disposal for her personal requirements. She must dress neatly, and then there are petty vanities that every woman likes to indulge, no matter what her station may be. The woman clerk is rarely frivolous in her demeanor. She cannot afford frivolity; the mere fact of her self-dependence invests her with a certain outward dignity that one sees seldom displaced even when brought into collision with the powerful exuberance of youthful animal spirits. Not that she is prim and puritanical. She does not eschew legitimate pleasure nor regard amusement as superfluous. But she seems impressed by the consciousness that being forced to trust her mental resources for whatever she now has and is destined to enjoy in the future constitutes an inspiring duty that is not the less evident or sacred because it happens to devolve entirely upon herself. Temptations descend and threaten her, temptations whose very existence is ignored by those who, in the peaceful serenity of home and protected from the world, are dimly aware of the actual meaning of life, and faintly appreciate the devastating force that lurks about, seeking so-called "independence" for its prey.

If individual fidelity marks an interesting step on the road to progress, a great deal also depends upon judicious coöperation. There are several clubs and societies in New York that are maintained by clerical workers for the purpose of mutual advancement. One or two of these admit men as well as women to membership. These associations offer much that is both attractive and useful. A clerk, typewriter or stenographer who is out of employment can practice at the club rooms. At a stated evening of each week literary exercises are conducted for the benefit of those who desire to attend, and once a month some distinguished lecturer is invited to address the society. The initiation fee is one dollar, and additional monthly dues of fifty cents are demanded. . . .

The matrimonial achievements of women clerks have become a species of national pleasantry. So many women employed in offices and mercantile houses have married men with whom they would hardly have come in contact in another sphere, that the subject has long ceased to be a matter of speculation, and has gradually drifted from witty comment to the more sober attention that bespeaks a recognized fact. . . .

From all I am able to gather the girls make good wives. There is nothing in clerical training that detracts from the finest womanly qualities, and men have outgrown their admiration for feminine helplessness and have come to look upon independence as something worth having. Clerical training educates the mind to accuracy in details, punctuality in the daily affairs of life, economy in the adjustment of time and quickness of perception. Perhaps this is the reason why so many men choose a wife amid the deft-fingered clerks in preference to the society misses. The woman clerk has studied the value of concentration, learned the lesson that incites to work when a burden bears heavily upon her strength. She knows the worth of self-reliance, and the fine courage that springs from the consciousness that a good result has been accomplished by a well-directed effort.

Samuel Gompers on Why Married Women Should Not Work, 1906

In undertaking to answer the question as to whether the wife should help to support the family, I take it that what is meant is the wife of a mechanic, a laborer, a workman, not the well-to-do or the fairly well-to do, for among the latter there is not even the false pretense of necessity. Taking, then, my conception of what is implied by the question, I have no hesitancy in answering, positively and absolutely, "No." . . .

Imagine the wife leaving her home and children unprotected and uncared for during the working hours, which among women generally, by reason of their comparative lack of organization, are much longer than the day's work of men. . . .

It is not for any real preference for their labor that the unscrupulous employer gives work to girls and boys and women, but because of his guilty knowledge that he can easily compel them to work longer hours and at a lower wage than men. It is the so-called competition of the unorganized, defenseless woman worker, the girl and the wife, that often tends to reduce the wages of the father and husband, so that frequently in after years, particularly in factory towns, the combined wages of the husband and wife, the father and daughter, have been reduced to the standard of the wages earned by the father or husband in the beginning.

I contend that the wife or mother, attending to the duties of the home, makes the greatest contribution to the support of the family. The honor, glory, and happiness that come from a beloved wife and the holiness of motherhood are a contribution to the support and future welfare of the family that our common humanity does not yet fully appreciate.

It is with keen gratification that observers have noticed in recent years that the wife of the wage-earner, where the husband has been a fair bread-winner for the family, has taken up beautiful needlework, embroidery, and the cultivation of her better, but heretofore latent, talents.

There is no reason why all the opportunities for the development of the best that women can do should be denied her, either in the home or else-where. I entertain no doubt but that from the constant better opportunity resultant from the larger earning power of the husband the wife will, apart from performing her natural household duties, perform that work which is most pleasurable for her, contributing to the beautifying of her home and surroundings. . . .

Harriet Brunkhurst on the Home Problems of "Business Girls," 1910

That the girl who goes to business frequently faces home problems more difficult than those she meets in an office is a fact that comparatively few people recognize. The status of the girl in the home changes when she becomes a breadwinner, yet there are many homes where the new order not only is not accepted, but is also stoutly combated. Perhaps the main difficulty arises from the fact that although the girl is out in the world and may develop capabilities and breadth unattainable to the one whose life lies in a narrower groove, yet she is still but a girl, shrinking, sensitive, pos-sessed of all the whims, fancies and weaknesses that have marked her sex from the beginning of things.

The mother whose daughter goes to business, as do the husband and sons, finds it difficult to realize that anything is changed beyond the mere fact that the girl is away all day. When she returns she slips into her old place; not "all in a minute" can the mother bring herself to acknowledge that the daughter's position in the home is, in fact, precisely like that of her brother. If the mother is long in recognizing this so is the rest of the world. Meanwhile the daughter may be having a hard time.

A certain little woman whose daughter is the household provider has a grievance that seems to her almost insupportable. The daughter, Rose, is advertising manager in a big store; she has a private office, a stenographer, errand-boys and clerical workers to assist her; she employs no heavier im-plement than pen or scissors; her hours are from nine to five, six, seven—possibly ten at night, as the occasion may demand. She earns a comfortable salary, and she pays into the family exchequer whatever sum is necessary, with never a question as to where the money goes.

The mother is careful in her expenditure and an excellent housekeeper; she refuses to keep a maid because they have no room for her, but the rough work is done by outside hands. Her ideas of housekeeping demand rising at five-thirty A. M. She sleeps lightly, having a midday siesta, and she prefers to do her work in the early morning. She is ready for breakfast at six-thirty. There is no necessity for Rose to breakfast before eight, but the mother begins each day with a complaint at the late breakfast hour. This point of difference, trivial in itself, causes continual irritation.

Rose, capable executive head of a big department though she is, simply cannot fight the matter to a finish. The same girl who calmly gives orders right and left, once the office is reached, chokes with tears and has not a word to say when the little mother, who does not know even the rudiments of business, tells her that she is indolent and selfish. Rose knows that she herself is right—that she must have recreation and rest; deprivation of her morning sleep might be serious to the point of a breakdown—and she must not be ill, for she is the breadwinner. It is the principle of the thing, the mother avers, and she means just the best in the world, of course. But there is only one right way, and that is her way.

This mother is overlooking some very pertinent facts, even excluding the unhappiness she causes her daughter. Rose is actually, by right of her earnings, the head of the house; yet the mother, who would yield without question to husband or son occupying the same position, debates Rose's every movement simply because she is a girl. Were Rose to take her courage in her own hands and face her mother it would avail nothing. So she accepts an unnecessary unhappiness simply because she can see no solution. If the mother could see things in their true light she would be appalled.

There is another mother whose daughter, Cecil, carries a similar burden in the home. The latter finds that many little economies are necessary in order to conduct the home liberally. With fingers as nimble as her brain she finds a woman's innumerable tasks about her wardrobe—lace to be mended, fresh ribbons needed, a stitch here and there that she may be immaculate and insure the longest possible service from her clothing. When Cecil returns from her work, however, she is too weary to attempt any sewing. If she is to remain bright and alert, hold her position and not become ill, she must have relaxation in the evening. She goes to the theater, opera, concerts, has friends to see her, or spends a quiet evening with a book. At nine in the morning she is at her desk, bright-eyed and with a clear brain.

That their support is absolutely dependent upon Cecil's remaining "fit" the mother knows; but that recreation is necessary to maintain the condition she cannot grasp. Consequently, when Cecil takes Sunday morning for the little fussy tasks about her wardrobe the mother sees only sheer perversity, to say nothing of incipient depravity, about it. And there is the incontrovertible fact that Cecil "has all her evenings free." Moreover the mother wails: "She never has time to do anything for me!" It does not occur to her that she is asking of Cecil, whose strength already is fully taxed, more than she would ask from a man. She is the type of woman who would say of her husband: "John is so tired when he returns from work!" That Cecil may be tired she never considers. . . .

One of the most difficult phases of the situation appears with the subject of housework. While going to business absolves the daughter, even as it does the husband and sons, it is a fact not so fully recognized as it might be. To the mother seven or eight hours of work followed by complete release appear so easy in comparison with her own lot that a few additional duties seem no more than fair. Moreover there is the family, its relations and friends, to make the contention should the mother take a different view of the matter.

Maud's mother, for instance, is criticised severely by her relatives for her careful fostering of her daughter's strength.

"It is perfectly ridiculous for you to iron Maud's shirtwaists," declared an elderly aunt. "She doesn't work half as hard as you do, and it wouldn't hurt her a bit to do her ironing in the evening. We used to do ours, and we were none the worse for it."

Maud's mother made no reply as she hung the sixth white blouse in a row with its mates. The years had gifted her with a sweet wisdom the other had not attained, and she knew well the futility of argument.

"I did my own fine ironing at home," she said afterward, "but there was never an afternoon or a morning when I could not go out if I chose. A task in the evening, unless it was for our pleasure, we never knew. Maud goes to the office in sun and in storm; she has never a day or an afternoon, except holidays, when she is free to do as she pleases. Days of headache or other slight indisposition, when I would have been on the sofa or comfortably in bed, she trudges bravely away. Often she is too tired even for recreation, to say nothing of work, when she returns in the evening."

"But six white shirtwaists!" exclaimed the listener.

"She works in an office where the furnishings are of mahogany, with rich rugs, polished brass and other things in harmony. How long could she hold her position were she to appear in a soiled blouse?"

Now that was only plain, practical good sense, clear-eyed recognition of pertinent facts; but astonishingly few people can boast it.

Mabel's mother, for example, takes a different and a more usual view of a similar situation. True, her work is far heavier than is that of Maud's mother, but Mabel works eight hours a day while Maud works seven. She is home in time to assist in preparing dinner, she helps with the dishes afterward, and there are innumerable little "odd jobs" that frequently keep her busy until nine o'clock. If she goes out there is a mad rush to finish the dinner work and be dressed sufficiently early. She does not go out very much, however, for she must rise at six-thirty, assist with the preparation of breakfast, and be at the office by eight-thirty o'clock.

That Mabel is fagged continually is inevitable. "I am so tired, Mother," she said once, when an additional bit of work was suggested.

"Aren't you ashamed to say that when you see how your mother works?" demanded the father.

Mabel did the required work with no further comment, although the tears smarted in her eyes, her heart ached with the injustice of the taunt, and her weary little body seemed ready to fail her. She could earn her own living, but she could not fight her own battles. . . .

The problems these girls face are delicate, whichever way they are viewed. Perhaps part of the trouble arises from non-recognition of arrival at "years of discretion." We are all of us individuals first, and members of a family afterward. The family fosters and develops, but it may hamper freedom as well. There must be dependence upon one another, there must be community of interests; but in the successful home there must also be a clearly-defined recognition of individual existence. The girl attains her "majority" when she goes to business, and the home must learn when to "let go." It is not a question of independence—a word often misapplied and misunderstood—but simply one of self-reliance, and acknowledgment of the girl's right to it.

Fannie Barrier Williams, "The Problem of Employment for Negro Women," 1903

It can be broadly said that colored women know how to work, and have done their full share of the paid and unpaid service rendered to the American people by the Negro race. This is a busy world; the world's work is large, complicated, and increasing. The demand for the competent in all kinds of work is never fully supplied. Woman is constantly receiving a larger share of the work to be done. The field for her skill, her endurance, her finer instincts and faithfulness is ever enlarging; and she has become impatient of limitations, except those imposed by her own physical condition. In this generalization, colored women, of course, are largely excepted. For reasons too well understood here to be repeated, ours is a narrow sphere. While the kinds and grades of occupation open to all women of white complexion are almost beyond enumeration, those open to our women are few in number and mostly menial in quality. The girl who is white and capable is in demand in a thousand places. The capable Negro girl is usually not in demand. This is one of the stubborn facts of to-day. . . .

In the city of Chicago domestic service is the one occupation in which the demand for colored women exceeds the supply. In one employment office during the past year there were 1,500 applications for colored women and only 1,000 of this number were supplied. Girls of other nationalities do not seem to compete with colored women as domestics. It is probably safe to say that every colored woman who is in any way competent can find good employment. Her wages for general housework range from four to seven dollars per week, while a good cook receives from seven to ten dollars. Now what is the condition of this service? The two most important things are that the wages paid are higher than those given for the same grade of intelligence in any other calling; and that colored women can command almost a monopoly of this employment.

It might be safe to presume that as our women are so much in demand for this service they give perfect satisfaction. In considering that it is important to bear in mind that there are two kinds of colored women who perform domestic service:—First, there are those who take to the work naturally and whose training and habits make them perfectly satisfied with it; and second, those who have had more or less education and who are ambitious to do something in the line of "polite occupations." The women of the latter class do not take to domestic service very kindly. They do not enter the service with any pride. They feel compelled to do so this work because they can find nothing else to do. They are always sensitive as to how they may be regarded by their associates and friends, and shrink from the term servant as something degrading "per se." . . .

It is of course an easy thing to condemn our young women who have been fairly educated and have had good home training, because they prefer idleness to domestic service, but I am rather inclined to think we must share in that condemnation. If our girls work for wages in a nice home, rather than in a factory or over a counter, they are ruthlessly scorned by their friends and acquaintances. Our young men, whose own occupations, by the way, will not always bear scrutiny, will also give them the cut direct, so that between the scorn of their associates and the petty tyranny of the housewife, the colored girls who enter domestic service are compelled to have more than ordinary strength of character.

But after all is said, I believe that it is largely in the power of the young woman herself to change and elevate the character of domestic service. She certainly cannot improve it by taking into it ignorance, contempt, and inefficiency. There is no reason why a woman of character, graciousness, and skill should not make her work as a domestic as respectable and as highly regarded as the work of the girl behind a department-store counter. For example, if by special training in domestic service, a girl can cook so well and do everything about a house so deftly and thoroughly that she will be called a real home helper and an invaluable assistant, it is in her power, with her intelligent grasp upon the possibilities of her position, to change the whole current of public opinion in its estimate of domestic service. . . .

When domestic service becomes a profession, as it surely will, by the proper training of those who follow it, what will be the condition of colored girls who would participate in its benefits? It is now time to prepare ourselves to answer this question. In my opinion, the training for this new profession should be elevated to the dignity and importance of the training in mathematics and grammar and other academic studies. Our girls must be made to feel that there is no stepping down when they become professional housekeepers. The relative dignity, respectability, and honor of this profession should first be taught in our schools. As it is now, the young woman in school or college knows that if she enters domestic service, she loses the relationships that she has formed. But schools of domestic science cannot do it all. The everyday man and woman who make society must change their foolish notions as to what is the polite thing for a young woman to do. The kind of stupidity that calls industrial education drudgery is the same kind of stupidity that looks upon the kitchen as a place for drudges. We must learn that the girl who cooks our meals and keeps our houses sweet and beautiful deserves just as high a place in our social economy as the girl who makes our gowns and hats, or the one who teaches our children. In what I have said on this particular phase of our industrial life, I do not wish to be understood as advocating the restriction of colored girls to house service, even when that service is elevated to the rank of a profession. My only plea is that we shall protect and respect our girls who honestly and intelligently enter this service, either from preference or necessity. . . .

There is still another consideration which suggests the importance to the colored people of taking the lead in helping to improve and elevate this service. Race prejudice is kept up and increased in thousands of instances by the incompetent and characterless women who are engaged in this work. While there are thousands of worthy and really noble women in domestic service who enjoy the confidence and affection of their employers, there is a large percentage of colored women who, by their general unworthiness, help to give the Negro race a bad name, for white people North and South are very apt to estimate the entire race from the standpoint of their own servant girls. When intelligence takes the place of ignorance, and good manners, efficiency, and self-respect take the place of shiftlessness and irresponsibility in American homes, one of the chief causes of race prejudice will be removed.

It should also be borne in mind that the colored girl who is trained in the arts of housekeeping is also better qualified for the high duties of wifehood and motherhood.

Let me say by the way of summary that I have dwelt mostly upon the opportunities of domestic service for the following reasons:—

1. It is the one field in which colored women meet with almost no opposition It is ours almost by birthright.
2. The compensation for this service, in Northern communities at least, is higher than that paid for average clerkships in stores and offices.
3. The service is susceptible of almost unlimited improvement and elevation.
4. The nature of the work is largely what we make it.
5. White women of courage and large intelligence are lifting domestic service to a point where it will have the dignity of a profession, and colored women are in danger, through lack of foresight, of being relegated to the position of scrub women and dishwashers.
6. The colored girl who has no taste or talent for school teaching, dressmaking, or manicuring is in danger of being wasted in idleness, unless we can make domestic service worthy of her ambition and pride.
7. There can be no feature of our race problem more important than the

saving of our young women; we can perhaps excuse their vanities, but idleness is the mildew on the garment of character.

8. Education has no value to human society unless it can add importance and respectability to the things we find to do.

9. Though all the factories and offices close their doors at our approach, this will be no calamity if we are strong enough to so transform the work we must do that it shall become an object of envy and emulation to those who now deny us their industrial fellowship.

❖ E S S A Y S

The University of Michigan's Leslie Tentler looks in the first essay at the experiences of young women employed in factories, arguing that the nature of their work culture reinforced traditional views of gender roles. In the second selection, Margery Davies, an independent scholar, reaches a similar conclusion after examining the new office workers. But Susan Porter Benson of the University of Missouri, who contends that her findings could apply in other settings as well, asserts in the final essay that the young women working as department store sales clerks were able to subvert the ends of their employers and, in the end, to "manage the managers" to some extent.

Work Culture in Factories

LESLIE TENTLER

Before the Second World War, and particularly before 1930, a sizeable majority of women who worked outside the home were young and single. Fully 55% of women at work in cities of more than 100,000 in 1920 were between the ages of sixteen and twenty-four. Married women in 1920 accounted for only 21.2% of the female nonagricultural labor force. And because older women and many married women tended to choose different occupations than the young and single, most young women found at work a markedly age-segregated environment. The Bureau of Labor, for example, in an investigation of factory and sales occupations in five cities in 1908, discovered that approximately 75% of female factory workers and 63% of the retail sales workers studied were under the age of twenty-five, with the largest group of workers those between sixteen and nineteen years of age.

The youthful female work environment stood in marked contrast to the work world experienced by most men, for the male labor force was dominated numerically by men in middle life. And young, single males did not generally gravitate to different occupations and places of work than older

Leslie Woodcock Tentler, *Wage-Earning Women: Industrial Work and Family Life in the United States, 1900–1930*, 58–80. Copyright © 1979 by Oxford University Press, Inc. Reprinted by permission.

married workers. Adolescent boys, then, entered the work world as a minority population, necessarily deferential to those to whom experience and seniority gave status. For boys, the world of work was the world of their fathers.

Young women, however, found at work a preponderantly adolescent world, and the workroom social life they enjoyed provided them with some important freedoms. It also communicated to most of them very conservative ideas about their identities and destinies as women. Young women created workroom social life in the context of a sexually hierarchical work situation, and their communal social life of necessity recognized and reflected the sexual inequities of the work world. And workroom social life was importantly influenced by the relative absence of older women workers, women whose experience might serve to counter the conservatism of adolescent fantasies about romance and marriage.

Nevertheless, the hours of work also provided many young women with unusual social freedom. The most effective industrial discipline was unable to regulate completely workroom sociability, and, particularly in the absence of large numbers of older workers, young women at work were often less supervised in certain aspects of personal behavior than they were in most nonwork situations. Since working-class girls, unlike their brothers, seemed to have no permanent street-corner groups and few single-sex social clubs, the workroom provided many young women a unique place of refuge from family and neighborhood surveillance and an opportunity for free sociability with peers. It provided a chance to explore, however tentatively, new styles of speech and manners, and the chance to learn, from the more worldly-wise, about the possibilities of social and sexual experimentation open to the Americanized adolescent.

Indeed, many young women learned at work to want more freedom in social life and management of wages than the typical working-class family would willingly countenance. The romantic preoccupations of the work group, moreover, encouraged many young women to choose an early marriage as the most desirable route to freedom from parental control. But many working-class parents not only opposed early marriage for the wage-earning young, they were doubtful about the propriety of matches that had not been mediated by the older generation.

Work group associations thus facilitated conflict between parents and working daughters. Indeed, the preoccupations of the woman's work group defined the central problem in young female lives as the struggle with parents for social freedom. And these preoccupations shaped decisively most young women's responses to their work. For many, the frustrations, disappointments, and physical agonies of the job were alleviated through an intense involvement with social life and workroom personal relations, although in this respect women were much the same as men. But the female work group, reflecting the special needs and narrow experiences of very young, unmarried women, endorsed an understanding of the job that placed work at far remove from the central concerns of life. The struggles that mattered were the struggles for adolescent autonomy; the essential victories were romantic conquests. The very success of the work group in facilitating adolescent rebellion served to deflect worker dissatisfaction from overt political expression.

Much in the nature and content of work-group sociability thus reinforced a marginal work role for women and served to integrate young women into a domestic adult role. The values of the work group were not generally conducive to unionization or other forms of direct political action, nor did the group support unconventional visions of women's life possibilities. Young women brought to the job conservative values about femininity learned at home and in school. And in their very struggle for adolescent independence, they reinforced for one another an ultimately conservative orientation to their lives as women.

In their own work communities, then, young women internalized and legitimized the assumptions about male and female that undergirded the sex-segregated world of work. But this is not to argue that the creation of the work community was not an important achievement, or that this community failed to function for women in essential protective ways. The work community, particularly because of its youthful composition, failed to challenge the sexual hierarchy of the job, but it did provide women with a refuge from workroom authority, which was most often male. The work community often provided the basis for limited resistance to supervisory pressure and innovation, though the ethos of that community was generally supportive of work discipline. The work community represented a social world where women could express individuality and independence, though group values rarely sanctioned competition with men for better jobs and wages. The work community facilitated something of a social and sexual revolution for many young women, and yet it functioned too as a bridge to conventional adulthood. As we examine more closely the nature of the social environment of women's work, we must keep in mind the contradictions between the liberating and the restrictive effects of workroom social life. For the complexities of the work community teach us how subtly and deftly a culture transmits sexually stereotyped roles and values.

Most observers of women at work, and the women themselves, were impressed by the vigor of workroom social life; women formed work friendships even under difficult conditions. Some women's work, mainly handwork such as millinery sewing or flower making, encouraged group association, but women also created elaborate social worlds in shops where the conveyor belt or noisy machinery erected formidable barriers to interaction: "We used to talk very loudly so as to be heard above the roar of the machines," Agnes Nestor remembered of her work in Chicago glove factories. Even piecework did not generally deter sociability, despite the premium on rapid production and the competitive situation piecework fosters. Women working under pressure often sang together to ease tensions, and work groups frequently enforced informal sanctions against excessive production competition. The most stringent supervision proved impotent in prohibiting all workroom social life: "You can hear talkin' all over our room when the forelady goes out." Since a prohibition against laughing and talking was not necessarily conducive to maximum worker productivity, in many shops rules against on-the-job socializing were not rigorously enforced.

Indeed, a lively workroom social environment often supported effective work discipline. The small but significant freedoms of workroom social life made less onerous the petty controls of supervision. Group life endowed tedious unskilled labor with the drama of personal interaction; it created loyalties to fellow workers which often worked against the development of hostility to the employer. And where socializing on the job was officially forbidden, challenges to the rules could provide pleasurable and effective release for anger and frustration. . . .

A supportive work group, although immensely important as a source of job satisfaction, also embodied an oblique protest. The work group normally asserted, to what extent it could, the priority of human needs over the demands of production. In a cohesive work group, for example, newcomers and slow workers were often aided in their work by more competent mates. Group loyalties were thus demonstrably more important than competitive, achievement-oriented values. Similarly restrictions on excessive production placed the interests of the group above those of the ambitious individual. But the success of the work group as a community based on values antithetical to those that governed production generally served to minimize overt conflict with work authority. "Even in the shop I was happy. My neighbors were very kind. Each one would help the other out of difficulties in the work," an immigrant garment worker in New York remembered. Their kindness was at once a conscious criticism of the values symbolized by piecework production and real assistance to the employer in sustaining production and amicable labor relations.

Men's work groups, of course, generally sanctioned similar values. But for women the ethic of work-group solidarity was probably less ambiguous than it was for men, because women were not enjoined by the larger society to achieve as individuals through their work, and they saw fewer opportunities for such achievement. Working-class men were shielded by the work group from the injunction to achieve, but they were rarely deaf to it. Since women enjoyed especially strong cultural supports for work-group solidarity, there were powerful inducements for them to understand the indirect protest of the work community as satisfying and sufficient. That the protest embodied in the work community did not facilitate mobility for the individual or the group was often of little importance to women. There were men, certainly, for whom this was also true. But for many men, even some who never joined a union or went on strike, the satisfactions of such limited protest were probably less complete. That women were widely reported to be more docile workers than men may reflect, to some extent, the greater satisfactions women obtained from highly indirect forms of work protest. . . .

And the values of the women's work community were enormously successful in integrating into group life a wide variety of women workers. It is significant that severe interethnic conflict on women's jobs was apparently rare, for in the trades where women found work, it was not usually possible to minimize ethnic contacts through job stratification based on nationality. . . . Contemporary reports suggest that open and disruptive ethnic conflict among working women was rare. The bonds of age and sex usually served to transcend the divisions of ethnicity. For as young women of various national groups pursued as fellow workers their common goals of a thoroughly American personal style and unprecedented freedom from parental control, they often had reason to feel that they had more in common with one another than with the older generation. Through their work experience, reinforcing as it did a heightened identification with mass popular culture, these young women were creating for themselves a common identity that we can call working-class.

A workroom little divided by occupational rivalries supported the evolution of a common identity. Only a few trades had skill hierarchies open to women. Garment sample-makers, chocolate dippers, and millinery trimmers, for example, were skilled workers and were accorded the envy and respect of their workmates. These aristocrats of women's labor often formed separate social groups within the factory. But, normally, opportunities for genuine mobility in women's jobs were limited, and serious competition among women for achievement and promotions was not common. Instead, the values of the work community focused women's competitive energies on social relations, conventionally the one acceptable arena of female competition. Thus, while diminished competition for status on the job contributed to work-group solidarity, it discouraged women from the individualistic ambition characteristic of the economically and socially mobile male.

The basically conservative functions of the women's work group are revealed in the normal preoccupations of workroom social life. The essence of conformity in many shops was enthusiastic discussion of off-the-job social activities: "Say, you got a feller?" was a standard overture in new work situations, according to one New York investigator. Many observers of women's work emphasized the universal importance of social life as a workroom topic; no other concern rivaled it—not wages, hours, or conditions of work. Beaus, social events, clothing, and the romantic prospects of workmates provided more welcome diversions from the monotony of the long day. . . .

Young women's interest in social life is hardly surprising, and no one doubts that men at work devote a good deal of time to the discussion of sex. What is significant, however, is that the meaning of femininity—and of masculinity—is being transmitted to young working women in highly romanticized, decidedly adolescent terms. Of significance too is the illusion of intimacy and solidarity that personal gossip inevitably creates—"illusion," because hurried confidences about boyfriends and struggles with parents were rarely sufficient to create friendships capable of sacrifice, especially among a highly mobile work force. But young women cherished the illusion of intimacy; it gave meaning and dignity to their working lives. An organizational drive within a shop put work friendships to a severe test. Rather than jeopardize the comforts of easy companionship, women often declared off-limits such potentially troublesome topics as unions and politics. Indeed, it was an unwritten rule in some women's workrooms that while the most complete confidences about social life were expected, women never revealed to one another what wage they were earning.

The romantic preoccupations of the work group enhanced the prospect of marriage as the logical means to material prosperity for women, as well as to freedom from parental control. Many observers, especially those who hoped to organize women, noted the exaggerated expectations of marriage that many young working women entertained. Dorothy Richardson found that her coworkers in a New York box factory constantly discussed the heroes of popular novels and endowed their own prosaic boyfriends with similar characteristics. These women also adopted romantic pseudonyms from sensational fiction. Frances Donovan noted that Chicago waitresses considered expensive downtown restaurants the most desirable work places because they believed that wealthy businessmen sometimes married attractive women who served them. And contemporary testimony is virtually unanimous that young working women looked forward to marriage as a desired rite of passage to adult freedom. Presumably, few women anticipated that marriage would mean for them the cramped and stringent home life they had experienced as children. Perhaps collective fantasies about the possibilities of matrimony helped to obscure for the young the still harsh realities of early twentieth-century working-class life, endowing domesticity with a romantic glow. "Marriage is for all these girls the final and greatest adventure of adolescence," noted Ruth True of young workers in Manhattan. "They do not look past the adventure at the responsibilities which lie beyond. The question of children is waved aside as scarcely worth a hearing."

A passionate interest in social life generated conflict with parents while it minimized conflict with the employer. Many young women learned at work to want and expect the freedom of city nightlife. But many parents, especially those of the immigrant generation, could not sanction the sexual autonomy implied by an unrestricted social life for women, nor could they tolerate the allegiance of daughters to the alien norms of urban mass culture. In an important way, the experience of work proved liberating to the young, for it introduced many of them to an exciting adolescent world. And it was parents, not the boss, who were perceived as frustrating the wage earner's freedom.

Work group norms also generated ambitious standards of dress and personal display. Louise Odencrantz noted that immigrant women refused to wear "old country" clothing in the factory; for many, the workplace provided the first American models of fashionable female dress. Mary MacDowell of the University of Chicago settlement claimed that many young women in the "Back of the Yards" district dressed for work as stylishly as possible, because going to work was for them an important social event. Robert Woods of Boston's South End House reported that store clerks in the neighborhood consciously imitated the dress of their most prosperous customers.

But this interest in dress, rather than creating widespread and articulated dissatisfaction with low wages, served mainly to cause conflict with parents over control of the young woman's wage. (In most working-class families it was customary for an unmarried daughter to surrender all or most of her wage to her mother, and the mother determined what limited amount of pocket money would be returned to the girl.) Again, it was the parent and not the employer who was seen as the obstacle to happiness. "The girls were not so much interested in the amount earned as in the amount given back for spending money," noted Hazel Ormsbee in 1927 of young factory workers in New York, "and an increase in weekly wage interested many of them only if it resulted in more spending money."

The romantic preoccupations of the youthful work community significantly shaped women's attitudes toward work and achievement. The work community provided little support for job-related ambitions; rather, the group endorsed the tendency of most women to understand their work as temporary and extraneous to their adult lives. The work community discouraged competitiveness, directed emotional energies away from individualistic ambition toward personal relations, and emphasized the precedence of group loyalties over private achievement. . . .

The work behavior of most women reflected the high value they placed on personal relationships and group solidarity. Job choice, for example, was often dictated by friendship rather than private economic advantage. Young women often sought work in the company of friends, and sometimes even changed jobs together, although group pursuit of employment lessened women's chances of securing particularly advantageous and well-paying jobs. The low-wage neighborhood shop with an abundance of openings for unskilled workers was usually most willing to accommodate a group of friends. Similarly, investigators noticed that women sometimes objected to transfers within the factory, even where it signalled a promotion or a wage increase, because the transfer meant separation from friends. Some women were reported reluctant to accept rare promotions to positions of authority, possibly because supervisors were often lonely workers, thrust outside workroom social life.

The same priorities bolstered conservative attitudes among women toward job competition with men. In many trades, real advancement for women meant challenging male domination of skilled and high-paying jobs, yet women generally accepted without protest prevailing definitions of male and female employment. Contesting the sexual hierarchy of the work world required a higher valuation of work achievement and its rewards than the rewards of conventional femininity. Most young women, anticipating early marriage, were not eager to incur male hostility through open competition for jobs. And the rewards of a successful competition were mixed at best. In return for higher wages and increased job status, real advancement for women would have meant promotion into the intense loneliness of a male occupation. Hence, most women accommodated the rigid sexual hierarchy of the work world, and in so doing verified the conservative view of femininity endorsed by the larger society. . . .

Women were certainly capable of direct collective action to improve wages and working conditions. But more often than not, these were spontaneous, disorganized actions of short duration, the highly emotional reactions of a temporarily aroused group and not the calculated action of a disciplined and self-interested collectivity. There is evidence that spontaneous work stoppages over accumulated grievances were fairly common in some shops. But generally these actions were brief, lasting only until group emotion was spent. Sometimes immediate objectives were achieved, especially since work stoppages most commonly occurred over sudden violations of standard workroom practice: a reduction in the piece-rate, a sudden spate of overtime work, a change in job procedure. Thus Agnes Nestor's diary records on November 12, 1900: "The power stopped twice to begin with today. This afternoon we went on a strike about being cut down on 60¢ work and we won." Victories achieved through spontaneous direct action, however, were usually precarious, because women rarely followed a successful action with permanent organization. Just so, Agnes Nestor's shop failed to unionize in the year 1900, and Agnes herself betrayed in the year's diary no interest in permanent organization or trade unions. . . .

The typical women's work community, then, was a youthful, sex-segregated social world where important conservative values about femininity were reaffirmed by women themselves. Among their peers, young working women were encouraged to seek future security and mobility through marriage rather than employment. They learned to accept a work world that defined women as dependent and marginal employees. Not all women, of course, acceded without struggle; on rare and moving occasions, workroom social ties provided the solidarity necessary for long and bitter strikes. But these moments of sustained conflict were exceptional. Most women, in their brief working lives, found in the work community the pleasures and sustenance of friendship and support as they moved from the years of work to the decades as wives and mothers.

Work Culture in Offices

MARGERY DAVIES

The period from 1870 to 1930 witnessed profound changes in clerical work. By 1930 the fundamental characteristics that it still has today had been established. Clerical workers could be divided analytically into two basic groups: lower-level employees who executed routine tasks in a manner increasingly controlled and prescribed by employers; and, on a higher level best typified by private secretaries, those responsible for a wide variety of tasks who were encouraged to exercise a relatively greater degree of initiative and independence. Furthermore, clerical workers, who prior to 1870 had practically all been men, were by 1930 predominantly women. This feminization of the clerical labor force was related to the reorganization of clerical work.

Prior to 1870, offices were quite small, in general employing no more than a few clerks; consequently the division of clerical labor within them was rudimentary. Only four different kinds of employees can be distinguished—copyist, bookkeeper, office boy, and clerk. With the exception of the copyist who was hired purely to transcribe letters and other documents, these workers engaged in a wide variety of tasks and were able to learn a great deal about the workings of their firm. Furthermore, until at least the early nineteenth century, many clerks were specifically working as apprentices as a means of learning the business. After their apprenticeship, many went on to own and operate firms themselves. Much of the office work at this time was organized as an integrated whole—clerks were in a position not only to gain experience in the entire range of office work, but also to understand precisely how a particular task was related to overall office operations. Such employees were a far cry from scientifically managed clerical workers whose jobs had been reduced to the deadening repetition of a few steps in the labor process, and who had no opportunity to grasp how their tasks fit into the workings of the office on the whole.

Before 1870 relations between employer and employee were quite personal. That a clerkship was often seen as an apprenticeship meant that the employer often took a paternal role vis-à-vis his clerks. The small size of offices and the lack of codified bureaucratic procedures allowed an employer's personal idiosyncrasies to have a very large effect on the tenor of office relations. A harsh or ill-tempered employer could make life miserable for his clerks; with a lenient or kindly one things could be much more pleasant. Whether or not a clerk was trustworthy seems to have been very important to employers—an indication that they were forced to rely on the personal merits of their office help and were relatively unprotected by formal rules or bureaucratic procedures.

After 1870, however, political-economic changes had a profound effect on the organization of office work. Capitalist enterprises began to expand and to consolidate, resulting in much larger corporations whose operations covered a much wider geographic area. Moreover, other ancillary institutions expanded. Witness, for instance, the expansion in both size and scope of law offices, as well as municipal, state, and federal governments. Because of their need for more record-keeping and correspondence, these growing firms and institutions experienced a dramatic increase in the volume of office work. Naturally, the demand for office workers rose rapidly as well. This increasing need was the impetus for both the feminization and the reorganization of clerical work. Some employers soon found that in order to cope with the mounting paperwork, it was not sufficient merely to multiply the number of bookkeepers, copyists, office boys, and clerks. Furthermore, their burgeoning workforce was becoming more difficult to supervise. For both of these reasons, employers found it necessary to reorganize office work.

The primary characteristic of that reorganization was an elaboration of the division of labor, with the restructuring of firms into functionally defined departments being basic. The effect on clerical jobs was immediate. Confined to working in a single department, a clerical employee was now at best able to understand only how things were done in that one department. No longer was he or she doing a job whose vantage point afforded a picture of the entire operations of a firm. Departments were often divided and subdivided into their component parts, a process that served only to further the isolation of any single office job.

The scientific management of office work systematized the division and redivision of clerical labor. Although it was by no means universal, scientific management was in the vanguard of developments in office organization. Its two major characteristics were that each component step in the labor process should be executed using the cheapest possible labor, and that most clerical workers were to be divested of as much control as possible over their work, and relegated to the execution as opposed to the conception of their tasks. The first of these tenets was often termed "efficiency" by scientific managers, who thought it wasteful to expend the more highly paid labor of a "skilled" worker on a task which could just as easily be done by a lower-paid "unskilled" worker. But, as Harry Braverman has observed, the motive force behind the change was the drive for as much profit as possible, rather than some abstract concern for "efficiency."

The detailed division of labor was one of the ways in which scientific managers controlled clerical labor, for through its application they restricted the scope of clerical jobs and defined in very precise ways exactly what office workers were to do. Such restrictions further diminished the control that office workers exercised over their work. Placed in a position where they were unable to explore beyond the narrow confines of their individual jobs, and denied knowledge of how their own work fit into the firm's overall labor process, clerical workers could neither understand nor intelligently control their work.

Scientific management methods of control and supervision were not exclusively indirect or structural in character. Scientific managers dictated to the minutest degree imaginable the manner in which clerical workers were to execute their tasks; concocted a variety of premium and bonus schemes to induce their staff to produce up to and over the management-dictated standard; and arranged their offices so that employees would produce as much work and waste as little time as possible.

It is sometimes argued that machines caused the routinization of office work and the restriction of the office worker to a few limited tasks. But nothing inherent in the typewriter, for instance, dictated that an individual clerical worker must operate it eight hours a day at a given rate of productivity. It was instead the particular organization of the office that tied an employee to the typewriter to the exclusion of any other duties. The successful invention and manufacture of the typewriter was a result of developments in the growth and organization of office work that made an automatic writing machine useful. As a general rule, technological inventions followed in the wake of changes in capitalism and in the reorganization of the labor process.

A second characteristic of the reorganization of office work was the growth of hierarchical structures of authority. These tended to replace the idiosyncratic, personal control of owners and managers with codified, impersonal rules. The existence of codified procedures for decision making meant that clerical workers had fewer opportunities to make decisions, and their control over their jobs was consequently diminished. A legion of rules covering all areas of office life accompanied this formalization of office hierarchy—rules about the degree of punctuality required, proper office attire, and what constituted "businesslike" behavior. The point is not that these features of office work were never dictated by employers in the small, pre-1870 office, but that the direct personal control of employers over their clerical employees was being replaced by the impersonal control of hierarchical structures and codified rules.

The elaboration of the division of labor and the creation of hierarchical structures of authority affected low-level clerical workers most directly. But the reorganization also brought into being the private secretary, whose work was typical of higher-level clerical workers.

Unlike the scientifically managed clerical worker, the private secretary was expected to take the initiative in his or her work, which consisted of an almost infinitely wide variety of tasks. The private secretary and the executive for whom he or she worked divided between them all of the duties involved in the latter's job. The governing principle of the division was that the executive's time, attention and energy should be saved for the "important," creative aspects of the task, with the private secretary doing the menial parts. In practice, of course, the division of labor varied a good deal. A private secretary might be restricted to specific tasks because the executive liked to see to all details himself, or a private secretary might do most of the executive's work. In either case, the secretary was the executive's personal servant, with tasks defined by his personal choice. . . .

Economic forces, which were responsible for this reorganization of office work, also prompted changes in the work force itself. The feminization of clerical work was simply the result of the exigencies of demand and supply. The rapid expansion of capitalist firms and government agencies, accompanied by the growth of correspondence and record keeping, led to a mounting demand for clerical labor. That demand was met, in part, by the availability of literate female labor. A number of factors contributed to the existence of this labor force. The economic instability of small farm and small business families both released women's labor to the paid labor force and made the income women could earn more important. Clerical work was more desirable than other working-class jobs, both because of the higher wages it offered and the comparatively high status it enjoyed. The decline of productive work in the home also released women's labor to the labor force, and few other jobs specifically requiring literacy were open to women. Furthermore, the supply of literate male labor was being tapped not only for

the burgeoning clerical field, but also for management and professional positions, which rapidly increased in number with late nineteenth-century
capitalist expansion. These factors, rather than technological innovation,
explain the changes in clerical work.

Technological change did, however, facilitate the feminization of clerical work. New office machines, the most prevalent form of technological
change, were gender-neutral. Being new, they had not been associated with
the male-dominated early nineteenth-century office. Consequently, women
hired to operate them were not met by the argument that they were employed at "men's" machines or encroaching upon "men's work." The lack
of such protest facilitated their entry into clerical jobs associated with new
machines. This in no way suggests, it must be emphasized, that various
office machines were more "suited" to female labor than to male. Although
many made this claim, notably in the case of the typewriter, the fact that,
outside the United States, typists were often men suggests otherwise. It was
not because the typewriter was more "suited" to female labor, but because
it was gender-neutral that women's entry into the office was facilitated.

Other factors also facilitated the feminization of clerical workers. Perhaps the most important was the reorganized division of labor. Many clerical
jobs, relatively integrated prior to 1870, were subjected to a radical division
of labor as offices expanded. This resulted in a large number of routine,
repetitive, low-level, dead-end clerical tasks, often filled by women. Thus
the degradation of clerical work included a shift from one sex to another.
Following an office reorganization, a male nineteenth-century bookkeeper
would not, in all likelihood, find himself demoted to a low-level job in the
bookkeeping department. Instead, he would probably be gracefully retired,
or else put in charge of the bookkeeping department, with that department's
low-level jobs very likely being filled by women. Since they were not directly
competitive with the male bookkeepers, potential opposition to them doing
men's work in this department would be muted. Reorganization thus frustrated the possibility of women directly pushing men out of jobs, a development that might have served as a deterrent to feminization.

A third factor that eased women's employment as office workers was
their recruitment as clerks in the Treasury Department during the Civil War.
This radical wartime "experiment" provided an often cited precedent for
hiring women clerical workers that the expanding businesses of the late
nineteenth century followed.

Finally, patriarchal social patterns help to explain why women were
concentrated in the clerical, as opposed to managerial, positions in the expanding office sector. In a society where men were dominant and women
subordinate, it seemed only natural that men occupied the higher-level jobs.

The patterns of patriarchy also affected the extent to which office workers saw themselves as belonging to the "clerical class." By and large, employers and managers were men while clerical workers were women. This
was the case with private secretaries by 1930; and even the low-level clerical
workers whose immediate supervisors were women were likely to see only
men as they looked up the ladder of the office hierarchy. Thus there was a

tendency, particularly obvious in the literature on private secretaries, for bosses to be seen as males first and as employers or managers second. Theirs was often perceived as predominantly a male, rather than as a class, authority.

To the extent that female clerical workers hesitated to challenge their male employers and supervisors *because* they were men, the gender-specific character of office hierarchies served to stabilize class relations. Women reared in a male-dominated society and shaped by patterns of male dominance in a variety of ways, both subtle and direct, were trained to submit to male authority. Thus the feminization of clerical labor meant a docile workforce and helped to stabilize the power relations between office workers and management.

The fact that female clerical workers were often identified as women first and as workers second reinforced the assumption, probably shared by many of them, that a woman's primary role in life was to marry and raise a family. Such a perception tended in itself to distract women from their membership in the clerical class. And female office workers who gave primacy to their domestic role were likely to leave the office and the labor force when they married or, at the latest, started having children.

It should not be thought that women, voluntarily or by their "natures," chose to emphasize their gender instead of class identification. This was a question not of choice but of women's structural position in society. Their place in a variety of institutions made women more likely to submit to male authority rather than to challenge it openly. Certainly up until 1930, most families in the United States were dominated by systems of male authority that allowed women little formal power. It was not until 1920 that women even had the right to vote in federal elections. Women did not necessarily choose to submit to male authority; rather, they were both trained to do so from birth and, in many cases, simply denied the right to do anything else. The lack of promotional opportunities and the degrading nature of many of the jobs offer further evidence of the structural, as opposed to voluntary, basis for female clerical workers' identification with their gender rather than with their class. Such conditions tended to push women out of the clerical labor force. A woman who had to choose between a life of domestic work and working at a deadening low-level clerical job or as an executive's personal servant earning no public recognition whatsoever was not given much of a choice. Instead of arguing that women were simply "choosing" to leave the office in order to go home and tend the hearth, it makes more sense to maintain that their structural position in the office as well as in society at large pushed them out of the clerical labor force after a relatively short tenure within it.

Aspects of the organization of clerical work itself also militated against the development of class identity among clerical workers. The relationship between a private secretary and his or her employer was, in some ways, deeply personal. The secretary was in effect a servant, expected to be trustworthy beyond reproach and to carry out many non-business errands for him. Such duties and such a relationship militated against secretaries perceiving their work situation in structural or class terms. They were more likely to assess it in terms of their individual employer, than in terms of the conditions they shared with other private secretaries. Much as in a nineteenth-century office, the behavior of the individual employer loomed large: if he was "nice," considerate, and so on, then the job could be enjoyable or at least not oppressive; if he was a tartar or treated his secretary like a doormat, then the job could be unbearable. That private secretaries were actively encouraged to identify their interests with their employers rather than with other private secretaries also contributed to such a perception. And it could only be enhanced by the fact that private secretaries, working alone in individual offices, were isolated from other members of their class.

Low-level clericals usually did not work in the same degree of isolation. But there were other factors discouraging them from seeing their situation in class terms. First of all, the private secretary and the low-level clerical worker were not always distinguished from each other, a confusion that was probably shared by some low-level clerical workers themselves. Furthermore, the job of private secretary was often considered the ultimate promotional goal of these workers, and one that was by no means unattainable. Consequently, thinking of themselves as future private secretaries, they identified with private secretaries and were thereby discouraged from perceiving their situation in class terms.

Competition among clerical workers, fostered by management, also retarded the development of a common class perception. The institution of bonus and premium plans, the attempts to foster a "spirit of friendly rivalry," and even the creation of finely delineated (and sometimes meaningless) hierarchical levels within clerical work all encouraged clerical workers to compete with one another. Although management often initiated these competitive schemes in order to prod clerical workers to higher levels of productivity, they also had the effect of disguising clerical workers' common class position.

But clerical workers grouped together in large work units had more opportunity to observe their common class interests. Indeed, David Lockwood found that the size of a firm was the best indicator of whether or not a clerk in Britain was likely to join a union—the larger the firm, the more likely the clerk was to be a union member. Clerical workers who worked in the relative isolation of small offices were likely to attribute their situation to the peculiarities of their firm, rather than to their structural position.

We return in the end to the significance of the feminization of the clerical labor force. It meant that the degradation of clerical work and the proletarianization of office workers was disguised. To the extent that female office workers were seen as women first and workers second, the decline in their position relative to their nineteenth-century predecessors' was masked. Instead of the process being seen as proleterianization, the shift merely appeared to be from male to female office workers. Among the many assumptions about women that identified them as women a very strong first and as workers a very weak second was the idea that women were primarily concerned with being or becoming wives, mothers, and housewives. Hence their jobs were considered relatively unimportant to them—a means of filling time and earning a little extra money until marriage. Furthermore, it was often assumed that women, in part because of their past or future familial roles, were meant to be subservient to men. Finally, they were believed uniquely suited to boring, menial tasks where qualities of leadership or independence were totally unnecessary. Such beliefs could become self-fulfilling prophecies. If a woman saw that her future in office work was limited, she might well perceive marriage and domestic life as a welcome alternative. Had office work been more promising, with job possibilities offering challenges and a certain degree of power, she might have been more reluctant to marry or to quit work upon marriage. But such was not the case, and if they had the chance many women left office employment after a few years, thereby lending support to the claim that they cared mainly about being wives, mothers, and housekeepers. The process of degradation that had taken place throughout much of office work from the nineteenth to the twentieth centuries was thereby disguised. The nineteenth-century clerk had not turned into a proletarian; he had merely turned into a woman.

Work Culture Among Sales Clerks

SUSAN PORTER BENSON

When a woman chose—for whatever reason—to become a department-store saleswoman, she moved into the orbit of a powerful work culture which helped to shape and define daily working life. The world of women's work intersected with the world of the department-store industry on the selling floor, and the culture which emerged from that conjunction built upon both elements. The heart of saleswomen's lives from every perspective was skill in social interaction. As women, they had been socialized to become adept at interpersonal relations and—lacking formal authority—to use influence. As clerks they were trained to be masters of the complex social situation involved in persuading someone of another class background to make a purchase. As members of occupational and departmental groups, they used their social skills to forge a resilient and cohesive work culture.

Saleswomen, no less than managers and customers, had their own ideas about how they should do their work. Observers of workers' conduct on the shop floor have long recognized that custom and informal rules compete with employer's prescriptions to govern day-to-day life on the job. Building on the insights of observers such as Stanley Mathewson and Frances Donovan, labor historians are now writing the history of these shop-floor practices and of the ideology and social organization which support them. Frequently focusing on a single industry or workplace, detailed studies recapture the complex history of the social relations of production as they developed through daily contact among and between workers and managers. When a third element—the patient in a hospital, for example, or the customer in a department store—enters into the equation, the possibilities for workers to manipulate the situation become that much greater. Labor history written from this point of view focuses on daily interaction within the workplace rather than upon formal union organization and dramatic events such as strikes.

The concept of work culture—the ideology and practice with which workers stake out a relatively autonomous sphere of action on the job—is a useful tool for analyzing these interactions. A realm of informal, customary values and rules mediates the formal authority structure of the workplace and distances workers from its impact. Work culture is created as workers confront the limitations and exploit the possibilities of their jobs; it is transmitted and enforced by oral tradition and social sanctions within the work group. Generated partly in response to specific working conditions, work culture includes both adaptation and resistance to these structural constraints. More than simply reactive, work culture embodies workers' own definition of a good day's work, their own sense of satisfying and useful labor. While condemning oppressive aspects of the job, it also celebrates the skill it demands and the rewards it brings. Work culture is very much an in-between ground: it is neither a rubber-stamp version of management policy nor is it a direct outcome of the personal—class, sex, ethnic, race, age—characteristics of the workers. It is the product of these forces as they interact in the workplace and result in collectively formed assumptions and behaviors.

The study of work culture opens the way to a fuller understanding of the formation of workers' consciousness and of the strategies through which they resist and accommodate to employers' demands. Both processes are currently the subject of much discussion among students of the labor process; the writings of Harry Braverman, Michael Burawoy, and Leslie Tentler show the range of the debate. Braverman and Burawoy, devoting their closest attention to male workers, maintain that forces inside the workplace are the prime shapers of consciousness; Braverman ignores and Burawoy discounts the influence of life beyond the factory gates. Tentler, focusing on women factory workers, argues that consciousness is formed most powerfully by gender, particularly by women's experience in the family and the home, and that women's labor-force experience only reinforced their progress toward "conventional maturity." For Braverman and Burawoy changes in the labor process are controlling; for Tentler, they are incidental to the central fact of women's workplace subordination. All three agree that, ultimately, workers' submission to the conditions of their jobs surpasses their resistance: Braverman assumes that the process of rationalization crushes workers; Burawoy affirms the transformation of resistance into consent; Tentler argues that women abandoned their grueling and demeaning jobs for the higher status and greater satisfactions of marriage and the family. In the end, of course, it is difficult to fault their shared judgment that workers' accommodation in whatever form has outweighed workers' resistance, but for students of work culture the process is as interesting as the result, the study of the small struggles, victories, and losses of daily life equal in significance to the exploration of the larger political context.

My discussion of the work culture of department-store saleswomen departs from two common assumptions, often all the more powerful because implicit, made by writers on labor and the labor process. First, I view skill not as an objective category but rather as a judgment based on social and economic imperatives which may be far removed from the nature of the work itself. In studies of the working class, the notion of skill has been biased in favor of men's work and artful manual work, with jobs performed by men labeled as more skilled than those performed by women, and the highest skill attributed to those engaged in custom production. All workers, in fact, whatever the level of skill attributed to their jobs, shape their workplace experience in ways that revise and expand managers' notions of the job, using the special "working knowledge" they develop. In the case of women workers, this working knowledge is often grounded in social interaction—as it is in retailing—and is thus doubly devalued. Second, I find that the family consciousness/work consciousness dichotomy distorts and oversimplifies the process by which forces both within and outside the workplace shape the outlook of male and female workers alike. Department-store saleswomen's work culture reflected a consciousness of themselves as workers, as women, and as consumers, reflecting the complexities and contradictions of their lives. . . .

Managers' efforts to rationalize the selling floor created the ideal conditions for the flourishing of saleswomen's work culture. Typically, department stores had conflicting lines of authority: members of the buying, operations, advertising, personnel, accounting, and sales promotion staffs all had some degree of leverage over the salespeople. In theory, this meant more thorough supervision, but in practice it meant that authority was hopelessly fragmented and frequently inconsistent. Saleswomen's work culture both exploited this weakness and mediated the contradictions in the situation. Management's decision to increase productivity by encouraging more and larger sales through "personal" or "skilled" or "suggestive" selling rather than resorting to self-service further enhanced the power of salespeople; managers relied increasingly on their initiative, originality, and skills at social interaction. This policy had a powerful double potential, since the skilled saleswoman could manipulate not just her customers but also her relationship with her bosses and her coworkers. The most valued employee could also be the most subversive.

Class and gender also played an important role in work culture. When managers tried through training and discipline to erase signs of working-class origins and to apply a veneer of middle-class or elite culture to the saleswomen, they raised the issue of class in a persistent and emphatic way. It would have been difficult for a saleswoman to avoid learning the lesson: that she was different from bosses and customers, that she and her peers formed a group apart. On the other hand, by encouraging clerks to form a womanly rapport with women on the other side of the counter, store managers set the stage for saleswomen to ally with customers and other saleswomen in ways that hurt the store's profits. Managers tried to harness class and gender to further their own ideas of selling efficiency, but in fact they unwittingly encouraged connections that could as easily do the opposite. . . .

Departmental work culture helped to manage the ties of interdependence between saleswomen and their buyers. Although the formal structure of the store defined clerks as simply subordinate to buyers, in fact the two were linked by almost feudal ties of dependence, loyalty, and obligation. The buyer bought the merchandise—but depended upon saleswomen to sell it. The buyer could provide the merchandise information for which saleswomen were eager—but saleswomen controlled the shop-floor knowledge about customers' wishes and demands which was vital to buyers' success. As a rule, saleswomen disliked classroom-type training and preferred to receive information from their buyers, whom they regarded as more expert than staff executives such as training directors. A good buyer was one who helped them learn about the stock; a bad buyer was one who did not. They disliked written materials and classroom lectures because their work culture and their entire work lives depended upon oral tradition and persuasion and they preferred to sharpen their skills through similar means. Older saleswomen whose stock-in-trade was experience rather than formal education especially resisted the classroom setting. Saleswomen perceived merchandise training as useful information; they scorned salesmanship training as an insult to their shop-floor skills. When training was given in a dictatorial or condescending fashion, they simply ignored it.

Buyers, for their part, came to saleswomen to learn what was selling, what customers were saying about the merchandise, what the department needed, what trends they observed in customer demand. This information was enormously important to buyers in planning for the future, in solving problems before they crippled the department, and in petitioning upper management for more merchandise, space, or personnel. Saleswomen, predictably, gave buyers this information in a way that reflected well on themselves and worked in their best interests. Merchandise managers and general managers eager to break the power of buyers and salespeople alike tried to switch the source of shop-floor knowledge from salespeople to accounting figures so that "[s]alespeople can't hornswoggle [buyers] any more with threats and cajoleries." But simple figures lacked the subtleties and the qualitative information saleswomen could provide. This exchange of knowledge about merchandise and customers formed a powerful link between buyers and saleswomen. Buyers could reward faithful and effective saleswomen with good recommendations and performance reports, juicy store gossip, and perquisites such as out-of-town buying trips and special bargains on merchandise.

Buyers and saleswomen were also involved in a tacit alliance against other managers. The buyers acted as a buffer between saleswomen and floorwalkers or upper-level management. She could shield her clerks from harassment by other executives and enforce rules in a lax manner. When salespeople clashed with upper management, buyers often pleaded their cases. Saleswomen in one department at Filene's appealed the store's decision to deny them supper money on a technicality. The general manager argued to the Board of Arbitration that the sales force was uncooperative about giving overtime: "the people should be willing to do a little of the giving and not demand the last drop of blood every time anything special comes up." The department head objected angrily to the "drop of blood" phrase, asserting that "[t]his is a question of justice." Such advocacy earned the loyalty of department members; they could, moreover, reciprocate by protecting the buyer from her superiors. Managers understood that a good way to get saleswomen's compliance with a storewide procedure or rule was to make it a test of cooperation with and loyalty to the buyers. Filene's top management learned the hard way that salespeople would resist anything that smacked of betrayal of the buyers; in 1922, the store announced a "Complete Stocks" contest offering workers a 50¢ prize for each report of an article or size that was out of stock. In the first two weeks of the contest, they received only nine reports because salespeople were well aware that incomplete selections reflected badly on a buyer. Only after A. Lincoln Filene himself met with the buyers and convinced them that the information would not be used against them did the reports come rushing in—eight hundred in a single week.

The gossip columns of the *Echo* are filled with notices about department parties including buyers. Sometimes the saleswomen were the hostesses— as when the suit department saleswomen held a reception for their buyer on her return from a European buying trip—and sometimes the buyer was—as when the cotton waist buyer entertained the department at her home in honor of one who was leaving to marry. One particularly beloved buyer, after casually remarking that she needed three horseshoes for good luck on the opening of her department in the new store building, found her new office filled with three huge horseshoes made of flowers, a gift from her saleswomen. But however warm department relations, a buyer was still well advised to keep her place. A little selling on the floor was fine, a sign of her willingness to work along with the rest, but any buyer who competed with saleswomen for sales or spoke disparagingly of them to customers incurred lasting enmity.

Other managers—floorwalkers, staff executives, and those above buyers in the merchandising hierarchy—were equally aware of saleswomen's work culture but tended to see it as evidence of stupidity, stubbornness, or indifference to self-interest rather than as a sign of workers' informal self-government. Not unlike the slave owners of the antebellum South, they interpreted the actions of their subordinates in a self-serving fashion, refusing to acknowledge explicitly what most dimly perceived: the existence of an oppositional set of rules which simultaneously challenged and sustained the functioning of the store. On one hand, work culture helped the store to run smoothly by arbitrating interdepartmental conflicts, socializing new members, and fostering selling skill; on the other, it sanctioned the stint and various kinds of insubordination, its influence countering management's authority. To crush saleswomen's work culture would have damaged selling service by angering and alienating the saleswomen; to ignore it would have damaged selling service by giving free rein to the stint and departmental sociability. Most managers chose a middle ground which focused limited efforts on specific offenses.

Saleswomen bent rules at every turn, showing that they sensed their employers' hesitancy. Bosses and floorwalkers constantly complained of high spirits and boisterous sociability in the departments and did their unsuccessful best to stamp out loud laughing, talking, singing, and horseplay. Saleswomen openly ridiculed petty regulations and simply refused to comply with managers' demands that they complete "want slips" for every customer request they were unable to fill. They intentionally omitted their numbers from sales checks so that returned goods could not be subtracted from their sales totals. Rule-breaking was a way of life at Filene's; the *Echo* contained many exhortations to employees to be more conscientious. Saleswomen so frequently violated the dress rules with improprieties such as sleeveless dresses and sheer blouses that management began in the mid-1920s to send them home to change clothes and to dock their pay for time lost. They exploited the seasonal rhythms of retailing; twice as many arrived late for work during the summer doldrums as during the busier spring season. When an antitardiness campaign pushed too hard on the rank and file, a wit in the *Echo* suggested that the Tardiness Committee would have to hire Mechanic's Hall, a large auditorium, to hear all the cases of executive tardiness.

Saleswomen most dramatically defied managers when they felt that their dignity had been attacked or their prerogatives undermined. Such was the case in a drapery department in a Pittsburgh store. When the display department assumed the task of decorating the department, saleswomen viewed it as an insult to their abilities; they criticized the display department's work and ostentatiously refused to straighten out displays which became disarranged during the day. A saleswoman whom an executive offended spread the word among her co-workers, and "in a few minutes all the salespeople [were] aroused and doing all they [could] to ignore or annoy him." In dealing with staff personnel, floorwalkers, and upper management, saleswomen maintained a stern unity.

Management's major offensive against saleswomen's work culture was an effort to break the hold of the stint through incentive systems of payment. Saleswomen, like skilled craftsmen and less skilled factory operatives, resisted these tactics. Managers found to their sorrow that these plans might raise sales levels only to cause other problems. Saleswomen became more ruthless about weeding out those whom they supposed to be lookers and concentrated on the most likely prospects, particularly those who appeared to be more prosperous. They became fixated on their books; as one rueful manager put it, they "look at the records their sales are going to show this month, and they do not look at *the customer*." They shunned stock work as if to point out to management that they would play the game of higher sales with a vengeance, to the exclusion of other aspects of their work. They kept a wary eye out for any among them who might take the incentives too seriously and become a grabber. They ignored less popular merchandise and sold along the lines of least resistance, leaving large portions of the stock untouched until it had to be marked down. And, perhaps most alarming of all, they administered collectively what was designed to be an individualistic system. One manager reported that "[t]here was a tendency for some sales-people who had no prospects of making their quota to turn their sales over to someone who had made their quota and split the commission." Despairing of material incentives, one harried buyer simply resorted to pitting one saleswoman against another with vicious gossip in order to foster a competitive selling spirit. She succeeded in the short run, but in the long run she was left with a foul-tempered and backbiting department that was unable to deliver good selling service.

As universally as managers complained about the power of sales-women's work culture, no boss testified to the successful and total elimination of its practices. Dire threats and draconian discipline might break its grip on an individual: the manager of an Ohio store told of his year-long battle to get one saleswoman to sell occasionally in other departments. She stood firm in her refusal, affirming "I'm a coat girl," invoking work culture's pride in and identification with her merchandise. Only his threat to fire her forced her to sell other merchandise, and even then he hedged his bets by demanding that she sign a letter promising to sell anywhere in the store. But more impressive are tales of saleswomen's small, quiet, collective victories against management. In 1915, for example, a desperate floorwalker mounted a major offensive against an obstreperous and temperamental department. He succeeded in subduing the saleswomen temporarily and in whipping them on to higher sales levels, but his success was short-lived. The store manager, faced with imminent insurrection among the saleswomen, finally had to transfer him to another floor. Even in the depth of the Depression, managers lost their battles with work culture. A retailing student reported on an extremely cohesive women's shoe department where the saleswomen enforced the stint rigorously, flaunted the dress code by wearing large hoop earrings, unilaterally extended their lunch hour from forty-five minutes to an hour, and resolutely ignored all storewide activities. Not even the specter of Depression-era unemployment deterred them. . . .

The nature of saleswomen's work culture shows their notable ability to exploit a flexible and ambiguous situation. Because there was no rigid formula for successful selling, clerks could liberally interpret employers' rules and instructions with relative impunity. For example, managers urged sales-women to help one another, and they went overboard in forming close-knit work groups which subverted management goals. Managers emphasized selling skill, and saleswomen made those skills the basis of a resourceful work culture. Management encouraged saleswomen to use their domestic knowledge and women's culture in the store, and they went a step further in forming the "clerking sisterhood." Management encouraged clerks to become adept at social interaction, and they huddled on the selling floor, using their social skills with their peers as well as with their customers. Management emphasized the importance of fashion, and saleswomen used their arguments to justify insurrections against dress rules.

Saleswomen's techniques for disciplining unruly customers were similar to their ways of dealing with their bosses. They withheld their knowledge about merchandise from customers, and often sullenly withheld the merchandise itself. Clerks had enormous discretion in dealing with customers as well as in dealing with their employers: they could calculatingly fawn over or condescend to them; they could terrorize them or kill them with kindness; they could ignore them or overwhelm them with attention.

The study of saleswomen's work culture not only illuminates the lives of those legions of women who were part of it, but also suggests ways of revising the history of women workers in particular and life on the shop floor in general. At least one group of women workers, and doubtless others, developed a shop-floor culture that combined a keen sense of themselves as workers and as women. Both elements contained contradictions. As workers, saleswomen developed an appreciation of the skill of selling but an unwillingness to use that skill as their employers wished. As women, they integrated both a traditional home-and-family outlook and a more critical feminist stance into their work culture. The long-standing assumption that women's consciousness is overwhelmingly the product of domestic imperatives oversimplifies the complicated dynamic of women workers' daily lives.

The tactics of saleswomen's work culture were those long familiar to male skilled workers, but now mobilized to protect interpersonal and consumer skills rather than artisanal or mechanical ones. It is time to ask if these tactics are less specific to skilled workers than generalized among workers under conditions of capitalist production. All workers have a knowledge of the work they do that surpasses the prescriptions of their employers; to understand the modes by which workers protect and expand their knowledge can help to fix the boundary between the struggle and the acquiescence that are part of every worker's life.

One of male skilled workers' major weapons was conspicuously absent from saleswomen's work culture: the labor union. Until the CIO-sparked drives of the middle and later 1930s, barely a handful of the nation's saleswomen carried union cards. The Retail Clerks' International Protective Association (RCIPA), the principal pre-CIO retail union, claimed only two thousand female members in the mid-1920s—an insignificant .4 percent of the nation's women sales workers, many of them in small-town shops rather than in urban department stores. The organizing efforts of the late 1930s brought the unionized proportion nearer 5 percent. For most of the half-century between 1890 and 1940, then, labor unions had very little impact on the day-to-day life of the selling floor.

Far from surprising, this fact is doubly predictable because of the tendency of both women and white-collar workers to organize less often than men and blue-collar workers. Virtually all of the factors which conspire against women's unionization converged in department-store selling: high labor turnover; possibilities for upward mobility for the longer-term worker; a union (the RCIPA) which was at best paternalistic and often outright hostile to the organizing of saleswomen; and managers who were especially ruthless in firing union sympathizers uncovered by their pervasive and effective spy networks. Given the array of circumstances undermining unionization, it is remarkable not how little but how often saleswomen tried to organize. First during the pre–World War I burst of women's militancy, then after World War I, and again during the late 1930s, some department-store saleswomen saw unionization as desirable and possible. As historians begin to ask not why women fail to organize but why they sometimes try and succeed, the motivations, victories, and failures of this minority will be recaptured for the historical record.

One of the questions a study of department-store saleswomen's union efforts will have to consider is that of the relation of saleswomen's work culture to labor unions. Recent writers have argued both that work culture fed into union strength and that it thwarted it; an understanding of saleswomen's work culture suggests that the two possibilities coexisted and that work culture was indeed a flexible resource. Work culture fostered persuasive skills and ease at dealing with the public which served saleswomen well in their union struggles; news reports frequently note the energy and verve that saleswomen brought to the picket line and support meetings. Even as they displayed workers' militancy, however, saleswomen could still act out their pride in their white-collar status and their vision of themselves as the arbiters of fashion and consumption: during the 1937 San Francisco strike saleswomen from the carriage-trade stores showed up for picket duty dressed to the nines, making the strike action look "like a fashion show."

Seen from another point of view, of course, work culture was a hindrance to and an inferior substitute for unionization. Reinforcing the fragmentation of the store into departments, work culture's base in the departmental work group could undercut the storewide solidarity required to build a union. The aspects of work culture which provided channels for expressing hostility toward managers and customers could legitimate that anger, but could also defuse it by allowing saleswomen to act out their workers' consciousness in the sheltered context of the department rather than taking the enormous risks of union activity. Moreover, sales work did not involve the dyadic worker-manager relationship of the factory; the complex saleswoman/customer/manager triangle obscured and transformed the content of class conflict on the selling floor. It was not always clear who the enemy was. Finally, and perhaps most important of all, work culture functioned in an informal, customary fashion while unions adopted formalized legalistic agreements; shop-floor action was not always readily transferable to the bargaining table or the grievance procedure. Labor unions might regularize management practice, but work culture protected the "perks," and the two could clash as well as reinforce each other. It would be equally inappropriate to romanticize saleswomen's work culture and to blame it for their failure to unionize. Work culture in itself cannot insure dignity and justice for workers, but it did shape the daily lives of thousands of saleswomen, providing organizing principles and a sense of right even as it lacked the authority to enforce them. Placed alongside the cultural factors inhibiting the organization of white-collar women, the impotence of the RCIPA, and the grimly anti-union policies of their employers, saleswomen's work culture pales into insignificance as a block to unionization. . . .

❖ *FURTHER READING*

Faye Dudden, *Serving Women: Household Service in Nineteenth-Century America* (1983)

Sarah Eisenstein, *Give Us Bread But Give Us Roses* (1983)

Nancy Schrom Dye, *As Equals and as Sisters: Feminism, The Labor Movement, and the Women's Trade Union League of New York* (1981)

Martha Fraundorf, "The Labor Force Participation of Turn-of-the-Century Married Women," *Journal of Economic History*, XXXIX (1979), 401–18

Dee Garrison, *Apostles of Culture: The Public Librarian and American Society, 1876–1920* (1979)

Claudia Goldin, "The Work and Wages of Single Women, 1870–1920," *Journal of Economic History*, XL (1980), 81–88

Tamara Hareven, *Family Time and Industrial Time* (1982)

Barbara Harris, *Beyond Her Sphere: Women and the Professions in American History* (1978)

Joan Jensen and Sue Davidson, eds., *A Needle, A Bobbin, A Strike* (1984)

Jacqueline Jones, *Labor of Love, Labor of Sorrow: Black Women, Work, and the Family from Slavery to the Present* (1985)

David Katzman, *Seven Days a Week: Women and Domestic Service in Industrializing America* (1978)

Alice Kessler-Harris, *Out to Work: A History of Wage-Earning Women in the United States* (1982)

Kathy Peiss, *Cheap Amusements* (1986)

Joanne Reitano, "Working Girls Unite," *American Quarterly*, XXXVI (1984), 112–34

Elyce Rotella, *From Home to Office: United States Women at Work, 1870–1930* (1981)

Barbara Miller Soloman, *In the Company of Educated Women* (1985)

Meredith Tax, *The Rising of the Women: Feminist Solidarity and Class Conflict, 1880–1917* (1981)

Mary Roth Walsh, *Doctors Wanted: No Women Need Apply* (1977)

Winifred Wandersee, *Women's Work and Family Values, 1920–1940* (1981)

CHAPTER

12

After Suffrage:

Gender, Race, and Politics

In 1920 the goal women had been seeking since 1848 was finally won—the Nineteenth Amendment was formally added to the Constitution, and women could vote at last. But the achievement that suffragists expected to be a way station en route to further political triumphs turned out to have been the pinnacle of success itself. After suffrage was obtained, the coalition that had fought so long and hard to achieve it collapsed. Without one overriding aim, feminists could not agree on a top priority for action: social feminists like Florence Kelley continued to emphasize the need for protective labor legislation; the National Woman's Party (NWP) started on the path that would lead it to propose the Equal Rights Amendment; and black feminists placed their major stress on combating the racial discrimination they suffered in concert with their black male counterparts.

Even acknowledging the disagreements, though, the demise of the powerful movement that had been so effective seems to require additional explanation. Historians have been attempting to understand the dynamic processes that worked to defeat a subsequent feminist agenda in the 1920s. No definitive, widely accepted answer has yet emerged from those efforts. To what extent did the dropping of a single-sex approach to politics lead to the decline of the women's movement, and to what extent was its demise connected to the lack of interrelatedness with other social movements after suffrage was obtained? How did these considerations affect black women in relation to the feminist movement?

❖ DOCUMENTS

In October 1920, in an effort at interracial cooperation, the Women's Council of the Methodist Episcopal Church, South, issued a statement supporting a number of reforms desired by black women. Conspicuously absent from their list, however, was suffrage—an omission not lost on the Southeastern Federation of Colored Women's Clubs, which pointedly responded to the white women's statement in June 1921; these statements appear here as the first selection. In the second document, published the following year in *The Nation* magazine, Elsie Hill of the National Woman's Party called for the elimination of all legal distinctions between

men and women. In the same issue of the same magazine, Florence Kelley
criticized the NWP's lack of attention to the concerns of black and working-class
women. Excerpted in the fourth selection is Dorothy Dunbar Bromley's article
"Feminist—New Style," which rejected many of the tenets of the suffragists. And
in 1931, a decade after the vote had been won, Emily Newell Blair—a former vice-
chairman of the Democratic Party—expressed her discouragement at women's lack
of progress in politics, as revealed in the final document.

Two Statements on Race Relations

Women's Council of the Methodist Episcopal Church, South, 1920

We, a company of Southern white women, in conference assembled on the
invitation of the Commission on Inter-Racial Cooperation, find ourselves
with a deep sense of responsibility to the womanhood and childhood of the
Negro race, and also with a great desire for a Christian settlement of the
problems that overshadow the homes of both races. . . .

We recognize and deplore the fact that there is friction between the
races, but we believe that this can be largely removed by the exercise of
justice, consideration and sympathetic cooperation.

In order that the results of this conference may be perpetuated and
enlarged, we recommend:

That a Continuation Committee be appointed to devise ways and means
for carrying out the work considered by this conference; that this committee
be composed of one woman from each denomination and Christian agency
here represented, and that it be empowered to add to its membership as may
seem necessary; that each local community form a Woman's Inter-Racial
Committee, which may include representatives from all religious, civil and
social service bodies working in the community, and that this Continuation
Committee recommend plans by which this may be accomplished.

Desiring that everything that hinders the establishment of confidence
peace justice and righteousness in our land shall be removed in order that
there shall be better understanding and good will in our midst, we call
attention to the following points as possible causes of friction, which if
corrected, may go far toward creating a better day.

Domestic Service. We acknowledge our responsibility for the protection
of the Negro women and girls in our homes and on the streets. We therefore
recommend: That the domestic service be classed as an occupation and
coordinated with other world service in order that better relations may be
established by both employer and employee.

Child Welfare. We are persuaded that the conservation of the life and
health of Negro children is of the utmost importance to the community. We
therefore urge: That day nurseries and kindergartens be established in local
communities for the protection, care and training of children of Negro
mothers who go out to work; that free baby clinics be established and that
government leaflets on child welfare be distributed to expectant mothers,
thus teaching the proper care of themselves and their children; that adequate

playgrounds and recreational facilities be established for Negro children and young people.

Sanitation and Housing. Since good housing and proper sanitation are necessary for both physical and moral life, we recommend: That a survey of housing and sanitary conditions be made in the Negro section in each local community, followed by an appeal to the proper authorities for improvements when needed.

Education. Since sacredness of personality is the basis for all civilization, we urge: That every agency touching the child life of the nation shall strive to create mutual respect in the hearts of the children of different races. We are convinced that the establishment of a single standard of morals for men and women, both black and white, is necessary for the life and safety of a nation. We therefore pledge ourselves to strive to secure respect and protection for womanhood everywhere, regardless of race or color. Since provision for the education of Negro children is still inadequate, we recommend: More equitable division of the school fund, suitable school buildings and equipment, longer school terms, higher standards and increased pay for teachers.

Travel. Since colored people frequently do not receive fair treatment on street cars, on railroads and in railway stations and recognizing this as one of the chief causes of friction between the races, we urge: That immediate steps be taken to provide for them adequate accommodations and courteous treatment at the hands of street car and railway officials.

Lynching. As women, we urge those who are charged with the administration of the law to prevent lynching at any cost. We are persuaded that the proper determination on the part of the constituted officials, upheld by public sentiment, would result in the detection and prosecution of those guilty of this crime. Therefore we pledge ourselves to endeavor to create a public sentiment which will uphold these officials in the execution of justice.

Justice in the Courts. We recommend: That our women everywhere raise their voices against all acts of violence to property and person, wherever and for whatever cause occurring. We further recommend: That competent legal assistance be made available for colored people in the local communities in order to insure to them the protection of their rights in the courts.

Public Press. Since the public press often gives undue prominence to the criminal element among Negroes, and neglects the worthy and constructive efforts of law-abiding citizens, we pledge ourselves to cooperate with the men's committees in endeavoring to correct this injustice, and to create a fair attitude to Negroes and Negro news. . . .

Southeastern Federation of Colored Women's Clubs, 1921

We desire to state our position on some matters relating to the welfare of colored people, and to enlist the sympathy and cooperation of Southern white women in the interest of better understandings and better conditions, as these affect the relations between white and colored people.

THESIS

We take this opportunity to call to your attention certain conditions which affect colored women in their relations with white people and which if corrected will go far toward decreasing friction, removing distrust and suspicion and creating a better atmosphere in which to adjust the difficulties which always accompany human contacts.

Conditions in Domestic Service. The most frequent and intimate contact of white and colored women is in domestic service. Every improvement made in the physical, moral and spiritual life of those so employed must react to increase the efficiency of their service to their employers.

We, therefore, direct your attention to: Long and Irregular Working Hours; (1) lack of provision for wholesome recreation; (2) undesirable housing conditions. We recommend, therefore, (1) definite regulation for hours and conditions of work; (2) sanitary, attractive and wholesome rooming facilities; (3) closer attention to personal appearance and deportment; (4) provision for and investigation of character of recreation.

Child Welfare. The large burden of economic responsibility which falls upon many colored women results in their prolonged absence from home and the consequent neglect of the children of the homes. We direct your attention to: Child Welfare—(1) neglected homes (irregularity in food, clothing, conduct, training); (2) truancy; (3) juvenile delinquency. We therefore recommend—Welfare Activities—(1) day nurseries, play grounds, recreation centers; (2) home and school visitation; (3) probation officers and reform schools.

Conditions of Travel. Race friction is perhaps more frequent in street cars and railroad trains than in any other public places. To reduce this friction and remove causes for just complaint from colored passengers we call your attention to: (1) seating accommodations on street cars; (2) unsanitary surroundings, at stations and on trains; (3) toilet facilities, at stations and on trains; (4) difficulty in securing tickets, Pullman accommodations and meals; (5) abuse of rights of colored passengers by train crew and white passengers occupying seats while colored passengers stand, smoking, profane language, overcrowding; (6) As corrective measures we suggest provision of equal accommodations in all public carriers and courteous treatment at the hands of street car and railway officials, for all passengers.

Education. Without education for all the children of all the people we cannot sustain a democracy. Ignorance and crime are the twin children of neglect and poverty. We urge your increasing effort for better educational facilities so that there may be provided: adequate accommodations for all Negro children of school age, vocational training in all secondary schools, improved rural schools—longer terms, suitable buildings, training schools for teachers, adequate salaries for teachers.

Lynching. We deplore and condemn any act on the part of any men which would tend to excite the mob spirit. We believe that any man who makes an assault upon any woman should have prompt punishment meted out to the limit of the law, but not without thorough investigation of the facts and trial by the courts. The continuance of lynching is the greatest menace to good will between the races, and a constant factor in undermining respect for all law and order. It is our opinion that mob violence incites to crime rather than deters it; and certainly it is less effective in discouraging crime than the watchful, thorough and deliberate processes of a fair and just trial.

Toward the suppression of this evil, we appeal to white women to: (1) raise their voices in immediate protest when lynchings or mob violence is threatened; (2) encourage every effort to detect and punish the leaders and participants in mobs and riots; (3) encourage the white pulpit and press in creating a sentiment among law-abiding citizens and urge outspoken condemnation of these forms of lawlessness.

The Public Press. In the great majority of cases the white press of the South gives undue prominence to crime and the criminal element among Negroes to the neglect of the worthy and constructive efforts of law-abiding Negro citizens. We feel that a large part of friction and misunderstanding between the races is due to unjust, inflammatory and misleading headlines, and articles appearing in the daily papers. We suggest that white women include in their local community program a united effort to correct this evil and to secure greater attention to worthy efforts of Negro citizens.

Suffrage. We regard the ballot as the democratic and orderly method of correcting abuses and protecting the rights of citizens; as the substitute of civilization for violence. As peace loving, law-abiding citizens we believe the ultimate and only guarantee of fair dealing and justice for the Negro, as well as the wholesome development of the whole community, lies in the peaceful, orderly exercise of the franchise by every qualified Negro citizen. We ask therefore, that white women, for the protection of their homes as well as ours indicate their sanction of the ballot for all citizens as representing government by the sober, reasoned and deliberate judgment of all the people.

In these articles offered at your request we are stating frankly and soberly what in our judgment, you as white women may do to correct the ills from which our race has so long suffered, and of which we as a race are perhaps more conscious now than ever. We recall how in the recent days of our nation's peril so many of us worked side by side for the safety of this land and defense of this flag which is ours as it is yours. In that same spirit of unselfishness and sacrifice we offer ourselves to serve again with you in any and every way that a courageous facing of duty may require as you undertake heroically this self-appointed yet God-given task. We deeply appreciate the difficulties that lie before you, but as you undertake these things which are destined to bless us all, we pledge you our faith and loyalty in consecration to God, home and country.

Elsie Hill on Why Women Should Have Full Legal Equality, 1922

The removal of all forms of the subjection of women is the purpose to which the National Woman's Party is dedicated. Its present campaign to remove the discriminations against women in the laws of the United States is but the beginning of its determined effort to secure the freedom of women, an integral part of the struggle for human liberty for which women are first of all responsible. Its interest lies in the final release of woman from the class of a dependent, subservient being to which early civilization committed her.

The laws of various States at present hold her in that class. They deny her a control of her children equal to the father's; they deny her, if married, the right to her own earnings; they punish her for offences for which men go unpunished; they exclude her from public office and from public institutions to the support of which her taxes contribute. These laws are not the creation of this age, but the fact that they are still tolerated on our statute books and that in some States their removal is vigorously resisted shows the hold of old traditions upon us. Since the passage of the Suffrage Amendment the incongruity of these laws, dating back many centuries, has become more than ever marked. . . .

The National Woman's Party believes that it is a vital social need to do away with these discriminations against women and is devoting its energies to that end. The removal of the discriminations and not the method by which they are removed is the thing upon which the Woman's Party insists. It has under consideration an amendment to the Federal Constitution which, if adopted, would remove them at one stroke, but it is at present endeavoring to secure their removal in the individual States by a blanket bill, which is the most direct State method. For eighty-two years the piecemeal method has been tried, beginning with the married women's property act of 1839 in Mississippi, and no State, excepting Wisconsin, where the Woman's Party blanket bill was passed in June, 1921, has yet finished. . . .

The present program of the National Woman's Party is to introduce its Woman's Equal Rights Bill, or bills attaining the same purpose, in all State legislatures as they convene. It is building up in Washington a great headquarters from which this campaign can be conducted, and it is acting in the faith that the removal of these discriminations from our laws will benefit every group of women in the country, and through them all society.

Florence Kelley Explains Her Opposition to Full Legal Equality, 1922

"The removal of all forms of subjection of women is the purpose to which the National Woman's Party is dedicated."

A few years ago the Woman's Party counted disfranchisement the form of subjection which must first be removed. Today millions of American women, educated and uneducated, are kept from the polls in bold defiance of the Suffrage Amendment. Every form of subjection suffered by their white sisters they also suffer. Deprivation of the vote is theirs alone among native women. Because of this discrimination all other forms of subjection weigh a hundred fold more heavily upon them. In the family, in the effort to rent or to buy homes, as wage-earners, before the courts, in getting education for their children, in every relation of life, their burden is greater because they are victims of political inequality. How literally are colored readers to understand the words quoted above?

Sex is a biological fact. The political rights of citizens are not properly dependent upon sex, but social and domestic relations and industrial activities are. All modern-minded people desire that women should have full political equality and like opportunity in business and the professions. No enlightened person desires that they should be excluded from jury duty or denied the equal guardianship of children, or that unjust inheritance laws or discriminations against wives should be perpetuated.

The inescapable facts are, however, that men do not bear children, are freed from the burdens of maternity, and are not susceptible, in the same measure as women, to poisons now increasingly characteristic of certain industries, and to the universal poison of fatigue. These are differences so far reaching, so fundamental, that it is grotesque to ignore them. Women cannot be made men by act of the legislature or by amendment of the Federal Constitution. This is no matter of today or tomorrow. The inherent differences are permanent. Women will always need many laws different from those needed by men.

The effort to enact the blanket bill in defiance of all biological differences recklessly imperils the special laws for women as such, for wives, for mothers, and for wage-earners. . . .

Why should wage-earning women be thus forbidden to get laws for their own health and welfare and that of their unborn children? Why should they be made subject to the preferences of wage-earning men? Is not this of great and growing importance when the number of women wage-earners, already counted by millions, increases by leaps and bounds from one census to the next? And when the industries involving exposure to poisons are increasing faster than ever? And when the overwork of mothers is one recognized cause of the high infant death rate? And when the rise in the mortality of mothers in childbirth continues?

If there were no other way of promoting more perfect equality for women, an argument could perhaps be sustained for taking these risks. But why take them when every desirable measure attainable through the blanket bill can be enacted in the ordinary way? . . .

Is the National Woman's Party for or against protective measures for wage-earning women? Will it publicly state whether it is for or against the eight-hour day and minimum-wage commissions for women? Yes or No?

Dorothy Dunbar Bromley, "Feminist—New Style," 1927

Is it not high time that we laid the ghost of the so-called feminist?

"Feminism" has become a term of opprobrium to the modern young woman. For the word suggests either the old school of fighting feminists who wore flat heels and had very little feminine charm, or the current species who antagonize men with their constant clamor about maiden names, equal rights, woman's place in the world, and many another cause . . . *ad infinitum.* Indeed, if a blundering male assumes that a young woman is a feminist simply because she happens to have a job or a profession of her own, she will be highly—and quite justifiably insulted: for the word evokes the antithesis of what she flatters herself to be. Yet she and her kind can hardly be dubbed "old-fashioned" women. What *are* they, then?

The pioneer feminists were hard-hitting individuals, and the modern young woman admires them for their courage—even while she judges them for their zealotry and their inartistic methods. Furthermore, she pays all honor to them, for they fought her battle. But *she* does not want to wear their mantle (indeed, she thinks they should have been buried in it), and she has to smile at those women who wear it to-day—with the battle-cry still on their lips. . . .

Numbers of these honest, spirited young women have made themselves heard in article and story. But since men must have things pointed out to them in black and white, we beg leave to enunciate the tenets of the modern woman's credo. Let us call her "Feminist—New Style."

First Tenet. Our modern young woman freely admits that American women have so far achieved but little in the arts, sciences, and professions as compared with men. . . . So far as the arts are concerned, it cannot be stated categorically that women lack creative power, in view of their original work in fiction, poetry, and the plastic arts. As for their status in the professions, it might fairly be claimed that they have scarcely had time to get a running start. And their limited success in business would prove that they have not yet cast off their age-old habit of over-emphasizing detail and, as a consequence, they have not yet learned to grasp the larger issues.

But it remains true that a small percentage of women have proved the capacity, even the creative power of the feminine mind. Or have they not rather proved the fallacy of drawing a hard and fast distinction between the quality of men's minds and the quality of women's minds? . . . But whether or no the masculine mind is biologically superior to the feminine mind, it is obvious that women in America are progressing much faster in their mental evolution than men are. And that is the reason, no doubt, why the average man is either on the defensive or on the fence, as regards his relationship with the modern woman.

Second Tenet. Why, then, does the modern woman care about a career or a job if she doubts the quality and scope of women's achievement to date? There are three good reasons why she cares immensely: first, she may be of that rare and fortunate breed of persons who find a certain art, science, or profession as inevitable a part of their lives as breathing; second, she may feel the need of a satisfying outlet for her energy whether or no she possesses creative ability; third, she may have no other means of securing her economic independence. And the latter she prizes above all else, for it spells her freedom as an individual, enabling her to marry or not to marry, as she chooses—to terminate a marriage that has become unbearable, and to support and educate her children if necessary. . . .

In brief, Feminist—New Style reasons that if she is economically independent, and if she has, to boot, a vital interest in some work of her own she will have given as few hostages to Fate as it is humanly possible to give. Love may die, and children may grow up, but one's work goes on forever.

Third Tenet. She will not, however, live for her job alone, for she considers that a woman who talks and thinks only shop has just as narrow a horizon as the housewife who talks and thinks only husband and children— perhaps more so, for the latter may have a deeper understanding of human nature. She will therefore refuse to give up all of her personal interests, year in and year out, for the sake of her work. In this respect she no doubt will fall short of the masculine ideal of commercial success, for the simple reason that she has never felt the economic compulsion which drives men on to build up fortunes for the sake of their growing families.

Yet she is not one of the many women who look upon their jobs as tolerable meal-tickets or as interesting pastimes to be dropped whenever they may wish. On the contrary, she takes great pride in becoming a vital factor in whatever enterprise she has chosen, and she therefore expects to work long hours when the occasion demands. . . .

Fourth Tenet. Nor has she become hostile to the other sex in the course of her struggle to orient herself. On the contrary, she frankly likes men and is grateful to more than a few for the encouragement and help they have given her.

In the business and professional worlds, for instance, Feminist—New Style has observed that more and more men are coming to accord women as much responsibility as they show themselves able to carry. She and her generation have never found it necessary to bludgeon their way, and she is inclined to think that certain of the pioneers would have got farther if they had relied on their ability rather than on their militant methods. To tell the truth, she enjoys working with men, more than with women, for their methods are more direct and their view larger, and she finds that she can deal with them on a basis of frank comradeship.

When she meets men socially she is not inclined to air her knowledge and argue about woman's right to a place in the sun. On the contrary, she either talks with a man because he has ideas that interest her or because she finds it amusing to flirt with him—and she will naturally find it doubly amusing if the flirtation involves the swift interplay of wits. She will not waste many engagements on a dull-witted man, although it must be admitted that she finds fewer men with stagnant minds than she does women. . . .

Fifth Tenet. By the same corollary, Feminist—New Style professes no loyalty to women *en masse,* although she staunchly believes in individual women. Surveying her sex as a whole, she finds their actions petty, their range of interests narrow, their talk trivial and repetitious. As for those who set themselves up as leaders of the sex, they are either strident creatures of so little ability and balance that they have won no chance to "express themselves" (to use their own hackneyed phrase) in a man-made world; or they are brilliant, restless individuals who too often battle for women's rights for the sake of personal glory. . . .

Sixth Tenet. There is, however, one thing which Feminist—New Style envies Frenchwomen, and that is their sense of "chic." Indeed, she is so far removed from the early feminists that she is altogether baffled by the psychology which led some of them to abjure men in the same voice with which they aped them. Certainly their vanity must have been anaesthetized, she tells herself, as she pictures them with their short hair, so different from her own shingle, and dressed in their unflattering mannish clothes—quite the antithesis of her own boyish effects which are subtly designed to set off feminine charms. . . .

Seventh Tenet. Empty slogans seem to Feminist—New Style just as bad taste as masculine dress and manners. They serve only to prolong the war between the sexes and to prevent women from learning to think straight. Take these, for instance, "Keep your maiden name." "Come out of the kitchen." "Never darn a sock." After all, what's in a name or in a sock? Madame Curie managed to become one of the world's geniuses even though she suffered the terrible handicap of bearing her husband's name, and it is altogether likely that she darned a sock or two of Monsieur Curie's when there was no servant at hand to do it. . . .

Eighth Tenet. As for "free love," she thinks that it is impractical rather than immoral. With society organized as it is, the average man and woman cannot carry on a free union with any degree of tranquillity.

Incidentally, she is sick of hearing that modern young women are cheapening themselves by their laxity of morals. As a matter of fact, all those who have done any thinking, and who have any innate refinement, live by an aesthetic standard of morals which would make promiscuity inconceivable. . . .

Ninth Tenet. She readily concedes that a husband and children are necessary to the average woman's fullest development, although she knows well enough that women are endowed with varying degrees of passion and of maternal instinct. Some women, for instance, feel the need of a man very intensely, while others want children more than they want a husband, want them so much, in fact, that they vow they would have one or two out of wedlock if it were not for the penalty that society would exact from the child, and if it were not for the fact that a child needs a father as much as a mother.

But no matter how much she may desire the sanction of marriage for the sake of having children, she will not take any man who offers. First of all a man must satisfy her as a lover and a companion. And second, he must have the mental and physical traits which she would like her children to inherit. She has seen too many women engulfed in tragedy simply because they let their instincts rush them into an ill-advised marriage and into the bearing of one child after another, each one handicapped by a bad physical or moral heritage. Instincts are an excellent thing in their place, but they must be guided by reason if disaster is not to follow. . . .

If Feminist—New Style finds it practicable to have children she will resolve from the start not to sacrifice everything to them—for their sake as well as her own. During the years of their babyhood she may find it necessary to give up her work, either partially or wholly; but as soon as possible she will organize the family life so as to resume her own interests.

This business of combining two careers presents its grave difficulties. In fact, it is a bigger job than any man has ever attempted. But because it *is* a

big job, and because she has seen a few women succeed at it, Feminist—
New Style will rise to the challenge, provided that she has a normal amount
of physical energy. . . .

Tenth Tenet. But even while she admits that a home and children may be
necessary to her complete happiness, she will insist upon *more freedom and
honesty within the marriage relation.*

She considers that the ordinary middle-class marriage is stifling in that it
allows the wife little chance to know other men, and the husband little
chance to know other women—except surreptitiously. It seems vital to her
that both should have a certain amount of leisure to use exactly as they see
fit, without feeling that they have neglected the other. . . .

Finally, Feminist—New Style proclaims that men and children shall no
longer circumscribe her world, although they may constitute a large part of
it. She is intensely self-conscious whereas the feminists were intensely sex-
conscious. Aware of possessing a mind, she takes a keen pleasure in using
that mind for some definite purpose; and also in learning to think clearly and
cogently against a background of historical and scientific knowledge. She
aspires to understand the meaning of the twentieth century as she sees it
expressed in the skyscrapers, the rapid pace of city life, the expressionistic
drama, the abstract conceptions of art, the new music, the Joycian novel.
She is acutely conscious that she is being carried along in the current of
these sweeping forces, that she and her sex are in the vanguard of change.
She knows that it is her American, her twentieth-century birthright to
emerge from a creature of instinct into a full-fledged individual who is capable of molding her own life. And in this respect she holds that she is becoming man's equal.

If this be treason, gentlemen, make the most of it.

Emily Newell Blair, "Why I Am Discouraged About Women in Politics," 1931

Five years ago I wrote an article on women in politics in which I said that
women were already participating in politics to some extent, and that the
promise was good that they would participate more and more. My conclusions were based upon the situation as it appeared then. After the first five
years of woman suffrage I was encouraged. The beginning was good. The
future looked bright. Since then the going has been bad. Having expressed
my optimism, I must now in fairness to myself report my pessimism and its
causes.

Let me note at the outset two things. I am not disappointed in those
women who have succeeded in politics. I am disappointed with what politics
has done for women. I am not discouraged because I feel that I have been
ineffective as a politician, for I do not. I am discouraged because I have been
ineffective in politics as a feminist.

To me the aim of woman suffrage was to make women co-partners with
men in government. I thought it would make it possible for women with
ambition and political ability to enter politics as a career without disqualifi-

cation because they were women. I never had any illusions that women would "clean up" politics, for I never believed that women were better than men. Also, I knew enough about politics to understand that its ethics and practices were caused by other conditions than the dominance of men. But I did think woman suffrage would widen the opportunities of women.

I hoped to see women candidates exemplifying women's right to participate with men in politics and to have enough of them elected to accustom men and women to women in office, and thus serve to overcome the prejudice against women in positions of importance. . . .

Now at the end of ten years of suffrage, I find politics still a male monopoly. It is hardly any easier for women to get themselves elected to office than it was before the Equal Suffrage Amendment was passed. Women still have little part in framing political policies and determining party tactics.

Far from participating equally with men in politics, they participate in leadership hardly at all—less, as a matter of fact, than they did in 1920. To realize this, I have only to recall the national political conventions of 1920, when candidates for the presidential nominations selected as women-managers leaders of women, when they emphasized in their campaign literature their sympathy with the recognition of women, when women spoke from the convention rostrums on debatable planks, when women delegates cast their votes without advice from men associates, when men on the Resolutions Committees conferred with and kept in touch with leaders of women, and women in the delegations kept in touch with the same leaders and forced their members of the Resolutions Committee to vote for the measures they favored. Since then I have attended two national conventions of my own party and one of the other party, and at no one of them have I seen women, as feminists, of so much importance.

If this is not convincing that there has been a decline in the participation of women in politics, let us turn to the political party organization and see what has happened there. When it appeared that women might be given the right to vote before the next national election, politicians of both parties rushed to place women on their party committees. In their choice, the men paid women a high compliment. They believed, it was evident, that women would want the highest type of women to represent them. And in their eagerness to capture the women's votes for their party they put this type on their committees. They also believed that women would want women on these committees who could lead women. They therefore named women whose leadership had been tried and tested. And then these men listened to these women whom they had chosen: even when they did not have a vote on the committees, their opinions had weight. And why? Because the men saw them as powerful leaders of women.

Since then, women have come officially to have a place on party committees. They are elected to them as are the men. But in too many cases these first women have been succeeded by a different type, who give their proxies at committee meetings to the men by whose influence they have been elected, who do what they are told by these men to do, and who are without achievement or previous leadership of women. . . .

.Such women never bother with so-called women's measures or movements. They have no use for feminism. The League of Women Voters, for
instance, is anathema to them. And so they do nothing to forward the participation of women in politics. Small wonder that politicians think woman
suffrage a success. The bogie of the feminine influence, of the woman-vote,
has been laid.

But there are also women on these committees who went into politics
desirous of representing women and strengthening their position in politics. I
was one of them once myself. I owed my election to the National Committee
and my subsequent position with the committee in Washington to the fact
that I had been associated with women in pre-suffrage activities. For I was
elected to this committee and position in the days when men still feared
women's votes and it was thought that I would have influence with women
and so win them to the support of the party. But once in politics I found
myself entirely surrounded by men. . . .

Unfortunately for feminism, it was agreed to drop the sex line in politics.
And it was dropped by the women. Even those who ran for office forgot that
they were women. "I am not running as a woman, but as a Democrat (or as a
Republican)!" How many times have I heard it! No appeal to women to put
a woman into office, no argument as to her right to hold office, but a
minimizing always of her sex. And yet thousands of votes were cast against
her, for no other reason than that she was a woman. For let us not think,
because we cease to talk of it, that the prejudice against women in public
office has been overcome. . . .

Of all the women the country over who have been elected to office, I
know of only one who went into politics as a feminist; that is, who made an
appeal to women to support a woman, organized women to back her because
she was a woman, stressed the right of women to hold office, thus making
that an issue in her campaign, and owed her election to a following of women
instead of a political following dominated by men. I refer to Florence Allen,
Judge of the Supreme Court of Ohio. There are probably others scattered
about the country in state legislatures and county offices, but their number is
without doubt small. . . .

❖ E S S A Y S

Estelle Freedman of Stanford University, addressing a question that has puzzled
historians for years—Why did the feminist movement apparently disappear after
suffrage was won?—hypothesizes in the first essay that in the 1920s feminism lost
touch with its "woman-centered" roots and failed to maintain a distinctively female
identity. Conversely, Nancy F. Cott, who teaches at Yale University, argues in the
second selection, her study of the National Woman's Party, that perhaps a too-nar-
row focus on specifically "feminist" concerns led to the party's failures. In the
third essay, Rosalyn Terborg-Penn of Morgan State University, like Cott, points
out that white feminists refused to accord their black counterparts full equality
within their own movement. These authors all agree that there was a definite decline in the feminist movement during the 1920s but disagree on its cause.

What Happened to Feminism in the 1920s?

ESTELLE FREEDMAN

Most explanations of the decline of women's political strength focus on either inherent weaknesses in suffragist ideology or on external pressures from a pervasively sexist society. But when I survey the women's movement before suffrage passed, I am struck by the hypothesis that a major strength of American feminism prior to 1920 was the separate female community that helped sustain women's participation in both social reform and political activism. Although the women's movement of the late nineteenth century contributed to the transformation of women's social roles, it did not reject a separate, unique female identity. Most feminists did not adopt the radical demands for equal status with men that originated at the Seneca Falls Convention of 1848. Rather, they preferred to retain membership in a separate female sphere, one which they did not believe to be inferior to men's sphere and one in which women could be free to create their own forms of personal, social, and political relationships. The achievements of feminism at the turn of the century came less through gaining access to the male domains of politics and the professions than in the tangible form of building separate female institutions.

The self-consciously female community began to disintegrate in the 1920s just as "new women" were attempting to assimilate into male-dominated institutions. At work, in social life, and in politics, I will argue, middle-class women hoped to become equals by adopting men's values and integrating into their institutions. A younger generation of women learned to smoke, drink, and value heterosexual relationships over female friendships in their personal lives. At the same time, women's political activity epitomized the process of rejecting women's culture in favor of men's promises of equality. The gradual decline of female separatism in social and political life precluded the emergence of a strong women's political block which might have protected and expanded the gains made by the earlier women's movement. Thus the erosion of women's culture may help account for the decline of public feminism in the decades after 1920. Without a constituency a movement cannot survive. The old feminist leaders lost their following when a new generation opted for assimilation in the naive hope of becoming men's equals overnight. . . .

Unfortunately, the rhetoric of equality that became popular among men and women (with the exception of the National Woman's Party) just after the passage of the Suffrage Amendment in 1920 subverted the women's movement by denying the need for continued feminist organization. Of course, external factors significantly affected the movement's future, including the new Freudian views of women; the growth of a consumer economy

Reprinted from Estelle Freedman, "Separatism as Strategy: Female Institution Building and American Feminism, 1870–1930," *Feminist Studies*, V 1979, 514–15, 521–24, by permission of the publisher, *Feminist Studies*, Inc., c/o Women's Studies Program, University of Maryland, College Park, MD 20742.

that increasingly exploited women's sexuality; and the repression of radicalism and reform in general after World War I. But at the same time, many women, seemingly oblivious that these pressures necessitated further separate organizing, insisted on striving for integration into a male world—sexually, professionally, and politically.

Examples of this integrationist approach can be found in the universities, the workplace, and politics. In contrast to an earlier generation, the women who participated in the New York World's Fair of 1937 had no separate building. Woman, the Fair Bulletin explained, "will not sit upon a pedestal, not be segregated, isolated; she will fit into the life of the Exposition as she does into life itself—never apart, always a part." The part in this World's Fair, however, consisted primarily of fashion, food, and vanity fair. In the universities, the success of the first generation of female academics did not survive past the 1920s, not only because of men's resistance, but, as Rosalind Rosenberg has explained, "Success isolated women from their culture of origin and placed them in an alien and often hostile community." Many academics who cut off their ties to other women "lost their old feminine supports but had no other supports to replace them."

The lessons of women's politics in the 1920s are illustrated by the life of one woman, Emily Newell Blair, who learned first hand the pitfalls of rejecting a separatist basis for feminism. Blair's life exemplified the transformation of women's roles at the turn of the century. Educated at a woman's college, Goucher, this Missouri born, middle-class woman returned to her hometown to help support her family until she married and created her own home. Between 1900 and 1910 she bore two children, supported her husband's career, and joined in local women's club activities. In her spare time, Blair began writing short stories for ladies' magazines. Because she found the work, and particularly the income, satisfying, she became a free lance writer. At this point, the suffrage movement revived in Missouri, and Blair took over state publicity, editing the magazine *Missouri Woman* and doing public relations. Then, in World War I, she expanded her professional activities further by serving on the Women's Council of the U.S. Council of National Defense. These years of training in writing, feminist organizing, and public speaking served Blair well when suffrage passed and she entered politics.

In 1920, women faced three major political choices: they could become a separate feminist political force through the National Woman's Party, which few did; they could follow the moderates of the NAWSA into the newly formed, nonpartisan League of Women Voters, concentrating on citizen education and good government; or they could join the mainstream political parties. Emily Newell Blair chose the last, and rose through the Democratic Party organization to become national vice-chairman of the party in the 1920s.

Blair built her political life and her following on the belief that the vote had made women the political equals of men. Thus, the surest path to furthering women's goals was through participation in the party structure. Having helped to found the League of Women Voters, Blair then rejected nonpartisanship, while she urged women not to vote as women but as citizens. In a 1922 lecture on "What Women May Do with the Ballot," Blair argued that "reactions to political issues are not decided by sex but by intellect and emotion. . . ." Although she believed that lack of political experience and social training made women differ from men temporarily, she expected those differences to be eliminated after a few years of political activity. To hasten women's integration into the mainstream of party politics, Blair set up thirty "schools of democracy" to train the new voters during the early twenties, as well as over one thousand women's clubs. Her philosophy, she claimed, was one of "Boring from Within." Blair rejected the "sex conscious feminists" of the Woman's Party and those who wanted "woman cohesiveness." Although she favored the election of women, she wanted them to be chosen not as women but as politicians. "Give women time," she often repeated, and they would become the equals of men in politics.

By the late 1920s, however, women had not gained acceptance as men's political equals, and Blair's views changed significantly. Once she had claimed that the parties did not discriminate against women, as shown by her own powerful position. After she retired from party office in 1928, however, Blair acknowledged that the treatment of women by the parties had deteriorated since the years immediately after suffrage passed. As soon as male politicians realized that there was no strong female voting block or political organization, they refused to appoint or elect powerful women, and a "strong masculine prejudice against women in politics" surfaced. Now they chose women for party office who seemed easiest to manage or who were the wives of male officeholders.

By 1931, Blair's former optimism had turned to disillusionment. She felt herself "ineffective in politics as a feminist," a term that she began to use positively. Blair realized that women could not command political power and the respect of their male colleagues unless, like the suffrage leaders, they had a visible, vocal following. "Unfortunately for feminism," she confessed, "it was agreed to drop the sex line in politics. And it was dropped by the women." In the pages of the *Woman's Journal,* Blair called for a revival of feminism in the form of a new politics that would seek to put more women into office. Reversing her former stance, she claimed that *women* voters should back *women* candidates, and use a *women's* organization to do so. They could remain in the parties, but should form "a new organization of feminists devoted to the task of getting women into politics."

The development of Emily Newell Blair's feminist consciousness may have been unique for her time, but it is a familiar process among educated and professional women today. Having gained access to formerly male institutions, but still committed to furthering women's struggles, today's "new women" are faced with political choices not dissimilar to the generation that achieved suffrage. The bitterness of Stanton and Anthony in their advice to the younger generation in 1881, and the strategy that Emily Newell Blair presented in 1931, may serve as lessons for the present.

The strength of female institutions in the late nineteenth century and the weaknesses of women's politics after the passage of the Suffrage Amendment suggest to me that the decline of feminism in the 1920s can be attributed in part to the devaluation of women's culture in general and of separate female institutions in particular. When women tried to assimilate into male-dominated institutions, without securing feminist social, economic, or political bases, they lost the momentum and the networks which had made the suffrage movement possible. Women gave up many of the strengths of the female sphere without gaining equally from the man's world they entered. . . .

Thesis

The National Woman's Party

NANCY F. COTT

The National Woman's Party (NWP) is not well known. For a long time it has stood under a pall, its history obscured by being recounted from its opponents' point of view when recounted at all. The minority faction among suffragists, it became an even more embattled minority among activist women in the 1920s because of its invention of the equal rights amendment. Insofar as it is known, the party has a paradoxical image. In histories of the suffrage movement in the 1910s, it appears as the militant, "left" wing; in histories of women's reform movements of the 1920s, it appears as a clique of prosperous business and professional women, repellent to the Left. The one organization of women that openly declared itself feminist, it has attracted most of historians' blame for the "demise" of feminism after woman suffrage was obtained. The whole story of feminism's fate after 1920 is more interesting than ever because of possible parallels between the 1920s and the 1980s, and an internal examination of the NWP and a clearer interpretation of it are necessary if we are to begin to understand the earlier decade.

The NWP grew from the Congressional Union, the suffrage organization Alice Paul and Lucy Burns founded when they broke with the leadership of the National American Woman Suffrage Association (NAWSA) early in 1913. Paul and Burns distinguished their approach from the mainstream in several ways that persisted as the Congressional Union evolved into the Woman's Party (1916) and the NWP (1917). A group of, by, and for women, it concentrated on the federal (rather than state) government and aimed to amend the United States Constitution to gain woman's rights; it used flamboyant publicity tactics, including street marches, open-air meetings, and eventually picketing of the White House and the Capitol; and it employed a "political" (rather than simply educative) strategy, attempting to marshal women's votes (in the states where women were enfranchised) to punish "the party in power," the Democratic party, until a woman suffrage amendment was passed. Between 1914 and 1919 the group took risks; it stood as

Cott, Nancy F., "Feminist Politics in the 1920s: The National Woman's Party," *Journal of American History*, 71 (June 1984), 43–68. Copyright Organization of American Historians, 1984.

"the party of youth" regardless of its members' chronological age; its leaders did not fear and did not fail to rankle the stalwarts of the mainstream suffrage association. The party appealed to working-class women and inadvertently or advertently to left-wing women with its militant tactics, opposition to the government during wartime, and sidestepping of gentility at the same time it appealed to wealthy socialites with its newsworthiness and its strategy of lobbying the president and national legislators in addition to exhorting the man on the street. In 1914 Alva Belmont (widow to Vanderbilt and Belmont millions) became the party's financial angel and an important voice.

Only a fractional craft on the prosuffrage sea, the NWP made waves beyond its size because of the variety, devotion, and vigor of its organizers and members. The organization charted a course with no contingencies, its orientation constantly toward a constitutional amendment for woman suffrage; and its heterogeneous membership worked toward that goal under control from above. "There is no difference of opinion in regard to Alice Paul in the Woman's Party," wrote Inez Haynes Irwin, the group's historian. "With one accord, they say 'She is the Party.' They regard her with an admiration which verges on awe." Paul seems never to have imagined any other than a tightly knit, ideologically pure, vanguard party. Though V. I. Lenin was probably far from her ken or sympathy, Paul's leadership style might be called "Leninist"; indeed, NWP organizer Doris Stevens thought in 1919 that Paul "must possess many of the same qualities that Lenin does, according to authentic portraits of him—cool, practical, rational, sitting quietly at a desk and counting the consequences." By virtually all accounts of the 1910s, Paul was charismatic. . . .

By July 1920, a month before the final ratification of the Nineteenth Amendment, Belmont was stressing the need for the NWP to continue as an organization to "obtain for women full equality with men in all phases of life and make them a power in the life of the state," and Paul had enunciated as a worthy goal some form of "blanket" legislation that would remove all legal discriminations against women. From September 1920 through February 1921, the party's inner circle, the National Executive Committee, met monthly to hash out resolutions to present at the grand convention in February, where the future form and goals (if any) of the party were ostensibly to be decided by the delegates present. While Paul gave many of her followers the impression that she was too exhausted to go on leading them, her predilections guided preparations. In December she told the National Executive Committee that Sue Shelton White (a lawyer and vigorous party worker since 1917), who had been surveying sex discriminations in state legal codes, had drawn up a "blanket bill" that "could be introduced in Congress and each legislature to sweep away these discriminations" and "could be offered at the final convention as a possible piece of work for the future." Despite the contrary efforts of a few who wished for a broader-ranging program—especially Edith Houghton Hooker, a longtime social-hygiene proponent from Baltimore—the leadership moved undeviatingly toward the majority resolution offered at the convention: that the NWP disband but immediately regroup under the same name, with its "immediate work" being "the removal of the legal disabilities of women." . . .

The NWP's new priorities, and Paul's ruthlessness in paring away "diversions," were clarified in a little-known controversy over black women voters at the convention. Despite early links between the woman's rights and the antislavery movements, the suffrage movement after 1890 failed to take a stand against the oppression of blacks, knuckling under to the racism of the surrounding society, sacrificing principle and the interests or pride of black people, if that seemed advantageous to white women's obtaining the vote. Whether the NWP was more honorable on that score than was the NAWSA is debatable. The NWP's insistence on the constitutional route to woman suffrage seemed especially aimed against the South, where racist fears of the black vote combined with archaic notions of white womanhood and the concern of textile manufacturers for a manipulatable female labor force to stymie woman suffrage attempts at the state level. During its "militant" years the NWP sought and gained the support of some black women, including two outstanding leaders, Ida B. Wells-Barnett and Mary Church Terrell. Nonetheless, the NWP may have deserved the bitter assessment early in 1919 of Walter White, director of the National Association for the Advancement of Colored People (NAACP), following a wrangle with Paul, that "if they could get the Suffrage Amendment through without enfranchising colored women, they would do it in a moment."

When the February 1921 convention was announced, Mary White Ovington, a white socialist, feminist, and founding member of the NAACP, wrote to all members of the NWP National Advisory Council whom she knew personally, urging them to arrange for a black woman to address the group. Describing how prospective black voters in the South were being terrorized, Ovington stressed that black women would never vote unless their rights were upheld by all other women. She urged that the convention appoint a committee to investigate and take action on this issue. Although several National Advisory Council members endorsed Ovington's proposal, the response from the NWP headquarters was negative. Headquarters secretary Emma Wold, writing for Paul, explained that the convention could give the podium only to groups with legislative programs for women or with feminist aims. The point was to ensure that the NWP, in choosing its goals, did not duplicate another group's work. Since Mary C. Talbert of the National Association of Colored Women's Clubs, the speaker whom Ovington recommended, represented a group with a "racial," not "feminist," intent, she could not be featured. Wold emphasized that it was the definition of the convention program rather than lack of concern about blacks that caused this refusal. She encouraged the appointment of black women as delegates who could speak from the floor. Headquarters did make efforts to facilitate the inclusion of blacks in state delegations, and when a black woman from Virginia, probably fearing segregation, inquired "how will the arrangements be for the colord delegates in this convenchion," Wold replied for Paul that black delegates would have exactly the same arrangements as white delegates and would be seated with their state delegations. Paul also conferred with Hallie Brown, Terrell, and other black women leaders about representation of the National Association of Colored Women's Clubs at the ceremony unveiling the sculptures and reached agreement on a "representation of their race" satisfactory to the black women, according to Paul.

Black women's formal presentation of their concerns at the convention was more significant, however, and here there was no satisfaction. Talbert, appreciating Ovington's efforts, confessed, "I do not believe that Alice Paul is at all sincere, I doubt her very much on the color line." Ovington herself, while trying to reverse the decision, judged that "Miss Paul unquestionably is more influenced by her southern white constituency than by those northerners who believe in working for the colored woman." When Florence Kelley, leader of the National Consumers' League and a member of the NWP National Executive Committee, intervened on behalf of Ovington's plea, Paul gave her a more complicated explanation. Next on the NWP's agenda, Paul said, and "by far the most important item of their immediate program" was to push for legislation "enforcing" woman suffrage by means of federal penal sanctions against any state registration or election official who discriminated against women. The proposed legislation was presumably aimed at southern states that disfranchised black women. Paul gave Kelley the impression that she feared Talbert's "inflaming" the southerners at the convention, once the enforcement bill became known. Kelley concluded that "Miss Paul, as a Quaker woman is of course entirely in sympathy with Mrs. Talbert and her work" but "as a tactician" denied the request for Talbert to speak from the podium. The NWP did in fact have an enforcement bill introduced to Congress, on December 30, 1920, by Wesley Jones, Republican senator from Washington.

A group of black women subsequently took up the second part of Ovington's request, for an investigation of voting rights violations. Early in February a large delegation claiming to represent five million black women in fourteen states called on Paul to point out violations of black voting rights in 1920 and to ask for opportunity to call the NWP's attention to that travesty of the Nineteenth Amendment. Paul gave them only the same opportunity other individuals had—to speak as delegates from the convention floor. At the convention Ella Rush Murray, a white delegate from New York and member of the National Advisory Council, managed to present a minority resolution directing the NWP to form a committee to pressure Congress to investigate violations of the Nineteenth Amendment. (Mysteriously, her resolution, first moved at the National Advisory Council's meeting on January 28, was left out of that meeting's minutes and did not appear in the convention issue of the party's newspaper, the *Suffragist*.) The resolution was voted down. In the *Nation* Kirchwey asserted that "Miss Paul was indifferent to" the appeal of the black women and "resented the presence of the delegation." Kirchwey reported that black delegates were denied use of the elevator at the convention; moreover, she voiced a rumor that the NWP had agreed not to raise the race issue as a price for the ratification of woman suffrage in the South.

Paul's view of the matter differed entirely. In a lengthy letter to the

Nation (never printed and perhaps not even sent) and in letters to her intimates, Paul denied all of Kirchwey's damaging allegations. The elevator story was a mistake: black women had been asked by the elevator boy to use the stairs but so had all the white women, until someone complained, whereupon everyone was allowed to use the elevator. Paul asserted, more significantly, that the NWP had never made a "deal" to ignore the racial question in the South but always as a *general* policy ignored *all* issues outside the woman suffrage amendment. She maintained that she had made sure, after receiving the black delegation, that they had the same opportunity everyone else did to present their views from the convention floor, although she anticipated southern white delegates' hostility. Indeed, the entire white delegation from North Carolina at first refused to register, in protest against the black women's presence, and only with difficulty were persuaded to attend at all; they stayed away from the ceremonial dinner, where they would have had to eat with black women, and one member refused to receive her "picket pin" because Terrell was awarded one at the same ceremony. In Paul's view no discrimination and no "machine" had operated. The convention had passed over black voting rights, as it had passed over disarmament and birth control, because its consensus genuinely formed around another goal, that of eliminating women's legal disabilities.

Complaints surfaced from a few. Kelley expressed chagrin that the party had "welshed on the Negro question." Agnes Chase joined the reorganized party with the caustic protest that its circulars ought to have said "for white women" rather than "women." Murray declined to serve on the party's new National Advisory Council, "in view of certain phases of the recent convention," and ended her subscription to the party newspaper. After the convention the issue of the enforcement bill slipped from sight and was dropped entirely at a meeting of the National Executive Committee in May 1921 attended only by Hill and three southerners.

It was a great credit to Paul and her immediate lieutenants that they asserted the ongoing need for an association dedicated to women's power, not to social service or to good government, but to "the removal of all remaining forms of subjection" of the female sex. The treatment of black women's concerns at the convention forewarned, however, that the party's interpretation of equal rights would narrow, rather than expand, its purview and its constituency. Paul presumed that equality of legal rights was, like woman suffrage, a "purely feminist" program on which women could unite regardless of their disagreements on other issues. Instead of encompassing the issue of black women's voting rights in the circle of women's legal equality, Paul regarded it as a diversion, and she regarded it as a diversion because black women were suffering an injustice imposed, not by sex, but by race—black men were similarly disfranchised. A diversion on which there might be controversy could not be taken up, for fear of compromising the goal on which presumably all women could agree. That Paul's outlook was at least as much due to her conception of the viability of single-issue politics as it was to racism is strongly suggested by her similar attitude at the convention toward birth control as a "diversion" from the principal route. The party's refusal to declare on any issue besides the woman suffrage amendment had been consistent with heterogeneity among its membership during the suffrage campaign, and Paul envisioned no difference in procedure for the future. But in the case of black women's voting rights, Paul's newly defined "simple, concrete object" excluded a group of women. The black women's question at the convention was the first clear indication that in claiming to make equal rights—intrinsically so much thornier to define and to pursue than suffrage was—stand for and speak to all women, the NWP would stand for and speak to fewer and fewer women. . . .

To translate "the removal of legal disabilities" into legislation was the prime task. Paul had been experimenting with forms for a constitutional amendment to end sex discrimination in law even before the convention gave its mandate. As a sequel to their strategy in the suffrage campaign, NWP leaders clearly preferred the "clean sweep" approach of amending the Constitution. (It should be noted, of course, that many reformers who did not support an equal rights amendment in the 1920s sought the route of constitutional amendment to accomplish other reforms, from the abolition of child labor to the outlawry of war.) Party leaders began surveying state legal codes for sex discriminations, conferring with lawyers, drumming up attendance for a delegation to President Warren G. Harding, and drafting numerous versions of equal rights legislation and amendments for the state as well as the federal level. . . .

The "clean sweep" approach seemed all the more appealing to NWP leaders as their lobbyists working on state legislatures made little headway between 1921 and 1923 in eliminating specific sex discriminations. By analogy with the suffrage struggle, frustration at the state level fueled the rationale for a constitutional amendment. At a grand conference staged in Seneca Falls, New York, in November 1923 to commemorate the seventy-fifth anniversary of Stanton's Declaration of Sentiments, the NWP introduced an equal rights amendment stating, "Men and women shall have equal rights throughout the United States and every place subject to its jurisdiction." The amendment was introduced into Congress on December 10, 1923.

Forging ahead, the NWP cut its links with most women connected to the labor movement, who remained convinced of the need for sex-specific protection. The few NWP members with strong labor attachments, such as Blatch, insisted that trade union organizing, not special legislation, should protect women workers' interests. The NWP presented its opposition to sex-based legislation as a positive program of industrial equality, but only a handful of working-class activists agreed. Representatives of the AFL and of several international unions as well as a lengthy list of women's groups voiced opposition at the first Senate subcommittee hearings on the equal rights amendment. Mary Anderson, director of the Women's Bureau of the Department of Labor, fiercely opposed the NWP and threw the bureau's weight against the amendment.

The arguments against the equal rights amendment offered by the various groups overlapped. They assumed that an amendment would invalidate sex-based labor laws or, at least, throw them (and welfare laws designed for mothers and widows) into the courts for protracted argument, during which time women would lose needed benefits. They argued that sex discriminations would be more efficiently and accurately removed from legal codes by attacking each case. Opponents of the amendment asserted that women workers, wary of employers' freedom to exploit them, valued sex-based labor legislation and that maximum-hour laws for women had benefited men, too, in factories where male workers could not continue operations once female employees had left for the day. If protective laws hampered job opportunities for some small minority of working women, then the proper tactic was to exempt some occupations, not to eliminate the laws altogether. They declared that only the elite who did not have to work at all or professional women whose conditions of work were entirely different could possibly denigrate the benefits of protective laws. They regularly accused the NWP of being the unwitting tool (at best) or the paid servant of rapacious business interests, although no proof was ever brought forward.

In the NWP's view the equal rights amendment was the logical sequel to woman suffrage, the fulfillment of Susan B. Anthony's vision. The many differences in state codes and practices in sex discriminations made a constitutional amendment the most direct route to equal rights. Protective laws that classed women with children as "the industrial and political wards of the state" only manifested women's long history of economic dependence and served to preserve the most lucrative and interesting jobs for men. (With reason the NWP accused the AFL of supporting sex-based protective legislation in order to keep women from competing for men's jobs.) By eliminating "anachronism" in the law, the amendment would encourage women to become self-respecting citizens, to slough off their history of subservience and their embedded psychology of the unpaid worker. Women workers' real interests lay in obtaining equal access to job opportunities and to trade union organization, the NWP maintained. The party became the champion of working women materially hurt by protective legislation, such as printers or railroad conductors or waitresses hampered by hours limitation, or cleaning women fired and replaced by men after the passage of minimum-wage laws. At the same time, the NWP expressed no opposition to protective labor legislation as such or to protection of motherhood, so long as neither legally treated women "as a class."

This is not the place to analyze the controversy over the equal rights amendment in its full complexity, except to say that the opponents' attempts to portray the amendment as "class" legislation were simplistic, just as the proponents' attempts to portray it as legislation affecting only sex equality understated the case. Neither side acknowledged the real ambiguities and complications of the workings of sex-based protective legislation at the time. While the antiamendment side was right, in that protective laws had improved conditions for the great majority of women in industry, the proamendment side was also right, in that the laws had limited women's opportunities in the labor market and had helped to sustain the notion that women were dependent and secondary wage earners. Supporters of protective legislation did not see that their expectations of women, rooted in biological and customary notions of women's place and purpose, helped to confirm women's second-class position in the economy. Nor did advocates of the equal rights amendment recognize the need protective legislation addressed or acknowledge that their program of equal rights would not in itself free women's economic opportunity from the stranglehold of the domestic stereotype.

When the Supreme Court in 1923 used reasoning consonant with the NWP's to invalidate the minimum-wage law covering women in the District of Columbia, the party's new newspaper, *Equal Rights,* applauded but deferred: "It is not within the province of the Woman's Party, as a purely feminist organization, to discuss the constitutional question involved or to discuss the merits of minimum wage legislation as a method of bettering labor conditions. On these points we express no opinion." Just as black voting rights had been judged outside the "purely feminist," so was the betterment of labor conditions. That single-mindedness made the NWP virtually anathema to labor and the Left. In the 1920s context of Republican domination, with business in the saddle and with labor interests losing out in both trade union organization and state protection, to express no policy but equal rights for women was to affirm the status quo in every other respect. Although NWP members did not hold consistently laissez-faire views, the single-mindedness of their espousal of equal rights made them appear to. While the NWP was able to hold on through the 1920s to a few of its longtime members who had vital interests in changing conditions for the working masses, it could not recruit new ones with its insistence on "purely feminist" claims. . . .

The NWP . . . , left out process entirely and focused single-mindedly on its *goal* of equal rights, conceived ever more abstractly. The equal rights amendment, supposed to be the first step in an agenda to end women's subjection, became itself the panacea. Stevens recognized this when in an acid critique of 1946 she wrote, "To my way of thinking the NWP in its direction since 1923 has lost more [and] more of that great feminist tradition handed on to our care from the 18th century. We are bogged down in legal formalism." The "dead hand" of Paul prevented anyone from "revitalizing the feminist climate": "the sad, bleak truth is that AP [Alice Paul] dislikes people . . . can't be bothered with members. . . . No sooner does a struggling state org[anization] show signs of life than, I am told, AP picks off their best workers for money and 'lobbying' . . . men on whom they have no claim. . . . One of our pioneers said lately, 'if AP had died 25 years ago, we'd now have the amendment.' "

The failure to ratify the equal rights amendment in the 1980s indicates how obstacle-ridden the path of the amendment has been and thus how wrong, in one respect, that commentator on Paul was; yet Stevens's lament had a firm basis. Certainly a mix of historical factors in the 1920s conditioned the NWP's fate: the impasse over sex-based protective legislation was one; the defensive antisocialist trend of American politics was another; the panache of self-seeking in the younger generation was a third—not to speak of the deep-rootedness of gender hierarchy in the culture at large. But the NWP just as certainly had its dynamic, forged in the suffrage struggle and applied and misapplied obsessively after that. Though a full and fair treatment of the NWP would require richer detailing of its members, leaders, and activities, that dynamic is clear. It is not to dismiss the NWP's efforts—its carrying the banner of equal rights at state, federal, and international levels, its sustenance of a community of interest among its members, its serving as a resource for women seeking feminist affiliation—to acknowledge that after 1928 its once-envisioned vanguard role was no more. Considering its very small numbers and the odds against it, one can be amazed at what the NWP did in fact accomplish toward equal rights legislation in the interwar period, all the while it became less and less able or likely to lead a movement of women.

Initiated in a vision of inclusiveness, a stand for all women, the NWP campaign for equal rights developed into a practice of exclusiveness and a defense of the status quo with regard to everything but the gender question. That devolution owed in great part to Paul's assumption that equal rights (like suffrage, in her view), a demand relevant to all women, was separable from all other issues. Paul posed women's political options in either-or, rather than both-and, terms: "work for women" (which meant equal rights) or something else. Within that framework NWP loyalists chose equal rights. Women who had any other priority were "followers of men, worms of the dust," in the vitriolic words of Caroline Spencer, "who cannot see that the tyranny of half the race over the other half is the first wrong to be righted, and its overthrow, the greatest revolution conceivable."

As a result of its construction of the gender imperative, the NWP made equal rights an abstract goal, because placing it in the context of social reality would have required stands on social and political issues that affected women but that were not strictly gender questions. (The suffrage battle might have provided a different lesson, regarding the separability of women's rights from politics in general, but perhaps only long retrospect allows us to see that feminist movements flourish best in the midst of other reforming politics and in alliance with other reforming aims.) With some justice Mary Anderson accused the NWP of putting the "woman question" first and of demanding that "the solution of all others should be determined solely by what is done with women's problems." A tremendous irony lies here. The NWP set out to erase legislation that treated women "as a class" but predicated its feminism on construing women as a class, that "other half" of the human race. Its dilemma was the dilemma of twentieth-century feminism, that it required gender consciousness for its basis while it aimed for the dissolution of prescribed gender roles.

Discontented Black Feminists

ROSALYN TERBORG-PENN

On the eve of the passage of the Nineteenth Amendment, black women leaders could be counted among other groups of women who had worked diligently for woman suffrage. At least ninety black women leaders endorsed woman suffrage, with two-thirds of these women giving support during the decade immediately before passage of the amendment. Afro-American women organized suffrage clubs, participated in rallies and demonstrations, spoke on behalf of the amendment, and wrote essays in support of the cause. These things they had done since the inception of the nineteenth-century woman's rights movement. However, the largest woman suffrage effort among black women's groups occurred during the second decade of the twentieth century. Organizations such as the National Federation of Afro-American Women, the National Association of Colored Women (NACW), the Northeastern Federation of Colored Women's Clubs, the Alpha Kappa Alpha Sorority, and the Delta Sigma Theta Sorority actively supported woman suffrage. These organizations were national or regional in scope and represented thousands of Afro-American women. Some of the women were from the working class, but most of them were of middle-class status. Across the nation, at least twenty black woman suffrage organizations or groups that strongly endorsed woman suffrage existed during the period.

Three examples provide an indication of the diversity in types of woman suffrage activities among black women's organizations. In 1915 the Poughkeepsie, New York, chapter of the Household of Ruth, a working-class, black women's group, endorsed woman suffrage by sending a resolution to the New York branch of the National Woman's Party (NWP) in support of the pending state referendum on woman suffrage. With the need for an intelligent female electorate in mind, black women of Texas organized voter leagues in 1917, the year Texas women won the right to vote. Among these was the Negro Women Voters' League of Galveston. Furthermore, in 1919, the Northeastern Federation of Colored Women's Clubs, representing thousands of women from Montreal to Baltimore, petitioned the National American Woman Suffrage Association (NAWSA) for membership.

The enthusiastic responses of black women to woman suffrage may seem astonishing when one realizes that woman suffrage was a predominantly middle-class movement among native born white women and that the black middle class was very small during the early twentieth century. Furthermore, the heyday of the woman suffrage movement embraced an era that historian Rayford Logan called "the nadir" in Afro-American history,

Rosalyn Terborg-Penn, "Discontented Black Feminists: Prelude and Postscript to the Passage of the Nineteenth Amendment," in *Decades of Discontent: The Women's Movement, 1920–1940,* Lois Scharf and Joan M. Jensen, Eds. (Contributions in Women's Studies, No. 28, Greenwood Press, Inc., Westport, CT 1983), 261–68. Copyright © 1983 by Lois Scharf & Joan M. Jensen. Abridgement and reprinting with permission.

characterized by racial segregation, defamation of the character of black women, and lynching of black Americans, both men and women. It is a wonder that Afro-American women dared to dream a white man's dream—the right to enfranchisement—especially at a time when white women attempted to exclude them from that dream.

The existence of a double standard for black and white women among white woman suffragists was apparent to black women on the eve of Nineteenth Amendment passage. Apprehensions from discontented black leaders about the inclusion of black women as voters, especially in the South, were evident throughout the second decade of the twentieth century. During the early years of the decade, black suffragists such as Adella Hunt Logan, a club leader and suffragist from Tuskegee, Alabama; Mary B. Talbert, president of the National Association of Colored Women; and Josephine St. Pierre Ruffin, a suffragist since the 1880s from Boston and the editor of the *Woman's Era,* a black women's newspaper, complained about the double standard in the woman suffrage movement and insisted that white suffragists set aside their prejudices to allow black women, burdened by both sexism and racism, to gain political equality. . . .

By 1919, the year before the Nineteenth Amendment was adopted by Congress, antiblack woman suffrage sentiments continued to plague the movement. Shortly before the amendment was adopted, several incidents occurred to further disillusion black feminists. Mary Church Terrell, a Washington D.C., educator and national leader among black club women, reported that white suffragists in Florida discriminated against black women in their attempts to recruit support for the campaign. In addition, the NAACP, whose policy officially endorsed woman suffrage, clashed with Alice Paul, president of the NWP because she allegedly said "that all this talk of Negro women voting in South Carolina was nonsense." Later, Walter White, the NAACP's assistant to the executive secretary, complained to Mary Church Terrell about Alice Paul and agreed with Terrell that white suffrage leaders would be willing to accept the suffrage amendment even if it did not enfranchise black women.

Within a week after receiving Walter White's letter, Mary Church Terrell received a letter from Ida Husted Harper, a leader in the suffrage movement and the editor of the last two volumes of the *History of Woman Suffrage*, asking Terrell to use her influence to persuade the Northeastern Federation of Colored Women's Clubs to withdraw their application seeking cooperative membership in the NAWSA. Echoing sentiments expressed earlier by NAWSA president Carrie Catt, Harper explained that accepting the membership of a black organization was inexpedient for NAWSA at a time when white suffragists sought the cooperation of white southern women. Harper noted that the major obstacle to the amendment in the South was fear among whites of the black woman's vote. She therefore asked federation president Elizabeth Carter to resubmit the membership application after the passage of the Nineteenth Amendment.

At its Jubilee Convention in Saint Louis in March 1919, the NAWSA officially catered to the fears of their southern white members. In response to a proposal by Kentucky suffragist Laura Clay that sections of the so-called Susan B. Anthony amendment that would permit the enfranchisement of black women be changed, the convention delegates agreed that the amendment should be worded so as to allow the South to determine its own position on the black female vote.

During the last months before the passage of the Susan B. Anthony amendment, black suffragists had been rebuffed by both the conservative wing of the suffrage movement, the NAWSA, and by the more radical wing, the NWP. Why then did Afro-American women continue to push for woman suffrage? Since the 1880s, most black women who supported woman suffrage did so because they believed that political equality among the races would raise the status of blacks, both male and female. Increasing the black electorate, they felt, would not only uplift the women of the race, but help the children and the men as well. The majority of the black suffragists were not radical feminists. They were reformers, or what William H. Chafe calls social feminists, who believed that the system could be amended to work for them. Like their white counterparts, these black suffragists assumed that the enfranchised held the key to ameliorating social ills. But unlike white social feminists, many black suffragists called for social and political measures that were specifically tied to race issues. Among these issues were antimiscegenation legislation, jim crow legislation, and "lynch law." Prominent black feminists combined the fight against sexism with the fight against racism by continuously calling the public's attention to these issues. Ida B. Wells-Barnett, Angelina Weld Grimke, and Mary Church Terrell spoke out against lynching. Josephine St. Pierre Ruffin and Lottie Wilson Jackson, as well as Terrell and Wells-Barnett took steps to challenge jim crow facilities in public accommodations, and antimiscegenation legislation was impugned by Terrell, Grimke, and Wells-Barnett. . . .

The inability of the NAACP to protect the rights of black women voters led the women to seek help from national woman suffrage leaders. However, these attempts failed also. The NWP leadership felt that since black women were discriminated against in the same ways as black men, their problems were not woman's rights issues, but race issues. Therefore, the woman's party felt no obligation to defend the rights of black women.

That they would be abandoned by white female suffragists in 1920 came as no surprise to most black women leaders. The preceding decade of woman suffrage politics had reminded them of the assertions of black woman suffrage supporters of the past. Frederick Douglass declared in 1868 that black women were victimized mainly because they were blacks, not because they were women. Frances Ellen Watkins Harper answered in 1869 that for white women the priorities in the struggle for human rights were sex, not race. By 1920 the situation had changed very little, and many black suffragists had been thoroughly disillusioned by the machinations of the white feminists they had encountered.

Afro-American women continued to be involved in local and national politics during the post–World War I years. However, few organized feminist activities were apparent among the disillusioned black feminists of the period. Afro-American women leaders and their organizations began to focus on issues that continued to plague both the men and the women of the race, rather than upon issues that concerned white feminists. The economic plight of black women kept most of them in poverty and among the lowest of the working classes. Middle-class black women were still relatively few in number. They were more concerned about uplifting the downtrodden of the race or in representing people of color throughout the world than in issues that were limited to middle-class feminists. Hence, during the 1920s there was little concern among black women over the Equal Rights Amendment debate between the more conservative League of Women Voters (LWV) and the more radical NWP. Although the economic roles of many white American women were expanding, the status of black women remained basically static between the wars. As a result, black feminists identified more with the plight of Third World people who found themselves in similar oppressed situations. Former black suffragists were more likely to participate in the Women's International League for Peace and Freedom (WILPF) or the International Council of Women of the Darker Races than in the LWV or the NWP. . . .

A look at the 1920s reveals that most of the black women's organizations that were prominent during the woman suffrage era remained so. Nonetheless, new groups were organized as well. Elizabeth Carter remained president of the Northeastern Federation of Colored Women's Clubs, which celebrated its twenty-fifth anniversary in 1921. The leadership of the NACW was in transition during the 1920s. Mary B. Talbert retired as president and was succeeded by a former suffragist, Hallie Q. Brown, in 1922. In the middle of the decade Mary McLeod Bethune assumed the presidency. In 1922 several NACW leaders organized the International Council of Women of the Darker Races. Margaret Murray Washington, the wife of the late Booker T. Washington and the first president of the National Federation of Afro-American Women, was elected president.

In addition to these established black women's organizations, there was the women's arm of Marcus Garvey's United Negro Improvement Association (UNIA). At its peak, in 1925, the UNIA had an estimated membership of 2 million and can be considered the first mass movement among working-class black people in the nation. Amy Jacques Garvey, Marcus Garvey's wife, was the articulate leader of the women's division and the editor of the women's department of the UNIA official newspaper, *Negro World*. A feminist in the international sense, Amy Jacques Garvey's feminist views embraced the class struggle as well as the problems of Third World women. A black nationalist, Garvey encouraged women of color throughout the world to organize for the benefit of themselves as well as their own people. Although she gave credit to the old-line black women's clubs, Garvey felt their approach to the problems of Third World women was limited. A Jamaican by birth, she called for revolutionary strategies that did not merely reflect the reform ideas of white middle-class women. Instead Garvey called upon the masses of black women in the United States to acknowledge that they were the ''burden bearers of their race'' and to take the lead in fighting for black independence from white oppression. Amy Jacques Garvey combined the UNIA belief in the power of the black urban working class with the feminist belief that women could think and do for themselves. The revolutionary implications of her ideas are reflected in the theme of the women's pages of *Negro World*—"Our Women and What They Think." Garvey called for black women's dedication to social justice and to national liberation, abroad as well as at home.

Garvey was a radical who happened to be a feminist as well. Her views were ahead of her time; thus, she would have fit in well with the mid-twentieth century radical feminists. However, the demise of the UNIA and the deportation of Marcus Garvey in 1927 shattered much of Amy Jacques Garvey's influence in the United States and she returned to Jamaica. In the meantime, the majority of black feminists of the 1920s either joined the white social feminists, such as Jane Addams and the WILPF, or bypassed the feminists altogether to deal with race issues within black organizations.

The leadership of the WILPF was old-line and can be characterized as former progressives, woman suffragists, and social feminists. Jane Addams presided over the organization before U.S. entry into World War I and brought black women such as Mary Church Terrell, Mary B. Talbert, Charlotte Atwood, Mary F. Waring, and Addie W. Hunton into the fold. Terrell had been a member of the executive committee since 1915. As a league representative, she was elected a delegate to the International Congress of Women held in Paris in 1919. Upon her arrival, Terrell was impressed with the conference delegates but noticed that there were none from non-western countries and that she was the only delegate of color in the group. As a result, she felt obliged to represent the women of all the nonwhite countries in the world, and this she attempted to do. At the conference meeting in Zurich, Switzerland, Terrell agreed to represent the American delegation and did so by speaking in German before the largely German-speaking audience. In addition, she submitted her own personal resolution to the conference, despite attempts by American committee members to change her wording. "We believe no human being should be deprived of an education, prevented from earning a living, debarred from any legitimate pursuit in which he wishes to engage or be subjected to humiliations of various kinds on account of race, color or creed." Terrell's position and thinking were in keeping with the growing awareness among black women leaders in the United States that Third World people needed to fight oppression together.

Although Mary Church Terrell remained an active social feminist, her public as well as her private views reflected the disillusionment of black feminists of the woman suffrage era. In 1921 she was asked by members of the WILPF executive committee to sign a petition requesting the removal of black troops from occupied German territory, where they were alleged to be violating German women. Terrell refused to sign the petition because she felt the motives behind it were racist. In a long letter to Jane Addams, the executive committee chairman, Terrell explained why she would not sign the petition. She noted that Carrie Catt had investigated the charges against the black troops and found them to be unfounded. The troops, from French colonies in Africa, were victims, Terrell contended, of American propaganda against black people. Making a dramatic choice between the feminist organization position and her own loyalty to her race, Terrell offered to resign from the executive committee. Addams wrote her back, agreeing with Terrell's position and asking her not to resign. In this case, when given the choice between the politics of feminism and race pride, Terrell felt that her energies were needed most to combat racism, and she chose to take a nationalist position in the controversy.

Several other attempts were made at interracial cooperation among women's groups during the early 1920s, but most of these efforts were white-dominated and short-lived. An exception was the Cooperative Women's League of Baltimore, founded in 1913 by Sarah C. Fernandis. This group maintained relations with white women's civic leagues in connection with local health and sanitation, home economics, art, and education projects. In 1925 the league initiated its twelfth annual program. This organization was quite conventional, a far cry from feminist—black or white. However, the activities were, like most black women's group activities of the times, geared to strengthen local black communities.

Other black-white cooperative ventures on a grander scale included the Commission on Inter-Racial Cooperation of the Women's Council of the Methodist Episcopal Church South. In October 1920 the commission held a conference on race relations. Only four black women were invited and they were selected because of their husbands' prominence, rather than for their feminist views. The conference pledged a responsibility to uplift the status of black women in the South, calling for a reform of the conditions under which black domestics worked in white homes. The delegates passed resolutions supporting improved sanitation and housing for blacks, fair treatment of blacks in public accommodations, the prevention of lynching, and justice in the courts. Significantly, no mention of protecting black women's suffrage was made. Several months later, the National Federation of Colored Women's Clubs met at Tuskegee, Alabama, and issued a statement that seemed to remind the Methodist Episcopal women of their pledge and called for increased cooperation and understanding from southern white women. Interestingly, the black women included suffrage in their resolution.

Nothing came of this attempt at interracial cooperation, for neither the social nor the economic status of black women improved in the South during the 1920s. The trend toward interracial cooperation continued nevertheless, and in 1922 the YWCA appointed a joint committee of black and white women to study race problems. Once again, only four black women were invited to participate. Principles were declared, but little came of the gathering.

In the meantime, most black women's organizations had turned from attempts to establish coalitions with white women's groups to concentrate upon pressing race problems. Lynching was one of the major American problems, and black women organized to fight it. On the national front, black women's groups used political strategies and concentrated their efforts toward passage of the Dyer Anti-Lynching Bill. In 1922 the Northeastern

Federation of Colored Women's Clubs appointed a delegation to call on Senator Lodge of Massachusetts to urge passage of the Dyer bill. In addition, the Alpha Kappa Alpha Sorority held its national convention in Indianapolis and sent a telegram to President Warren Harding urging the support of his administration in the passage of the bill. Also that year, the NACW met in Richmond and appointed an antilynching delegation to make contact with key states needed for the passage of the Dyer bill in Congress. In addition, the delegation was authorized to meet with President Harding. Among the black women in the delegation were veteran antilynching crusader Ida B. Wells-Barnett, NACW president Hallie Q. Brown, and Rhode Island suffragist Mary B. Jackson.

Perhaps the most renowned antilynching crusader of the 1920s was Spingarn Medal winner Mary B. Talbert. In 1922 she organized an executive committee of 15 black women, who supervised over 700 state workers across the nation in what Talbert called the Anti-Lynching Crusade. Her aim was to "unite a million women to stop lynching," by arousing the consciences of both black and white women. One of Talbert's strategies was to provide statistics that showed that victims of lynching were not what propagandists called sex-hungry black men who preyed upon innocent white women. The crusaders revealed that eighty-three women had been lynched in the United States since Ida B. Wells-Barnett had compiled the first comprehensive annual report in 1892. The Anti-Lynching Crusade was truly an example of woman power, for the crusaders believed that they could not wait for the men of America to stop the problem. It was perhaps the most influential link in the drive for interracial cooperation among women's groups. As a result of its efforts, the 1922 National Council of Women, representing 13 million American women, resolved to "endorse the Anti-Lynching Crusade recently launched by colored women of this country."

Although the Dyer bill was defeated, it was revised by the NAACP and introduced again in the House of Representatives by Congressman Leonidas C. Dyer of Missouri and in the Senate by William B. McKinley of Illinois in 1926. That year the bill failed again, as did similar bills in 1935, 1940, and 1942. However, it was the effort of blacks and white women organized against lynching that pressed for legislation throughout the period. Without a doubt, it was the leadership of black women, many of whom had been active in the late nineteenth-century women's club movement and in the woman suffrage movement, who motivated white women in 1930 to organize the Association of Southern Women for the Prevention of Lynching. Although a federal antilynching bill never passed the Congress, by the end of the 1940s public opinion had been sufficiently convinced by the efforts of various women's groups that lynching was barbarous and criminal. Recorded incidents of lynching ceased by 1950.

Even though interracial cooperation in the antilynching campaign was a positive factor among black and white women, discrimination against black women by white women continued to plague feminists. In 1925, for example, the Quinquennial of the International Council of Women met at the Washington Auditorium in the District of Columbia. The council sought the cooperation of NACW president Mary McLeod Bethune and arrangements were made to have a mass choir of black women perform. The night of the concert, black guests were placed in a segregated section of the auditorium. Mary Church Terrell reported that when the singers learned of what was happening, they refused to perform. Foreign women delegates were in the audience, as well as white women from throughout the nation. Many of them were angry because the concert had to be cancelled. Terrell felt that this was one of the most unfortunate incidents of discrimination against black women in the club movement. However, she agreed with the decision of her black sisters not to sing.

National recognition of black women did not really come until 1936, when Mary McLeod Bethune was appointed director of the Division of Negro Affairs, National Youth Administration, under the Franklin D. Roosevelt administration. The founder of Bethune-Cookman Institute in Daytona, Florida, Bethune had been a leader in the black women's club movement since the early 1920s. NACW president from 1924 to 1928, she founded the National Council of Negro Women (NCNW) in 1935. What feminist consciousness Bethune acquired was thrust upon her in the mid-1930s because for the first time, a black woman had the ear of the president of the United States and the cooperation of the first lady, who was concerned not only about women's issues, but about black issues. In 1936 Bethune took advantage of her new status and presented the concerns of the NCNW to Eleanor Roosevelt. As a result, sixty-five black women leaders attended a meeting with Eleanor Roosevelt to argue the case for their greater representation and appointments to federal bureaus. They called for appointments of professional black women to the Children's Bureau, the Women's Bureau, and each department of the Bureau of Education that dealt with the welfare of women and children. The NCNW also wanted the appointment of black women to administrative positions in the Federal Housing Administration and Social Security Board. In addition, they called for enlarging the black staff of the Bureau of Public Health and for President Roosevelt to suggest to the American Red Cross that they hire a black administrator.

The NCNW requests reflect two trends among middle-class women in the mid-1930s. First, they were calling for positions that black women had never held, nor would achieve until a generation later; consequently, their ideas were revolutionary ones in terms of federal policies. Second, they were calling for policies to benefit not only their sex, but their race; hence, the NCNW reflected the position established by black feminists a generation before. . . .

Although President Roosevelt made good his promise to Mary McLeod Bethune, so that by 1945 four black women had received outstanding federal appointments, the political viability of black women in the early 1940s was bleak. The list of black elected officials from 1940 to 1946 included no women. Agents of white supremacy continued to subvert what vestiges of political influence blacks held. For example, in 1942 Congressman Martin Dies, chairman of the congressional committee investigating un-American activities, attempted to link several national black leaders to the Communist party. Among the group was Mary McLeod Bethune, who remained the only black woman prominent in national politics.

Hence, over twenty years after the passage of the Nineteenth Amendment racial discrimination festered in most areas of American life, even among feminists and women in political life. Prejudice did not distinguish between middle-class and working-class black women, nor between feminists and nonfeminists who were black. Although black women continued to use what political rights they maintained, the small number of those politically viable made little impact upon public policies.

❖ FURTHER READING

Susan D. Becker, *The Origins of the Equal Rights Amendment* (1981)

William Chafe, *The American Woman: Her Changing Social, Economic, and Political Roles, 1920–1970* (1972)

Nancy F. Cott, *The Grounding of Modern Feminism* (1987)

Richard J. Evans, *The Feminists: Women's Emancipation Movements in Europe, America and Australasia 1840–1920* (1977)

Paula Fass, *The Damned and the Beautiful: American Youth in the 1920s* (1977)

Estelle Freedman, "The New Woman: Changing Views of Women in the 1920s," *Journal of American History,* LXI (1974), 372–93

Peter Geidel, "The National Woman's Party and the Origins of the Equal Rights Amendment, 1920–1923," *The Historian,* XLII (1980), 557–82

Paula Giddings, *When and Where I Enter: The Impact of Black Women on Race and Sex in America* (1984)

Patrice M. Hummer, *The Decade of the Elusive Promise: Professional Women in the United States 1920–1930* (1981)

Joan Hoff-Wilson and Marjorie Lightman, eds., *Without Precedent: The Life and Career of Eleanor Roosevelt* (1984)

J. Stanley Lemons, *The Woman Citizen: Social Feminism in the 1920s* (1973)

Christine Lunardini, *From Equal Suffrage to Equal Rights: Alice Paul and the National Woman's Party, 1913–1928* (1986)

Rosalind Rosenberg, *Beyond Separate Spheres: Intellectual Roots of Modern Feminism* (1982)

Lois Scharf and Joan Jensen, eds. *Decades of Discontent: The Women's Movement 1910–1940* (1983)

Frank Stricker, "Cookbooks and Lawbooks: The Hidden History of Career Women in Twentieth-Century America," *Journal of Social History,* X (1976–77), 1–19

Susan Ware, *Beyond Suffrage: Women in the New Deal* (1981)

———, *Partner and I: Molly Dewson, Feminism, and New Deal Politics* (1987)

CHAPTER
13

World War II and Its Aftermath

After the United States entered World War II in late 1941, the nation devoted most of its resources to wartime production. Because so many men were called into the armed forces, as early as mid-1942 the country needed to tap its large pool of potential female employees. Historians once thought that "Rosie the Riveter"—the classic image of the female war worker—was an unemployed housewife before the war. But now it is clear that many of the "Rosies" who sought high-paying positions in defense industries had previously worked in typical, poorly paid "women's jobs." The women who flocked to the plants and shipyards to make airplanes, weapons, tanks, and other necessary equipment for the military, or who moved into other nontraditional areas of employment, faced persistent discrimination on the basis of sex (and race) and received lower wages than their male counterparts. Even so, most did better financially than ever before.

Still, what was their attitude toward their work? Did they seek such jobs primarily because of patriotism, or because they wanted the money? Did their wartime experiences have a long-term impact on their lives, or did they regard their war work as a temporary aberration? After the war had been won, did they willingly turn their jobs (now reconverted to civilian production) over to the returning veterans who were their husbands, brothers, and fathers? Did they freely choose postwar lives as housewives and revert to sex-typed employment without protest, or were they forced from their more lucrative positions by the bias of male employers and fellow workers? Such questions have attracted the attention of a number of historians.

✥ DOCUMENTS

In August 1942, the *Ladies Home Journal* article "This Changing World for Women," reprinted as the first document, described the daily routines of four young female workers in a Baltimore airplane factory. Two months later, in the same magazine, a female psychiatrist explored the problems faced by employed mothers. Dr. Leslie Hohman's emphatic "yes" to the question, "Can Women in War Industry Be Good Mothers?" (the second selection) broke sharply with prewar wisdom on the subject. The third document is *Life* magazine's July 1943 account of

350

the "girl pilots" training in Texas to ferry airplanes for the Army Air Corps. And in the spring of 1944, Mrs. Norma Yerger Queen, the wife of a Utah doctor, responded to the Office of War Information's questions about the difficulties encountered by working women in her region; her reply is reprinted as the fourth document. These documents show how women adjusted to the demands of the time, often taking what were thought to be men's jobs. But for married working women, child care and household responsibilities became pressing issues that competed with their wartime jobs for their time and energy.

The *Ladies Home Journal* on "This Changing World for Women," 1942

Marjory Kurtz, *just 20, was a $15-a-week secretary in Absecon, N.J. Now she works in the Martin plant stock rooms.*

Virginia Drummond, *30, ran a beauty shop in Punxsutawney, Pa. Today she wields an electric drill on the bomber assembly line.*

Tommy Joseph, *24, of Clanton, Ala., wife of a young Army lieutenant in the Pacific, now drills bulkhead webs for Army planes.*

Margaret Kennedy, *22, a Lancaster, Pa., schoolteacher till January, now works the midnight shift at the Glenn Martin plant.*

When brisk Ginny Drummond and her cover-girl roommate of the silky black hair and gentian-blue eyes, Tommy Joseph, sink dog tired into bed these evenings, often as not a lively jive party is just starting in the adjoining room. Getting eight hours' sleep a night to bolster aching arms and feet for another eight hours' stand on the Glenn Martin aircraft-assembly line is practically impossible when four girls, sharing the same cramped one-bedroom apartment on Baltimore's sweltering Mt. Royal Avenue, keep working hours that stretch right around the clock.

Ginny and Tommy work six days in seven from 8:45 A.M. to 4:15 P.M. Their two other roommates, twenty-year-old Marge, daughter of a small-town mayor, and ex-schoolteacher Margaret Kennedy, are on the midnight shift, from 12:30 to 8:15 A.M. While waiting until it's time to leave for the plant, they try to subdue their chatter for the benefit of the two day-shift girls sharing the same lumpy bed in the next room. But long before the doorbell starts its nerve-shattering jangle over the bedroom door, and friends crash upstairs to drive Marge and Kennedy to work, the two sleepers are thoroughly awake.

"Daylight" nights pose even a greater problem for Marge and Kennedy. By the time these two are back, at 9:30 the following morning, the double bed is invitingly made up again, albeit with the same sheets. But by then the sun is warm and bright, and dawdling on the white front stoop is an irresistible temptation. All too often it's late afternoon before Marge and Kennedy drop into bed. By seven the apartment is filled with the rich odors of Ginny's cooking, and by the time everyone has eaten and the dishes are washed, a horde of swains has arrived to keep them chattering and jiving way past the day shift's ten-o'clock bedtime.

Since March, Marge and Kennedy have found getting sufficient rest for working days a problem—days off they often get none at all. In a tolerant, baffled kind of way, Ginny and Tommy fret over their two younger roommates. "They haven't reached the point we have," they explain, "where we realize we're not missing an awful lot if we don't go out every time a boy asks us for a date. Anyway, we couldn't. We'd drop in our tracks." Ginny even went so far as to buy vitamin pills for the youngsters, but ended up by apologetically swallowing them herself while the others remained as full of brash high jinks as ever.

All the girls' boy friends are Martin workers, but on the job, except for a few gleeful catcalls and whistles from the men as a pretty girl swings through the gate, both sexes tend strictly to business. It's a tough proposition working on aircraft assembly, where one slip can mean thousands of dollars of damage and perhaps a flier's life.

"You'll do a man's job and you'll get a man's pay check," Glenn L. Martin tells his 4000 women employees, "but you'll be treated as the men are treated."

This means a full six-day week, taking the night shift when so assigned and, in the case of Tommy and Ginny, spending the forthcoming Thanksgiving, Christmas and New Year's holidays amid the terrific hubbub of hammers, cranes and electric drills.

Eighty per cent of the women at Martin are on the "small parts" assembly line, with a handful skilled enough to do the highly paid final installation jobs. From 3 to 5 per cent are engineers and inspectors. In aircraft manufacture for the United States as a whole, fewer than 2 per cent of the workers are women, compared with 40 to 80 per cent in some aircraft plants in Great Britain. But as more and more men are being taken into the armed forces, opportunities for women are booming. At least 2,000,000 women who have never drawn any kind of pay check in their lives—schoolgirls and housewives—will be in factories within the next year or two. They must be, if the war of production is to go forward.

Most Martin workers are between eighteen and twenty-four, although a few are over forty. Tommy, Ginny, Marge and Kennedy started off at the usual beginner's pay of 60 cents an hour with a guaranty of 75 cents an hour within three months. Already the older girls are doing skilled work such as drilling on bulkhead webs—part of the frame of a plane—and, with two raises, now net $32.67 a week. Marge and Kennedy are in the stock rooms. Although they both proudly wear bright nail polish, their hands are red and sore from handing out countless nuts, screws and bolts. (A Martin bomber has 50,000 small parts, and each is nearly as important as a wing or propeller when a bomber goes into action.) They are now earning around $28 a week: "When we think what we used to make, that sure isn't hay."

An assembly-line worker has to buy her own tools, including electric hand drills, an investment that runs to about $30 cash if she's properly equipped. Tommy and Ginny say there are tools in their work kit they still don't know how to use—but they will before they're through at Martin: "There's no chance to get fed up with any particular job. The minute you've mastered one, they switch you to something harder."

Nobody at Martin has any doubt about the outcome of this war. When they watch those sleek-winged bombers line up, row on row, they feel they're helping to win it right now.

Only Tommy has a few bad moments when she gets a long-delayed batch of mail from her soldier husband in the South Pacific, begging for planes and more planes. Tommy married stunningly handsome Lt. Franklin Joseph, University of Alabama track star, class of '39, just two years ago. When he got his orders to sail, shortly after the Hawaii debacle, Tommy brooded until she nearly went mad. Now she's where she wants to be, with the chance to work desperately hard at the one thing she's sure will help bring beloved Joe back to her side.

Blond and gay Virginia Drummond, looking five years younger than her alleged thirty, was much too ambitious and concerned about the war to remain in an upstate Pennsylvania beauty shop. Now her quick, slim fingers handle screw drivers and pliers instead of hairpins.

Marge Kurtz was used to airplanes before she got past her multiplication tables, the result of her ex-mayor father's interest in an Absecon, New Jersey, airport. She still wants to learn to fly. Meanwhile, it's no more likely that she'll go back into secretarial work than that her special pal Kennedy will go back to teach spelling in a Lancaster, Pennsylvania, grammar school.

And when the war is over? Some of the girls, and certainly the men they work beside, wonder just what all these women are going to do when the boys come home. Some, of course, will quit to get married. But not all of them will have husbands, because some of these boys aren't coming back. Tommy has faced that stark possibility with grim and self-searching courage. She, like many other of the women workers, may go on to a big supervisory job in aircraft production. As for the younger girls, "When the war's over we'll probably go home again and wash dishes."

"We'd better," Ginny advises with a wry smile. "It's the only way we'll ever get our hands clean again."

Dr. Leslie Hohman Asks, "Can Women in War Industry Be Good Mothers?", 1942

The task of working women who are mothers, too, involves unquestionable difficulties which we must face squarely. Yet it gives women and their husbands a chance to prove dramatically and quickly where their deepest interests are.

If I had had any doubts on the question, my trip to the Hartford home of Fred and Mary Berckman would have converted me. Their whole household teems with evidence that their children are to them the most important consideration in the world. Their unflagging interest is the solid foundation for the first of the specific rules to be drawn from their highly successful experience.

The first rule is that mothers who are working must deliberately and determinedly plan to spend ample time with their children. To Mary this is not in the least burdensome. She delights in helping with the lessons of all her merry brood—second-grader son Junie, and the daughters Eileen, Fredrica and the eldest, Catherine, in the fifth grade. Mary sings with them, laughs with them, tells them stories in her fine Irish brogue of County Mayo, where she was born and lived until she came to America nineteen years ago.

"We make things interesting in this house," Mary said—an excellent boost for girls and boys along the road to happiness and security.

With all her fondness for her children, Mary could not accomplish so much time with them if both she and Fred had not organized their days carefully with that very purpose in mind. Her early shift at the Colt arms plant brings her home in the afternoons about the time the children arrive from school. She mixes them a malted milk, does preliminary work on dinner, then lies down for an hour until the children call out that their father is home from work. Fred is there at noon, too, from the Royal Typewriter plant just across the street, to help the youngsters prepare the lunch that has been arranged by Mary before she left for work.

Not much is to be gained by a detailed study of the exact schedule Fred and Mary use. Each working mother will have to arrange a schedule according to her individual working hours and her individual problems. We can be sure in advance that those who haven't the will to succeed will seek excuses for not doing so well as Fred and Mary—such as, "Neither my husband nor I can come home at noon." We can be equally sure that those who sincerely try will find some way to make certain that their children are well cared for while they are at work.

One mother I know who has an important executive position and commutes every working day to her desk rises much earlier every morning than she otherwise would have to, so that she can have breakfast and a long chat with her daughter. In the evenings, also, she always manages to spend some time with the child. They talk gaily of topics which interest the little girl. Their companionship is far closer than that of most daughters with mothers who haven't any outside work to do.

A writing assistant on a daily radio program who has few unfilled hours at home during the week still arranges to find brief and happy intervals for her young son every day. The main feature of her admirable plan comes every Sunday. The entire day is her son's. Any reasonable suggestion he makes on how they shall spend his day, she follows merrily. They have grand fun. The scheme often means that she and her husband decline week-end invitations, but they hold to their plan and enjoy themselves more than they would on the missed parties. The result is that the son is held to his parents by the strongest possible bonds of wholesome affection.

The general attitude of mothers—and fathers too—is a more powerful influence than the actual number of hours they spend with their children.

Couples who want to act childless and who find association with their children irksome and dull, do not fool their children by staying home and snapping at them. Fewer hours and more companionship would be much better.

A child's sense of security is fostered psychologically by stability in his environment. Despite all protestations of love at odd moments, young children in a harum-scarum household are likely to develop unstable emotional habits and a feeling of insecurity.

I am convinced that jobs for mothers outside the home generally help to create the stability of environment that is so essential. The gain usually more than offsets the loss of the hours in which the mother has to be away. Besides the scheduling of household routine imposed by regular employment, there is the added advantage for children that the inefficient mothers whose home management is hit-or-miss and disturbingly unreliable will learn to be more efficient by working where efficiency is required.

The skill and willingness in housework which Fred acquired when he took it over completely while his heart would not permit more strenuous exertion, makes him an ideal partner for a working wife. This suggests still another flat rule:

If children are to be reared successfully in families with employed mothers who haven't enough money for nursemaids and servants, it is absolutely necessary for husbands to help their wives with home duties and with the children's training.

Many unemployed wives would say offhand that their husbands could never learn. They probably would be pleasantly surprised. An outside job for a wife usually seems to cause a striking improvement in the husband's domesticity. Every husband of a working wife to whom I have mentioned the problem assured me that he felt obligated to help. "I never did before my wife got a job," several said. "After all, why should I when I had done my part and she had nothing else to do?" Not taking the husbands' statements of their own virtues as final, I made extensive inquiries among employed wives I knew. With hardly any exceptions, they cited their husbands for extraordinary household accomplishments.

Even when father knuckles down to do his share, there will be plenty of chores left for children in homes where both parents have outside jobs and abundant assistance cannot be hired. That is a great good fortune for the children. If we had enough working mothers, there would be a reinstatement of work training and early feeling for useful accomplishment. Too many young boys and girls are missing this valuable training.

Watching the Berckman children, I thought how much more fortunate they were than the ten-year-old son of an idle, prosperous mother who recently sought my advice because she saw, at last, that something was going wrong with him. Something had been going wrong since infancy. His mother and nursemaid and later his whole family waited on him hand and foot. An important part of my prescription was that useful chores be found for him.

The family is having a hard time following the prescription after its long habit of spoiling the boy.

The troubles of mothers who have jobs will be greatly lessened if they and their husbands enforce good training while they are at home. Mary and Fred established a cornerstone by affectionate discipline from infancy, not shying from occasional punishment when it was necessary to stop the development of traits that would handicap their children.

Merely the presence of a mother in the house will not make children behave—as harried neighbors can testify. Mothers cannot incessantly watch children old enough to go out and play, and it would be harmful to the children's self-reliance if they could. The best guaranty is the trained-in reliability and independence that enable Mary to say confidently: "My children never have done anything I told them not to do. I can trust them completely."

War or no war, outside work should never be undertaken by mothers until adequate care and training of their young children are assured. The arrangements frequently are hard to make, but rarely impossible. Where there is money enough, a qualified woman can be paid to come in and take charge. In most neighborhoods where money is not too plentiful, some woman who has proved her skill with her own children will be glad to augment the family income a little by taking care of one or two more for eight or nine hours a day.

No story of the problems and difficulties that working mothers meet could give a complete picture without prominent mention of the intangible gain that is nearly always overlooked. With few exceptions, women are made more interesting to their girls and boys by an outside job. Mary Berckman is a shining example. She is in brisk step with the world of today. She has sorted out her values under the test of stern realities. She has no time to be bored, no time for gossip. She always has time for companionship. It is not surprising that she, with Fred's excellent help, fills her children's lives with happiness.

Life Magazine Looks at the Training of "Girl Pilots," 1943

The time-honored belief that Army flying is for men only has gone into the ash can. At Avenger Field, near Sweetwater, Texas, girls are flying military planes in a way that Army officers a year or so ago would never have thought possible. These girls, who so joyously scramble into the silver airplanes of the Women's Flying Training Detachment each day, fly with skill, precision and zest, their hearts set on piloting with an unfeminine purpose that might well be a threat to Hitler. Each month scores of them complete their training in Texas and go to the Ferry Command to relieve fighting men for combat duty.

"Girl Pilots: Air Force Trains Them at Avenger Field, Texas," *Life*, XV, No. 3 (July 19, 1943), 73, 75, 80. Copyright © 1943, Time, Inc., reprinted with permission.

Behind the Army decision to train girl pilots was the personality of a smart and pretty woman, Miss Jacqueline Cochran, a famous pilot herself. Miss Cochran's proof of practicability of using America's 3,000 licensed women pilots came after her ferry flight to England in 1941 and close study of what women fliers were doing there. Shortly after, she demonstrated [the] ability of U.S. girl pilots by taking 25 with ample flying experience to England for the R.A.F. ferry setup. About the time that Nancy Love and a score of others with lots of flight hours formed the Women's Auxiliary Ferrying Squadron, Miss Cochran offered the U.S. Air Force a training plan for developing U.S. girl pilots with limited flying time to meet Army needs. That the plan is working is attested by the W.F.T.D. program now flourishing under Major General Barton K. Yount, commanding general of the Flying Training Command, and by the new job General "Hap" Arnold gave Miss Cochran last week—director of all women in the Army Air Forces and special assistant to Major General Barney Giles of the air force staff in Washington.

Under present requirements, any girl pilot with 35 hours flying time in light planes, who is between ages 21 and 34 and has a high-school education, is eligible for the Women's Flying Training Detachment after passing the regular Army Air Force physical examination and a personal interview test. After assignment to Avenger Field, new trainee is under Army supervision but remains a civilian. Upon graduation she is competent to fly any size Army trainer and has the ground work for flying fast combat planes. One curious fact has come out of mass training of girl pilots: the instructors say that girls are faster on instruments than boys, more smooth and gentle in flying characteristics. But on the male side of the ledger goes credit for less mechanical flying and better memory for details. . . .

Girls are very serious about the chance to fly for the Army at Avenger Field, even when it means giving up nail polish, beauty parlors, and dates for a regimented 22½ weeks. On the go from 6:15 in the morning till 10 at night, they follow a stepped-up version of the nine-month course developed for male aviation cadets, learning every thing that regular Army pilots master except gunnery and formation flying. Every morning after straightening barracks and marching to breakfast, half of them have calisthenics or drill and attend three classes of ground school, while the other half reports to the flight line to take off in primary Fairchilds, basic Vultures or advanced planes of single and twin-engine types. Every afternoon the schedule is reversed. Every evening girls study in the barracks or are on night-flying assignment. For the whole course under Army command the trainee's life revolves around living and talking one thing—flying.

Though the program is physically strenuous, Avenger Field girls thrive on it, eating more heartily than ever before and sleeping like babes, even in short snatches between flights. On rainy days when they can't fly, they are skittish with excess energy that is turned to editing a newspaper called *The Avenger,* organizing plays or concerts, and writing gay parodies on modern songs. After dinner each evening trainees linger in the recreation hall, playing ping-pong, singing or dancing. On weekends, they sunbathe or swim and see movies in Sweetwater—that is, if flight schedules are up to date. If not, they stay home and fly. Fly first, then relax is the unwritten rule for trainees, most of whom have immediate relatives on active duty with the Army and Navy. That flying agrees with them anyone can see as Uncle Sam's sun-tanned girl pilots march along at Avenger Field, lustily singing the Air Corps'

Off we go into the wild blue yonder,
Climbing high into the sun!

Mrs. Norma Yerger Queen Reports on the Problems of Employed Mothers in Utah, 1944

My dear Mr. Hart [of the Office of War Information],

In reply to your questions about women working I should like to say that from March 1, 1943 to July 31, 1943 I was the Day Care Worker for our county and as such tried to learn the needs of day care for children of working mothers and to make possible the employment of women. Since then as child welfare worker for our county, I have continued to keep in touch with the need for women working, their problems & the attitudes of the community about it. We opened a day nursery for preschool children June 15th & closed Oct. 31st because it was never sufficiently used. It was more than well publicized but we finally decided that really not enough women with preschool children were employed to warrant keeping it open.

The people of this community all respect women who work regardless of the type of work. Women from the best families & many officers' wives work at our hospital. It is not at all uncommon to meet at evening parties in town women who work in the kitchens or offices of our hospital (Army-Bushnell-large general). The city mayor's wife too works there.

The church disapproves of women working who have small children. The church (L.D.S.) has a strong influence in our county.

For the canning season in our county men's & women's clubs & the church all recruited vigorously for women for the canneries. It was "the thing to do" to work so many hrs. a week at the canneries.

I personally have encouraged officers' wives who have no children to get out and work. Those of us who have done so have been highly respected by the others and we have not lost social standing. In fact many of the social affairs are arranged at our convenience.

Some husbands do not approve of wives working & this has kept home some who do not have small children. Some of the women just do not wish to put forth the effort.

The financial incentive has been the strongest influence among most economic groups but especially among those families who were on relief for many years. Patriotic motivation is sometimes present but sometimes it really is a front for the financial one. A few women work to keep their minds from worrying about sons or husbands in the service.

In this county, the hospital is the chief employer of women. A few go to

Ogden (20 miles away) to work in an arsenal, the depot, or the air field. When these Ogden plants first opened quite a few women started to work there, but the long commuting plus the labor at the plants plus their housework proved too much.

Many women thoroughly enjoy working & getting away from the home. They seem to get much more satisfaction out of it than out of housework or bringing up children. Those who quit have done so because of lack of good care for their children, or of inability to do the housework & the job.

We definitely found that having facilities for the care of children did not increase the number of women who worked. In 1942, the women kept saying they couldn't go to the canneries because they had no place to leave their children. In 1943 everyone knew we had the day nursery & private homes available & still there was difficulty in recruiting. One of the big reasons we got the nursery was to help in our canning & poultry seasons.

Most all jobs are secured thro our U.S.E.S. so I assume people know about it. It runs frequent stories in our local paper.

I am convinced that if women could work 4 days a week instead of 5½ or 6 that more could take jobs. I found it impossible to work 5½ days & do my housework but when I arranged for 4 days I could manage both. These days one has to do everything—one cannot buy services as formerly. For instance—laundry. I'm lucky. I can send out much of our laundry to the hospital but even so there is a goodly amount that must be done at home—all the ironing of summer dresses is very tiring. I even have to press my husband's trousers—a thing I never did in all my married life. The weekly housecleaning—shoe shining—all things we formerly had done by others. Now we also do home canning. I never in the 14 yrs. of my married life canned one 1 jar. Last summer I put up dozens of quarts per instructions of Uncle Sam. I'm only one among many who is now doing a lot of manual labor foreign to our usual custom. I just could not take on all that & an outside job too. It is no fun to eat out—you wait so long for service & the restaurants cannot be immaculately kept—therefore it is more pleasant & quicker to cook & eat at home even after a long day's work. I've talked with the personnel manager at the hospital & he agrees that fewer days a week would be better. The canneries finally took women for as little as 3 hrs. a day.

This is a farming area & many farm wives could not under any arrangements take a war job. They have too much to do at their farm jobs & many now have to go into the fields, run tractors & do other jobs formerly done by men. I marvel at all these women are able to do & feel very inadequate next to them. Some do work in Ogden or Brigham during the winter months.

Here is the difference between a man working & a woman as seen in our home—while I prepare the evening meal, my husband reads the evening paper. We then do the dishes together after which he reads his medical journal or cogitates over some lecture he is to give or some problem at his lab. I have to make up grocery lists, mend, straighten up a drawer, clean out the ice box, press clothes, put away anything strewn about the house, wash bric a brac, or do several of hundreds of small ''woman's work is never done stuff.'' This consumes from 1 to 2 hrs. each evening after which I'm too weary to read any professional social work literature & think I'm lucky if I can keep up with the daily paper, Time Life or Reader's Digest. All this while my husband is relaxing & resting. When I worked full time, we tried doing the housecleaning together but it just didn't click. He is responsible for introducing penicillin into Bushnell & thus into the army & there were so many visiting brass hats & night conferences he couldn't give even one night a week to the house. Then came a mess of lectures at all kinds of medical meetings—he had to prepare those at home. I got so worn out it was either quit work or do it part time.

This has been a lot of personal experience but I'm sure we are no exception. I thought I was thro working in 1938. My husband urged me to help out for the war effort—he's all out for getting the war work done & he agreed to do his share of the housework. He is not lazy but he found we could not do it. I hope this personal experience will help to give you an idea of some of the problems.

❖ E S S A Y S

Alan Clive's study of women who worked in Michigan war industries convinced him that their lives were little altered by the experience: they resisted placing their children in day-care centers during the war and readily returned to their prewar lives once the emergency had ended. His research is presented in the first essay. In contrast, Nancy Gabin of Purdue University contends in the second selection that after the war female workers in Michigan defense plants vigorously resisted the efforts of male managers and fellow employees to force them out of their hard-won jobs. In the third essay, Karen Tucker Anderson, who teaches at the University of Arizona, points out that black women, who were even more discriminated against in employment than were white women and black men, were rarely allowed to hold the better-paying jobs in the first place. Having gained so little by the war, they had less to lose after it was over. These essays reveal American society's resistance to the notions that mothers could work outside the home and that women could hold jobs not traditionally defined as ''women's work.'' To what extent did employed women themselves accept such ideas?

Women's Conservative Choices During and After the War

ALAN CLIVE

The war's impact on working women reveals much about the scope and limits of change in American society. The most obvious indicator of the wartime change is the great increase in female employment that took place during the conflict. From 14,600,000 in 1941, the number of employed

Alan Clive, ''Women Workers in World War II: Michigan as a Test Case,'' *Labor History*, XX (1979), 44–72.

women in the United States had increased by 1944 to 19,370,000, far more than a third of the labor force. Women took jobs of all descriptions and skills in war industry. But what did the rise in the female labor force signify, beyond the fact that more women were at work? Did the war experience generate new attitudes toward women and their status? . . .

An examination of women and war in a single state affords the opportunity of testing national-level generalizations on a specific test community. Few states better qualify for such a study than Michigan. With 4 per cent of America's population, the state obtained better than 10 per cent of the nearly two hundred billion dollars in prime war supply and facilities contracts awarded by the US government and the Allies from 1940 to 1945. Only New York state outranked Michigan in this category. Hundreds of companies in dozens of other communities across the state fashioned every conceivable item required by an embattled nation. The automobile industry, which had made the name of Detroit world-famous in a more peaceful era, naturally led all Michigan manufacturers in the output of war goods. Most of the automakers' national total of twenty-nine billion dollars worth of vehicles, engines, guns, shells, and additional assorted material was produced in such prewar industry centers as Detroit, Pontiac, Flint, Lansing, Saginaw, and Muskegon. . . .

The proportional rise of female employment in the state ultimately was more striking than that for the nation; from 391,600 in March 1940 (24.8 per cent of the nonfarm workforce), the number of employed women in Michigan more than doubled by the war peak in November 1943 to 799,100 (34.8 per cent of the nonfarm workers). The proportion of males employed in manufacturing in the Detroit labor market area rose from 56 per cent to 71 per cent between 1940 and 1943, but the percentage of Detroit women in industry increased from 22 per cent to 33 per cent of all employed females in the area during the same period. In October 1940 there were only 5.7 women per one hundred production workers in the automobile industry; four years later, the rate reached 24.4. Examining Detroit war plants in March 1943 investigators for the United Automobile Workers (UAW) found that women composed 30 per cent of the workforce at Briggs, 32 per cent at Bendix's Wayne division, and 27 per cent of all persons employed at Willow Run.

A Women's Bureau survey disclosed that fully 51 per cent of the 387,000 women at work in Detroit during late 1944 and early 1945 had been employed before Pearl Harbor. They had shifted from jobs as waitresses, sales clerks, and maids into manufacturing and, to a lesser extent, into government work. The war years also witnessed the emergence of a new female worker: the same study reported that 28 per cent of the Detroit female labor force were housewives, and 18 per cent had been students prior to the declaration of war (the remaining 3 per cent were then seeking work). The demographic balance of the female labor force altered radically with the entrance of these new workers in vast numbers. Once dominated by single women under thirty years of age, the female labor force now contained substantially larger proportions of older and married women. The Women's Bureau found Detroit's female workers evenly divided at 45 per cent each between single and married women, the remaining 10 per cent being widowed or divorced. Only 44 per cent of the women were in the prime employment age group of twenty-nine years, in contrast to the 41 per cent of women workers over thirty. . . .

Women worked for many reasons. Some responded to propaganda that stressed the link between their jobs and the lives of their men in combat. "Since I have found the place where I can serve my country best, I should feel as if there were blood on my hands—his blood—if there were no oil on my hands today," a begrimed woman worker proclaimed from a 1943 recruiting advertisement.

Women took jobs out of patriotism or as a way of escape from the tedium of separation from husband or fiancé. They sought to enlarge their economic opportunities, but in many instances, women worked simply to maintain a standard of living equivalent to or even lower than that to which they had become accustomed before the war. Service wives often experienced long delays in receiving government allotment checks or found that the monthly stipend did not stretch far enough. The Women's Bureau estimated that more than 70 per cent of Detroit's married female workers contributed at least 50 per cent of their earnings toward the maintenance of a family group. The majority of the women worked to live.

Despite the declared manpower emergency, Michigan industry welcomed women with something less than enthusiasm. Lansing employers, confronted in late 1942 with a dwindling labor pool, refused to admit the need to recruit female workers, and Flint industry did not undertake mass hiring of women until August 1943. Manufacturers insisted that women simply were not the equal of men in factory work. Women did not understand machinery and were not trainable. Employers complained of the added costs of adjusting equipment used by women and of providing such facilities as separate washrooms and the like.

Such negative attitudes, however, could not bar the new female workers from the shop floor, and once the women arrived, recalcitrant employers discovered that the necessary accommodations did not bring on bankruptcy and often promoted productivity. Observers noted that women's absentee rate was generally lower than that of men and that female motivation was generally higher. Briggs and Packard were among the many firms that hired women to act as counselors to the female workers. The counselor's mandate varied from plant to plant, but her duties usually included advising women of company policy and assisting them with personal or work-related problems. The UAW trained female stewards to take on similar responsibilities in several factories. Experience convinced management that women, after all, could learn quickly and well. Much was made of the ability of tiny feminine hands to deal with intricate components and of women's presumed aptitude for dull, repetitive tasks. "There isn't a thing women can't do here when we divide a job into small parts," said a superintendent at Cadillac. Such an assessment, of course, applied to many a raw male recruit as well, and not infrequently the praise bestowed by management on women workers carried a condescending undertone implying that women would never match men in industrial competition.

Employers made no secret of their unwillingness to hire black women, whom management often regarded as so many refugees from *Porgy and Bess* or Harlem's Cotton Club. The first major breakthrough in black female hiring in Detroit did not come until the end of 1942, when, after a vigorous campaign by black protest organizations, token numbers of black women began work at Willow Run, Kelsey-Hayes, and Murray Body. The total black female labor force in the four-county Detroit metropolitan area rose from 20,170 in 1940 to 50,215 in 1944, a rise of 150 per cent and a rate of increase triple that of white female workers. Thousands of black domestics abandoned their positions as household servants for more lucrative factory work. Black women eventually constituted between 35 and 75 per cent of the workforce in certain small Detroit plants. Black females, however, remained concentrated in such low-wage positions as janitors, sweepers, and material handlers. And employer discrimination continued: in early 1944 a Detroit firm hired black females in order to demonstrate their incompetence as industrial employees, only to discover that the new workers were equal to their tasks.

Women workers of all races faced a variety of discriminatory practices. Industry upgraded and promoted women much more slowly than men. Separate seniority lists often confined a woman's upward occupational mobility within a single all-female department. It was the wage issue, however, that caused the most controversy. Manufacturers customarily placed women in the lowest-paying jobs and paid them less for the performance of work traditionally done by men. Michigan state law guaranteed women equal pay for "similar" work, but the statute was so vague that it was virtually unenforceable. "In the plant I come from, we have thousands of women who in the past have been working on jobs that are practically identical with men's work, and yet because there was the word 'similar' in there, we have never been able to break this thing down," complained Irene Young, a worker from the General Motors (GM) Ternstedt plant in Detroit, in 1942. In late September of that year, the War Labor Board (WLB) ruled against GM in an equal-pay case brought by the UAW and the United Electrical Workers, and WLB General Order 16, issued in November, permitted companies to equalize male and female pay on a voluntary basis without reference to Washington.

The voluntary clauses of the WLB's order, together with qualifications later placed on the original GM decision, vitiated the Board's original initiative. Organized labor failed to mount a sustained campaign on the equal-pay issue. Employers proved adept in maintaining the sexual pay differential by such means as giving different titles to similar jobs or by changing job classifications from skilled to semi-skilled. The Michigan Regional WLB issued a murky directive in August 1944 forbidding employers to pay lower rates to women because of slight changes in job content, but the same ruling stated that women were not entitled to equal pay *per se,* especially when costs were increased in order to hire them. Despite government laxity, union indifference, and employer evasion, women's average weekly wages in Michigan rose $14.40 between October 1942 and August 1944, while male wages increased only an average of $9.90 per week. By August 1944 women in the state's engine turbine industry earned 94.3 per cent as much as men, and female in the automobile industry had closed to within 89 per cent of the male wage average. But the weekly wage gap at that time favored males by $15.22, or more than seven hundred dollars a year.

Male workers and union leaders did not go out of their way to welcome women employees. Men vociferously protested and sometimes went on strike against policies favorable to women, such as the movement of women to better shifts that they were not entitled to by strict seniority. Speaking before a New York City meeting of female unionists in October 1943, UAW president R. J. Thomas scored women for an alleged inability to think through problems; for their "ingratitude" in refusing to support unions, which were responsible for their high wages; and for their dependence on men for leadership. . . .

The woman worker may not have been the beloved of labor and management, but she was the undoubted darling of the press and public. According to a typically gushing newspaper report of mid-1943, every Rosie who riveted at Detroit's N. A. Woodworth Company looked "like a cross between a campus queen and a Hollywood starlet." The press closely scrutinized "the girls," their parties, and their late-night meetings with male coworkers at local bars. Such glamorization may have served a useful purpose insofar as it attracted women to war work by assuring them that they would not lose their "feminine" qualities in so doing. But some of the publicity, with its constant emphasis on beauty and its sexual innuendo, deprecated the woman worker as a person. . . .

The working woman of World War II was concerned with far more than the decency of her dress. An employee in plant or office, she was, in many instances, also the manager of a household. She shared with other citizens the discomforts of crowded housing and transportation, but manpower and supply shortages particularly frustrated her efforts to maintain a home. Too often, she found empty shelves or locked doors at neighborhood groceries. A WPB study of August 1943 estimated that 75 per cent of female absenteeism in one plant could be attributed to inadequate laundry service. The Detroit WPB office announced in February 1943 the appointment of local socialite and Presidential in-law Dorothy Kemp Roosevelt as special coordinator for both female recruitment and for women's out-of-plant problems; little, however, was ever heard from her. In seeking to solve war-related community problems, the federal government rarely distinguished between matters of concern to the entire community and those that impinged especially upon women. This attitude was described by Mary Anderson, one of the wartime directors of the Women's Bureau, who noted "a great tendency among governmental officials to speak about 'the people' as a whole, but when they spoke of 'the people,' they meant the men."

The sudden entrance of thousands of women into industrial life raised many issues, and none carried more far-reaching social implications than the question of whether mothers should work, and the subsidiary problem of care for their children. Some mothers had always worked outside the home, but *Detroit News* women's advisor Nancy Brown stated the prevalent opinion about the practice in a 1940 reply to a woman undecided about seeking a job: "Your children are still of school age. In spite of your assertion to the contrary, they do need you. It would not be possible for you to carry on two jobs, one outside your home and one inside."

Throughout the war, government agencies, social workers, educators, and politicians echoed this sentiment in varying words. Mothers who worked, it was maintained, might do enormous psychic harm to their young children and irreparable damage to the family, the primary social unit. The WMC released its first official statement on the working-mother question during the spring of 1942: "The first responsibility of women with young children in war, as in peace, is to give suitable care in their own homes to their children."

Even when the state reached the height of its manpower demand in November 1943, Governor Harry Kelly observed: "I have yet to find any emergency that should call mothers away from home to the detriment of our youth. For the good of the Michigan of tomorrow, I ask mothers of young children to pause and consider before they seek outside employment. . . . Consider your children."

Among the arguments mustered on behalf of working mothers was the contention that their employment in war industry might reduce migration into congested areas (there is no evidence, however, that such a relationship actually developed). The economic imperative certainly weighed heavily upon the woman who had to support her family while her husband was in the service. Even the 1942 WMC directive cited above insisted that no bar to employment be placed in the way of mothers with young children and that "the decision as to gainful employment should, in all cases, be an individual decision made by the woman herself. . . . When certain Michigan factories attempted to exclude younger mothers, management invariably discovered that many women lied about their family status rather than lose the chance for work. Since women workers were being recruited and since an increasingly large number of mothers intended to work in spite of pleas to the contrary, something had to be done about their children, from whom they would be separated for a large part of each working day. . . .

The most popular type of facility was the day nursery for two-to-five-year-old children. Practices varied from area to area, but most centers operated continuously for twelve hours, from six-thirty or seven o'clock in the morning onward. They served three meals a day, offered organized recreation directed by nursery teachers and volunteers, and provided cots or beds for afternoon naps. Extended school services allowed mothers to leave children six to fourteen years of age for care immediately before and after school. These centers or "canteens" usually were located within the school building itself. A center for night care proved unsuccessful in Detroit, but similar centers apparently worked well in Ypsilanti and Saginaw. Several communities sought to obtain care for infants by encouraging nonworking women to become foster mothers, taking perhaps three or four infants into their homes for more individualized attention. In addition to sponsoring such programs, four Michigan cities ran counseling services to guide mothers to the best available child care, and the Wayne County committee organized an elaborate information clearinghouse, the Children's War Service (CWS), in April 1943.

Day care advocates supported their demands with a flood of statistics suggestive of a great unmet need. The Wayne County committee estimated in early 1943 that local war plants and civilian industry employed some sixty thousand mothers, who had forty-five thousand children potentially in need of care. On the basis of this and other surveys, the Michigan WMC devised a formula that calculated that one child required day care for every seven women employed in Michigan industry (the ratio was projected to be 1:5 for women entering manufacturing for the first time). The friends of day care also noted many pathetic instances of individual deprivation. Thousands of children roamed the streets of industrial communities unable to enter homes locked for the day by their war-worker parents. More fortunate youngsters carried the house key on a string fastened around the neck.

A need clearly existed, yet day care centers were strikingly under-utilized both in Michigan and across the country. Nationally, Lanham Act programs served a mere hundred thousand children, perhaps a tenth of those eligible, and far fewer than the total of youngsters served by Great Britain's more elaborate system of child care. To be sure, the number of day care children in Michigan steadily increased, reaching 6,024 in early 1945 (4,501 in metropolitan Detroit), while the number of employed women steadily declined. But the same surveys that seemed to affirm the necessity for day care consistently reported that no more than 5 to 10 per cent of the presumably needy youngsters were actually enrolled in nursery school programs. . . .

Day care specialists spent most of the war years attempting to explain the seeming maternal indifference that even the minimal use of day care appeared to signify. The UAW claimed, with much justification, that many women simply could not afford to pay the fees charged for day care. Weekly costs for day care in Detroit varied from six dollars at a city-run center to sixteen dollars for a foster home, no small sums for that majority of working women who made less than the average of $47 per week earned by Detroit female employees in 1943. Other observers emphasized the apathy of working mothers or their lack of knowledge. The Detroit Board of Education discovered that a three-month lag existed between the time a center opened and the generation of a large-scale response from the nursery's expected clientele. Women often resented having to deal with social workers and counselors; middle-class mothers especially perceived day care, with its WPA antecedents, to be a welfare measure and shied away from mixing their children with youngsters from the lower classes.

At base, most women rejected day care services because they preferred to have their children cared for by relatives, neighbors or friends—or not at all—rather than by strangers in a nursery or a canteen. Despite the horror stories about "latch-key" children, most mothers were able to make arrangements that the mothers apparently regarded as satisfactory. The Women's Bureau 1944–1945 survey reported that 92 per cent of Detroit working women with children under fourteen years of age claimed to have made some provision for regular care, with only a meager 2 per cent relying on day nurseries. When an interviewer asked a group of Detroit working mothers why they did not avail themselves of the local day care program, she received such replies as the following: "I wouldn't have a stranger"; "No one could be better than my mother"; and, "The baby might catch a disease in a nursery."

With the exception of a few lay activists, it was the child welfare professional, not the mother, who demanded day care in World War II. . . .

The army of newly employed women added greater uncertainty to already uncertain postwar economic calculations, as evidence accumulated to document female intentions of remaining at work. The Women's Bureau reported in May 1945 that 75 per cent of all Detroit working women desired some form of postwar employment. The percentage rose to 80 per cent among women employed before Pearl Harbor and fell to no less than 60 per cent among former housewives.

Such surveys, of course, indicated only what women wished to do, not what they would do after V-J Day. Many female workers probably wanted to remain in their high-paying industrial jobs but did not really expect to do so. A large number of women declared against future employment if their husbands could support them or if men were in need of work. A national consensus, moreover, developed rapidly and strongly in support of the contention that women should not remain at work in their wartime numbers once peace returned. Opinion polls found solid majorities opposed to female employment that jeopardized jobs for men. The Federal government took pains to emphasize the temporary nature of war work and did nothing to encourage women in their aspirations for peacetime jobs. A spate of books and articles appeared, increasing in volume as victory neared, picturing a happy future for women in wedded bliss and in homes chock-a-block with long-unavailable consumer goods.

Betty Allie, chairwoman of the Michigan Unemployment Compensation Commission, spoke for the majority when she said in November 1943: "When the period of postwar adjustment comes, and their men come home, . . . you will see women returning naturally to their homes. A woman's first interests are her home, her husband, and their children. . . ." Women without family ties or who had lost husbands during the war were entitled to employment, Allie continued, "but there need be no fear that all [women] will compete for the postwar job. They will look on this period in their lives as an interlude. . . . Women will always be women."

When production cutbacks accelerated during the spring and summer of 1945, women were severed from employment at a rate approximately double that of men. Women composed one of the largest elements in the low-seniority pool ordinarily laid off first, but management had other ways of ridding itself of unwanted females. A government survey of conditions in

Michigan as of September noted that some employers were shuffling work assignments to give women the sort of heavy-lifting jobs that they were either legally barred from performing or that they might not want. One GM plant in Flint violated seniority altogether to put all women on the midnight shift. The majority of women who worked prior to the war could return to being waitresses, shop clerks, or maids, but they could not remain in industry.

Those women who turned for help to their unions found little comfort. The UAW was preoccupied with assimilating the returning veterans and with its forthcoming confrontation with General Motors. Walter Reuther warned the Women's Conference in 1944 that women could expect no "special privilege" to enable them to hold on to their jobs; rather, they must fight for a full employment economy. By November 1945 Michigan's nonfarm female workforce stood at 525,000, a quarter of a million less than the wartime peak, but still higher both proportionately and absolutely than in 1940. Female manufacturing employment in Detroit, however, fell from 124,000 in March 1945 to sixty-six thousand by year's end, one-quarter of the wartime high and a mere twenty thousand more than in 1940. Only a handful of women workers protested the treatment accorded them.

When America entered the war, leaders of some of the prominent women's organizations expressed cautious optimism that the nation would respond to the female contribution to victory with the grant of equality. As V-J Day dawned, however, it was difficult to determine the actual extent of change. The volume of female employment had risen, but women's status had not. The government, so generous in its praise of female America, still evinced no willingness to grant women an effective voice in political or economic decision-making. Neither business, labor, nor any other major organized segment of society supported a significant change in women's role based on wartime accomplishments. There had been no revolution in attitudes, only a series of expedient measures, often implemented grudgingly in the face of national emergency. The genteel club leaders and lady college presidents who functioned as spokeswomen for their sex submitted, with more or less grace, to male notions of women's place. . . .

Americans wanted affirmation, not change. The pride of the nation before 1929 had been its industrial machine, exemplified best by the automotive factories of Detroit and Michigan. To that machine, and not to a transforming doctrine, the nation turned in 1941 for the key to victory. Among the most hallowed of American institutions to be protected and affirmed was the traditional concept of womanhood. It was during World War II that the apotheosis of the unliberated woman, Miss America, rose to national prominence and respect. At times it appeared that every nubile young woman was competing for a place in the pin-up parade. Most women failed to grasp whatever opportunity for emancipation the war afforded. As Straub observes, they "saw it as a matter of production and military strategy rather than a contest of values and ideals." Women perceived World War II very much as men did, and by and large, expected no more than a better life for themselves and their families in a nation renewed and once more confident.

Women's Protests After the War

NANCY GABIN

The dramatic advances made by women workers in the United States during the World War II years and the setbacks they experienced in the immediate aftermath of the war have been the subject of considerable historical interest in recent years. Stressing the extent to which the war did not challenge basic assumptions about woman's role in society, recent works dealing with the experience of women in the 1940s have attributed the withdrawal of women workers from basic industries during reconversion to the power of ideology about gender. The attitudes and behavior of women workers themselves, historians William Chafe and Alan Clive argue, conformed to the dictates of the decade's conservative consensus. According to this view, women workers continued to view their primary role as that of wife and mother and perceived their employment in previously male-dominated industries as responsive to the needs of a war economy. Instead of defining their economic interests as workers, it is argued, women acquiesced in the loss of their wartime jobs during reconversion, choosing more conventional forms of employment in the postwar era.

Recent scholarship on this subject has devoted considerable attention to the auto industry. Yet historians have largely overlooked or ignored the fact that women workers in Detroit area auto plants actively contested efforts to exclude them from the postwar automotive labor force during the reconversion period. Women's protests ranged from individual grievances to picket lines outside plant employment offices and the headquarters of the United Automobile Workers (UAW). Analysis of the causes of these actions indicates that the withdrawal of women from basic industries after World War II resulted not from the war's failure to change women's attitudes toward work, but rather from management and union discrimination.

Women who were unwilling to relinquish the benefits of industrial employment and expected that the seniority they had accumulated during the war would enable them to return to the plants after reconversion found that discriminatory practices in transfers, layoffs, and recalls violated and abrogated their seniority rights. Because the manner in which women were ousted from their wartime jobs seriously threatened their chances of reclaiming their positions in the postwar period, the restoration of the prewar occupational distribution of women in the labor force in the years following World War II should be read as evidence of the extent to which women were unable to make their own decisions regarding employment. It does not indicate their preference for traditionally female jobs.

The protest actions of women auto workers during reconversion are important not only because they offer evidence regarding the organization of

Reprinted from Nancy Gabin, " 'They Have Placed a Penalty on Womanhood' ": The Protest Actions of Women Auto Workers in Detroit-Area UAW Locals, 1945-1947," *Feminist Studies,* VIII (1982), 373–97, by permission of the publisher, *Feminist Studies,* Inc., c/o Women's Studies Program, University of Maryland, College Park, MD 20742.

the sexual division of labor in post–World War II America, but also because they counter the prevailing view of the working women of the 1940s as passive and socially conservative. The strength of opposition to the continued presence of women in the industry, the rapidly diminishing number of women in the plants, and the absence of a feminist movement to lend additional legitimacy to the protest of female auto workers minimized the prospects for an industry-wide challenge to sexual discrimination. Although protest activity was neither typical nor widespread, the evidence suggests that conditions in Detroit area auto plants and UAW locals mitigated the factors that precluded or inhibited female protest elsewhere. An examination of how women mobilized to defend their right to postwar employment in the plants, and the extent to which their mobilization changed the UAW's policies on issues of concern to women auto workers, indicates the importance of the industrial unions as arenas for female activism and the ways in which trade union membership may serve as a resource as well as a constraint for working women's collective action. . . .

The rapid reduction of the female labor force in the auto industry after World War II was in part an unavoidable consequence of the race to reconvert the industry to consumer production. In the first week following the surrender of Japan, one-half of the workers in plants under contract with the UAW were laid off, and layoffs of both women and men continued as the cancellation of war contracts eliminated many of the jobs held by workers during the war. Women represented a disproportionate number of those laid off in the industry, and they were also discriminated against in transfers and recalls. The treatment accorded women in the auto industry during reconversion indicated that management, having viewed the employment of women during the war as a temporary and undesirable expedient, did not include them in its postwar plans. Although managers had praised the performance of women workers during the war and had taken advantage of their presence to simplify production processes and reduce wages on jobs ordinarily performed by men, their desire to exclude women from the postwar automotive labor force and the renewed availability of a male labor supply precluded any examination of the possible economic benefits of employing women.

The Ford Motor Company was unabashedly vigorous in its efforts to eliminate women from plants after the war. During the war, the company employed nearly one-quarter of all the women working in the auto industry, and women comprised 22 percent of the Ford work force. The proportion of women workers was even higher in some plants, such as the one in Highland Park, Michigan, where, at the peak of wartime employment in 1944, 43 percent of the 13,500 workers were women. By January 1946, less than six months after V-J day, only forty-nine hundred women, representing just 4 percent of all Ford employees, were working in company plants. Although some women voluntarily left their jobs and others, who had accumulated little seniority, were among the first to be laid off, many women who were laid off had seniority equal to or greater than male employees who were retained on their jobs. The methods used by management to discharge these female employees violated and abrogated their seniority rights, thereby generating not unwarranted fears that the company would exclude women from its postwar labor force. . . .

Although tireless in its efforts to exclude women from postwar employment in auto plants, management was not solely responsible for the tenuous position of women workers during reconversion. The reluctance of the UAW to take concerted action against management practices in effect sanctioned discrimination. The union's ambivalent attitude toward women auto workers meant that the opposition of male unionists and plant managers to the continued presence of women in the plants went largely unchallenged. When codified in jointly negotiated contract clauses that provided women with seniority rights unequal to those of men, union prejudices not only protected management from liability for discrimination, but also facilitated and expedited the expulsion of women from Ford plants.

Agreements that provided for non-interchangeable occupational group seniority had onerous consequences for women who were transferred, laid off, or recalled to jobs they were physically unable to perform. Although obviously inspired by the company's desire to eliminate its female employees, the practice could not be assailed as a violation of the contract. In March 1945, Local 400 attempted to negotiate a plant-wide, interchangeable occupational group seniority agreement with management that would have permitted women who were unable to perform a job in their occupational group to "bump" an employee with less seniority on an appropriate job in another group. Refusing to accept the local's plan, the management had it revised to restrict seniority to the occupational group or to the labor pool. In a decision that the local union president later admitted was a "serious blunder," the membership voted to ratify the agreement.

Management curtailed work in the bomber wing press shop in April 1945 and transferred 103 women with the least seniority of all employees in the occupational group to work loading boxcars, the only job in the labor pool to which their seniority entitled them. Because they were physically unable to perform the job, management discharged the women as "quits." As a result, the women were not only deprived of seniority, but also could not qualify for unemployment compensation. In his decision on a policy grievance filed by the local on behalf of the 103 women, Harry Shulman explained that it was not within his power "to decree some wise solution for the difficult problems involved." "By the parties' own choice," he observed, "my power is limited to their contracts and to a determination of what those contracts require." Although the local protested that management had manipulated the seniority agreement in order to discharge both female and elderly or disabled male employees, Shulman, unable to read into the contract what was not there, decided that the protested practice was in accord with the local seniority agreement and did not violate any agreement between the company and the union.

To meet problems caused by non-interchangeable occupational group seniority, the Ford-UAW contract that was negotiated during the late fall of 1945, and ratified by the membership in March 1946, included a provision for a single, plant-wide seniority list. Although the provision guaranteed women who were transferred, laid off, or recalled access to a wider variety of jobs, the contract also provided for two types of seniority. Those employees hired before June 20, 1941, were permitted, in the event of layoffs, to retain and exercise their accumulated seniority for a period of up to four years. Those hired after June 20, 1941, however, were entitled to a "break period" equal only to their accumulated seniority; if they were not recalled within a period of time equal to their accrued seniority, they were removed from plant seniority lists. The significance of the two types of seniority becomes evident when it is noted that Ford had begun hiring women for war production jobs beginning in 1942. A number of the women laid off during reconversion had acquired three years of seniority, but most had accumulated less. The longer management delayed in recalling women who had been laid off during the first months of reconversion, the slimmer their chance became of returning to work in the plants.

In response to the discriminatory treatment accorded them in Ford and other auto company plants during reconversion, women appealed to the union to live up to its wartime promises to female members who, by 1945, represented 28 percent of the UAW's 1 million members. During the war, the UAW had established a record of progressive action on issues regarding women in the auto industry. Acknowledging the problem of sexual discrimination, it had, for example, successfully prosecuted an equal-pay-for-equal work case against General Motors before the National War Labor Board in 1942, sought the elimination of separate seniority lists for men and women, and devised a model maternity clause to be included in contracts. The efforts of women activists and their male allies to make the UAW responsive to the needs of the female membership had culminated in the spring of 1944 in the creation of the Women's Bureau as a department of the union's War Policy Division. R.J. Thomas, president of the UAW, explained in a letter to the local unions that the bureau was designed to deal with the special employment problems of the union's female membership, such as daycare, the enforcement of state and federal laws regulating the hours and conditions of women's work, equal pay for equal work, and the opposition of management and male workers to the idea of women working.

The placement of the bureau in the War Policy Division, however, indicated the limited and short-range character of the UAW's commitment to its female members. The comment made by James Burswald of Local 329 in response to a Women's Bureau survey of local union policies toward women was characteristic of the attitude of male unionists. "Our first interest is in interesting male members in Union activity," he remarked, "since women very likely will not be employed in our shop after the war." Policies adopted by the union during the war further illustrate the nature and extent of resistance to the introduction of women in auto plants. When, for example, the War Policy Division in 1944 issued its suggested policy for filling job openings, it strongly urged the elimination of job classification by sex "so management can't claim any job or classification strictly for women and use this, especially after the war." By the end of the war, the issue of veterans' seniority and job rights and the prospect of a return to the high unemployment levels of the 1930s reinforced the view of male unionists that women were a threat to wage standards and competitors for a limited number of jobs. Although women insisted that they did not wish to displace veterans who, by virtue of previous employment in the industry or length of service in the armed forces, had greater seniority, the male membership and leadership were not generally supportive of the desire of women auto workers to pursue postwar employment in the plants.

Having defined its postwar membership as male, the union ignored indications that women auto workers, contrary to expectation, would not acquiesce in the loss of their jobs after the war. In February 1944, C.G. Edelin, president of Local 51, criticized the International Executive Board (IEB) for its refusal to address the issue of postwar jobs for women and warned that "if a long-range policy covering female workers cannot be worked out before peace is declared abroad . . . we may find ourselves in some very warm water." A survey conducted by the union's research department in the spring of 1944, which revealed that 85.5 percent of female UAW members wanted to keep their wartime jobs, confirmed Edelin's suspicions. . . .

The response of the Local 400 Women's Committee at the Ford Highland Park plant to the plight of the 103 women who were unfairly discharged and deprived of their seniority rights in April 1945 demonstrated how determined women were to resist the loss of their wartime jobs. In response to their request for assistance, John Carney, the local union president, asked management to change the women's discharge slips to read "laid off" rather than "quit" so that they could retain their seniority in the event of a recall and be eligible for unemployment compensation. When the management refused to comply with his request, Carney directed the union building chairman and committeeman to file grievances with management for the 103 women on the grounds that men with less seniority than the women were working on jobs that women could perform.

It soon became apparent that the women did not have the full support of their local leadership. The building chairman and committeeman refused to write up grievances for the women. Consequently, Carney performed the task himself, giving the reports to the committeeman for processing. Pat McLean, chairwoman of the Women's Committee, later reported to the IEB, however, that when they inquired about the progress of the grievances, the women were informed that the grievance reports had been stored in a committeeman's locker and that "all the grievances, 103 in all (triplicate copies), had mysteriously disappeared from the locker." This act of sabotage by the men enabled management to stand by its position, the head of Labor Relations in the plant refusing to respond to the grievances until the union's triplicate copies had been presented.

Angered by the resistance of the male leadership and its complicity with management, the Women's Committee called a plant-wide meeting for May 6. In the flyer they distributed at plant gates to advertise the meeting, they were careful to include an appeal to male workers. Condemning the efforts by management "to turn women workers in the Highland Park plant against the union by carrying through a policy of discrimination," the authors of the flyer promised that "we [women] intend to stick with our union and fight" and warned that management's violation of the seniority rights of the 103 women would set a precedent that could eventually threaten male employees as well. "The first step in fighting these company tricks," the organizers of the meeting explained to women, "is to get together—to learn the facts, and to plan the fight! Let nothing stop you from attending the meeting Sunday! OUR JOBS ARE AT STAKE!" When the meeting was held, the women devised an alternative strategy for registering their protest against management. With the approval and assistance of Richard Leonard, director of the UAW Ford Department, they filed a police grievance against management with the UAW-Ford umpire in July.

Experiences similar to those of women in Local 400 inspired five women from four other Detroit area locals to request an appearance before the July IEB meeting in Minneapolis, Minnesota, to address the problems confronting women in the plants. Charging that the union was failing to defend its female membership, the women demanded that there be greater female representation on the international level and that the union deal more effectively with discrimination on the local level. The women also urged the IEB to act on the union's commitment to women workers and voice its opposition publicly to the precedent established by the War Labor Board in its favorable ruling on an agreement between the Michigan Tool Company and the Mechanics Educational Society of America (MESA) that sanctioned the surrender by women workers of their seniority rights in return for four weeks of severance pay. . . .

The women's protest during the spring and summer of 1945 did have an effect on union policy. Although they lost their campaign to elect a woman to the IEB, their strategic emphasis on the threat that violations of women's seniority posed to the principle of seniority was successful. In August 1945, the UAW submitted a statement to the Detroit War Labor Board protesting the board's ruling in the Michigan Tool Company and MESA case. In a letter to George Taylor, chairman of the National War Labor Board, Thomas explained that although the UAW was aware that it had no standing in the case, it nevertheless believed that it would be "unfortunate if the government in any way dilutes its own policy relating to non-discrimination against women workers." In its statement on the case, the union expressed concern "lest the ruling . . . be considered as having established a precedent for the handling of similar cases in the future. . . . We believe it obvious that the company is seeking to reinstitute its pre-war discriminatory hiring policy against women and is using an ill-conceived device for the purpose." In a letter addressed to all local union presidents, regional directors, and international representatives, Thomas outlined the union's position on the MESA agreement and explained its implications for the UAW.

> This action [he declared] focuses the attention on one of the major problems facing local unions today, that of zealously protecting seniority rights in the transfer, lay off and rehire of all members without prejudice because of race, creed, national origin, sex or marital status. In a sense, this is a test period in

which we are being called upon to make a reality of our principles of equality of membership rights. . . .

Their dissatisfaction with the response of the UAW to the plight of women workers having increased during the winter of 1946, women unionists voiced their anger at the UAW convention in March 1946. On the first day of the convention, the delegates approved a resolution urging the passage of a Full Employment Act, federal legislation providing equal pay for equal work, and the institution of government-supported daycare centers. Despite this action, female delegates were suspicious of the international's motives in advocating federal and state action against discrimination. McLean called the resolution an attempt "to pass the buck on to the United States Government rather than setting a policy within our own union." Reporting that the seniority rights of women at the Ford River Rouge plant were being abrogated in layoffs and recalls, Minnie Jones, a Local 600 delegate, condemned the callous attitude of men in the local that women war workers belonged back in the home and cited the example of war widows with children who needed to work in the auto plants where wages were higher than those in traditional women's jobs. "Other women throughout America still have jobs," she noted, "and certainly we are not going to work to organize the union and then go back to work for $15.00 a week." Inez Walker, a delegate from Local 927, supported the resolution, but asked "what happened to all the wonderful resolutions we passed at the [December 1944] Women's Conference? They have never been executed. . . . I should like to see this resolution not only adopted but actually worked on and carried into effect."

Following the floor discussion of the resolution, several women organized the Council of Women Delegates to draft a second resolution demanding union action against sex discrimination. The resolution, which was unanimously adopted by the Resolution Committee and approved by the delegates in the closing minutes of the convention, condemned the collusion between local union leaders and management in discriminating against women in transfers, layoffs, and recalls, urged the incorporation of a model fair practices clause in local union contracts, and directed the international leadership to instruct regional directors to disapprove any contract that discriminated against women.

By making the IEB responsible for the implementation of the resolution on women's rights, the Council of Women Delegates remedied a major weakness in the UAW's approach to the problem of sexual discrimination. The reconversion crisis had revealed the extent of the male opposition to the presence of women in the plants. By obstructing grievance procedures, ignoring violations of contract provisions that protected women's rights, and complying with agreements and practices that discriminated against women, male unionists had facilitated management efforts to exclude women from the post-war automotive labor force. The international leadership had demonstrated its own ambivalence by failing to do much more than inform the locals in writing of its preference for fair and equal treatment. Although the resolution did not stipulate any penalties for noncompliance by local unions, it eliminated any ambiguity about the union's commitment to women auto workers and made the IEB responsible for implementing the agreed-upon policy. In June 1946, the IEB granted the Women's Bureau, which had been in limbo since the dissolution of the War Policy Division, permanent status by incorporating it into the newly established Fair Practices and Anti-Discrimination Department. The action of the IEB symbolized its recognition of the legitimacy of the protests made by women within the union during the previous eighteen months. . . .

Historians have argued that women workers were essentially uninterested in challenging the sexual segregation of occupations and so voluntarily left their wartime jobs in basic industries after World War II. It is likely that a proportion of those women employed in the auto industry during the war simply did not plan to seek continued employment in the plants in the postwar period. Some women had never intended to continue working after the war, and others were content to return to jobs in the traditionally female employment sectors. Many women viewed their wartime experience in the automobile industry as temporary and saw no reason to participate in protest actions when they were laid off. Dorothy Haener, who worked in the Willow Run Ford plant during the war and later served as an international representative for the UAW, recalls that as a young woman in the early 1940s, she, like many other women, considered every job temporary. She viewed her experience at Willow Run as no exception, although at the time she was aware that her job paid higher wages than the traditionally female jobs she had held prior to the war. "I really expected to do what everyone else, every woman who . . . grew up under the circumstances I did, with the conditions and the culture we had [did]," she remarked. "I really expected to get married and not have to work anymore."

Although the prevalence of these attitudes undoubtedly inhibited solidarity among women workers and confirmed the sentiment among male unionists that women did not belong in the auto plants after the war, it is important to recognize that many women may have chosen not to protest because to do so appeared futile. Mildred Jeffrey, noting the hostility of men and the general public toward women workers, claims that this had its negative impact on women. "It was attitude setting," she notes, "it was the environment—it created a lot of pressures on women not to pursue their grievances."

The treatment accorded those who did protest probably further discouraged women from seeking postwar employment in the auto plants. The male rank and file and the local union leadership occasionally expressed their hostility toward women workers by sabotaging the processing of grievances. The hostility or, more commonly, the disinterest of the international leadership deprived women of much needed support and influence in their confrontations with management. Company managers were tireless in their efforts to exclude women from plants in the postwar period; there were reports that Ford management even threatened women with the loss of unemployment compensation if they did not acquiesce in the treatment accorded them. Jeffrey recalls that "it was just so hard for women, although we had women who got their heads bloodied, figuratively speaking . . . they had a hell of a time! It was really, really rough getting equal rights!''

The comments of Haener and Jeffrey indicate that the relationship between the attitudes and behavior of women who worked in basic industries like auto manufacturing during the war was more subtle and elusive than historians have acknowledged. The ambiguous character of that relationship suggests the contingencies involved in working women's collective action in the immediate postwar period. In contrast to the experience of women in other industries and unions, the UAW's antidiscrimination policies and its commitment to the hard-won principle of seniority provided women auto workers with a legitimate platform for contesting the loss of their jobs during reconversion. The initiative for challenging the violation of their rights as union members, however, lay with the women themselves. The prospects for mobilizing a campaign both within the union and against management were as a result most favorable in those auto plants and UAW locals where there were women like Pat McLean, Della Rymer, and Grace Blackett who had acquired organizational and leadership skills during the war, and women's committees such as those in Locals 400 and 600 which had been established before the war's end and could serve as bases for protest activities. With these resources, women in Detroit area auto plants overcame the factors that inhibited or precluded female protest elsewhere.

The strength of opposition to the continued presence of women in the plants and the absence of a feminist movement outside of the plants, which, by challenging the ideology of woman's proper place, would have given the protest of female auto workers additional and much-needed legitimacy, made it difficult even for the women in Detroit to secure postwar employment in the industry. The rapid reduction of the female labor force and the consequent loss of women leaders as a result of layoffs during reconversion further detracted from the success of their efforts. Grace Blackett, for example, whom Jeffrey calls a ''fireball'' and an ''agitator,'' was laid off from the union staff of region four in August 1945, and soon after from her job at the Ford Willow Run plant. ''We tried to have demonstrations of women,'' Jeffrey remembers. ''That was kind of depressing because here we had worked so hard trying to develop leadership, but when it came to this period, it wasn't there. There weren't enough women.''

Although the protest actions of women unionists in Detroit area auto plants during reconversion changed the UAW's policies on issues of concern to female auto workers, and in some instances prevented plant managers and male unionists from discriminating against women in transfers, layoffs, and recalls, alone they could not effect a transformation of the sexual division of labor in the auto industry. Given the political weakness of women unionists and their male allies and the obstacles that prevented women from retaining or reclaiming their wartime jobs, the restoration of the sexual division of labor in auto plants after the war is not surprising. One historian has stated that ''most women failed to grasp whatever opportunity for advancement the war afforded,'' but in light of the experience of women auto workers, it seems more appropriate to stress the extent to which women simply were not given the chance to make their own decisions regarding employment in the post–World War II period.

Persistent Discrimination Against Black Women

KAREN TUCKER ANDERSON

As a result of the increasing demand for workers in all categories of employment, and especially in the high-paying manufacturing sector, the full employment economy of World War II posed the most serious challenge in American history to the traditional management preference for white male labor in primary-sector jobs. The war years were especially important for blacks, who benefited from an expanding labor force, changing racial values, a revitalized migration out of the rural South, and the attempted enforcement of equal employment opportunity under a presidential executive order. Although scholars have given some attention to the labor-force fortunes of blacks in the war economy, few have considered the impact of the wartime expansion on black women, who constituted 600,000 of the 1,000,000 blacks who entered paid employment during the war years. Those who have focused on black women have stressed the degree to which the war opened new job categories and fostered mobility. William Chafe, for example, contends that the opportunities generated by the wartime economy and the long-term changes they fostered constituted a "second emancipation" for black women. According to Dale L. Hiestand, occupational shifts by black women workers during the 1940s promoted substantial income improvement.

A careful examination of the labor-force status of black women during the 1940s brings into question such sanguine pronouncements. Focusing on the wartime experiences of black women provides insight into the nature of prejudice as manifested and experienced by women and into the sources and mechanisms of labor-force discrimination in a particular historical context. It also facilitates an examination of the relative importance of managerial intransigence and coworker prejudice in perpetuating discriminatory employment practices. In addition, it gives an indication of the importance of tight labor markets in fostering economic mobility for minority group women.

Labor force statistics support the contention that the war marked an important break with the historic allocation of work by race and sex. Between 1940 and 1944 the proportion of employed black women engaged in domestic service declined from 59.9 percent to 44.6 percent, although their share of jobs in this field increased because white women exited from private household work in even greater proportions. In addition, the percentage of the black female labor force in farm work was cut in half, as many from the

---

Karen Tucker Anderson, "Last Hired, First Fired: Black Women Workers During World War II," *Journal of American History,* 69 (June 1982), 82–97. Copyright Organization of American Historians, 1982.

rural South migrated to urban areas in response to the demand for war workers. The shift of large numbers of black women from work in farms and homes to work in factories resulted in the proportion of black females employed in industrial occupations rising from 6.5 percent to 18 percent during the war. A comparable expansion also occurred in personal service work outside of the private household, which claimed 17.9 percent of black women workers in 1944.

To stress only the improvement wrought during the war, however, is to understate the extent to which discrimination persisted and to ignore the fact that the assumptions of a historically balkanized labor force continued to determine the distribution of the benefits of a full employment economy. When faced with a shortage of white male workers, employers had various options. They could seek workers from other areas of the country, hoping that this would enable them to minimize the changes produced by the wartime expansion, or they could rely on underutilized elements of the local labor supply—workers in nonessential employment, women, blacks, and older and younger workers. If unable to secure large numbers of white male in-migrants and unwilling to modify hiring patterns too dramatically, they could limit production, sacrificing output to prejudice.

Those who decided to employ substantially increased numbers of women and/or minorities established a complex hierarchy of hiring preferences based on the composition of the local labor force and the nature of the work to be done. In light industries, women workers became the first recourse of employers unable to recruit large numbers of white males. In the airframe industry, for example, women constituted 40.6 percent of the employees by November 1943, while blacks claimed only 3.5 percent of airframe jobs. Employers in heavy industries, by contrast, sought minority males as a preferred source of labor, with the result that the level of utilization of women depended on the minority population of an area. In Baltimore, for example, blacks comprised up to 20 percent of the shipbuilding workers while women represented only 4 percent. Seattle, which had only a small black population, relied on women for 16 percent of its shipyard employees.

Whatever the hierarchy of preference, however, black women could always be found at the bottom. The dramatic expansion of jobs for women did not necessarily mean the opening up of new categories of employment for minority group women. A survey conducted by the United Auto Workers (UAW) in April 1943 found that only 74 out of 280 establishments that employed women in production work were willing to hire black women. Similarly, a 1943 study by the National Metal Trades Association revealed that only twenty-nine out of sixty-two plants that used women workers had black women in their employ. Moreover, most of them used black women only in janitorial positions. Even some employers willing to hire white women and black men in large numbers balked at including black women in their work forces. At the Wagner Electric Corporation in Saint Louis, for example, 64 percent of the employees were white women, 24 percent were black males, and 12 percent were white males. The company refused to hire

black women throughou   er
from the President's Co   to
cease all discrimination.

Because of the mol   1e
military, the availability   1e
nature of the jobs being   u-
dice against black wome   ly
flexible than the female labor force. While the number ot all blacks employed
in manufacturing increased 135 percent between April 1940 and January
1946, the number of black women in such work rose only 59 percent. Blacks
made their greatest wartime gains in heavily male-employing industrial
fields; by January 1945 they constituted 25 percent of the labor force in
foundries, 11.7 percent in shipbuilding, and 11.8 percent in blast furnaces
and steel mills. By contrast, nonwhites accounted for only 5.8 percent of
employees in aircraft and 2.7 percent of those in electrical equipment production. In the traditional female fields of clerical and sales, the gains of
black women were negligible—their share of female clerical jobs rose from
0.7 percent to 1.6 percent while their proportion in the female sales force
declined from 1.2 percent to 1.1 percent.

One of the most important and obdurate of the industries that fought the
employment of black women during the war was the auto industry. Led by
the negative example of the Ford Motor Company, which refused to hire
nonwhite women in any but token numbers, the auto companies persisted in
rejecting trained black female applicants or in limiting their employment to a
few work categories until very late in the war. When referred to the automakers by the United States Employment Service (USES) in response to
calls for women workers, black women found that the white women accompanying them would be hired immediately while they would be told to await
a later call, a call that would never come. When Samella Banks, along with
five white women, applied to Cadillac Motor Company in November 1942,
she was told that there might be a janitress opening in a day or two while
they were hired as welder trainees. As a result, much of the expansion of the
female labor force in industrial work occurred before economic or political
pressures necessitated the hiring of black women. By February 1943 nonwhite women had claimed only 1,000 of the 96,000 jobs held by women in
major war industries in Detroit. Consequently, most nonwhite females were
confined to work in low-paying service and other unskilled categories, and
those who landed industrial jobs had so little seniority that their postwar fate
was guaranteed.

As was generally the case with wartime racial discrimination in employment, the most frequent employer rationale for excluding nonwhite women
was the fear that white opposition to the change might cause work slow-
downs or strikes. An examination of the nature and goals of coworker prejudice during the war years provides some possible answers to the question of
whether such prejudice is rooted in an aversion to social contact in a context
of equality or is primarily a calculated attempt on the part of whites to
maintain an exploitative economic advantage. When the former issue is the

basic concern, it is manifested in a desire to exclude blacks altogether or to segregate them on the job. When the latter is the wellspring of white workplace prejudice, it is evidenced, not in a wish to segregate black workers, but in an attempt to prevent the hiring of blacks or to limit them to particular low-paying job categories.

During the war years, white male hostility to expanded job opportunities for black men focused primarily on the issue of promotion rather than on hiring or segregation. Although some strikes occurred when black men were admitted to entry-level jobs or over the issue of integrating the workplace, most white-male hate strikes took place when black male workers were promoted into jobs at higher skill and pay levels. This was a product of the fact that black men had been employed as janitors and unskilled laborers in many defense industries prior to the war and sought promotions as opportunities expanded. White males thus seemed to be concerned primarily with maintaining their advantaged economic position. Moreover, their resistance to the elimination of discrimination was more tenacious and more effective than was the opposition of white women to the opening of opportunities for black women. Control over labor unions, whose opposition to black entry into previously white jobs proved an effective barrier to change in many cases, gave white males more power to translate prejudice into employer discrimination.

For women workers, on the other hand, the desire to maintain social distance, rather than a wish to safeguard economic prerogatives, seemed to be the dominant motivation in many cases. White female workers frequently objected to working closely with black women or sharing facilities with them because they feared that blacks were dirty or diseased. Work stoppages occurred in several places after the introduction of black women into the female work force. More than 2,000 white women employed at the U.S. Rubber plant in Detroit walked off the job in March 1943, demanding separate bathroom facilities. A similar walkout occurred at the Western Electric plant in Baltimore in summer 1943. In both cases management refused to segregate the facilities and appealed to patriotic and egalitarian values to persuade the striking workers to return to their jobs. Significantly, the one hate strike by white women workers that focused on upgrading as well as integration, the Dan River strike in 1944, was in a traditional female-employing industry. . . .

As a result of the idiosyncratic nature of employer practices during the war, some areas and some employers offered greater employment opportunities for black women than others. Aircraft plants in the Los Angeles area, for example, began hiring black women for production work relatively early by comparison with similar operations in other areas of the country. As a result, by 1945 black women could be found doing industrial work in all Los Angeles aircraft plants; 2,000 were employed by North American Aviation alone. Among the automakers, the Briggs plant in Detroit deviated from industry patterns and hired substantial numbers of black women. In Saint Louis, where defense industry discrimination against black women was the general rule, the Curtiss-Wright Company and the U.S. Cartridge Company eased the situation somewhat by providing industrial jobs for hundreds of nonwhite women. These examples, however, were not typical of employer response; restrictive hiring and segregation remained the rule, even in industries faced with severe labor shortages. Nowhere was this truer than in the South, where traditional practices remained virtually unchanged.

Even when defense employers broke with tradition and hired nonwhite women, they generally segregated them from other women workers and employed them only for certain kinds of work, usually that which was arduous, dirty, hot, or otherwise disagreeable. A cursory study of black women workers done by the Women's Bureau of the United States Department of Labor in 1945 revealed that in many cases nonwhite women were disproportionately represented among women employed in outside labor gangs, in foundries, and in industrial service work. On the ore docks of the Great Lakes, for example, the survey found women, predominantly black, shoveling the leavings of ore from the bottoms of ships onto hoists. According to the USES, the meat-packing industry in Detroit resorted to black women in large numbers during the war years to take jobs others had spurned. On the railroads minority group women found employment in substantial numbers as laborers, loaders, car cleaners, and waitresses. The city of Baltimore first broke with its policy of hiring only whites for street-cleaning work in the immediate prewar period when it began hiring black males; by 1943, when the black male labor force was completely exhausted, the city turned to the only labor reserve left—the large numbers of unemployed and underemployed black females.

The insistence by some employers on segregated work arrangements and facilities served as a rationale for excluding black women altogether or limiting their numbers to conform to physical plant requirements. The Glenn Martin Aircraft Company, for example, hired the same proportion of nonwhite women for its integrated plant in Omaha, where the black population was quite small, as it did for its Baltimore operations, where black women constituted a substantial proportion of the local labor supply. In Baltimore, however, their numbers were limited because they had to be assigned only to a small separate subassembly plant. A small aircraft parts firm in Los Angeles asserted that it could not hire black women because it separated workers by sex as well as by race and could not further complicate its managerial and supervisory difficulties. At the Norfolk Navy Yard, management excluded black women from most production jobs on the grounds that women workers had to be segregated by race, although the racial integration of male workers was an accomplished fact. As a result, black men worked in a wide variety of jobs at all skill levels in the yard while the jobs assigned to women were virtually monopolized by whites. . . .

The major agency charged with enforcing equal opportunity in employment regardless of race, religion, or national origin was the FEPC, an agency created in 1941 by executive order of President Franklin D. Roosevelt in response to a threatened march on Washington by civil rights groups protesting discriminatory policies by war contractors. Although the FEPC could theoretically recommended the removal of war contracts from those who continued to discriminate and the WMC could restrict work permits to enforce federal hiring policies, the federal government was not inclined to hamper the production of essential war materials in order to foster racial equity. As a result, the agency had to rely on behind-the-scenes negotiations and the possibility of adverse publicity generated by public hearings. Although effective in some cases, such tools proved ineffectual against recalcitrant violators, whose ranks included some major war industries. The large volume of complaints and the bureaucratic delays inherent in the situation facilitated evasion, even on the part of blatant violators officially ordered to cease restrictive hiring practices. Moreover, the reliance on individual, documented complaints rather than on employer hiring patterns as the basis for action hampered effective enforcement.

The decision by Roosevelt to place the FEPC under the jurisdiction of the WMC in July 1942 also handicapped the agency in its efforts to end employment discrimination. WMC head Paul McNutt, never enthusiastic regarding the FEPC's goals and afraid that they were incompatible with his agency's responsibility for allocating scarce manpower within war industries, canceled scheduled FEPC hearings on discrimination by the railroads and generally made racial equity a low priority within WMC. Even after the FEPC was removed from the WMC in May 1943, it was hampered in its efforts to enforce the law by the unwillingness of southern representatives of the WMC and the USES to cooperate in reporting and seeking to change discriminatory practices. Although the USES had agreed in September 1943 to refuse to fill employer requests for workers when they included racial restrictions, its agents in the South frequently disregarded this directive. Thus, when blacks with defense training applied for appropriate work, they were often referred to jobs outside the area. The persistence of discrimination, despite a federal commitment to eliminate it, hampered the ability of all blacks, male and female, to find industrial employment in the region that still claimed a majority of the black population.

In its official policies the FEPC treated discrimination against black women as seriously as discrimination against black males, although its rate of success in enforcing compliance in women's cases lagged somewhat behind the rate for men. After its 1944 hearings in Saint Louis, the FEPC ruled that a company that hired black males while discriminating against black women was still in violation of the executive order, noting that "partial compliance is partial violation." Despite pressure from civil rights groups on behalf of black women workers and occasional threats of strikes by black male workers, the equal opportunity machinery of the government proved unable to aid minority women in any substantial way. By the time the agency had investigated, negotiated, or held hearings, much valuable time had been lost. For women, this could be especially damaging because it meant that anything beyond token conformity could be jeopardized by employer unwillingness to expand the female work force late in the war.

The Carter Carburetor Company in Saint Louis, for example, managed a minimal compliance with an FEPC order to cease discriminating when it came to black men, but refused in April 1944 to hire any black women on the grounds that it had no intention of hiring any more women. Although the government continued to pressure the company, it stood by its policies. The Allied Tent Manufacturing Company in New Orleans claimed to have instituted a nondiscriminatory policy regarding women workers when it announced its intention in June 1945 to replace all its women machine operators with men (white and black), having decided that women workers had proved themselves "unsatisfactory." Federal enforcement officials thus found that labor-market forces late in the war provided a rationale and a means for continued resistance by those employers intent on circumventing federal hiring policies regarding black women.

The organization that was most cognizant of persisting discrimination against black women and most active in fighting against it was the National Association for the Advancement of Colored People (NAACP). As early as August 1942, Detroit NAACP officer Gloster Current wrote to McNutt of the WMC, complaining that the Ford Motor Company was discriminating against black females as it hired thousands of whites for work at the Willow Run Bomber Plant. In March 1943 the Detroit NAACP cooperated with the United Auto Workers Inter-Racial Committee in staging a large rally to protest continued discrimination against black women in hiring and black men in promotion on the part of Detroit's war industries. Thereafter both groups continued to pressure employers and government officials at all levels on the issue. In a statement prepared for presentation to the House manpower committee, the NAACP evinced its awareness that the situation was not unique to Detroit but was a national problem resulting in the serious underutilization of black womanpower. . . .

Job retention was a serious issue for those women who landed industrial work during the war. The persistence of discrimination and the late entry of black women into production work, rather than their on-the-job conduct, meant that nonwhite females were more likely than others to experience layoffs resulting from contract completions or seasonal cutbacks. Once fired, they faced great difficulties in finding comparable work. According to an official of the Baltimore Urban League, white women there with industrial experience were easily reabsorbed by war industries while black women were being referred by the USES to work as maids, counter girls, and laundry pressers. As would be the case for all unemployed women after the war, those who turned down such jobs faced the possibility of losing their unemployment benefits for refusing suitable work. Black women thus experienced a much greater degree of job discontinuity than others during the war, hampering their ability to accumulate seniority.

Once the war was over and American industry began its postwar contraction, those black women who had held industrial jobs during the war found that their concentration in contracting industries, their low seniority, and their sex contributed to employment difficulties in the postwar period. American women, black and white, were overrepresented among those experiencing layoffs in durable good industries. When management began rehiring workers in the reconversion period, it reinstituted most prewar discriminatory policies regarding working women, even to the point of disregarding their seniority rights, a practice facilitated by union acquiescence.

USES officials reinforced employer policies by denying unemployment benefits to those women who refused referrals to jobs in traditional female-employing fields. To a greater extent than white women, black women were victimized by the postwar eviction of women from jobs in durable goods industries. . . .

In other work categories black women fared somewhat better in the postwar years. Although some apparently lost employment in service, sales, and clerical work as a result of competition from displaced white women, most managed to maintain their hold on lower-level jobs in the female work force. Despite attempts by USES officials in some local offices to force black women to return to domestic service work by threatening to withhold unemployment compensation benefits, enough job opportunities in other categories remained available to prevent a massive return to household work. Even so, domestic service remained the primary occupation of black women, providing employment to 782,520 in 1950, 40 percent of the black female work force.

As a result of the wartime experience, black women made substantial progress in the operatives occupational category, although their position in this area deteriorated somewhat in the late 1940s. One of the most important areas of expansion for nonwhite women was the apparel industry, which witnessed a 350 percent increase in black female employment during the 1940s. By 1950, it offered employment to 56,910 black women and ranked second in the operatives category behind laundry and dry cleaning establishments, where 105,000 black females were employed. Other major sources of industrial work for women, including textiles, remained virtually closed to blacks during the 1940s. In the durable goods industries, which had experienced the greatest wartime expansion, black women were a rarity in the postwar period. In 1950, only 60 black women held jobs as operatives in aircraft plants, while 2,730 claimed similar positions in the auto industry.

In the long run, the greatest benefit of the wartime experience for black women workers derived from their movement in large numbers out of the poverty of the rural South to the possibilities provided by an urban, industrialized economy. The extent to which those possibilities were realized in the decade of the 1940s can be overstated, however. Both during and after the war, black women entered the urban female labor force in large numbers only to occupy its lowest rungs. Largely excluded from clerical and sales work, the growth sectors of the female work force, black women found work primarily in service jobs outside the household and in unskilled blue-collar categories. Although many experienced some upward mobility during the war, their relative position within the American economy remained the same.

Wartime circumstances illustrate the extent to which an economic system that had historically allocated work according to race and sex could tolerate a high level of unemployment and underemployment even in a time of labor shortage in order to minimize the amount of change generated by temporary and aberrant conditions. By stressing the modification of traditional patterns fostered by rapid economic growth, scholars ignore the degree to which prejudices inhibited change and constrained the rate of economic expansion even in the face of strong patriotic, political, and economic incentives favoring expanded output at all cost. For black women, especially, what is significant about the war experience is the extent to which barriers remained intact.

❖ *FURTHER READING*

Karen Tucker Anderson, *Wartime Women: Sex Roles, Family Relations, and the Status of Women during World War II* (1981)

M. Joyce Baker, *Images of Women in Film: The War Years, 1941–1945* (1981)

D'Ann Campbell, *Women at War with America* (1984)

William Chafe, *The American Woman: Her Changing Social, Economic, and Political Roles, 1920–1970* (1972)

Maurine Weiner Greenwald, *Women, War, and Work: The Impact of World War I on Women Workers in the United States* (1980)

Susan Hartmann, *The Home Front and Beyond* (1982)

Maureen Honey, *Creating Rosie the Riveter: Class, Gender, and Propaganda during World War II* (1984)

Ruth Milkman, *Gender at Work: The Dynamics of Job Segregation by Sex during World War II* (1988)

Marc Miller, "Working Women and World War II," *New England Quarterly,* LIII (1980), 42–61

Paddy Quick, "Rosie the Riveter: Myths and Realities," *Radical America,* IX (1975), 115–32

Leila Rupp, *Mobilizing Women for War* (1978)

Mary Schweitzer, "World War II and Female Labor Force Participation Rates," *Journal of Economic History,* XL (1980), 89–95

Karen Beck Skold, "The Job He Left Behind: American Women in the Shipyards during World War II," in *Women, War, and Revolution,* ed. Carol Berkin and Clara Lovett (1980), 55–75

Sheila Tobias and Lisa Anderson, *What Really Happened to Rosie the Riveter?* MSS Modular Publication no. 9 (1973)

CHAPTER 14

Feminism and Civil Rights
in the 1960s

The history of the quest for women's rights in the United States has long been in-
tertwined with the quest for black equality. In the 1840s and 1850s, many of
those who joined the women's rights movement had first been active abolitionists.
In the late 1860s, the refusal of Republican party leaders to include provisions
explicitly protecting women in the Reconstruction amendments to the Constitution
led to the founding of an independent women's-suffrage organization. During the
final push for the Nineteenth Amendment early in the twentieth century, advocates
of women's suffrage constantly had to confront the issue of voting rights for blacks
—both men and women. So, too, in the 1960s, when feminism was reborn,
the connection of the two movements remained intricate and inescapable.

There were two sides to feminism in the 1960s, and both had links to civil
rights. The more conventional feminists sought legal and constitutional victories of
the sort that blacks had begun to win, starting with the school-desegregation deci-
sion (Brown v. Board of Education) in 1954. Such activists, most of whom were
older, married, white, and middle class, were in many ways the heirs of the Na-
tional Woman's Party. They formed the National Organization for Women (NOW)
in 1966, adopting the National Association for the Advancement of Colored People
(NAACP) as one of their models. Members of the second set of feminists, younger
and far more radical, created small ''consciousness-raising groups'' rather than
large formal organizations. Many of these young women, also the product of white,
middle-class homes, had been active in civil rights organizing in the South—es-
pecially under the auspices of the Student Non-Violent Coordinating Committee
(SNCC)—or in Students for a Democratic Society (SDS) and other radical student
organizations in the North. The two branches of the women's movement often
argued over tactics and goals, but together they helped to bring about massive
change in attitudes toward the role of women in American society. Why were the
feminist and civil rights movements so closely related to each other? In what ways
might they come into conflict? How did NOW members, radical feminists, and black
feminists arrive at their respective positions?

❖ D O C U M E N T S

In 1961, in its decision in *Hoyt* v. *Florida,* excerpted as the first document, the same Warren Court that had worked a revolution in blacks' civil rights adhered to a traditional vision of women's place in society, refusing to apply the standards it had developed in cases involving racial bias to a woman claiming sex discrimination. Two years later Betty Friedan, one of the founders of the contemporary feminist movement, described "The Problem That Has No Name" (the second selection) in the first pages of her influential book, *The Feminine Mystique.* Also in 1963, President Kennedy's Commission on the Status of Women refused to endorse the Equal Rights Amendment, as revealed in the third document. In the fourth selection, Mary King, a white civil rights worker, complained loudly but anonymously in 1964 about the discrimination she and other women suffered while working for SNCC. In 1966, the founding statement of NOW (extracted in the fifth document) laid out the organization's central premises. Note the striking contrast between that statement and the final selection, the "Redstockings Manifesto" of 1969, a creation of the more radical wing of the feminist movement.

Hoyt v. *Florida,* 1961

Mr. Justice Harlan delivered the opinion of the Court.

Appellant, a woman, has been convicted in Hillsborough County, Florida, of second degree murder of her husband. On this appeal from the Florida Supreme Court's affirmance of the judgment of conviction, we noted probable jurisdiction to consider appellant's claim that her trial before an all-male jury violated rights assured by the Fourteenth Amendment. The claim is that such jury was the product of a state jury statute which works an unconstitutional exclusion of women from jury service.

The jury law primarily in question is Fla Stat, 1959, § 40.01 (1). This Act, which requires that grand and petit jurors be taken from "male and female" citizens of the State possessed of certain qualifications, contains the following proviso: "provided, however, that the name of no female person shall be taken for jury service unless said person has registered with the clerk of the circuit court her desire to be placed on the jury list."

Showing that since the enactment of the statute only a minimal number of women have so registered, appellant challenges the constitutionality of the statute both on its face and as applied in this case. For reasons now to follow we decide that both contentions must be rejected.

At the core of appellant's argument is the claim that the nature of the crime of which she was convicted peculiarly demanded the inclusion of persons of her own sex on the jury. She was charged with killing her husband by assaulting him with a baseball bat. . . . As described by the Florida Supreme Court, the affair occurred in the context of a marital upheaval involving, among other things, the suspected infidelity of appellant's husband, and culminating in the husband's final rejection of his wife's efforts at reconciliation. It is claimed, in substance, that women jurors would have been more understanding or compassionate than men in assessing the quality of appellant's act and her defense of "temporary insanity." No claim is made that the jury as constituted was otherwise afflicted by any elements of supposed unfairness.

Of course, these premises misconceive the scope of the right to an impartially selected jury assured by the Fourteenth Amendment. That right does not entitle one accused of crime to a jury tailored to the circumstances of the particular case, whether relating to the sex or other condition of the defendant, or to the nature of the charges to be tried. It requires only that the jury be indiscriminately drawn from among those eligible in the community for jury service, untrammeled by any arbitrary and systematic exclusions. . . .

In the selection of jurors Florida has differentiated between men and women in two respects. It has given women an absolute exemption from jury duty based solely on their sex, no similar exemption obtaining as to men. And it has provided for its effectuation in a manner less onerous than that governing exemptions exercisable by men: women are not to be put on the jury list unless they have voluntarily registered for such service; men, on the other hand, even if entitled to an exemption, are to be included on the list unless they have filed a written claim of exemption as provided by law.

In neither respect can we conclude that Florida's statute is not "based on some reasonable classification," and that it is thus infected with unconstitutionality. Despite the enlightened emancipation of women from the restrictions and protections of bygone years, and their entry into many parts of community life formerly considered to be reserved to men, woman is still regarded as the center of home and family life. We cannot say that it is constitutionally impermissible for a State, acting in pursuit of the general welfare, to conclude that a woman should be relieved from the civic duty of jury service unless she herself determines that such service is consistent with her own special responsibilities. . . .

This case in no way resembles those involving race or color in which the circumstances shown were found by this Court to compel a conclusion of purposeful discriminatory exclusions from jury service. There is present here neither the unfortunate atmosphere of ethnic or racial prejudices which underlay the situations depicted in those cases, nor the long course of discriminatory administrative practice which the statistical showing in each of them evinced. . . .

Finding no substantial evidence whatever in this record that Florida has arbitrarily undertaken to exclude women from jury service, a showing which it was incumbent on appellant to make, we must sustain the judgment of the Supreme Court of Florida.

Affirmed. [unanimously]

Betty Friedan on "The Problem That Has No Name," 1963

The problem lay buried, unspoken, for many years in the minds of American women. It was a strange stirring, a sense of dissatisfaction, a yearning that women suffered in the middle of the twentieth century in the United States. Each suburban wife struggled with it alone. As she made the beds, shopped for groceries, matched slipcover material, ate peanut butter sandwiches with her children, chauffeured Cub Scouts and Brownies, lay beside her husband at night—she was afraid to ask even of herself the silent question—"Is this all?"

For over fifteen years there was no word of this yearning in the millions of words written about women, for women, in all the columns, books and articles by experts telling women their role was to seek fulfillment as wives and mothers. Over and over women heard in voices of tradition and of Freudian sophistication that they could desire no greater destiny than to glory in their own femininity. Experts told them how to catch a man and keep him, how to breastfeed children and handle their toilet training, how to cope with sibling rivalry and adolescent rebellion; how to buy a dishwasher, bake bread, cook gourmet snails, and build a swimming pool with their own hands; how to dress, look, and act more feminine and make marriage more exciting; how to keep their husbands from dying young and their sons from growing into delinquents. They were taught to pity the neurotic, unfeminine, unhappy women who wanted to be poets or physicists or presidents. They learned that truly feminine women do not want careers, higher education, political rights—the independence and the opportunities that the old-fashioned feminists fought for. Some women, in their forties and fifties, still remembered painfully giving up those dreams, but most of the younger women no longer even thought about them. A thousand expert voices applauded their femininity, their adjustment, their new maturity. All they had to do was devote their lives from earliest girlhood to finding a husband and bearing children. . . .

The suburban housewife—she was the dream image of the young American women and the envy, it was said, of women all over the world. The American housewife—freed by science and labor-saving appliances from the drudgery, the dangers of childbirth and the illnesses of her grandmother. She was healthy, beautiful, educated, concerned only about her husband, her children, her home. She had found true feminine fulfillment. As a housewife and mother, she was respected as a full and equal partner to man in his world. She was free to choose automobiles, clothes, appliances, supermarkets; she had everything that women ever dreamed of.

In the fifteen years after World War II, this mystique of feminine fulfillment became the cherished and self-perpetuating core of contemporary

Betty Friedan, selected excerpts from "The Problem That Has No Name" from *The Feminine Mystique*, 11–16, 21–22, 27. Reprinted by permission of W. W. Norton & Company, Inc. Copyright © 1963, 1974 by Betty Friedan.

American culture. Millions of women lived their lives in the image of those pretty pictures of the American suburban housewife, kissing their husbands goodbye in front of the picture window, depositing their stationwagonsful of children at school, and smiling as they ran the new electric waxer over the spotless kitchen floor. They baked their own bread, sewed their own and their children's clothes, kept their new washing machines and dryers running all day. They changed the sheets on the beds twice a week instead of once, took the rug-hooking class in adult education, and pitied their poor frustrated mothers, who had dreamed of having a career. Their only dream was to be perfect wives and mothers; their highest ambition to have five children and a beautiful house, their only fight to get and keep their husbands. They had no thought for the unfeminine problems of the world outside the home; they wanted the men to make the major decisions. They gloried in their role as women, and wrote proudly on the census blank: "Occupation: housewife."

For over fifteen years, the words written for women, and the words women used when they talked to each other, while their husbands sat on the other side of the room and talked shop or politics or septic tanks, were about problems with their children, or how to keep their husbands happy, or improve their children's school, or cook chicken or make slipcovers. Nobody argued whether women were inferior or superior to men; they were simply different. Words like "emancipation" and "career" sounded strange and embarrassing; no one had used them for years. When a Frenchwoman named Simone de Beauvoir wrote a book called *The Second Sex,* an American critic commented that she obviously "didn't know what life was all about," and besides, she was talking about French women. The "woman problem" in America no longer existed.

If a woman had a problem in the 1950's and 1960's, she knew that something must be wrong with her marriage, or with herself. Other women were satisfied with their lives, she thought. What kind of a woman was she if she did not feel this mysterious fulfillment waxing the kitchen floor? She was so ashamed to admit her dissatisfaction that she never knew how many other women shared it. If she tried to tell her husband, he didn't understand what she was talking about. She did not really understand it herself. For over fifteen years women in America found it harder to talk about this problem than about sex. Even the psychoanalysts had no name for it. When a woman went to a psychiatrist for help, as many women did, she would say, "I'm so ashamed," or "I must be hopelessly neurotic." "I don't know what's wrong with women today," a suburban psychiatrist said uneasily. "I only know something is wrong because most of my patients happen to be women. And their problem isn't sexual." Most women with this problem did not go to see a psychoanalyst, however. "There's nothing wrong really," they kept telling themselves. "There isn't any problem."

But on an April morning in 1959, I heard a mother of four, having coffee with four other mothers in a suburban development fifteen miles from New York, say in a tone of quiet desperation, "the problem." And the others knew, without words, that she was not talking about a problem with her husband, or her children, or her home. Suddenly they realized they all shared the same problem, the problem that has no name. They began, hesitantly, to talk about it. Later, after they had picked up their children at nursery school and taken them home to nap, two of the women cried, in sheer relief, just to know they were not alone.

Gradually I came to realize that the problem that has no name was shared by countless women in America. As a magazine writer I often interviewed women about problems with their children, or their marriages, or their houses, or their communities. But after a while I began to recognize the telltale signs of this other problem. I saw the same signs in suburban ranch houses and split-levels on Long Island and in New Jersey and Westchester County; in colonial houses in a small Massachusetts town; on patios in Memphis; in suburban and city apartments; in living rooms in the Midwest. Sometimes I sensed the problem, not as a reporter, but as a suburban housewife, for during this time I was also bringing up my own three children in Rockland County, New York. I heard echoes of the problem in college dormitories and semi-private maternity wards, at PTA meetings and luncheons of the League of Women Voters, at suburban cocktail parties, in station wagons waiting for trains, and in snatches of conversation overheard at Schrafft's. The groping words I heard from other women, on quiet afternoons when children were at school or on quiet evenings when husbands worked late, I think I understood first as a woman long before I understood their larger social and psychological implications.

Just what was this problem that has no name? What were the words women used when they tried to express it? Sometimes a woman would say "I feel empty somehow . . . incomplete." Or she would say, "I feel as if I don't exist." Sometimes she blotted out the feeling with a tranquilizer. Sometimes she thought the problem was with her husband, or her children, or that what she really needed was to redecorate her house, or move to a better neighborhood, or have an affair, or another baby. Sometimes, she went to a doctor with symptoms she could hardly describe: "A tired feeling . . . I get so angry with the children it scares me . . . I feel like crying without any reason." (A Cleveland doctor called it "the housewife's syndrome.") . . .

Most men, and some women, still did not know that this problem was real. But those who had faced it honestly knew that all the superficial remedies, the sympathetic advice, the scolding words and the cheering words were somehow drowning the problem in unreality. A bitter laugh was beginning to be heard from American women. They were admired, envied, pitied, theorized over until they were sick of it, offered drastic solutions or silly choices that no one could take seriously. They got all kinds of advice from the growing armies of marriage and child-guidance counselors, psychotherapists, and armchair psychologists, on how to adjust to their role as housewives. No other road to fulfillment was offered to American women in the middle of the twentieth century. Most adjusted to their role and suffered or ignored the problem that has no name. It can be less painful for a woman, not to hear the strange, dissatisfied voice stirring within her.

It is no longer possible to ignore that voice, to dismiss the desperation of so many American women. This is not what being a woman means, no matter what the experts say. For human suffering there is a reason; perhaps the reason has not been found because the right questions have not been asked, or pressed far enough. I do not accept the answer that there is no problem because American women have luxuries that women in other times and lands never dreamed of; part of the strange newness of the problem is that it cannot be understood in terms of the age-old material problems of man: poverty, sickness, hunger, cold. The women who suffer this problem have a hunger that food cannot fill. It persists in women whose husbands are struggling internes and law clerks, or prosperous doctors and lawyers; in wives of workers and executives who make $5,000 a year or $50,000. It is not caused by lack of material advantages; it may not even be felt by women preoccupied with desperate problems of hunger, poverty or illness. And women who think it will be solved by more money, a bigger house, a second car, moving to a better suburb, often discover it gets worse.

It is no longer possible today to blame the problem on loss of femininity: to say that education and independence and equality with men have made American women unfeminine. I have heard so many women try to deny this dissatisfied voice within themselves because it does not fit the pretty picture of femininity the experts have given them. I think, in fact, that this is the first clue to the mystery: the problem cannot be understood in the generally accepted terms by which scientists have studied women, doctors have treated them, counselors have advised them, and writers have written about them. Women who suffer this problem, in whom this voice is stirring, have lived their whole lives in the pursuit of feminine fulfillment. They are not career women (although career women may have other problems); they are women whose greatest ambition has been marriage and children. For the oldest of these women, these daughters of the American middle class, no other dream was possible. The ones in their forties and fifties who once had other dreams gave them up and threw themselves joyously into life as house-wives. For the youngest, the new wives and mothers, this was the only dream. They are the ones who quit high school and college to marry, or marked time in some job in which they had no real interest until they married. These women are very "feminine" in the usual sense, and yet they still suffer the problem. . . .

If I am right, the problem that has no name stirring in the minds of so many American women today is not a matter of loss of femininity or too much education, or the demands of domesticity. It is far more important than anyone recognizes. It is the key to these other new and old problems which have been torturing women and their husbands and children, and puzzling their doctors and educators for years. It may well be the key to our future as a nation and a culture. We can no longer ignore that voice within women that says: "I want something more than my husband and my children and my home."

President Kennedy's Commission on the Status of Women Opposes the ERA, 1963

Equality of rights under the law for all persons, male or female, is so basic to democracy and its commitment to the ultimate value of the individual that it must be reflected in the fundamental law of the land. The Commission believes that this principle of equality is embodied in the 5th and 14th amendments to the Constitution of the United States.

The 14th amendment prohibits any State from depriving any person of life, liberty, or property without due process of law and from denying to any person the equal protection of the laws. Essentially the same prohibitions apply to the Federal Government under the due process clause of the fifth amendment.

In the face of these amendments, however, there remain, especially in certain State laws and official practices, distinctions based on sex which discriminate against women. Both the States and the Federal Government may classify persons for the purpose of legislation, but the classification must be based on some reasonable ground. There exist some laws and official practices which treat men and women differently and which do not appear to be reasonable in the light of the multiple activities of women in present-day society.

The Commission considered various proposed methods of achieving greater recognition of the rights of women:

• Test litigation seeking redress from discrimination under constitutional safeguards looking to ultimate review by the U.S. Supreme Court.

• Amendment to the U.S. Constitution—the proposed equal rights amendment provides, in part, that *Equality of rights under the law shall not be denied or abridged . . . on account of sex.*

• State legislative action to eliminate discriminatory State laws.

Divergent viewpoints on these methods, particularly among national women's organizations and labor union groups, were made known in documents lodged with the Commission and in oral presentations at two hearings.

Since the Commission is convinced that the U.S. Constitution now embodies equality of rights for men and women, we conclude that a constitutional amendment need not now be sought in order to establish this principle. But judicial clarification is imperative in order that remaining ambiguities with respect to the constitutional protection of women's rights be eliminated.

Early and definitive court pronouncement, particularly by the U.S. Supreme Court, is urgently needed with regard to the validity under the 5th and 14th amendments of laws and official practices discriminating against women, to the end that the principle of equality become firmly established in constitutional doctrine.

Accordingly, interested groups should give high priority to bringing under court review cases involving laws and practices which discriminate against women.

At the same time, appropriate Federal, State, and local officials in all branches of government should be urged to scrutinize carefully those laws, regulations, and practices which distinguish on the basis of sex to determine whether they are justifiable in the light of contemporary conditions and to the end of removing archaic standards which today operate as discriminatory.

The Commission commends and encourages continued efforts on the part of all interested groups in educating the public and in urging private action, and action within the judicial, executive, and legislative branches of government, to the end that full equality of rights may become a reality.

Mary King on the Position of Women in SNCC, 1964

1. Staff was involved in crucial constitutional revisions at the Atlanta staff meeting in October. A large committee was appointed to present revisions to the staff. The committee was all men.
2. Two organizers were working together to form a farmers league. Without asking any questions, the male organizer immediately assigned the clerical work to the female organizer although both had had equal experience in organizing campaigns.
3. Although there are women in Mississippi project who have been working as long as some of the men, the leadership group in COFO is all men.
4. A woman in a field office wondered why she was held responsible for day to day decisions, only to find out later that she had been appointed project director but not told.
5. A fall 1964 personnel and resources report on Mississippi projects lists the number of people in each project. The section on Laurel however, lists not the number of persons, but "three girls."
6. One of SNCC's main administrative officers apologizes for appointment of a woman as interim project director in a key Mississippi project area.
7. A veteran of two years work for SNCC in two states spends her day typing and doing clerical work for other people in her project.
8. Any woman in SNCC, no matter what her position or experience, has been asked to take minutes in a meeting when she and other women are outnumbered by men.
9. The names of several new attorneys entering a state project this past summer were posted in a central movement office. The first initial and

last name of each lawyer was listed. Next to one name was written: (girl).

10. Capable, responsible and experienced women who are in leadership positions can expect to have to defer to a man on their project for final decision making.

11. A session at the recent October staff meeting in Atlanta was the first large meeting in the past couple of years where a woman was asked to chair.

Undoubtedly this list will seem strange to some, petty to others, laughable to most. The list could continue as far as there are women in the movement. Except that most women don't talk about these kinds of incidents, because the whole subject is not discussable—strange to some, petty to others, laughable to most. The average white person finds it difficult to understand why the Negro resents being called "boy," or being thought of as "musical" and "athletic," because the average white person doesn't realize that *he assumes he is superior*. And naturally he doesn't understand the problem of paternalism. So too the average SNCC worker finds it difficult to discuss the woman problem because of the assumption of male superiority. Assumptions of male superiority are as widespread and deep rooted and every much as crippling to the woman as the assumptions of white supremacy are to the Negro. Consider why it is in SNCC that women who are competent, qualified and experienced, are automatically assigned to the "female" kinds of jobs such as typing, desk work, telephone work, filing, library work, cooking and the assistant kind of administrative work but rarely the "executive" kind.

The woman in SNCC is often in the same position as that token Negro hired in a corporation. The management thinks that it has done its bit. Yet, every day the Negro bears an atmosphere, attitudes and actions which are tinged with condescension and paternalism, the most telling of which are when he is not promoted as the equally or less skilled whites are. This paper is anonymous. Think about the kinds of things the author, if made known, would have to suffer because of raising this kind of discussion. Nothing so final as being fired or outright exclusion, but the kinds of things which are killing to the insides—insinuations, ridicule, over-exaggerated compensations. This paper is presented anyway because it needs to be made known that many women in the movement are not "happy and contented" with their status. It needs to be made known that much talent and experience are being wasted by this movement when women are not given jobs commensurate with their abilities. It needs to be known that just as Negroes were the crucial factor in the economy of the cotton South, so too in SNCC, women are the crucial factor that keeps the movement running on a day to day basis. Yet they are not given equal say-so when it comes to day to day decision making. What can be done? Probably nothing right away. Most men in this movement are probably too threatened by the possibility of serious discussion on this subject. Perhaps this is because they have recently broken away from a matriarchal framework under which they may have grown up. Then too, many women are as unaware and insensitive to this subject as men, just as there are many Negroes who don't understand they are not free or who want to be part of white America. They don't understand that they have to give up their souls and stay in their place to be accepted. So too, many women, in order to be accepted by men, on men's terms, give themselves up to that caricature of what a woman is—unthinking, pliable, an ornament to please the man.

Maybe the only thing that can come out of this paper is discussion— amidst the laughter—but still discussion. (Those who laugh the hardest are often those who need the crutch of male supremacy the most.) And maybe some women will begin to recognize day to day discriminations. And maybe sometime in the future the whole of the women in this movement will become so alert as to force the rest of the movement to stop the discrimination and start the slow process of changing values and ideas so that all of us gradually come to understand that this is no more a man's world than it is a white world.

NOW's Statement of Purpose, 1966

We, men and women who hereby constitute ourselves as the National Organization for Women, believe that the time has come for a new movement toward true equality for all women in America, and toward a fully equal partnership of the sexes, as part of the world-wide revolution of human rights now taking place within and beyond our national borders.

The purpose of NOW is to take action to bring women into full participation in the mainstream of American society now, exercising all the privileges and responsibilities thereof in truly equal partnership with men.

We believe the time has come to move beyond the abstract argument, discussion and symposia over the status and special nature of women which has raged in America in recent years; the time has come to confront, with concrete action, the conditions that now prevent women from enjoying the equality of opportunity and freedom of choice which is their right as individual Americans, and as human beings.

NOW is dedicated to the proposition that women first and foremost are human beings, who, like all other people in our society, must have the chance to develop their fullest human potential. We believe that women can achieve such equality only by accepting to the full the challenges and responsibilities they share with all other people in our society, as part of the decision-making mainstream of American political, economic and social life.

We organize to initiate or support action, nationally or in any part of this nation, by individuals or organizations, to break through the silken curtain of prejudice and discrimination against women in government, industry, the professions, the churches, the political parties, the judiciary, the labor unions, in education, science, medicine, law, religion and every other field of importance in American society. . . .

There is no civil rights movement to speak for women, as there has been for Negroes and other victims of discrimination. The National Organization for Women must therefore begin to speak.

WE BELIEVE that the power of American law, and the protection guaranteed by the U.S. Constitution to the civil rights of all individuals, must be effectively applied and enforced to isolate and remove patterns of sex discrimination, to ensure equality of opportunity in employment and education, and equality of civil and political rights and responsibilities on behalf of women, as well as for Negroes and other deprived groups.

We realize that women's problems are linked to many broader questions of social justice; their solution will require concerted action by many groups. Therefore, convinced that human rights for all are indivisible, we expect to give active support to the common cause of equal rights for all those who suffer discrimination and deprivation, and we call upon other organizations committed to such goals to support our efforts toward equality for women.

WE DO NOT ACCEPT the token appointment of a few women to high-level positions in government and industry as a substitute for a serious continuing effort to recruit and advance women according to their individual abilities. To this end, we urge American government and industry to mobilize the same resources of ingenuity and command with which they have solved problems of far greater difficulty than those now impeding the progress of women.

WE BELIEVE that this nation has a capacity at least as great as other nations, to innovate new social institutions which will enable women to enjoy true equality of opportunity and responsibility in society, without conflict with their responsibilities as mothers and homemakers. In such innovations, America does not lead the Western world, but lags by decades behind many European countries. We do not accept the traditional assumption that a woman has to choose between marriage and motherhood, on the one hand, and serious participation in industry or the professions on the other. We question the present expectation that all normal women will retire from job or profession for ten or fifteen years, to devote their full time to raising children, only to reenter the job market at a relatively minor level. This in itself is a deterrent to the aspirations of women, to their acceptance into management or professional training courses, and to the very possibility of equality of opportunity or real choice, for all but a few women. Above all, we reject the assumption that these problems are the unique responsibility of each individual woman, rather than a basic social dilemma which society must solve. True equality of opportunity and freedom of choice for women requires such practical and possible innovations as a nationwide network of child-care centers, which will make it unnecessary for women to retire completely from society until their children are grown, and national programs to provide retraining for women who have chosen to care for their own children full time.

WE BELIEVE that it is as essential for every girl to be educated to her full potential of human ability as it is for every boy—with the knowledge that such education is the key to effective participation in today's economy and that, for a girl as for a boy, education can only be serious where there is expectation that it will be used in society. We believe that American educators are capable of devising means of imparting such expectations to girl students. Moreover, we consider the decline in the proportion of women receiving higher and professional education to be evidence of discrimination. This discrimination may take the form of quotas against the admission of women to colleges and professional schools; lack of encouragement by parents, counselors and educators; denial of loans or fellowships; or the traditional or arbitrary procedures in graduate and professional training geared in terms of men, which inadvertently discriminate against women. We believe that the same serious attention must be given to high school dropouts who are girls as to boys.

WE REJECT the current assumptions that a man must carry the sole burden of supporting himself, his wife, and family, and that a woman is automatically entitled to lifelong support by a man upon her marriage, or that marriage, home and family are primarily woman's world and responsibility—hers, to dominate, his to support. We believe that a true partnership between the sexes demands a different concept of marriage, an equitable sharing of the responsibilities of home and children and of the economic burdens of their support. We believe that proper recognition should be given to the economic and social value of homemaking and child care. To these ends, we will seek to open a reexamination of laws and mores governing marriage and divorce, for we believe that the current state of "half-equality" between the sexes discriminates against both men and women, and is the cause of much unnecessary hostility between the sexes.

WE BELIEVE that women must now exercise their political rights and responsibilities as American citizens. They must refuse to be segregated on the basis of sex into separate-and-not-equal ladies' auxiliaries in the political parties, and they must demand representation according to their numbers in the regularly constituted party committees—at local, state, and national levels—and in the informal power structure, participating fully in the selection of candidates and political decision-making, and running for office themselves.

IN THE INTERESTS OF THE HUMAN DIGNITY OF WOMEN, we will protest and endeavor to change the false image of women now prevalent in the mass media, and in the texts, ceremonies, laws, and practices of our major social institutions. Such images perpetuate contempt for women by society and by women for themselves. We are similarly opposed to all policies and practices—in church, state, college, factory, or office—which, in the guise of protectiveness, not only deny opportunities but also foster in women self-denigration, dependence, and evasion of responsibility, undermine their confidence in their own abilities and foster contempt for women.

NOW WILL HOLD ITSELF INDEPENDENT OF ANY POLITICAL PARTY in order to mobilize the political power of all women and men intent on our goals. We will strive to ensure that no party, candidate, President, senator, governor, congressman, or any public official who betrays or ignores the principle of full equality between the sexes is elected or appointed to office. If it is necessary to mobilize the votes of men and women who believe in our cause, in order to win for women the final right to be fully free and equal human beings, we so commit ourselves.

WE BELIEVE THAT women will do most to create a new image of women by *acting* now, and by speaking out in behalf of their own equality, freedom, and human dignity—not in pleas for special privilege, nor in enmity toward men, who are also victims of the current half-equality between the sexes—but in an active, self-respecting partnership with men. By so doing, women will develop confidence in their own ability to determine actively, in partnership with men, the conditions of their life, their choices, their future and their society.

Redstockings Manifesto, 1969

I. After centuries of individual and preliminary political struggle, women are uniting to achieve their final liberation from male supremacy. Redstockings is dedicated to building this unity and winning our freedom.

II. Women are an oppressed class. Our oppression is total, affecting every facet of our lives. We are exploited as sex objects, breeders, domestic servants, and cheap labor. We are considered inferior beings, whose only purpose is to enhance men's lives. Our humanity is denied. Our prescribed behavior is enforced by the threat of physical violence.

Because we have lived so intimately with our oppressors, in isolation from each other, we have been kept from seeing our personal suffering as a political condition. This creates the illusion that a woman's relationship with her man is a matter of interplay between two unique personalities, and can be worked out individually. In reality, every such relationship is a *class* relationship, and the conflicts between individual men and women are *political* conflicts that can only be solved collectively.

III. We identify the agents of our oppression as men. Male supremacy is the oldest, most basic form of domination. All other forms of exploitation and oppression (racism, capitalism, imperialism, etc.) are extensions of male supremacy: men dominate women, a few men dominate the rest. All power structures throughout history have been male-dominated and male-oriented. Men have controlled all political, economic and cultural institutions and backed up this control with physical force. They have used their power to keep women in an inferior position. *All men* receive economic, sexual, and psychological benefits from male supremacy. *All men* have oppressed women.

IV. Attempts have been made to shift the burden of responsibility from men to institutions or to women themselves. We condemn these arguments as evasions. Institutions alone do not oppress; they are merely tools of the oppressor. To blame institutions implies that men and women are equally victimized, obscures the fact that men benefit from the subordination of women, and gives men the excuse that they are forced to be oppressors. On the contrary, any man is free to renounce his superior position provided that he is willing to be treated like a woman by other men.

We also reject the idea that women consent to or are to blame for their own oppression. Women's submission is not the result of brainwashing, stupidity, or mental illness but of continual, daily pressure from men. We do not need to change ourselves, but to change men.

The most slanderous evasion of all is that women can oppress men. The basis for this illusion is the isolation of individual relationships from their political context and the tendency of men to see any legitimate challenge to their privileges as persecution.

V. We regard our personal experience, and our feelings about that experience, as the basis for an analysis of our common situation. We cannot rely on existing ideologies as they are all products of male supremacist culture. We question every generalization and accept none that are not confirmed by our experience.

Our chief task at present is to develop female class consciousness through sharing experience and publicly exposing the sexist foundation of all our institutions. Consciousness-raising is not "therapy," which implies the existence of individual solutions and falsely assumes that the male-female relationship is purely personal, but the only method by which we can ensure that our program for liberation is based on the concrete realities of our lives.

The first requirement for raising class consciousness is honesty, in private and in public, with ourselves and other women.

VI. We identify with all women. We define our best interest as that of the poorest, most brutally exploited woman.

We repudiate all economic, racial, educational or status privileges that divide us from other women. We are determined to recognize and eliminate any prejudices we may hold against other women.

We are committed to achieving internal democracy. We will do whatever is necessary to ensure that every woman in our movement has an equal chance to participate, assume responsibility, and develop her political potential.

VII. We call on all our sisters to unite with us in struggle.

We call on all men to give up their male privileges and support women's liberation in the interest of our humanity and their own.

In fighting for our liberation we will always take the side of women against their oppressors. We will not ask what is "revolutionary" or "reformist," only what is good for women.

The time for individual skirmishes has passed. This time we are going all the way.

July 7, 1969

❖ E S S A Y S

Carl M. Brauer, a researcher at Harvard University, in the first essay describes the peculiar conjunction of circumstances that led to the addition of the crucial word "sex" to Title VII of the Civil Rights Act of 1964—a victory with undertones of racism that occurred before the "new feminism" and, indeed, largely under the direction of the veteran politicians of the National Woman's Party. In the second selection, the University of Minnesota's Sara Evans looks at the consciousness-raising experiences of white and black women who participated in SNCC during 1964 and 1965, identifying the origins of the radical feminism that appeared later in the decade. Both these essays disclose the interconnectedness of the women's and civil rights movements—how they fostered each other and how they clashed with each other, sometimes simultaneously.

The "Old Feminism" and the Civil Rights Act of 1964

CARL M. BRAUER

Title VII of the 1964 Civil Rights Act prohibited discrimination in employment on the basis of sex as well as on the bases of race, color, religion, and national origin. This prohibition was added to the civil rights bill through an amendment on the floor of the House of Representatives by Howard Worth Smith of Virginia, an ardent opponent of the legislation as a whole. Because his motives in proposing the amendment were questionable, because of the occasionally facetious tone of the debate on the amendment, and because women's rights were generally not taken seriously then, the prohibition of sex discrimination originally tended to be lightly regarded, even after it became law. The Equal Employment Opportunity Commission (EEOC), established by Title VII to administer the law against employment discrimination, initially treated the ban on sex discrimination as something of a joke. Others, however, did not. In the first two years of enforcement, over four thousand charges of sex discrimination were lodged, representing roughly one-quarter of all complaints. EEOC's languid record of enforcement precipitated formation of the National Organization for Women in 1966, an important institutional development in the birth of the women's rights movement. Pressure from this and other groups and individuals, along with a changing consciousness about sex roles, led in time to more rigorous enforcement and generally sympathetic court rulings. By 1975 legal experts on women's rights could aptly characterize Title VII "the most comprehensive and important of all federal and state laws prohibiting employment discrimination."

Although the sex amendment eventually developed legal and practical significance that few, including its sponsor, seemed to anticipate in 1964,

Brauer, Carl M. "Women Activists, Southern Conservatives, and the Prohibition of Sex Discrimination in Title VII of the 1964 Civil Rights Act," *Journal of Southern History,* XLIX (1983), 37–56.

some people who played a critical, though generally unrecognized, role in its enactment relished the outcome. They were women—members of the National Woman's party (NWP) or members of Congress. Their advocacy of women's rights in 1963 and 1964 both foreshadowed the new women's rights movement and provided it with its most important legal tool to date. Able and committed though these pioneers were, they lacked numbers and power. Without a social movement behind them, they had to work for women's rights from marginal, rather than central, positions in politics, riding the forces unleashed by the powerful social movement of the time, the movement for black civil rights.

The campaigns for civil rights for blacks and for women in America have long been intertwined, sometimes complementing one another, at other times clashing. The fascinating story of the sex amendment's inclusion in the 1964 Civil Rights Act reflects a modern version of a historic ambiguity. In this recent instance the civil rights movement opened the door for women's rights, but it was the opponents, not the supporters, of federally mandated civil rights for blacks who escorted them across the threshold. Women's rights advocates requested and welcomed this act of chivalry; they were pragmatic, taking whatever assistance they could get. In doing so, they created an important legal basis for women in the future to claim equal rights with men, allowing them to become less dependent both upon men and chivalry.

With the burgeoning of the civil rights movement in the late 1950s and early 1960s some veteran women's rights advocates from the National Woman's party early saw a connection that might be forged between the rights of blacks and the rights of women. When Congress considered civil rights legislation in the late 1950s Alice Paul, the key figure in the National Woman's party since its founding in 1913, unsuccessfully promoted the idea of including women's rights. Shortly after President John Fitzgerald Kennedy asked Congress to enact sweeping new civil rights legislation in June 1963 some members of NWP again thought of connecting the two issues. "So much of the racial discussion, even that on the most elevated and inspired level," Mary F. Anderson wrote Alice Paul, "seems to assume that everybody but the Negro in this country has full equality." She hoped to see two birds, the "woman problem" and the "Negro problem," killed with one stone. An NWP loyalist from Richmond likewise was thrilled to hear Fulton Lewis, Jr., a conservative radio commentator, criticize Kennedy's omission of sex discrimination from his legislative proposals on civil rights.

At this time most of the NWP's several hundred active members were elderly, middle- or upper-class women, many of them either former suffragists or relatives of suffragists. Very few NWP members came from working-class backgrounds, and the party accepted no men. Often party members were lawyers, businesswomen, or other professionals. Typically, they revered their leader Alice Paul, who had as a young woman led some of America's most militant suffragist demonstrations. The historic Alva Belmont House in Washington served as headquarters, gathering place, and hotel for NWP members. Although other women's organizations, such as the National Federation of Business and Professional Women's Clubs, supported women's rights, NWP members alone and with pride called themselves feminists. NWP had one overriding objective—passage of the Equal Rights Amendment (ERA) to the federal Constitution. In that objective and in its embrace of feminism NWP served as a link between the women's rights movement that preceded World War I and the one that came into being in the mid-1960s. In other respects, however, NWP tended to look backward rather than forward. Its overwhelmingly and perhaps exclusively white membership evinced little concern for racial or economic equality. More of its members appeared to be politically conservative or reactionary than liberal or radical. Yet their friendships with conservative politicians proved invaluable in 1964.

The rise of the civil rights movement and the existence of a feminist organization with ties to conservative politicians constituted two essential ingredients in the story of the 1964 sex amendment, but the immediate precipitant came from the division that had existed among women activists over the Equal Rights Amendment ever since the National Woman's party had begun to promote it in the early 1920s. Proponents of ERA believed that it would eliminate all legally based barriers to women's advancement. Opponents feared its blanket effect. Though it would do some good, in their view, it would also do great harm by eliminating laws that favored women, such as those that set minimum wages and maximum hours, which they believed aided working-class women in particular. The debate over ERA had distinctly class, interest-group, and ideological overtones, pitting affluent, business-oriented, and politically conservative women against poor, union-oriented, and politically liberal women. The sources of congressional support for and opposition to ERA from the 1920s through the mid-1960s have not been systematically studied, but it is probably safe to say that most prounion congressmen were anti-ERA and most antiunion congressmen were pro-ERA.

The long-standing division among women over ERA accounted in part for the creation of the President's Commission on the Status of Women in 1961. Like other presidential candidates before him, Kennedy endorsed ERA during his campaign. This troubled Esther Peterson, an early Kennedy partisan and labor advocate, whom he appointed director of the Women's Bureau and assistant secretary of labor, and who was the most influential woman in his administration. Although she opposed ERA because it would void protective labor laws, Peterson had long advocated equal economic opportunities for women. For that reason she wanted a national commission to educate the public and promote legitimate change in this area. She hoped, too, that such a commission would focus attention on important, attainable objectives and divert it from agitation for ERA, which she regarded as misguided and futile.

Peterson largely determined the composition of the President's Commission on the Status of Women, which Eleanor Roosevelt chaired until her death in 1962. Seeking a viable compromise between supporters and opponents of ERA, the commission declared that equality of rights under law was already embodied in the Fifth and Fourteenth amendments and urged appropriate test cases to vindicate this principle. The commission, therefore, concluded in its report on October 11, 1963, that "a constitutional amendment need not now be sought in order to establish this principle." Although the inclusion of the word "now" represented something of a concession, NWP's leaders were enraged. "Esther Peterson loaded the Commission against equality," Emma Guffey Miller, the eighty-nine-year-old president of NWP and a prominent Democrat, wrote an ally. "But instead of informing the public that some members were for the Equal Rights Amendment they issued what they term a compromise, but it is really what [Walter] Reuther and Peterson wanted."

Had the commission endorsed ERA, Paul and the National Woman's party would probably have been content, at least for the moment, but the commission's refusal to do so angered and frustrated them, for what was the most prestigious national panel ever to report on the status of women had rejected their primary objective of the previous forty years. Including women in the coverage of the civil rights bill then pending thus presented a logical and available alternative. Perhaps, too, it was NWP's revenge. According to Paul's lieutenants, in her scheme to have sex added to the civil rights bill Paul hatched the idea either alone or in consultation with Emma Guffey Miller. The earliest documentary evidence are letters from her lieutenants to Howard W. Smith proposing the idea. On December 10, 1963, Butler Franklin wrote Smith that "This single word 'sex' would divert some of the high pressure which is being used to force this Bill through without proper attention to all of the effects of it." Five days later Nina Horton Avery wrote Smith in similar terms.

Paul called upon Franklin and Avery because they both knew Smith. Franklin, a constituent of Smith's, had worked successfully with him in establishing a national park in Fredericksburg, her hometown. The widow of a diplomat, Franklin had been encouraged by Paul to organize the wives of retired diplomats to lobby for improved widows' pensions. Avery, a former president of the Virginia Federation of Women's Business and Professional Clubs and a longtime member of NWP, had graduated from the University of North Carolina in 1917. Forty years later, after a career with a railroad where she encountered rank sexual discrimination, she became a lawyer. Both women were devoted to Paul, and neither appears to have had much sympathy for the civil rights bill. In the case of Avery one letter reveals blatant hostility to it. Paul herself, it should be noted, was probably not unsympathetic to black civil rights. Her Quaker background and her friendships with successful black women at least would so imply. Paul's only prejudice, one friend has noted, was the one she held against anyone opposed to ERA.

The choice of Smith as sponsor made sense for several reasons. He was chairman of the House Committee on Rules, which was preparing to consider the civil rights bill for clearance to the floor. Even more important, he was one of the most influential southern conservatives and had a background of support and friendship for NWP, for Alice Paul herself, and for the Equal

Rights Amendment. As far back as 1945 he had served as a sponsor of ERA. Probably not coincidentally, he had a long record of opposition to labor unions. Butler Franklin has also recalled that Paul fully expected Smith to welcome the opportunity to subject the civil rights bill to ridicule by adding sex to it.

The National Woman's party did not confine its lobbying to Smith, however, nor did it refrain from framing its appeal in implicitly racist, anti-Semitic, and xenophobic terms. On December 16 NWP unanimously adopted a resolution calling for inclusion of sex in the civil rights bill. ". . . the Civil Rights Bill would not even give protection against discrimination because of 'race, color, religion, or national origins,' to a *White Woman,* a *Woman of the Christian Religion,* or a *Woman of United States Origin,* according to the construction that appears to have been placed on the words . . . in Orders and Statements by Government officials," the resolution declared. . . .

The evidence on Smith's motives for deciding to offer a sex amendment is conflicting. On the one hand, he was adamantly opposed to the civil rights legislation and was a wily legislator. "I am a conservative and I have been scrambling and scratching around here for 32 years now," Smith told a reporter around this time, "and I have always found that when you are doing that you grasp any snickersnee you can get hold of and fight the best way you can." That the sex amendment was merely such a weapon in Smith's hand was implied by the light tone of his comments on the House floor. Martha Wright Griffiths, who defended Smith's amendment in the floor debate, has recalled Smith's explicitly telling her that the amendment was a joke.

On the other hand, Smith repeatedly claimed, during the debate and afterward, that he was sincere. Two of his former assistants have agreed, asserting that Smith fully expected the civil rights bill to become law and insisting that he simply did not sponsor or vote for things in which he did not believe. In an oral-history interview in 1973 Alice Paul recalled Smith's cautioning her that were he to sponsor the sex amendment, it would be handicapped since people would question his motives. Although no one will ever be able to say for sure, it is probably safe to guess that Smith's motives were mixed. He saw an opportunity to take a swipe at the civil rights bill, but as a chivalrous old southern gentleman he also believed that it was only fair that women, specifically white women, be granted the same legal protections that the government was preparing to afford black men. . . .

According to Nicholas deBelleville Katzenbach, deputy attorney general and the administration's principal manager of the legislation, the administration "believed, wrongly, that including sex might overburden the legislation." Although she was concerned about a sex amendment's possible effect on protective labor laws, Esther Peterson opposed an amendment primarily because she was worried that it might impede passage of the legislation. She believed that blacks, not women, faced the greatest discrimination, and she distrusted the amendment's proponents, Smith and the

National Woman's party. Consequently, she wrote a letter to Emanuel Celler opposing any sex amendments, citing the recent report of the President's Commission on the Status of Women which had recommended against including "sex" in an executive order on discrimination in federal employment. ". . . discrimination based on sex, the Commission believes," Peterson quoted, "involves problems sufficiently different from discrimination based on the other factors listed to make separate treatment preferable."

Although the administration succeeded in persuading Edith Green of its case, it failed to win over Martha Griffiths. A Democrat from East Lansing, Michigan, Griffiths was a shrewd, effective legislator and the first woman member of the powerful Ways and Means Committee. Long aware of discrimination against women, Griffiths joined the National Woman's party in 1955 but came to regard it as an ineffectual organization on Capitol Hill. Contrary to an assertion by Alice Paul, Griffiths insists that she planned to introduce a sex amendment to the civil rights bill on the floor of the House if Smith did not. She has recalled that she deferred to Smith simply because he would command many more votes, probably over a hundred more than she could. In addition to being knowledgeable on the Hill, Griffiths was a skilled debater and was not reluctant to speak her mind. Interestingly, she was also attuned quite early to the white backlash against civil rights that was developing in the North. Just prior to the 1962 election her sharp warnings helped persuade President Kennedy to delay issuing his executive order against discrimination in federally assisted housing until after the election. . . .

In his initial remarks Smith provoked considerable laughter on the floor by reading from a letter he had received from a woman in Omaha, Nebraska. She had facetiously proposed that he also offer an amendment correcting the imbalance between the number of men and women in the United States. "Just why the Creator would set up such an imbalance of spinsters, shutting off the 'right' of every female to have a husband of her own, is, of course, known only to nature. But I am sure you will agree that this is a grave injustice," Smith read to general amusement. Several times Smith insisted that he was serious about his amendment, but his comments appear to have been aimed at satirizing the logic behind the civil rights bill, which, in the view of Smith and many conservatives, was attempting to defy human nature. Smith did not dispute the perception of mock seriousness by presenting substantive arguments on behalf of his amendment. He did not, for example, cite data provided by the NWP of discrimination against women in employment.

Emanuel Celler argued against his amendment in somewhat the same fashion. He protested that women were not in the minority in his own house, that although during nearly fifty years of happy marriage he usually had the last two words, those words were "Yes, dear." He quoted from Esther Peterson's letter and then questioned the notion of establishing blanket legal equality between the sexes. Celler, who long kept the Equal Rights Amendment bottled up in his committee, directed most of his fire at ERA, not against Smith's much more limited proposal: "Would male citizens be justified in insisting that women share with them the burdens of compulsory military service? What would become of traditional family relationships? What about alimony? Who would have the obligation of supporting whom? Would fathers rank equally with mothers in the right of custody to children? What would become of the crimes of rape and statutory rape? Would the Mann Act be invalidated? Would the many State and local provisions regulating working conditions and hours of employment for women be struck down?" Celler apparently regarded Smith's amendment merely as the entering wedge toward adoption of the Equal Rights Amendment.

The two elderly chairmen then exchanged expressions of good-humored dismay at the other's position on the amendment and the bill, and they were soon joined by John Dowdy, Frances Payne Bolton of Ohio, a Republican and the senior woman in the House, and Ross Bass, a Democrat from Tennessee. They supported Smith's amendment, but in a light vein. The mood shifted, however, when Martha Griffiths spoke. ". . . I presume that if there had been any necessity to have pointed out that women were a second-class sex, the laughter would have proved it," she pointedly observed. ". . . I rise in support of the amendment," she declared, "primarily because I feel as a white woman when this bill has passed this House and the Senate and has been signed by the President that white women will be last at the hiring gate."

Griffiths questioned Celler sharply, posing hypothetical cases to try to show that colored women would be protected by the legislation as written but that white women would not. In the abstract, it was a weak contention that Celler might have exposed through a hypothetical case of his own, such as one where a large trucking company that employed only white male drivers was sued for a job first by a qualified black man and then by an equally qualified black woman. If the company agreed to hire the black man but refused to hire the black woman it could have argued reasonably that it was not discriminating against her on the basis of race but on the basis of sex. Griffiths stood on firmer ground when she defended Smith's amendment on the practical grounds that without it black women would at least have some legal recourse, whereas white women would have none. Seeking victory, however, neither side confined its arguments to reason and practicality. Celler had raised the specter of the disintegration of the family and a revolution in sex roles. Griffiths now appealed to the emotions of opponents of the legislation as a whole. ". . . a vote against this amendment today by a white man is a vote against his wife, or his widow, or his daughter, or his sister," she warned.

Three other congresswomen defended Smith's amendment, Katharine St. George, a Republican from New York, Catherine Dean May, a Republican from Washington, and Edna Kelly, a Democrat from Brooklyn. They emphasized the facts of job discrimination against women, called for equal treatment of women, and argued that the amendment would not rescind protective labor laws in the states. Nine southern men, including Smith, supported their cause on grounds of chivalry, equity, practicality, and emotion. Faced with a choice between hiring a white woman and a black woman of equal qualifications, Smith maintained, employers would choose the "colored woman" to prevent the government from suing them. "Some men in some areas of the country might support legislation which would discriminate against women," said James Russell Tuten of Georgia, "but never let it be said that a southern gentleman would vote for such legislation." "It is incredible to me that the authors of this monstrosity," Lucius Mendel Rivers, a senior South Carolinian, declared, ". . . would deprive the white woman of mostly Anglo-Saxon or Christian heritage equal opportunity before the employer."

Edith Green led opposition to the amendment, questioning the motives of its southern defenders. She did not know whether she would be called an "uncle Tom" or an "aunt Jane" for her stand; in self-defense, she cited her past record as an advocate of women's rights. "For every discrimination that has been made against a woman in this country," she asserted, "there has been 10 times as much discrimination against the Negro of this country." The amendment, she said, would "clutter up the bill and it may later— very well—be used to help destroy this section of the bill by some of the very people who today support it," she warned. She also read a letter opposing the amendment from the legislative representative of the American Association of University Women. Green's position was supported by four leading members of the bipartisan coalition working for the civil rights bill, Frank Thompson, Jr., a Democrat from New Jersey, James Roosevelt, a Democrat from California, John Vliet Lindsay, a Republican from New York, and Charles McCurdy Mathias, Jr., a Republican from Maryland.

When the vote was taken Martha Griffiths demanded tellers, and the amendment was approved 168 to 133. Reportedly, a woman in the gallery, which held a large representation from the NWP, cheered and was escorted out of the chamber. Unfortunately, no roll call was demanded, but Griffiths, who along with Celler was a teller, has recalled that most of the amendment's supporters were southerners and Republicans. Most nonsouthern Democrats voted against it. The amendment proved to be the only substantive change in the employment title made on the House floor. Interestingly, Smith's amendment inadvertently failed to insert "sex" in several places in Title VII, so two days later Frances Bolton offered a correcting amendment that the House accepted without objection, though Edith Green pointed out that the mistake illustrated that the original amendment had been ill-considered. Finally, Congressman Robert Paul Griffin, a Republican from Michigan, introduced an amendment that would have required that an individual filing a charge of sex discrimination certify that his or her spouse was unemployed and was unemployed at the time of the discriminatory act. This amendment provoked no debate and was defeated by a wide margin.

The National Woman's party rejoiced in the victory, sealed on February 10 when the House approved the civil rights bill, and claimed sole credit for itself. The press gave the amendment only light-hearted treatment, if any at all. "Finally, the Southerners were wearing down—but not that other compulsively rhetorical segment of U.S. society: The Women," reported *Newsweek,* sarcastically noting the approval of the "May Craig Amendment (named for the frilly-bonneted Maine reporter seen so often on TV) . . . ." The result, the Washington *Post* commented lightly in an editorial, demonstrated "who's head of the house up there on the Hill."

Some of the amendment's opponents, on the other hand, were dismayed. Griffiths has recalled that Jack Thomas Conway, a high-ranking official of the United Auto Workers, was furious at her. Esther Peterson reportedly said the amendment "might jeopardize the Civil Rights bill" and also had some harsh words for Griffiths, according to Griffiths. "This is the apples-and-bananas fallacy," Alexander Mordecai Bickel, the eminent constitutional lawyer from Yale, commented in the *New Republic.* "It is burdening with the regulation of bananas an agency already sufficiently overwhelmed with the problem of apples. That isn't the way to ensure adequate regulation of bananas; it is a way only to ensure less effective regulation of apples."

Approval by the House was, of course, only the first of two critical steps the amendment needed to take, so the women who had fought for it in the House continued their efforts in the Senate. Martha Griffiths has written that she called Elizabeth Sutherland ("Liz") Carpenter, an assistant to President and Mrs. Johnson, "and asked her to tell the President that if that amendment came out of that bill, I would send my speech door to door in every member's district who had voted against it, and in my opinion, those who voted against it would never return to Congress." Members of NWP lobbied in the Senate, with both opponents and supporters of the civil rights bill as a whole. Emma Guffey Miller tried unsuccessfully to persuade James Oliver Eastland of Mississippi, chairman of the Committee on the Judiciary and a prominent opponent of the legislation, whom she regarded as "a great friend of Equal Rights for Women," to propose sex amendments to other parts of the civil rights bill.

Liz Carpenter has no recollection of Griffiths' threat, but she has recalled that Johnson was always sympathetic to women's rights and that he had high regard for the women legislators with whom he had served. She has also said that at this point Esther Peterson lobbied hard for the amendment's retention. Peterson herself has explained her reversal simply by reflecting that once the amendment had cleared the House she could see no harm in leaving it in. Peterson's papers provide no additional evidence of her change in position, but Margaret A. Hickey, who knew Peterson well and who was head of the Citizens' Advisory Council on the Status of Women, has explained that Peterson believed in using every means available to help women. Peterson and Hickey opposed ERA because it threatened protective legislation, but it was unclear that adding sex to Title VII would also threaten protective legislation, contrary to Emanuel Celler's argument.

Hobart Taylor, Jr., a black assistant to Johnson and a friend of Martha Griffiths, has recalled Johnson's asking him about the sex amendment and his recommending that it be retained. Johnson also received pleas from a number of women activists from his home state of Texas and elsewhere asking him to support women's rights in the civil rights bill. Responding to these petitioners on his behalf on March 27, Peterson wrote that it was not practical to add further amendments to the bill, implying that Johnson would not seek the elimination of the present one. A month later Johnson himself signed a letter explicitly accepting Title VII as amended.

Given the positive support for the amendment as well as the lack of significant opposition to it, Johnson's decision to accept the work of the House is understandable, especially in light of the larger legislative struggle. The House bill was the strongest one Johnson might hope to have enacted. Most important, if the Senate approved a bill substantially the same as the House version, it would remove the necessity of sending the legislation to conference. A conference might well have effectively postponed action until the next Congress convened in 1965. Much of Johnson's efforts, therefore, as well as the efforts of his allies in the upper chamber, were directed at getting the Senate to keep the House bill substantially intact. They fully expected it to be subjected to an onslaught of weakening amendments there and did not want to encourage that process. In their eyes the sex amendment must have failed to warrant a potentially damaging fight. The prudent course was simply to let it be. When an aide to Hubert Horatio Humphrey, Jr., floor manager of the bill in the Senate, briefed him before an appearance on "Meet the Press" in early March, he noted that May Craig, who was "responsible for the women's equal rights provision . . . may ask about that." He suggested that Humphrey say, as he had said before, "I'm all for women," which is what Humphrey did. Peterson's reversal is, of course, also understandable in view of the larger legislative strategy. Thus, much as opposition to the civil rights bill proved decisive in adding the sex amendment in the House, the forces favoring the bill proved decisive in retaining the amendment in the Senate. . . .

The prohibition of sexual discrimination in employment, therefore, represented a convergence of conflicting, unrelated, and sometimes inherently ambiguous aims. It came about in the first place because of the rise of the civil rights movement, which led Presidents Kennedy and Johnson to seek legislation banning racially discriminatory practices. The ban on sex discrimination was merely an amendment to that legislation. Secondly, it resulted from the efforts of women activists, from both the feminist National Woman's party and from women in Congress, who sought the ban on its merits and who made the most out of the limited means they had available to them. Thirdly, it went through the House because of the support it received from southern opponents of the legislation as a whole, most notably from Howard Smith. Their motives are the hardest to determine precisely, but appear to have involved a combination of a desire to thwart or at least ridicule the legislation and a feeling of chivalry toward white women. Finally, the amendment also survived in the Senate because of legislative strategy, but this time the strategy of the legislation's supporters who wanted to get it approved as quickly and surely as possible, though here again women activists played an important role. Thus, the ban on sex discrimination came about because of both opposition to and support for the goals of the civil rights movement and because of the determination and skill of a relatively small number of women activists who anticipated the women's rights movement by several years.

The "New Feminism" and SNCC, 1964–1965

SARA EVANS

Black women struck the first blow for female equality in SNCC. Their half-serious rebellion in the spring of 1964 signaled their rising power within the organization. On the front lines black women received their share of beatings and incarceration, but back at the headquarters—the "freedom house"—they still, along with the white women, did the housework; in the offices they typed, and when the media sought a public spokesperson they took a back seat. Gradually they began to refuse this relegation to traditional sex roles. Ruby Doris Smith Robinson, no longer a daring teenager, was on the way to becoming one of the strongest figures in SNCC. Donna Richards reclaimed her maiden name after marrying Bob Moses, one of the most highly respected and influential men in the organization. Few understood her abrasive rejection of the slightest hint of sex stereotyping, though many remember it.

The patterns set by such women prepared the way for a new generation of black women who joined SNCC in 1964 and 1965 firmly believing that a woman could do anything a man could do. Fay Bellamy, Gwen Patton, Cynthia Washington, Jean Wiley, Muriel Tillinghast, Annie Pearl Avery—according to Gwen Patton they were equal to any man in SNCC. Taking women like Diane Nash and Ruby Doris Smith Robinson as models, they asserted themselves in unmistakable terms. Perhaps at some cost. Gwen Patton felt that they had to be "superwomen" to maintain their standing. Others pointed out that anyone who was effective in SNCC in those days— whether male or female—had to work long hours, take incredible risks, and refuse to be pushed around by anyone. Such toughness in women exacted a personal toll: "Probably if you looked at all our personal lives, we've probably had a very difficult personal life in terms of relations with men. Many of us made decisions not to go with SNCC men, because in some kind of way we didn't need to be fucked . . . it was very confusing." Patton's fumbling effort to explain the dilemma is revealing. She did not mean that women had no sexual needs, though they may have had to set them aside temporarily. The slang usage of "to be fucked" meant to be abused or taken advantage of. Women found it difficult to be tough and vulnerable at the same time.

Sara Evans, "Black Power Catalyst for Feminism" in *Personal Politics*, 83–101, copyright © 1979 by Sara Evans. Reprinted by permission of Alfred A. Knopf, Inc.

White women on the SNCC staff shared many of the tensions and ambiguities that affected black women. For a moment it seemed that their perceptions might coincide as the summer of 1964 raised sexual tensions to new heights. During the summer a group of women led by Ruby Doris Smith Robinson, and including Mary King, Casey Hayden, and Mary Varela, sat down to write a paper on the movement's failure to achieve sexual equality. Yet King, Hayden, and Varela lacked the self-assurance of Robinson, and they were "reluctant, and even afraid to sign" their own document. As white women they were in an increasingly ambiguous position in a black-led movement. Compared to the black women's growing power, whites were losing ground. Women like Hayden and King understood that their roles in many ways had to be supportive, that the movement must be led by blacks. Yet they also wanted to be taken seriously and to be appreciated for the contributions they made. To fresh recruits they appeared to be in a powerful position. They had an easy familiarity with the top leadership of SNCC, which bespoke considerable influence, and they could virtually run a freedom registration program; but at the same time they remained outside the basic political decisionmaking process. Staughton Lynd observed the contradiction during the summer of 1964. It was, he said, as if "they had power but they didn't have power." Mary King described herself and Hayden as being in "positions of relative powerlessness." To the extent that they were powerful, it was because they worked very hard. According to King, "if you were a hard worker and you were good, at least before 1965 . . . you could definitely have an influence on policy."

Thus white women, sensing their own precariousness within the movement, held back from a direct engagement on the issue of sex roles and instead raised it anonymously, thereby inadvertently drawing on the growing strength of black women. Racial tension and controversy swirled ominously about the November 1964 SNCC staff retreat at Waveland, Mississippi, where thirty-seven papers were presented on staff relations, SNCC's goals and ideology, organizing, decisionmaking, and race relations among the SNCC staff. On the mimeographed list of paper titles, Number 24 read: "SNCC Position Paper (Women in the Movement)"; the authors' names "withheld by request." Casey Hayden and Mary King had written it in discussion with Mary Varela. They debated whether to sign it, but concluded that they "wouldn't want it to be known at that point that [they were] writing such a thing." Thus they invited a fight but stayed out of the ring.

The paper indicted SNCC in strong "scrappy" language. "The woman in SNCC," Hayden and King charged, "is often in the same position as that token Negro hired in a corporation. The management thinks that it has done its bit. Yet, every day the Negro bears an atmosphere, attitudes and actions which are tinged with condescension and paternalism . . ." They used their own anonymity as an example: "Think about the kinds of things the authors, if made known, would have to suffer because of raising this kind of discussion. Nothing so final as . . . outright exclusion, but the kinds of things which are killing to the insides—insinuations, ridicule, over-exaggerated compensations." . . .

ked in among dozens of papers at the Waveland conference, the one
en in the movement provided a certain relief as the butt of ridicule
culation about its authorship, but otherwise went unnoticed. Many in
attendance at the conference have no memory of it at all. Others recall
sitting out on the dock after a day of acrimony and rocking with laughter at
Stokely Carmichael's rebuttal: "The only position for women in SNCC is
prone."

But this was the same conference at which Donna Richards reclaimed
her maiden name and her husband, Bob Moses, joined her, publicly adopting
his mother's maiden name, Parris. The issues asserted themselves in many
forms. Speculation about the authorship of the paper on women centered on
black women, particularly Ruby Doris Smith Robinson. Soon it was common knowledge among the white women who cared to remember that
Robinson had presented the paper herself. This myth has become a staple in
accounts of feminism in the civil rights movement. Its pervasiveness recognized an important truth: that black women occupied positions of growing
strength and power which challenged sexual discrimination. Their example
inspired white women outside SNCC's inner circles, who believed that if
anyone could be expected to write such a paper, it would be black women.
In particular the myth honored the memory of Robinson, and it took on
reality as tales of the memo and of Carmichael's response generated feminist
echoes throughout the country.

Carmichael's barb was for most who heard it a movement in-joke. It
recalled the sexual activity of the summer before—all those young white
women who supposedly had spent the summer "on their backs." The impact of the freedom summer, then, had both raised the issue of sex roles and
infused the issue with racial tensions. For a moment black and white women
had shared a feminist response to the position of women in SNCC, but
objectively black and white women lacked the trust and solidarity to call
each other "sister."

Soon after the summer, some black women in SNCC confronted black
men with the charge that "they could not develop relationships with the
black men because the men didn't have to be responsible to them because
they could always hook up with some white woman who had come down."
Deeply resentful of the attraction of white women to black men, they began
to search for definitions of femininity that included blackness. Robinson
herself hated white women for a period of years when she realized that they
represented a cultural ideal of beauty and "femininity" which by inference
defined black women as ugly and unwomanly.

The black women's angry demand for greater trust and solidarity with
black men constituted one part of an intricate maze of tensions and struggles
that were in the process of transforming SNCC and the civil rights movement as a whole. By the winter of 1965 SNCC had grown from a small band
of 16 to a swollen staff of 180, of whom 50 percent were white. The earlier
dream of a beloved community was dead. The vision of freedom lay crushed
under the weight of intransigent racism; of disillusionment with electoral
politics, the system, and nonviolence; and of the differences of race, class,

and culture within the movement itself. The anger of black women toward white women was only one element in the rising spirit of black nationalism. . . .

In addition, the summer that motivated young whites to explore their own potentials for courageous action and to build a new vision of social equality also exposed the weakness of a movement whose impulse was fundamentally moral. As they watched their idealism dashed upon the realities of power in American society, SNCC and CORE workers became bitter and disillusioned. The summer project had been built on the assumption that massive registration of black people in Mississippi, accomplished through publicity and the protection of the federal government against blatant repression, would create real power for black people. It was a naïve if noble attempt to force the political process to live up to the democratic ideals it professed.

Those hopes were crushed repeatedly. The federal government continued its policy of protecting people's rights by writing down whatever happened to them. Again and again the FBI and the Justice Department officials would stand by and take notes while demonstrators were beaten and illegally jailed. Finally, at the Atlantic City Democratic Convention the Mississippi Freedom Democratic Party (MFDP) brought the summer to a climax by offering a delegation to challenge the all-white representatives of the state Democratic machine. Fannie Lou Hamer testified to the Credentials Committee that she had been denied the right to vote, jailed, and beaten. At a rally the next day she repeated her story and pleaded: "We are askin' the American people, 'Is *this* the land of the free and the home of the brave?' "

The "compromise" that Democratic officials offered—to seat the white delegation if they would take a loyalty oath and to give delegate-at-large status to two from the MFDP—seemed to those who had spent the summer in Mississippi unthinkable. That they should be asked to give up so much to white racists after all they had suffered showed them, finally, that those in power could not be compelled by moral considerations. "Atlantic City was a powerful lesson," according to James Forman, "not only for the black people from Mississippi but for all of SNCC. . . . No longer was there any hope . . . that the federal government would change the situation in the Deep South." . . .

In the fall of 1964 tensions within the movement were massive and still growing, and SNCC's anarchic lack of structure served only to magnify them. When the staff met in October, eighty-five new members were voted in, most of them summer volunteers who had decided to stay on and work in Mississippi. The meeting was chaotic and alienating. Many recognized that the power base that had been built in Mississippi over the summer would soon be lost, because no one could agree on an internal structure for SNCC, much less build a unifying mass organization for Mississippi. Swollen in size, increasingly diverse, SNCC had split into mutually suspicious factions.

The dominant group in the fall meetings came to be known as the "freedom high" faction. Based largely in Mississippi, it represented a strange amalgam of the oldest and the newest elements in the southern movement.

The position they represented was an exaggerated version of "Let the people lead themselves," focusing on individual freedom, reacting against the least suggestion of authority, and romanticizing the local people. James Forman charges that this faction represented the northern middle-class students, black and white, who had come south in 1964. The middle-class idealism and moralism of these youth, added to their own cultural rebellion against the world their parents represented, led them to take ideas like "participatory democracy" to logical extremes. They were frequently the people who challenged any decision not made by the whole group or reached by consensus, who were continually suspicious of anyone they perceived as powerful. They prefigured the anarchist factions of SDS and the counterculture's "do your own thing" focus on lifestyle and drug culture. Jack Newfield described them more sympathetically as emerging from the summer of 1964 "in the image of Camus' existential rebel," with a "mystical and transcendental faith in the inherent goodness of the poor, even in their infinite wisdom." This was not simply a set of ideas imported from the north. Rather, it was the final distillation of the "beloved community" in the face of too frequent defeat. The informal leadership of the "freedom high" faction was made up not of northern students but of black and white southerners who had been in the movement from 1960. For them the issues were fundamentally moral, and the validation of the individual's sense of personal worth within the movement was the prerequisite for effective action outside it. Racial hostility and a formal, hierarchical structure within the movement thus represented a betrayal of the beloved community, the vision which now formed a core of their identity. And it came at the moment when the physical and psychological damage they had sustained in three or four years of constant work left them desperately in need of a warm, loving, sustaining community.

The "freedom highs" were opposed by the "structure faction," generally longtime field staff whose growing militance and nationalism was born of a disillusion with whites, the impatience of frustrated anger, and a wish to bring coherence and order to the movement, to shift from moral issues to questions of power. James Forman and Ruby Doris Smith Robinson led the fight against hiring the eighty-five new staff members, arguing that SNCC should be black-dominated and black-led and that SNCC staff should undergo both careful training and security checks before being hired.

The southern black field workers carried with them wounds that refused to heal and that intensified the atmosphere of suspicion and recrimination: bitterness that the press was outraged when whites were murdered and hardly noticed when blacks died in the struggle; awareness that the country reveled in stories of blue-eyed blondes living with poor blacks and ignored blacks who had been working in Mississippi for years:

> Didn't anyone care about Willie Peacock, born and raised on a Mississippi plantation, who couldn't go back to his home town because he was an organizer for SNCC and the white people would kill him if he went to see his mother? Apparently not.

Hostility toward whites in the movement also reflected a rising militance and impatience with nonviolence, magnified by events outside the south. In 1964 there was the Harlem riot; in 1965 Watts erupted. African nations were demanding and winning their independence with slogans about colonialism, pan-Africanism, and African socialism. Malcolm X began to voice anti-white attitudes that American blacks had previously expressed only to each other or had been afraid to acknowledge at all. Many were attracted to his angry words; many more were jolted by his violent death in the spring of 1965. Alienation from the concept of nonviolence and "black and white together" was completed with the Selma campaign that same spring, when the breach between SNCC militants and the more traditional approach of SCLC moderates became unbridgeable. As Julius Lester put it:

> Each organizer had his own little techniques for staying alive. Non-violence might do something to the moral conscience of a nation, but a bullet didn't have morals, and it was beginning to occur to more and more organizers that white folks had plenty more bullets than they had conscience.

By February 1965, the "structure faction" gathered its forces and prevailed in a "stormy," "traumatic," and "confusing" SNCC staff meeting. The road to "black power" was clear.

When Mary King asserted that "if you were a hard worker and you were good, at least before 1965 . . . you could definitely have an influence on policy," the key phrase in the quote was "at least before 1965." By 1965 the position of whites in SNCC, especially southern whites whose goals had been shaped by the vision of the "beloved community," was in painful decline. Whites were less and less welcome in any part of the civil rights movement. An activist in CORE and COFO described the situation:

> Hostility against white faces was such that even those few white organizers who had earned the respect of their black co-workers found it impossible, and unnecessarily disagreeable, to operate any longer within existing movement organizations. . . . Many had been questioning their own roles for a long time, and . . . their approach had always been that of consciously working toward their own elimination from leadership positions.

Most northerners simply returned home, changed but confused, fearful that in their attempt to do right they had done wrong. The two northern white women in the inner circles of the SNCC staff, Betty Garman and Dottie Miller Zellner, sided with the "structure faction" and finally agreed that they too must go. But for southern white women who had devoted several years of their lives to the vision of a beloved community, the rejection of nonviolence and the shift toward a more ideological, centralized, and black nationalist movement was disillusioning and made them bitter. One southern woman felt that she "could understand [the movement] in Southern Baptist terms like 'beloved community,' but not in Marxist terms—that was someone else's fight and someone else's world." And Mary King recalled:

> It was very sad to see something that was so creative and so dynamic and so strong [disintegrating]. . . . I was terribly disappointed for a long time. . . .

> I was most affected by the way that the black women turned against me. That hurt more than the guys. But it had been there, you know. You could see it coming. . . .

Many women had simply "burned out" and left the deep south. Jane Stembridge had withdrawn quietly to write. SSOC provided an institutional context within which other whites like Sue Thrasher, Cathy Cade, and Cathy Barrett could continue to function. But for Casey Hayden and Mary King, there was no alternative. Their lives had centered in SNCC for years and they could neither imagine leaving nor give up the moral idealism of the "beloved community"—the south was home. What would they do here without the movement?

In the fall of 1965 King and Hayden spent several days of long discussion in the mountains of Virginia. Both of them were on their way out of the movement, although they were not fully conscious of that fact. Finally they decided to write a "kind of memo" addressed to "a number of other women in the peace and freedom movements." In it they argued that women, like blacks,

> . . . seem to be caught up in a common-law caste system that operates, sometimes subtly, forcing them to work around or outside hierarchical structures of power which may exclude them. Women seem to be placed in the same position of assumed subordination in personal situations too. It is a caste system which, at its worst, uses and exploits women.

King and Hayden set the precedent of contrasting the movement's egalitarian ideas with the replication of sex roles within it. They noted the ways in which women's positions in society determined such roles in the movement as cleaning house, doing secretarial work, and refraining from active or public leadership. At the same time, they observed,

> having learned from the movement to think radically about the personal worth and abilities of people whose role in society had gone unchallenged before, a lot of women in the movement have begun trying to apply those lessons to their own relations with men. Each of us probably has her own story of the various results. . . .

They spoke of the pain of trying to put aside "deeply learned fears, needs, and self-perceptions . . . and . . . to replace them with concepts of people and freedom learned from the movement and organizing." In this process many people in the movement had questioned basic institutions such as marriage and child rearing. Indeed, such issues had been discussed over and over again, but seriously only among women. The usual male response was laughter, and women were left feeling silly. Hayden and King lamented the "lack of community for discussion: Nobody is writing, or organizing or talking publicly about women, in any way that reflects the problems that various women in the movement come across. . . ." Yet despite their feelings of invisibility, their words also demonstrated the ability to take the considerable risks involved in sharp criticisms. Through the movement they had developed too much self-confidence and self-respect to accept subordinate roles passively.

The memo was addressed principally to black women—longtime friends and comrades-in-nonviolent-arms—in the hope that "perhaps we can start to talk with each other more openly than in the past and create a community of support for each other so we can deal with ourselves and others with integrity and can therefore keep working." In some ways it was a parting attempt to halt the metamorphosis in the civil rights movement from nonviolence to nationalism, from beloved community to black power. It expressed Casey Hayden and Mary King's pain and isolation, as white women in the movement. The black women who received it were on a different historic trajectory. They would fight some of the same battles as women, but in a different context and in their own way.

This "kind of memo" represented a flowering of women's consciousness that articulated contradictions felt most acutely by middle-class white women. While black women had been gaining strength and power within the movement, the white women's position—at the nexus of sexual and racial conflicts—had become increasingly precarious. Their feminist response, then, was precipitated by loss in the immediate situation; but it was a sense of loss heightened against the background of the new strength and self-worth the movement had allowed them to develop. Like their foremothers in the nineteenth century they confronted this dilemma with the tools the movement itself had given them: a language to name and describe oppression; a deep belief in freedom, equality, and community—soon to be translated into "sisterhood"; a willingness to question and challenge any social institution that failed to meet human needs; and the ability to organize.

It is not surprising that the issues were defined and confronted first by southern women, whose consciousness developed in a context that inextricably and paradoxically linked the fate of women and black people. These spiritual daughters of Sarah and Angelina Grimké kept their expectations low in November 1965. "Objectively," they said, "the chances seem nil that we could start a movement based on anything as distant to general American thought as a sex-caste system." But change was in the air and youth was on the march. In the north there were hundreds of women who had shared in the southern experience for a week, a month, a year, and thousands more who participated vicariously or worked to extend the struggle for freedom and equality into northern communities. Thus the fullest expressions of conscious feminism within the civil rights movement ricocheted off the fury of black power and landed with explosive force in the northern, white new left. One month later, women who had read the memo staged an angry walkout from a national SDS conference in Champaign-Urbana, Illinois. The only man to defend their action was a black man from SNCC.

✢ *FURTHER READING*

Lois W. Banner, *Women in Modern America* (1984)
Maren Lockwood Carden, *The New Feminist Movement* (1974)
William Chafe, *Women and Equality* (1977)
Robert Daniel, *American Women in the Twentieth Century* (1987)

Barbara Deckard, *The Women's Movement* (1983)

John D'Emilio, *Sexual Politics, Sexual Communities: The Making of a Homosexual Minority in the United States, 1940–1970* (1983)

Jo Freeman, *The Politics of Women's Liberation* (1975)

Cynthia Harrison, "A 'New Frontier' for Women: The Public Policy of the Kennedy Administration," *Journal of American History,* LXVII (1981), 630–46

Judith Hole and Ellen Levine, *Rebirth of Feminism* (1971)

Gloria Joseph and Jill Lewis, *Common Differences: Conflicts in Black and White Feminist Perspectives* (1981)

Nancy McGlen and Karen O'Connor, *Women's Rights* (1983)

Mary Rothschild, "White Women Volunteers in the Freedom Summers: Their Life and Work in a Movement for Social Change," *Feminist Studies,* V (1979), 466–95

Leila Rupp and Verta Taylor, *Survival in the Doldrums: The American Women's Rights Movement, 1945 to the 1960s* (1987)

Nancy P. Weiss, "Mother, the Invention of Necessity: Dr. Spock's *Baby and Child Care,*" American Quarterly, XXIX (1977), 519–46

Gayle Graham Yates, *What Women Want: The Ideas of the Movement* (1975)

CHAPTER
15

Feminism and Antifeminism
in the 1980s

After the successes of the late 1960s and 1970s, feminism appeared to founder in the 1980s. Two things symbolized the feminist movement's inability to achieve its goals: the failure of a sufficient number of state legislatures to ratify the long-sought Equal Rights Amendment, which had finally been adopted by Congress in 1972, and the election of Ronald Reagan as president in November 1980. As the representative of a New Right backlash that challenged everything feminism stood for, Reagan's strength seemed to point up feminism's weaknesses. He and his supporters emphasized what they called "traditional family values," which included opposition to abortion and to the employment outside the home of mothers with young children. They characterized feminists as selfish individuals who were abandoning women's true calling. The evidently strong appeal of these ideas among the American people led a number of feminist scholars and activists to reflect on what had gone wrong. Why had the promise of the 1970s not been wholly fulfilled? Are prolife and profamily issues used as fronts by conservatives to gain more power? Why has the family become such a focal point for politics in the eighties? In what ways does Friedan help or hinder the women's movement by placing so much emphasis on family, and by including men in it? What fears in women does Schlafly appeal to? What bearing might "the feminization of poverty" have on the future of feminism?

❖ DOCUMENTS

The first document, the Equal Rights Amendment, approved by Congress in 1972 and sent to the states for ratification, used simple wording first proposed by Susan B. Anthony in the nineteenth century. In 1973, the U.S. Supreme Court's divided opinion in *Frontiero* v. *Richardson* (the second selection) reflected the continuing unwillingness of a majority of its members to apply to the circumstances of women the strict tests established to judge racial discrimination. Nevertheless, the language of the opinion written by Justice Brennan contained the strongest indictment of sex discrimination the court has yet endorsed. That same year saw the issuing of the still highly controversial opinion in *Roe* v. *Wade* (excerpted in the third document), which restricted the states' authority to pass laws prohibiting abortion. In the fourth selection, Phyllis Schlafly, "the sweetheart of the silent majority," explored what she saw in 1977 as the inherent differences between men and women. In the fifth document, which appeared in 1980, the Reverend Jerry Falwell gave his views on the potential destructiveness of the ERA. The last selection is Betty Friedan's 1981 reflections on the feminist movement, proposing that it should begin its "second stage."

The Equal Rights Amendment, 1972

[Sent to the states, 1972]

Section 1   Equality of rights under the law shall not be denied or abridged by the United States or by any State on account of sex.

Section 2   The Congress shall have the power to enforce, by appropriate legislation, the provisions of this article.

Section 3   This amendment shall take effect two years after the date of ratification.

Frontiero v. *Richardson*, 1973

Mr. Justice Brennan announced the judgment of the Court and an opinion in which Mr. Justice Douglas, Mr. Justice White, and Mr. Justice Marshall join.

The question before us concerns the right of a female member of the uniformed services to claim her spouse as a "dependent" for the purposes of obtaining increased quarters allowances and medical and dental benefits on an equal footing with male members. Under these statutes, a serviceman may claim his wife as a "dependent" without regard to whether she is in fact dependent upon him for any part of her support. A servicewoman, on the other hand, may not claim her husband as a "dependent" under these programs unless he is in fact dependent upon her for over one-half of his support. Thus, the question for decision is whether this difference in treatment constitutes an unconstitutional discrimination against servicewomen in violation of the Due Process Clause of the Fifth Amendment. A three-judge District Court for the Middle District of Alabama, one judge dissenting, rejected this contention and sustained the constitutionality of the provisions of the statutes making this distinction. We reverse. . . .

Appellant Sharron Frontiero, a lieutenant in the United States Air Force, sought increased quarters allowances, and housing and medical benefits for her husband, appellant Joseph Frontiero, on the ground that he was her "dependent." Although such benefits would automatically have been granted with respect to the wife of a male member of the uniformed services, appellant's application was denied because she failed to demonstrate that her husband was dependent on her for more than one-half of his support. Appellants then commenced this suit, contending that, by making this distinction, the statutes unreasonably discriminate on the basis of sex in violation of the Due Process Clause of the Fifth Amendment. In essence, appellants asserted that the discriminatory impact of the statutes is twofold: first, as a procedural matter, a female member is required to demonstrate her spouse's dependency, while no such burden is imposed upon male members; and, second, as a substantive matter, a male member who does not provide more than one-half of his wife's support receives benefits, while a similarly situated female member is denied such benefits. Appellants therefore sought a permanent injunction against the continued enforcement of these statutes and an order directing the appellees to provide Lieutenant Frontiero with the same housing and medical benefits that a similarly situated male member would receive.

Although the legislative history of these statutes sheds virtually no light on the purposes underlying the differential treatment accorded male and female members, a majority of the three-judge District Court surmised that Congress might reasonably have concluded that, since the husband in our society is generally the "breadwinner" in the family—and the wife typically the "dependent" partner—"it would be more economical to require married female members claiming husbands to prove actual dependency than to extend the presumption of dependency to such members." Indeed, given the fact that approximately 99% of all members of the uniformed services are male, the District Court speculated that such differential treatment might conceivably lead to a "considerable saving of administrative expense and manpower.". . .

There can be no doubt that our Nation has had a long and unfortunate history of sex discrimination. Traditionally, such discrimination was rationalized by an attitude of "romantic paternalism" which, in practical effect, put women, not on a pedestal, but in a cage. . . .

Our statute books gradually became laden with gross, stereotyped distinctions between the sexes and, indeed, throughout much of the 19th century the position of women in our society was, in many respects, comparable to that of blacks under the pre–Civil War slave codes. Neither slaves nor women could hold office, serve on juries, or bring suit in their own names, and married women traditionally were denied the legal capacity to hold or convey property or to serve as legal guardians of their own children. And although blacks were guaranteed the right to vote in 1870, women were denied even that right—which is itself "preservative of other basic civil and political rights"—until adoption of the Nineteenth Amendment half a century later.

It is true, of course, that the position of women in America has improved markedly in recent decades. Nevertheless, it can hardly be doubted that, in part because of the high visibility of the sex characteristic, women still face pervasive, although at times more subtle, discrimination in our educational institutions, in the job market and, perhaps most conspicuously, in the political arena. . . .

Moreover, since sex, like race and national origin, is an immutable characteristic determined solely by the accident of birth, the imposition of special disabilities upon the members of a particular sex because of their sex would seem to violate the basic concept of our system that legal burdens should bear some relationship to individual responsibility. . . ."

And what differentiates sex from such nonsuspect statutes as intelligence or physical disability, and aligns it with the recognized suspect criteria, is that the sex characteristic frequently bears no relation to ability to perform or contribute to society. As a result, statutory distinctions between the sexes often have the effect of invidiously relegating the entire class of females to inferior legal status without regard to the actual capabilities of its individual members. . . .

With these considerations in mind, we can only conclude that classifications based upon sex, like classifications based upon race, alienage, or national origin, are inherently suspect, and must therefore be subjected to strict judicial scrutiny. Applying the analysis mandated by that stricter standard of review, it is clear that the statutory scheme now before us is constitutionally invalid. . . .

Mr. Justice Stewart concurs in the judgment, agreeing that the statutes before us work an invidious discrimination in violation of the Constitution.

Mr. Justice Rehnquist dissents for the reasons stated by Judge Rives in his opinion for the District Court.

Mr. Justice Powell, with whom The Chief Justice and Mr. Justice Blackmun join, concurring in the judgment.

I agree that the challenged statutes constitute an unconstitutional discrimination against servicewomen in violation of the Due Process Clause of the Fifth Amendment, but I cannot join the opinion of Mr. Justice Brennan, which would hold that all classifications based upon sex, "like classifications based upon race, alienage, and national origin," are "inherently suspect and must therefore be subjected to close judicial scrutiny." It is unnecessary for the Court in this case to characterize sex as a suspect classification, with all of the far-reaching implications of such a holding. . . .

There is another, and I find compelling, reason for deferring a general categorizing of sex classifications as invoking the strictest test of judicial scrutiny. The Equal Rights Amendment, which if adopted will resolve the substance of this precise question, has been approved by the Congress and submitted for ratification by the States. If this Amendment is duly adopted, it will represent the will of the people accomplished in the manner prescribed by the Constitution. By acting prematurely and unnecessarily, as I view it, the Court has assumed a decisional responsibility at the very time when state legislatures, functioning within the traditional democratic process, are debating the proposed Amendment. It seems to me that this reaching out to pre-empt by judicial action a major political decision which is currently in process of resolution does not reflect appropriate respect for duly prescribed legislative processes.

There are times when this Court, under our system, cannot avoid a constitutional decision on issues which normally should be resolved by the elected representatives of the people. But democratic institutions are weakened, and confidence in the restraint of the court is impaired, when we appear unnecessarily to decide sensitive issues of broad social and political importance at the very time they are under consideration within the prescribed constitutional processes.

Roe v. *Wade,* 1973

Mr. Justice Blackmun delivered the opinion of the Court.

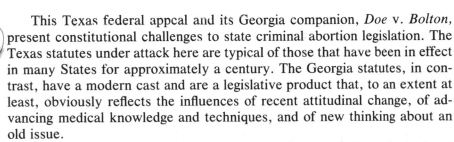

This Texas federal appeal and its Georgia companion, *Doe* v. *Bolton,* present constitutional challenges to state criminal abortion legislation. The Texas statutes under attack here are typical of those that have been in effect in many States for approximately a century. The Georgia statutes, in contrast, have a modern cast and are a legislative product that, to an extent at least, obviously reflects the influences of recent attitudinal change, of advancing medical knowledge and techniques, and of new thinking about an old issue.

We forthwith acknowledge our awareness of the sensitive and emotional nature of the abortion controversy, of the vigorous opposing views, even among physicians, and of the deep and seemingly absolute convictions that the subject inspires. One's philosophy, one's experiences, one's exposure to the raw edges of human existence, one's religious training, one's attitudes toward life and family and their values, and the moral standards one establishes and seeks to observe, are all likely to influence and to color one's thinking and conclusions about abortion.

In addition, population growth, pollution, poverty, and racial overtones tend to complicate and not to simplify the problem.

Our task, of course, is to resolve the issue by constitutional measurement, free of emotion and of predilection. We seek earnestly to do this, and, because we do, we have inquired into, and in this opinion place some emphasis upon, medical and medical-legal history and what that history reveals about man's attitudes toward the abortion procedure over the centuries. . . .

It perhaps is not generally appreciated that the restrictive criminal abortion laws in effect in a majority of States today are of relatively recent vintage. Those laws, generally proscribing abortion or its attempt at any time during pregnancy except when necessary to preserve the pregnant woman's life, are not of ancient or even of common-law origin. Instead, they derive from statutory changes effected, for the most part, in the latter half of the 19th century. . . .

Three reasons have been advanced to explain historically the enactment of criminal abortion laws in the 19th century and to justify their continued existence.

It has been argued occasionally that these laws were the product of a Victorian social concern to discourage illicit sexual conduct. Texas, however, does not advance this justification in the present case, and it appears that no court or commentator has taken the argument seriously. . . .

A second reason is concerned with abortion as a medical procedure.

When most criminal abortion laws were first enacted, the procedure was a hazardous one for the woman. . . . Thus, it has been argued that a State's real concern in enacting a criminal abortion law was to protect the pregnant woman, that is, to restrain her from submitting to a procedure that placed her life in serious jeopardy.

Modern medical techniques have altered this situation. Appellants and various amici refer to medical data indicating that abortion in early pregnancy, this is, prior to the end of the first trimester, although not without its risk, is now relatively safe. Mortality rates for women undergoing early abortions, where the procedure is legal, appear to be as low as or lower than the rates for normal childbirth. Consequently, any interest of the State in protecting the woman from an inherently hazardous procedure, except when it would be equally dangerous for her to forgo it, has largely disappeared. Of course, important state interests in the area of health and medical standards do remain. . . .

The third reason is the State's interest—some phrase it in terms of duty—in protecting prenatal life. Some of the argument for this justification rests on the theory that a new human life is present from the moment of conception. The State's interest and general obligation to protect life then extends, it is argued, to prenatal life. Only when the life of the pregnant mother herself is at stake, balanced against the life she carries within her, should the interest of the embryo or fetus not prevail. Logically, of course, a legitimate state interest in this area need not stand or fall on acceptance of the belief that life begins at conception or at some other point prior to live birth. In assessing the State's interest, recognition may be given to the less rigid claim that as long as at least *potential* life is involved, the State may assert interests beyond the protection of the pregnant woman alone. . . .

The Constitution does not explicitly mention any right of privacy. In a line of decisions, however, the Court has recognized that a right of personal privacy, or a guarantee of certain areas or zones of privacy, does exist under the Constitution. . . .

This right of privacy, whether it be founded in the Fourteenth Amendment's concept of personal liberty and restrictions upon state action, as we feel it is, or, as the District Court determined, in the Ninth Amendment's reservation of rights to the people, is broad enough to encompass a woman's decision whether or not to terminate her pregnancy. The detriment that the State would impose upon the pregnant woman by denying this choice altogether is apparent. Specific and direct harm medically diagnosable even in early pregnancy may be involved. Maternity, or additional offspring, may force upon the woman a distressful life and future. Psychological harm may be imminent. Mental and physical health may be taxed by child care. There is also the distress, for all concerned, associated with the unwanted child, and there is the problem of bringing a child into a family already unable, psychologically and otherwise, to care for it. In other cases, as in this one, the additional difficulties and continuing stigma of unwed motherhood may be involved. All these are factors the woman and her responsible physician necessarily will consider in consultation.

On the basis of elements such as these, appellant and some amici argue that the woman's right is absolute and that she is entitled to terminate her pregnancy at whatever time, in whatever way, and for whatever reason she alone chooses. With this we do not agree. Appellant's arguments that Texas either has no valid interest at all in regulating the abortion decision, or no interest strong enough to support any limitation upon the woman's sole determination, is unpersuasive. The Court's decisions recognizing a right of privacy also acknowledge that some state regulation in areas protected by that right is appropriate. As noted above, a State may properly assert important interests in safeguarding health, in maintaining medical standards, and in protecting potential life. At some point in pregnancy, these respective interests become sufficiently compelling to sustain regulation of the factors that govern the abortion decision. The privacy right involved, therefore, cannot be said to be absolute. . . .

We, therefore, conclude that the right of personal privacy includes the abortion decision, but that this right is not unqualified and must be considered against important state interests in regulation. . . .

The appellee and certain amici argue that the fetus is a "person" within the language and meaning of the Fourteenth Amendment. In support of this, they outline at length and in detail the well-known facts of fetal development. If this suggestion of personhood is established, the appellant's case, of course, collapses, for the fetus' right to life is then guaranteed specifically by the Amendment. The appellant conceded as much on reargument. On the other hand, the appellee conceded on reargument that no case could be cited that holds that a fetus is a person within the meaning of the Fourteenth Amendment.

The Constitution does not define "person" in so many words. Section 1 of the Fourteenth Amendment contains three references to "person." The first, in defining "citizens," speaks of "persons born or naturalized in the United States." The word also appears both in the Due Process Clause and in the Equal Protection Clause. "Person" is used in other places in the Constitution. . . . But in nearly all these instances, the use of the word is such that it has application only postnatally. None indicates, with any assurance, that it has any possible prenatal application.

All this, together with our observation, supra, that throughout the major portion of the 19th century prevailing legal abortion practices were far freer than they are today, persuades us that the word "person," as used in the Fourteenth Amendment, does not include the unborn. . . .

Texas urges that, apart from the Fourteenth Amendment, life begins at conception and is present throughout pregnancy, and that, therefore, the State has a compelling interest in protecting that life from and after conception. We need not resolve the difficult question of when life begins. When those trained in the respective disciplines of medicine, philosophy, and theology are unable to arrive at any consensus, the judiciary, at this point in the development of man's knowledge, is not in a position to speculate as to the answer. . . .

With respect to the State's important and legitimate interest in the health of the mother, the "compelling" point, in the light of present medical knowledge, is at approximately the end of the first trimester. This is so because of the now-established medical fact that until the end of the first trimester mortality in abortion may be less than mortality in normal childbirth. It follows that, from and after this point, a State may regulate the abortion procedure to the extent that the regulation reasonably relates to the preservation and protection of maternal health. . . .

With respect to the State's important and legitimate interest in potential life, the "compelling" point is at viability. This is so because the fetus then presumably has the capability of meaningful life outside the mother's womb. State regulation protective of fetal life after viability thus has both logical and biological justifications. If the State is interested in protecting fetal life after viability, it may go so far as to proscribe abortion during that period, except when it is necessary to preserve the life or health of the mother. . . .

To summarize and to repeat:

1. A state criminal abortion statute of the current Texas type, that excepts from criminality only a *life-saving* procedure on behalf of the mother, without regard to pregnancy stage and without recognition of the other interests involved, is violative of the Due Process Clause of the Fourteenth Amendment.
   a. For the stage prior to approximately the end of the first trimester, the abortion decision and its effectuation must be left to the medical judgment of the pregnant woman's attending physician.
   b. For the stage subsequent to approximately the end of the first trimester, the State, in promoting its interest in the health of the mother, may, if it chooses, regulate the abortion procedure in ways that are reasonably related to maternal health.
   c. For the stage subsequent to viability, the State in promoting its interest in the potentiality of human life may, if it chooses, regulate, and even proscribe, abortion except where it is necessary, in appropriate medical judgment, for the preservation of the life or health of the mother. . . .

Mr. Justice White, with whom Mr. Justice Rehnquist joins, dissenting.

At the heart of the controversy in these cases are those recurring pregnancies that pose no danger whatsoever to the life or health of the mother but are, nevertheless, unwanted for any one or more of a variety of reasons—convenience, family planning, economics, dislike of children, the embarrassment of illegitimacy, etc. The common claim before us is that for any one of such reasons, or for no reason at all, and without asserting or claiming any threat to life or health, any woman is entitled to an abortion at her request if she is able to find a medical advisor willing to undertake the procedure.

The Court for the most part sustains this position: During the period prior to the time the fetus becomes viable, the Constitution of the United States values the convenience, whim, or caprice of the putative mother more than the life or potential life of the fetus; the Constitution, therefore, guarantees the right to an abortion as against any state law or policy seeking to protect the fetus from an abortion not prompted by more compelling reasons of the mother.

With all due respect, I dissent. I find nothing in the language or history of the Constitution to support the Court's judgment. The Court simply fashions and announces a new constitutional right for pregnant mothers and, with scarcely any reason or authority for its action, invests that right with sufficient substance to override most existing state abortion statutes. The upshot is that the people and the legislatures of the 50 States are constitutionally disentitled to weigh the relative importance of the continued existence and development of the fetus, on the one hand, against a spectrum of possible impacts on the mother, on the other hand. As an exercise of raw judicial power, the Court perhaps has authority to do what it does today; but in my view its judgment is an improvident and extravagant exercise of the power of judicial review that the Constitution extends to this Court. . . .

Phyllis Schlafly on the Differences Between Men and Women, 1977

The first requirement for the acquisition of power by the Positive Woman is to understand the differences between men and women. Your outlook on life, your faith, your behavior, your potential for fulfillment, all are determined by the parameters of your original premise. The Positive Woman starts with the assumption that the world is her oyster. She rejoices in the creative capability within her body and the power potential of her mind and spirit. She understands that men and women are different, and that those very differences provide the key to her success as a person and fulfillment as a woman.

The women's liberationist, on the other hand, is imprisoned by her own negative view of herself and of her place in the world around her. This view of women was most succinctly expressed in an advertisement designed by the principal women's liberationist organization, the National Organization for Women (NOW), and run in many magazines and newspapers and as spot announcements on many television stations. The advertisement showed a darling curlyheaded girl with the caption: "This healthy, normal baby has a handicap. She was born female."

This is the self-articulated dog-in-the-manger, chip-on-the-shoulder, fundamental dogma of the women's liberation movement. Someone—it is not clear who, perhaps God, perhaps the "Establishment," perhaps a conspiracy of male chauvinist pigs—dealt women a foul blow by making them female. It becomes necessary, therefore, for women to agitate and demonstrate and hurl demands on society in order to wrest from an oppressive male-dominated social structure the status that has been wrongfully denied to women through the centuries.

By its very nature, therefore, the women's liberation movement precipitates a series of conflict situations—in the legislatures, in the courts, in the schools, in industry—with man targeted as the enemy. Confrontation replaces cooperation as the watchword of all relationships. Women and men become adversaries instead of partners.

The second dogma of the women's liberationists is that, of all the injustices perpetuated upon women through the centuries, the most oppressive is the cruel fact that women have babies and men do not. Within the confines of the women's liberationist ideology, therefore, the abolition of this overriding inequality of women becomes the primary goal. This goal must be achieved at any and all costs—to the woman herself, to the baby, to the family, and to society. Women must be made equal to men in their ability *not* to become pregnant and *not* to be expected to care for babies they may bring into the world.

This is why women's liberationists are compulsively involved in the drive to make abortion and child-care centers for all women, regardless of religion or income, both socially acceptable and government-financed. Former Congresswoman Bella Abzug has defined the goal: "to enforce the constitutional right of females to terminate pregnancies that they do not wish to continue."

If man is targeted as the enemy, and the ultimate goal of women's liberation is independence from men and the avoidance of pregnancy and its consequences, then lesbianism is logically the highest form in the ritual of women's liberation. Many, such as Kate Millett, come to this conclusion, although many others do not.

The Positive Woman will never travel that dead-end road. It is self-evident to the Positive Woman that the female body with its baby-producing organs was not designed by a conspiracy of men but by the Divine Architect of the human race. Those who think it is unfair that women have babies, whereas men cannot, will have to take up their complaint with God because no other power is capable of changing that fundamental fact. . . .

The third basic dogma of the women's liberation movement is that there is no difference between male and female except the sex organs, and that all those physical, cognitive, and emotional differences you *think* are there, are merely the result of centuries of restraints imposed by a male-dominated society and sex-stereotyped schooling. The role imposed on women is, by definition, inferior, according to the women's liberationists.

The Positive Woman knows that, while there are some physical competitions in which women are better (and can command more money) than men, including those that put a premium on grace and beauty, such as figure skating, the superior physical strength of males over females in competitions of strength, speed, and short-term endurance is beyond rational dispute. . . .

Does the physical advantage of men doom women to a life of servility and subservience? The Positive Woman knows that she has a complementary advantage which is at least as great—and, in the hands of a skillful woman, far greater. The Divine Architect who gave men a superior strength to lift weights also gave women a different kind of superior strength.

The women's liberationists and their dupes who try to tell each other that the sexual drive of men and women is really the same, and that it is only societal restraints that inhibit women from an equal desire, an equal enjoyment, and an equal freedom from the consequences, are doomed to frustration forever. It just isn't so, and pretending cannot make it so. The differences are not a woman's weakness but her strength. . . .

The new generation can brag all it wants about the new liberation of the new morality, but it is still the woman who is hurt the most. The new morality isn't just a "fad"—it is a cheat and a thief. It robs the woman of her virtue, her youth, her beauty, and her love—for nothing, just nothing. It has produced a generation of young women searching for their identity, bored with sexual freedom, and despondent from the loneliness of living a life without commitment. They have abandoned the old commandments, but they can't find any new rules that work.

The Positive Woman recognizes the fact that, when it comes to sex, women are simply not the equal of men. The sexual drive of men is much stronger than that of women. That is how the human race was designed in order that it might perpetuate itself. The other side of the coin is that it is easier for women to control their sexual appetites. A Positive Woman cannot defeat a man in a wrestling or boxing match, but she can motivate him, inspire him, encourage him, teach him, restrain him, reward him, and have power over him that he can never achieve over her with all his muscle. How or whether a Positive Woman uses her power is determined solely by the way she alone defines her goals and develops her skills.

The differences between men and women are also emotional and psychological. Without woman's innate maternal instinct, the human race would have died out centuries ago. There is nothing so helpless in all earthly life as the newborn infant. It will die within hours if not cared for. Even in the most primitive, uneducated societies, women have always cared for their newborn babies. They didn't need any schooling to teach them how. They didn't need any welfare workers to tell them it is their social obligation. Even in societies to whom such concepts as "ought," "social responsibility," and "compassion for the helpless" were unknown, mothers cared for their new babies.

Why? Because caring for a baby serves the natural maternal need of a woman. Although not nearly so total as the baby's need, the woman's need is nonetheless real.

The overriding psychological need of a woman is to love something alive. A baby fulfills this need in the lives of most women. If a baby is not available to fill that need, women search for a baby-substitute. This is the reason why women have traditionally gone into teaching and nursing careers. They are doing what comes naturally to the female psyche. The schoolchild or the patient of any age provides an outlet for a woman to express her natural maternal need. . . .

Finally, women are different from men in dealing with the fundamentals of life itself. Men are philosophers, women are practical, and 'twas ever thus. Men may philosophize about how life began and where we are heading; women are concerned about feeding the kids today. No woman would ever, as Karl Marx did, spend years reading political philosophy in the British Museum while her child starved to death. Women don't take naturally to a search for the intangible and the abstract. The Positive Woman knows who she is and where she is going, and she will reach her goal because the longest journey starts with a very practical first step.

Jerry Falwell on the ERA, 1980

I believe that at the foundation of the women's liberation movement there is a minority core of women who were once bored with life, whose real problems are spiritual problems. Many women have never accepted their God-given roles. They live in disobedience to God's laws and have promoted their godless philosophy throughout our society. God Almighty created men and women biologically different and with differing needs and roles. He made men and women to complement each other and to love each other. Not all the women involved in the feminist movement are radicals. Some are misinformed, and some are lonely women who like being housewives and helpmeets and mothers, but whose husbands spend little time at home and who take no interest in their wives and children. Sometimes the full load of rearing a family becomes a great burden to a woman who is not supported by a man. Women who work should be respected and accorded dignity and equal rewards for equal work. But this is not what the present feminist movement and equal rights movement are all about.

The Equal Rights Amendment is a delusion. I believe that women deserve more than equal rights. And, in families and in nations where the Bible is believed, Christian women are honored above men. Only in places where the Bible is believed and practiced do women receive more than equal rights. Men and women have differing strengths. The Equal Rights Amendment can never do for women what needs to be done for them. Women need to know Jesus Christ as their Lord and Savior and be under His Lordship. They need a man who knows Jesus Christ as his Lord and Savior, and they need to be part of a home where their husband is a godly leader and where there is a Christian family.

The Equal Rights Amendment strikes at the foundation of our entire social structure. If passed, this amendment would accomplish exactly the opposite of its outward claims. By mandating an absolute equality under the law, it will actually take away many of the special rights women now enjoy. ERA is not merely a political issue, but a moral issue as well. A definite violation of holy Scripture, ERA defies the mandate that "the husband is the head of the wife, even as Christ is the head of the church'' (Ep. 5:23). In 1 Peter 3:7 we read that husbands are to give their wives honor as unto the weaker vessel, that they are both heirs together of the grace of life. Because a woman is weaker does not mean that she is less important.

Betty Friedan's Second Thoughts on Feminism, 1981

Around 1969, when that anti-man, anti-family, bra-burning image of ''women's lib'' was built up in *Newsweek* and *Time* cover stories exaggerating the antics of the most extremist voices in the movement, I remember the helpless feeling shared by the founding Mothers of NOW: ''But that's not what we meant, not at all.'' For us, with our roots in the middle American mainstream and our own fifties' families, equality and the personhood of women never meant destruction of the family, repudiation of marriage and motherhood, or implacable sexual war against men. That ''bra-burning'' note shocked and outraged us, and we knew it was wrong—personally and politically—though we never said so, then, as loudly as we should have. We were intimidated by the conformities of the women's movement and the reality of ''sisterhood is powerful,'' as we never would have been by ''the enemy.''

But in the late sixties and the seventies, young radical women, scarred early by the feminine mystique, and without firm roots in family or career, gave vent to their rage in a rhetoric of sexual politics based on a serious ideological mistake. And they, and later daughters who based personal and political strategies on their distortion, locked themselves and the movement into a reaction that perpetuates, in reverse, the very half-life they were reacting against.

Consider, for instance, the personal reality of some of those valiant women who produced fantasies of mounting Amazonian armies against men, wrote SCUM manifestos (Society for Cutting Up Men), or would shock and titillate suburban matrons at meetings of the League of Women Voters and the National Conference of Christians and Jews by proclaiming, ''All married women are prostitutes,'' and ''Only honest prostitutes are heroines.'' Consider the ones who said women would never be free unless the family was abolished and women forswore motherhood and sexual intercourse with men. ''Let babies be bred in test tubes!'' they cried. Or they created elaborate rationales reducing every relation of man to woman, and the military and economic depredations of the nation, to rape. The rhetoric ranged from the ridiculous (the members of the consciousness-raising group deciding that if they go home and sleep with their husbands, from now on they must be ''on top''; the belief that masturbation or sex with a woman was superior to any ''submission'' to man's penis) to the sublime (the high preaching of the new feminist theologians against every manifestation of ''God, the father,'' or Mary Daly's image of man as vampire who feeds ''on the bodies and minds of women . . . like Dracula, the he-male has lived on woman's blood''). ''The personal is political'' was the motto: not shaving your legs or underarms, refusing to go to the beauty parlor or wear makeup, not letting him pay the restaurant bill or hold the door open, not making his breakfast or dinner, or washing his socks. . . .

The rhetoric of sexual politics resonated and dignified the mundane, daily buried rage of countless ''happy'' suburban housewives and sweetly efficient secretaries, nurses and stewardesses. But its origin was the extreme reaction of the ''chicks'' and ''earth mothers'' of the radical student movement of the sixties against their own situation in the so-called revolutionary counterculture where, in fact, the feminine mystique reached its apogee.

The position of women in that hippie counterculture was, as a young radical black male leader preached succinctly, ''prone.'' Tom Hayden and others might like to forget it now, but those early male leaders of the radical student movement and counterculture of the sixties, white and black, were more blatantly male chauvinist pigs than their conservative fathers. From the communes of Haight-Ashbury and Big Sur and Vermont to the seized and trashed academic fortresses of Harvard and Columbia, women were supposed to wash the pots and pans and cook the spaghetti and be good girls at the mimeograph machine—the ''woman trip''—while the men made the revolutionary decisions, smoking their pot around the commune fire and taunting ''the pigs'' under the television lights.

And when these radical ''chicks'' were finally infected by our first feminist stirrings, and saw through the feminine mystique in the radical movement itself, and introduced their resolutions for ''women's liberation'' at Berkeley or Cornell, the radical young men just laughed. So the women walked out of the larger radical ''movement'' and formed their separate ''women's lib'' groups—like black separatism, right? No men allowed; man was the *enemy*.

Their personal truth as women in the counterculture or radical student movement of the sixties was doubly humiliating when viewed through the lens of revolutionary equality: the ideology of class warfare they had learned to apply to oppressed races and masses, black, brown and pink.

They made a simple, though serious, ideological error when they applied the same political rhetoric to their own situation as women versus men: too literal an analogy with class warfare, racial oppression. It was heady, and made headlines, to vent the venom earlier directed against ''whitey'' or ''boss finks'' against *men*—your own man and the whole damn sex—and use all that sophisticated Marxist jargon to make a new revolutionary case for destruction of ''the patriarchal nuclear family'' and the ''tyranny'' of sexual biology as the source of all oppression. The media seized on the rhetoric. A ''revolutionary in every bedroom'' was both sexier and less threatening to vested economic and political interests (it was not political at all, merely personal) than the mainstream actions of the women's movement: breaking through sex discrimination in employment, professions, education, the church; gaining women some measure of the economic independence and self-respect they so desperately needed, control over their own bodies and reproductive process and simple, nonhumiliating police protection against rape. . . .

The women's movement has for some years been the scapegoat for the rage of threatened, insecure housewives who can no longer count on husbands for lifelong support. Recently I've been hearing younger women, and even older feminists, blame the women's movement for the supposed increase of male impotence, the inadequacy or unavailability of men for the "new women." Some even suggest that the recent explosion of rape, "battered wives," "battered children" and violence in the family is a reaction to, or byproduct of, feminism.

The women's movement is being blamed, above all, for the destruction of the family. Churchmen and sociologists proclaim that the American family, as it has always been defined, is becoming an "endangered species," with the rising divorce rate and the enormous increase in single-parent families and people—especially women—living alone. Women's abdication of their age-old responsibility for the family is also being blamed for the apathy and moral delinquency of the "me generation."

Can we keep on shrugging all this off as enemy propaganda—"their problem, not ours"? I think we must at least admit and begin openly to discuss feminist denial of the importance of family, of women's own needs to give and get love and nurture, tender loving care.

What worries me today is the agonizing conflicts young and not-so-young women are facing—or denying—as they come up against the biological clock, at thirty-five, thirty-six, thirty-nine, forty, and cannot "choose" to have a child. I fought for the right to choose, and will continue to defend that right, against reactionary forces who have already taken it away for poor women now denied Medicaid for abortion, and would take it away for all women with a constitutional amendment. But I think we must begin to discuss, in new terms, the choice to *have* children.

What worries me today is "choices" women have supposedly won, which are not real. How can a woman freely "choose" to have a child when her paycheck is needed for the rent or mortgage, when her job isn't geared to taking care of a child, when there is no national policy for parental leave, and no assurance that her job will be waiting for her if she takes off to have a child? . . .

This uneasy sense of battles won, only to be fought over again, of battles that should have been won, according to all the rules, and yet are not, of battles that suddenly one does not really want to win, and the weariness of battle altogether—how many women feel it? What does it mean? This nervousness in the women's movement, this sense of enemies and dangers, omnipresent, unseen, of shadowboxing enemies who aren't there—are they paranoid phantoms, and if so, why do these enemies always win? This unarticulated malaise now within the women's movement—is something wonderful dulling, dwindling, tarnishing from going on too long, or coming to an end too soon, before it is really finished?

Though the women's movement has changed all our lives and surpassed our dreams in its magnitude, and our daughters take their own personhood and equality for granted, they—and we—are finding that it's not so easy to *live,* with or without men and children, solely on the basis of that first feminist agenda. I think, in fact, that the women's movement has come just about as far as it can in terms of women alone. The very choices, options, aspirations, opportunities that we have won for women—no matter how far from real equality—and the small degree of new power women now enjoy, or hunger for, openly, honestly, as never before, are converging on and into new economic and emotional urgencies. Battles lost or won are being fought in terms that are somehow inadequate, irrelevant to this new personal, and political, reality. I believe it's over, that first stage: the women's movement. And yet the larger revolution, evolution, liberation that the women's movement set off, has barely begun. How do we move on? What are the terms of the second stage?

In the first stage, our aim was full participation, power and voice in the mainstream, inside the party, the political process, the professions, the business world. Do women change, inevitably discard the radiant, enviable, idealized feminist dream, once they get inside and begin to share that power, and do they then operate on the same terms as men? Can women, will women even try to, change the terms?

What are the limits of the true potential of women's power? I believe that the women's movement, in the political sense, is both less and more powerful than we realize. I believe that the personal is both more and less political than our own rhetoric ever implied. I believe that we have to break through our own *feminist* mystique now to come to terms with the new reality of our personal and political experience, and to move into the second stage.

All this past year, with some reluctance and dread, and a strange, compelling relief, I've been asking new questions and listening with a new urgency to other women again, wondering if anyone else reads these signs as beginning-of-the-end, end-of-the-beginning. When I start to talk about them, it makes some women, feminists and antifeminists, uncomfortable, even angry.

There is a disconcerted silence, an uneasy murmuring, when I begin to voice my hunches out loud:

The second stage cannot be seen in terms of women alone, our separate personhood or equality with men.

The second stage involves coming to new terms with the family—new terms with love and with work.

The second stage may not even be a women's movement. Men may be at the cutting edge of the second stage.

The second stage has to transcend the battle for equal power in institutions. The second stage will restructure institutions and transform the nature of power itself.

The second stage may even now be evolving, out of or even aside from what we have thought of as our battle.

I've experienced before the strange mix of shock and relief these hunches arouse. It happened twenty years ago when I began to question the feminine mystique. It happened before when I put into words uncomfortable realities women had been avoiding because they meant we'd have to change. Even the makers of change, self-proclaimed revolutionaries, women no less than men, resist change of the change that has become their security, their power.

If we put these symptoms I have hinted at to the test of full conscious-ness—as I intend to do in this book—facing clearly, openly, publicly what they mean, will we find that the women's movement is, in fact, harboring some incurable cancer, dooming it to imminent death? Inconceivable—never has the women's movement, and the movement of women in the largest sense, seemed stronger, more endurable, irreversible. Three genera-tions of women, millions upon millions, in this and other lands, are living, moving, changing, frantically grasping a new life, or trying to hold on to life, in terms of feminism.

I and other feminists dread to admit or discuss out loud these troubling symptoms because the women's movement has, in fact, been the source and focus of so much of our own energy and strength and security, its root and support, for so many years. We cannot conceive that it will not go on forever the same way it has for nearly twenty years now. But we can't go on denying these puzzling symptoms of distress. If they mean something is seriously wrong, we had better find out and change direction yet again—as much as we ourselves resist such change now—before it is too late.

"How can you talk about the second stage when we haven't even won the first yet?" a woman asks me at a Catholic college weekend for house-wives going back to work. "The men still have the power. We haven't gotten enough for ourselves yet. We have to fight now just to stay where we are, not to be pushed back."

But that's the point. Maybe we have to begin talking about the second stage to keep from getting locked into obsolete power games and irrelevant sexual battles that never can be won, or that we will lose by winning. Maybe only by moving into the second stage, and asking the new questions—political and personal—confronting women and men trying to live the equal-ity we fought for, can we transcend the polarization that threatens even the gains already won, and prevent the ERA from being lost and the right to abortion and the laws against sex discrimination reversed. . . .

✤ *E S S A Y S*

In 1981, Rosalind Pollack Petchesky, currently Coordinator of Women's Studies and a professor of political science at Hunter College of the City University of New York, analyzed the rise of the New Right and its connections to the anti-abortion movement, linking the strength of both directly to the continuing impact of feminism; her views appear in the first essay. Sarah J. Stage, a historian at the University of California at Riverside, in 1983 looked at feminism and its problems, as embodied in the writings of Betty Friedan and Phyllis Schlafly. In the second selection she concluded, like Petchesky, that all was not yet lost—that feminism could still attain its goals if the movement could once again find a basis for unification.

Antiabortion and Antifeminism

ROSALIND POLLACK PETCHESKY

Soon after the 1980 elections, it became all too clear that American society and the state were plunging day by day more deeply into conservative reactionism. Throughout its regime, the Reagan administration presented a power structure and political culture that were openly racist, antifeminist, and also antiliberal. To characterize such a basic political shift in terms of the conspiratorial maneuvering of a tightly organized New Right seems tempting but simplistic, given the pervasiveness of the conservative pull. For the 1980s threatened not only a well-orchestrated right-wing offensive, but also the demise of the liberal state and, along with it, some of its more progressive ideas—ideas such as individual freedom, "equality," and the responsibility of the state to provide for social welfare needs—in short, the tenets of bourgeois democracy. In practice, these ideas have historically stood in marked contrast to a capitalist, racist, and male-supremacist society. Although they were never either carried to their logical conclusions or made real for large groups of people, they nevertheless, until now, had a widespread ideological legitimacy, and as such were taken up and transformed by progressive movements, sometimes effectively, in the fight for radical social change. The antiliberal reaction obviously poses serious contradictions for socialists, feminists, gay rights activists, and others who have fought to transform the liberal state; at the same time, the attack on liberal reforms pushes those groups to organize on a much broader basis than they have done in the recent past.

Clearly, the New Right is not alone in abandoning liberalism. The dogma that social programs for the poor and working people represent "intrusiveness" and "overregulation" by the state, and that feminism and the sixties' counterculture represent "permissiveness" and "hedonism" (or "narcissism") in the society, emanates not only from the Moral Majority, but also from the dominant media and intellectual organs, the centers of corporate and state power, and even from some self-defined leftists. It is important to recognize the generality of these trends and also that Reagan's election and reelection cannot be read as a popular "mandate" for conservatism. And yet it is still the case that the New Right *is* an identifiable political reality, which had visible success in mobilizing conservative voters and in creating an effective organizational machine in the 1980s. Above all, I shall argue that what has given the New Right both ideological legitimacy and organizational coherence in this period has been its focus on reproductive and sexual issues. If there is anything genuinely "new" about the current right wing in the United States, it is its tendency to locate sexual, reproductive, and family issues at the center of its political program—not as

Reprinted (updated) from Rosalind Pollack Petchesky, "Antiabortion, Antifeminism, and the Rise of the New Right," *Feminist Studies,* VII (Summer 1981), 206–46, by permission of the publisher, *Feminist Studies,* Inc., c/o Women's Studies Program, University of Maryland, College Park, MD 20742.

manipulative rhetoric only, but as the substantive core of a politics geared, on a level that outdistances any previous right-wing movements in this country, to mobilizing a nationwide mass following. The politics of the family, sexuality, and reproduction—and most directly, of abortion—became a primary vehicle through which right-wing politicians achieved their ascent to state power in the late 1970s and the 1980s. My purpose here is to analyze the role of antiabortion and antifeminist politics in that rise to power. . . .

If the embodiment of absolute evil for an earlier generation of the Right was international communism, the Left, and labor movements in the United States, in the recent period, it is feminism and homosexuality—both representing movements for transcendance of a patriarchal form of family and for sexual liberation. This shift is not surprising given the weakness of the Left and labor movements at the present time; whereas the women's liberation movement in the 1970s has become the most dynamic force for social change in the country, the one most directly threatening not only to conservative values and interests, but also to significant groups whose way of life is challenged by ideas of sexual liberation. And of all feminist demands, the *right to abortion* is that which somehow appears most threatening to traditional sexual and social values.

The antiabortion movement, which began in the Catholic church and, despite disclaimers, has remained an essentially *religious* movement, has been the main vehicle through which the New Right has crystallized and developed both its mass base and its mass ideology. This particular crusade—which existed before the New Right and, I would argue, in many ways laid the groundwork for it—has provided the existing right wing with the perfect issue to "freeze" the political process into an absolute struggle between good and evil; an intensely palpable symbol of martyrdom, something "positive to fight for." But, while the religious, moralistic, and often mystical terms in which this crusade is couched resonate for many of its followers, religion should not be mistaken for the *content* of right-wing politics. Religion provides an "apocalyptic framework which validates [moral] absolutism," but the content of this framework is political in the most conventional sense: it has to do with how and by whom power is exercised—in the economy, the state, the family, and the churches.

From this perspective, it becomes clear that the major role of organized religion for the Right during elections has been to serve as a major organizational infrastructure, a nationally and locally established institutional network, one that exists outside the framework of the Democratic and Republican party structures, but which would give the Right access to an organized mass constituency. The two main institutions comprising this infrastructure, and around which New Right organizing strategy has revolved, are, first, the conservative wing and hierarchy of the Catholic church; and, second, the fundamentalist Protestant churches, particularly those affiliated with the Moral Majority. Both of these groups are already organized through the "right-to-life" movement, as well as through their own internal congregations and networks—a reality on which the New Right has sought to capitalize. Through a vigorous use of these conservative religious organizations, the New Right—and indirectly the Reagan forces—sought to achieve certain key ingredients of political power: votes and funds; active recruits and foot soldiers; and legitimacy (through association with a morally righteous cause). Already by 1978, its spokesmen were claiming that this base would give them potential access to one hundred million voters, and they were confident of commanding sufficient votes in the elections to give them control over the Senate, the Republican party, and, indeed, the presidency. Regardless of how one analyzes the deeper causes of the right-wing electoral victories in 1980, it is undeniable that a key element in the Right's strategy was to use the churches and particularly the "right-to-life" movement as an organizational model and base.

The "right-to-life" movement was originally a creation of the Family Life division of the National Conference of Catholic Bishops (NCCB), the directing body of the Catholic church in America. Immediately following the Supreme Court decision in *Roe* v. *Wade,* the NCCB Pro-Life Affairs Committee declared that they would not "accept the Court's judgment," and called for a major legal and educational battle against abortion. Since then, in numerous documents the bishops have summoned Catholics, both lay and clergy, to enter the antiabortion struggle: to defeat liberal abortion laws and proabortion candidates, and to work for a constitutional amendment that would, in accordance with Roman Catholic doctrine, declare the fetus a full human person from the moment of fertilization, and abortion thus a homicide. In 1975, the NCCB presented a detailed strategy for the church's antiabortion crusade, its "Pastoral Plan for Pro-Life Activity." It called for the establishment of a network of "prolife committees" based in the parishes, that would (1) effect the passage of a "prolife" amendment; (2) elect "prolife" sympathizers to local party organizations; (3) monitor officials on their abortion stands; and (4) "work for qualified candidates who will vote for a constitutional amendment and other prolife issues." In other words, from the outset, the "right-to-life" movement was set up to be a political action machine to influence national and local elections, but working primarily through the churches and the financial and organizational leadership of the hierarchy. . . .

The New Right could not help but be drawn to these winning ingredients: a tightly controlled organization geared to recruiting and influencing voters across party lines; an alleged eleven million members and three thousand chapters throughout the United States; and a sense of moral righteousness on behalf of conservative values and "a cause." It would seem that the "right-to-life" movement became for the New Right a *model* for building a mass base. In addition, the New Right has been the direct beneficiary of mass antiabortion organizing, which has helped to create a constituency and a consciousness that is both responsive to the New Right's "profamily" ideology (see below) and committed to participating in the electoral process. In a political climate in which the majority of liberals and radicals are disaffected nonvoters, such political socialization undoubtedly contributed to the Right's margin of victory.

In 1978, the New Right began to take the "prolife" message outside of the "right-to-life" committees, setting up its own network of "prolife" Political Action Committees (PACs), "leadership conferences," and "conservative Christian" organizations, all under the rubric of the "profamily" movement. The strategy adopted in 1977 was to absorb "groups devoted to preservation of the traditional social roles of the family, the churches, and the schools" (that is, groups that were antiabortion, antibusing, anti-ERA, and antigay rights) into a single coalition organized around four main planks: "prolife," "profamily," "promoral," and "pro-American," with "family" as the keystone. New Right organizers launched direct-mail campaigns aimed at politicizing the country's fundamentalist preachers and organized a series of "leadership conferences" and religious coalitions. In addition to the highly publicized Moral Majority, conferences and groups with names like Religious Roundtable, Christian Voice, and American Family Forum proliferated, with the same speakers and leaders appearing continually on their rosters. . . .

The main constituency "profamily" leaders sought to organize was the estimated fifty million "born-again" Christians in this country, reached through both the evangelical church pulpits and, even more directly, the vast broadcasting network (thirteen thousand radio stations, thirty-six television shows) to which the evangelical churches have access. As in the "right-to-life" movement, the key to this strategy was the *preachers,* but particularly the nationally known Bible-preaching broadcasters. For millions of evangelical Protestants, who are the most frequent listeners to religious broadcasts, radio and television have taken the place of the local church, reaching people in their cars and homes, not only on Sunday, but on every other day all across America. Religious broadcasting for right-wing political purposes has long been a tool of right-wing preachers. But today the use of high-wave frequencies and satellite technology magnifies the potential impact of such broadcasting, and its costs, tremendously. What is of interest here, of course, is not the high-powered technology of the fundamentalist broadcasters, but the large financial backing which allows the application of that technology on a massive scale; and the political and ideological purposes for which the "electronic church" was created. An important example is Rev. Jerry Falwell, founder of the "profamily" Moral Majority, which has a mailing list of seventy thousand pastors. Falwell broadcasts *daily* over 300 television stations and 280 radio stations in thirty-one states. The message he communicates through the electronic church is the essence of "profamily" ideology: antihomosexuality ("the bisexual and homosexual movements in America are antifamily, . . . the number one offender . . . in traditional man-woman relationships"); antifeminism ("we believe in *superior* rights for women"); antiabortion and antidivorce. . . .

An alliance between Protestant fundamentalist preachers and the political right wing is far from new. This writer remembers only too well growing up in Tulsa, Oklahoma, in the 1950s, where Anita Bryant was the football queen of our rival high school one year, where the fundamentalists (Oral Roberts, Billy James Hargis) maintained their headquarters, where "Athletes for Christ" made regular rounds of the high schools and where, above all, the connection of these groups with anticommunism and the John Birch Society were commonly known. That connection is documented in an article published in 1962 by David Danzig, who describes "extreme Protestant fundamentalism," linked to ultra-Right organizations, as "a growing socio-religious force in America." In the early 1960s, American fundamentalism was still fiercely anti-Catholic, but cut across various Protestant sects, uniting them in a general belief in the Bible's "inerrant truth" as literally interpreted, in "salvation by faith alone and the pre-millennial return of Christ." These beliefs, as David Danzig points out, lend themselves to both "an anti-historicism which readily supports the conspiracy theory of social change," and an "apocalyptic conception of the world" which sees everything in terms of "the unending struggle between God and the devil." Fundamentalist thinking is thus ripe to be won over by a political ideology that is similarly absolutist and apocalyptic, projecting a vision of society as ridden by demons (communists, homosexuals, "liberated women") from whom the innocent and God-fearing must be saved. By the late 1950s and early 1960s, the *class base* of Protestant fundamentalism in the South and Southwest (where it was still largely contained) had changed. It was no longer mainly the rural poor, but included the wealthy beneficiaries of what later would be known as the "sun belt revival":

> Many fundamentalist churches are modern and imposing, financed by wealthy oilmen from Texas and Oklahoma and prosperous farmers in the wheat and corn belts. Rich and influential lay leaders . . . now make their influence felt in the power structure of the community and state. The fundamentalists also operate a vast network of colleges, training schools, Bible institutions, Bible prophecy conferences, prayer meetings, and study groups. They have many large publishing houses which blanket small towns with conservative tracts and pamphlets.

The fundamentalists thus developed a formidable base of financial and corporate support. The main purpose of "profamily" organizing prior to 1980 was to mobilize the growing social force of Christian fundamentalism into conservative political activity, and to weld it to the already politicized and Catholic-dominated "right-to-life" movement. An alliance between conservative Catholics and Protestants would be historically unprecedented in the United States; and New Right leaders believe that the politics of "morality"—that is, conservative family and sexual politics—is the key to forging such an alliance, and thus to uniting a potential "100 million Americans" into right-wing political identity and votes. Their method is to tap—as the "right-to-life" movement has done so successfully—both religious guilt and emotional vulnerability to all the symbolic meanings of "family" and "morality." The "profamily" movement promises not only to save fetuses, but to save "the family" itself and the moral foundations of "Christian civilization." Through citation of scripture and an urgent appeal to Christian conscience ("out of the pew, into the precinct"), Christians are urged to get involved in politics for the sake of the family and morality. But the vision implied in Moral Majority rhetoric transcends the family. It is one of a

Christian theocracy, a transformed political system in which the (conservative) clergy is at the center of state power, and the state is avowedly "Christian"—and patriarchal.

Yet, the relationship between the group of conservative politicians and political promoters who call themselves the New Right and the right-to-life movement is a complicated one, involving both close ties and potentially deep divisions. From its origins in the early 1970s, the right-to-life movement has been courted by and wedded to a whole series of right-wing political veterans, whose affiliations include the John Birch Society, the Young Americans for Freedom, the World Anti-Communist League, and the Conservative Caucus. These relations have developed into a symbiosis in which New Right organizers lend to prolife groups their expertise in direct mailings, targeting candidates, and managing PACs, in return for securing a mass base of voters and local organizers. Rhonda Copelon, attorney for the plaintiffs in *Harris* v. *McRae,* speculates that the New Right politicos see the right-to-life movement as genuinely broad-based and thus a vehicle through which conservative forces can make inroads into the (majority) liberal-democratic electorate. Although less successful in 1984, in the 1980 elections, the New Right succeeded in combining its direct-mail fundraising techniques with the church-based electoral machinery of the "prolife" movement to elect an impressive number of conservatives to national office, and to defeat liberals.

At the same time, the New Right's political aims go well beyond the abortion issue. The goal of their electoral strategy is to get rid of legislators considered liberal on *any* of the Right's favorite issues, including environmental regulation, welfare, defense spending, and civil rights. It is this connection of abortion to a much larger and more traditional set of rightist political ends that has sown the seeds of difference between hardcore "right-to-lifers" and their New Right and fundamentalist patrons. Even prior to 1980, some antiabortion leaders expressed suspicion of the New Right's motives and were reluctant to let their "single-issue" focus become absorbed in the larger "profamily"/"pro-America" agenda. Indeed, much of the rhetoric and organizing of the NRLC has attempted to appeal to liberal and "humanist" religious people who identify with the poor and the oppressed, to connect the "rights of the unborn" to other human rights issues. (There is even a "Prolife Feminists" caucus which meets at the NRLC national convention, as well as a small, "left" wing of the movement which opposes population control and nuclear power and favors welfare benefits.)

While the actual ideas and priorities of the antiabortion movement contradict the appearance of liberalism and grass-roots populism (to say nothing of feminism), the desire to maintain that appearance, in order to win on the abortion issue, is very real. A too-close association with the New Right could be damaging to the "right-to-life" movement's support among liberal Catholics and others who identify with humanist and pacifist traditions, who strongly favor many of the services and institutions (daycare, labor unions, environmental protection laws) that the New Right loudly condemns. In an

editorial in early 1976, the liberal Catholic journal *Commonweal* gave pro-
phetic warning to the Church hierarchy about the fellows it was bedding
down with in the antiabortion campaign:

> The anti-abortion amendment is a right-wing issue, and the bishops will quickly
> become the tools of conservative so-called "pro-life" (and perhaps anti-busing,
> anti-'welfare chiselers,' pro-arms race, pro-CIA) candidates in the 1976 elec-
> tions. The effort will fizzle and the church will have been had.

The New Right found in the antiabortion movement not only an efficient organizational network, but also the source of its ideological coherence
and legitimacy. As previously suggested, the abortion issue resonates many
social and political meanings—about the family, sexuality, the position of
women—that go far beyond the status of the fetus; and thus *the organized
opposition to abortion has never, in fact, been a "single-issue" movement.*
The underlying message of the crusade against abortion—the message
which the New Right itself has embraced as its ideological centerpiece—is
that conveyed in the defensive response by Dr. J. C. Willke, when he was
president of the NRLC, to accusations about firebombings and harassment
of abortion clinics:

> It is they who are doing violence to our beloved nation by their systematic
> undermining of the basic unit of our society, the family. They do violence by
> their so-called sex education which is encouraging sexual promiscuity in our
> children and leading to more and more abortions. They do violence to us by
> driving wedges, barriers, and suspicion between teenagers and parents. They do
> violence to marriage by helping to remove the right of a husband to protect the
> life of the child he has fathered in his wife's womb.

Abortion, Willke suggested, is just the opening wedge in an avalanche of
"moral" assaults on the traditional nuclear family, including sex education,
teenage sexuality and autonomy, and the sexual and reproductive freedom
of women. Preservation of the fetus, note, is not the central issue here, but
rather the patriarchal dominion of the husband over "his wife's womb." . . .

Sexual and family politics, beginning with abortion, became for the New
Right intrinsic elements in a larger program that encompassed more traditional right-wing aims: anticommunism, antidetente, antiunionism, racial
segregation and antifederalism. Election propaganda appealing to potential
constituents typically listed many targeted issues on which every member of
the Christian Right was expected to share a common view, interlacing
"moral" questions with economic and foreign policy questions: "abortion,"
"family," "ERA," "homosexuality," "pornography," moving on to
"public school prayer," "government intervention in your private Christian
school," "the right to bear arms" (gun control), "high taxes," "balanced
budget," and "America's failing military strength."

Yet if we are to understand the specificity of New Right politics, we
need to analyze the complex relationships between "economic," "political," and "moral" issues in their thinking. What I want to argue is, first,
that the politics of the New Right seek legitimation from a common ideological core, the idea of *privatization*; and second, that the "privatization"

impulse itself cuts in two interrelated directions: against social welfare and the poor, and against feminism and women. What is particularly important here is the ideology of the "private sphere" and its relation to both the family and states' rights. The New Right in its "profamily" program invokes deep fears of loss of control over what is considered most "private," most "personal." Historically, the concept of "privacy" for American conservatives has included not only "free enterprise" and "property rights," but also the right of the white male property owner to control his wife and his wife's body, his children and their bodies, his slaves and their bodies. It is an ideology that is patriarchal and racist, as well as capitalist. Part of the content of the formal appeal to "states' rights" is the idea of the family as a private, and above all male-dominated, domain. Control over families (one's wife and children) and control over local and state power structures are closely related conservative values, insofar as the latter is the means whereby the former is sought as an end. Thus what appear to be attacks on federalism are simultaneously attacks on movements by women, blacks, and young people to assert their right to resources, services, and a viable existence outside the family and the ghetto. . . .

The New Right must be understood as a response to feminist ideas and to their strong impact, in the 1970s, on popular consciousness. Joined by major segments of the corporate capitalist and state power structures, the New Right is trying to designate the private as "private" once again, but in a particular sense. The aim is surely to *reprivatize* every domain of social, public intervention that has been created through the struggles of working people, blacks, the poor, and women for the last twenty years. Not only abortion, sex education, and domestic violence services, but health care, education, the right to equal education, legal services, health and safety at work, access to the broadcasting media are all being pushed back into the unregulated anarchy of the private sector. The legitimation for this massive attempt to destroy the meager reforms that were won from the liberal state in the 1960s and 70s is the myth of "privatism"—the idea that what's wrong with busing or medicaid abortions or the Occupational Safety and Health Administration (OSHA) or the Environmental Protection Agency is that the federal government is "meddling in our 'private' business"; that, indeed, there even exists some private, safe, secure place—our neighborhoods, our churches, above all, the family—that would give us everything we needed if only the government would stay out.

But, although the language of New Right ideology evokes the sentiment of personal freedom from state interference, what distinguishes that ideology from classical conservatism is that it is spoken on behalf of *corporate* bodies rather than individuals. It is, in other words, corporate privatism—in the service of business, church, private school, and patriarchal family—that is intended, not individual privacy. In this regard, the New Right's appeal to privatism is much closer to fascism than to classical libertarian doctrine and is thus perfectly compatible, in theory as well as practice, with a program of massive state control over individuals' private lives. Of course, the fact that this ideology is being propagated widely in a period of severe economic crisis and recession is not particularly surprising. My argument here is that it is the context of a popular feminist movement and an antifeminist backlash that has, in this historical period, fueled that ideology and given it a certain popular momentum. In that context, by focusing on those realms which still have the greatest *appearance* as "private," or "personal," in our culture—sexuality, abortion, the relations between parents and children—the New Right has been able to achieve a much greater ideological legitimacy for its politics of racism and fiscal conservatism than it could have by calling things by their right names. . . .

Antiabortion ideology has been taken up by the right wing not only for its "profamily" and prochurch message, but also for its support of conservative sexual values. The "right-to-life" doctrine of the fetus's "personhood" and the aborting woman's "selfishness" is directly akin to the antihumanist philosophy of the "profamily" movement. Antihumanism, as professed by the "right-to-life" and "profamily" movements, pits itself squarely against every intellectual and philosophical tradition that grew out of the Enlightenment and secularism. Marxism and feminism both are clearly denounced by the "right-to-life"/"profamily" movement, but so are all philosophies, including radical Christian movements, whose central focus is social change on this earth or even human as opposed to divine, or scriptural, ends. When Weyrich describes the Moral Majority as "a Christian democratic movement rooted in the authentic Gospel, not the social gospel," he is attacking, and distinguishing his politics from, those Christian and Catholic movements in the United States and Latin America who ally with the poor to change oppressive social conditions. All social movements—including labor movements, peasant uprisings, anticolonial struggles, civil rights, antinuclear protests—would thus be categorized by the New Right under "materialistic, atheistic humanism," charged with the sin of making human life and human pleasure on earth the measure of all value.

But a very particular condemnation is reserved for feminism and the movement for sexual liberation. It is this branch of humanism that the New Right associates most closely with hedonism, equated with "doing whatever feels good," with "moral perversity and total corruption." If a woman can control her pregnancies, there is no built-in sanction against her having sex when, how, and with whom she pleases—and this, for the "profamily"/"prolife" movement, is the heart of the matter. As Ellen Willis once put it, "the nitty-gritty issue in the abortion debate is not life but sex." The fetus itself, its "innocence," symbolizes asexuality. . . .

Over and over again in antiabortion and "profamily" literature, one is struck with a defiantly traditional middle-class morality regarding sexual behavior and an undisguised antipathy toward *all* forms of sexuality outside the marital, procreative sphere. Male homosexuality, lesbianism, extramarital sex, divorce—all are targets of the New Right's modern "purity crusade." But more than anything else, the subject that excites "prolifers" is premarital sex among teenagers. Increasingly it appears that antagonism to abortion stems less from concern for protecting the fetus than from a desire to prevent teenage sexuality. "Right-to-life" advocates assume as a matter of course that there is a causal relationship between legalized abortion and a rise in sexual promiscuity and illegitimacy, particularly among teenagers. Not only abortion but also birth control and sex education programs sponsored by clinics and schools are seen as giving official government sanction to "illicit" sex—and, therefore, as interfering with parents' control over the moral behavior and values of their children. Conversely, the way to eliminate premarital sexuality, it is thought, is to eliminate abortion, teenage contraceptive programs, and sex education. . . .

The theme of protecting children has also been applied in the movement's virulent, active campaign against homosexuals and lesbians. On the false pretext that male homosexuals and lesbians are child molesters, New Right legislative and political offensives have sought, with some success, to defeat local gay rights ordinances in cities around the country; to deny federally funded legal services to homosexuals; to bar homosexuals from teaching in the public schools (as in the defeated Briggs Amendment campaign in California); and to revive the ideology (abandoned even by the American Psychiatric Association) that homosexuality is "pathological" and "perverse." A longer-range goal is to prohibit the employment of homosexuals not only in education, but in *any* "public sector" or "high visibility public jobs"; as well as to prohibit federal funding of any organization that even "suggests" that homosexuality "can be an acceptable lifestyle." Conservatives both within and outside the Reagan administration have cruelly exploited the AIDS epidemic as "God's curse" on homosexuals, a pretext for discrimination and, in some quarters, proposals for quarantine.

The ideas behind the New Right's antihomosexual campaign are revealing of the political values that motivate the "profamily" movement, including the movement against abortion. They suggest that, while it may be true that "prolifers" are hostile to sexuality as such, it is really the social aspects of traditional gender identities—and particularly the position of male paternal and heterosexual authority—that they are determined to protect. Homosexuality is characterized by "profamily" representatives as "unnatural," "evil," and psychologically "perverse"; but male homosexuality is even more dangerous than female, in the "profamily" view, because it signals a breakdown of "masculinity" itself—or what one right-wing ideologue calls the "male spirit," or "the male principle." Thus, what is at stake in the New Right campaign against homosexuality is the very idea of what it means to be a "man" or a "woman," and the structure and meaning of the traditional family. These two concepts are clearly related, for the meaning of "masculinity" (as of "femininity")—that is, of gender itself—has been defined historically through the structure of the family and dominant position of the father within it. Paul Weyrich, a leader of the "profamily" movement, expresses an awareness of this reality when he says that

> there are people who want a different political order, who are not necessarily Marxists. Symbolized by the women's liberation movement, they believe that the future for their political power lies in the restructuring of the traditional family, and particularly in the *downgrading of the male or father role in the traditional family.*

The aim of the "profamily" movement is to restore heterosexual patriarchy, the control of men over their wives and children. Teenage sexuality; homosexuality; the freely determined sexuality of women as wives and daughters; abortion and contraception, insofar as they promote sexual freedom; even "test-tube babies," which hold out the prospect of totally removing procreation from heterosexual monogamy—all are a direct threat to male authority and the identification of men as heads of families. Given this, it is not surprising that all these activities have become the central target of a movement that is led by middle-class conservative men. The men of the "profamily" movement, mainly upper-middle-class professionals, are not immune to the sense of personal loss and threat provoked by feminism and by recent changes in the family and women's work. Weyrich again captures the essence of this middle-class patriarchal *ressentiment* when he proclaims: "The father's word has to prevail." With this unambiguous call to arms, Weyrich speaks not only as a New Right general, but also as a husband and a father. And he speaks, too, as a leading patriarch in his church, aware of the Sonia Johnsons and the Sister Theresa Kanes and the other believing women who would perhaps turn traditional church governance upside down.

In the case of the Catholic Church, one could argue that it is feminism itself, within the church as outside it, that explains the singlemindedness and fury with which the church hierarchy has engaged in the current crusade against birth control and abortion. The hierarchy and the pope have evidenced strong concern about feminist and Marxist stirrings within the church's own ranks and the need to impose "discipline" and patriarchal authority in its own house. This was made clear in the pope's visit to the United States in 1979 and his outspoken endorsement there, and during the recent Synod of Bishops, of the most conservative views on women, birth control, sexuality and marriage—even in the face of widespread lay nonconformism and public appeals by nuns for a more modern approach. Feminism represents to the church a threat of insubordination, but also a threat of depopulation: not only have Catholic birth rates gone down as much as other groups', but Catholics today both approve of and *practice* abortion in nearly as large numbers as do other groups in the United States. Declining enrollments in parochial school may play no small part in motivating church attacks on birth control, abortion, and women's control over pregnancy.

Taking feminist ideas more seriously than do many liberals, the doctrinal leaders of the New Right relate women's sexuality to their place in society—only reversing the feminist vision. Connie Marshner, another prime mover behind the "profamily" movement and director of its "Library Court" legislative group, assures women that all they need is "to know 'that somebody will have the authority and make the decision, and that your job is to be happy with it.' " This is exactly what Schlafly and her anti-ERA forces have been vociferously promoting since 1973—the idea that it is women's "right" to be dependent, cared for, subordinate to men, and defined by marriage and motherhood. At the center of anti-ERA ideology is the assumption that it is destructive of the family for married women to work outside the home. From this follows their opposition to federally funded childcare programs and their support for "protective" legislation that would exclude women from certain jobs, due to their "physical differences and family obligations," or would "give job preference . . . to a wage-earner supporting dependents" (meaning men). Most fundamentally of all, however, "prolife" and "profamily" ideology represent the urge to restore the values of motherhood as they have been propagated since the late eighteenth century: as woman's true destiny, her "calling," that which defines her above all else and so must take priority above all other tasks or commitments. Clearly, this is the underlying message of the antiabortion movement, that women who seek abortions are "selfish" because they attempt to deny the "life" of "their own child" and therefore their own "destiny" (both "natural" and God-given) to procreate, nurture, and suffer. One could speculate at length on the deeper cultural and psychological roots of the "promotherhood" backlash, yet it obviously touches something very profound—in men, a long-ingrained expectation of being taken care of, which feminism seems to threaten; in women, a long-ingrained vulnerability to guilt, which antifeminism evokes.

"Profamily"/"prolife" organizers understand all too well that the main threats to maintaining a traditional family structure in which men dominate women and children, and women seek their identity in motherhood, are women's economic independence from husbands and the existence of a strong feminist movement. The massive rise in women's labor force participation, particularly among married women; and, on a much smaller but still important scale, the existence of feminist alternatives outside the home (battered women's shelters, lesbian communities, "returning women's" programs in colleges, feminist health networks), create the possibility for women to imagine existing outside of traditional married life. For married women too, these possibilities have changed how they think about marital relations and motherhood, whether or not they remain married or remarry (which most of them do). Far more than an opportunistic appeal to the "irrational," the New Right represents a highly conscious conservative response to these broad and changing social conditions. It is a response that advocates a return to the values of privatism; that would throw the welfare and education of individuals back onto the resources of the family and the church; that would confine sexuality within the strict bounds of heterosexual marriage, and women within a patriarchal version of self-denying motherhood.

Describing the ideology and political program of a social movement is not at all the same as understanding the consciousness of the masses of people who make up that movement, much less the material and social conditions that bring a particular consciousness to light. We have to consider why that ideology is able to have a broad impact on people's consciousness; why, in this case, the resurgence of patriarchal authority, in its "prolife" and "profamily" incarnations, has come to play such a central role in American politics and its current bend to the right.

First, the simplest and most obvious explanation for the "prolife" movement's existence and its success in developing a mass-based organization is that the political values and social changes its members are fighting against are real and pervasive. Both the women's and gay liberation movements, on the one hand, and the structural changes in the family that have been both cause and effect of those movements, represent a genuine threat to the type of family system and the sexual morality that the New Right is seeking to preserve. While New Right language and symbolism often take a mystical and irrational form, their ends are nevertheless coherent and clear; the conflict between the values of the New Right and those they oppose, as they perceive better than many liberals, broaches no compromise. In this sense, the antiabortion/antigay/anti-ERA/"profamily" current is indeed a backlash movement, a movement to turn back the tide of the major social movements of the 1960s and 1970s. This backlash is aimed primarily at those organizations and ideas that have most directly confronted patriarchal traditions regarding the place of women in society and the dominant norms of heterosexual love and marriage. But it is also a reaction to the New Left and the counterculture generally, which many white middle-class parents experienced as having robbed them of their children, either literally or spiritually. The strength and determination of this backlash—particularly in regard to abortion, homosexuality, and the ERA—is in part a measure of the *effectiveness* of the women's and gay movements, the extent to which their ideas (and various commercial distortions of their ideas) have penetrated popular culture and consciousness, if not public policy. This ideological impact has, of course, been double-edged because it has brought with it a great deal of uncertainty about what will replace the old forms that are being challenged, and even about people's own identities. But it is also true, as Zillah Eisenstein has argued elsewhere, that there is no corner of the society where the basic liberal feminist idea of women's "equality" with men has not touched people in their daily relationships.

Second, the "profamily" movement is reacting to very real, dramatic changes in family life that have occurred most sharply during the past twenty years. The kind of family model the New Right would like to restore—in fact, to make morally and legally mandatory—has become practically extinct in America. By the early 1980s, fewer than 10 percent of all households were composed of husband-wife families with children where the husband was the sole "breadwinner." The majority of women with school-age children were working outside the home, increasing proportions of them (50 percent of Black families, 15 percent of white) as the primary supporters of their households.

These changes have been accompanied by much greater openness about homosexuality, nonmarital heterosexuality, living arrangements, and child-rearing arrangements that fall outside the traditional heterosexual-married-household pattern. Further, the whole pattern and social context of motherhood has changed as a result of these shifts. While most women will raise one or two children in their lives, they will do so in a context of nearly continuous work outside the home; and, for many, of decreasing economic dependence on husbands or other men.

The New Right's "prolife," "profamily" campaign thus cannot easily be written off as either religious fanaticism or mere opportunism. It has achieved a mass following and a measure of national political power because it is in fact a response to real material conditions and deeplying fears, a response that is utterly *reactionary,* but nevertheless attune. It is not only those conditions and fears, however, that have given the New Right its leverage, but also the failure of the Left and feminist movements to develop an alternative vision, based on socialist and feminist values, that gives people a sense of orientation in dealing with the kinds of personal insecurity and disruption brought by recent changes in the family and sexual norms. The disjunctions in relations between parents and teenagers illustrate this lack of vision painfully. For the concerns of parents about their children getting pregnant, having abortions, being encouraged toward "sexual freedom," without any social context of sexual and reproductive responsibility, are rational and real and neither the Left nor the women's movement has offered a model for a better, more socially responsible way for teenagers to live. The "prolife" movement's critique of a certain kind of "hedonism," the cult of subjective experience and "doing whatever feels good," with no sense of values outside the self, is in part a response to the moral failure of contemporary capitalist culture.

In addressing these cultural dislocations, the New Right answers with the reassurance of moral absolutism: to deal with the problems of abortion, teenage sexuality, conflicts in female-male relations, simply abolish them. There are no decisions to make, no hard choices, no ambiguities. You have only to listen to "the word"—of the priest, of the husband, of the father. But this is a nonmorality, because it absolves human beings (especially those lacking patriarchal authority) of moral agency, and thus plays on people's weakness and insecurity. Moreover, it puts its own followers—for example, the activist women of the "right-to-life" movement—in a terrible dilemma, because the meaning of political activism, to which they are being called, is to think, to act, to be responsible. Indeed, the most stinging contradiction embodied in the "prolife" movement may be that confronting its apparently large numbers of female rank and file, most of them white, middle class and middle aged. On the one hand, we may speculate that these are the very women for whom the loss of a protective conjugal family structure and the idea of motherhood as the core of woman's fulfillment is a truly menacing specter. On the other hand, what can it mean to be active as a woman in a political movement, or a church, that stands for women's passivity and subordination? How will the women of the New Right begin to confront this dilemma?

Anita Bryant, for three years national symbol and leader of the anti-gay rights movement and a devout fundamentalist, may be a harbinger of a gathering storm. Finding herself divorced, jobless, and denounced by the male-dominated church that has made millions of dollars off her name, Bryant now claims to "better understand the gays' and the feminists' anger and frustration." She sees "a male chauvinist attitude" in "the kind of sermon [she] always heard" growing up in the Bible belt—*"wife submit to your husband even if he's wrong"*; and thinks "that her church has not addressed itself to women's problems":

Fundamentalists have their head in the sand. The church is sick right now and I have to say I'm even part of that sickness. I often have had to stay in pastors' homes and their wives talk to me. Some pastors are so hard-nosed about submission and insensitive to their wives' needs that they don't recognize the frustration—even hatred—within their own households.

But there are also material contradictions that, I believe, will undo the "prolife" movement in the long run. The New Right's rejection of the now dominant ideology of the "working mother," their determination to bring women back into the home, represents a basic misunderstanding of current economic realities, including the long-range interests of the capitalist class as a whole, which continues to rely heavily on a (sex-segregated) female labor force. Emma Rothschild has cogently pointed out that the only real "growth" industries in the American economy in the current period— "eating and drinking places," "health services," and "business services"—are those whose labor force is predominantly women. Corporations are unlikely to fill these low paid, part-time, unprotected, high-turnover jobs with male workers; they are, in the existing division of labor, "women's work."

Finally, neither the practice of abortion and birth control nor the expression of sexual desire has ever been successfully stamped out by repressive religious or legal codes. As Jill Stephenson comments with regard to the failure of Nazi "promotherhood" ideology to raise the German birthrate:

> The long history of birth control in Germany, with widespread resort to abortion if contraception had been unavailable, or had failed, could not be eliminated from popular consciousness by a few laws and even a mass of propaganda. . . . Repression could only drive these practices underground, where popular demand ensured that, somehow, they survived.

In the United States in the 1980s and 1990s, social needs and popular consciousness will also assure the survival of these practices. But whether survival will transform into political struggle will depend on the existence and strength of an organized popular movement.

Feminism in the 1980s

SARAH J. STAGE

The contemporary women's movement, observers say, is in trouble, perhaps dying. Obituaries for the feminist movement, however, are not new. As early as 1968 critics pronounced the women's movement dead. Each internecine fight, each judicial or legislative setback, has been greeted as the death knell for feminism. So it came as no surprise that in the final months of the losing battle for the Equal Rights Amendment obituaries flew thick and

Sarah J. Stage, "Women [in the 1980s]," *American Quarterly*, XXXV (1983), 169–90, copyright 1983, American Studies Association.

fast. What was surprising was that this time they came not from the Phyllis Schlaflys, but from women on the inside, the advocates and instigators of the contemporary women's movement.

Months before the defeat of the ERA, Betty Friedan in *The Second Stage* announced "if not the beginning of the end," the "end of the beginning" of the women's movement. At the opposite pole of feminism's political spectrum Barbara Ehrenreich, writing in *Radical America,* conceded that "the women's movement has peaked" at the same time that a second women's movement, this one antifeminist, had gained ground. Neither writer judged the women's movement as beyond resuscitation; in fact each offered a prescription for its recovery. Yet both agreed it would take drastic measures to keep feminism alive in the 1980s.

Just how drastic became clear when Friedan outlined her strategy for feminism's survival: the women's movement, she argued, must become coed. "Men," she predicted, "may be at the cutting edge of the second stage." Ehrenreich, far from Friedan on most issues, agreed in substance, calling for "a new, non-separatist notion of sisterhood."

Under fire by the New Right, which uses antifeminism as a mainstay for its "profamily politics," and attacked by a growing segment of the Left, which dismisses women's struggle for autonomy as a symptom of cultural malaise and narcissism, some feminists are desperately trimming sail. The temptation to jettison embarrassing baggage from the sixties (epithets like "male chauvinist pig") and sail under the rose-colored banner of coed sisterhood is hard to resist.

Even before the backlash, segments of the women's movement willingly sacrificed ideological coherency to respectability in the hope of attracting a broader constituency. Initially their efforts met with success. Feminism was the only mass movement born in the sixties to survive and gain ground in the seventies.

In the eighties the women's movement faces a crisis of consciousness: it must counter increasingly virulent attacks from its critics, Left and Right, with no strong ideological identity to inform or sustain it. As a result, feminists risk mistaking appeasement for adaptation, capitulation for compromise. In their haste to meet criticism they may be tempted to abandon not only the outdated slogans of the sixties, but the developing core of feminist theory as well. If this happens, the women's movement will fall victim not to its enemies, but to its own failure of nerve.

To many Americans Betty Friedan and feminism are synonymous. As feminism's gray eminence, the author of *The Feminine Mystique* and the founder and first president of the National Organization for Women (NOW) commands a wide popular audience. For this reason, *The Second Stage* is perhaps as dangerous as it is specious. Styled as one woman's soul-searching recognition of the failures of feminism, *The Second Stage* is a wholesale distortion of the contemporary feminist movement written by a woman who knows better.

The women's movement from its outset was not a single, unified political or social movement any more than, say, was the progressive movement in American politics. Rather, it was a spontaneous reaction against barriers placed in the path of women—legal barriers, social barriers, and psychological barriers. During the 1960s feminism developed simultaneously on a number of fronts and drew support from a number of sources: women professionals angry at discrimination that relegated them to second-class status within government and the professions; housewives and mothers tired of being told fulfillment came only through husbands and children; and women activists in civil rights and student politics sick of the reality behind the jibe that the only position for women in radical politics was prone. Never was nascent feminism limited to one constituency and rarely did it speak with one voice. Yet, as the Women's Strike of 1969 demonstrated, by the end of the decade a substantial number of women, however different their backgrounds and their organizational strategies and allegiances, saw themselves as part of a larger women's movement.

In Friedan's rewrite, however, the feminists of the sixties emerge not as the tough professional women in government, who, in a brilliant piece of political legerdemain, tricked the Congress into adding bans against sex discrimination to Title VII of the 1964 Civil Rights Act. Nor are they the frustrated housewives of *The Feminine Mystique,* struggling to escape the "comfortable concentration camp" of suburbia. Least of all are they the political activists in the civil rights movement and the New Left who began to analyze women's own oppression. No, Friedan's feminist pioneers are styled as "women with our roots in the middle American mainstream and our own fifties families," women "shocked and outraged" by the "antics" or "anti-man, anti-family, bra-burning" "extremists." "[W]e knew it was wrong," writes Friedan, ". . . though we never said so, then, as loudly as we should have." In her belated *mea culpa* Friedan trots out all the clichés used to discredit the women's movement and embraces them in an attempt to diffuse criticism of the movement and recapture its leadership.

Granted Friedan's brand of feminism has always differed from that of radical and socialist feminists. Nevertheless, the differences between those strains of the women's movement contemporary analysts dichotomized and variously labeled women's rights/women's liberation, reformist/radical, egalitarian/liberationist can be overemphasized. Differences in age and style obscured similarities in substance during the late sixties, when age and style themselves became politicized, when liberals were branded "fascists" and students "revolutionaries."

The National Organization for Women was never as radical as its conservative, antifeminist critics claimed; but neither was it as hopelessly "establishment" as its more radical sisters charged. NOW's Statement of Purpose, adopted in 1966, included, in addition to the often quoted promise "to take action to bring women into full participation in the mainstream of American society NOW," an attack on traditional notices of woman's place. The Statement challenged assumptions about marriage and the family by calling for "a different concept of marriage" and an "equitable sharing of responsibilities of home and family." It attacked as demanding and destructive the "false image" of women pervasive in American society, and it firmly rejected the antifeminist dogma that women's problems were their own individual responsibility, and not "a basic social dilemma which society must solve."

NOW toughened its stance less than a year after its founding by enacting a Bill of Rights which included the two highly controversial planks endorsing the Equal Rights Amendment and asserting a woman's right to safe, legal abortion. Enacted in 1967, at a time when the ERA was considered a dead letter and when abortion was not yet recognized as a feminist issue, NOW's Bill of Rights marked a landmark in the history of contemporary feminism.

Friedan consistently downplays NOW's early radicalism in *The Second Stage*. Her view of history is warped by her desire to mend fences in middle America. Mercilessly caricatured as an abrasive exponent of "women's lib," Friedan tries desperately throughout the book to change her image and present herself as the homegrown champion of respectable, middle-American feminism. She rarely misses a chance to remind us she was born in Peoria. Yet she would like us to forget that abortion, along with the ERA, emanated from the National Organization for Women. Ignoring her own active role in NOW's endorsement of the ERA and abortion rights, she blames a cabal of radical feminists for "[making] it easy for the so-called Moral Majority to lump ERA with homosexual rights and abortion into one explosive package of licentious, family-threatening sex."

While it is incontrovertible that Friedan presided over the coupling of abortion and the ERA in the NOW Bill of Rights, no one can accuse Friedan of lumping feminism with lesbianism. From the first she viewed lesbian issues as a "lavender herring" introduced to discredit the women's movement. Her advice to lesbian feminists is and has always been to stay in the closet, presumably for the good of the movement. In the mid-seventies, when it appeared her homophobia might cost her a voice in the women's movement, she momentarily waffled and spoke in support of the sexual preference resolution at the National Women's Conference in Houston. Now that the political winds have shifted, she is more than willing to recant, to jettison lesbian rights and back off on abortion, blaming "distorted sexual politics" for coupling these issues with the ERA in the first place.

In Friedan's lexicon "sexual politics" is reduced to an epithet. When Kate Millet coined the term as the title of her book in 1970, she provided the feminist movement with more than a catch-phrase. The recognition that the personal is itself political constituted feminism's major contribution to the understanding of social reality, one that grew out of a phenomenological approach to women's liberation. Women met in small groups, later called consciousness-raising groups, to discuss their own experiences. As women talked, they began to see that what they had considered personal failings or individual problems were part of a larger pattern of women's oppression extending into all areas of women's experience, including sexual experience. The phrase "sexual politics" signalled the extent to which women became politicized. Women came to recognize that problems traditionally viewed as personal or sexual were in essence political and they began to call for structural and institutional solutions. In *The Second Stage* Friedan willfully misuses the term to indict what she judges the "distorted priorities" of radical feminists. Lumping together groups with very different theoretical, tactical, and ideological approaches, Friedan creates an all-purpose radical-lesbian-socialist-feminist bogeywoman. The radicals' focus on "sexual battles," she charges, "took energy away from the fight for the equal rights amendment [sic] and kept us from moving to restructure work and home so that women would have real choices."

At the same time Friedan faults "radicals" for sabotaging the ERA, she charges that they slowed down attempts to restructure work and the home. This second charge is particularly unfair. It was the radical and socialist feminists who insisted that the ERA alone could not liberate women and who called for major structural changes in the home and workplace. Friedan's smear of sexual politics not only misrepresents radical feminism; it attempts to co-opt its critique of liberal, mainstream goals. In her rewrite it is the radicals who are to blame for "obsessive careerism," that is, for believing that women's equality rests in "trying to beat men at their own old power games and aping their strenuous climb onto and up the corporate ladder. . . ." It will come as a surprise to women who fought Friedan's bourgeois feminism with the slogan "Out of the mainstream and into the revolution," to read that they, and not the author of *The Feminine Mystique,* peddled professionalism to women as a cure-all. Friedan's distortion of sexual politics signals the emergence of a pseudofeminist Newspeak.

There is little new or original in *The Second Stage.* In her earlier book, *It Changed My Life* (1976), Friedan mounted the same criticisms of the feminist movement she reiterates in *The Second Stage.* No one paid much attention to her critique of the women's movement in 1976, the palmy days when it looked like the ERA was sure to pass and liberation was just around the corner. Obviously times have changed. Once again Friedan mounts her campaign to regain control of the women's movement, this time armed with a set of half-digested ideas from writers as diverse as Christopher Lasch, Jean Bethke Elshtain, and yes, even Phyllis Schlafly. What these writers share is the view that feminism is inimical to the family. In what Friedan evidently considers a brilliant strategical move, she attempts to counter their criticism of contemporary feminism simply by capitulating to their charge. The first stage of feminism, she tells us, has come to a "dead end" because it denied "the importance of family." In rhetoric as calculated as it is offensive, Friedan warns feminists that to abandon the family to the Right, "aborts our own moral majority."

Friedan offers to dismantle the women's movement altogether, to declare the first stage of feminism over—the stage in which, presumably, women gained the trappings of equality—and to move on to a second stage where harmony will reign. Harmony is the key word in the second stage; harmony between men and women, between feminists and right-to-lifers, between "women-as-individuals" and women as "servers-of-the-family." By fiat Friedan declares an end to conflict. Faced with what appear irreconcilable differences, she counters with optimism and appeasement.

The Second Stage is feminism's Atlanta compromise. It marks a retreat in women's fight for economic, social, and psychic equality. Whereas one can argue that for blacks in 1895, the Atlanta Compromise constituted a concession made in the cause of survival, the same cannot be said for feminism. The Moral Majority has not yet taken to lynching uppity women. Friedan's capitulation rests not on the exigencies of survival, but on her own failure to understand that feminism is not simply a program but a wholesale critique of the power relationship between men and women.

No wonder *The Second Stage* has found few champions. Critics hostile to the women's movement have greeted the book with "I-told-you-so" glee. Feminists, on the other hand, are understandably indignant. One has already taken to calling Friedan, "Aunt Betty." Yet as a statement of the failure of nerve of liberal feminism, *The Second Stage* is a significant document. It points to the inability of Friedan's brand of feminism to come to terms with questions essential to the survival of the women's movement, not the least of which is the family. . . .

Feminists have always argued that far from forming a model of loving community, the family traditionally has rested on a form of domination—patriarchy. They have begun, systematically, to study the relationship between oppression in the family and in other institutions. Critics who charge that feminism has turned the family into a battleground overlook the extent to which, historically, the cost of quiescence has been women's individuation.

Whether the family can be stripped of its patriarchal trappings and remain intact is a question troubling to feminists, who are no more immune to transhistorical needs for love, stability, and intimacy than are their profamily critics. Yet they insist that the family must be treated as a social institution and not a "catch-all synonym for intimate community." Part of feminism's crisis of consciousness comes from the difficult task of trying to reconcile women's struggle for autonomy and the gains it promises with the need for secure and coherent intimate human relations. The answer to the dilemma of women and the family involves more than the denunciations of family popular with radical feminists in the early seventies and more than Friedan's attempt to "transcend" the issue and proclaim a new era of harmony in the eighties.

One of the most disheartening aspects of the antifeminist backlash is the support it receives from women. "It is as if," writes one feminist, "at the height of the civil rights movement, a large percentage of blacks had suddenly organized to say: 'Wait a minute. We don't want equal rights. We like things just the way they are.' " The existence of large numbers of women who not only dissociate themselves from the women's movement, but who actively work to oppose abortion and the ERA, should come as no surprise to those familiar with the history of women's movements in the nineteenth and early twentieth centuries. During the fight for suffrage, both in England and the United States, feminists found their sisters arrayed against them. Although it is a matter of record that organized antifeminism always draws a good deal of its financial and organizational clout from association with conservative males, it would be folly to dismiss antifeminism as merely a conspiracy of the Right. If Phyllis Schlafly and her historical cohorts did not speak to women's very real fears and apprehensions, no amount of conservative capital could keep them afloat.

In *The Power of the Positive Woman* (1977), Schlafly attacked the ERA, claiming it was a trojan horse designed by the women's movement to ruin the housewife. The charge that the ERA would make the housewife obsolete proved much more damaging than Schlafly's tirades against coed toilets and a women's draft. The ultimate effect of the ERA, according to Schlafly, would be to drive women out of the home, forcing those who lack the credentials for "careers" into low-paying, drudge jobs. Why leave your own nice, comfortable kitchen to go to work as a cook or waitress? Why indeed?

Schlafly has always been less an antifeminist than a right-wing ideologue. Her attack on the ERA was fueled by her belief that it constituted part of a liberal plan to drive America to dictatorship—to force women out of the home and children into state indoctrination camps cleverly camouflaged as child care centers. Initially she spurned the anti-ERA movement, preferring to focus her fire on Henry Kissinger and the eastern internationalist establishment. Her leadership in STOP ERA came only after she became convinced the women's movement was linked to a larger liberal conspiracy. Ironically, just as feminists view Schlafly as a tool of the Right, Schlafly dismisses feminism as no more than a front for a liberal plot to extend the powers of the federal government, weaken America's defense, and undermine the free enterprise system.

Schlafly's politics went largely unnoticed in the seventies by her audience of middle-class housewives. Although some no doubt shared her concern over the perfidy of liberalism, many responded to her charge that the ERA threatened marriage and with it their livelihood. Their fears were not groundless. For those women who work full-time in the home and have no independent income, economic survival in a very real sense depends on the health of their marriages.

Schlafly was quick to point out that feminism, by urging women to find jobs, made it easier for husbands to escape their financial obligations and their marriages. Further, she charged that by bringing women into every level of the work force, feminism threatened marriages by throwing men and women together, whether in the boardroom or in the firehouse. Finally, she warned that the Courts interpreted equal rights legislation to the detriment of women, using sex-blind provisions to question women's traditional right to child custody and men's responsibility for alimony and child support.

Feminists found Schlafly's arguments hard to refute. It did no good to point out that inflation more than feminism pushed women into the work force, that women already worked side by side with men in jobs where their powerlessness made them targets for sexual harrassment, and that the Courts had a history of arbitrarily interpreting legislation designed to protect women.

Although Schlafly ignored the majority of women who already worked outside the home, her message struck a chord with them as well. Like it or not, the sad economic truth for women in the seventies was that they earned fifty-nine cents for every dollar a man earned; that on the average a male high school dropout earned more than a woman college graduate working full time; that women composed only ten percent of those who earned over ten thousand dollars per year; that sex segregation in the work force pushed women into pink collar ghettoes where "equal pay for equal work" was a meaningless phrase; that the proportion of women-headed households below the poverty level was six times that of male-headed households; that half the American women over sixty-five had incomes below three thousand dollars per year; that only fourteen percent of women divorced or separated were awarded alimony by the Courts, and of that group only forty-six percent collected regularly; that of the forty-four percent of divorced mothers awarded child support, over half did not receive regular payments. Despite charges of "reverse discrimination," affirmative action has yet to improve substantially women's economic status. As economist Diana Pearce discovered, after a decade of feminist agitation the major macroeconomic trend for women was the alarming "feminization of poverty."

Worsening economic conditions have done little to strengthen the women's movement. The economic reality behind Wilma Scott Heide's observation that the average woman is "only one man away from welfare" acts for many women more as a caution than a call to action. The shocking increase in woman-headed households below the poverty level speaks eloquently to women's fear of divorce. Schlafly is seductive because she promises women who are afraid of anything that threatens the fragile security of marriage that if they play by the old rules, if they keep their virginity before marriage and their priorities after marriage, putting their husbands and children first, they will be rewarded: men will live up to their end of the bargain by marrying and supporting women for life. In a world in which marriage is still a woman's major source of economic security, Schlafly's facile formula for "positive womanhood" is as pathetically appealing as it is meretricious. . . .

Feminism addresses the problems facing working women, both housewives and women working outside the home. Demands for equal pay for equivalent work, child care centers in the workplace, income and social security benefits for housewives, flextime and jobsharing for women who wish part-time work, and men's equal sharing of housework and parenting responsibilities all address the needs of contemporary women. Yet it is difficult for many women to recognize that feminism speaks to them. Too many women see the women's movement as something that serves only the interests of young, upwardly mobile career women. The image of the bra-burning radical of the sixties has been superseded in the seventies and eighties by that of the silk blouse feminist. On the newsstands, in magazine ads, on television, and in the movies the feminist is portrayed invariably as under forty, dressed for success, slim, trim, and on her way up in the world. The movies present a feminist caricature, either a homewrecking monster like Faye Dunaway in *Network,* or a sexy klutz like Jill Clayburgh in *An Unmarried Woman* and *It's My Turn.* The uniform never varies. Skirted, suited, high-heeled, with the obligatory briefcase and string of sexual partners, the media feminist's only concession to the sixties image of radical feminism is the obvious lack of a bra under her silk blouse. It would be difficult to conjure up an image more inimical to the working wife and mother, the beleaguered single parent, or the middle-aged housewife. . . .

A concerted effort was made to broaden the base of the women's movement in the mid-seventies by pushing aside divisive ideological and political issues. The price of inclusiveness was an ideological flabbiness that gave rise to pseudo-feminism. Women who had never experienced the politicization of consciousness-raising too often mistook "dress for success," assertiveness training, or negotiating skills for feminism. Magazines like *Savvy* and *New Dawn* compounded the problem by peddling a spurious self-help for feminist politics.

In the eighties the lack of focus in the women's movement is catching up with it. The movement's diversity begins to look alarmingly like balkanization. Programs like rape crisis centers and shelters for battered women which receive funding from grants and government are going under as they compete against each other for an increasingly smaller piece of what is fast becoming a nonexistent pie. At the same time emphasis on creating a "woman-centered culture," which garnered support from among lesbian feminists, appears to have backfired. However well intentioned, it has impeded efforts at outreach. Women's centers too often have become havens for the already committed, rather than forums for educating and politicizing women. A younger generation of women has grown up taking for granted gains earlier feminists fought hard to win.

The virulent opposition to feminism mounted by the New Right, which threatens to sweep away the limited advances the women's movement gained in the seventies, is also taking a toll. Feminists lost a last-ditch battle for the ERA at the same time they had to mount a campaign against the Human Life Amendment. Meanwhile the Left, when it does not indict feminism for narcissism, castigates it for seeking to integrate women into "an already bankrupt model of welfare or bureaucratic capitalism" which, some observers insist, is now in its death throes.

The socialist revolution the Left so ardently desires cannot be purchased at the cost of women's retreat back into the patriarchal family any more than the New Right can restore the past by imposing patriarchy by law. Since the family seems destined to be a primary focus of politics, Left and Right, in the eighties, the women's movement must confront the issue and articulate a feminist family politics. Friedan's attempt to diffuse the issue by embracing the specious profamily rhetoric of the Right will not work. Instead, feminist family politics must underscore the link between oppression in the family and in other institutions. Without a consistent, coherent ideology, the women's movement will remain unarmed in the face of its opposition, unable to articulate its own vision of the future and win support for its cause. So long as women fail to advance such an ideology, American society surely will not. . . .

A broad-based, cross-class alliance among women has long been the goal of feminists, who insist that women are disadvantaged as a gender in ways that unite them across class lines. Divisive racial, class, and ethnic tensions historically have posed obstacles to such an alliance and indeed will surely continue to do so. However, as women increasingly recognize they are disadvantaged *as women,* a recognition the feminization of poverty serves to sharpen, women may be more willing to forge such an alliance.

Clearly the women's movement has a role to play in proposing measures to secure economic viability for women. It is here that the issues addressed by feminism under the rubric of sexual politics become crucial. For no simple economist stance can deal adequately with women's economic plight, precisely because women's economic position is a function of their social position. Despite the fact that more and more women are primary earners for themselves and their children, society continues to assign women a secondary earner status, presuming that a woman's work outside the home comes second both to her husband's job and to her home and family responsibilities. For growing numbers of women heading households, societal expectations that reduce them to secondary earner status are clearly dysfunctional and almost guarantee poverty. Feminism, by urging both social and economic independence for women, challenges traditional notions about women's secondary status and calls for changes not only in the workplace but in the family, which will allow women full autonomy. Any prescription for a cure for the feminization of poverty that leaves out the larger social dimension of women's plight simply will not work.

The women's movement, far from being dead, may be about to enter a new and dynamic phase in the eighties. However, it must first reject Friedan and others who would argue that women can achieve equality without addressing women's need for social and economic independence. For women, sexual politics is the only viable politics.

❖ *FURTHER READING*

Mary Frances Berry, *Why ERA Failed* (1986)
Janet Boles, *The Politics of the Equal Rights Amendment* (1979)
Jane DeHart-Matthews and Donald Mathews, *The Equal Rights Amendment and the Politics of Cultural Conflict* (1988)
Bonnie Thornton Dill, "Race, Class, and Gender: Prospects for an All-Inclusive Sisterhood," *Feminist Studies,* IX (1983), 131–50
Barbara Ehrenreich, *The Hearts of Men* (1983)
Zillah Eisenstein, *The Radical Future of Liberal Feminism* (1981)
Carol Felsenthal, *Sweetheart of the Silent Majority: The Biography of Phyllis Schlafly* (1981)
Janet Giele, *Woman and the Future* (1978)
Joan Hoff-Wilson, ed., *Rites of Passage: The Past and Future of the ERA* (1986)
Bell Hooks, *Ain't I a Woman? Black Women and Feminism* (1981)
Ethel Klein, *Gender Politics* (1984)
Kristin Luker, *Abortion and the Politics of Motherhood* (1984)
Jane Mansbridge, *Why We Lost the ERA* (1986)
James Mohr, *Abortion in America* (1980)
Rosalind Pollack Petchesky, *Abortion and Woman's Choice* (1984)
Ann Snitow et al., eds., *Powers of Desire: The Politics of Sexuality* (1983)
Carol Vance, ed., *Pleasure and Danger: Exploring Female Sexuality* (1984)